SCHOLASTIC JOURNALISM

Eleventh Edition

SCHOLASTIC JOURNALISM

THOMAS E. ROLNICKI

C. DOW TATE

AND

SHERRI A. TAYLOR

© 2007 by Thomas E. Rolnicki, C. Dow Tate, and Sherri A. Taylor

BLACKWELL PUBLISHING
350 Main Street, Malden, MA 02148-5020, USA
9600 Garsington Road, Oxford OX4 2DQ, UK
550 Swanston Street, Carlton, Victoria 3053, Australia

First edition *Scholastic Journalism* copyrighted 1950 and carried through four printings. Revised from *Exercises in Journalism*, first copyrighted 1939 and continued through nine printings.
Second edition published 1957
Third edition published 1962
Fourth edition published 1968
Fifth edition published 1972
Sixth edition published 1978
Seventh edition published 1984
Eighth edition published 1990
Ninth edition published 1996
Tenth edition published 2001
Eleventh edition published 2007 by Blackwell Publishing Ltd

4   2009

Library of Congress Cataloging-in-Publication Data

Rolnicki, Tom.
  Scholastic journalism / Thomas E. Rolnicki, C. Dow Tate, and Sherri A. Taylor. – 11th ed.
    p. cm.
  Includes bibliographical references and index.
    ISBN 978-1-4051-4415-5 (hardback : alk. paper) – ISBN 978-1-4051-4416-2
(pbk. : alk. paper)   1. Journalism, School.   2. Journalism.   I. Tate, C. Dow.
II. Taylor, Sherri A.   III. Title.
LB3621.E52 2007
373.18′97–dc22
                                                                                2007003755

A catalogue record for this title is available from the British Library.

Set in 9.5/12.5pt Sabon
by Graphicraft Limited, Hong Kong
Printed and bound in the United States
by Sheridan Books, Inc.

The publisher's policy is to use permanent paper from mills that operate a sustainable forestry policy, and which has been manufactured from pulp processed using acid-free and elementary chlorine-free practices. Furthermore, the publisher ensures that the text paper and cover board used have met acceptable environmental accreditation standards.

For further information on
Blackwell Publishing, visit our website:
www.blackwellpublishing.com

Contents

Preface

What does it take to be a student journalist today? Is the skill set that distinguishes a journalist from someone else any different than it was five or ten years ago?

To really answer those questions, you need to see what is being published today in schools, how it is published and who is publishing it. The answers may open some eyes and provide more credence to Indiana University Professor Jack Dvorak who said more than a decade ago: "Journalism kids [still] do better."

The tools of the trade have changed at the professional level of journalism and high schools have picked up many, if not all, of these changes. The ease of use and relatively low cost of these digital and electronic gizmos have even blurred the line between who is a journalist and who isn't; students publish at home on their own website independent of their school or the school-established media. Broadly speaking, anyone who publishes a website with any kind of news or opinion content is a journalist today. These sites are sometimes called "blogs" (web logs or an online journal) and those who publish them are "bloggers." With this new form of journalism in mind, the definition of who is or is not a journalist is expanding.

Just ten years ago, the technical skills needed to be a blogger belonged only to true programmers or "techies." Now, anyone who knows how to use a computer and access the Web can be one of these new breed of independent journalists.

News media published in the schools – from traditional print and broadcast to online and DVD – employs much or all of the new digital technology in their formal classroom or informal, after-school group programs. The near universal use of most or all of these new tools by students has changed the face of student media and publishing processes. The skills needed to effectively use these digital devices are seemingly easy to master by young people who have only lived in a microchip world. Students ten years ago didn't have wireless options and their phones didn't take pictures.

Yet if you strip away the digital cameras, cell phones, iPods, wireless laptops, the most recent versions of PhotoShop and InDesign, you begin to see that the student journalist of today is not all that different from the one ten years ago with this exception – today's journalism "kids" are more savvy about what they report.

Today's student journalists still need all the basics: knowledge of news values, journalism ethics and press law; how to write a good news story and a headline; how to design a page that attracts readers; how to shoot an event and edit a photo for visual impact; and how to edit content following standard journalistic style. The basics apply to all media, even online and broadcast, although with some modifications given the differences of each medium. To these, you can add the specialty reporting areas of sports, features and opinion writing and other forms of visual communication, such as graphics and illustration. It doesn't do a photographer much good to have an expensive digital camera unless he or she first knows the news value of what they are shooting Likewise, it doesn't matter if a reporter uses a wireless laptop to submit a story unless he or she knows how to write a good story lead. Yesterday, today and tomorrow, the basics of journalism remain as core essentials.

Widely reported lapses in ethics in the commercial press, including plagiarism and fabrication, are not absent, unfortunately, in the student press. With the credibility of all news media at stake when these violations are revealed, today's student journalists must be even more aware of what plagiarism, fabrication and copyright are than their predecessors were. The internet is a great source of temptation to those who look for shortcuts and steal someone else's work. Today's journalist knows that ignorance is no excuse for the twin evils of plagiarism and fabrication.

Knowledge of press law has also become increasingly important and marks another difference between today's student journalist and those of the past. Censorship, threatened and actual, and prior review of content before publication undermine the learning process and show a lack of trust in the students' ability to abide by the standards of good journalism. Students need to know about libel, privacy, obscenity, copyright and freedom of information laws before they publish for the first time.

Another difference between students of today and those of the past decade is one that is troublesome to many in the media: the public spends less time with news media although there are more choices for news than ever before. Students are busier than ever with less time to read, listen to or watch news media. This means that today's newspaper, yearbook, magazine, broadcast and online publications need to do a better job than ever with designing and packaging their product. Visual journalism now nearly matches verbal journalism in importance. The student reporter who has just finished the most important and well-written story of her career may fear that few will read it unless it is accompanied by a photo, has an enticing headline and is displayed in an eye-catching page design.

A quick look at what today's students have published (for example, the many articles, designs, photographs and art reproduced in this book) will show the growing professionalism of the student press. The stories reported, the sophistication of the layout design, the quality of the photos and graphics underscore this assertion. Just as Professor Dvorak said, "Journalism kids are doing better," and we add, "better and better" all the time.

For more than 55 years, teachers have relied on *Scholastic Journalism* to help them teach the essentials of journalism to their students. The book is a comprehensive resource for beginning and advanced journalism classes and for more short-term instruction if class time is shared with other modules. The text covers reporting, writing, editing and design for newspapers and yearbooks, with updated sections on the internet and its use as a reporter's tool and as a place to publish. Chapters on photography, advertising, ethics, press law and other pertinent subjects show the book's depth. Those who teach journalism education classes at colleges and universities also adopt *Scholastic Journalism* as the class textbook. There are also many useful chapters for those who teach broadcast journalism. For many teachers, it's the only book they say they need to teach journalism and produce a high-quality product.

This edition maintains the integrity and commitment to diversity and journalism excellence established long ago by the founding authors Clarence Hach and Earl English. The text's long-standing position as the preeminent text for high school journalism is the impetus for the present authors to keep the book fresh and vital. As student journalism has changed, *Scholastic Journalism* has changed.

The authors of this edition are indebted to the students, advisers and others who shared their work and their helpful advice so that another generation of students can continue the tradition of student-published media in secondary schools. It's a tradition that is one of the most beneficial, practical and personally rewarding activities and courses of study within the school.

What does it take to be a student journalist today? Armed with this textbook, it's up to you, the reader, to help answer that question. We expect you to be one of those "kids" who do better.

T.E.R.
C.D.T.
S.A.T.

Acknowledgments

We'd like to thank a long list of teachers, colleagues, friends and corporations who helped us in the preparation of the tenth and eleventh editions: Their support, insight and help in providing permission to use material from their newspapers and yearbooks have been invaluable in producing this textbook.

Robert Adamson, Ridley High School, Folsom, Pa.
Logan Aimone, Wenatchee High School, Wenatchee, Wash.
Martha Akers, Loudoun Valley High School, Purcellville, Va.
Jim Allen, Lancaster High School, Lancaster, Calif.
American Society of Newspaper Editors, Washington, D.C.
Olaina Anderson, Torrey Pines High School, San Diego, Calif.
asap, Associated Press, New York, N.Y.
Judy Babb, (formerly) Highland Park High School, Highland Park, Texas
Austin Bah, Tamalpais High School, Mill Valley, Calif.
Susan Baird, Bellevue East High School, Bellevue, Neb.
Brother Stephen V. Balletto, Chaminade High School, Mineola, N.Y.
Sue Barr, South Eugene High School, Eugene, Ore.
Kathryn Barton, Oak Hall School, Gainesville, Fla.
Marjorie Bell, (formerly) Bakersfield High School, Bakersfield, Calif.
Robert and Penny Belsher, Ferris, Texas
Lew Bernes, Birmingham High School, Van Nuys, Calif.
Kathy Beyer, McMinnville High School, McMinnville, Ore.
Laurie Bielong, Belleville Township High School, Belleville, Ill.
Don Bott, Amos Alonzo Stagg High School, Stockton, Calif.
John Bowen, (formerly) Lakewood High School, Lakewood, Ohio
Jan Bowman, Walt Whitman High School, Bethesda, Md.
Diane Boyle, (formerly) Parkway Central High School, Chesterfield, Mo.
Wayne Brasler, University High School, Chicago, Ill.
Deanne Brown, Westlake High School, Austin, Texas
Renee Burke, William R. Boone High School, Orlando, Fla.
Michelle Burress, Plainfield High School, Plainfield, Ind.
Pam Carlquist, Park City High School, Park City, Utah
Meg Carnes, Robert E. Lee High School, Springfield, Va.
Judi Coolidge, Bay High School, Avon Lake, Ohio
Charles Cooper, National Press Photographers Association, Durham, N.C.
Sandra Wilson Coyer, Puyallup High School, Puyallup, Wash.
Jeff Currie, (formerly) Oak Park and River Forest High School, Oak Park, Ill.
Kathy Daly, (formerly) Overland High School, Aurora, Colo.
Albert DeLuca, James Madison University, Harrisonburg, Va.
Cynthia Dewes, Crown Point High School, Crown Point, Ind.
Kay Dillard, Abilene High School, Abilene, Texas
Drake University, Des Moines, Iowa

Jon Paul Dumont, San Francisco, Calif.

Terry Durnell, Lee's Summit North High School, Lee's Summit, Mo.

Jennifer Dusenberry, Dallas, Texas

Ray Elliott, University High School, Urbana, Ill.

Brenda Feldman, (formerly) Coral Gables High School, Coral Gables, Fla.

Brenda Field, Plainfield High School, Plainfield, Ind.

Karen Flowers, (formerly) Irmo High School, Columbia, S.C.

Maureen Freeman, Montgomery Blair High School, Silver Springs, Md.

Jared Freibel, Hinsdale Central High School, Hinsdale, Ill.

Bob Frischmann, Hazelwood Central High School, Florissant, Mo.

Katherine Gazella, St. Petersburg Times, St. Petersburg, Fla.

Lora Geftic, Hasbrouck Heights High School, Hasbrouck Heights, N.J.

Mark Goodman, Student Press Law Center, Washington, D.C.

Brenda Gorsuch, West Henderson High School, Hendersonville, N.C.

Peggy Gregory, Greenway High School, Phoenix, Ariz.

H.L. Hall, (formerly) Kirkwood High School, Kirkwood, Mo.

Sandy Hall-Chiles, (formerly) Highland Park High School, Dallas, Texas

Randy Hamm, East Bakersfield High School, Bakersfield, Calif.

Jack Harkrider, L.C. Anderson High School, Austin, Texas

Nancy Hastings, Munster High School, Munster, Ind.

Bobby Hawthorne, Austin, Texas

Alan Heider, Minneapolis, Minn.

Brother Peter Heiskell, Chaminade High School, Mineola, N.Y.

Andrea Henderson, Torrey Pines High School, San Diego, Calif.

Dr. J. Henery, Wooster High School, Wooster, Ohio

Diane Herder, Laingsburg High School, Laingsburg, Mich.

Betty Herman, Putnam City North High School, Oklahoma City, Okla.

Patricia Hinman, Robinson Middle School, Fairfax, Va.

Jane Hirt, Red Eye, Chicago Tribune Publishing Co., Chicago, Ill.

Dean Hume, Lakota East High School, Liberty Township, Ohio

Mark Johnston, City High School, Iowa City, Iowa

Jim Jordan, Del Campo High School, Fair Oaks, Calif.

Paul Kandell, Palo Alto High School, Palo Alto, Calif.

Linda Kane, Naperville Central High School, Naperville, Ill.

Marilyn Kelsey, Bloomington High School, Bloomington, Ind.

Jack Kennedy, (formerly) Iowa City High School, Iowa City, Iowa

Linda Kennedy, (formerly) Hinsdale Central High School, Hinsdale, Ill.

Jason King, Kansas City Star, Kansas City, Mo.

David Knight, Lancaster, S.C.

Mitchell Koh, Crossroads School, Santa Monica, Calif.

Nancy Kruh, Dallas Morning News, Dallas, Texas

Patricia Ladue, McClintock High School, Tempe, Ariz.

Pete LeBlanc, Center High School, Antelope, Calif.

Gary Lundgren, Jostens, Minneapolis, Minn.

Steven Lyle, West High School, Davenport, Iowa

Chris McDonald, (formerly) Viking Shield, Spring Valley High School, Columbia, S.C.

Jim McGonnell, Findlay High School, Findlay, Ohio

Elizabeth McNamara, Dallas, Texas

Susan Massy, Shawnee Mission Northwest High School, Shawnee, Kan.

John Mathwin, Montgomery Blair High School, Silver Spring, Md.
Steve Matson, Charles Wright Academy, Tacoma, Wash.
Jennifer Moffitt, Lowell High School, San Francisco, Calif.
Cathy Molstad, Wausau, Wis.
Pat Monroe, Burges High School, El Paso, Texas
Peggy Morton, Hill Country Middle School, Austin, Texas
Mark Murray, (formerly) Lamar High School, Arlington, Texas
Jeff Nardone, Grosse Pointe South High School, Grosse Pointe Farms, Mich.
Sarah Neblett Nichols, (formerly) Danville Community High School, Danville, Ind.
Libby Nelson, Lenexa, Kan.
Kathy Neumeyer, Harvard–Westlake School, North Hollywood, Calif.
The Newseum, Washington, D.C.
Newspaper Career Guide, Newspaper Association of America, Vienna, Va.
Casey Nichols, Rocklin High School, Rocklin, Calif.
Matt Okerlund, Roosevelt High School, Sioux Falls, S.D.
Janet Owens, Gresham High School, Gresham, Ore.
Jane Pak, Dallas, Texas
Gary Pankewicz, Hasbrouck Heights High School, Hasbrouck, N.J.
Joe Pfeiff, Mountain Ridge High School, Glendale, Ariz.
Marci Pieper, Clayton High School, Clayton, Mo.
Pizza Hut, Inc., Dallas, Texas
Wayna Polk, Abilene High School, Abilene, Texas
David Porreca, University High School, Urbana, Ill.
Betsy Pollard Rau, H.H. Dow High School, Midland, Mich.
Mary Pulliam, Duncanville High School, Duncanville, Texas
Red Eye, Chicago Tribune Publishing Co., Chicago, Ill.
Carol Richtsmeier, (formerly) DeSoto High School, DeSoto, Texas
Tim Roberts, San Dieguito High School Academy, Encinitas, Calif.
James Rogers, Ferris, Texas
Polly Rolnicki, Wausau, Wis.
Rod Satterthwaite, Dexter High School, Dexter, Mich.
John Scott, Thomas Downey High School, Modesto, Calif.
Natalie Sekicky, Shaker Heights High School, Shaker Heights, Ohio
Susan Sloan, McLean High School, McLean, Va.
Margaret Sorrows, Bryant High School, Bryant, Ark.
Paul Spadoni, Peninsula High School, Gig Harbor, Wash.
Howard Spanogle, Asheville, N.C.
Dot Stegman, (formerly) Kapaun Mt. Carmel High School, Wichita, Kan.
Heather Stockdell, Southport High School, Indianapolis, Ind.
Jim Streisel, Carmel High School, Carmel, Ind.
Edmund Sullivan, Columbia Scholastic Press Association, New York, N.Y.
Katharine Swan, Lowell High School, San Francisco, Calif.
Becky Tate, Shawnee Mission North High School, Overland Park, Kan.
C. Dow Tate, Shawnee Mission East High School, Prairie Village, Kan.
Lee Terkelsen, Golden West High School, Visalia, Calif.
Barbara Thill, Lyon's Township High School, LaGrange, Ill.
David Thurston, Allen High School, Allen, Texas
TLP Advertising, Dallas, Texas
Cindy Todd, Westlake High School, Austin, Texas

Bernadette Tucker, (formerly) Redwood High School, Visalia, Calif.
Tina Turbeville, Crossroads School, Santa Monica, Calif.
Randy Vonderheid, Frisco Centennial, Frisco, Texas
Harvey Wehner, Live Oak High School, Morgan Hill, Calif.
Alan Weintraut, Annandale High School, Annandale, Va.
David Weisenburger, Gahanna Lincoln High School, Gahanna, Ohio
Lorraine Wellenstein, Schurr High School, Montebello, Calif.
Ray Westbrook, St. Mark's School of Texas, Dallas, Texas
Tony Willis, (formerly) Carmel High School, Carmel, Ind.
Dave Winter, Henry W. Grady High School, Atlanta, Ga.
Scott Winter, (formerly) Bismarck Century High School, Bismarck, N.D.
Esther Wojciki, Palo Alto High School, Palo Alto, Calif.
Kristie Yellico, (formerly) Arvada High School, Arvada, Colo.
Mitch Ziegler, Redondo Union High School, Redondo Beach, Calif.
Clay Zigler, Rockwood Summit High School, Fenton, Mo.
Kathleen D. Zwiebel, Tide Lines, Pottsville Area High School, Pottsville, Pa.

Note on Authors

Tom (Thomas) E. Rolnicki teaches business writing and communications at the Minnesota School of Business. He was the executive director of the National Scholastic Press Association and the Associated Collegiate Press for 26 years. During that time, he edited the association's magazine, newsletter, guidebooks and the annual "Best of the High School Press." He taught high school journalism in Wisconsin and Iowa, and has spoken at journalism conferences, workshops and conventions throughout the United States and Canada and in other countries, including Croatia, South Korea, Germany, the Czech Republic, Finland and Slovenia. He has a bachelor's degree in journalism and secondary education from the University of Wisconsin, Madison, and a master's degree in journalism and mass communication from Iowa State University, Ames. He was the editor of his high school newspaper at Newman High School, Wausau, Wis. He has received the Carl Towley and Medal of Merit awards from the Journalism Education Association and the Gold Key from the Columbia Scholastic Press Association.

C. Dow Tate is a journalism teacher at Shawnee Mission East High School in Prairie Village, Kansas, and the director of the Gloria Shields All-American Publication Workshop sponsored by Dallas County Schools. He was inducted into the Scholastic Journalism Hall of Fame at the University of Oklahoma and was named a Texas Legend, as one of the most influential people in the state's 75-year scholastic journalism history. His students' publications have earned the nation's highest honors, including the National Scholastic Press Association's National Pacemaker and the Columbia Scholastic Press Association's Gold Crown. Tate has been named the Dow Jones Newspaper Fund's National High School Journalism Teacher of the Year as well as the Texas Max R. Haddick Teacher of the Year.

Sherri A. Taylor teaches graphic design in the Visual and Interactive Communications Department of the S.I. Newhouse School of Public Communications at Syracuse University in Syracuse, New York. She is the director of the Empire State School Press Association for New York schools and directs the School Press Institute, a summer journalism workshop for scholastic journalists. She was formerly an award-winning publications adviser and journalism teacher in Irving, Texas. She was inducted into the Scholastic Journalism Hall of Fame at the University of Oklahoma and received the Gold Key award from the Columbia Scholastic Press Association and the Pioneer Award from the National Scholastic Press Association. She has judged Gold Crown and Pacemaker awards for high school publications and has been a judge for the Society of News Design's international competition. At Syracuse, she is the adviser to an award-winning yearly magazine, *MPJ*. In addition to teaching, she has advised students on two book projects. The first, *Eyes on the World* (2006), is based on 15 years of documentary photography from the Alexia Foundation for World Peace and Cultural Understanding, and the second, *Life Going On 9/11/02*, was produced by the Eddie Adams Barnstorm Workshop.

SCHOLASTIC JOURNALISM

Eleventh Edition

Understanding News

The president of the United States played golf yesterday. You played golf yesterday too. Today, your city newspaper has a picture of the president playing golf on an inside news page; there is no picture of you on the golf course, even though you got a hole-in-one on the ninth, and the president, reportedly, rarely breaks 100 on 18 holes. Why wasn't your achievement reported?

The difference has to do with what news is and what it isn't. Understanding news is fundamental to writing for a news medium, be it a newspaper, magazine, yearbook, broadcast station or internet site. It is important because it enables a reporter to sort and prioritize information and help readers distinguish between what is relevant – what they need to know – and what is less important, even though readers may be interested in the subject. This understanding of news is also useful to reporters so they can make all stories appealing to readers. Faced with busy readers who can get their news from print, broadcast and internet sources, a reporter who knows what news is will likely write better than one who doesn't. Delivering information fast and first are two goals of most news organizations today, but the consumer will rely upon and trust that source that delivers it with accuracy and relevance.

The president made news by golfing and you didn't simply because he is the president and you aren't. That's called *prominence*, and it's just one of the many aspects of the definition of news to be explored here.

A DEFINITION OF NEWS

The president as a golfer and why he made news is easily understood, but this is only one part of a more complex definition of news. News, by definition, isn't an orderly, exact list of "it's always this, but never that." Circumstances and nuances can change almost anything into news.

To arrive at an understanding of news, the following points are important to know:

1. News must be factual, yet not all facts are news.

2. News may be opinion, especially that of a prominent person or an authority on a particular subject.

3. News is primarily about people, what they say and do.

4. News is not necessarily a report of a recent event.

5. What is important news to one community or school may be unimportant or have little or no news value in another community or school.

6. What is news in one community or school may be news in every community or school.

7. What is news today is often not news tomorrow.

8. What is news for one person may not be news for another.

9. Two factors necessary to news, interest and importance, are not always synonymous.

Of these nine points, numbers 4 and 9 may need further explanation.

The full text of a news story need not be about a recent occurrence. Often only the first paragraph and one or several follow-up paragraphs contain the facts or opinions that make an old story news again. An event that happened months or even years ago may be news if it has just been disclosed. In the midst of a political campaign, for example, often something in a candidate's past is revealed. Events that have not yet happened may be news.

Interest and importance are not always synonymous because the most important news story is not often the most interesting or compelling one. For example, two stories appear on page 1: the school board announces the building of a new gymnasium for the school and the school's athletic director is being sued for sexual harassment by one of the school's coaches. If you didn't know about either event before the stories were published, which one would you read first? Which would be more interesting to you? Which would be more important and have a greater impact on you? If you think the sexual harassment suit is more interesting than building a new gym, but you think the new gym will have a greater impact on your life, then this illustrates the conflict between important and interesting regarding news value. There are many variables, and personal preference is one of them.

Occasionally a story that receives the most display in a newspaper or time on television or radio is often not very important to most readers or listeners. However, editors decided to devote extensive space or time to the story because it has one or more unique characteristics, sometimes involving a conflict. For example, a story about the rescue of a mountain climber stranded on Mount Everest may not be important to the majority of readers or viewers, but it is interesting to many because of the man against nature conflict that is a big part of the story. When planning their lead or most prominently displayed stories, editors for all media will consider both importance and interest and then choose stories with both elements for the prime, lead-off positions.

HARD NEWS AND SOFT NEWS

News can further be defined as either hard or soft; the difference, to the news consumer, is sometimes obvious and sometimes not.

Hard news has significance for relatively large numbers of readers, listeners and viewers about *timely* events that have just happened or are about to happen in government, politics, foreign affairs, education, labor, religion, courts, financial markets and the like.

Soft news is usually less important because it entertains, though it may also inform, of course, and is often less timely than hard news. It includes human interest and feature stories that may often relate to hard news. It appeals more to emotions than the intellect and the desire to be informed.

For example, the announcement by a software company of its plans to issue public stock is a hard news story. A companion story about the person who started this same software company and her collection of motorcycles is soft news.

Hard news, despite its importance, usually attracts fewer readers, listeners or viewers because it unfortunately is less interesting to many or is often more difficult to understand than soft news, particularly if one has not been following a continuous story every day. Though reporters always "fill in" some essential background, readers need to think about the information presented to comprehend its significance. As a result, much straight reporting of facts for hard news has given way to interpretive reporting in which the reporter explains the significance of facts and gives the background necessary for people to understand what they read, hear or see. Often, this type of story is written by an experienced reporter who is an expert, for example, in foreign affairs or in science. This interpretation, which sometimes borders on informed opinion, usually carries the writer's byline.

In radio and television, this type of interpreted news will be presented by a commentator or by a specialist in the type of news such as in politics. Many reporters and commentators become well known, and their bylines are sought by readers, listeners and viewers who wish to hear or read stories by certain news analysts or specialists. Today there are special television and radio shows and internet sites devoted exclusively to discussions of news events. *Meet the Press*, *Crossfire* and *Washington Week in Review* are just a few of the many broadcast and cable television shows that feature journalists analyzing the news. These shows are comparable to the editorial pages in print newspapers and appeal to those who wish to be well informed and hope to learn different points of view.

Most large newspapers have reporters whose expertise lies in the reason that make news – government, foreign affairs, law, education, science, finance, religion, entertainment and the like. Smaller papers depend on the Associated Press, Reuters, United Press International or a syndicate, such as the Tribune Media Services, for example, for nonlocal stories of significance. Many large radio and television stations and some internet news and magazine sites have reporters expert in certain fields, such as state government. Reporters are stationed in the state capitol during legislative sessions. Smaller broadcast stations depend on nationally syndicated experts whose services, particularly news or features on health, entertainment and money matters, are purchased by the station. The television and cable news networks have their own specialists.

Many stories combine hard and soft news elements. Hard news about personal conflict may trigger an emotional response from the reader, listener or viewer. Skillful writers will often highlight a human angle to a story about an important subject – softening the hard news – with the hope of attracting a wider audience. For example, a news story about Congress lowering federal income tax rates will usually be written predominately as hard news, but some soft news elements, such as a description of how the change affects typical persons with specific incomes, will be prominently featured, humanizing an important but mostly uninteresting story. The human or personal angle will often be the lead or one of the follow-up paragraphs. By doing this, the writer indirectly tells readers why this story is important or relevant to them. Writers also try to add a local element to a national or international story for the same reason – to connect the important story to some aspect of the local reader's, viewer's or listener's experience.

CONNECTING FACTS, INTERESTS AND THE AUDIENCE

The basis for all news is fact, and there is a dependent relationship between fact and audience (reader, viewer, listener), fact and interest, and interest and audience. Essentially, the job of a reporter is to make facts interesting to a particular audience. Therefore a reporter for a school news medium should write all stories for those particular readers. A story would be written somewhat differently for a school newspaper than for a city paper. The audiences for each, though they may overlap some, are mostly different.

News, which must be factual, is based on actual occurrences, situations, thoughts and ideas. Yet, as already written, not all facts are news.

News must also be interesting, but not all facts are interesting to everyone. The degree and breadth of interest will vary. One story may have a high degree of interest for only a small number of people. Another story will have some interest for a great many. Still another story will have great interest for large numbers. This story, especially if it is also very important, will be the number 1 story and given the lead position on page 1 of the paper or will be the first story read on a news broadcast.

The death of Diana, Princess of Wales, in 1997 led to unprecedented international news coverage. Her death was clearly an example of a story of great interest, but not necessarily of great importance, to a large number of people worldwide. Though tragic and a personal loss to many, her death had little consequence for most people in the world. A hard news story with many elements of soft news, it was interesting to many because of her fame and prominence and the circumstances of her death. The war in Kosovo in 1999, though of great importance, was not of great interest to many unless their fellow citizens were somehow affected by the war. It was a hard news story, and reporters sought to add more interest to the facts by including personal accounts from the war's victims.

Editors realize that their papers, web sites or broadcast news programs should have broad appeal even for a target audience. They select a mixture of stories of varying degrees of interest and importance in the hope of reaching every audience member with at least one story of particular importance to that person. Simply, newspapers and news programs have something for everybody. Smart editors know the demographics of their audience and publish content to meet its needs and wants.

NEWS IS DIFFERENT FROM OTHER FORMS OF WRITING

News must be accurate. Factual accuracy means that *every* statement, name and date, age and address, and quotation is a verifiable fact. This unwavering commitment to accuracy is essential to a news medium's credibility and a journalist's personal integrity.

Accuracy means correctness not only of specific detail but also of general impression – the way the details are put together and the emphasis given. It is very easy to distort the importance of a particular fact by giving it major importance when in reality it is a minor detail. It is also easy to "play down" an important fact. A reporter's judgment is always involved. That's why complete objectivity really does not exist. That is also one reason readers should think as they read.

Accuracy is difficult to achieve because of the myriad facts that go into a story, the speed involved in modern journalism, and the many people who help to produce the finished story – the copyreader, the editors and the anchorpersons in radio and television whose vocal inflections may even distort the facts. Use of the internet as a news medium, with its speed and global reach, makes the conflict between the time needed for checking for accuracy and the ability to get the news out quickly even greater than ever before. Every news medium wants to be the first to break a story, but does it do this at the expense of accuracy? That is debated today by many media critics.

Reporters must work painstakingly to achieve accuracy. They must check *every* note, particularly such specific details as names, dates, ages, times and addresses. Nothing must be taken for granted, even a name pronounced smith. Is it Smith, Smithe, Smythe? Or is it Schmidt, Smeeth or even Psmythe? Is Friday, April 26 – the night of the National Honor Society induction – really Friday, or is the 26th Saturday?

Reporters must learn to question sources carefully. Informants sometimes misinform, rarely intentionally. School reporters often do not ask enough questions to get all the facts necessary to write an accurate story, especially if they don't understand their assignment and have not thought it through before conducting the interview. A reporter needs to "talk out" a story with the assignment editor and ask pertinent questions to develop the main idea or focus for the story. Only then will a reporter be able to ask intelligent questions to fill in the details pertaining to the main idea or focus.

For beginners, it is helpful if a reporter writes the main idea of the story in sentence form before going on the interview. The "bottom line" is that a reporter must understand clearly what a story is about before preparing for the interview. One of the weaknesses of the student press is that student reporters often rely on their informants to tell them the story rather than ask enough questions during interviews to "dig" it out.

News is balanced. Balance in a news story is a matter of emphasis and completeness. It is a reporter's giving each fact its proper emphasis, putting it into its proper relationship to every other fact and establishing its relative importance to the main idea or focus of the story.

A sports reporter could have every statement in a story correct, but if only the action of his or her school team was covered, the reporter would be guilty of imbalance and incompleteness. A reporter who covered a teacher strike by only talking to striking teachers and not the school board would be equally guilty.

News is usually considered balanced and complete when a reporter informs readers, listeners or viewers of all important details of a news event in proper relationship. Balance and completeness do not mean reporting every little detail. Rather, balance is the selection of *significant* details as a result of informed judgment. The purpose of balance is to give a reader, listener or viewer a fair understanding of an event, not a detailed account of every fact.

Balance is related to objectivity to some degree. Since a reporter is not in reality completely objective, it is important, especially for controversial subjects, for the reporter to at least consider information and opinions from sources who may be opposed to the mainstream or majority viewpoint. At the same time, a reporter has to use common sense and dismiss the views or statements of "crackpots" or fringe elements whose positions are implausible and too extreme. For example, a story about a racial conflict at school would not have to include the opinions of a white supremacist or neo-Nazi group just for "balance" if no such group was involved in the racial incident being reported.

News is as objective as it can possibly be. News is the factual report of an event, not the event as a prejudiced person might see it or as the reporter or assignment editor might wish it to be seen. For the reporter and editor, staying out of a story means relying on the most knowledgeable sources for all pertinent information (Fig. 1.1).

A reporter should report news as impartially and honestly as possible. That's always a worthy goal.

Because the world is so complex, people often cannot understand all factual stories unless facts are interpreted and evaluated against background information. This situation has led to an offshoot of news,

Self-scheduling made easier with color codes

In brief

■ Colored sheets prevented students from staying in arena for long periods of time

■ Extra effort was needed to correct computer errors

By Jessica Qu

ADMINISTRATORS, teachers and students believe that use of colored program sheets made this semester's self-scheduling process easier than in previous years.

The implementation of the colored program sheets enabled teachers and administrators to prevent students from staying in the arena longer than their designated time period, according to assistant principal Gloria Bogdanoff, who added that it made the self-scheduling process in the arena run more smoothly.

"It makes us feel good that the students are moving at the right pace," Bogdanoff said.

Italian teacher Judy Branzburg said that she believed the new system made an improvement in he overall scheduling process. "At least we know which group the kids belong to and how long they're suppose to stay in the arena," she said.

Freshman Jason Siu agreed. "It went well," he said. "It wasn't too chaotic afterall, and I got all the teachers I wanted even though I was at the end of the rotation."

However, the system was not as easily accomplished.

The counseling department had to print the labels to attach to each program sheet, instead of ready-to-go, single-colored program sheets that the school received in the past from the school district. Because of the extra time and labor required to attach labels to the program sheets, the administration ordered the labels before distributing class verification sheets to students, and counselors were not be able to correct computer system mistakes.

"The burden was on all of us," Bogdanoff said. "The district refused to help us, so we had to do it on our own. I felt sorry that we couldn't ensure the kids their classes on their program sheets."

Computer system errors were so serious that some students did not have a single class listed on their verification sheets.

Bogdanoff, who spent two days correcting the errors on the labels, felt that it was "a waste of time" and "should never happen again."

"We have to leave time between the distribution of verification sheets and the ordering of labels," she said. "This is something that we definitely need to improve next time, if we are to continue using the colored sheet system."

---

interpretative reporting or, as it is also called, news analysis. Sometimes giving background information may mean reporting opinions or facts at variance with those given by a source.

Objectivity, an essential principle of news practice, is often difficult to achieve. A reporter's own opinions and emotions can easily interfere with factual presentation in stories about which strong biases are held. Being aware not only of prejudices but also of responsibilities will help. If a reporter is too close to the story (knows the sources intimately or has expressed strong opinions about some aspect of it), it might be better to reassign the story to another reporter to avoid any questions of bias.

News is concise and clear. For a newspaper most hard news stories follow the inverted pyramid form (see Chap. 3) and are written concisely and simply so that the meaning is clear to an average reader. There are other forms, however, that may fit the story better, such as beginning with the inverted pyramid form and, after the lead and follow-up paragraphs, changing to a chronological or storytelling form for the rest of the story. This combination of forms is often used for covering sports. Other forms used for most features, sports and interview stories are discussed in later chapters.

Although newswriting is concise – every word counts – it is still lively, with strong and colorful verbs. Subjects are complete and specific, opinion is attributed to the source and direct quotes rise above ordinary comments and vague information. With a writer's best efforts, newswriting can be as creative and descriptive as any other form of writing.

Usually, news is recent. Timeliness is of the greatest importance in this era of fast communication. Other facts being equal, a news editor will choose one story over another because of its timeliness.

Fig. 1.1. For this story, the reporter interviewed sources who were relevant authorities and involved with the self-scheduling process at the school. *The Lowell*, Lowell High School, San Francisco, Calif.

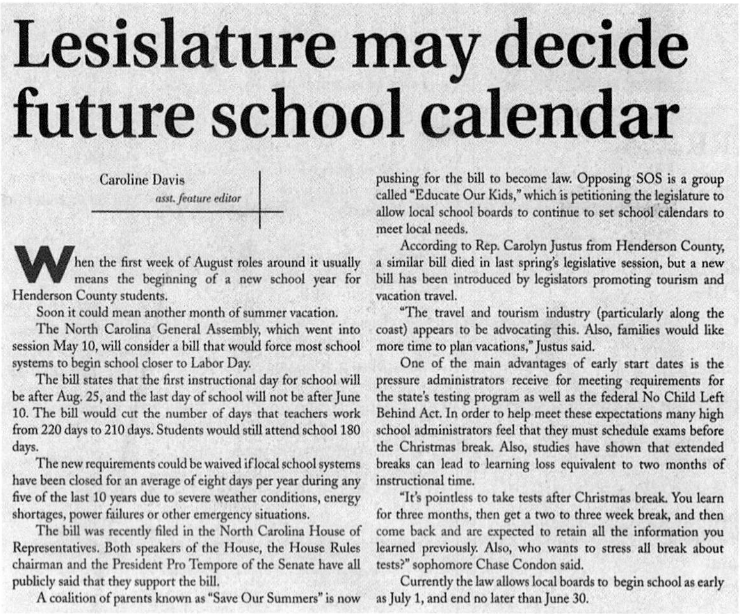

Lesislature may decide future school calendar

Caroline Davis
asst. feature editor

When the first week of August roles around it usually means the beginning of a new school year for Henderson County students.

Soon it could mean another month of summer vacation.

The North Carolina General Assembly, which went into session May 10, will consider a bill that would force most school systems to begin school closer to Labor Day.

The bill states that the first instructional day for school will be after Aug. 25, and the last day of school will not be after June 10. The bill would cut the number of days that teachers work from 220 days to 210 days. Students would still attend school 180 days.

The new requirements could be waived if local school systems have been closed for an average of eight days per year during any five of the last 10 years due to severe weather conditions, energy shortages, power failures or other emergency situations.

The bill was recently filed in the North Carolina House of Representatives. Both speakers of the House, the House Rules chairman and the President Pro Tempore of the Senate have all publicly said that they support the bill.

A coalition of parents known as "Save Our Summers" is now pushing for the bill to become law. Opposing SOS is a group called "Educate Our Kids," which is petitioning the legislature to allow local school boards to continue to set school calendars to meet local needs.

According to Rep. Carolyn Justus from Henderson County, a similar bill died in last spring's legislative session, but a new bill has been introduced by legislators promoting tourism and vacation travel.

"The travel and tourism industry (particularly along the coast) appears to be advocating this. Also, families would like more time to plan vacations," Justus said.

One of the main advantages of early start dates is the pressure administrators receive for meeting requirements for the state's testing program as well as the federal No Child Left Behind Act. In order to help meet these expectations many high school administrators feel that they must schedule exams before the Christmas break. Also, studies have shown that extended breaks can lead to learning loss equivalent to two months of instructional time.

"It's pointless to take tests after Christmas break. You learn for three months, then get a two to three week break, and then come back and are expected to retain all the information you learned previously. Also, who wants to stress all break about tests?" sophomore Chase Condon said.

Currently the law allows local boards to begin school as early as July 1, and end no later than June 30.

Fig. 1.2. Current facts and a "what could happen next?" angle combine to make this story relevant. *Wingspan*, West Henderson High School, Hendersonville, N.C.

Timeliness does not necessarily mean that all the events or facts of a news story are current. It may mean only that the story is appropriate at the time it is printed or broadcast. For example, a story about the last time an American president visited Russia may appear in connection with the announcement of the current president's trip to Russia. Recentness alone does not determine the timeliness of every news story.

Because school papers are not published daily and rarely published weekly, timeliness is a factor very different from that for a daily or weekly paper. For a paper published monthly, *current* may be a better word than *timely* as a factor for news. Journalists for these infrequent publications can also capitalize on timeliness from a different perspective by writing the advance story about what is going to happen soon (Fig. 1.2). News sites on the internet, with the capability to change content within minutes, can take full advantage of timeliness as a key factor in writing news that is important to readers.

A NUMBER OF NEWS ELEMENTS MAKE FACTS INTERESTING

Immediacy or *timeliness* is the most essential element of most news. A reporter usually emphasizes the newest angle. For daily papers and broadcast and online news, the words *yesterday*, *last night*, *today* and *tomorrow* characterize most stories. Occasionally a story will concern events that happened in the past. In this case, the reporter tries to seek a "today" angle to the previous event. For example, on Nov. 9, 1999, the 10th anniversary of the fall of the Berlin Wall made the news pages of many newspapers, was aired on many news broadcasts and was published on internet news sites. The *news angle* was the anniversary. Most stories were presented in a form other than the inverted pyramid and included a summary of the changes that have occurred in Germany and former communist countries in Europe since the wall was torn down.

Another example:

The old angle

West High girls' basketball center Lori Harris hurt her right knee Saturday while skiing at Alpine Village.

The team's trainer said that Harris is recovering quickly but may not be able to play in Friday's game.

Harris is the only player injured.

The new angle

Girls' basketball center Lori Harris will not play in tonight's game between West High and conference rival East High because of a knee injury she sustained last saturday when she fell while skiing at Alpine Village.

All other members of the team are in good physical condition according to Coach Dave Adams.

The team trainer said that Harris is recovering quickly from her skiing accident.

The most significant difference between these two stories is that the second one begins with the most recent development, Harris' inability to play during tonight's game. Leading off with this angle keeps the story more timely, more immediate. Six days after it happened, her injury is no longer "news," bat the consequences of it are.

Editors need to seek ways of keeping school print, online and broadcast news *timely* and therefore interesting. This is especially important for printed publications, which have deadlines a week or longer before the publication date. Online and radio and television broadcast sites have the ability to update, edit and delete stories quickly, sometimes within minutes before they are uploaded on the internet or broadcast.

For printed newspapers, hardly any stories are breaking or spot news because of early deadlines. Consequently, many school papers publish background and analysis pieces about major news events (Fig. 1.3). Many of these takes are more in-depth, with many sources and sidebar, or companion, stories clustered together. These in-depth stories have a broader time implication than the yesterday, today or tomorrow angles of many news stories. Despite the restriction of early deadlines, news stories can still be written, but the latest development or consequence should be in the lead. The advance news story, writing about what is soon to happen, is also a way for print papers to be vital and interesting.

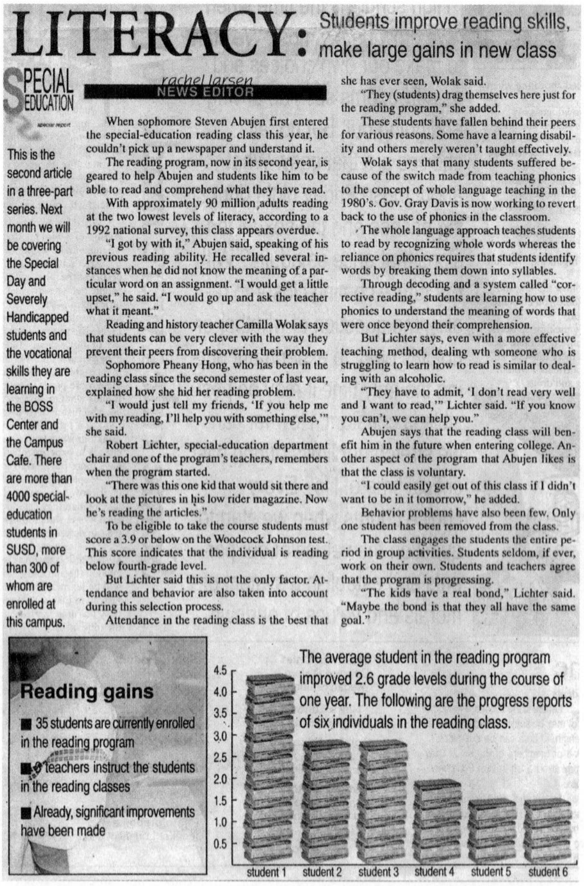

LITERACY: Students improve reading skills, make large gains in new class

SPECIAL EDUCATION

rachel larsen
NEWS EDITOR

This is the second article in a three-part series. Next month we will be covering the Special Day and Severely Handicapped students and the vocational skills they are learning in the BOSS Center and the Campus Cafe. There are more than 4000 special-education students in SUSD, more than 300 of whom are enrolled at this campus.

When sophomore Steven Abujen first entered the special-education reading class this year, he couldn't pick up a newspaper and understand it.

The reading program, now in its second year, is geared to help Abujen and students like him to be able to read and comprehend what they have read.

With approximately 90 million adults reading at the two lowest levels of literacy, according to a 1992 national survey, this class appears overdue.

"I got by with it," Abujen said, speaking of his previous reading ability. He recalled several instances when he did not know the meaning of a particular word on an assignment. "I would get a little upset," he said. "I would go up and ask the teacher what it meant."

Reading and history teacher Camilla Wolak says that students can be very clever with the way they prevent their peers from discovering their problem.

Sophomore Pheany Hong, who has been in the reading class since the second semester of last year, explained how she hid her reading problem.

"I would just tell my friends, 'If you help me with my reading, I'll help you with something else,'" she said.

Robert Lichter, special-education department chair and one of the program's teachers, remembers when the program started.

"There was this one kid that would sit there and look at the pictures in his low rider magazine. Now he's reading the articles."

To be eligible to take the course students must score a 3.9 or below on the Woodcock Johnson test. This score indicates that the individual is reading below fourth-grade level.

But Lichter said this is not the only factor. Attendance and behavior are also taken into account during this selection process.

Attendance in the reading class is the best that she has ever seen, Wolak said.

"They (students) drag themselves here just for the reading program," she added.

These students have fallen behind their peers for various reasons. Some have a learning disability and others merely weren't taught effectively.

Wolak says that many students suffered because of the switch made from teaching phonics to the concept of whole language teaching in the 1980's. Gov. Gray Davis is now working to revert back to the use of phonics in the classroom.

The whole language approach teaches students to read by recognizing whole words whereas the reliance on phonics requires that students identify words by breaking them down into syllables.

Through decoding and a system called "corrective reading," students are learning how to use phonics to understand the meaning of words that were once beyond their comprehension.

But Lichter says, even with a more effective teaching method, dealing wth someone who is struggling to learn how to read is similar to dealing with an alcoholic.

"They have to admit, 'I don't read very well and I want to read,'" Lichter said. "If you know you can't, we can help you."

Abujen says that the reading class will benefit him in the future when entering college. Another aspect of the program that Abujen likes is that the class is voluntary.

"I could easily get out of this class if I didn't want to be in it tomorrow," he added.

Behavior problems have also been few. Only one student has been removed from the class.

The class engages the students the entire period in group activities. Students seldom, if ever, work on their own. Students and teachers agree that the program is progressing.

"The kids have a real bond," Lichter said. "Maybe the bond is that they all have the same goal."

Fig. 1.3. The newsworthiness of this story is not tied to an event that occurred on a specific date. It's timely in a broader sense, relating to a situation that has occurred for some time. *Stagg Line*, Amos Alonzo Stagg High School, Stockton, Calif.

If the principal resigns on Nov. 1 and the public was informed, you cannot expect readers of your school newspaper to be as interested in that fact on Nov. 13, when the next issue of your paper is published. The governor visits your school and speaks at an all-school assembly on Nov. 3. A speech coverage story, reporting the highlights of the governor's talk, would be a good, timely news story if the paper came out one or a few days after the event. However, the Nov. 13 publication date makes the speech story less vital than it seemed the day after it occurred. The *timeliness* or *immediacy* aspect of the news is mostly gone.

In addition to solving this print news problem with more advance, background, analysis and in-depth stories, a reporter can develop a "nose for news," which can also be a solution to potentially "tired" news.

If the reporter has a nose for news, he or she will find out something about the principal's resignation or future plans that hasn't already been reported (see Fig. 1.4). The governor's talk may be tied to pending legislation or a trend in national politics. The talk may have led to students becoming involved in some

Armstrong to retire, plans move to Hawaii

by Jessica Silver-Greenberg

If you need to find Mrs. Armstrong next year, you should check out the senior tennis circuit in Hawaii. You may find her playing a match on the sun-speckled courts of Waikiki. For at the conclusion of the school year, Emmy Lou Armstrong, assistant head of upper school and employee of the school for 23 years, will retire and move to Hawaii.

Armstrong had been debating the move over the summer and made the final decision over winter break. "I decided this was the time to go," Armstrong said.

Since her first visit in 1950, Armstrong has always harbored a deep love for Hawaii, and promised herself that one day she would live there. Both her granddaughter and her daughter live in Hawaii and Armstrong visits about three times a year.

"I am just going to kick back and chill out for a long while," Armstrong said.

It is an opportunity for Armstrong to finally pursue her aspiration of playing on the senior tennis circuit.

"That is what I have wanted to do for a long time," she said. "I haven't

Emmy Armstrong

been able to because they start on Thursdays and I work."

Although she is excited about her future in Hawaii, Armstrong laments having to leave the students.

"It was really scary making the decision because I love it here so much," Armstrong said.

If she misses teaching while residing in Hawaii, Armstrong plans on substituting at local high schools. She hopes to maintain the close relationships she has developed with students and faculty members over the years.

Fig. 1.4. Despite infrequent publication, school newspapers can still break news even if some facts are already known. In this story, the retirement of the school official is likely known, but what she will do once she retires probably is not widely known. *Chronicle*, Harvard–Westlake High School, North Hollywood, Calif.

community action program, or it may be part of a re-election campaign. Anything the reporter finds out about these stories that hasn't already been reported will be *new* (*timely*) to readers – and therefore news. Many news stories have the potential for an update or further reporting if the reporter persists.

During a public school board meeting and in a letter to parents, the school announces that it will change its class schedule effective next year. Students are also given a letter with the announcement during a homeroom period. Therefore a straight news story in the school paper reporting the same details would have little interest and would not be timely. A background story, however, relating the reasons for the change, the history of the present class and time structure, an account of how the new schedule works at schools already using it, and student and faculty opinions about the change would be a timely and interesting update of the original announcement.

Proximity or *nearness* refers not only to geographic nearness but also to interest nearness, sometimes called *impact*. In other words, what effect will the story have on its readers, listeners or viewers? What will it mean to readers? Impact can come from many interesting quotations from sources interviewed for the story. For example, a story about the change in the dress code, with direct and indirect quotes from proponents and opponents, can be more interesting to readers, more compelling than even a spot news story announcing the adoption of the dress code. Often interpretation or explanation is part of the news story announcing the most important fact, the reason for the story.

Usually a reader is more interested in an event geographically near than in one far away. School readers are usually more interested in events of their own school than in those of a neighboring one. Yet an incident in Kosovo during the 1999 war between NATO and Yugoslavia involving emails sent between a teenager in Kosovo and one in California may not have been near geographically but may have been of great interest to students at almost every school in the United States. This is *interest nearness*, or *impact*.

Allegedly drunk driver strikes student

By Matt Franks
ASST. EDITOR-IN-CHIEF

A TPHS student was injured in a collision with an allegedly drunk driver along Highway 78 Saturday morning at 6:55 a.m.

Kristen Rife (11) and David Richardson ('04) were driving around a bend in the road in Richardson's Ford Explorer when a Chevy Silverado driving on the wrong side of the road collided with them. Witnesses put the Silverado at 70 miles per hour.

The driver of the other car, a 26-year-old male, was killed instantly. Rife and a male passenger from the Silverado were airlifted to Scripps Memorial Hospital. Richardson was ambulanced to Palomar Hospital, and a female passenger from the Silverado was ambulanced to Sharp Memorial Hospital. With the exception of the allegedly drunk driver, all victims sustained major injuries.

Rife sustained a fracture in her right lower leg, a broken right arm, a lacerated left arm, a broken collar bone, a fractured left cheek bone, a fractured nose, several other broken bones and external cuts. She is expected to make a full recovery and will be released from Scripps today.

Richardson, who was released from Palomar on Sunday, sustained a broken wrist, a broken ankle, a fracture in his back, and several cuts. Both Richardson and Rife were wearing seatbelts at the time of the accident.

Richardson and Rife were driving to Ocotillo Wells to go off-roading. They were driving behind students Corey Chin (12) and Ryan Collins (12), and in front of Alex Carter (12), none of whom were involved in the collision.

Within the last month, three other accidents have occurred at the same bend in the road, according to local residents.

Principal Rick Schmitt sent an e-mail to the counseling staff and Rife's current teachers Monday notifying them of the accident.

According to the National Highway Traffic Safety Administration, drunk driving is the nation's most frequently committed violent crime, responsible for killing someone every 30 minutes.

The naming of a graduate of a school to the president's cabinet or the Baseball Hall of Fame is news to the school's paper and online and broadcast sites; it is also an example of interest nearness. A graduate winning the mayoral election in the same town the school is located in is an example of geographic nearness.

A reporter emphasizes a local or school angle of a story whenever possible (Fig. 1.5). For example, when President Clinton signed into law the National Service Program, which allows students to do public service work in exchange for tuition and living allowances, many school papers had stories that interested many students. The stories were a way of making facts about a federal government program interesting to high school readers. They "drove the story home." They added *impact*.

Stories in school print, broadcast and online media are usually restricted to school activities and classroom academics; the activities and opinions of students, faculty and other school personnel; and those community, state, national and international events and issues that concern readers and in which they should be interested. Some of these stories did not originate on the school's campus, but some readers may have a connection to the event or social issue, and students and others are talking about it on campus. These off-campus, student interest stories have recently been reported in the high school press: abortion, nutrition, sexuality, road rage, gun violence, alternative medicines, breast cancer, censorship of the internet and legal restrictions on personal freedoms. The key to getting students to read stories like these is accurate reporting, the use of expert sources and lively writing, always with a student angle. Interesting displays, with graphics and photography or other art, will likely increase readership.

Consequence is another important element of news. It pertains to the breadth of appeal – to *importance* – and to the effect a story will have on readers. In other words, *impact*.

A story that affects every student in the school – one on a change in graduation requirements – will have more interest than one affecting only members of one class – the destination for the senior class trip. Since the audience for the medium is usually wider than one class, the reporter should emphasize the angle of the story that will interest most readers, listeners or viewers. Sometimes the reporter will need to interpret the significance of a story. For example, will a change in the school's graduation requirements affect seniors, or will the changes affect only incoming freshmen? The reporter considers all possible reader questions and then tries to find the most knowledgeable authorities to give the answers.

Consequences that affect a person's well-being will make the news story more important to readers. How many people will be affected and how badly are

Fig. 1.5. A story that reports a nonschool news event that involved students has impact. *Falconer*, Torrey Pines High School, San Diego, Calif.

considered by the reporter when the story is developed and by the editor when determining how much display the story gets in print and online media or how much time it gets on a news broadcast. Sometimes the *impact* is good – every student gets one more vacation day during spring break this year.

Prominence, as a news element, includes persons, places, things and situations known to the public by reason of wealth, social position, achievement or previous positive or negative publicity.

Generally, names make news. Reporters should always include as many names as possible in their stories. The more well known a particular name, place, event or situation, the more interest the story will have. The president's golf game, discussed at the beginning of this chapter, is news because the president of the United States is a prominent person. Princess Diana's death made news worldwide because of her prominence rather than because of the circumstances that caused her death.

At a high school, the principal and other top administrators, teachers and student leaders and those students who excel in some endeavor are prominent, and what they do may be more newsworthy because of their status. The principal's resignation makes page 1 in the school newspaper and leads on the school's broadcast news show; a teacher's resignation will likely not get the same treatment because the teacher is not as prominent as the principal. A star athlete gets a football scholarship to a Big Ten university; another student, not an athlete, gets a scholarship based on academic achievement to the same Big Ten university. The athlete's scholarship and decision to attend the university is usually news, and the nonathlete student's scholarship achievement may only be included in a composite story, a list of who received scholarships and where they are going to college. Again, prominence makes the difference.

Drama adds vitality and color to a news story and is another ingredient of news. A reporter always tries to find picturesque background and dramatic action. Often the more picturesque and dramatic a story, the more appealing it is to the audience. However, since this is news, all the colorful details and dramatic action are true.

Mystery, suspense, comedy, the unusual and even the bizarre are the chief elements of drama. If the facts of a story have one or several of these elements, the reporter should develop the story to take full advantage of them. The storytelling method of development would seem the best way to relate the facts to the reader. Yet relating dramatic facts in the storytelling form isn't all a

reporter can do to attract readers. Reporting the story as a human experience – someone's personal story – will usually enhance the story even more.

Three hikers in Yosemite National Park are lost for four days during a blizzard. The park rangers and others search around-the-clock and eventually find all three alive, cold and hungry, huddled in a makeshift shelter. To keep awake and prevent themselves from freezing to death, they played trivia games. This story has suspense, a colorful setting, possible dire consequences and even some humor. It can best be reported as a personal survival story, through the eyes of one or all three hikers, with all the suspense that chronological storytelling can facilitate.

Oddity, or *unusualness*, almost always helps to make facts interesting. The greater the degree of unusualness in a story, the greater its value as news. A first-time or last-time event often is more interesting to the audience. One-of-a-kind or rarely happening events are news. Solar and lunar eclipses are news. The last baseball game in old Detroit Municipal Stadium was news in 1999, at least in Michigan, and the outcome of the game didn't matter as much as the fact that it was the last game ever to be played there. The end of the century, end of the millennium on Dec. 31, 1999, also was a significant story because of its unusualness. The first baby born each year in many cities becomes a news story. The birth of a panda bear in a zoo in North America is news because pandas are rare outside of their native China.

Some stories depend almost entirely on this element. The persons involved are not prominent, the impact on others is negligible, and timeliness is only important in some cases such as the birth of the first baby born in the new millennium in a city. Yet readers, listeners and viewers usually love these kinds of human interest stories.

Conflict is one of the most basic and important news elements. It is the news element that appears most frequently in news media. An examination of the front page of a daily paper or the content of a radio or television news program will illustrate this point.

Conflict is inherent in all sports stories; all news of war, crime, violence and domestic disputes; much news of government bodies such as city councils, state legislatures and Congress; and all stories involving differences of opinion.

Much news of conflict involves other news values, such as drama and oddity, and therefore has emotional impact, a factor that appeals to many people and sometimes causes media to overplay this news element.

Conflicts can be both physical and mental. Even stories of one person's ideas versus another's are colored by this important ingredient. The more prominent the opponents, the bigger the news.

Conflicts can involve human versus human, human versus animal, human versus nature, human versus environment, human versus space or animal versus animal. For example, a story about the first all-women expedition, led by Ann Bancroft, to the North Pole, is a story primarily about human versus nature. Because it involved a "first," it also had the oddity element. Another conflict story example would be a space shuttle launch, human versus space.

If a reporter really understands news and the elements that it contains and knows who the audience is and what its interests are, the reporter can sometimes inject conflict into a story and therefore make it a story of wide appeal. It involves how the facts are presented, how the story is told. For example, a school newspaper story about the resignation of a principal could be told in several ways, usually as a prominence story but also, perhaps, as a conflict story, if facts reveal that the principal's ideas or work was opposed by a school board member, the superintendent of schools or the teachers' union. In this sense, a reporter can be creative and not rely solely on facts given out in a statement or press release. The reporter digs deeper to see if there is some conflict, some more facts. That's why a reporter really needs to understand a story well before going on an interview.

Sex, an integral force in human life, is the news value in stories of romance, marriage, divorce and other relationships. The treatment of sex varies widely, particularly in different types of print, broadcast and online media. For print and other media with visual components to news, photography and video have helped media to focus attention on sex and sometimes exploit it. School media journalists should be aware of their community standards and audience ages when sex is an element in a story. Sex can be reported maturely in an informative and nonsensational way.

Emotions and *instincts* as news elements involve the desire for food, clothing and shelter; the universal interest in children and animals; and the elements of fear, jealousy, sympathy, love and generosity.

The public likes stories that appeal to its emotions. For example, the international group Habitat for Humanity, which builds houses for the poor in various countries, is news. The elements of generosity, sympathy

and even prominence (President Jimmy Carter is actively involved with this group) are key to these stories. Each year, broadcast news media report from food shelters and facilities that feed the homeless at Thanksgiving. These stories appeal to viewers' emotions. Stories about asteroids striking earth appeal to people's fears, and stories about births in zoos appeal to people's love of animals, especially young or helpless ones.

For high school media, stories with emotions and instincts as ingredients include those about student or faculty deaths or serious illnesses, food drives, charity events, community volunteerism, new fashions and fads, students who have pets, animal shelters, organ transplants and organ donations, homelessness and lottery winners, among others.

Stories with emotional elements are generally the most widely read in print media and watched or listened to on broadcast news and public affairs programs. Editors who realize this high audience potential will assign several emotionally involving stories for each edition of the paper or news program. A yearbook, which is an ideal medium for feature writing, will also benefit from a large number of stories that are emotions and instincts based.

Progress, another news element, involves any significant change for the betterment of humanity. It may refer to achievements in a research laboratory, a business, a legislative body, and other concerns from the multinational to one-person homes.

Progress may refer to advances in the treatment of breast cancer or HIV/AIDS; cleaning toxic waste sites; multinational space stations and exploration; acceptance of alternative medicines by the mainstream public; and growth of global communications, among other wide interest topics. Progress, as a key news element, may also refer to schoolwide stories such as the physical expansion of the school, changes in the school's graduation requirements, or adding new courses to the curriculum.

TEN ELEMENTS OF NEWS

1. Immediacy or timeliness

2. Proximity or nearness

3. Consequence or impact

4. Prominence

5. Drama

6. Oddity or unusualness

7. Conflict

8. Sex

9. Emotions and instincts

10. Progress

JOURNALISTS MODIFY THE IMPORTANCE OF NEWS ELEMENTS IN PRACTICE

Why one newspaper, online site or broadcast station reports a story differently than another, or whether it publishes it all, depends, in part, on the policy of the news medium regarding news and its elements. The policy may increase or diminish the importance of a story or kill it entirely.

The political and religious beliefs of the news medium's owner or management may alter news value. A story on abortion or gay civil rights would probably get different treatment and display in a Catholic newspaper than it would in a nonsectarian metropolitan daily. Even in a nonsectarian newspaper, whether or how a story is reported can be influenced by the political, religious or other biases of the publisher and the top editors.

The attitude of the news medium toward labor, agriculture, gun control or particular racial, ethnic or sexual orientation groups may change news value. For example, a story on the number of blacks in Congress or in federal judgeships would likely be reported differently in the *Chicago Defender*, a newspaper read primarily by blacks, than it would in one of the other Chicago dailies. A story about farm subsidies might receive more display in the *Star Tribune* (Minneapolis) than in the *Baltimore Sun*.

Demographics, a scientifically done profile that reveals many aspects of a target audience such as its education level, racial and ethnic mix, family income and median age, among others, determines largely what is news for most newspapers, magazines, online news sites and broadcast stations. Media owners want to know who their audience is and as much about how it lives and uses media as possible. This information not only relates to coverage but also to potential advertising income.

Although demographic studies aren't important for high school news media, it is helpful for editors to know generally the ethnic, racial, religious and sexual orientation of their audience so they can report stories of importance to these groups. This population profile should be done at the beginning of the school year for it to be useful in long-range planning.

Special interest groups, such as racial, labor, religious, sexual orientation and others, often have their own community or national newspapers, magazines, web sites and broadcast programs and networks. On cable, there is the Black Entertainment Television Network, the *Christian Science Monitor* is a popular newspaper with religious ties and *Today's Education* is a magazine representing the work and views of the National Education Association, a labor union.

A news source aligned with a particular political party or other special interest groups may also publish news and commentary in opposition to its own positions. Nationally syndicated columnists representing a wide range of backgrounds and opinions are often published in newspapers or included on public affairs news shows to diversify the content of the medium.

School media may want to achieve the same diversity by inviting guest commentators who represent minority groups within the school to write for the school print media or speak on broadcast shows. Additionally, editors and advisers should try to recruit minority students to join the staff. Staff diversity will usually broaden coverage and better serve a diverse school population.

The amount of space given to a story in a print or online medium or the amount of time on radio or television determines whether a story is told briefly or in detail. An online news site mostly prints brief to medium length stories; the medium itself – the computer monitor and method of accessing stories – is more suited to shorter rather than longer stories. Broadcasters have the benefit, as do online media, of adding content quickly. They can break into regular programming at any time with a news bulletin.

Timing often alters the value of a story. All news must be judged in competition with the news available at the moment it is to be published or aired. All other stories, for example, "took back seats" on the day Princess Diana died in 1997. Had Princess Diana not died on that August day, some other story would have been number one.

Previous publication or broadcast of a story changes its value. A story published in an early edition of a paper or broadcast will rarely receive the same attention later. Other events will likely have preempted its importance. At the very least, a paper, online news site or broadcast station will update the story, reporting the newest or more timely angle.

With the ability of online and broadcast media to publish and air stories within minutes of when they happen, print media today, especially newspapers, have to compensate for their inability to break much news to the public. Few newspapers today will publish an "extra" edition when a major story breaks. Rather, the papers focus more on the "why" and "how" of news, since the "who," "what," "when" and "where" are often known already by the public. Newspapers will publish more news analysis and background stories. They will also concentrate more on local news, which may be easier to break to the public.

School print media have the same lag time problem as their commercial counterparts. School newspapers, which publish monthly or less frequently, can also emphasize the "why" and "how" of a news story, as well as publish advance stories. *Timeliness* is mostly lost for school papers as a news value, with the exception of the advance story. News is either packaged as news briefs or presented as a news-feature, with other news elements, such as emotions or prominence, as the focus.

Print media can compensate in another way for their inability to compete with other media on *timeliness*. A newspaper can create a companion web site on the internet and refer readers to its electronic version for updates, breaking news and other materials cut from the print version or created especially for the online version.

Censorship can also change news value, especially during war or national crisis for nonstudent media. Sometimes stories are not published or broadcast for years later. Reports involving the CIA and FBI, even of American involvement in the Persian Gulf War and the bombing of U.S. embassies in Africa in 1998, are examples of government censorship. Often, private papers of prominent persons, including presidents, are not made available to the public and the press until after their deaths or even years longer.

Censorship can take other, less direct forms, including an absence of presidential press conferences in order to keep a president from answering questions about events or decisions. Occasionally a news medium may ignore a story, even a rather explosive one. Some of these permanently or temporarily censored stories are ones with sex and prominence as news values.

Although there is a Freedom of Information Act, which allows the public and the press access to most government information, sometimes government officials hamper the press and others from finding this information. The press, as one of its functions, is the watchdog on government. In that capacity, it sometimes finds itself in an adversarial position with regard to government. This can also interfere with the free flow of information.

DEVELOP A SENSE FOR NEWS

Students who want to be journalists should develop a "nose for news," a sixth sense. They should develop a curiosity about people, what they do and what makes them act as they do. Student journalists should have the ability to recognize a newsworthy event. Understanding the news elements already explained will help a student journalist develop an instinctive nose for news, which many of the best professional journalists have.

A reporter for a newspaper, yearbook, web site or broadcast program should begin to think of everything that happens that is of interest to students, whether at school or in the community, as a possible story. Reporters should tell their editor about all possible ideas. If they interest both the reporter and editor, they probably will interest others.

EXERCISES

1. Bring copies of your city's (or nearby city's) daily newspaper for five consecutive days to class. Examine page 1, especially the lead or top story for each day. Which of the elements of news can be found in each page 1 story?

2. Record one of the broadcast network's evening television newscasts. Show the recording in class, list all the stories and identify the elements of news in each story.

3. Analyze a news story on page 1 of a daily newspaper. Identify any opinion that is in the story. Is the opinion expressed by the reporter who wrote the story, or is it attributed to someone else whom the reporter quoted, indirectly or directly?

4. As a class, list five major news events from the past 10 years. For example, the 2003 war in Iraq could be one. Discuss how each of these events could again be a page 1 newspaper story or be reported on a broadcast news show.

5. Get two or more newspapers from different cities that were published on the same day. Examine page 1 to see what stories are covered. If there are different stories on page 1, how do you account for the differences? Which of the elements of news could have been considered by the editors that might explain the differences?

6. As a class, list all of the events that occurred during the past week at your school. Which ones are newsworthy and why? Rank the events from the most to least newsworthy.

7. Consider the idea that what is news for one person isn't news for another. As the publisher of a news medium, how could you provide news that would interest each subscriber? The news medium can be print, broadcast, online or other.

8. Why are these elements of news seemingly so interesting to so many people: prominence, sex and oddity? Do stories with mainly these elements in them deserve to be reported? Cite some examples from recent newspapers or broadcasts. Is coverage of these stories overshadowing coverage of other stories that have other elements of news in them?

Gathering News

Sitting in a newsroom in Phoenix, a reporter writes a story about the discovery of dinosaur bones in Africa's Sahara desert. At Chicago's O'Hare International Airport, another reporter, using a laptop computer, is filing a story to a newspaper in Atlanta about the just-announced selection of new inductees into the Rock and Roll Hall of Fame in Cleveland. In Dallas, a 16-year-old reporter completes a story on school shootings nationwide for the high school newspaper. While in Eugene, Ore., another teen reporter files a story on a proposed dress code for the school.

In 24 hours, this slice of journalism life is repeated by hundreds of thousands of journalists worldwide, including thousands reporting for high school media. There never is a "no news" day, and the work done by reporters for print, broadcast and online media never stops. With global telecommunications and massive amounts of information available to all reporters, regardless of age, a reporter has more sources available than ever before. Distance, cost, time and politics are no longer barriers for most reporters, even high school students. Daring the 1999 war in Kosovo, a high school broadcast journalist in California reported the war in a unique way through his email source, another teenager, in Kosovo. It is possible today to have the world as a news beat without ever leaving home.

For those who work in news media, there are three core considerations:

1. What is the story?

2. Where do I find the facts?

3. How do I report it?

With so much information available, a journalist has to distinguish what is news and worth reporting and what isn't. What is the story? In Chapter 1 of this textbook, news is defined as information that has one or more of these elements: immediacy or timeliness; proximity or nearness; consequence or impact; prominence; drama; oddity or unusualness; conflict; sex; emotions and instincts; and progress. A reporter looks at information with these elements in mind. If this information has at least one, but usually many, of these elements, it is newsworthy and may even be selected for publication. Not all news is published in every news medium because of space and time limitations.

PRIMARY VERSUS SECONDARY SOURCES

What often separates a good story from a better one is the quality of the sources used by the reporter, both in gathering the facts and in what is later published. To use the best possible sources is the goal, but sometimes a reporter, who can't always be on the scene or has limited time, has to settle for less. But less doesn't mean inferior or insufficient.

Two kinds of information sources are tapped by journalists, primary and secondary sources. Primary sources are eyewitnesses to an event or are the creators of an original work – a physical or intellectual property. Primary source information can be in print or other recorded form. A secondary source is a person who has some knowledge but didn't get it through personal involvement or is a published work that cites the words of others, words that have already been published in a primary source. Published work isn't restricted to print on paper, but includes tape, film and electronic files.

Journalists often get their information from both primary and secondary sources. Access and time may limit a reporter, but lack of either or both does not necessarily harm a story. Even though an eyewitness to a devastating flood in Texas lives 1,000 miles from a reporter, that reporter can conduct a phone interview with the eyewitness, who is a primary source of information. Even though a reporter has less than 10 hours to write a long story about the hurricane damage in North Carolina and the reporter lives 1,000 miles away and is writing for a Michigan newspaper, the reporter can get plenty of facts on previous hurricanes that damaged North Carolina from various internet databases. This retrieval of background or secondary source information takes minutes.

The quality of the primary and secondary sources is also a factor. Credibility and degree of involvement of eyewitnesses are worth considering. Are they the most expert persons available? Were they actively involved in the event being reported or did they just observe it from the sidelines? Is their age or some physical characteristic a factor? There are many ways to categorize and rank the potential credibility of the primary source, and the reporter will have to choose the best available source based on his or her judgment. Ideas, opinions and other intellectual property can be good primary sources if they are cited from the original works.

Other primary sources for news media include leaders and spokespersons for organizations, associations, political and social causes and government agencies, among others. Often, these persons are contacted regularly to get facts for a story and comments. These primary sources are sometimes part of a beat system (see below).

Some secondary information sources, such as the weekly newsmagazines *Time* and *Newsweek*, are cited by young journalists as sources of information for stories. Although these magazines are well written and credible, they are not the best secondary sources or the only sources easily available to students. Generally, student journalists should not get their story facts from or quote an expert's opinion published in newsmagazines or other popular culture periodicals. It's better to go to more scholarly sources. For example, a student reporter who is writing a story on teens and HIV infection rates can get information from a scholarly journal, such as the *New England Journal of Medicine*, or directly from in-person interviews or bulletins from the Center for Disease Control in Atlanta. For this reporter's story, these primary sources are better than the secondary sources *Time* and *Newsweek*.

A BEAT SYSTEM AND HOW IT WORKS

Not all news stories come knocking on the newsroom door. Reporters have to find them, and that's done through a systematic and routine procedure called the *beat system* (Fig. 2.1).

A beat system is a plan to cover routinely all potential news sources in a specific area. Each contact or information source is called a beat. For high school news media, beats can include these:

- Each academic department and its chair
- Each extracurricular or cocurricular activity, its faculty sponsor and its student leader
- The athletic department and its director
- The student activities department and its director
- The school principal
- The school's superintendent and district office
- The school board chair
- The guidance and counseling office
- The discipline office and director
- Student government officers
- Drama director
- Vocal and instrument music directors
- Cafeteria or food service director
- School transportation director
- School maintenance director

- Directors of any special, in-school programs such as for student mothers and their children

- Athletic conference office or director

- State education department office (public information and legislative affairs)

- City government youth liaison office; youth recreation; youth employment

- City organizations with youth outreach programs such as the Urban League

Beats can also be topical and not specially tied to a location or spokesperson. These kinds of beats require the reporter to make multiple contacts, perhaps in many distant locations. Some of these beats are

- The environment

- Popular music

- Fine arts

- Juvenile justice

- Presidential politics

- Travel

- Medicine, health, nutrition

- Money and finance

- Religion

- The internet

- Law

- Fashion

Debut intramural sports week a success

By Meredith Pierce
ENTERTAINMENT EDITOR

For the first time at TPHS, students and staff participated in Intramural Sports week to promote and encourage participation in intramural sports.

"It's a way to advertise and promote the program to the students. Since most intramural sports are after school, [the week] gives students who can't do it after school a chance to do it during lunch," Ashley Carrick (11), Commissioner of Intramural Sports, said.

Intramural Sports week was put on by the Associated Student Body for the duration of this week. Participants played ultimate Frisbee on Monday, soccer on Tuesday, Hula-Hoop and jump rope on Wednesday, plastic pin bowling today and they will have to traverse an obstacle course tomorrow.

"This year was an experimental year. We tried to do it last year but it was too short notice," Carrick said.

Carrick estimates around 15 people participated on Monday, increasing to 25 by Tuesday.

"The whole point [of intramural sports] is that Torrey Pines sports are so competitive and to get on a team is so ridiculous, that [intramural sports] allow students to play in a noncompetitive environment, play whenever they want, meet new people and even play sports they didn't make the team for," Carrick said.

The next intramural event will be volleyball, held on Mar. 26 in the gym.

PHOTOS BY MEREDITH PIERCE/FALCONER

CATCH IT IF YOU CAN: Brendan Boerbaitz (12) and Bryan Dworsky (11) play ultimate frisbee during lunch on Monday as a part of Intramural Sports week, held by the Associated Student Body. This is TPHS' first Intramural Sports week, held in hopes of promoting participation in intramural sports. Today at lunch there will be plastic pin bowling and tomorrow there will be an obstacle course.

Fig. 2.1. News beats, such as the school's district administrative office (Governor's proposed cuts story), athletic or school activities office (Intramural sports week story), school counselors' office (New SAT story) and curriculum director's and school administrator's offices (Pending Saturday classes story) can be a regular source of timely and significant stories. *Falconer*, Torrey Pines High School, San Diego, Calif.

All of these, and others, have student angles and are often of great interest to teen readers. High school reporters who cover these beats usually need a local or school tie-in to increase the relevance and potential impact of the story. For example, a travel story could focus on popular destinations for students during spring break. A story with a religion base could be about student missionaries or students who do church-related volunteer work.

These beats and others that may be unique to a community can be regular sources of information and possibly news for high school media. For example, a call or visit to the athletic director could lead to information about an upcoming sports banquet or changes in the composition of the athletic conference; a call or visit with the school's food service director could lead to information about menu

Fig. 2.2. To make newspapers that publish infrequently more timely and relevant, some yet-to-happen, advance stories are necessary ("Laugh-In opens Thursday"). *The A-Blast*, Annandale High School, Annandale, Va.

changes or statistics on food costs or wastage; a call or visit to the city's youth liaison office could lead to information about a summer employment program for teens; a call or visit with the school board office could lead to an advance copy of the agenda for the next meeting; and a call or visit to the state education department office could lead to information about a newly proposed, statewide testing program for all high school juniors.

To make a beat system work, one reporter should be assigned to each beat. If the staff is small, a reporter could cover more than one beat. Several weeks before each deadline and just before the content is finalized for the next edition of the paper or other news outlet, the reporter should phone or visit the beat's spokesperson and ask for any new information. Although the reporter is not conducting an interview, he or she should probe for as much information as possible, especially if it's a follow-up on a tip. The reporter should try to develop a cordial relationship with the spokesperson so information is given readily and completely.

A good reporter will get some information from a beat every time a contact is made. As the source or spokesperson gets to know the reporter, it is likely he or she will start collecting information to save for the reporter.

With the nearly universal use of email, a beat reporter can check with the source more frequently and even more quickly in some cases than with a phone call. However, personal contact is important too. Relying only on email could preclude the special rapport that often develops between two persons when they meet in person or talk on the phone. A mix of phone calls, personal visits and emails could be a workable goal. Good rapport between a reporter and regular source can be invaluable when a story is being developed that requires more than the usual amount of information.

When the news staff gathers to plan an issue of the newspapers or the next broadcast news program, each beat reporter can share story leads received from the beat spokesperson. Then the editors can decide if the information has enough news value to warrant a story.

A reporter who enjoys a particular beat, one that has a nonschool counterpart such as city government, nurtures sources and learns as much as possible about the subjects and contacts related to the beat, can begin a life-long career extending from high school journalism through the world of commercial media (Fig. 2.2).

OTHER CONTACTS AND INFORMATION SOURCES

Although beats are good for story tips, information and primary source interviews, there are other sources for news tips and information.

A master calendar of all school activities is likely kept in the school's office. At the beginning of the school year, the news staff should get a copy of this calendar. Each month, or even weekly, it should be updated. The calendar, or "datebook" as it is sometimes called, should be reviewed as each issue of the school newspaper, each broadcast news program and each update of an online news site is being planned. Since the reporting of future events – what will happen – is vital for monthly newspapers, it may even be useful to look more than one month ahead. Events scheduled on the calendar can be reviewed as potential stories.

The school's handbook is another useful reference for student journalists. An up-to-date version is necessary. It can provide background and may be cited as a source for a variety of stories such as ones about dress code, tardy and absence policies, and emergency building evacuation, among other topics. Since policies may be updated after a new school year has begun, it is important to verify the contents with school officials if information from the handbook is being cited in a story. The handbook can also be reviewed for possible opinion columns, editorials or other stories that examine school rules that may be ignored or not enforced.

A current student, faculty and staff directory is also useful to identify and locate sources. Although the directory may be reliable, a student journalist would be wise to double-check spellings of names with a phone directory to avoid errors, which may be embarrassing or even result in legal problems. The school may maintain its directory online. A directory published at the start of the school year may not be inclusive of all students and others as the year progresses; the newsroom should ask for an updated version periodically. There may be some privacy issues about the identification of sources: names and class affiliation are acceptable; home addresses are mostly unnecessary and are not published.

Bulletins from the school administrative, counseling, activities and other offices will likely be sources of news. These are often posted in the main or guidance office or in a public area. All student media should request a mailbox in the main office and request copies of these bulletins when they are distributed to the faculty and others.

Minutes from school board meetings, press releases and bulletins from the school's district office should also be reviewed by student journalists for possible story ideas and sources. With the exception of personnel records, these documents are open to the public and should be available to students.

Other resources that may be helpful to student journalists include, either in print, online or in CD or DVD form: telephone and city directories, zip code directory, encyclopedias, world almanac, biographical dictionary, various government databases and other books useful for copyediting.

School and city libraries have several other useful resources, especially to find background facts for a story. These are the indexes of magazine articles and include the *Readers' Guide to Periodical Literature* and the *Education Index*.

Press releases and bulletins from colleges, universities, technical schools, the armed forces, scholarship-granting agencies, U.S. government agencies, businesses (computer hardware and software and telecommunications are especially relevant), charities (volunteer opportunities) and other sources can also be leads for news and feature stories. Student journalism should usually not publish these releases without some verification of the information, editing and localizing the angle with some original interviews. A new lead should also be written. Press releases are often slanted to put the business or sponsor in the most favorable light. Consequently, journalists should be wary of accepting the content without some scrutiny. The journalist should ask: Is there legitimate news value in this information?

Back issues of the school newspaper and yearbook and tapes of previous broadcast news shows can be valuable sources of information for a reporter. Many stories are updates of some event or issue reported earlier. Other stories can be better reported if some relevant background – what happened in the past to lead up to this new development? – is included. If the story is essentially about a school-related event, then the most comprehensive account should have been published in a previous edition of the paper or news broadcast. Back issues of the school paper, a set of back volumes of the school yearbook and a tape library of former broadcasts should remain in the staff newsroom for this research purpose. Some papers are storing their back issues electronically; an electronic library is easily accessible and takes less storage space than print.

THE INTERVIEW

The most important and common way for a reporter to get information is through an interview with a person, called the "source." Facts can be found in previously published documents, available in print and online

Fig. 2.3. A mixture of inside-school ("Teachers wear blue" story) and outside-school ("Financial problems" story) comprises the content on page 1. *The Lowell*, Lowell High School, San Francisco, Calif.

form, but almost every story needs one or more primary sources. Fact-based reporting is more credible, professional and important to readers if there is evidence of firsthand reporting. If the reporter did not witness the event, then did he or she talk to those who did? This is an important reader expectation, and journalists need to satisfy it for the reader.

An interview can be as informal as asking someone in a crowd one question or a series of questions on the phone or through email. Or an interview can be formal, with an agreed-upon time and place and much advance research work by the reporter. Many stories combine every possible approach.

Student journalists must realize that writing a news or other journalism story is not like writing a term paper or essay for another class, where secondary source information sources may be all that is necessary to complete an assignment. For journalists, the secondary sources, though important, only provide background or some of the necessary information for a story.

Before any interview, other than spontaneously asking someone at the scene of an event a question or two, the reporter needs to do some research and even prepare questions. Exploration of any story begins at a news staff meeting when the story is assigned. The assignment editor, reporter and others brainstorm for potential information sources, including personal interviews, and angles for development of the story. Even a story that may be slotted as a "news brief" – restricted to one or a few paragraphs – will likely mean the reporter has to talk with at least one source. Longer stories, with many facts and different angles to develop, will usually lead the reporter to multiple sources and several personal interviews (Fig. 2.3).

Once the story has been discussed and especially if the reporter knows little or nothing about the subject, the reporter needs to research at least the basic, established facts, if any exist. This research will help the reporter frame the questions that will be asked during the interviews. The research will also help during the writing stage following the interviews. In addition to researching the subject, a reporter may also find it useful to research the person being interviewed, especially if he or she is noteworthy and is connected in more than a circumstantial way to the subject.

Depending upon the complexity of the subject and the anticipated depth of the interview, the reporter prepares a list of questions following the initial research of the subject and the interviewee. Doing this does not mark the reporter as a beginner; veteran journalists often do this to help ensure a successful interview.

Prepared questions help a reporter conduct a complete interview. Fear and nervousness could cause a reporter to forget some or all of the questions. If they are written, it is less likely that this will happen; it also means the reporter will only have to write the source's responses.

The prepared list should begin with one or several easy questions that help establish a comfortable, trusting rapport between the reporter and the source. Even before the first question is asked, it is acceptable and often beneficial for a very brief amount of "small talk" to happen. The reporter could comment on the weather or note something interesting about the location or some items in the room. These openers or icebreakers often help the interviewee feel at ease. However, some powerful, tightly scheduled persons want to get right to the point of the interview. The reporter needs to be flexible. The reporter also needs to be in control of the interview: If the source wanders off the topic and the new information isn't newsworthy, the reporter needs to bring the source back to the topic at the first opportunity.

Often, the interviewee expects the reporter to know the basics of the subject and will be displeased if time is "wasted" with background questions.

Interview questions often relate to the basic reader questions, the "5 *W*'s and *H*" – what, who, where, when, why and how. Although all six of these basic questions should give the reporter facts, it is the "why" and "how" that need to be emphasized during the interview. Answers to these will more likely give quotable material and a more interesting insight of the topic. As a reporter writes the prepared questions, the "5 *W*'s and *H*" should all be considered.

Questions that could result in a yes, no, maybe or "I don't know" response should be rewritten to potentially get a more complete answer with concrete details:

Poor
Will the benefit dance raise money for the school's athletic budget?

Better
What programs will benefit financially from the money raised at the dance?

The first question will likely get a yes or no response. The reporter should know the answer to this before the interview takes place. The second question will likely get concrete details. The first question would be acceptable if a "What programs will benefit?" follow-up question was asked.

To avoid sounding stiff and too formal, a reporter should not actually read the questions word for word. Rather, the reporter can glance at the prepared questions, note some key words and then casually ask it while looking at the source rather than at a piece of paper. As a reporter does more interviews, this becomes easier to do.

During the course of the interview, the reporter, even while taking notes, must have passing eye contact with the source and listen carefully to the responses. Listening is something reporters have to do well. A reporter should not try to impress a source with how much he or she knows; the purpose of the interview is to find out what the source knows.

Even though a reporter has prepared questions, the need to ask new questions to follow up an unexpected, unclear or incomplete comment made by the source is always possible. Veteran reporters say that some of their best stories have come from unexpected or new information that came up during routine questioning. Reporters need to be ready to deviate from their prepared list of questions and pursue a new area; they can return to the original list later.

For accuracy, a reporter needs to take notes during an interview. If the source agrees, the interview can be taped or digitally recorded. Doing both may be desirable. The notes will help the reporter write the story more quickly than can be done if only a tape recorder is used. The recording will be especially helpful for the accuracy of direct quotes. Many reporters develop their own note-taking shorthand. They may leave out the articles "a," "an" and "the," spell words without vowels or abbreviate long words – whatever helps them take notes efficiently and quickly. Immediately following an interview, a reporter should review the notes to complete sentences and add missing details. The story should be written as soon as possible after all interviews have been completed.

The time to verify facts and opinions given during an interview is during the interview. If something is unclear or incomplete, if statistics are too complex or given too quickly by the source, or if the opinion given is unusual or potentially controversial, the reporter should repeat the fact or statistic or read the statement back to the source and ask if it is correct. It is also acceptable to follow up an interview with a phone call to verify information and statements. It is not professional to show a completed story to a source for approval before publication. If a source retracts a statement – denies making it originally – that contradiction could be used as part of the story. It is important for reporters to take accurate notes and to save these notes and any recordings for some time following publication of the story.

Tips for conducting a successful interview:

- Research the subject and the source (interviewee).

- Make an appointment.

- Prepare a list of questions.

- Create some shortcuts for note-taking, including abbreviations.

- Bring a pocket-size recorder; make sure it has fresh batteries and it works.

- Bring a notebook – something with a hard surface so you can write on your lap – and two pens (one may run out of ink).

- Wear clean, suitable clothes. Shower and wear deodorant but don't wear cologne or perfume (distracting and possibly offensive).

- Arrive on time or a few minutes early. If you are going to be unavoidably late, phone and give an estimated time of arrival.

- Introduce yourself as a reporter (always) and give the name of your news medium.

- Smile and say something friendly to break the ice. Don't sit until you've been invited to sit or ask where you may sit.

- If you brought a recorder, ask permission to record the interview.

- Turn on the recorder, open your notebook, make eye contact with the source and begin.

- Ask one or two easy questions, ones that aren't threatening to the source.

- Ask the tougher questions. Make eye contact.

- Ask follow-up questions to get examples or explanations: "Could you give me an example?" "Could you explain that?" These are not on your prepared questions list, but they need to be asked.

- Follow up unanticipated responses or new information with new, spontaneous questions. Quickly add these new questions (using some shorthand) to your questions list in your notebook.

- Ask the source to repeat any facts, statistics you don't understand or information you missed because the source was talking too quickly. Check the spellings of names given by the source in his or her responses.

- Ask the source if you can repeat something he or she said if you think it is unusual or controversial or if you want to quote it in your story. You want to get it right.

- Ask your last question.

- Ask the source if she or he has anything else to say.

- Quickly check your list of prepared questions to verify that you asked all of them. This is especially important if the source wandered off the topic.

- If you agreed upon a time limit for the interview, try to respect that agreement or ask if you could have a few more minutes.

- Quickly note the setting and any incidentals in the location that could add color to the story or reveal something more about the source. This observation could lead to a new question or two.

- Thank the source. Make eye contact and smile.

- Give the source your phone number or email address and ask the source to call you if he or she has anything more to say.

- Turn off your recorder and take your notebook and recorder with you.

Some sources are reluctant to talk or are shy. Public officials have a duty to talk to the media; private persons don't have to. By looking professional and being polite and considerate, a reporter will likely put the uncomfortable source at ease. Brief small talk also helps. When an interview appointment is made, ask the source when it would be best for him or her to be interviewed; that will also reduce some tension. Being punctual will also help. Sometimes some charm or a compliment can disarm an unfriendly source. Tough questions – ones that may reflect negatively on the source – should be asked carefully and in a respectful tone of voice. If the source does not answer, the tough question could be rephrased and asked again. Probably the question should not be pursued if no answer is given after two attempts. In the story, the reporter can write that the source "declined" to comment on whatever the subject was; writing "refused" to comment is harsh and has a different connotation than "decline."

Reporters should be especially careful when they interview a source who is involved in a personal tragedy. Media, especially broadcast, have a tendency to be intrusive during large-scale disasters and small but violent accidents. A reporter should respect the wishes of the immediate survivors and the dignity of the dead as much as possible and still report the event. By being courteous, showing appreciation for the dire circumstances and asking questions politely and gently, a reporter may get access more easily to information from survivors and others close to the event than reporters who are uncaring and confrontational.

Phone and in-person interviews are somewhat alike. In a phone interview, a reporter will not be able to include details about the person's appearance, mannerisms or surroundings. However, phone interviews save time and are a common way all reporters get information and comments. Phone interviews can be taped, but in many states it is illegal to tape people over the phone without their permission. It may be just as important, depending upon the availability of the source, to make an advance appointment for a phone interview. As in every interview situation, the reporter identifies himself or herself by name and as a reporter for a specific news medium. Phone interviews are usually not long; interviews for long stories, especially personality profiles, are best done in person.

Interviews can also be conducted by email on the internet. In some ways they are like phone interviews; usually you are not observing the source and are unable to note physical details. However, the email interview has advantages: Responses are already written, thus eliminating note-taking, and the responses can be made at a time when it is convenient for the source. The email responses may also be more carefully written and so more coherent than answers given in person or over the phone. This can be good and troublesome. Responses may have more substance, but they also may be less conversational, more formal. Readers may not find the resulting interview story as "human" as one that followed an in-person interview.

An email interview can be followed up with a phone call to the source to verify important facts and unusual or controversial comments. A reporter may want to verify that the person who responded to the email was really the source; some email names and addresses are cryptic.

Reporters can assume that an interview is "on the record" (for publication) as long as they identify themselves as a reporter. Sometimes a source will say that something is "off the record" (not for publication). The reporter has to decide whether to accept this change. There is no rule all journalists follow. However, if a reporter agrees to listen to something that is off the record, then the reporter should clearly understand exactly when the interview is back on the record. When a source is talking on the record, everything that is said can be quoted directly or indirectly and attributed by name to the source. However, just because there is an assumption that the interview is on the record doesn't mean that the reporter is obligated to use all of the facts and comments given by the source during the interview.

INFORMATION ON THE INTERNET

The internet links reporters to information stored on computers throughout the world. What used to take reporters hours and days to find in libraries, court houses, print reference books and through phone calls now takes minutes to find on the internet. The blessing: speed and a wealth of information. The curse: too much, often unedited information for most users, some of the sources are unreliable and some information isn't true.

No one can deny that the vast amount of information now easily accessible to reporters has enriched stories published in print, online and broadcast. More and better statistics from databases representing a wide variety of government and other public and private agencies have added more depth to stories. Student reporters for the *Falconer* newspaper at Torrey Pines High School in San Diego have the same access to these available databases as the reporters for the San Diego *Union-Tribune*, a commercial newspaper. The internet is the great equalizer.

The internet is also a useful communications link for a reporter and a source. Once information pertinent to a story is found by a student reporter in a database on the internet, that reporter can contact a person connected to the information through email or a phone call. A student in Mountlake Terrace, Washington, can email an official in Washington, D.C., and ask questions about teenagers incarcerated in federal prisons for a story on capital punishment. A traffic accident resulting in a death led a reporter for the *Pilot's Log* student newspaper in Hasbrouck Heights, N.J., to the internet for information on all vehicle accidents involving pedestrians in Hasbrouck Heights in one year (Fig. 2.4). Once the information is found in public records, the reporter can phone or email a city official to verify the facts. This internet search resulted in a sidebar to the main story in the *Pilot's Log*.

While reporters have increasingly used the internet as a tool for reporting, they haven't abandoned the other methods of gathering information. Reporters still

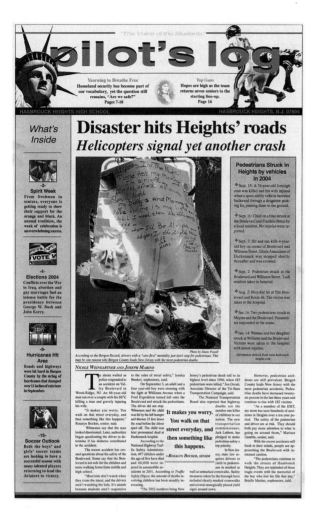

Fig. 2.4. The reporter found relevant information on the internet for this story and sidebar. *Pilot's Log*, Hasbrouck Heights High School, Hasbrouck Heights, N.J.

conduct in-person and telephone interviews and still consult print resources (a phone directory for example) for information. The internet has added to a reporter's "bag of tricks" and not decreased it.

To take advantage of all the information available on the internet, a reporter needs to know where to look. Many journalists who work at commercial media have access to the subscription database Nexus Lexus. For a price, a journalist can find specific information easily. Few student journalists have access to Nexus Lexus or similar dedicated pay-for-access services.

The reporter for the *Pilot's Log* went directly to the town's website where public information such as traffic accident statistics are available. However, if a specific web address is not known or if a reporter wants to see if more information is available other than at the known address, a journalist will go to a "search engine" (a website with an electronic researcher) that finds information. There is often a list of other websites that include everything from a brief reference to extensive information on the subject. Various search engines are available and each prioritizes its search results according to its own standards. Depending upon the breadth of the search, the results could number into the thousands or more. How to conduct a worthwhile search and manage, interpret and trust the results are important things for a journalist to learn.

Using a search engine to find information is usually one of the early steps a reporter takes in gathering news. Often, with the advice of an editor, the story is first framed for its news value and direction and narrowed in its scope, though not at the risk of overlooking new and maybe more important facts uncovered during the reporting process. Once the story is framed, the reporter can go to a search engine and ask some questions or enter some key words to learn more about the subject and find some useful sources to contact.

Although Google (www.google.com) is the most popular search engine, the following search engines should also be checked: Yahoo (www.search.yahoo.com), MSN (www.search.msn.com), AltaVista (www.altavista.com), HotBot (www.hotbot.com), Ask Jeeves (www.ask.com) and Lycos (www.lycos.com). AOL has a search feature, but it uses a Google database. Other search engines are also on the internet. Different search engines will likely provide some different results.

To do a search on one of these internet search engines, it's wise for a reporter to save time – there could be millions of references – and do the following:

1. If the search engine offers any shortcuts or "help" advice in its menu, the reporter should try them. This can save time, especially if the search is wide and could yield abundant leads.

2. Choose the keyword or keywords or plain-English (standard language) sentence search method. Be precise or try alternate ways to refer to something or someone.

3. Even though a search engine presents a list of web addresses in some hierarchical form, it's wise to review the entire list or at least several dozen. A reporter who has a good sense of what news is, and what facts may be important, will likely be a better judge of the site's value than a new reporter.

4. Review the site's domain addresses given in the search. Addresses that end in "gov" (government) may be the best sites to go to first if the reporter is looking for a senator's voting record or the number of Native Americans living in a particular state, for example. Depending upon what kind of information the reporter is searching for, an examination of the sites' addresses can steer him or her to the best source, although all sites could be reviewed if the reporter has enough time. Web addresses include:

- com (commercial businesses and some personal sites)

- biz (commercial businesses)

- edu (educational institutions)

- net (internet networks such as EarthLink and some personal sites)

- gov (government agencies)

- org (nonprofit organizations and some personal sites)

- mil (U.S. military facilities)

- coop (nonprofit cooperatives)

- info (information)

- name (individual)

- pro (accountants, lawyers, physicians)

For other domains, including new ones, the reporter can check with the website of the group that assigns domains, the internet Corporation for Assigned Names and Numbers: www.icann.org.

The internet is international, so some websites are at computers outside the United States. Many of these web addresses end in a two-letter abbreviation for the country. For example, "ca" is Canada, "uk" is the United Kingdom and "es" is Spain. Some search engines allow the user to search by domain, including countries.

If the reporter doesn't already know the web addresses, selection of the keyword or words or plain-English sentence for the search is one of the most important steps toward using the internet successfully in news gathering.

On Google, the reporter can follow these suggestions for an easier and more direct keyword search:

1. For a plain-English question, ask it directly and precisely, using as many words as necessary. For example: "When was the iPod first sold?"

2. For a phrase search, type the phase surrounded by double quotation marks. For example: "iPod sales"

3. For a multiple words and phrases search, in which each must be present (an "and" search), type the words (or phrases in quotation marks) separated by a space, without any special punctuation and use a plus sign (+) only if one of the words is a common word but important to the search. Common words are called "stopwords" by Google and they are ignored. For example: Steve Jobs "iPod introduction" or +about iPod Steve Jobs

4. For a multiple words and phrases search, any one of which may be present (an "or" search), type words or phrases with no quotation marks but separated by "OR" in all caps. For example: iPod OR digital music players

5. For a search to exclude a word or phrase (a "not" search), use a minus sign (−) directly in front of the word to be excluded. For example: iPod −"Steve Jobs"

6. For a date search – information within a specific time range – choose from within the last three or six months or one year. The reporter can find this on the Google menu under advanced search options.

These are some of the ways the reporter can use Google effectively for keyword or question searches. Google has other search options and the other search engines offer similar help. Some search engines rely more heavily upon the first word of the keywords.

Reporters may also want to do a subject directory search on a search engine site if the site has this option. This type of search may help remove some of the irrelevant clutter that comes with keyword searches that may be too broad. Some professional reporters prefer to begin with a subject directory search.

Many websites have a "contact us" in their menu. To verify the truthfulness of the information on a site, the reporter should contact someone in an official capacity with the site's sponsor by email or a phone call and conduct an interview. This is an example of the reporter or the editor judging the site based on domain, or reputation of the site or sponsor and an assessment of the content found on the site. As with all stories, double-check important facts including spellings. If information from an internet search is used in a story, the story will likely be more credible if it also has facts and opinions gathered from in-person or phone interviews. Information from the internet should be attributed to the source as it would be done with information derived from an interview, press release, press conference or other means. For the internet, the attribution should be to the website, sponsor and the writer if known. Republishing some or all of a story from a website without copyright permission is plagiarism. Rewriting information found on the web without attribution is unethical.

Some useful websites for reporters, including students who localize national and international stories, include these:

www.splc.org/ltr_sample.html

Maintained by the Student Press Law Center, this site provides a sample letter for students to use to request public records from government bodies, with appropriate language for each state.

www.census.gov/star_abstract

Maintained by the U.S. Census Bureau, this site helps journalists get a wide range of statistics on various economic and social aspects of the U.S. population.

www.congress.org

Learn about and contact all U.S. Senators and Representatives

www.firstgov.gov

Directory and search engine for all federal and state governments.

www.thomas.loc.gov

Named after Thomas Jefferson, this site contains all federal legislation, voting records of members of congress and their email addresses, among other useful information.

www.nytimes.com

The New York Times is a good resource for background information on all national and international events.

www.profnet.com

Database of professionals and experts on a wide range of subjects who can be contacted as sources for stories.

www.robertniles.com

Advice on how to use the internet to research a story.

www.journaliststoolbox.com

Online resources for reporters and editors.

www.espn.go.com

This cable sports network site is a good resource for reporters who write about professional, collegiate and other sports.

www.ncaa.org

Maintained by the National Collegiate Athletic Association, this site can be used for information for sports stories about college athletics and eligibility standards.

www.billboard.com

Reporters who write about popular music and concerts will find this site to be a helpful resource.

These and many other websites with specialized information can be useful during all the reporting and writing stages. Since new sites are added to the internet daily, it is advantageous for a reporter to periodically update his or her list of web contacts.

Student reporters should bookmark and regularly check the websites for their local and state capital newspapers, state and local governments and their own schools; these can be valuable resources for current and archival information for stories with local and state roots.

Websites maintained by scholastic press groups, including the National Scholastic Press Association, Journalism Education Association, Columbia Scholastic Press Association and Quill and Scroll, may also have information that could assist a reporter.

Reporters can subscribe to electronic mailing lists or "Listservs" from a wide variety of special interest groups, government bodies and others. Not all the information or postings sent are going to be reliable; as always, a reporter should verify any information received this way with other sources. However, an electronic mailing list can be another valuable source. To locate the most useful lists for a story or beat, a reporter can go to the www.reference.com website and search by keyword for the most appropriate ones to subscribe to. On the site's home page, select electronic mailing list directory.

Newsgroups and Google groups are sites on the internet where persons with similar interests can gather electronically and enter messages about related topics. These groups operate on the internet's Usenet system and on Google (www.groups.google.com). This can be useful for a reporter to find sources and experts, gather background information, pose questions and generally gauge the current interest and opinions on various issues. Newsgroups and Google groups are unlike Listservs in one important way: once a person subscribes to a mailing list, messages are automatically sent to the subscriber's email box; to participate in a newsgroup, the person has to actively go to the site on the internet to read the posted messages and add any new ones.

Newsgroups are organized on the internet into categories:

- alt (alternative newsgroups; fringe groups)
- biz (business related)
- comp (computer related)
- misc (catch-all, jobs, sales and more)
- news (concerns about Usenet network only)
- rec (recreation and hobbies)
- sci (science related)
- soc (social issues, concerns, popular culture).

Google, Yahoo, AOL and other search engines have special interest groups or communities that can be tapped as resources by journalists.

To help a reporter find the most appropriate newsgroup to join and monitor, there is another search engine other than Google, Yahoo or AOL to check: www.cyberfiber.com.

EXERCISES

1. Plan a beat system for your school newspaper. List 12 or more different sources of information, departments or offices in your school, a contact person or spokesperson for that beat, and the contact's phone number and email address.

2. Prepare a beat system for six specific interest groups outside of the school, such as MADD (Mothers Against Drunk Driving), travel or intercollegiate sports. List a contact or spokesperson for each group and that person's phone number and email address.

3. Prepare a list of six things you should not do during an in-person interview. Share your list with the class and discuss, as a class, the "dos and don'ts" of an interview. Do two short mock interviews in class, with one demonstrating several mistakes and the other done correctly.

4. As a class, select a popular topic, one that is "in the news," such as assisted suicides or the legalization of marijuana for the treatment of illnesses. Each person in the class should randomly select another person in the class to interview about the topic. Each student should write five prepared questions and then conduct an interview. Follow-up and new questions should be encouraged. Each student will be an interviewer and interviewee.

5. Each student should select one person within the school or in the community who is a leader or spokesperson for a department, special interest group, organization or other agency to interview either in person or on the phone. Acting as a news staff, the class should discuss each "story" and suggest angles and sources of background information to help the "reporter" prepare questions. Following

this "news staff meeting," each student should prepare for the interview by researching the person and topic, writing advance questions and calling the person for an appointment. The student should conduct the interview. Afterward, the student should submit to the teacher for evaluation the advance questions, the responses received during the interview and any new or follow-up questions and responses (a transcript of the interview). Later, following the completion of Chapter 4, "Writing the News Story," the student could write a story based on this interview.

6. Using print or online resources, students should find these facts: (1) the came of the 36th president of the United States; (2) the population of France; (3) the highest-grossing film of 1999 and amount; (4) the NBA (basketball) team with the most championship titles; (5) the names of three special interest groups that focus on the environment; (6) the spelling of the name of the president of South Africa; (7) the number of time zones on earth; (8) how the Roman Catholic pope is selected; (9) all the countries bordering Hungary; (10) stock market abbreviations for Microsoft, General Electric and Sony; (11) the meaning of the abbreviation GMT; (12) three possible or alternate spellings for the surname Anderson.

7. List 10 web sites that have information on pregnancy rates among unmarried teens in the United States in the last five years.

8. List three newsgroups that posted messages within the last two years about anorexia.

9. Develop a strategic search for information on teenage suicides in the United States for a story you could write for your school newspaper. List as many resources as you can, including several persons you could interview either in person, on the telephone or through email and 10 or more print and online sources of information.

10. Review the web sites of these two organizations and write a brief summary of what they do and what they offer on their web sites: Center for Investigative Reporting and National Institute for Computer-Assisted Reporting.

Writing News Leads

Except for the barely audible drone of the computer and someone talking on a mobile phone in another cubicle, the newsroom is silent. A reporter sits in front of a glowing monitor, impatient keyboard and restless mouse. An empty window waits, offering a wealth of choices on its menu. It's a window of opportunity for the reporter, who is about to begin writing. Newly on the job and armed with copious notes, the reporter momentarily wonders where to begin.

Begin at the beginning: Write the lead – that's what the reporter wants to do. It's the logical place to start. And like all good stories, this one needs to begin with the right words and a tantalizing hook that will, it is hoped, attract some readers or listeners. The reporter knows that there are thousands of other stories that will be written today, and all of them will be waiting for an audience. As the reporter writes, the audience is getting busier and more distracted than ever.

Given the nearly universal complaint today – too many choices, not enough time – it's no wonder that print media are in fierce competition with broadcast and electronic media for readers, listeners and viewers. For print media to compete successfully with other, more immediate information services, they have to package their content in a visually appealing way. When it comes to packaging writing, it means beginning a story with something that will grab the reader's attention due to its relevance or unique personal appeal. A reporter must rise to this challenge with each story.

A headline, accompanying photo or other art can bring a reader to the story, but there will have to be some carefully chosen words to make the reader continue into the body of the story and even reach the story's end. These first words – typically less than 40 – form the lead (pronounced *leed*) of the story. Many veteran news writers think the lead is the most important element of a news story. At the very least it is pivotal in the goal of achieving high readership of a story.

Simply, if you want someone to read your story, write a great beginning.

In daily newspapers, most timely and featured news stories are written in the traditional news form, the inverted pyramid. Facts are presented in decreasing order of importance. The inverted pyramid wasn't always the form of choice for the daily press: The narrative form – often called "storytelling" – was popular through the mid-19th century. During the Civil War, news bulletins from the battlefronts, with timely updates on the war's progress, were received at newspaper offices and printed at the top of the story. The "older" news fell a few notches lower in the story.

Eventually, prioritizing the facts from the latest information and often the most important to the less timely information and often least important became the common practice. The beginning or lead for the inverted pyramid story was almost always a brief summary of the most up-to-date and important facts. The news summary lead remains a popular choice today for those who write for the daily press.

High school print media, especially newspapers, are mostly published monthly; some are published weekly. This frequency factor, compared with dailies, means the inverted pyramid, with its characteristic news summary lead, has limited value.

One Story, Six Possible Leads

The *who* beginning:

Los Angeles Board of Education members agreed today to extend the current school year for some one million area public school students until July 20. The 15 additional school days were added to make up for the time when schools were closed due to the October earthquake.

The *what* beginning:

The current school year will be extended until July 20 as the result of a vote today by the Los Angeles Board of Education. Some one million area public school students will have to spend 15 more days in school due to the school closure following last October's earthquake.

The *where* beginning:

In Los Angeles today, the Board of Education extended the current school year until July 20 for some one million area public school students. The 15 additional school days were added to make up for the time when schools were closed due to the October earthquake.

The *when* beginning:

Today, the Los Angeles School Board extended the current school year until July 20 for some one million area public school students. The 15 additional school days were added to make up for the time when schools were closed due to the October earthquake.

The *why* beginning:

To make up for the time when schools were closed due to last October's earthquake, the Los Angeles Board of Education agreed today to extend the current school year to July 20 for some one million area public school students. Fifteen more days were added to the school calendar.

There are few breaking news stories in the school newspaper and perhaps none in the yearbook. School news web sites may break news if they update content frequently. If school newspapers use the news summary lead and a traditional inverted pyramid form for stories that already happened a week or more before the paper is published, they risk low readership. The central issue: Who wants to read old news, especially if it hasn't been updated? However, the inverted pyramid, with its signature news summary lead, is a useful form for advance stories in the school paper and, in a modified form, for most other stories.

Here is a story in inverted pyramid form with a news summary lead.

SGA members hold votes on School Council

Two seniors hold voting seats on the School Council, Lee's largest governing body.

SGA president Patricia Lopez and SGA member Alison Douglass attend weekly council meetings after school and vote equally with other members.

Lopez said all council members encourage the students to give their input because they often have ideas different from adult members.

"They have one way of thinking, and we have another," Lopez said.

According to Council Chair Mike Cooley, both students see things from a student's angle that adult members may not see.

"They give us a student perspective on issues around the school," Cooley said. "We often ask for their opinions and are given insight we wouldn't have."

Cooley said they were instrumental in approving student surveys, a duty of the School Council. One survey had been approved by all adult members, but when read by both students, neither understood it. The council then asked for changes to be made.

"If the students didn't understand it, what's the sense of putting it out?" Cooley said.

Although both students have been present for discussions such as B lunch, MU, the school plan and a time-out room policy, the only issue the School Council has formally voted on this year has been the teacher of the year. Government teacher Adrienne Green was selected.

The School Council is a school governing body, comprised of 13 faculty members, one parent and two students, the SGA president and another student selected from the SGA class.

The School Council makes decisions on issues such as the three-year school plan, which will be submitted to Area 1 before Dec. 21.

Lance
Robert E. Lee High School
Springfield, Va.

In the above story, the most important information – two students serve on an important, decision-making council – is in the lead, the first paragraph of the story. The next most important information – the names of these two students – is in paragraph two. Usually, the first thing a reader wants to know is "what happened?" The next natural question is "who was involved?" The first two, brief paragraphs in this story answer both of these questions. The other paragraphs in this story answer other, less important questions and further describe what happened through the "voices" of those who are involved.

THE NEWS SUMMARY LEAD

Also called a "direct" or "hard news lead," the news summary lead gets readers immediately to the main point of the article. A well-written news summary lead gives structure to the rest of the story.

To write an effective news summary lead, the reporter needs to review all the facts and opinions gathered for a story. Six important reader questions must be answered in each news story:

1. *What* happened? *What* will happen next?

2. *Who* was involved?

3. *Where* did it happen?

4. *When* did it happen?

5. *Why* did it happen?

6. *How* did it happen?

The news writer may even organize his or her notes in an informal outline form, writing these questions and then answering them. Once the writer is satisfied with the answers, the news summary lead will be easy to write.

Usually, the *what* and *who* are the most important of these six questions. With this in mind, the writer can begin with either the *what* (what happened?) or the *who* (who was involved?) answers. If the person or persons involved are prominent – well known – then the *who* can begin the lead.

Here is a news summary lead that begins with *what* will happen for an advance story.

> **A meeting is to be held with administrators and parents today to discuss the switch from selling Coke to Pepsi on campus. The transition was made in compliance with a contract change that took effect this year.**

Stagg Line
Amos Alonzo Stagg High School
Stockton, Calif.

The main *what* fact in this lead is "a meeting." There are other *what* facts in the second sentence, including "Coke," "Pepsi" and "contract." The *who* facts, which follow the *what*, are "administrators" and "parents."

The *how* beginning:

By a vote today, the Los Angeles Board of Education extended the current school year to July 20 for some one million area public school students. The 15 additional days were added to make up for the time when schools were closed due to the October earthquake.

All of these leads are acceptable, but some are better than others. The *what* and the *why* are direct and begin with more important facts. The *who* and the *how* are somewhat important; the *when* and *where* are not very important.

In this lead and follow-up paragraph, a *who* fact begins the story.

> Area students now have the opportunity to receive high school credit by using the internet.
>
> The program offering the credit is called Virtual High School. It allows students to choose from more than 105 semester and year-long classes.

Lakewood Times
Lakewood High School
Lakewood, Ohio

The *who* in this lead, "area students," is general. The *what*, "an opportunity," is also not specific. The follow-up paragraph expands the *what* and provides more details. This is a common way to develop an inverted pyramid story with a news summary lead. This lead is also an example of the effectiveness of a simple, declarative sentence in newswriting. The subject ("students") is first, followed by the verb ("have") and then the receiver or object of the action ("opportunity"). Newswriting should be conversational in most cases.

Another news summary lead that begins with the *who* fact and expands on it with more details also answers nearly all of the essential reader questions.

> One of the most recognizable figures in women's basketball, Los Angeles Sparks center Lisa Leslie, will speak at the annual Women's History Assembly March 8. Leslie, a three-time collegiate All-American, Olympic gold medalist and WNBA all-star will be the first speaker in the school's history to high-light the increasing contributions of women in athletics.

Chronicle
Harvard–Westlake School
North Hollywood, Calif.

Many facts can be included in a news summary lead without it becoming too long, awkward to read and ineffective. In the following example, the *what* question is answered first, but the other reader questions are also answered.

> A policy designed to control all forms of school sponsored expression will be presented at the Peninsula School Board meeting Thursday, April 22, for possible implementation.

Peninsula Outlook
Peninsula High School
Gig Harbor, Wash.

News summary leads can begin with any of the other reader questions: *where*, *when*, *why* and *how*. An example of a lead that begins with the *where* angle:

> Nevada is getting its first taste of the impact of charter schools with the opening of the I Can Do Anything High School in Washoe County. Charter schools offer alternatives to traditional schools, although they are funded through the public school system.

Excalibur
Robert McQueen High School
Reno, Nev.

Beginning with the *where*, the location of what happened, is sometimes the best choice to open a story. Proximity or nearness is one of the key news elements. Localizing a story will make the facts at least seem more relevant to readers.

An example of a lead that opens with the *when* angle and a follow-up paragraph that shows effective parallel construction:

> April 20, the nation watched in horror as students in Littleton, Colorado, fled their blood-stained Columbine High School.
>
> April 21, two incidents at LHS involving threats prompted school officials to intervene, although principal Vince Barra said the Littleton incident was not the reason.

Lakewood Times
Lakewood High School
Lakewood, Ohio

An example of a lead that begins with the *why* angle, this is also called beginning with an **infinitive** ("To look . . ."):

> To look for suggestions to improve the outlook of the community, a public meeting May 10 at Naperville North High School will discuss the results of the Search Institute Profiles of Student Life.

Central Times
Naperville Central High School
Naperville, Ill.

An example of a lead that opens with the *how* angle, this is also called beginning with a **present participle** ("Rejecting . . ."):

> Rejecting an appeal to a school's expanded drug testing program, the Supreme Court ruled last month that schools have the power to extend drug-tests to all students involved in extracurricular activities.

Falconer
Torrey Pines High School
Encinitas, Calif.

The infinitive and present participle lead openers are called **subordinate clauses**. Although a subordinate clause delays briefly the subject–verb–object flow of the declarative sentence form, it is acceptable for news writers to use them. In addition to the infinitive and present participle openers, there are others writers can use.

Begin with a **prepositional phrase**: a group of words beginning with a preposition and not containing a subject and a verb.

> After two years of discussion, the banning of book bags will become a school policy effective at the beginning of next school year.

Blue & Gold
Findlay High School
Findlay, Ohio

Begin with a **gerund**: the *ing* form of noun becomes the subject.

> Flying planes has always been David Ashamalla's ('99) dream. Last year, Ashamalla competed in aviation at the Skills USA competition, another step towards becoming a pilot.

Lion
Lyons Township High School North Campus
LaGrange, Ill.

Begin with a **temporal** clause: a period of time is an important fact.

> After months of anticipation and the loss of half of the teacher's parking lot, construction on the new library, theater and other bond improvements officially began Wednesday, March 31.

Edition
L.C. Anderson High School
Austin, Texas

Begin with a **conditional** clause: express speculative interest or a condition. If *this* happens, then *that* will happen.

> If the Board of Education's planned budget is approved by the Dare County Board of Commissioners, a debt of approximately $19,000 created by the athletic department will finally be eliminated.
>
> According to Mary Ann Bohannon, finance officer for MHS, the debt has been accumulating for the past several years.

Sound to Sea
Manteo High School
Manteo, N.C.

Begin with a **concessive** clause, a subordinate clause that begins with *though* or *although* and expresses either circumstances that make a result unusual or difficulties overcome.

> Although former principal Jim Blanche left West to be superintendent of schools, some will probably be seeing his face

around the halls of West between now and the end of the year.

Except this time he might be a substitute teacher.

Beak 'n' Eye
West High School
Davenport, Iowa

A well-written news summary lead does not have to answer all of the reader's questions – *what*, *who*, *where*, *when*, *why* and *how* – in the first sentence or even the first paragraph. A second sentence in the lead paragraph or a follow-up paragraph can include facts that answer all or most of the remaining ones. Although *when* and *where* lead openers can be effective as the above examples illustrate, they are usually less important and less interesting than the *what*, *who*, *why* and *how* openers. To begin with a date that has no significance is usually a weak start. Writers should think about all the facts and select the most important one for the lead opener. This is sometimes called the **feature fact**. Knowledge of the elements of news, found in Chapter 1 of this book, is helpful in determining the feature fact.

Although reporters should not write according to a formula or follow too closely restrictive guidelines on structure, a good news lead is often about 35 words or one or two sentences. Certainly, good leads of one word to more than 35 words have been written, including some for the best, prize-winning stories in journalism history. However, short sentences and paragraphs are easier for people to read.

A news lead often cites the source of the news. This gives the story and the newspaper credibility.

Here is an example of a news lead with the source of the facts cited.

Stony Point High School has been completed three-fourths of the way and is set to be finished July 1, according to Ruben Whitney, campus principal.

Spitfire
Round Rock High School
Round Rock, Texas

In this example, the source of the facts is given in the second paragraph.

The computer lab has been upgraded by the addition of 28 new IBM compatible computers.

Technology Committee Chairman Al Bell said that the PC lab will help prepare students to use both IBM and Macintosh computers.

Blue & Gold
Findlay High School
Findlay, Ohio

It is necessary to not only identify the news source by name but by title too. For the facts to be believable to readers, the rank or authority position of the source is considered: the higher the source is in rank, the more credible the facts are likely to be or at least perceived to be by the reader. Citing only one source, no matter the rank of that source, is risky if the facts are being disputed or if the source's opinion is mixed in with the facts.

When citing a source, use the past tense verb "said" and add a time reference, such as "last week," "today," "recently" or a specific date. The time reference will help make the lead more complete.

If a student is cited as a source, the student's year in school is given after the name. For example: Alan Heider, '03, or Alan Heider, junior. A teacher cited should be identified with his or her subject or department. For example: Ann Tiffany, English, or Ann Tiffany, counselor.

If opinion is included in the lead, then the opinion is attributed to a source, a person. This is done to increase story objectivity and credibility.

Here's a lead that includes opinion attributed to a source.

A number one ranking for the boys' soccer team has evaporated under a recent rash of injuries, said coach Randy Freeman.

Smoky Hills Express
Smoky Hills High School
Aurora, Colo.

The attribution is needed in this lead because the potential inability to compete for the number one ranking is speculation, someone's opinion. The most credible or believable person to speculate would be the coach. The sports writer could not make this statement since he or she needs to remain objective. A writer's opinions are left out of the news or sports story.

Reporters who write for papers that publish infrequently need to also consider timeliness of the facts as they write their news summary lead. Leads can be revised at press time if a new development has occurred. The reporter may have to actively seek more information and interview again the story's sources to get an update.

Here's an example of a news lead with an updated *who* and *what* angle.

> The administration has decided not to take action against the senior class even though 24 percent of the class was absent on an unofficial senior skip day Jan. 25.
>
> *Lance*
> Robert E. Lee High School
> Springfield, Va.

This story was published in the *Lance* one month after the senior skip day. Since a month had passed since the skip day, the reporter made a wise decision to feature the latest development in the story's lead.

The news summary lead is frequently used because hurried readers who may not have time to read an entire story can still get the most important information by reading the story's headline and the first few paragraphs. Some who favor its use also say that it is logical when telling someone about an event to tell the most important facts first; others disagree and think methodically building a story from a set-the-scene introduction to its most important facts at the end is better.

Today, newspapers use both forms. Another advantage of the news summary lead and inverted pyramid form is that if an editor or page designer needs to cut a story to fit a layout, it may be easier to trim the final paragraph or two, since the lead and immediate follow-up paragraphs have the most important facts and the final paragraphs have the least important facts.

Writing a headline for an inverted pyramid story with a news summary lead may be easier since the main facts are presented in the opening paragraphs; the headline writer does not have to read the complete story to select the key words that accurately represent the key facts in the story.

As more people get their breaking or hard news as bulletins or short reports on television, radio or the internet, the need for the traditional news summary lead for an inverted pyramid story decreases. News-features, news background and analysis stories have increased in newspapers as a consequence, either pushing out hard news or turning those hard news stories into news briefs. For newspaper writers, the new content means fewer news summary leads and more creative choices. As already discussed in this book, the school newspaper is even more likely than a commercial daily to begin more of its stories with modified news summary leads, including many novelty or feature approaches.

THE MODIFIED NEWS LEAD AND THE NUT GRAPH

In the face of competition from other media, newspapers – those published daily and less frequently – have tried to make news and other information more interesting and relevant to readers to give them a good reason to keep buying and reading newspapers. Newspaper reporters have varied the form of their work, including writing more creative story leads. These leads are often less direct and less "formulaic" than the traditional news summary lead. Some journalists call these soft or indirect news leads.

The most obvious way to modify a news summary lead is to use only the feature fact or perhaps two of the *what*, *who*, *where*, *when*, *why* and *how* in the lead. By delaying some of the answers to these essential reader questions, the sentences can be short, and the writer can create a "hook" to catch or entice the reader to continue into the body of the story.

Sometimes the writer simply modifies the news summary lead by dividing the essential facts into two paragraphs, delaying complete disclosure of the main facts.

Here is a modified news summary lead.

> After taking her junior year off from the tennis team, Kari Olsen (12) is back as the number one singles player on the varsity team.
>
> She took the year off to concentrate on her own individual game and earn herself a twelfth place ranking in Southern California.

Since returning, she has helped the Falcons to another CIF team title.

Falconer
Torrey Pines High School
Encinitas, Calif.

In the first paragraph, the *who* and *what* are introduced. In the follow-up paragraph, the reader learns *why*, *how* and, generally, *where* and *when*. Together, they complete the news summary.

Another example of a modified lead shows a creative flair.

With last year's state championship still fresh in its mind, the boys' volleyball team began its season hungry for a second helping.

After losing seven seniors to graduation last year, the team enters the season unranked. But after several early victories, the boys earned a number 7 ranking from the *Chicago Tribune*.

Central Times
Naperville Central High School
Naperville, Ill.

Many writers use a brief anecdote as the first paragraph, or some suspended or delayed interest statement. The follow-up paragraph then is a more conventional summary of the main fact of the story. It answers the most important of the reader's questions. This follow-up is called the **nut graph**. It gets its name from a comparison of a nut to a news story. The nut, the follow-up paragraph, contains the hard news, the feature fact. *Graph* is simply an abbreviation of "paragraph." Another term for nut graph is **focus graph**.

In this example of a story that begins with an anecdotal lead and follows with a nut graph, the opening paragraph refers to prominent persons and places to create a memory flashback.

Growing up playing football in the backyards, going to Memorial Stadium, or listening to Kent Pavelka on the radio or Keith Jackson on ABC, many dreamed of wearing that red "N" on their helmets or being the next Tommie Frazier or Ricky

Williams. As people get older, however, those dreams start to fade away.

On Feb. 3, that dream became a reality for four Southeast football players as seniors Chris Loos, Ty Gifford, Sean Blue and Brandt Bacus all signed to play football for either Division I or II schools next fall.

Clarion
Southeast High School
Lincoln, Neb.

The first paragraph is soft and indirect, and the follow-up, the nut graph, is direct and summarizes the facts.

Another example of a story with a suspended interest lead and a follow-up nut graph has some shock value.

Justine Yeung always wanted a cat. She is now the proud owner of a dark male named Chimichanga. Unfortunately, Chimichanga is skinned and in a garbage can, and junior Yeung is preparing to remove its musculature.

These nightmarish scenes may offend the weak of heart, but in Ms. Rama's anatomy class, they have become the order of the day as the latest shipment of cat cadavers have arrived for dissection.

Day Times
Detroit Country Day School
Beverly Hills, Mich.

The nut graph answers other readers' questions: So what? Why should I read this story? If the anecdotal lead is used, it is important for writers and editors to remember to write a nut graph, even one that is one sentence long.

THE VIGNETTE LEAD

Commercial newspapers, such as the *Wall Street Journal*, have relied increasingly upon a form of the storytelling method of story development for story leads. As already mentioned, these leads are followed by a nut graph, which includes the feature fact and one or more of the other main facts of the story.

The **vignette lead**, as these brief anecdotes are called, often is used for reports on social, economic, political, environmental and other major issues to bring the stories to the human or personal level. Readers seem to relate to these "big" stories more easily if they begin with a personal story. A vignette is a brief descriptive sketch or story.

Vignette leads are longer than anecdotal–nut graph leads. A vignette may be many paragraphs long, but eventually the writer returns to a more conventional newswriting form to present the hard news facts and opinions in the story. The writer may return to the vignette later in the story, including in the ending. Usually the result, the final story, is a combination of two methods of development, (1) narrative or story-telling and (2) inverted pyramid.

Some stories are so broad (for example, drug abuse) or so complicated (for example, the federal budget) that use of the vignette is the first and only effective choice to begin the story. Since the reader may be asking "so what?" about all stories, the vignette may provide the most direct response when the stories are broad based.

Here is an example of a vignette.

> Senior Josh Bartlett gets home from school around 4 p.m. He squeezes in half an hour of homework – some sociology or maybe a little econ. At 7 p.m., after a workout, a shower and a quick dinner, he is ready to hit the books again, this time for advanced chemistry or calculus.
>
> "On a normal night I can do probably about three hours," he said.
>
> After he has finished his school assign-ments, Bartlett also has to prepare for a mock trial, model UN and an upcoming engineering competition. If he works straight through, he can be done by 10:30 p.m., but more often he shoots to finish at 11 and be in bed by 11:30. He rarely makes it.
>
> Bartlett is one of thousands of students in the United States being smothered by homework. According to researchers at the University of Michigan, kids are doing more school work than ever before and at much younger ages. In 1981, grade school students spent 84 minutes a week on homework. In 1997, that figure was up to 134 minutes per week. In 1997, junior high students were pounding out upward of three and a half hours of homework per week, compared to only two hours in 1981.

Update
Herbert Henry Dow High School
Midland, Mich.

In the above story, the four-paragraph vignette leads into a fact-filled, hard news paragraph. The sub-ject of the story, teens and homework, is, for the high school press, a significant, far-reaching story. Although the topic affects every student, the vignette brings it immediately to the personal level – one person's story is everyone's story. What *The Update* reporter has given readers is a short, descriptive sketch, complete with a direct quote, which paints a compelling picture.

To end the homework story, the writer brings the reader back to the vignette:

> Meanwhile Bartlett is finally ready for bed. On an average night he gets about six hours of sleep. The recommended amount is eight. But everything is done. His assignments are completed and his books are packed away.
>
> "Besides sleep and relaxing," he said, "I've managed to fit everything in."

Another example of a vignette opening is for a story about a major social issue, family time and meals.

> Every morning Ray Gautschy '01 eats breakfast before going to school. This alone is an impressive feat for many teenagers, but Gautschy doesn't stop there. He actually sits down to eat with his entire family.
>
> "We've been doing it forever," Gautschy said of his family's breakfast ritual. "We try to eat dinner together every night, too."

Tips for Writing the News Lead

- Ask yourself, "What do I want to tell my readers?" Can you write your answer in one or two sentences? Try it. This is a way to keep you focused on the purpose of the story.
- Organize your notes to answer the six basic reader questions: **what, who, where, when, why** and **how?**
- Decide which of the six reader questions is most important. Think about the elements of news from Chapter 1 of this textbook. Your choice is called the **feature fact** – the fact you are going to feature first in your lead. There can be several facts of equal importance in a news lead.
- Begin writing your lead in sentence form with the feature fact first. Then add a few more facts, a few more answers to the remaining reader questions to complete the sentence. Keep the sentence short.
- Use specific nouns and complete names. Use colorful, lively verbs. Adjectives and adverbs add opinion. Attribute opinion to the source.
- If the lead has some unusual or especially important facts, name the source of this information in your lead.
- A second sentence in the first paragraph can amplify or expand the facts given in the first sentence or answer more of the reader questions.
- If the lead paragraph is indirect or delays the feature fact, write a **nut graph** as the follow-up to the lead to tell the reader the feature fact.
- If you have written your lead in the S–V–O (subject–verb–object) sentence form and think it is effective, then continue developing the rest of the story. If you think the lead you have written will not attract many readers to your story, try one of the lead variations listed in this chapter.

Gautschy's family proves to be the exception rather than the rule, as many teens say they never eat together.

Lion
Lyons Township High School North Campus
LaGrange, Ill.

The remainder of this story about the demise of at-home family meals is built around comments from other students and a sociology teacher who serves as the "expert" source.

Another short vignette introduces a story about programs for teen mothers.

Senior Amanda Williams sat calmly in her chair among playing children, holding her sleeping son, 10-month-old Daniel.

"I didn't know what I was living for before I had him," Williams said.

She was at the Mommy and Me meeting held every Thursday at Lakewood Hospital. The program gives teen parents a chance to talk with other teen parents.

Lakewood Times
Lakewood High School
Lakewood, Ohio

Long or short, vignettes are a useful tool for news, sports and feature writers. They are also effective for broadcast features. Writers should always find real persons to sketch, to help set the scenes for the presentation of fact, figures and opinions that follow. Fabrication – making up a vignette – is unethical and unacceptable. (See Chap. 22.)

OTHER CHOICES FOR LEADS

In addition to the news summary, modified summary and vignette leads, the news writer has some other choices to consider as the lead is written.

Facts, opinions and other information gathered by the reporter for the story are considered when the story is written; not every lead type is suitable for every story. What a lead is called isn't important, especially to readers. What counts most is the creativity of a writer to see the possibilities in the facts and always anticipate reader interest.

A **descriptive**, or **background**, lead describes the story's setting or gives details leading up to the story itself. It can also include dialogue. Although it delays the introduction of the feature fact or answers to reader questions (*what, who, where, when, why* and *how*), it can be effective for a story setting that is unusual or contribute to the core news elements.

Here is an example of a descriptive lead.

Hundreds of thousands of televisions were tuned into the Weather Channel as the announcer spoke of destructive winds and massive waves. Awaiting the next update and hoping for a change

in course, vacationers and residents alike wondered if they should leave.

On Aug. 25 they got their answer.

Sound to Sea
Manteo High School
Manteo, N.C.

In this descriptive lead, dialogue is used to set the scene.

"Psssst! Have you heard the news?"

"She did WHAT?"

"So and So told me that he said . . ."

Sounds like the typical chatter of GLHS students as they switch classes each day. But these conversations, full of details that change as quickly as a child's game of telephone, will be brought to the stage Nov. 13 and 14 as the GLHS Theatre Department present *Rumors*, a farce by Neil Simon.

Lion's Roar
Gahanna Lincoln High School
Gahanna, Ohio

A **direct address** lead temporarily speaks directly to the reader by using the second person pronouns "you" and "your." After the lead, the body of the story is then written in third person. It is informal and is intended to involve the reader in the story. Here is an example of a direct address lead.

You may have seen Justin Lopez roaming through the halls and wondered "Should this guy be in college?" It turns out that this 6'6", 235 lb. giant is a sophomore.

Horizon
Westwood High School
Austin, Texas

Another direct address lead:

Minutes before your vocabulary quiz, cheat sheets are being passed around the room from student to student. Do you take one? Many of your peers feel you shouldn't.

Highlights
Coral Gables High School
Coral Gables, Fla.

Direct quotation leads are used infrequently, and only if the direct quote is brief. Sometimes a partial direct quote may be effective. A long direct quote slows readers and may inhibit comprehension of the facts.

- Review your lead once your story is done. If you began with the *when* angle as your feature fact ("This year . . ."; "On Feb. 23, . . ."), you might want to reconsider and rewrite it. Usually, the *when* fact, though often important, is not the most interesting way to begin a story. Would the *who*, *what* or *why* facts be better?
- Update your lead to include the latest development if your story is written a week or more before it is published. Keep your news as timely as possible.

Here is a direct quotation lead in question form. It can also be considered a descriptive lead, as it sets the scene and delays the feature fact.

> "When I say Colombia, what do you think of?" Pilar Gonzalez asks an intent group of Uni students.
>
> "Soccer," ventures one. There are a few giggles.
>
> "That's right, what else?" Drugs and coffee are added to the list. Gonzalez is a speaker from the Colombia Support Network, here to speak with the Spanish Club.

Gargoyle
University High School
Urbana, Ill.

Another infrequently used opener is the **question** lead. It can be effective if the question is the crux of the story. More than one or two question leads in one issue of the school newspaper is not recommended.

Here is an example of a question lead.

> What happens to all of that recycling? Blue bins have been placed in classrooms, and sometimes students remember to put their used paper in them, but when they fill up, what happens to all that stuff?

A-Blast
Annandale High School
Annandale, Va.

There are several kinds of **comparison** or **contrast** leads. A widely used one is a **time comparison** (then and now; yesterday and today). Two other ones are **size comparison** (macro to micro; global to home) and **cultural comparison** (Asian to European; liberal to conservative).

Here is an example of a time comparison lead.

> From the time she was a little girl, Sarah Harvey ('99) has loved flying in commercial jets. A year and a half ago, on her 16th birthday, Harvey sat in the cockpit of a Cessna 150 and began flying herself.

Academy Times
Charles Wright Academy
Tacoma, Wash.

Here is another time comparison lead, one with a cultural twist.

> Two-stepping and line dancing have slid out of physical education class. Now when students put their badminton rackets and basketball shoes aside, it is to do Tae-Bo.

Falcon's Cry
Jordan High School
Durham, N.C.

Here is a size comparison lead, going from a global to a home setting.

> While the media may focus on the battles in Kosovo, another war is being waged right here at OHS. It is the struggle between the fireants and the termites in US Government teacher Dale Reichard's classroom.

Lion's Tale
Oviedo High School
Oviedo, Fla.

This size comparison lead goes from a universe of "all" to a much smaller one of "eight."

> Unlike the rest of their classmates, eight seniors will not be attending college this fall. They are taking a year off to pursue special interests, volunteer, travel or do an internship.

Gargoyle
University High School
Urbana, Ill.

Novelty, or **oddity**, leads are a catch-all category. They are creative leads that likely succeed at attracting readers simply because they are different. They may be humorous or startling or make an allusion to some other existing writing.

Here are two novelty leads.

Most high school students have been told not to play with matches, but not all of them listened.

The five fires in February alone that scorched the Jordan bathrooms brought attention to a problem of trash can and paper dispenser fires that is neither new nor easily solved.

Falcon's Cry
Jordan High School
Durham, N.C.

It's a strange twist on an old classic.

The Disney-fied version presents a sweet blond in a dress and apron, but Thursday night at 7:30 the curtain goes up on The Charles Wright Players' production of *Alice in Wonderland* . . . in an insane asylum.

Academy Times
Charles Wright Academy
Tacoma, Wash.

All of these lead variations can also be effective to begin feature and other kinds of stories in school newspapers, yearbooks and online news websites.

EXERCISES

1. Select a news story from page 1 of your city newspaper. Identify the "five W's and H" in the first two paragraphs. Which one of these begins the story? Why do you think the reporter chose that one to begin the story?

2. Read the leads (opening paragraphs) for all the stories on page 1 of your city newspaper. Identify the kind of lead. Is there one kind that is used more than others? Do any of the leads include a nut graph? How long are the paragraphs in a story of your choice (number of sentences and words)?

3. Select one news story on page 1 of your city paper that has a news summary lead. Identify which one

of the "five W's and H" it is that begins the story. Rewrite the lead five times, with a different one of the five W's and H as the opener. Which one, including the original, do you think emphasizes the most important angle or feature? Which one features the most timely angle? Which one is the least important and why?

4. Select one news story from anywhere in your city paper that has a news summary lead and rewrite the lead using either a descriptive, comparison or contrast, question or direct address lead.

5. Look through all stories in your city newspaper and find an example of a story with a vignette lead and one with a modified news summary lead, which has a nut graph. Do you think these leads are effective and why?

6. Clip one lead from your city paper that begins with one of these types of clauses: infinitive, present participle, preposition, gerund and conditional.

7. Interview one of your classmates about either his or her hobbies or recreational interests. After reviewing your notes, select what you think is the most interesting or newsworthy fact or comment and write a one-sentence news summary lead for your story based upon that fact. Then, with the same fact, write another lead that is either a modified news summary lead or some other type presented in this chapter. Which one do you like better? Which one will likely appeal to more readers and why?

8. Analyze one issue of your school's newspaper or a section of your school's yearbook. Identify the kinds of leads written for all or most of the stories. If a variety of types are used, why might this be a good strategy?

9. Find one story that was reported in a print newspaper and also online on a news web site. Which is longer? Compare their leads. What are some similarities and differences between the two versions of the same story? Does the method of publication – print versus online – affect the telling of the story? Which medium do you prefer to get your news from and why?

Writing the News Story

"Hope of finding the three climbers missing for four days on Mount Rainier is fading."

Who are these climbers? Why is finding them so difficult? Who is giving up hope of finding them? These are just a few of the questions someone might have after reading this bulletin or news summary.

Even in a fast-paced, computer-driven world, where headline-style news is delivered within an instant to almost anyone, there remains the need for the fully developed news story. In the "information age," the need to be informed defines success. For every person who wants only the headlines and the one-paragraph summaries, there is someone else who needs all the facts. Journalists provide all three – the headline, the summary and the full story. Where the full story is published is secondary today; it can be read or heard almost anywhere on a variety of media. The print newspaper remains a primary outlet, but journalists can write for the new media – the internet for example – as well.

A journalist who understands the purpose of news and masters the art of newswriting will be prepared to work in both traditional and new media. No matter what type of reporting and writing is eventually done by a journalist, learning how to write a news story is fundamental.

Writing the news story is another step in the news dissemination process. First comes learning about what news is and what it isn't (Chap. 1). Then, the news reporter gathers all the information for the story (Chap. 2). Following the fact-finding stage, the reporter organizes his or her notes and writes the beginning of the story or the lead, which to many is the critical part of the story (Chap. 3). After the lead, the rest of the story, the body and the conclusion, is written. The result is a fully developed story, not just a one-paragraph summary.

The missing climbers on Mount Rainier in the hypothetical story above will be more than anonymous persons if the bulletin is developed into a fully developed news story. All or most of the reader's questions will be answered as the writer goes beyond the headline and the summary to tell the rest of the story. And it's likely someone will want to read it from beginning to end.

THE INVERTED PYRAMID FORM

Writing a news summary lead is the first step in writing a fully developed, inverted pyramid news story. The inverted pyramid form presents facts in descending order, from most important to least important. The most important facts, based on news values and selected by the reporter, are given in the opening, the first and sometimes the second paragraph. All of the succeeding paragraphs expand the lead by supporting it, explaining it or making it specific. Often some of the important reader questions, the five W's and H (*what*, *who*, *where*, *when*, *why* and *how*), are put into a second paragraph to keep the first paragraph as short as possible. Many hard news stories will have a two-paragraph lead.

Fig. 4.1. Significant news, including stories on school overcrowding, test scores and fighting discrimination marks this paper as professional and relevant. *Silver Chips*, Montgomery Blair High School, Silver Spring, Md.

Before and after writing the story's lead, the reporter studies all of his or her notes carefully to see the story as a whole, perhaps grouping the separate notes under topics that are the related areas of the interview and from other sources during the fact-finding stage. Some reporters may find it helpful to actually answer the basic reader questions – *what, who, where, when, why* and *how* – before the lead and the body of the story are written. This helps the reporter order the information from most to least important. It can also help in organizing all of the details and elaborations of the basic facts. As they organize their notes, reporters can actually put numbers – 1, 2, 3, etc. – opposite the facts to indicate decreasing order of importance.

Here's a news story that presents facts in descending order of importance, or in the inverted pyramid form.

Library provides internet access

Through the Montebello Unified School District Network (MUSD Net), students will have access to the internet for educational purposes.

"The majority of students don't have access at home so this is a great way for them to get up-to-date information," said Principal Terrance Devney.

Students can log on through the computers in the library by signing in at the desk with their IDs and stating a valid reason to use the internet.

Assistance will be available in the library for internet users. "We all need to be trained because there is more to the internet than looking up sites," said Librarian Randie Hayward.

The District internet Consent and Waiver Form for Students will be issued to students next week. Once the forms are returned to the Student Store, students will receive internet stickers that will be applied to their IDs.

"It is a tremendous tool for students," said Assistant Principal Russ Davis. Students can lose this privilege if they break any of the network access rules. The MUSD Net can be only used for purposes consistent with their approved curriculum and not for commercial profit services. Those who use the network illegally or improperly will lose their privileges.

"Every teacher will have the responsibility to supervise the use of the internet in the classroom," said Davis.

The Board of Education Policy and Administrative Regulations addresses disciplinary actions for vandalism of computer equipment, unauthorized access to information, computer piracy, hacking and any tampering with hardware or software. Students will be liable for damage or information loss. According to the policy, students may not use the network to annoy, harass or offend people.

"Internet misuse is serious because the district could be liable," said Hayward.

According to Davis, classrooms and offices have or will have internet access. MUSD Net links to various MUSD schools and offices. Students can also connect with businesses, major universities, national libraries and other schools and students around the world.

Spartan Scroll
Schurr High School
Montebello, Calif.

Writing a focus statement that states, in a sentence or two, what the story is about is not only helpful in writing a summary lead but it can also keep the writer on track as the rest of the story is developed.

For example, a possible focus statement for the *Spartan Scroll* news story about new internet access for students within the school could be: "Students will get access to the internet for the first time at school if they have permission from their parents or guardian." This one sentence summarizes the main point of the story and gives it direction for development. The reporter will then answer the reader questions – *what, who, where, when, why* and *how* – in a more journalistic style.

Some professional reporters write their leads last, but for a beginning reporter it is advisable to at least write a draft lead, a lead that can be edited, polished or even completely rewritten later. Even a draft lead will help the reporter stay focused on the essential facts of the story. Eventually, every reporter will do what works best; it's part of a reporter's style.

School papers that publish infrequently should consider the timeliness of all stories. A summary lead for an inverted pyramid story could feature the most recent development or an expected future development: What can the reader expect to see happen next?

The lead for the *Spartan Scroll* story on internet access opens with the answer to *how* and continues with the *who* and *what*. The lead reads: "Through the Montebello Unified School District Network (MUSD Net), students will have access to the internet for educational purposes." This brief, direct one-sentence summary lead tells the reader first *how* something will happen ("Through the Montebello Unified School District Network"), then tells *who* it will happen to ("students"), and finally *what* will happen ("will have access to the internet").

After the lead is written, the remaining facts should be reviewed again. If some of the five *W*'s and *H* have been omitted in the lead, they will need to be included in the body of the story. Additional details about the person or persons involved and more details about what happened will need to be considered and possibly added to the story. This is called "fleshing out" or expanding upon the summary facts in the lead. Opinions of those who are involved in the story are included with the facts to help explain and humanize the story. These opinions and explanations are either indirect or direct quotes.

The second paragraph of the *Spartan Scroll* story answers another one of the five *W*'s and *H* reader questions, the *why*. The second paragraph reads: " 'The majority of students don't have access at home so this is a great way for them to get up-to-date information,' said Principal Terrance Devney." The principal is quoted directly. Short direct quotes are preferable to multi-sentence ones in a news story.

The third paragraph in the *Spartan Scroll* story expands the *how* fact and tells the reader *where* it will happen. "Students can log on through the computers in the library by signing in at the desk with their IDs and stating a valid reason to use the internet."

Subsequent paragraphs – of various lengths but all brief – expand the story with more details. Various persons involved provide explanations and give their opinions. By including them in the story, the reporter adds a human element, which should increase reader interest. A story that is only a list of facts without attributed comments and explanations from those involved is not very interesting to most readers. All opinions are attributed to someone specific. The reader knows who said what. Some comments are quoted directly (" 'Every teacher will have the responsibility to supervise the use of the internet in the classroom,' said Davis"), and others are indirect quotes ("According to Davis, classrooms and offices have or will have internet access"). The reporter got facts from multiple sources for the story.

The last paragraph, about the wide range of internet connections students can now make from school, has the least important facts and could be cut from the story. This is characteristic of the inverted pyramid form. However, when writing, the reporter should not assume that the last paragraph of his or her story will be cut; facts or opinions of interest to readers should be included even though they aren't as important as the ones placed higher in the story.

The reporter who wrote the *Spartan Scroll* story used personal judgment in ranking the facts from most to least important. Every reporter does this. Later, in the copy-editing stage, another person will read the story and determine, among other things, if the facts are presented in a logical and relevant order. If the copy editor thinks they aren't, the lead or more may be rewritten for better emphasis or to highlight the most recent development in the story. Beginning writers may consult with an editor during the writing stage about emphasis and order.

Despite the notion that an editor could cut the last paragraph of an inverted pyramid story and the story wouldn't suffer, in recent years editors and reporter have resisted this practice. Now, they put more emphasis on the story ending. This change is also the result of editors' attempts to hold readers throughout the story. To do this, reporters sometimes save an especially interesting quote or fact until the end, or they answer a question posed at the beginning of the story that remains unanswered until the last paragraph. This deviation from the inverted pyramid form shows the ongoing evolution of journalistic writing, especially for newspapers.

Paragraphs in a news story are short, with usually one main fact or one person's opinions or explanation in a paragraph. Another main fact and another person's comment will be in a new paragraph. To avoid a monotonous pattern, the number of sentences in a paragraph should vary from paragraph to paragraph. Most paragraphs in a news story will have one to three sentences. Sometimes a reporter will write a series of one-sentence paragraphs for emphasis, but generally this is not done. However, this is a guideline or a rule; structure is secondary to content, but structure is still somewhat important. Because of the typically narrow column width in a newspaper, a paragraph with more than four sentences will look long and complex and may discourage readers from starting or finishing even an interesting story.

CONTINUITY

Paragraphs and sentences should follow one another smoothly. If they do, the story will have continuity, or achieve coherence. If a story coheres, it sticks together, making the development easy to follow. Besides putting related information together, continuity, or coherence, is achieved in the following ways.

PRONOUNS

In a news story, the writer uses third-person pronouns (*she*, *he*, *they*, etc.). First-person pronouns (*I*, *me*, *my*, *we*, *us*, etc.) and second-person (*you*, *your*) are only used (1) when they are in a direct quote or in an indirect, paraphrased quote, both attributed to a source, or (2) in a question or direct address lead (Chap. 3).

Sentences and paragraphs can be linked through the use of pronouns as well as demonstrative adjectives *this* and *that* and to refer to nouns in preceding sentences.

> Beginning next fall, teachers will have internet access in their classrooms. **This** will allow **them** to tap into resources available worldwide within minutes.

REPETITION OF A KEY WORD FROM THE PRECEDING PARAGRAPH OR SENTENCE

> In an attempt to boost its sagging treasury, the **Student Council** announced last week the sale of school mascot phone cards.

> About $2 of the $10 retail cost of the card will go directly to the **Student Council**. According to Caries Raimerez, **council** treasurer, card sales will begin in mid-January and could raise as much as $500 in profits the first month.

In the first two paragraphs of this hypothetical story, the key term "Student Council" is repeated, and the shorter version, "council," is also used.

USE OF A SYNONYM REFERRING TO A KEY WORD IN THE PRECEDING PARAGRAPH

> Two members of the **class of '01** were named to the **All-State Marching Band** following their appearance in a day-long competition in Madison last Saturday.

Senior band members Pam Tiffany and Robert Wilson received superior ratings in the tuba category to receive the **statewide honor**.

The synonym for "class of '01," given in the first paragraph, is "senior," which opens the second paragraph and otherwise identifies the two students by class. "All-State Marching Band," first paragraph, and "statewide honor," second paragraph, are also synonyms.

ELABORATION OF DETAILS IN LOGICAL SEQUENCE OR ORDER OF IMPORTANCE

New graduation requirements will affect the class of '03 if a proposal before the Medford School Board is passed at next week's meeting.

The changes include the addition of a second year of Spanish, reducing the physical education minimum to two years and eliminating World Literature as a required course.

The first paragraph introduces the fact that graduation requirements could change. The second paragraph elaborates on this, specifying the changes.

TRANSITIONAL WORDS

Special words and phrases can be used to tie paragraphs together and develop story continuity. These are called "transitions," and they point out the sequence of thought and help the reader move from paragraph to paragraph.

These transitional words show time: *then, now, shortly thereafter, meanwhile, afterward, later, soon, all this time, formerly, previously, at last, finally, following.*

With a ten-foot bonfire lighting the night sky, the annual Homecoming festivities began for some one thousand students and others at Parade Stadium last Friday night.

Later, during the half-time ceremonies of the football game, the glowing embers provided a backdrop for the crowning of Rita Mach, senior, as homecoming queen.

The transitional word *later* is used to begin the second paragraph to show progression of time and to link the two paragraphs. (Use of the word "embers" in the second paragraph is also a link to "bonfire" in the lead.)

These transitional words and phrases show emphasis: *similarly, furthermore, in addition to, especially, moreover.*

Lighted candles flickered in the breeze as 35 juniors and seniors were initiated into the National Honor Society May 13.

In addition to achieving high grade point averages, the new society inductees were recognized for their community service and participation in school activities.

The transition from the first to second paragraph is with the phrase *In addition to.*

These transitional words and phrases show contrast or change in viewpoint: *however, but, nevertheless, also, of course, instead, in another way, otherwise, in addition, in general, seriously, in a lighter view.*

Girls rule! At least they do on the honor roll for first semester. Girls outnumber boys 3 to 2 on the list, which was released last week.

However, the news isn't all bad for the boys. The number of boys who made the list rose by 12 percent.

The transitional word *however* is used to show contrast between (1) the statement and facts in the lead and (2) the fact in the follow-up paragraph.

These transitions show place: *here, there, near, opposite, beyond, adjacent to.*

Twelve students from West spent their spring vacation building a house in San Antonio with the Habitat for Humanity program.

The house, **near** the Alamo, was built in four days by the students and three supervising carpenters from the city.

The transition *near* is used to locate the site within the city of San Antonio. ("City" in the second paragraph refers to "San Antonio" in the first paragraph, an example of using a synonym to refer to a key word in the preceding paragraph.)

THE MODIFIED INVERTED PYRAMID

Occasionally, a news story takes a short step back into time to recap a past event that is related to the topic of the present story. This is often within the paragraph following the lead.

Bond project finally breaks ground

After months of anticipation and the loss of half of the teacher's parking lot, construction on the new library, theater and other bond improvements officially began Wednesday, March 31.

Two years ago, schools voted on what changes were to be made on their campuses with money from the bonds. In addition to the construction of new buildings, changes such as the expansion of the band hall, girls' dressing room, and the renovation of select classrooms are scheduled to take place at Anderson.

"(After the changes) we will have one of the finest high school campuses in the country," principal Dr. David Kernwein said. The changes are scheduled to take approximately 15 months, so the new buildings will be accessible to students at the end of next year. Though construction at other AISD schools has been running behind their expected schedules, construction field manager Craig Johnson said, "Even if we slide off a week or two, we have methods to make up the time."

Most of the construction will be done during normal working hours (7:30 a.m. to 3:30 p.m.), with interior work being done after school and on the weekends. The majority of the exterior work on the new buildings will take place over the summer. Kernwein does not expect construction to distract students.

"We have had contract work going on all year," Kernwein said. "They know how to do it." Though construction has blocked off much of the north parking lot, after the building is finished, Kernwein expects to lose only 15 spaces.

"I don't think it is right that we aren't allowed to park in the teacher parking lot after we have paid for a spot," sophomore Natalie Hopkins said.

The groundbreaking ceremony provided photo opportunities, such as Kernwein in an Anderson hard hat sitting in a tractor surrounded by students. Kernwein also introduced many of the people involved in the construction.

WSM architect Craig Estes took on the project not only for business reasons, but also because he had two daughters graduate from Anderson.

In addition to the changes included in the bonds, Anderson will get a new track around the football field over the summer. This project, funded by the district, is expected to be completed by July.

Edition
L.C. Anderson High School
Austin, Texas

Without disrupting the flow of this story, the second paragraph recaps what had happened earlier. This story also includes some examples of good transitions, including using the synonym "changes" for the noun construction "bond improvements" and the use of "In addition to the changes" to link the previous facts to the final ones. Paragraphs are short, and new paragraphs are used for most new quotes, including the indirect quote or paraphrase of the response from the WSM architect Craig Estes. The final paragraph also deviates from the inverted pyramid form by presenting some new information, facts that shouldn't be cut from the story.

ATTRIBUTION AND QUOTES

Attributing the source of facts and opinion in a news story – telling the reader where the information came from and who said what – is an essential aspect of establishing the person's professionalism and the medium's impartiality and credibility. Readers need to know that the reporter got his or her facts from the best possible sources and the opinions expressed and explanations given are not the reporter's own opinions.

By telling the reader the source of the facts, the reporter is also allowing the reader to make a judgment about the facts. The need to separate, in a news story, fact from opinion is also crucial. The reader deserves to know whose opinions are being expressed. A news story is not the place for a reporter to express his or her opinion, even a seemingly innocuous one such as: "Homecoming was a success." That may be true, but in a news story, the reporter has to tell the reader who thought the event was a success: "Homecoming was a success," Lisa Washington, senior class president, said. A reporter has an opportunity to express his or her opinion only in a signed opinion column or in an unsigned editorial.

Unattributed and attributed opinion in a news story is called **editorializing**. Reporters and editors who find unattributed opinion, even a single somewhat harmless adjective or adverb, should delete it from the story. For example, it may seem harmless to use the adjective "beautiful" in front of the noun "decorations" when writing a story about prom, but unless someone the reporter has interviewed said the decorations were beautiful, the adjective has to be deleted.

Sometimes opinion can be attributed to a general source if the assessment is generally accepted by most if not everyone who would read the story. For example: "Homecoming was a success, according to many who attended the parade, game and dance." The reporter has attributed the opinion, "success," to no one in particular, but to many persons. This can ethically only be done if the reporter actually asked a number of persons who participated in these Homecoming activities and the majority of them said they like or enjoyed the events, had a good time or called it a success.

Not every fact in a story needs to be attributed if the facts are all from the same source. Once the attribution of facts is made near the beginning of the story, the reader will likely assume the following facts are from the same source, However, additional attributions to the same source can be a good linking or transitional device. Some facts are general knowledge and also do not have to be attributed. Sometimes it will be obvious to readers that the facts are firsthand knowledge because the reporter witnessed the event. A reporter should use common sense in deciding which facts need attribution and which ones don't.

The preferred verb for the attribution of all direct and indirect quotes is *said*. Occasionally, the present tense *says* can be used. *Says* is a good choice when the quote, direct or indirect, is something a person repeatedly says or is a "signature" or "trademark" statement, identified with the person.

Fig. 4.2. Student newspapers report news originating from many sources, including local tie-ins to national issues such as security concerns. *Central Times*, Naperville Central High School, Naperville, Ill.

Direct quote with *said* in attribution:

"Violence will stop in school when students learn to respect their classmates who may be a different color or have a different religion, ethnic background or sexual orientation," school psychologist Marian Anderson **said**.

Indirect quote (paraphrase) with *said* in attribution:

Violence will stop in schools when students respect each other and ignore differences based on color, religion, ethnicity and sexual orientation, Marian Anderson, school psychologist **said**.

Use of verbs other than *said* in quote attributions is limited and often not recommended. *Stated* is very formal and should only be used if someone in authority issues a formal statement, either in person or on paper. Another possibility, *remarked*, is also formal.

News writers should not worry that frequent use of *said* is too repetitive or shows lack of creativity. Repeated use of *said* will likely not be noticed by readers, and this is the desired effect in most cases.

Opinions and facts should be quoted directly if the information is unusual and if the opinion is colorful and especially if it is controversial. Ordinary facts and "expected" opinions and explanations can be paraphrased (or left as they were said) and then attributed without quotation marks as indirect quotes. Learning what to quote directly and what to paraphrase comes with experience. If a reporter does quote someone directly – with quotation marks – the exact words must be used and in the intended context. An indirect quote – no quotation marks – is safer, but it still needs to be accurate.

Long quotes – more than one sentence – often interfere in the smooth flow of the story and can confuse readers. Short quotes, one sentence or even a phrase or word, are often more effective than long ones.

When deciding to quote someone directly or to paraphrase what was said, the reporter should ask: What would this direct quote contribute to my story? If the words are unique, controversial, colorful, poignant or in some other way memorable, then they should be quoted directly. If they are ordinary, then they shouldn't be.

Yet a story can be more interesting to readers if it has one or more direct quotes. During the interview stage, a reporter should ask questions that will possibly elicit quotable responses. If the initial interviews are finished and the reporter, as he or she is writing the story, has nothing worthy of a direct quote, the source could be asked additional questions; these new responses could provide memorable comments for a direct quote.

Effective news stories are often built around both facts and reactions to facts or opinions. A story with a fact, fact, fact flow, paragraph after paragraph, without the addition of a reaction or explanation provided by a source is usually not as interesting to readers or as effective. Most events need explanation for reader comprehension and relevance. As someone is reading a list of facts, he or she may ask: What does this mean and why should I care about it? A story with a pattern of fact, fact, quote, fact, quote, for example, may be more satisfying and effective than only a successive list of facts.

The following news story can be examined regarding its structure, transitions, use of direct and indirect quotes and attribution.

Program raises hopes for higher standards

With hopes of raising academic standards in all classes, the International Baccalaureate (IB) program is making a start here.

The IB program, coordinated by social studies teacher Carol Daiberl, consists of high level classes in not only core subjects such as English, math, social studies and science, but also in fine arts.

Although pieces of the program may be offered in various classes next year, the program won't officially start until Gresham is designated an "IB school."

To do this is a long process, according to Assistant Principal Paul Boly.

"We're in the application phase now," Boly said. The next step is for a representative of IB North America to come visit the school and community to "gauge the depth of the community's commitment to IB." This is expected to happen sometime between January and spring break.

The IB classes, which will be available to juniors and seniors, will officially be offered when current freshmen are juniors.

Boly hopes that at least one IB class will appeal to every student. "I'd like to see many of our kids as juniors and seniors take one or more of our classes," he said.

According to Jay Morris, one of the 16 teachers being trained to teach the curriculum of the IB program, IB has been a success for other schools and is expected to have a very positive effect here.

Boly also has high expectations for the program.

"[IB] is a very positive program," he said. "It helps students focus on academic achievement."

Morris thinks the IB program not only will benefit students while they are in high school, but also prepare them for the future.

"It's definitely going to help college-bound students," he said.

Both Morris and Boly also believe that besides helping students academically, IB will also act as a "magnet," attracting students from Barlow, where the program will not be offered. According to Boly, Gresham was chosen over Barlow to house the program since it is centrally located and has a smaller student population.

"Barlow will do a wonderful job preparing ninth and tenth graders," Boly said.

Boly also thinks the positive attitude of teachers such as Morris, combined with the high quality academic program here, will add to the effectiveness of the program.

"Students at Gresham High School are every bit as capable as students all over the world," Boly said.

Gresham Argus
Gresham High School
Gresham, Ore.

The *Argus* story represents many points about good news writing. Structurally, all the paragraphs are short, with no paragraph containing quotes from more than one person. There is a mix of indirect, direct and even partial direct quotes. "Said" is used most often for attribution. Three sources of information are cited, with two of them, misters Boly and Morris, cited more than once. Transitions between paragraphs are smooth, and there is good narrative explanation following most quotes. The story is a modified inverted pyramid, with a moderately interesting quote saved for the last paragraph. After reading this story, it is apparent that the facts and opinions were collected from several interviews.

A common mistake made by some beginning writers – trying to write the questions asked during an interview into the story – is not in the *Argus* story. The transitions and summaries between direct and indirect quotes make the reporter's questions apparent and unnecessary.

> *Wrong*
> When asked what she thought of the new graduation requirements, Rita Mach, principal, said they are an important step toward preparing students for a changing world.

> *Right*
> Principal Rita Mach said the new graduation requirements are an important step toward preparing students for a changing world.

Some reporters modify the inverted pyramid significantly by telling the story in a chronological way following the lead. The opening may be a news summary lead or a variation, possibly including a nut graph (Chap. 3). The lead usually features the most recent development, the most timely information. Following the lead, the story is then developed, with facts and attributed opinions, in a time sequence rather than most to least important.

The **time sequence** or **chronological news story form** is sometimes called **storytelling**. This form seems suited to certain kinds of topics. Some possibilities include accidents and natural disasters; anniversary commemorations and historical timelines; construction and renovation projects; competitions; and other stories with a step-by-step sequence. The sequential information should be interesting to readers; otherwise the traditional – most to least important facts – inverted pyramid form should be used.

BECOMING A BETTER NEWS WRITER

Although newswriting is meant to be direct and simple, good newswriting doesn't lack color, emotional appeal and occasionally drama. The topic may have inherent qualities that automatically attract readers, but even what would seem to be mundane can be reported with clarity and color. No story is too short to not merit a reporter's best writing.

Accuracy and fairness are the foundation of good newswriting. A good reporter checks facts and balances the story to provide a true account of what happened. This becomes second nature. But there is more to being a successful reporter than dedication to these two principles. What often separates a good reporter from a great one is how they use words.

To become a better news writer, the following points should be considered.

Begin each paragraph with a **significant** or **interesting fact** and use interesting, specific words. Avoid, if possible, beginning sentences with *It is*, *It was*, *It will be*, *There is*, *There are*, *There was* or *There were*.

> *Weak*
> **There will be a college fair next Tuesday in the gym.**

> *Better*
> **A college fair will be held in the gym next Tuesday.**

Sentences with the subject–verb–object order are direct and desirable for newswriting. However, sometimes a clause or infinitive phrase can precede the subject to emphasize some interesting or significant fact (opening the *why* or *how* of the five *W*'s and *H*).

> *Good*
> **Parking permits will be sold to students beginning next week.**

> *Better*
> **To raise money for the Student Council, parking permits will be sold to students beginning next week.**

Familiar, conversational words are usually better for newswriting than less common words found in scholarly work. Even greatly respected newspapers such as *The New York Times* and the *Wall Street Journal* report with simple, direct words.

Possible	conflagration
Better	fire
Possible	concept
Better	idea
Possible	proliferation
Better	spread
Possible	initiate
Better	begin
Possible	utilize
Better	use
Possible	finalize
Better	end
Possible	peruse
Better	read
Possible	endeavor
Better	try

"Say what you have to say as simply and concisely as possible and stop" is good advice to a news writer. However, **tight writing** is sometimes difficult and requires practice. By using one word for several and eliminating repetition of different words with the same meaning, a reporter can write more clearly and directly. Writers should always avoid wordy and unclear sentences.

Wordy	reached an agreement
Better	agreed
Wordy	submitted her resignation
Better	resigned
Wordy	held a meeting
Better	met
Wordy	put in an appearance
Better	appeared
Wordy	take into consideration
Better	considered

Redundant	end result
Better	end or result
Redundant	new record
Better	new or record
Redundant	close proximity
Better	close or proximity
Redundant	general public
Better	public
Redundant	true facts
Better	facts
Redundant	original founder
Better	founder

Wordy	The drama club won the one-act play contest that it entered last Saturday.
Better	The drama club won the one-act play contest last Saturday.
Wordy	The program for the spring band concert will include a Sousa march.
Better	The band's spring concert will include a Sousa march.
Wordy	Bob Schmidt, who is a member of the social studies department faculty, was named Teacher of the Year.
Better	Social Studies teacher Bob Schmidt was named Teacher of the Year.

Vigorous, exact verbs that suggest action and precisely state it will often improve a story. However, verbs should be familiar ones, ones used in everyday conversation. Most people don't use verbs such as sauntered, sped or ambled, even though they are fine words to have in one's vocabulary. When choosing a verb, the writer should ask: Is this something I would say or is it something I would hear? If not, consider another choice.

Active-voice verbs are often a better choice than passive-voice verbs for news stories. They are more direct. However, sometimes the passive-voice is the only workable choice. For example, when a story begins with the *who* element of the five W's and H, the passive voice is often the only choice, as in: "Joe DeLuca was elected president of the Student Council."

Passive
The football **was kicked** by George Taylor 40 yards through the goal posts.

Active
George Taylor **kicked** the football 40 yards through the goal posts.

Passive
Salt Lake City **was selected** as the site of the 2002 Winter Olympics.

Active
The Olympic committee **selected** Salt Lake City as the site of the 2002 winter games.

Concrete nouns will add more color to a story. They are precise and readily identified objects. Stories are often enriched with details. However, it is not necessary, and it can be annoying to cite brand names if they are mentioned too often or if they aren't necessary.

General	dog
Concrete	dachshund
General	book
Concrete	world atlas
General	food
Concrete	bagel
General	injury
Concrete	broken wrist
General	blue
Concrete	azure

Clichés and popular slang have limited value in a news story. If they are included in responses from sources, then they may be used in direct and indirect quotes. It is possible that a cliché or some slang could be included in an effective story lead, in an ending or within the body of the story, but it is unlikely that it would be more effective than original phrases and sentences from the news writer.

Some clichés are worse than others. For example, really tired ones to avoid include *breath of fresh air, leave no stone unturned, bite the dust, calm before the storm, proud parents, leap of faith, Mother Nature, Old Man Winter, storm of protest, true colors, heart of gold, Grim Reaper, light at the end of the tunnel* and *drop in the bucket*, among many others.

Occasionally, cliché can be a good choice, but only if it specifically applies. For example, a story about an antique or junk store could use the cliché "white elephant" if the store actually sold one.

Using a cliché or even a quote from a well-known book, song or other genre is really a question of opinion. Some journalists like to use them occasionally because they say readers identify with the cliché. They say a cliché is like "comfort food" (another cliché) for the mind. A story with more than one cliché is suspect. Writers who use them too often may be considered lazy by readers and their professional peers.

If a cliché is used in a story, it should not be put in quotation marks.

Language evolves. Each year, lexicographers (those who write dictionaries) add new words to dictionaries. These words are created by others who invent words to fit objects, actions, emotions or ideas. If enough people use the new word, it becomes part of the spoken language. Many new words were created for the information age of the 1990s: *web, cell phone, chat room, email* and *e-commerce*, among others. Journalists should use new words carefully and slowly. Newly coined words and jargon may not be understood by the general population. Newsrooms, including those in high schools, should buy a new dictionary and journalism stylebook every two years or sooner.

Slang or street language, especially coarse or sexually suggestive words, even though they may be in a dictionary, are usually not used by journalists – with some exceptions. For example, if a source is quoted directly or indirectly, slang or vulgar words may be necessary to publish for accuracy and fairness.

CHECKLIST FOR WRITING A GOOD NEWS STORY

- Do I have all the facts?
- Did I verify these facts with my sources?
- Have I checked the spelling of all names and are all persons identified?
- Have I certified all the dates with a calendar. Is May 13 a Friday as it is written?
- If a news summary lead is written, does it feature the most timely and important facts?
- If a soft or feature lead is written, is it followed by a nut or focus graph?
- Is the lead short?
- Are too many of the five W's and H in the first sentence? Should the lead be two sentences or two short paragraphs?
- Are the opening words interesting, good choices?
- Does the lead flow smoothly to the next paragraph?
- Do all paragraphs follow one another in logical order, with good transitions from one paragraph to the next?
- Are the paragraphs short? Do the paragraphs vary in length?
- Does each paragraph begin (the first few words) with significant or interesting facts worded in an interesting, specific way?
- Is the writing objective, with no editorializing?
- Is the story concise? Can any words be deleted or can any sentence be tighter?
- Is the story unified? Does it develop the focus statement?
- Have I included a mix of direct and indirect quotes from my sources?
- Are all direct and indirect quotes attributed? Is the attributive verb *said* used?
- Are my word choices simple, conversational and specific?
- Does the last paragraph have some fact or quote that is worth reading?
- Have I checked my story for all spelling, punctuation, subject–verb agreement and other possible style and grammatical errors?
- Am I satisfied with my story? Am I proud to have the story appear under my byline?

- Have I saved my notes? The accuracy of facts and quotes may have to be verified after the story is published.

EXERCISES

1. Clip a news story from your city newspaper that has a summary lead and has inverted pyramid story development. Write a one- or two-sentence focus statement for this story. Do you think the writer followed the focus statement throughout the story? Do you agree with the order, most important to least important listing of the facts? Could the last paragraph be cut from the story without losing anything interesting or important?

2. As a class, select one major news story from the past year. List as many facts as you can about the event without concern about order or importance. Next, relist these facts from most important to least important. Discuss why one fact may be more or less important than another fact. Separately, each student should write a summary lead for this story.

3. Before class, the teacher should select and photocopy one or more news stories from the city newspaper. Then, the original story should be cut into single paragraphs. During class, ask students to reassemble the story according to how they think it appeared in the paper. Compare their restructuring of the story to the original story as it was published.

4. To reinforce the need for attribution for direct and indirect quotes, and attributive verbs, the teacher should give each student a photocopy of the same news story from the city paper. Each student should circle each attribution. As a class, discuss the use of direct and indirect quotes in the story.

5. To reinforce the importance of transitions and the smooth flow of a story, the teacher should give each student a photocopy of the same news story from the city paper. Each student should circle the transitional words and phrases used to promote the flow of the story from one paragraph to the next.

6. To reinforce the need for objectivity in a news story, the student should clip one news story and one signed opinion column or unsigned editorial from the city paper. In about 250 words, the student should compare the two pieces and show how one is objective (the news story) and the other is subjective/the writer's opinions (the column). The student can note other differences too.

7. As a class, list different events at the school and in the community scheduled for one week. Discuss who the sources of information would likely be for each event. Assign one or two students to write a news story – either an advance story or a recap after the event – for each of these events. The story should be about 250–500 words and contain direct and indirect quotes from two or more sources. The story should conform to all newswriting guidelines and style. It should be written as if it was to be published in the school's newspaper.

8. Write a 250–500 word news story about one event you participated in during the last six months. The event could be school- or nonschool-related. It should be written in the third person, not first person. The inverted pyramid or a modified inverted pyramid (chronological) form should be used. It should conform to all news story guidelines and style. For example, a student who participated in a school play may want to write a news story about the play and cite him- or herself as the source. Remember: This is a news story, not an opinion column.

Writing Specialty Stories

Take a walk through the bookstore and notice the array of specialty magazines – everything from *Newsweek* to *Teen Star Hairstyles* to *Natural Health*. The cable television explosion brought hundreds more specialty shows. Newspapers have followed suit in creating more specialized beats in areas such as health and science. High school publications are covering an equally wide array of specialty stories.

HEALTH WRITING

For years, acne was the primary health concern of teens. The pimples haven't disappeared, but in the last decade, teens and school publications increasingly began taking an educated look at a wider variety of health issues – both physical and mental. Depression, AIDS and anorexia, among many others, have become teen health issues. A look at the causes, cures and stresses of health-related issues is now an important part of a publication's role of helping high school students understand their world (Fig. 5.1). Some of the stories covered by high school publications were

- Chemical dependency treatment centers and how they try to help adolescents overcome their addictions to everything from marijuana to heroin to inhalants

- A student's fight with brain cancer

- Biological brain differences in males and females. The story covers how boys and girls handle their emotions differently with examples such as what a kiss means and why guys won't cry

- The physical strains and hazards of wearing a heavy backpack

- The nutritional values and calories in school lunches

- Tips on preventing sunburning and skin cancer

- How students cope with attention deficit disorder

- The mental trauma of living in an abusive relationship. The story not only showed vividly how abusive relationships can be among boyfriends and girlfriends but also dealt with solutions for how to get out of the relationship and how to help a friend get out of the relationship.

- An anecdotal piece on how students cope with burnout

Health-related issues must be communicated with the utmost care because so much of the public's health knowledge comes from what it reads in newspapers and

Fig. 5.1. Health feature.
Silver Chips, Montgomery Blair
High School, Silver Spring, Md.

magazines rather than from what it learns from physicians or textbooks. A reporter who is inaccurate is like a doctor who gives bad advice.

The biggest pitfall for young health writers is writing about something they don't understand. Going into a world of medical jargon and complicated concepts can lead to writing such as this:

> Advil relieves pain. Body aches are caused when cells release a substance called prostaglandins, Dr. Foster said. Prostaglandins cause muscle stimulation which causes inflammation in the muscle. Advil is a nonsteroidal, anti-inflammatory drug. It goes to the cells that produce the prostaglandins and inhibits prostaglandins and inhibits prostaglandin synthesis and decreases muscle stimulation.

The writer later admitted he didn't understand what he was writing about. In trying to do a story about how pain medicine actually works, he succeeded only in confusing the reader.

Which leads us to this:

> Science Writing rule No. 1: Never try to explain something that you don't understand. Don't be shy about asking your sources to explain something again, if you don't get it the first time. And don't cop out by quoting the scientist's unhelpful explanation. If your scientist source is not a good explainer, ask him or her to refer you to somebody else, maybe one who teaches the field. Once you think you understand something, check yourself by saying it back to the scientist in your own words.

Boyce Rensberger
A Field Guide for Science Writers

Understanding the topic before interviewing will help you understand the doctor or scientist and in turn help you explain the story to the reader. Read books, medical pamphlets or magazine articles on the subject first. For subjects such as sleep deprivation or the athletic enhancement drug creatine, reading background material will provide knowledge of the specialized language and research. But do not use a lot of secondhand material in the reporting of the story. Health writing depends on interviews with local physicians, psychologists or students coping with the subject to make it relevant and real to the readers. Use interviews with firsthand sources to make sure you accurately understand the information. Do not avoid asking questions, even ones covering information you have already read about.

No question is dumb if the answer is necessary to help you understand something. There's a difference between not being prepared for an interview and feeling embarrassed about asking a question that you think may sound stupid or silly. Don't pretend to know more than you do in hopes of impressing a source. You need to know the information in order to write an accurate story.

The most important tool a journalist has is the ability to ask questions. Answers always raise more questions and you should keep asking them until you understand the subject.

Ronald Kotulak
A Field Guide for Science Writers

The point can't be emphasized enough: know what you are writing about before you write about it.

The following tips from professional science writers in *A Field Guide for Science Writers* should help the beginning health writer communicate complicated subjects to the average student.

1. **Do echo interviews**

   Mentioned earlier, the practice calls on the reporter to repeat the key information in his or her own words to the scientist to see if the interpretation is correct. The reporter gets an immediate check on how well he or she is grasping the material. For example, the reporter would listen to an answer and then say, "So my understanding of how Ritalin affects a teenager is . . ."

2. **Get the face behind the statistic or the issue, but make sure the personal story has relevance**

   Showing the reader a student who daydreams during a physics lecture, doesn't do his or her homework but makes an A on the test can help clarify a clinical psychologist's definition of a gifted person. The reporter must understand that the reader can relate to a story of an individual better than to a statistic or a medical description. A story on asthma should include a statistic on the number of people with asthma as well as a description of the challenges of the ailment. But a story on a student's

effort to control his breathing disorder while playing baseball gives life to the story.

A reporter should not assume that a student is an example of the larger story but should seek a professional's confirmation that this is the case. Just because a reporter finds a student who seems tired all the time does not mean he or she has found a person who suffers from chronic fatigue syndrome. Confirm the diagnosis with a doctor.

3. **Analogies, anecdotes, examples and metaphors are very effective in helping people understand any new ideas and concepts**

   Giving the reader specifics he or she can relate to is important to clearly communicate complex information. Here, the writer makes a comparison to clarify the dangers of a relatively unknown herbal cigarette.

   However, cloves include 60–70 percent tobacco and twice as much nicotine as the average Marlboro.

   In this next example, the author explains how small the chances are of contracting tuberculosis at a school where there is an infected student. Rather than making the vague statement that "the chances are rare," the writer follows up with this specific quote.

   "You have to breathe the same air as a person with TB in a small area," Dr. Goodman said. "You might contract TB if you lived in the some home as [an infected person] but classrooms are so large that it would be unlikely to catch it because that is a small amount of bacteria in a huge amount of air."

ACADEMIC WRITING

If a discussion between a mother and her 15-year-old daughter were the public's best source for academic coverage, there would be no reason to have this section.

"So what did you learn at school today?"
"Oh nothing."

B6 • Monday, May 2, 2005 **FEATURES** The Campanile

Tutors enrich educational experience, fight negative stigmas

BY ANJALI ALBUQUERQUE
Features Editor

Palo Alto High School junior Phil Jung views learning and getting good grades as a game. He plays the pawns carefully in his rage against the academic machine; a tutor gets him ahead of the other players in his Analysis H and Spanish 4 AP classes and he uses friends extensively as a resource. Despite Jung's talent for math and science, his tutor helps solidify concepts so he can better approach challenging problems on tests. However, Jung doesn't publicize his having a tutor, a pawn that puts him at an advantage in this academic game. The tutor business is kept out of the limelight, to prevent other academic players from becoming envious.

"People think if you have a tutor you have to be stupid," Jung said. "It's a dumb stereotype, because smart people can want an extra academic edge too. Tutoring is all about immersing yourself in a subject — learning and increasing your chance of getting good grades. It's helped me see how concepts fit together more coherently and I've been doing better."

However, other Paly students regard tutoring as implicit cheating, as it undermines individual-driven learning and the love of true knowledge while valuing manipulating the academic machine.

"If you're in an honors class, you are expected to be able to teach yourself," Paly junior Daniel Chew said. "Getting tutoring shows that you can't teach yourself and it deflects from the importance of initiative. If you have a tutor, chances are you can't apply much of what you learn to real life. You're just obsessed with bookwork, and can't think out of the box."

This stigma toward tutors undermines the learning environment and fuels the academic mindset that "natural geniuses" who do not have to work hard should be glorified while "hard workers" should be looked down upon.

"There's something so admirable about people that can get an 'A' on an Analysis test without studying compared to someone who has to slave away for a 'B'," Paly sophomore Natasha Whitney said. "Students and teachers romanticize it; it's hard to not romanticize it. It's hard to respect a student that drinks lots of coffee, is always stressed, but does mediocre when there's a chill person that doesn't do much but aces everything. But some people take it too far and consider the 'naturally talented as 'Gods'."

The lack of regard for "hard workers" who take advantage of academic opportunities like tutoring to

Paly senior Victor Zilinskas tutors sophomore Elise Mullen in the Academic Resource Center, where students can receive free academic tutoring from their peers without the fear that their academic potential will be questioned.

David Lehferes/The Campanile

improve their grades undermines the educational environment by convincing students that success is predestined.

"The stigma against tutors is very sad," SAT and math tutor Gus El Mashni said. "In life, there are some people who can absorb lots of material and there are some students who have to work twice as hard. People don't get to choose their IQs. The only thing people can really control is how hard they work. So it's sad when people don't admire the fact that some students are putting in all that effort and work. While it's easy for teachers to get caught up with the naturally talented, it's bad for them to neglect the others."

Neglecting others in a class and only teaching to the brightest students can make the lower segments of a class internalize feelings of inferiority and actually accomplish lower than their potentials. This situation puts students in a double bind, because they don't want to see a tutor and admit their feelings of inferiority, but at the same time their teachers don't give them much consideration, thus students start thinking less of themselves.

"When a teacher doesn't really care about you, it makes you feel stupid," junior Daniel Rosen said. "But seeing a tutor will make you feel more stupid, so it's not worth it. And on top of that, if you're truly stupid, why should you care? The school environment sends negative

messages all the time that can make people feel even more stupid."

The high level of pressure and expectations at Paly creates a game mentality, where students stop caring about 'true' learning — all that matters is mobilizing all resources that are available to ensure academic victory. It's commonplace for students to blame scapegoats for their own academic failure.

"I would do well in school, if it weren't for all the stupid people that the community thinks are actually smart that just work really hard," junior Martin Strauss said. "I'm not a genius, but I'm smarter than a lot of people. I have a tutor to help get me organized, but it's sad that the people that get the glory aren't truly intelligent."

However, tutors dispute the view that 'valid success' occurs without hard work. The academic machine is not an equal playing field, but neither is life.

"Obviously, the 'real smart people' never need tutors, and they are true leaders," El Mashi said. "Our community shouldn't be respecting people who just learn by working really hard and having a tutor dictate to them. They are like robots."

El Mashi believes in a more holistic approach to teaching, especially in light of teachers that undermine educational justice by only caring about the 'smarties.'

"The way to make the educational process more fair is by encouraging people to accomplish to their true potential," El Mashi said. "I think there's a confidence factor that goes into this stereotype about tutors. People need to feel comfortable asking for help, and people who 'get it' need to get over themselves."

Tutors provide students with more individualized help and aren't different from a parent that's trained in calculus and helps enrich their student. While not everyone can afford a tutor, not everyone can have a parent that can help. People are forced to take advantage of their dispositions to ensure they can get the most of their environment. Tutors' consensus is getting a grasp on life and maximizing one's chance for success is not morally reprehensible.

"In high pressure environments, students and parents feel they need to have a tutor to deal with the unequal playing field," El Mashi said. "There is some validity to it. From my perspective, the goal is to learn as much as you can. I don't see anything intrinsically wrong with getting help outside the classroom in an environment where it's easier to learn. There's no difference in principle in reading a book twice or getting a tutor to explain a concept. It's not cheating to study longer than someone else who's competing with you for a grade. But invariably, people should care more about the material."

Students may truly enjoy learning but there are still considerations that shape all students' lives: college plans, parental pressure and careers. However, a true love for knowledge and skillful moves in the academic game are not mutually exclusive.

"I'm really interested in math and science," Jung said. "And why doing well in school may be a 'game' at times, it's important to work hard so you can truly foster your interests later. It's about long term versus the short term."

A short-term goal may be to navigate the Paly academic system. However, long term, students can kindle passions about specific academic interests; a true love for learning is the long-term 'rage against the machine'. While the academic game can get out of control, the learning process is not a white and black issue. Generalizations that ignore the grey areas concerning the usefulness of tutors are dangerous to other students' psychological well-being.

"Sure you can call the academic environment machine-like," Jung said. "And that may be bad, but it's equally bad to stress 'natural talent' too much. Tutors are legitimate."

Fig. 5.2. Academic feature.
The Campanile, Palo Alto High
School, Palo Alto, Calif.

The answer is an easy escape from having to talk to your mother, but it is an exaggeration. Academics are a huge part of the school experience that should not be ignored in the high school publication. As a high school writer, your ability to see and cover what's going on in classrooms is critical. The publication can help students learn more about their education and make them more responsible for their own learning. Coverage can bring up curriculum issues that need to be debated so the public makes sure the students are getting a strong education.

Coverage should include

- Changes in graduation requirements and standardized testing

- Updates on student body progress – failure rates, testing rankings

- Creative or interesting assignments or projects in the classroom

- Curriculum issues such as the elimination of a class on jewelry making or the addition of the study of religion

- Education issues such as the introduction of block/alternative scheduling or the lengthening of the school year

Here are a few examples of academic stories covered in high school publications.

- A feature on the ways grades are weighted – honors classes, advanced placement classes and the like – combined with interviews of faculty and students

- A feature on mainstreaming in which less able students are in classes with those of average or better than average ability

- A feature story on the techniques teacher use to make academic classes interesting

- A news-feature story on the science class's project to study the school's garbage to show what it throws away

- A story on the impact the state's tougher graduation plans are having on electives

- A feature story about students who are finding easier routes for admission to academically rigorous universities (Fig. 5.3)

- An informative feature on girls-only classes and whether girls participate more and learn better in these classes

- A how-to piece on college application essays told through interviews with college admissions officers and high school alums

- A feature story on how to work effectively in group projects

- A feature story on a physical science class trip in a hot air balloon to study Charles' Law and Archimedes Principle

Fig. 5.3. A feature story about students who are finding easier routes for admission to academically rigorous universities. *Chronicle,* Harvard–Westlake High School, North Hollywood, Calif.

All of these stories are appropriate in school newspapers. How well they are read, of course, depends on how well they were investigated, written and displayed. Most, of course, are not hard news stories dependent on a spot news peg (a timely, newsworthy event or element), although academic stories are often related to a recent event such as a school board meeting or a topic of high reader interest such as grades.

Stories of interesting classroom activities, such as a business law mock trial, should not be neglected. Sometimes a class has speakers whose comments would have interest beyond the classroom. Occasionally a field trip can be developed into an interesting story (Fig. 5.4).

Yearbook academic sections or spreads should highlight interesting activities and issues of the year. Typically features, the yearbook academic stories should highlight interesting class assignments, teachers and educational issues. But they should do so through vivid storytelling that revives the reader's memories of the wobbly desk in science class and that faint whiff of formaldehyde.

Keep the student in mind when covering academics. If the story's about changes in science curriculum, make sure to get examples to show the student reader how

In the Flesh

Biology II and Anatomy students get a look at a real autopsy at a local morgue

BY SAMANTHA THOMPSON
Staff Writer

As they walk into the room the students shiver at the temperature. After all, this room is 10 degrees colder than most. It's a large room with muted colors and is surprisingly homey... compared to what most students were expecting.

One wall is covered with sinks, presumably to wash the bodies out. There is a large vacuum hose also.

The students in Al Frisby's Biology II and anatomy classes are in the Jackson County Examiner's office to watch human autopsies.

Frisby began offering the program about eight years ago when he started calling professionals he knew in the area. He then set up times for his students to come in and observe the professionals in their daily routine.

"A lot of students want to go into a medical field and this gives them the opportunity to see what it's like before they invest the time and money," Frisby said.

The program has grown so much that he is able to set up visits to a private doctor's practice, four different surgeons, three veterinarians, two physical therapists, three hospital operating rooms and an electron microscope specialist.

For the past two years, students have worked with Dr. Sam Gulino. Gulino decided to allow students to come watch him perform autopsies because he wanted students to understand what his career really is about.

"Most people don't understand the true service we provide," Gulino said. "As long as people have a true interest in the field and not just a morbid fascination, we like to have them come in."

Gulino was hoping that students would realize from the experience that the information they are learning from the textbook they will use later in life.

"When I was in school, I took physics and I thought I would never use what I learned," Gulino said. "It's amazing what I use everyday whether it involves car crashes or people falling out of buildings."

To be eligible for this program students simply have to be in one of the two classes, Biology II or Anatomy, and be on code six.

McGowen was a member of the first group to observe Gulino performing six autopsies.

Though McGowen doesn't want to go into the medical profession in the future, she does plan to become a biologist. She thought the experience would be educational.

"I thought it would be neat to see what an actual human body looked like, and to see what the organs really looked like," McGowen said.

Juniors Kiley McGowen and Jennifer Parrott take a first look at the body and react to the corpse.

McGowen was nervous that seeing the dead bodies would make her sick, but said that she did pretty well considering that one cadaver had its eyes open and another was beginning to turn green.

"It was really cool," McGowen said. "I was expecting it to be really medical, but it was just a room."

McGowen said that the experience was very strange and unusual. The room was very cold and she just couldn't get over how fake the bodies looked. Though she said that the outside looked like wax, she was positive the inside was real.

"They take out the organs and weigh them and find out the cause of death," McGowen said. "Then they put them in a bag and put them back into the guy, that was weird."

McGowen thought her time was well spent and that the whole experience was very interesting.

"I'd like to go back, I just can't see why anyone would want to do that as a profession," McGowen said.

Junior Andrey Hicks also attended the autopsy. Hicks, who is currently planning to go into the medical field as a pediatric cardiologist, thought the experience would be valuable. He discovered that he could handle at least a small part of being a doctor.

"I was reassured that I wasn't going to faint if I saw blood or someone died," Hicks said. "It was interesting to see the inside of the body. It really looked a lot like the inside of a cat's body."

There were some interesting moments in the morgue; the worst part of viewing the autopsy for Hicks was when he saw the corpse that was turning green. He found the most interesting part of the autopsy to be when the pathologist cut the frontal lobe of the brain. In most cases, the brain is not cut open during an autopsy, but the deceased had fallen and hit his head prior to death, so the pathologist had to run tests on the brain.

"It gave me a better understanding on a part of my field," Hicks said. "I got to see the gray and white matter of the brain. It just gives you a better understanding when you see it first hand."

Even if these students are not planning to become medical examiners, the experience is something they won't forget soon.

"(Going to the morgue) was a one time thing. A medical examiner is definitely not the career choice for me," Hicks said.

Junior Jennifer Parrot, senior Elizabeth Marvel and junior Andrey Hicks react when viewing the first cut through the skin of the body of a woman's corpse.

Fig. 5.4. Academic story. *Northwest Passage*, Shawnee Mission Northwest High School, Shawnee, Kan.

---

the classes will be different. Don't just republish the dry text of the district's mandates. If the story's about new science lab computers, get anecdotes from students who felt like real surgeons using the virtual operating room software in anatomy and physiology class. Don't just tell the reader how many computers the district is installing and "how excited" the science teachers are.

DEATH COVERAGE

In the middle of all the emotion of a death, a student publication must maintain a sense of objectivity. Guidelines or a policy set up before such an event happens may outline tough ethical questions for tough circumstances. Guidelines should cover what news-judging criteria to use in deciding whether to do an obituary, a straight news story or a eulogy-like news-feature. Considerations are the deceased's impact on students and the school, the nature of the death and often the time of death in relation to the deadline.

Yearbooks should be wary of dedicating books to a student who has died during the year. The practice can lead to fairness questions if another student dies after the final deadline, the student has moved away or a new student dies in a car accident. One yearbook staff simply places a gray bar across the student's name in the class section with the date of birth and death placed underneath. Others cover the death as a story and base coverage on news value. Allow family or friends to purchase an ad to increase coverage if they want.

News or feature death coverage should be free of editorialization. Any expressions of sympathy from the writer or staff should be reserved for the opinion section. A reporter should avoid euphemisms such as "passed away" and "Death's call." Simply use "died," unless as a religious-affiliated school the publication uses another term.

Accuracy of facts is always important, but in an obituary it is even more so. Common facts included in an obituary are full name (make sure of correct spelling), identification, age, date of death, cause of death, biographical details, survivors, date, time and place of funeral, and memorials. These facts appear in a news-feature story along with more anecdotes and quotes surrounding the student's or teacher's life. Those quotes come from family, friends, teachers or the minister who presided.

Fig. 5.5. Death story. *Panther Prints*, Duncanville High School, Duncanville, Texas.

School remembers classmate
Life Skills student David Whitley dies in his sleep

By Deidra Dallas
Panther Prints asst. editor

All David Whitley wanted was to go to Prom and to graduate.

"For the past four years he's really been looking forward to graduation. Every year he would ask someone new to go to Prom with him," Life Skills teacher Glenn Smith said.

David, a junior Life Skills, passed away Oct. 8 in his sleep. His death has been determined to be of natural causes, most likely relating to his breathing and heart problems.

"It was so sudden," junior Stephanie Mekhjian said. "We just didn't understand how this could happen. It made me realize how fleeting life is."

David was afflicted with Prader Willie syndrome, a mental retardation dealing with chromosome 15, which also leads to an eating disorder.

People with Prader Willie have one-third fewer nerve endings than a healthy person. This lessens the power in muscles throughout the body including the lungs, and also leads to obsessive overeating as they cannot tell when they are full.

Due to his disorder, David was obese and had difficulty breathing, causing him to need a tracheotomy, a tube inserted in his trachea to assist with breathing.

David Whitley

With enough structure, help and medication, David was able to control his overeating, though there were still some problems.

"We were very worried about his weight gain," Mr. Smith said. "He had gained a considerable amount of weight over the summer and was also having increasing amounts of trouble with his breathing."

Despite his condition, David always had a smile on his face.

"David was always very friendly, very social. He talked to everybody everywhere he went," Mr. Smith said. "He loved to sing and pretend to preach."

When David was off his medication, he sometimes had behavioral problems, another symptom of Prader Willie.

"He made really good prog-

ress over his past four years at the high school. He's grown up a lot," Mr. Smith said.

Conveying the information about David's death to the special education students was challenging.

Mr. Smith, who had been out due to minor surgery, came to school to tell the class of David's passing.

"He walked in and gave everyone a hug and said 'hi.' Then he told them to look around the room and notice that someone was missing," senior support counselor Renee McNeely said. "He said that David had simply gone to sleep and not awakened."

According to Mrs. McNeely, however, the Life Skills students didn't fully comprehend.

"But they knew that it was

(see David Whitley on page 3)

In the news-feature coverage of the death of Duncanville, Texas junior David Whitley, the *Panther Prints* writer clearly explains the complications of the Prader Willie syndrome Whitley was born with and the role the condition may have had in his death. The story also sensitively covers how teachers explained Whitley's death to his special education classmates.

While asking those questions, especially of family, is often awkward for reporters, Chip Scanlan, Director of Writing Programs for Poynter Institute, has suggestions. Scanlan said that he rang the doorbell of a victim's home to talk to the father.

> I said, without thinking, that I was a reporter and that I was very sorry to intrude at this time, "But I just didn't want you to pick up the paper Sunday and say "Couldn't they at least have asked if we wanted to say anything." It was as if I had said, "Open Sesame." Within moments, we were standing in their daughter's room. On the bed was an unopened package that had come in the mail that day. It was a set of pots and pans for her hope chest. That single detail still haunts me and I think really conveyed what the victim and those who

• David Whitley

(continued from page 1)

sad," she said.

Through the tears and confusion, Mrs. McNeely said there was one thing that stood out in her mind.

"It was refreshing to be in there. It's been awhile since I have been able to see the love teachers and students have for each other," she said. "It was very obvious they are a family."

David's death affected more than the just the Life Skills classes.

"It's very sad anytime you lose a kid," soccer coach Bill Manning said. "But it's different with the special ed. kids. I think I spend more time with them than I do my own. David will be missed, but he's in a better place."

Students from the Theatre Department also keenly feel David's absence.

Last year during the production *The Boys Next Door*, cast and crew members were able to spend time getting to know the special education students.

"Though I only knew him for a day, I got attached to him," junior Tyler Larson said. "He was a real great kid to be around."

Other theatre students also

said they will miss David.

"Although I didn't know him as much as I wished I had, just knowing that a hug everyday would bring a smile to his face filled me with an indescribable joy," sophomore Rebecca McPherson said.

Theatre director Robert Shepard said he and his students will miss David.

"Spending time with David and the Life Skills classes, we all developed a wonderful bond," he said. "They showed us that we are all the same. We all want to love, be loved, be needed. We want to laugh, smile, and in the end we all cry."

Theatre teacher Bruce Garner said David was his neighbor in building 9.

"For two years I got to see him everyday," Mr. Garner said. "With David, you got exactly what you saw. There was no pretense about him. He was a real human being. Some may place value on his life, but it was his life and I'm sorry he doesn't have it anymore. He was one of our kids. I feel like a part of my life is now missing."

Donations are being accepted by switchboard operator Carol Jackson to help David's family with funeral expenses.

loved her lost. In that way, I think I was able to honor the legitimate journalistic reasons without greatly re-victimizing the family.

Following is a hard news story on the death of a student, an excellent example of straight objective reporting.

Steve Mitchell, a senior, died early Wednesday morning, October 8, of a gunshot wound he had received two days earlier.

Mitchell, who was 17 years old and lived at 1416 Park St., had been shot in the head when he and three other youths "were fooling around with a gun" in a house at 1700 Marshall St., according to a police report.

The other three youths said the shooting was accidental, according to the report, but police did make an arrest in the case. Arrested was a 17-year-old youth, also a Central High student, who resides at the 1700 Marshall St. address.

Police said the shooting happened at 3 p.m. Monday, October 6.

Tiger
Little Rock Central High School
Little Rock, Ark.

This story appeared in the *Tiger* two days after the young man's death. It is strictly a news story. Had the story not been published until the following week, it probably would have been a news-feature, one perhaps with a feature lead since the spot news would have been common knowledge. The reporter could have researched the story to find significant facts of the young man's life. Outstanding or interesting activities he engaged in, achievements, anecdotes and recollections of friends and teachers can make for a good feature story. Details of the funeral service; comments from the minister, priest or rabbi; and other human interest details can be part of the story as well.

ADVANCE STORIES

Giving readers advance notice of a meeting or an assembly is an important role of the high school publica-

tion. Not all the news has already happened. Give the readers information about events that they can enjoy or participate in. The advance story is simply a story published prior to an event.

The advance story can be a news or a feature story. The reporter can use an inverted pyramid lead or a feature lead. The impact or an interesting aspect of the event makes up the lead. While in either form the time, day and place are not the first things to mention, they are covered early in the story.

THE ADVANCE MEETING STORY

Students often have opinions about issues such as a proposed change in the dress code or use of $5,000 raised by the senior class. The high school publication must play a role in helping students understand how and where to voice those opinions. An advance meeting story informs the readers of all sides of an issue so they can play an enlightened role in the democratic process (Fig. 5.6).

The reporter should find out the primary purpose of the meeting or the issue on the agenda that has the most impact on readers. If a series of events will take place at a meeting or a number of decisions will be made, the reporter will select the most important as a possible feature.

The basics included in an advance meeting story are (1) the purpose of the meeting, (2) the time and place (these are especially important in an advance story – double-check to be sure you are right), (3) the name of the organization, (4) the persons who will lead or participate, (5) any background information about the speaker or speakers, (6) the kind of meeting, (7) the feature angle.

Avoid wordy, dull beginnings, such as "There will be a meeting of . . ."; "The purpose of the meeting will be . . ."; "At 3:30 this afternoon the club will . . ." Also avoid saying, "Everybody is invited." It's assumed that the meeting is open to the public if the story reports the time and date. If the meeting is closed to the public, tell readers so.

FOLLOW-UP STORY

A follow-up story is simply a news or news-feature story that reports on an event after it has taken place. The time delay from the event to the date of publication dictates the way the story is covered. The city council's passage of a teen curfew three weeks before a publication's deadline makes the straight news lead obsolete. A lead summarizing the unanimous approval of an 11 p.m. curfew for those under 17 probably doesn't tell readers much new. Instead the reporter searching for a story angle may look for the newest information, such as a petition circulating to change the curfew to 1 a.m. The news-feature angle of the impact the curfew is having on students who work late hours or those who have been ticketed or detained by police for curfew violations makes for a more interesting story.

News staffs, however, need to be alert to events that should be covered. A teachers' strike, for example, would be covered by the local newspaper, radio, or television in the community as a hard news story, yet there are a number of stories available for the school paper. One might be how days missed are to be made up, another how graduation would be affected if the strike is a prolonged one, and still another how students and parents feel about the strike. There are many other news-features, feature stories, even editorials that the school paper could provide on this event. A number of issues can probably be covered in one follow-up story that simply refers to the existing strike.

Sometimes, of course, the strike can be over before the newspaper comes out. Should the newspaper then ignore the event as though it had never happened? In that case even the results of the strike would have been covered in other media. The important principle for a school newspaper staff is not to publish "old news" but to handle events in different ways so that there will be reader interest: news-features, feature stories and sometimes in-depth reporting. See Chapters 4, 6 and 9 for those types of stories.

WRITING FOLLOW-UP STORIES

Leads in a follow-up story should be timely or significant information. The information can be delivered in a summary inverted pyramid style or in a feature style.

The key is giving readers something they don't already know (Fig. 5.7).

If the school band wins an area contest, the story should cover how the win makes it eligible for the state contest in two weeks, or it should cover the band's 1 a.m. practice the night before the contest. When the deadline comes two days if not two weeks after the contest, the band's win has already been on school announcements and has spread by word of mouth.

Follow the lead with the tie-in, or the nut graph – one or more paragraphs briefly summarizing what has gone before. The tie-in, or nut graph, enables the reader who has not followed the story to this time to understand what it is all about. It also helps the reader who has followed the story to identify it.

Follow the tie-in, or nut graph, with facts to explain or build on the lead. The structure of this part may be chronological or

Board considers freshmen wing

Vanessa VanAtta

Reporter

A new addition to the high school has been proposed to the board of education, and may be voted on at Monday's meeting.

"The new wing would include 16 new classrooms, eight on each floor (two of which would be science rooms) and two rest rooms. It will be built where the modular classrooms are sitting right now.

"The three corner classrooms on each floor will have operational walls which could be removed for open lectures ," Board of Education Member Marty Rothey said.

There are a variety of reasons the new addition is needed.

"We have taken existing rooms and made them computer labs, open enrollment is also increasing the number of students at the high school," Rothey said.

According to the enrollment report, the high school population has increased by 111 students in one year.

The new addition will be a freshmen wing, but will not segregate them from the rest of the school.

"They (the freshmen) are getting the best of both worlds. They are not totally separate, they will be connected to the building and will not have all of their classes in the new wing," Principal Dr. Kathleen Crates said.

Though students will not spend all their time in the new wing, they may feel segregated.

"The new wing would relieve a lot of congestion in the halls and would allow the new freshmen to get to know each other better. It's a really good idea because the high school is crowded," Sophomore Kristy Coppes said.

Now that the new wing has been discussed, the board of education is searching for a way to finance the addition.

"At the last meeting (Superintendent) Mr. (Robert) Lotz discussed different ways of paying for the new wing. We want to lease a purchase with a bank (take out a loan). Now we are waiting on comments from the public," Rothey said.

Fig. 5.6. Advance meeting story. *Blue & Gold*, Findlay High School, Findlay, Ohio.

Water rushes down Coldwater Canyon and accumulates in deep puddles at the south gate of Harvard-Westlake Jan. 11.

Rain aftermath still causing delays

by Ashling Loh-Doyle

Nearly a month after record rainfall and the closure of both campuses for two consecutive days, upper school students are still inconvenienced by the rainstorm's destruction. Mulholland Drive, east of Coldwater Canyon Drive, is still closed to eastbound traffic, affecting some students' commute to school. It will be reopened March 5, according to the Los Angeles Department of Transportation.

"Because Mulholland is still closed, I have to leave ten minutes earlier to get to school in the morning. It's a pain because I have to come north on Coldwater to get to school, and it's so slow," Alex Hofbauer '06 said.

The closure of school Jan. 11 and 12 was the result of the closure of the canyon roads that serve upper and middle school families.

Despite damage to the roads, no damage was reported on either campus.

In the five-day storm preceding the closure of both campuses, more than 11 inches of rain fell, according to National Oceanic and Atmospheric Administration.

Laurel Canyon Boulevard closed because of a collapsed house Jan. 10, and various mud slides closed Coldwater Canyon Drive.

In addition, part of Mulholland Drive gave way in a mud slide onto Coldwater Canyon, and fallen trees closed Beverly Glen Boulevard throughout Jan. 10 and 11. Everyday roughly 1,000 Harvard-Westlake students commute between the San Fernando Valley and the Westside by utilizing these roads.

After receiving news of the closures and consulting the Los Angeles Department of Transportation on the evening of Jan. 10, Headmaster Thomas C. Hudnut decided to close both campuses. Parents and students were notified of school's closure through the Telephone Tree and a message from Hudnut on the school's emergency hotline.

"Everybody from the San Fernando Valley was trying to funnel through the 405 and Sepulveda, and at various times those were both closed. It didn't make much sense to have school with roughly 1,000 of our students on both campuses who have to go over the hill one way or another each day. We couldn't get to school. So why put an extra 1,000 people on the roads?" Hudnut said. Because of the transportation issues and the forecast for Jan. 11, Hudnut decided to close school for a second day. Although there was little rainfall that day, Laurel Canyon Boulevard, Coldwater Canyon Drive and parts of Mulholland Drive remained closed.

Hudnut consulted a number of administrators from other local area schools, which also closed Jan. 11.

"City Hall had recommended that people stay off the streets unless it was essential they drive. I could argue that school is essential, but I'm not going to argue that with houses fallen and mud slides blocking roads. When the roads are impassable, school is impossible," Hudnut said. The closure of school came at the end of the first semester, and for ninth to 12th-graders, at the beginning of the first week of finals. This was a concern to administrators, who felt that students would not be sufficiently prepared to take their exams.

"After the closure of school for the second day, we were wondering if we should change the exam schedule and give people extra time to review," Head of Upper School Harry Salamandra said. After consulting the department heads, the upper school administration decided not to change the exam schedule and to suspend free periods and double periods Jan. 13 and 14 in order to give students adequate classroom review time before their first final Jan. 15. "Some students came back and said, in some respects, it was advantageous to have that time off because they were able to organize study materials, which they may not have been able to do if they had been in school," Salamandra said.

Fig. 5.7. Follow-up story. *The Chronicle*, Harvard–Westlake High School, North Hollywood, Calif.

narrative or an inverted pyramid style, depending on the story.

The following story is a hard news story because the newspaper from which it was taken is a weekly with an all-night print shop. Therefore, a story happening Thursday evening could easily be in Friday's newspaper.

The tie-in paragraph, or nut graph, is the second paragraph, with background information that had already appeared in the newspaper the week before.

The remaining four paragraphs are in the order of decreasing importance. Notice that the final paragraph doesn't end abruptly with the least significant fact; it cites a significant quote from the local sponsor of the contest.

Andy Kende became the top science student in the United States when he won the Westinghouse Science Talent Search Tuesday night in Washington, D.C.

Originally one of 3,161 entrants, Andy went to Washington last Friday as one of 40 finalists to compete for the nation's top science award. Each entrant submitted a project demonstrating ability to do scientific research and took a comprehensive examination.

Andy won a $20,000 scholarship. Gretchen Warvel, a New York City high school girl, won second place and a $15,000 scholarship.

According to Mr. Sailsbury, biology teacher who supervised Andy's project, "Andy definitely has what it takes to excel in science, for he performed his project with the ease and skill with which a trained housewife boils water."

Andy's winning thesis and project was on "Grignard Reagents Synthesizing Organic Compounds." Andy discovered 18 new reagents not published in science literature before.

Summing up what he believes is Andy's most significant characteristic, Mr. Sailsbury said, "He is simply one of those unusual people who are highly motivated. He really can't think of any reasons why he shouldn't do almost everything."

Note particularly how the tie-in paragraph, or nut graph, gives the reader the necessary background that preceded this story and relates it to the preceding stories.

Because Andy had not yet returned from Washington, D.C., when the story had to be written, the story is a hard news story that appeared in a weekly paper. If Andy had returned before the story was written and even more time had elapsed before its publication, how might you have handled the story? What would you have included that is not in this story?

The following is another type of follow-up story, one that shows staff initiative. Some reporters would think that because there is not to be a spring honors assembly there would be no story. The writer of the following dug into the reasons for the decision not to have an assembly and followed up with an interesting story.

U-High's annual spring honors assembly is no more. Both the Student Legislative Coordinating Council (SLCC) and Principal Margaret Fallers felt the program should not be continued, citing last year's restless and unsympathetic audience.

"It was nice for the recipients but not for the student body," SLCC President Erwin Chemerinsky observed.

"It was organized," Mrs. Fallers said.

She is, however, seeking an alternative to the assembly because she feels "it is suitable for a school to recognize a special service given to the school."

The Senior Service Award and similar citations in past years announced at the assembly probably will be given this year, Mrs. Fallers said, though she is not certain when and where.

Awards have disappeared not only from the school calendar but also from the first floor trophy cases which formerly housed athletic, debate, journalism, language and math awards. They now house displays of student work and exhibits arranged by the library staff.

Advisers of activities which have received several awards this year generally do not feel an assembly or trophies are necessary to honor recipients.

"Only debaters understand debate awards," Debate Coach Earl Bell said. He feels recognition of excellence is important, and provides incentive but would like to see useful books and briefcases replace trophies as awards.

Music Teacher Gisela Goettling said she enters her students in contests so they can gain experience, not to win awards. She feels an honor itself is relatively unimportant.

Publications Adviser Wayne Brasler said, "Awards play an important role in high school journalism because they single out the excellent from the vast amount published.

"I'm against the school publicizing awards through assemblies and trophy displays, however. The number of awards an activity receives can be a misleading indication of its merit. Take drama, for example. Because of its teamwork nature the students and teachers involved have felt awards would do more harm than good. So you don't hear about awards to drama, yet it's probably the outstanding activity in the school."

Karen Uhlenhuth
U-High Midway
University High School
Chicago, Ill.

When the follow-up story is about a meeting, give the reader the point of the meeting and its meaning in the lead. Avoid beginning with time or place unless either is extremely unusual. Avoid a lead like this: "The Academic Decathlon team met Monday." Time, place and group name are included in the story, but not in the opening words.

SPEECH STORIES

The speech story is not as prevalent in high school publications as it is in professional publications. Still,

Malcolm X's daughter dares students to bridge racial gaps

by Angelica Baker

The eldest daughter of civil rights activist Malcolm X urged students to overcome social injustice and bridge the gap between "them" and "us" by making an effort to understand the beliefs and cultures of others at the Black History Month Assembly Feb. 14.

Attallah Shabazz, a producer, writer and the Ambassador of International Cultural Affairs and Project Development for Belize spoke at the assembly shortly after flying in from New York.

Shabazz began her speech by reminding students that privilege is not a joke but a gift to be shared before moving on to discuss her father's childhood and the extent to which his principles and theology shaped her own, stopping after each thought to demand of her audience: "Am I clear?"

Though portrayals of Malcolm X often begin with his teenage years and portray him as a gang member or pimp, Shabazz emphasized that her father had been an honor student, class president, and even a nerd before becoming "a hip brother from the street."

Shabazz's grandfather was killed by the Ku Klux Klan in 1935, at which point Malcolm and his seven siblings were separated in the foster care system.

Malcolm ended up in Boston, where he soon became part of a gang. At age 19, he was sent to prison.

"He always said that, as thrilling as it was to attempt to get away with something, by the time he was caught he breathed a sigh of relief," Shabazz said.

"He said that a part of him was so grateful when he was sent to prison because he had always lived with the shame and fear of what his mother would say if she ever found out what he was doing," she added.

Shabazz went on to discuss her father's involvement with the Nation of Islam.

"Theology belongs to everyone," she said. "Religion has no color. The Nation of Islam's intent was to nurture Black folks into feeling like citizens of this land," she said.

"The Muslim religion is a hot button issue now, but that doesn't make me want to be any less what I am. But growing up, I was not indoctrinated with the Nation of Islam."

In every response to a student question, Shabazz emphasized the fact that her father she knew and loved differed in many ways from the radical, combative image of Malcolm X that has endured over the years.

She stressed that her father had never advocated breaking the law and in fact had expressly discouraged it, discounting the common belief that he encouraged violence and civil disobedience.

She clarified his popular cry, "by any means necessary," by explaining that it was not merely an endorsement of violence — it was an acknowledgment of the fact that, if someone is hurting your loved ones, you must do what you can to stop them.

"I was his oldest child. If my father had any loathing in his system, I would have had it," Shabazz said.

"To many people Malcolm X is an

Attallah Shabazz spoke to students about her father's life and legacy Feb. 14.

image, a function, a philosophy," she said.

"For me personally, he is a father missing. But simply to have a living father, I would not have traded who he was," she said.

"To have had him as my first buddy, to have had him to listen to me, to know that he was who he was even when it wasn't popular — that is what sustains me," Shabazz said.

Shabazz continually spoke of the mentality of "them" versus "us" and how it feeds social injustice, insisting that education and exposure are the only effective ways to achieve unity.

Shabazz instructed the audience members to turn to their left and right, introduce themselves to their neighbor, and wish their neighbors success.

"I pronounce us all brothers and sisters," she said.

"Dare to dream, dare to behold people, and dare to achieve — by any means necessary."

Fig. 5.8. Speech story. *The Chronicle,* Harvard–Westlake High School, North Hollywood, Calif.

the speech story should be written when someone knowledgeable speaks to a group about a timely and relevant issue (Fig. 5.8). A gubernatorial candidate speaks to a teacher's group. A Vietnam War vet talks to a history class. Both could have insightful points to make or interesting stories to tell that readers would like to hear.

Preparing to cover a speech varies based on the background of the person speaking. The reporter should gather information about the person's background. The gubernatorial candidate will have a resumé, background information provided by his campaign staff, stories on past speeches and possibly a copy of the upcoming speech. A Vietnam War veteran may have some of the same prepared information but, more than likely, the reporter will have to depend upon the history teacher for background. In either case, the reporter should know as much as possible about the speech topic, whether it is state standardized testing reforms or a comparison of the Vietnam War with the war in Iraq. In either case, the reporter should know as much as possible about the speech topic, whether it is private school vouchers or a comparison of Eastern European ethnic cleansing of the 1990s with the Holocaust of the 1940s.

The reporter needs to make sure of the time, day and place of the speech so that he or she can arrive early to cover it. Even if the reporter has a copy of the speech, being there to hear what exactly the speaker says is a necessity since some speakers change drafts at the last minute. Being in a position to hear the speaker clearly and to take plenty of notes is important.

Here's where the skills discussed in Chapter 2 take over. The reporter will not have to take down every word but must have a good ear for news value. Identifying the primary focus and main points is important but may be difficult if the speaker rambles. The quotes the reporter will want to write down will be the ones that mean the most to the audience, the most descriptive ones or the most insightful ones. Remember that direct quotes mean you record the speaker's exact words. Listening before writing will help.

Other considerations for assessing what to quote directly are

- Listen for statements that emphasize a speaker's main points. Summarize others in your own words.

- Note references to your school or community. Often such statements, although perhaps of no great importance as far as the speech is concerned, do have considerable reader interest.

- Listen for references to topics of current interest to readers.

- Watch audience reaction carefully. What an audience applauds or jeers may make a good quotation.

Once the speech is over, have follow-up questions ready to ask. The questions should be for the speaker and for the audience. Ask follow-ups to points he or she made during the speech. Clarify any possible misunderstandings from the speech. Get the speaker's reaction to how the speech went or to the audience's reaction. Check the audience's reaction yourself. Once all reporting is done, read over notes as quickly as possible to make sure they are clear and understandable. Fill in missing information while the speech is still fresh.

The writing process begins with organizing the material around the primary focus of the speech. The lead will typically come from an interesting summarizing point or anecdote of the speaker. The lead can take a summary or feature approach. Give the reader something interesting about the speech in the lead. The basic information answering the five W's and H should always be high in the story.

> Thomas Meier ('97) had just graduated from high school, had just won the World Championships for close-up magic as "probably the youngest person ever to do that" and was planning to attend the University of Southern California on a full scholarship. Despite this recognition, Meier suffered from deep depression. By incorporating Buddhist thought into his life, he was able to find personal happiness.
>
> Meier shared his experience with students Nov. 2 in Chalmers East. He began his talk with a card trick, dazzling the audience with his magical talent as well as his heartfelt messages.

> Nancy Pak
> *Chronicle*
> Harvard–Westlake High School
> North Hollywood, Calif.

Notice how the author suggests the oddity of the speaker's story in the lead through specifics from the speaker's life and speech. Then the reporter inserts the basic information in the second paragraph.

A summary of the speaker's main conclusions, especially when he or she calls for change, can make a good lead.

Here the basic information is blended into the opening two paragraphs.

> A complete reorganization of the school's guidance services is the number one need of Georgetown High School, Dr. Jan Gray, superintendent of the Georgetown schools, informed the PTA at its annual meeting last Friday.
>
> In an address at the PTA's annual business meeting in the auditorium, Dr. Gray . . .

While rarely is a direct quote strong enough to open the lead, an indirect quotation stressing a significant or interesting point can make for a solid lead.

> Actress and recovering drug addict Jamie Lee Curtis told parents that if they didn't want their kids to drink alcohol they shouldn't drink it in front of them at a Parents' Association forum Jan. 31 that quickly dissolved into a chaotic discussion of fears about Saturday's semiformal after-party.

> Peter Jackson and Max Fifkind-Barron
> *The Chronicle*
> Harvard–Westlake High School
> North Hollywood, Calif.

In your lead, avoid stating the simple fact that a person spoke:

> District superintendent Nick Belsher spoke to the National Honor Society Friday.

The reader's response is "who cares," and then he or she is off to the next story.

Typically, organize the body of the story in order of decreasing importance. The points do not have to be presented as they were in the person's speech. However, make sure not to distort the meaning of the speech if you change the order of the points. Clearly connect the points together and the primary focus of the speech.

Fig. 5.9. Civic journalism. *Stinger*, Irmo High School, Columbia, S.C.

A few more tips to speech story writing are

- Be careful not to distort the speaker's meaning by taking quotations out of context.

- Normally, do not quote grammatical errors, awkward sentences, slips of the tongue or dialect unless there is some significant reason to do so. Rephrase these statements in your own wards. If there is a reason to use a grammatical error or slip of the tongue, use *sic* in brackets [*sic*] or parentheses if brackets are not available. In Latin *sic* means "thus" or "exactly as stated." This device can weary your readers; don't overuse it.

- Avoid letting your own opinions and prejudices color your report.

CIVIC OR PUBLIC JOURNALISM

Print and broadcast media not only cover the community but are a part of it. In the same way, high school journalists are also members of the student body, and they have a stake in the well-being of their school. Understanding this connection is at the center of a movement known as "civic journalism" or "public journalism."

Civic or public journalists believe it's not enough to report on a problem. They also must work to stir public conversation and problem-solving. When covering conflict, public journalists work "to frame" issues in ways to promote understanding and compromise, rather than hostility and intolerance. They also don't limit their work to the opinion page; they figure out ways to encourage attention and involvement in every section of the newspaper.

If, for example, a school is besieged with a high number of fights, public journalists not only would cover the incidents but would also explore the motivating factors, report on efforts at other schools to decrease similar violence, perhaps even convene a representative group of students to discuss possible solutions and then cover the get-together. When the district is faced with hiring a new principal, civic journalists would canvass students, teachers, parents and other members of the community, seeking each group's shared and conflicting perspectives on what qualities a new principal should have. When the school board calls a bond election – a topic that may seem like a snore on the surface – civic journalists would show

Since 1918

Palo Alto Senior High School

The Campanile

The largest circulation of any high school newspaper in the Bay Area

Palo Alto High School
50 Embarcadero Road
Palo Alto, CA 94301
NON-PROFIT ORG
Bulk Rate
U.S. Postage
PAID
Permit #44
Palo Alto, Calif.

Vol. LXXX No.4   http://voice.paly.net   Thursday, December 18, 2003

Campanile poll results reveal cheating at Paly

BY SARAH RIZK
Editor-in-Chief

While it is tempting to believe that we live in a world of integrity, a recent *Campanile* poll indicates otherwise. Of those polled, 23 percent admitted to copying answers on a test at least once in the past year; 16 percent admitted to plagiarizing; 60 percent indicated that they had shared information about a test; and 73 percent indicated that they had copied homework.

The poll was administered to random sophomores, juniors and seniors through the

Social Studies department in November. Freshmen were not polled, as the questions related to behavior within the past year, when these students were not at Palo Alto High School

A total of 447 students were polled: 191 of whom stated that they were not enrolled in any honors or Advanced Placement classes, and 256 of whom were. Due to human error in counting the polls, there is roughly a five percent margin of error in the results.

The poll contained questions not only about copying or sharing information about

SEE EDITORIAL
PAGE A2

tests, homework and essays, but also questioned subjects about use of online summaries as substitutes for reading novels as well as dishonesty toward teachers dealing with work previously, but not actually turned in.

Fifty-eight percent of students admitted to using online summaries instead of reading an assigned book, and 20 percent indicated that they had lied to a teacher about "completed" work.

The poll also indicated that cheating is more prevalent among students not enrolled in honors classes. Plagiarism, for example,

was reported 11 percent higher among the students not in honors classes. Cheating on tests was similarly seven percent higher among students not enrolled in honors classes. However, students enrolled in honors classes reported lying to teachers about assignments four percent more than those not in honors classes.

If caught, repercussions for a first offense include an F on the assignment, while for the second offense the student receives an F in the class in which the dishonest act

Cheating   *continued on page A8*

Cheating at Paly

- 58 percent of students surveyed have read an online summary instead of reading the assigned book

- 63 percent of students surveyed have received details about a test from someone who had taken it

- 73 percent of students surveyed have copied a homeword assignment

- 23 percent of students surveyed have copied answers from a peer's test

---

how the vote has a direct impact on the lives of students and why they should care. In Figure 5.9, the *Stinger* staff reacted to a letter to the editor by creating a focus group of students to discuss the racial and cultural concerns facing the school. The staff also ran an editorial and poll results on the issue.

Civic or public journalists, by the way, do not consider this practice a special genre of journalism. In fact, they see it as journalism fulfilling its highest calling to public service.

POLL STORY

After a series of school shootings, a *New York Times* poll showed that 87 percent of teenagers still felt at least "somewhat safe" in their schools. Were students so naïve that they believed this wouldn't happen in their school? Were they so resilient that they refused to be frightened by these well-publicized incidents?

We are naturally curious as to whether others think as we do. The poll story or a story based on a survey of the school population is a good way to assess the pulse of the community (Fig. 5.10).

In news and in-depth stories, high school writers often want to write "Many students believe . . ." after talking to only two or three students. The only accurate

Fig. 5.10. Poll story. *The Campanile*, Palo Alto High School, Palo Alto, Calif.

Poll yields information on cheating at Paly

Cheating   *continued from front page*

occurred. The third offense results in an F in the class and suspension from school.

However, most students who cheat aren't caught. In fact, in the past year, the administration filed cheating offenses for less than one percent of all students, according to Assistant Principal Doug Walker.

The poll indicated that of those who cheat at least twice in any given area, a relatively large number have cheated at least six times. In all categories, the number of students who had cheated five times, but not six times or more, was low: ranging from five to zero percent.

In contrast, the percent of students who had cheated at least six times was, in most categories, relatively high: ranging from two to 27 percent.

On some questions, students were slightly more likely to admit to a passive role in cheating than an active one; there

was a three percent discrepancy between those who admitted to hearing information about a test at least once in the past year, and those who admitted to telling others information.

On other questions, students were more likely to admit to aiding a peer in cheating than to having personally used others' work; seven percent more students admitted to having allowed others to take answers from their homework than those who admitted to copying someone else's.

Conversely, 21 percent admitted to giving a peer an answer to a test as compared to the 23 percent who had copied answers from another student's test.

In this category, students appear to be less likely to aid their peers cheat because giving answers on a test is treated more harshly by teachers than sharing homework, and the repercussions are the same for both students involved.

Campanile poll on cheating

Poll administered to 447 sophomores, juniors and seniors in November, 2003

1. Are you taking any AP or honors classes? If so, how many?

2. How many times within the past year have you read online summaries as a substitute for reading an assigned book?

3. How many times within the past year has someone else given you specific information about questions on a test you haven't taken?

4. How many times within the past year have you told someone else specific information about questions on a test they haven't taken yet?

5. How many times within the past year have you taken answers from a peer's homework assignment rather than completing it yourself?

6. How many times within the past year have you allowed a peer to take answers from your homework assignment?

7. How many times within the past year have you told a teacher that you turned in something that you hadn't?

8. How many times within the past year have you used someone else's writing (including siblings or friends) in an essay without citing the source?

9. How many times within the past year have you taken answers from a peer's test?

10. How many times within the past year have you allowed someone to take an answer from your test?

way to assess if "many" believe a certain way is to do a poll story. The poll story is useful in connection with elections. Student poll stories often cover issues such as dress code changes and open campus decisions and entertainment choices, such as most popular TV show.

Accuracy in the polling procedure should be a consideration. A poll of 10 people can be very misleading when there are 300 people in the school. While a poll distributed to two classes may seem sufficient, if both classes are honors classes, the results may be skewed.

SELECTING RESPONDENTS

The group to be surveyed must be carefully defined. For example, if the survey is aimed at students who are eligible to vote in a forthcoming national election, age must be considered. If, however, the question involves lengthening the school day or awarding school letters on sweaters to students who participated in all extracurricular activities, then many more students need to be polled. Since it is not possible to interview everybody, a sample must be selected to represent the large group. Major pollsters such as Gallup have specific guidelines to make sure polls are scientific and report a specific margin of error. The goal in sampling is to give every member of the group an equal chance of being selected. A listing of all members in a directory or a school roster from the data clerk makes this much easier.

Researchers recommend polling at least 10 percent or 50 individuals, whichever is more. To make the poll somewhat accurate, choose every tenth name in a school list, for example. No name should be substituted. If the poll is for only one grade level, then again every tenth name should be used, or if there are not enough students in that grade, then perhaps every ninth or eighth name should be used. But it is important not to choose students arbitrarily. Distribution during English classes that include the varying demographics of the school is another suggestion. Make sure the sample has percentages that represent all grade levels, sexes, socio-economic groups and races.

Sampling error, or degree of confidence of the accuracy of the poll, defines the difference between those actually interviewed and the opinions of the entire group. The larger the sample the greater the confidence that the observed difference is real and not an accident. In the case of close percentages, such as a 45–55 division, determine if this is a real difference before making an arbitrary statement about the findings.

Choosing and phrasing questions can be the tricky part. Just because the writer phrased them with one meaning in mind does not mean the poll taker will interpret the question the same way. For example, one school asked teachers "Do you feel safer in the school now than you did five years ago?" Yes and no were the answer choices. The student pollster interpreted a teacher's no answer to mean that the teacher felt unsafe. However, some teachers answered no because they felt the same as they did five years ago. They felt safe then, and they feel safe now.

The best way to make sure questions are clear is to pretest the survey. Choose a variety of different people outside the journalism room to pretest the survey. After they take the survey, ask them what they thought each question meant and why they answered the way they did. Avoid asking the question "So did you understand everything?" Few people would readily admit they did not for fear of looking stupid.

The questions used in the survey can each have a different function.

- Filter questions eliminate those who are not in a position to respond meaningfully. For example, attitudes toward the cafeteria food may not be meaningful from someone who does not patronize the cafeteria.

- Background questions give information to help interpret the results of polling. For example, those who plan to go to college may give different responses to the ideal marriage age from those who do not.

- Closed questions are answered with a yes or no. While they offer easy statistical results, an open-ended question or multiple-choice question may follow to give more depth to the poll taker's opinion.

- Open-ended questions seek answers to what is thought about issues and events. The questions encourage detailed answers, and while they may elicit rich quotes for a survey story, they may be difficult to summarize with other findings.

- A multiple-choice or -range question will give the pollster easier results to tabulate but may not offer as much insight into the poll taker's thoughts as the open-ended question. Examples of the answers to this type of question are "strongly agree" to "somewhat agree" all the way to "strongly disagree." Add "don't know" and "no opinion" answers when they are relevant.

A poll can be conducted over the phone or by distributing the poll to classes. Design must be a consideration for distributed polls. A survey should have a headline to identify the poll topic. Make sure the questions are separated enough for readability. Make sure the questions are short. Too many questions will decrease the chance that the poll taker will complete the poll.

The poll story itself should offer some insight into the results. One paragraph may highlight the statistical finding that 55 percent disagree with a proposed change from a block schedule back to a seven-period day. The quote in the next paragraph may illustrate a sophomore's frustration that the change would not allow him to have enough classes to get in journalism and athletics. An anecdote may be included, but a follow-up interview with a poll taker may be necessary to fill in the holes of his or her story. The reporter needs to make sure that the focus of the story accurately matches the poll results. A 12 percent result of students who didn't feel safe in the school should not be the primary story focus since it does not accurately reflect the school opinion. The number of people selected and how they were selected, the questions they were asked and the margin of error should all be included in the story.

A survey can also be useful in

- Locating people to interview. If a reporter is doing a yearbook feature on people who take self-defense classes, a poll can help the reporter reach out beyond his or her small group of friends to increase the diversity of people represented in the story.

- Assessing who is reading the publication and what they are reading.

- Assessing the buying habits and power of the publication's readership. Information about how much money students make and spend as well as what they spend it on and where they spend it can be useful for an ad salesperson.

- Brightening up the design of the publication by putting the results into an information graphic.

EXERCISES

1. Clip and mount a health story from a major daily newspaper. Make a list of the specific terms or medical-related phrases that are used. What did the writer do to make them clear to the public? Was each of the phrases made clear? What could the writer have done to make the story clearer?

2. Invite the school nurse to discuss a teen health issue. Prepare questions to ensure that you understand the issue well enough to write a story. Work on questions that will elicit clear explanations, examples and anecdotes.

3. Discuss and list three of the top health issues facing students at your school. Develop a list of three story ideas for each. Pick one and write a story for your school publication.

4. Ask members of each classification (freshman through senior) to describe the three most creative or interesting assignments from their other classes. Pick the most interesting and write a story on it.

5. Discuss the three biggest academic concerns or issues for students at your school. In small groups, discuss what story ideas could come from those three issues. Pick a story, develop a list of sources for the story, and write the questions for the sources.

6. Write your own obituary.

7. Clip and mount an example of a well-written advance story and a well-written follow-up story from your school or daily newspaper. Opposite each make a list of the good story qualities that it illustrates.

8. Ask a member of a speech class to present a speech before your journalism class. Before the talk obtain the person's name and qualifications. (The teacher may make up some qualifications to fit the type of speech the person will give.) Take notes and write a good draft. Pair up with another member of the journalism class and read each other's story.

Discuss the answers to these questions with your partner: Is the lead appropriate for the story? Does the body of the story adequately support and expand the lead? Why does or doesn't the story create a unified and accurate impression of the speech? Rewrite an improved draft of the story.

9. Cover a speech at one of your assemblies or a public meeting in your community. Write the story and submit your notes and the finished story to your instructor.

10. In class, discuss several controversial school issues that may lend themselves to a poll or survey. Divide into small groups, with the group's size depending upon the number of issues that seem pertinent. Each group should discuss one issue, develop a questionnaire, pretest the questions and revise them before use. Using an appropriate school directory to decide upon the number of students (and/or teachers) to be polled to give valid results, each group should conduct its poll. Results of the poll should be shared by the group; members of each group will write their individual stories. Stories should be discussed within the group. Perhaps some of these stories can be used in the school paper.

Some topics may not be school issues but may be topics of real interest to students: the relationship of high school students to fast food restaurants, diet foods, bulimia and the need "not to look fat"; the concern for a healthy body – depression, carbon monoxide levels in the blood, heart rate, blood pressure, cholesterol level, nutrition and general fitness; the problem of drug use, especially steroids in bodybuilding and athletic performance; part-time jobs and their ramifications; the school community – a world of minorities and multicultural interests; political correctness issues; sexual harassment; SAT or PSAT scores (or if your state has state exams, what are the results for your school?).

Writing Feature Stories

The news story reports that 10 percent of the senior class did not pass the standardized graduation exam. The feature story tells how Brent hid his failure notice in the bottom of his dresser to keep his parents from finding out that he will be the first of their eight children who won't graduate.

The news story reports the shooting of 15-year-old freshman Mike Bodine outside the Dairy Queen. The feature story covers ways teens cope with death.

The feature story can show the excuses students give for not doing homework or the pain students go through when a childhood pet dies. Neither of the two stories is necessarily timely, but both have human interest.

While a feature may be timely and informative, the story's primary role is to bring an issue or a person to life. The feature story's goal can also be to entertain and appeal to the emotions. If connected to a timely event, the feature story puts it in a bigger perspective, helping explain the event's impact through anecdotes and examples. The best feature story is accurate storytelling that makes the reader understand and feel. Be careful, as a feature writer, not to get so caught up in making the reader feel that you create scenes or images that are not true. Feature writing is not fiction.

This chapter outlines a few types of feature stories. Concentrate on what makes for accurate and interesting storytelling. Let the story types serve as ways to help brainstorm ideas. Notice how many different types of stories are in the feature category.

A monthly high school publication may sacrifice timeliness, but it has the opportunity to give the reader more of the story.

Today even daily newspapers print more features and feature news because they know that radio, TV and web sites may provide readers more up-to-date coverage.

For the yearbook, the feature story is the staple form of copy.

THE FEATURE STORY IDEA

The feature story comes in all forms. The stories are as serious as date rape and gun safety. The feature story can be as informative as stories on steps to buying a car or the investigation of fire hazards of a crowded gymnasium. Or the feature can be as entertaining as a story on the impact that childhood toys make on a person or a sophomore's tales from her summer as a roadie on a concert tour.

Tying all these stories together are the ideas that

- They are factual, requiring reporting and interviewing.

- They are not filled with the writer's opinion.

- They have a beginning, middle and end.

- The organization is as varied as the story ideas. However, the inverted pyramid form, which is typically used in straight news stories, is rarely used in features.

As with all quality stories, coming up with a quality idea is the first step.

The feature idea comes from a keen sense of awareness of life around you. Talking to the kid in the Star Wars T-shirt who sits on the steps outside the cafeteria leads to a story on extremely shy teens. Listening to an announcement for the deadline to turn in National Honor Society community service hours leads to a story about juniors who tutor the kindergartners at the neighboring elementary school. Reading a news story on a bus accident in Paradise, Texas, prompts a story on bus safety, whether a publication's 10 miles or 2,000 miles away.

Timeliness factors into a feature story. A story describing the ways teens cope with death can be printed at any time of the year because many students can relate to the subject. However, when such a story is covered after the death of two students, the story will have a more powerful impact on the reader. Writing about a teacher who acts out one-man plays in front of the class or dances to old English tunes to teach literature may be worth a feature story. Doing the story when the teacher has been named the school's teacher of the year gives the reader one more reason to read the story. Even if this teacher has been performing in the classroom like this for 10 years, his story warrants coverage in a year-book academic spread when he's been given the award that year.

Listed below are a number of feature ideas and angles covered in high school publications. Look for relevant story angles at your school.

- Factors in a teenage relationship. With interviews of teen couples, parents and psychologists, the story looks at what holds relationships together and tears them apart, covering everything from college to parents to pregnancy.

- A month after two boys slashed the throat, ears and legs of a Westside High School senior leaving him to die, a story on the victim's recovery. The story covers his physical therapy and the mental trauma since the assault.

- Fake IDs. The story covers students' increased use of fake identification cards, complete with a student poll. Covering online fake identification card companies and do-it-yourself computer programs offers a fresh angle to an old story. Interviews with police, bouncers and club owners on the impact of the use of fake IDs rounds out a balanced story.

- A story on students who are wait-listed by colleges. What should the students do to get in? What are their chances of getting in?

- What happens to teens when they get fired? The story includes a discussion of how to keep a job.

- JROTC boot camps. A sights and sounds piece on the grueling obstacle courses and drills of cadets going through military service training

- A how-to story on creating a job resumé

- High school stress – what causes it? How harmful can it be? A discussion of how to relieve the stress

- The life of a 16-year-old living on his own. The story covers his struggle to pay bills with a monthly social security check without any chance to save money for college. His loneliness after his mother and grandmother died is also a part of the story.

- An informative feature on freshman initiation. The story delves into whether initiation is harassment or harmless tradition.

- A where-are-they-now piece on those alumni voted "Most Likely to Succeed"

- How honest are we? The story looks at people's thoughts and stories on stealing, lying and cheating. The package includes a sidebar on how the staff "lost" a wallet with $3 and an ID to see whether the wallet would be returned or not.

- A feature on a group of students at school who design their own clothes

- A story of a girl who was sexually abused by her father and how she coped

- A symposium feature with a group of male and female students discussing dating rules

THE FEATURE-WRITING PROCESS

Once a reporter collects the information for the story, the organization and writing process begins. Short reader attention spans and increasing amounts of information challenge the reporter to write a strong enough lead to get and keep the reader's interest.

The feature lead is not a summary of the story. The feature lead is often an example, an anecdote or a statement that sets the tone for the story. The vignette, descriptive, contrast or oddity leads discussed in Chapter 3 can apply when writing a feature story. When the reporter has completed interviews and observation, he should choose the lead by asking:

- What about this story did I react the most to?

- What anecdote would I go back and tell a friend about?

- What did I see that made me say, "That's what this story is all about"?

Typically, features will have a nut paragraph or focus paragraph following the lead. This nut, wrap or focus paragraph ties the lead into the focus of the story. The nut paragraph helps the reader understand the main point of the story and gives the reader a sense of why he or she is reading this story. A feature tied to a news event will establish the timeliness in the nut graph. For example, the bus safety feature will have mention of the recent accident in the nut graph.

Read these opening paragraphs of high school stories and see if you get a sense of what the story is about.

> In fifth grade, life made sense to John Brzozowski. He played soccer on Saturdays, attended church on Sundays and did his homework on weekdays. For one assignment, John wrote: "If I could get Santa to grant two wishes . . . (1) Get rid of all pollution. (2) Get rid of all the drug dealers and tell everyone that drugs kill."
>
> Somewhere down the road, however, his mother Linda said her middle child got lost. On a rainy day, Brzozowski was found dying in his car of a suspected heroin or cocaine overdose, ending a six year battle with drugs.

> Melissa Borden
> *DeSoto Eagle Eye*
> DeSoto High School
> DeSoto, Texas

In the simple opening sentence, the author alludes to the fact that at some point life is no longer going to make sense for John Brzozowski. Then she paints a picture of a normal child who is very aware of a prob-

lem. The idea that a child so aware of the dangers could find himself in his own six-year battle with drugs hooks the reader. The wrap graph in this one is subtle. It's the second paragraph. The reader knows that the story is about a kid becoming lost in a drug scene for six years. The reader has a focus and is now ready to read the rest of the story.

Another type of feature lead is the startling statement lead. The opening line is a stunning statement that sets the tone. The second sentence is the wrap graph. See if you can understand why.

> **Nothing says "I hate you, Mom" more than a stainless steel bar through your tongue. While most parents look at body piercing as a form of rebellion against them, pierced students tend to say that piercings are a form of expression.**

> **Michael Weisman**
> ***Valkrie***
> **Woodbridge High School**
> **Woodbridge, Va.**

While question leads are rare, this next one offers vivid images, especially to the reader who knows the area.

> Gastonia – city of redneck farmhands with limited vocabularies, wads of chewing tobacco and Dale Earnhardt T-shirts cruising down Franklin in lowriders? Undeniably, Gastonia is viewed differently by different people. However, a large number of both Gastonia residents and "them that ain't from 'round here" see the town as farm community populated by pick-up trucks with shotguns on the dashboard and rebel flags in the windows. On the other hand, others see it as an emerging suburb of Charlotte – one with smalltown charm yet lacking all big city headaches.

> John Woody
> *Wavelengths*
> Ashbrook High School
> Gastonia, N.C.

In the following leads, answer the following questions: What is the tone of the lead? Do you think it fits the story? How did the reporter get the lead? What are the best details in the lead?

> She knows she is facing an 8 percent chance of dying. She understands it could affect her ability to have children someday. She realizes there will be a large scar on the side of her waist.
>
> Yet despite the realities, senior Miriam Flores is ready and willing to donate one of her kidneys to her father.

Alice-Anne Lewis
Gopher Gazette
Gresham High School
Gresham, Ore.

> At first glance, senior Tu Dang's small bedroom, punctuated with framed photographs and cluttered corners, seems like that of any typical teenage girl. But wait – there's a $600 silver Gucci purse draped over a hook on the wall. And a $1,200 Louis Vuitton purse on her nightstand. Not to mention a matching $285 Louis Vuitton belt tangled in a pile of accessories next to the laundry basket.
>
> Dang has spent thousands of dollars building a wardrobe from high-end designer labels. She is among a number of Blazers who use their paychecks to indulge in extravagantly priced brand names. The temporary pleasure and even social status granted by these expensive purchases are a testament to the power of brand-name marketing.

Amanda Lee
Silver Chips
Montgomery Blair High School
Silver Spring, Md.

> The automatic doors opened and a student with heavy pockets entered Nelson's Food. He took a few short steps to the customer service desk and requested three tickets to the "Blackhawk" concert. The total was $68.25 or 273 quarters. Senior Dave Anderson unloaded 300 quarters onto the counter.
>
> Anderson, along with senior David Hoffman, is the owner of the Sweet Tooth Candy Company, which provides the 25-cent candy machines found in the eight classrooms and the library of Albert Lea High School. This enterprise began with only one machine and has now evolved into their major source of income. The profit of the machines is Anderson's and Hoffman's spending money.
>
> "We love being able to make ourselves money, and not have to have a boss pay us," Hoffman said.

Chrissy Thompson
Ahlahasa
Albert Lea High School
Albert Lea, Minn.

Feature stories can be organized in any form and written at any length. Writers often use a fiction device such as suspense, surprise, dialogue, description, narration and climax in the development of the body if the device is appropriate to the topic.

The entire goal is to keep the story and the reader moving. Organize the story so the reader can logically and smoothly move from point to point or anecdote to anecdote.

The organization possibilities are as varied as the feature story types. The feature story can be told chronologically. Or just as a movie sometimes has flashbacks, feature stories can move around in time, as long as the reader follows. If the writer is using suspense, the storytelling will build, teasing the reader with bits of information while keeping the reader interested – a most challenging task. Feature writers should organize and outline their structure before they write.

ELEMENTS OF FEATURE WRITING

Observation or firsthand reporting can help you create an accurate and descriptive written scene. Taking notes firsthand is easier than trying to get a subject to recreate the scene verbally. Good feature writing is *not* done over the phone. Reporting is best done when a reporter gets out of the journalism room, visits the subject of the story and uses all five senses to describe what he or she observes.

You're assigned a story on agriculture students and their life at the barn. As a good reporter, you will want to go to the barn and spend part of the day with agricultural students.

What can you observe with your five senses?

Sight

A 1,000-pound Hereford steer that lumbers toward his owner's blue Dodge Ram pickup.

Feel or Touch

The slick mud in the animal pens gripping your rubber boots.

Smell

The sour stench of fresh manure mixed with the syrupy sweet hint of feed molasses.

Sound

The yelped "Whoop"s and "Hi-ya"s of the boys herding the Angus bull.

Taste

The sweet chocolate taste of Yoohoo, pulled from the old-time drink machine, that the freshmen drink as they sit waiting for their parents to pick them up.

An interviewer talking to young agricultural students would have been challenged to ask enough follow-up questions to gather such detail. An observer can manage those details by developing a keen eye as well as an understanding of what observation is relevant to telling the story. A good reporter will make note of a great many more details than he or she will actually use. The story focus dictates the mass of details the reporter observes.

The following are the elements of a good story-telling feature.

PRECISE WRITING

Observation and reporting is best when it is precise. Precise writing means choosing an accurate and specific word. How important is precise writing? Let's say the writer simply states: "The dog jumped up on the boy." Replace "dog" with the more precise Saint Bernard, and the scene dramatically changes. Or if the reporter writes: "The officer ran past the gate when the dog turned on him." Rewriting the sentence with more precise nouns and verbs changes the scene. "The officer sprinted past the gate when the Chihuahua turned on him." Precise nouns and verbs help make good feature writing.

If the reporter has to use an adjective, it should be a specific one. It's better to write "the teacher put on his cashmere sweater" than "the teacher put on his nice sweater."

DETAILS

Details are the small, specific facts that help make a larger point or impression. The reporter must choose details that add to the overall focus of the story. For example, the use of the cashmere sweater in the example above would be good detail use if the story is about a teacher who won the lottery but still teaches. The cashmere sweater helps to show how the teacher's life changed. The detail becomes needless if the story is about the heater in the school breaking down.

PACE

A reader needs variety. Variety can be achieved through pace. Pace is the rhythm created by word choice, sentence length and construction, and paragraph lengths. A good pace keeps the reader moving through the story. Read the story aloud to hear the rhythm and pace. If you have to take a breath in the middle of a long sentence or the writing slows, go back and work on pacing. If all the sentences begin the same way, go back and change sentence construction.

Good pace can also help the reader feel the emotion of the moment through varied structures. For example, a series of three short sentences can help recreate the anxiety of a situation. Another way to vary pace is by writing a well-crafted longer sentence, then following it with a short sentence. The use of other writing elements discussed in this chapter such as details and dialogue can alter pace.

EXAMPLES

Examples are specific and typical cases or samples. The basic premise in feature writing is "Show Don't Tell."

Fig. 6.1. "Into the arms of love" by Katherine Gazella. *St. Petersburg Times,* copyright 1999.

Don't leave the reader guessing or filling in blanks left by vague words. A beginning writer might tell the reader that "it's different being home-schooled." But in the following lead, Sadie Grabill from Harrisonville, Md., writes:

> **Her freshman year of high school, it took Katharine Steinmetz ten seconds to get to school. It was a matter of getting from her bed to her kitchen table.**

The reader now understands at least one way that Steinmetz's life is different from most students – an example to which teenagers can relate.

DIALOGUE

A device borrowed from fiction, dialogue is the use of quotes and conversation. Dialogue is useful if the sentences say more than the writer can put into his or her own words. The dialogue must be specific and relevant. The quotes can reveal the character of the speaker. You must have a keen ear or use a tape recorder to capture and use long segments of dialogue. Quotes must be exact. Be wary of dialects. If you choose to try to capture that dialect in writing, be fair and balanced. You may hear the accent of someone from another state or country, but you must be a good reporter to hear the accent of people who speak as you do.

VOICE

In Roy Peter Clark and Don Fry's book *Coaching Writers: Editors and Reporters Working Together,* voice is described this way:

> **Writers often talk about "finding their voice." Readers and editors may talk about how a story "sounds." All are describing the same phenomenon: the illusion that a single writer is talking directly to a single reader from the page. This effect derives from the natural relationship between the writer's speech and prose and from artifice and rhetorical invention. All writing, even newswriting, has a voice, although the voice may be described as objective, dispassionate or neutral.**

Voice comes from the writer's combination of pace, word choice and use of examples, dialogue and details. Voice in a feature story helps the reader capture the feel of the subject, place and time.

In this *St. Petersburg Times* story, Katherine Gazella shows what young love is all about. As you read, take note of how she wrote the story. Where does she use a variety of sentences to achieve pace? What observations are the most vivid ones?

Interview with Katherine Gazella of the *St. Petersburg Times*

I was taken back by the wonderful job you did observing for the piece. What was your observation process for this story?

Gazella: I actually was in a really good position on this story because it happened to be the one girl's birthday party and her mother invited me to come to the party, so it was just a matter of writing down all these great details that were there. They played this music that I had to go around and ask the kids who the artists were and what the songs were. I felt old at this thing. ... The party itself was such a great forum because they had a disco ball and they had all these wonderful details. So for me it was just writing all these things down and later on deciding which ones I had room to use. There were a lot of great things that I just didn't have room for.

How important do you think observation is in your writing?

Gazella: I think it's key. I think it's the most important thing. I wanted to be at as many places I could with them in the short time that I had between the time that it was assigned to me and the time that I had to turn it in. It turned out that there were some great opportunities for that. But I think you just have to walk around and do things with people that they normally would be doing. One of the things that people will often say to me, and I said it in this story I believe too, is that they had to make time with me, to spend time with me. I said, "Don't do anything other than you would normally be doing." I just wanted to see them in their normal setting. Just what they're normally like when they get in and out of the car and go to basketball games together and go out on a date.

How do you put them at ease like that?

Gazella: They were amazing – these two kids in particular. With other kids it has been more difficult, but with them they liked the idea of having a reporter with them, and they were popular at school, so they were used to having attention. Their other friends at school were kind of jealous that they had the reporter. They kind of liked it because it was sort of a status thing for them. They were just really sweet about it too. They were both very nice kids. They were very talkative and pleasant. In that case I didn't have to do that much. The harder thing with this project was getting the parents to be at ease with it. In fact, I had set it up with a different teenage couple, but one of the moms said, "No, I'm not comfortable with my son even having a girlfriend, and I certainly don't want it in the newspaper."

Let's talk about the piece a second here. How and why did you choose that stuffed monkey battle for your lead?

Gazella: [Laughing] It was just sort of a light-hearted scene. Every time I saw them, they were holding hands or trying to be that much closer to each other, so that was a good representation of that. Also, the scene in the car. It was so funny. I mean they were on a date, but they had the dad in the front seat, and they had this little 9-year-old brother that they had to deal with. It was just not exactly the most romantic of scenes, so it seemed perfect for the kind of a relationship that they would have at the age of 14 – that they have to deal with these little kids shooting fake machine guns.

One of the things you do well in the story is you have great use of pace in your writing. When and how do you think about pace in your writing, or is that something you consider?

Gazella: I don't think about it ahead of time, but I'll try to read it out loud in my head when I'm done writing it, and I guess I listen for that. And sometimes I'll feel like I'm going "vroom" right through the story, and I'll try and slow it down a little bit if that happens.

Summarize what your typical reporting and writing process is like.

Gazella: For a story like this, try and spend at least a couple of days with the people involved just to get to know them and what their routines are like. As opposed to just interviewing them for a half hour like you might do on a daily story. When you're there, you can interview about the important things, but just to really observe what their life is like is key. I just try to write down everything I can. It's hard sometimes because they are saying something important and you are also noticing some detail about the way they walk or the kind of car that they drive. But those are just as important, if not more so, when you're writing the story than what people say. I just try to write down as much as I can and wade through it later.

For these two, it was like this gift was given to me. They were both very talky. They said a lot of funny things. A lot of things, you would expect a 13-year-old and 14-year-old to say and with the sort of syntax that they have, so the actual quotes were really great. But also the style of clothing that they wore. The way that they looked at each other and joked around with each other turned out to be really great things to write down.

What kind of rewriting and reinterviewing did you go through? Was this one of those pieces where you sat down and sort of blast-drafted the whole thing?

Gazella: For me finding the top of the story is one of the last things that I do, and I think that's atypical. So I didn't know what the top was going to be until almost the end. So first of all that came last. The scene at the birthday party, I knew that would be a separate scene, so I just sat down and wrote that. Once you have something on paper, it's sort of a relief that you have a piece of the story done. But that was so lively, so fun and so energetic that I just wrote that one and then added some other details in later like about her mom and things like that. And a lot of that came from phone calls that I made later on. [That's how I] found out how long she and Jessica's father had been divorced.

If there's an easy section to pull out like that, then I'll start with that one. There's no order beyond that, except that [I'm] trying to organize it in a way that makes sense. Some of the stuff on their date fit together with some of the history of their relationship, and so a lot of it I'll just sort of write in pieces, then figure out how to piece it together later. It's not the most organized way of going about things [*laughing*]. Often I'll have the last line of the story written way before I'll have the top of it written.

Is it just something that stands out at you?

Gazella: The kickers usually come to me before the top does for whatever reason. The scene in the car didn't come to me, not long before my deadline.

What points is she making with the details she chose? How would you describe her voice?

SAFETY HARBOR – They sit shoulder to shoulder in the back of the white Mercury minivan, her neatly manicured right hand locked in his left. Mike throws a stuffed monkey at Jessica with his free hand; she catches it with hers and whips it back. They won't let go of each other, not even to fight.

The moment is sweet but hardly intimate. In the middle seat, Mike's 9-year-old brother, D.J., and his friend Andrew cackle loudly and spray each other with imaginary machine guns. You can always count on a kid brother to destroy a romantic moment.

Mike's dad is behind the wheel, good-naturedly performing his duties as chauffeur. He is driving the couple to Steak 'n' Shake in Clearwater, where Mike and Jessica will sip milkshakes and Mike will steal strips of chicken from Jessica's plate and Jessica will gently stab Mike's hand with a fork. The last time they were there, they caught Mike's dad standing outside the restaurant, spying on them through the windows.

Let him look. Jessica Replogle, 14, and Mike Sharkey, 13, are in love, and they don't care who sees it – which is a good thing, because they are hardly ever alone. Theirs is a roller-rink-and-Gummi-bear romance. They talk on the phone for hours. He's slender and athletic, so naturally she calls him Chubby. They celebrate an anniversary every month. In classes at Safety Harbor Middle School, he writes her notes that begin, "Hey, Beautiful." She wears a charm necklace, a gift from him. "Taken," says the charm. (Should they ever break up, Mike jokes, he'll give her another charm: "Available.")

Jessica and Mike love being together and being in love.

On this day in the minivan, they have been going out – dating each other exclusively – for precisely four months and nine days, a fact Jessica has at her exquisitely decorated fingertips. It is an endurance record for each of them.

"Things are, like, perfect right now," Jessica says. How many people can say that about their relationships? But like any romance between eighth graders this one is fragile and probably fleeting. Perfect things often are. When we began working on this article, we met an eighth-grade girl from New Tampa who said oh, yes, she and her boyfriend would just love to tell us their story. But when we called to set up the interview, she made an excuse and backed out. Her mother later explained why. Ten minutes before we talked to her, the boy dumped her.

Mike has no such plans; he's smitten. Still, if we want to understand where love begins, we need to watch Mike and Jessica now, in this pristine moment.

At last the van arrives at Steak 'n' Shake. When it stops, Mike bolts out so he can open the restaurant door for Jessica, an act of chivalry she has come to expect from him. Their love is one of the sweetest and most uncomplicated they will ever know.

The great wall of hair

The list of perfect things in the relationship includes Mike's tucked-in shirt.

It is Monday afternoon and Mike and Jessica are in his bedroom getting ready for a date. The time they will spend here provides a clear picture of the relationship, right down to the banter about Mike's shirt.

Mike, a snazzy dresser who sometimes changes his clothes three times in a day, twists and turns in front of the bathroom mirror, looking from all angles at the plaid button-down shirt he just put on.

He pulls it out of his jeans a little in front, tucks it in a little more in back, checks the mirror again.

Mike is seeking what he calls The Perfect Tuck.

"It takes him, like, an hour to do," Jessica sighs.

While she waits, she obsesses over a few details of her own appearance. She flattens her red shirt against her small waist, glosses her lips and brushes her long, middle-parted, blond-streaked hair.

Finally, Mike puts the finishing touches on the tuck of the century.

"Jessica, do I have it?" Mike asks, holding his arms up like a gymnast after a dismount.

"Nope," she says, then fixes one part of the shirt that was uneven. "There."

In some ways, Jessica and Mike are like an old married couple; they know each other's bad habits and quirks. It drives her crazy when he twitches his knee. He jabs her in the side when she says "like," which is often. And she knows that even if she tells him to wait for her call, he will grow impatient and call her first.

"And have you seen his wall of hair?" Jessica says, poking her finger into his heavily-gelled 'do. They gained this knowledge by spending a lot of time together. They meet in the hallway after fifth period when she's leaving math and he's coming out of language. They study together after school. They attend school basketball games together – Mike as a point guard, Jessica as a cheerleader. Go, Warriors.

At night they talk on the phone for hours at a time, but none of the conversations goes too deep. They usually end these marathons with a debate: "I love you more," she'll say. "No, I love you more," and so on.

They're like an old married couple, yes, but without the lingering resentments, the deep affection, the cycles of pain and forgiveness. Their love is true but it's also lite.

And they know it. When they are out with friends, as they will be today, Jessica will playfully drape her arm around another boy's shoulders and Mike will hug other girls.

"We'll both flirt with other people," Jessica says. "I mean, we're going out. We're not dead."

Me, you – and Pooh

It is Jessica's 14th birthday, and 60 – that is not a typo – of her closest friends are jammed into her living room for a party. These are the children of the mid-'80s, Generation Y. They wear hair scrunchies on their wrists and platform sneakers and low-slung Tommy Hilfiger jeans. Their names are Meghan and Tyson and Justin and Kalyn.

They're a peculiar subspecies, 14-year-olds; somehow, they're both children and adults, yet neither children nor adults. Theirs is a world of love notes passed in the hallways at school and i's dotted with hearts. It is also a world of skimpy tank tops, provocative songs, sexual exploration and sultry dancing.

You can see some of that right here, in Jessica's living room. Everywhere you look, kids are grinding their skinny hips to techno music. On a makeshift stage in the corner, other kids sing along to the music of a rented karaoke machine, appearing free of all inhibitions as they perform.

"Oooh! Me so horny," they sing.

At the same time, Winnie the Pooh and Rugrats balloons drift side to side, as if they, too, are trying to keep the beat.

One girl goes into the kitchen, her arms folded across her chest, and asks

Jessica's mom to turn off the black light. One of the boys has announced that he can see her bra through her black sweater.

It's unlikely that any couple here has been dating more than a year, and chances are none will be together a year from now. And yet the songs they sing are all about grown-up romance, with all its passion and peril. On the karaoke stage, Jessica and eight other girls line up for one of the big numbers of the night.

"At first I was afraid, I was petrified," they sing.

The song is *I Will Survive*, the anthem of women's heartache and resilience. The girls belt out these words with dramatic flair, squinting to demonstrate pain, shouting loudly to portray passion. Jessica's mom, Beverly, smiles as she watches. She's 42 and surprisingly calm amid all these boisterous teenagers. Five years ago she and Jessica's father were divorced – for the second time. She doesn't want to discuss it.

On stage, Jessica and the girls are still shouting out their song. "I'm trying hard to mend the pieces of my broken heart," they sing. One girl places her right hand over her heart, which is doubtless as pink and tender as filet mignon.

"They have no idea," Beverly says.

Save the last dance for me

One of the kids keeps turning the light on and off, on and off, until finally someone tells him to stop it and the room goes dark.

"Ladies' choice!" one of the girls shouts. Most of the ladies choose to giggle and look at their shoes, too coy or bashful to ask a boy to dance. One girl pulls a girlfriend into the corner, in a whisper, asks whether she should approach the boy she likes.

But Jessica is not shy or uncertain, and just a few notes into the Aaliyah song *One in a Million* she makes her move. She walks over to Mike and playfully butts her head into his chest. He grins, folds his arms around her waist and whispers something only she can hear.

Aaliyah sings:

Your love is a one in a million.

It goes on and on and on

Several couples join them on the carpeted dance floor. Many of the girls tower over their partners, their arms slanting downward to rest on the boys' shoulders.

But this is not the case for Jessica and Mike. She is three inches shorter than he is, the perfect height for dancing in the way long favored by teenagers: Her arms clasped behind his neck, his behind her waist, leaving no airspace between them. They shuffle side to side, hugging more than dancing, careful not to step on each other's bare feet.

To have and, like, to hold

For eighth graders, Jessica and Mike have had their share of experience in love. Asked to count their past relationships, they realize they have both reached the double digits. Off the top of his head, Mike knows how many girlfriends he has had.

"Fourteen," he says after taking a sip of his chocolate milk shake at Steak 'n Shake. "Swear to God."

Jessica has to do some math. Steve was her first flame, in fifth grade. Later, there was that guy who thought they were going out but she never knew it, so she doesn't count him. Then there was the guy who was involved in the kissing accident.

"He didn't actually bite my tongue," she says. "He just scraped it."

In all, she has had 10 relationships, most of them lasting only a couple weeks.

"That's my usual – two weeks," she says, then turns to Mike and grins. "You got lucky."

Her count of 10 includes the first time she and Mike hooked up, back in the sixth grade.

He asked her out – that is, asked her to go steady – over lunch in the school cafeteria. Twelve days later they had their only real date, at an after-school dance. They arrived separately and paid 50 cents each to get in.

The afternoon did not go well for Jessica, who expected Mike to slow-dance with her, or at least acknowledge her existence. He did neither.

"I was just all aggravated with him," Jessica says.

Afterward, they went with some friends to Astro Skate Center in Tarpon Springs, where he continued to neglect her. Well, there's only so much a 12-year-old woman can take. She decided she would break up with him the next day.

But Mike had made a decision of his own. Jessica and Mike were skating on opposite sides of the rink when Mike's friend Steve – Jessica's fifth-grade boyfriend – skated over to talk to her.

"He came up to me and said, 'Yo, Mike doesn't want to go out anymore,'" she says, rolling her eyes.

Yo!

Now, at Steak 'n Shake, Mike tries to defend himself. "I knew she was gonna dump me the next day, so I got to her first."

Jessica smirks. "Yeah. Whatever."

She exacted her revenge the next year, in seventh grade. She flirted with him incessantly in hopes he would become interested in her again. It worked.

"He'd ask me out and I'd say, 'Nope!'" she recounts gleefully.

Her attitude changed this year. Once, in September, they talked on the phone late into the night. Near the end of the conversation, Mike asked her if she wanted to go out with him. She said she would tell him the next day after school.

"But I had volleyball practice that night, so I had to wait an extra two hours," Mike says. "She made me wait the whole day."

Jessica the secret agent slayer

Jessica and Mike are spending a rainy afternoon in Mike's bedroom, with the door open as always. House rule. Other 14-year-old kids are having babies or doing what it takes to get them, but Jessica and Mike are in a simpler time of life, one filled with talking and wondering but not with doing, not yet.

At this moment they are surrounded by all the things that matter to a 13-year-old boy: posters of Michael Jordan, his tongue wagging, his body defying physics. On the dresser is a gift from Jessica: A Halloween photograph of the couple dressed as Sandy and Danny from *Grease*, with the words "I love you Chubby" painted on the frame. Pictures of Sarah Michelle Gellar, who plays the title character on TV's *Buffy the Vampire Slayer*, adorn three of Mike's walls. There's Buffy on the cover of YM magazine, Buffy on a motorcycle, Buffy with big devil horns and blacked-out teeth. The last one was altered by Jessica.

Jessica and Mike sit side by side on Mike's twin bed, playing the Nintendo 64 game GoldenEye 007, which involves secret agents. Jessica barely knows how to play, and Mike, an expert, is taking advantage of that.

"Hey, wait, which one am I?" Jessica asks. "You keep changing the controls! Am I the guy on the top or on the bottom?"

Seconds later, her secret agent dies. She was, as it turns out, the character at the top of the screen – the one that was blown to pieces by Mike's secret agent.

"No fair!" Jessica says.

They elbow each other, pout and giggle, delighting in this perfect moment when being together is all that matters. And why shouldn't they enjoy it? Someday, whether or not they stay together, things will be far more complicated for Jessica and Mike. If they're like most people, sooner or later they'll build up a little scar tissue on their hearts. It's a hard thing, getting together and staying there. Just ask Jessica's mom. And yet you see Jessica and Mike and it gives you hope, if you didn't have it already.

Yes, things will be hard. But for now, this is the way it should be: lighthearted and carefree and set to the rat-a-tat-tat soundtrack of a video game shooting match.

After a while, Jessica and Mike put on their shoes to go outside. When Mike bends over to tie his sneakers, Jessica grabs one of the controls and slaughters his unsuspecting secret agent.

Mike lets out a yelp. "Oh! No way!" he shouts.

He gently strangles her, then puts her in a headlock. She pats his stomach and says, "I'm sorry, Chubby."

And with that, all is forgiven.

Katherine Gazella
St. Petersburg Times, copyright 1999
St. Petersburg, Fla.

The feature writer used all the elements discussed earlier: precise writing, details, pace, voice, examples and dialogue – all creating a vivid feature on junior high love.

A lesser writer would have written about young love in terms of "innocent" and "going out and having fun together." The same writer might have described how "they always hold hands" or "they like to do things such as going out to eat and roller skating." Then the reader would have to work to visualize Mike and Jessica's relationship. Gazella lets the reader live this relationship.

Let's look at several particular pieces. Notice the pace of the opening paragraph. Look at how in the second sentence the author uses a semicolon to tie the two thoughts together. The connection of the two thoughts makes Jessica's reaction seem quick and instinctive. The sentence paints a picture of two people who won't let go of each other, physically or emotionally. Then after two long sentences, the third sentence is short to emphasize the point of the opening scene.

Pace is used well again in the fourth paragraph. After explaining that they caught Mike's dad spying on them through the restaurant window, Gazella follows with the short sentence "Let him look." The sentence length emphasizes the proud defiance of a junior high couple. The details and observations are photographic. What details did the author use to show the naïveté of the relationship? What verbs are particularly vivid?

What dialogue and observations in the opening scene does the author use to make the point that Mike and Jessica are like an old married couple? What effect does pace help create in the third paragraph? What specific images does Gazella capture to contrast the innocent and not-so-innocent nature of the teenagers at the dance? What point do the mother's quotes make in the story?

FEATURE STORY TYPES

The breakdown of feature story types is anything but definitive. Just let the story types serve as ways to help you brainstorm ideas.

PROFILES

Alex Abnos' favorite color is blue, and he is into Superman underwear and Coldplay, but few people care. The profile is more than a list of facts about a person, but it is not necessarily as comprehensive as a biography. A profile captures a central focus of someone's life that others might find interesting or entertaining (Fig. 6.2). If Alex has the largest Superman underwear collection in the state, there's your profile focus.

The personality sketch related to a news story should not be overlooked. For example, the school board has appointed a faculty member as the new principal. The story of the board's action would be news, but here is a chance for a personality interview or sketch.

Readers would be interested in knowing that the new principal has just made his first hole-in-one this spring, that he bakes luscious lemon pies, and that as a college student he was a Big 12 gymnast. Readers would also be interested in his views on education, his plans and his goals. The reporter writing this story would want to enable readers to "see" as well as "hear" the new principal.

The profile is not an encyclopedic listing of the subject's life and accomplishments. Rather, the reporter should select facts that individualize the person and suggest the type of personality he or she has. The account of what makes the subject unique should permit readers to clearly know the person. Typically there is one dominant reason the publication is doing a feature profile on the person. The reporter should collect information and details relevant to that central reason. The central reason should be in the wrap or nut paragraph of the story.

In collecting the information, the reporter should interview the subject's friends, relatives, colleagues and sometimes enemies. Reading all previous stories about the person will give the reporter a good background to work from. Good interviews with others may lead to information the reporter will look for or ask about in the interview with the subject. Another teacher's stories about the volunteer work a coach does at a homeless shelter provide good insight. An All-State actress's mother may have great anecdotes about how her daughter used to dress up the dogs and act out movies. Both interviews may lead to good leads or good body development.

The point of the profile is to bring the person to life. The reporter should reveal personality through incident and anecdote rather than through a summary of the person's life and achievements. Permit the reader to see the subject in action. The person's appearance, dialect and words; others' words about the subject; as well as his or her actions should help give the reader a clear picture of the subject.

Observation is one way for the reporter to get such description. A student leans down to just 3 inches above an English assignment to read five sentences typed so large they cover the page. Showing the reader this observation gives a better understanding of that student's challenges. The observation works better than the words "severely sight impaired."

The description could easily become a lead for a story on how a freshman is working to overcome a visual impairment. The lead must clearly match the primary focus of the profile. The profile on a teacher who rides bulls on the weekends could begin with an anecdote about being saved by a rodeo clown but not an anecdote about an unrelated scene in her biology class.

Working last Saturday afternoon, Matt Vick [12] glues the frame onto the door of his 1951 Ford. Having already finished most of the body work, Vick only has a few minor adjustments left before he can put his pick-up on the road. His goal is to finish the interior by graduation.

Get your motor running, again

Vicks take on full restoration of 1950s Fords

Mason **FLINK**
features editor

A pair of black Reef sandals sticks out between the front axles of a rusty 1951 Ford pick-up. Tattered finished manuals and Internet printouts on basic welding litter the garage floor. Clad in work jeans and a worn gray tee, his face covered in grease, National Merit Semi-Finalist and amateur mechanic Matt Vick [12] crawls out from under the hood of his near-finished masterpiece.

"I'm almost done," Matt said. "It's taken about four years, and all I have to do is some pretty minor stuff, like hooking up the rest of the linkages."

The whole process and idea of rebuilding a vehicle came from his father.

"My dad worked on his car when he was a kid," Matt said. "He just wanted my brother and [I] to do the same thing."

Matt and brother Zach [10] each have their own cars to restore. While Matt's is a 1951, Zach's is a 1952 of the same make.

"We chose Ford really because it was the cheapest we could find," Matt said. "Mine was $1500 sitting in a guy's backyard, so we bought it, and I started rebuilding it."

While the pick-up had an engine when purchased, the suspension had to be replaced. It was also missing its flatbed and rear fenders. Some of the parts Matt purchased through various catalogs and others were harvested from another pick-up they found.

"We found a really beat-up junk car and stole a couple of parts off of it," Matt said. "The hardest part was rebuilding the bed from scratch. My dad designed it, and I just practiced welding until I got it."

While the exterior looks complete, the interior of the car is missing key elements.

"The inside has a speedometer and all of the gauges, but it's missing a seat," Matt said. "I guess right now I could drive it while standing up if I wanted to."

While the process may seem difficult to outsiders, Matt didn't consult a mechanic in the process.

"A lot of it is just trial and error," Matt said. "We have an original factory manual for the car, and there are also a lot of places on the Internet we can go whenever we get stuck."

Because Matt's car is so old, it isn't required to pass many of the more extensive tests mandated for vehicles today.

"It has different requirements because it is over 25 years old," Matt said. "It only has to pass the laws that were in place back then. I don't need to have seat belts and back-up lights."

Even though the truck isn't complete, Matt said he plans to drive it before he graduates.

"If things are going well, I should finish in three months," Matt said. "I'm not going to sell it. I want to take it with me to college."

While there, Matt wants to continue his career in tinkering with machines.

"I want to major in mechanical engineering," Matt said. "Past that, I don't really know what I could do with that kind of degree. I haven't gotten that far yet."

Even though he has done most of the work alone, father James was a part of each step of the process.

"I taught him at first how to weld," Mr. Vick said. "I helped him take it apart and glue it back together, but he learned the body work pretty much on his own. I still help him with some of the assembly and the painting."

According to Matt, even though he has invested a lot of time in his car, it has all been worth it.

Said Matt: "It's a really cheap way to have a cool car. It's even better that it's a family ordeal."

Fig. 6.2. Profile story. *The Bagpipe,* Highland Park High School, Dallas, Texas.

An indirect quotation, relevant description or pertinent anecdote can make for a strong lead on a profile. Direct quotations are used less than indirect ones by experienced reporters because interviewees do not often provide strong quotations that make the point as tightly and effectively as the reporter's own careful paraphrase can. The wrap graph of a profile will clearly identify the primary reason you're doing a story about this person. The story's body will vary as it will in all features.

Here are a few tips for profile writing.

- Use only the most descriptive or entertaining words of the interviewee as direct quotations. If you can say what the interviewee said more concisely and interestingly, then you should paraphrase.

- Weave characteristic expressions, mannerisms or gestures into the story if appropriate. Avoid paragraphs in which you describe personality. Show personality by including precise descriptive details throughout the story.

- Dialect can provide wonderful development of the subject's personality. However, you must be careful to use the subject's slang and dialect consistently and honestly in the piece.

- Avoid overworking the interviewee's name by using noun substitutes that apply, such as "the noted foreign correspondent," "the author," "the former Council president," "the Heisman trophy-winner," "the well-known educator," "the editor of the local paper," "the former Olympic champion," "the new lottery millionaire."

In the following example, the writer captures the random and humorous characteristics of a teacher. While the use of first person "I" is not typical or recommended in features, this feature uses it well.

> He's a terrible artist. When I walk into physics teacher Dan Harper's classroom, he's sitting alone sketching gazelles. The stick figure equivalent of several of the long-legged creatures covers his page, and he carefully pencils in the arched antlers of another.
>
> "One of my students said I needed practice," he says, frowning at the paper with the stick gazelles.

> In an effort to lighten the concepts of physics, Harper's classes have long employed the gazelle as their mascot to demonstrate linear momentum – how fast a gazelle is soaring through the air when it falls off a wall and other important measurements.
>
> A metal ball appears in his hands from nowhere, and he begins to trace its circumference on the gazelle paper.
>
> "What are you doing," I ask.
>
> Fidgeting, he looks up and admits he's worried because he doesn't know what to expect from this interview. The P.A. interrupts us, informing all teachers that if they want to eat before their in-service, they have only 10 minutes until the cafeteria closes.
>
> He mentions he's hungry and I suggest interviewing him later.
>
> "Maybe I won't be so nervous next time," he says.
>
> As I walk in the door for our second interview, Harper offers me his package of Oreos. I take a cookie and sit down, but he shoves the bag toward me.
>
> "Take more or I'll eat them all," he says. "I'm trying to lose 10 pounds."
>
> He sits across from me, and with no gazelle sketches in sight, crosses his hands and looks at me expectantly. He seems less edgy than he'd been at our last meeting, and I throw out a question about his goals.
>
> It seems I've approached guarded territory. He sighs.
>
> "I really hate these goal things," he says, scrunching up his face as if he's tasted rotten food. "You can write that down. I've had to think of goals during educational courses in the past. For most people they're good. But any time I think of a goal it sounds trivial. I look at it and think, "Is that really what I want?"

"I avoid making goals. That pretty much says a lot about me. I have a hard time completing tasks. It's not something I'd recommend for students. There are probably counselors for that."

"Intelligent. Hilarious. Random." is senior Julie Schwartz's response when I ask for a description of Harper.

"Once I was walking down the hall and I saw him skateboarding upside down on his hands," senior Elizabeth Poole said. "It's got something to do with physics — you know, perpetual motion."

He's been known to demonstrate Newton's laws by shooting plastic monkeys with a dart gun and encourage paper ball fights in the halls to teach about nuclear reactions. So what's his teaching philosophy?

"Okay, let me ramble a little," he says. "We can make the most dull thing fun if we try to. I try to make it as fun, interesting and different as possible. That involves students working with each other and being able to control their own learning. Students have to pretend they're interested in the subject when they are not."

Harper's students don't seem to do much pretending.

"He's so excited — he's even giddy — just to be teaching us. It actually excites him to put equations together," senior Chase Shryoc said. "And every lesson has a funny story from the farm."

With lessons that regularly draw incidents from Harper's cow-milking, sheep-shearing, fence-repairing days as a boy on a West Texas farm, he brings a new meaning to real-life problem solving.

"It's sort of a career by default," the 14-year veteran says of teaching. "I'm glad I decided to become a teacher but I don't know why I did."

Harper's upbringing in the "desolate desert" region of Texas ("I see more people now every day than I did in the first five years of my life") didn't call for elaborate plans for the future.

"I didn't give it any thought — I just didn't want to live out on a ranch. When you come from a poor background, you don't think about what you're going to do for college or for a career. You just do what happens to you."

While his parents hadn't graduated from high school, Harper sought to leave the farm life and headed for college. Where to?

"You should probably ask where I didn't go," he says.

After a short-lived stint at Abilene Christian University, Harper cringed at the costs of a private education compared to value and headed to UT-Permian Basin, where he earned a B.S. in biology. Up next came an Electronic Engineering Technology ("be sure to write down that technology part") degree from Texas A&M.

"People say that if you're stimulus-deprived as a child you grow up to be stupid," Harper says. "I don't believe in any of that but it affected my ability to socialize some."

"Mr. Harper doesn't talk a lot," senior Andrew Ketcham said, "but he's probably the best teacher at Westlake."

"Not only can I handle being alone — I have to be alone," Harper says. "I grew up out of the city and was alone a lot so I learned to entertain myself. I find things to occupy my time." We discuss bee keeping, his lifelong hobby that has assured that "people are afraid to come into my backyard." He talks about his garden and admits that he spends a good bit of his free time in the company of his television.

"I have endless projects," he says. "I built a wall this summer in my back yard."

A wall. As I ponder the usefulness of a backyard wall, he beats me to the question, sharing that he's often asked the purpose of the wall.

"I tell people it's a meditation wall, but of course I don't meditate there," he says, his voice lowering a bit as if it's a secret. "It's a small, strong wall. I just wanted a wall in my back yard."

And if there's a wall, it's possible to calculate the speed of a gazelle jumping off of it.

Corrie MacLaggan
Westlake Featherduster
Westlake High School
Austin, Texas

Notice how the reporter begins with something that establishes the physics teacher's character. Then she brings the story full circle when she refers back to her lead in her conclusion. The story is full of feature-writing elements such as dialogue, examples, voice and details. With your classmates discuss how she uses those elements. Also notice how she weaves into the story the background information on his teaching experience and his education.

HUMAN INTEREST STORY

The human interest story is a story without much news value other than offering a closer look at the oddities of life. These features appeal to the emotions with entertainment as the goal. The human interest story can be about almost anything: persons, places, animals, inanimate objects (Fig. 6.3). This type of feature can be about the track team's unofficial mascot, a rabbit who makes his home along the practice track. Or the human interest feature can be a story about how two band students discovered they were distant cousins.

Any major news event has a human interest angle. A new bridge dedication may bring to mind a story on

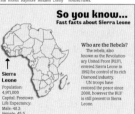

Fig. 6.3. Human interest feature. *Harbinger,* Shawnee Mission East High School, Prairie Village, Kan.

the first person to cross the bridge. The baseball fan who stood in line 18 hours to buy the first bleacher ticket becomes the human interest angle in connection with the start of the World Series.

Keen observation and intellectual curiosity will lead to most human interest stories. Learn to think of interesting little happenings as possible stories. No doubt there are little happenings or incidents in many of your classes that could be developed into good human interest stories that would amuse your paper's readers.

Consider possible story ideas in

- Any situation or incident that makes someone smile or laugh

- Any situation or incident that arouses someone's sympathy

- Any situation or incident that is unusual

The human interest feature usually is not written in the inverted pyramid order. Many follow the narrative or chronological order or a combination. Here are a few tips for the writing of the human interest feature:

- Select only the details necessary to develop that emotion. Don't overload your story.

- Try to present your story in an original, clever way to hold reader interest.

- Write to a particular reader, not just to anyone. That technique will help to create a conversational tone.

- Avoid presenting your story in the form of a condensed summary, which will not let your reader become involved. A reader must become part of an event if the story is to be successful. Do not say someone was angry, for example. Let us see the person in an actual scene.

- Follow the lead with concrete, actual details and examples.

- Try to include some dialogue if possible. The story becomes more personal because your readers will "hear" the persons.

INFORMATIVE FEATURE STORY

Informative features give the readers information about ordinary topics that they may deal with each day, in and outside of school (Fig. 6.4). Stories about college

---

Dumpster diving spiced up summer nights

Some Northwest students dug through various Dumpsters in the area this summer, fishing out anything that they found interesting.

By Allison Branch

After a summer night of watching Japanese films, Travis Arey, John Shafer and David Amir, seniors, found themselves plagued by boredom. Faced with plenty of time and nothing to do, Arey suggested a trip to the Dumpster behind an area bookstore.

"We went and found perfectly good books and took them out of Dumpsters," Arey said. "The books we found were basically John Grisham and Michael Crichton books or cheesy romances and self-help books."

What began as a temporary solution to boredom turned into regular raids on area Dumpsters throughout the summer. They call it "Dumpster diving."

Under cover of darkness the seniors and their friends slinked past unsuspecting stores and rummaged in the large metal bins behind them. They found both functional and unusual things hidden in these dark green treasure chests of trash.

"We found an old broken wheelchair one time and a bunch of random stuffed animals another time. It was all mostly a bunch of junk, but neat-looking junk," Amir said.

Most of the bounty was coverless books and old magazines,

but the guys also retrieved computer parts, mattresses, carpet squares, crutches, old TV sets and random pieces of furniture.

"People threw away good computer parts. I just scrounged those," Amir said.

The random dumpster dives became more organized as time went by, but many times the guys just cruised around town looking for interesting places to hit. Eventually the guys arranged a pretty efficient process during dives in order to grab the largest amount of items within a short amount of time.

"Two guys jumped in the Dumpster and passed books out, the rest formed an assembly line to run books to the car and come back for more," Shafer said.

The trio used the books they found in several creative pranks they referred to as "booking," in which the discarded literature was scattered on lawns and cars in parking lots.

In some areas Dumpster diving is illegal, but not in Shawnee. Still, the guys maintained a healthy fear of police, sometimes fleeing the scene if a police car passed them by during a dive.

"If you ask questions, it draws attention to it, so we're just going to let it lie since it's not actively against the law," Arey said.

With school in full swing and a host of other activities demanding their attention, the guys certainly have less time to go Dumpster diving. Nevertheless, Arey, Amir and Shafer may be seen later this year haunting area Dumpsters, searching for that perfect piece of trash.

"If there's any weekend where not much else is going on, it will probably start up again," Shafer said. "It's kind of a thrill to see what you can haul out of a Dumpster for free."

TRASH TRIVIA
(Clean Air Council)

- The average American produces 4.39 pounds of trash a day, up to 56 tons a year.
- Only 1/10 of solid garbage in the United States is recycled.
- The United States throws away enough trash to fill 63,000 garbage trucks a day.
- Each year, Americans create enough trash to build a 12-foot wall from Los Angeles to New York City.
- Businesses in the United States use about 21 million tons of paper a year, enough to equal 175 pounds for every American.
- The amount of glass bottles Americans throw away every 2 weeks can fill a space as large as the Twin Towers.
- Throwing away one aluminum can wastes as much energy as if it were 1/2 full of gasoline.
- The average American businessman goes through around 500 disposable cups a year.

RACHEL NELSON

Fig. 6.4. Human interest feature. *The Northwest Passage,* Shawnee Mission Northwest High School, Shawnee, Kan.

49% of students think that copying homework is not cheating 8% cheat on a regular basis

January 21 survey of 278 students

graphic by Mary Margaret Malloy

The newest modes of cheating include both downloading text or recording a soundtrack of spoken information onto iPods to refer to during a test.

Cheat sheets old-fangled

Faculty implements lessons to combat school dishonesty

Mason **FLINK**
features editor ▶

The huge math test covers topics more esoteric than tribal hunting rituals of African pygmies. The guy two desks ahead peeks at the formulas he wrote on the inside label of his water bottle, and the girl to the right turns her Livestrong bracelet inside out to view the formula that she had scribbled inside.

Regardless of what excuses fuel this predicament, teachers and students alike are aware of increased incidences of academic dishonesty.

"A lot of the cheating that I deal with is when students are under pressure, and they didn't study," assistant

principal Bobby Mabry said.

Assistant principal Marta Gott suggested every teacher address the issue with classes early in January, focusing on plagiarism.

"We are raising awareness and stimulating thought on a problem that is not only present in our school, but in the world," Gott said.

Gott said no spike in cheating caused the concern.

"There wasn't one incident that caused us to want to take a look at cheating," Gott said.

When teachers catch students cheating, the type of punishment is at their discretion.

"I talk to the student, call the parent, write a referral so it goes on record to the assistant principal and give a zero," said social studies department chair Skip Moran.

This year, of 606 disciplinary referrals, 20 have been for academic hon-

continued on page 3 ▶

Plagiarism places education at risk

continued from page 1 ▶

said.

esty, 3.3 percent.

According to counselor Jon Mamula, any disciplinary action can be released to prospective colleges.

"We do not voluntarily send the disciplinary record, but some schools ask for that information," Mamula said. "It could be a reason for outright denial."

Physics teacher Elizabeth Winslow said she is more disappointed than angry when she catches cheaters.

"It doesn't make me mad," Winslow said. "Students need to be responsible for their own education; it just saddens me."

The act of plagiarism, or copying another's work, has raised the most concern.

"The Internet makes it so easy to download papers," Gott said. "We need to talk more about how to avoid plagiarizing so our students don't go to college and get expelled. They need to know it's not okay to cut and paste."

According to the Center for Academic Integrity, a 2000-1 survey conducted of 4,500 high school students showed that 74 percent admitted to one or more instances of serious test cheating. 72 percent admitted to serious cheating on written assignments.

The website turnitin.com is one tool teachers employ to find out if a paper is not a student's original work; by typing in a paragraph from a student's paper, the website can search for a possible match.

Copying homework raises more eyebrows.

"Everyone cheats on homework," a junior girl said. "It is a waste of time anyway, and most of the time it is busy work and has no point."

US History teacher Janis Knott said cheating on homework hurts students in the long term.

"If they are using someone else's answers, they don't have an in-depth understanding of the [topic]," Knott

When her friends ask to borrow her homework, a freshman girl said she sometimes offers help.

"I think it's bad when people always take advantage of somebody and have other people do it for them," she said. "If it's one time, and they don't want a zero, I don't mind helping."

New technology has recently spawned even more cheating techniques. Cell phones and even iPods have been used to cheat on tests and quizzes.

Mallory Hughes [11] said that the attitude of a teacher has about academic dishonesty determines how much takes place in a class.

> "Everyone cheats on homework. It is a waste of time anyway.
> *a junior girl*"

"Teachers who do trust you and leave the issue alone make you not want to cheat," Hughes said. "It's those who freak out about it that make people almost want to."

Leslie Hunt [12] appreciates the respect students are given by calculus teacher Charles Tillerson, who regularly leaves the classroom during assessments.

"Dr. [Tillerson] trusts our integrity enough to leave us unattended, intending that we will be completely honest," Hunt said. "It's nice to know that a teacher trusts us enough to do that."

Gott admits that even with the faculty's best efforts, the issue will never completely go away.

"You look at the world around us: people cheating on taxes, speeding when highway patrolmen aren't around us, scandals like Enron; everyday there is dishonesty of some sort," she said. "Students are creative and smart, and they will know the ways to cheat. [But] when somebody cheats, it says a lot about his/her character."

Fig. 6.5. Informative feature. *The Bagpipe,* Highland Park High School, Dallas, Texas.

application tips or internet addiction are both informative features. While the topic may be timely, the story does not revolve around one central news event.

The informative feature often seems to overlap with the news-feature. The informative feature may not be as timely as a news-feature, but the informative feature may cover a recent issue. Internet addiction is certainly a relevant subject for an informative feature story. However, the same story would be a news-feature

if it comes after the school board's call for parents to limit their children's internet use.

The informative feature can be as everyday as taking care of your car or keeping a good friend. Coverage of lifestyle features is becoming more prevalent in professional and high school publications. Informative features on health, exercise and diet are part of the newspapers. Health story writing is covered more thoroughly in Chapter 5.

Some tips for informative feature stories:

- Talk to knowledgeable sources. Use in-school sources if knowledgeable but do not forget area college professors, businesspeople or professionals.

- Avoid using secondhand sources such as encyclopedias or books, other than as background for interviews.

- Use student quotes and anecdotes to bring life to the areas explained by professionals or knowledgeable sources.

- Be accurate. A reporter needs to make sure he or she understands the topic before informing the public.

OTHER TYPES OF FEATURES

A *community feature story*, usually of the informative type, relates the school to parts of the community with ties to students. Many of today's school newspapers have features on aspects of the juvenile court, the police department, the voter registration bureau, the emergency department of a hospital, the hospital itself (for example, care of drug addicts), mental health clinics, local colleges and universities, even nursing homes and other homes for the aged. If used, all these subjects must have a slant of interest to school readers.

Interpretative features explain various aspects of school, such as art exhibits, new courses, changes in graduation requirements, school financial problems, and the like. Art displays, for example, often need interpretation to help viewers understand the artist. Exhibits of work in home economics and industrial arts departments also lend themselves to interesting features that interpret the functions of the departments. The whys and wherefores of new courses and changes in graduation requirements will interest readers if they are handled informatively and are well written. A behind-the-scenes look at the school's financial structure can help readers understand where school money comes from and perhaps why the school is in financial trouble. Some school newspapers have published interesting statistical features on the cost of operating a school for one day, one week and one year. Interesting graphics could accompany such stories.

Historical feature stories are stories that bring the past to life. Historical coverage is usually tied to a timely event. For example, the school's fiftieth, seventy-fifth, or one-hundredth commencement would lend itself to a comparison and contrast feature, complete with pictures if records and files are available. Old yearbooks are often an excellent source for historical information.

The *symposium interview features* are written panel discussions on timely topics of interest to school readers (Fig. 6.6). Some examples are opinions on the counseling system, information kept on student records, merit pay for teachers, graduation requirements, the value of foreign languages, low enrollment in certain courses, censorship or prior review by administrators for school newspapers, or nonschool topics such as drugs, child abuse, divorce, police brutality, runaway teenagers, racial problems or classification of movies as PG, R or X. Background on the panelists should be included with the story.

There are many other types of feature stories – really beyond classification because types are limited only by the ingenuity and resourcefulness of a staff. One of the best ways to get ideas is to study exchange newspapers, particularly those that have been cited for imaginative feature coverage.

Fig. 6.6. Symposium interview feature. *Northwest Passage,* Shawnee Mission Northwest High School, Shawnee, Kan.

EXERCISES

1. Clip and mount on 8½ × 11-inch paper five different types of feature stories from school and daily newspapers. Label each. Beneath each type explain in detail what makes it a feature rather than a straight news story and what some of its best characteristics are.

2. Use the following categories to list possible feature story ideas.

   (a) List five topics for informative features. Indicate possible sources for each story. Try to have several that are related to timely events.

   (b) List five persons who would be excellent subjects for personality sketches or profiles. Opposite each indicate the reasons why each would make an interesting story.

3. Read and evaluate five different leads from the daily newspaper. Rank them. Which one does the best job of grabbing your attention? Why? Why did the writer choose the lead?

4. In small groups create a list of 10 things that interest students. Now develop at least two feature stories for each item on the list. Consider all types of features: profile, informative, human interest, community, interpretive historical and symposium review.

5. Find a major news story in a daily newspaper that has affected high school students. Create a list of possible feature story ideas based on the news story.

6. Interview a classmate on one of these experiences and write a feature story.

   (a) First or worst date

   (b) Scariest accident you've been in

   (c) The time your parent embarrassed you the most

   (d) Best holiday memory

   (e) Best or worst job experience

7. Pick a subject, such as the preparations for a Student Council bake sale or the school mascot at a basket-ball game, and observe. Use all your senses. Write down as much information as you can. Be precise and accurate. Based on your observations, decide what your focus would be for a story and circle the relevant details or dialogue to go with that focus.

8. Write a feature story from the following information.

The Student Council sponsor Amanda Webb is in her first year of teaching. She attended Eastfield Community College and then transferred to University of North Texas. Five years ago at Eastfield a friend of a friend asked her if she would like to join the rodeo club. The friend's friend was the club president.

She started going to the practice arena to learn how to ride a horse. She started riding with rodeo team members. Then one day, the president asked her to try chute dogging, a form of steer wrestling. She became the first female to steer wrestle for Eastfield. She still competes in rodeos on weekends. She's won several competitions that have earned her $420 in prize money, T-shirts and ribbons. Each competition during the rodeo season, she earns points for the grand prize, which is a belt buckle. She's never won a buckle. To pay for riding time, she has worked at the ranch repairing barbed wire fences, painting barns and repairing the rodeo arena's concession stand.

Quotes from an Amanda Webb interview

"I guess I've always wanted to do it. Ever since I was a little girl I've wanted to own horses. It's hard to explain; this is just something I love to do. The first time I went to the ranch, I rode a 20-year-old horse named Honey. He only walked in circles. I got bored pretty quickly. I was moved up to a horse named Star, and I would walk, trot and lope in circles with it. I was trying to teach the horse rein control. Walking in circles is good practice. I had to work at the ranch to get more riding time. Whatever it takes to be around the sport, I'll do. You can't be afraid of getting a little dirty. I've gotten manure in my hair so many times, I can't even count."

(on chute dogging): "It's actually easier for me than it is for some guys because of my size. I'm small enough to get up under the bigger steers, and I can use leverage to swing those big son-of-a-guns down. I'll battle one after the other. I'm not afraid of them. I've never been afraid of much. When I was 4 or 5, my mom said I'd walk right up to a barking Doberman."

"Anything a guy could do, I wanted to do. Anyway, it's the big ones (steers) that are easy. The little ones are the ones that will charge after you."

"The money and the scholarships don't mean anything. You compete for the buckle. It's all about the buckle."

Details

Webb is also the art teacher. She grew up in the city. She's 22. She's 5-foot 1 and 100 pounds. She wears cowboy boots with dresses to school. The average weight of a steer she wrestles is 600 pounds. She has a scrapbook with her ribbons in it. The scrapbook is decorated with cowhide drawings, cutout horses and cowboy hats made from construction paper. Her favorite song is Garth Brooks' song "Rodeo."

She has to drive 45 minutes to get to the rodeo arena.

In the chute dogging event, the competitor starts in the chute with the bull. The competitor grabs hold of the steer's horns. The gate opens. The steer is prodded with an electric device so that it runs out onto the floor of the arena. The wrestler's goal is to pull the steer off all four feet. The person who does so in the fastest time wins. Average time is five seconds.

9. Write a feature for the newspaper from the following information.

A group of Key Club members are helping teach kindergarten students. The students are from Virginia Bodine Elementary School. The Key Club is an all-boys club from the junior and senior class. The main activity the members participate in is reading to a class of 16 kindergartners. They go to Miss Kate Mider's class every Wednesday. Key Club sponsor Mary Tuttle said she has had 21 students who participate. She said four students volunteer to read more regularly than the others. Those who read regularly are Junior James Rogers, Senior Sam Jones, Junior Alan Ricks and Senior Alex Johnson. Some of the books that Key Club members have read are *Green Eggs and Ham, Fox and Socks, The Foot Book, The Armadillo from Amarillo, Chicka Chicka Boom Boom* and *The Very Hungry Caterpillar.*

Quotes

Sponsor Mary Tuttle

"I have two children. I thought of doing this after James (Rogers) came over this summer for a meeting and started reading a book to my youngest. He was great, and she loved him. So I called Kate and asked what she thought of the idea. She loved it, so we started about the second week of school. It's great for everyone. The kids will sit and listen to every word. These boys are role models for these kids. Afterwards, they want to talk to them. I saw little Kemble showing his football cards to James the other day. Then he wanted to talk about his dog. They hang on these boys' legs and climb all over them.

"I think it builds self-esteem for my Key Club kids because they see how much others care about them."

Kindergarten teacher Kate Mider

"These boys are great. When they started, they were a little timid. Then they got into it. My kids' favorite is *Green Eggs and Ham*. James decided one day he'd dress up to read it. He wore a long red and white hat and a red bow tie.

"He's quite an actor. He's created different voices for Sam-I-am and for the guy he's chasing around. He's great at bringing the book to life.

"Then there's Sam. Here's this guy who's 6–8 and about 230 pounds lying stretched out on the floor reading *The Very Hungry Caterpillar*. He may be three times their size, but he really relates to these kids. He gets down on their level, literally and figuratively."

Junior James Rogers

"I just remember how my mom used to act out all the books when I was little. I had this Dr. Seuss outfit that I wore for Halloween, so I thought the kids would get a kick out of it. Then I bought these toy eggs and ham and painted them green. We just have a good time. I was surprised that they'd really sit and listen to me. Their eyes get so big when you read to them. I could really see myself as a teacher. It's just neat to think I could help them want to read. They just hang on every word even though they've heard the same book at least five times. Now I'm really getting to

know some of the kids. Every time I go, Kemble and I have to talk about football cards. I don't have any brothers or sisters, so it's pretty cool to kind of have a little brother."

Senior Sam Jones

"At first, I was like, naw man. Then I did it once, and it was cool. The first time I did it, I stood up and read. They had to crane their necks to look up to me. So next time I laid down on the floor with them. I think they liked that. It put me on their level. They'll even climb on my back when I read.

"I go home and read to my brother now. I'll finish my homework, then I'll sit him on the couch with me, and we'll read. He's only three, but Miss Mider said I should point at the words as I read them and he'll learn to read that way.

"James is crazy, but he has great voices for the characters. I get to read *The Polar Express* next week, so I'm going to wear my big coat and hat."

Kindergartner Kemble White

"I like when they come to read. They're funny. I like it when James dresses up. He's crazy."

Details

Miss Mider has been teaching two years.

Senior Sam Jones is a starting center for the basketball team.

Junior James Rogers is the president of the Key Club. His mother is a teacher at Martin Luther King Jr. High School.

Key Club sponsor Mary Tuttle also teaches English I. Her two children are Heather, 5, and Thomas, 7.

Miss Mider's room is decorated like a rain forest, with lots of green leaves stapled to the ceiling and plants of all kinds sitting around the room. She decorated it like this because she's teaching about wild animals. She lays out blue gym mats for the kids to sit on during the reading time.

The first book that James read to the Tuttle children was Dr. Seuss' *Fox and Socks*.

Sportswriting

His clip-on tie barely covered the fourth button on his shirt. Still, the large figure known only as "Coach" standing before the young reporter was rather intimidating. Coach leaned across the desk and pounded his fist on the reporter's spiral notebook, emphasizing each word. "You can quote me on, this. We . . . are . . . going . . . to . . . give . . . it . . . one hundred . . . ten . . . percent."

Hearing the conviction in the coach's voice, the reporter just knew he had a zinger quote.

Suckered. Just like that, another cliché lives on in scholastic journalism sports reporting.

The ultimate goal in sportswriting is to give the reader a fresh approach to the struggles and the pain of the people who slip on a mesh uniform and strive to be better than the other team.

If the reporter does a two-minute interview where the only question is "How did you feel about the game?" then he or she can plan on coaches and players turning on the tape recorder in their brain to spit out all the clichés they've heard since they played Little League. "I think if we just play our game, we'll be okay." "We had better come to play today." If the reporter stops there, he or she doesn't have much of a story.

In developing a story that goes beyond the trite angles of the last 10 years to capture the real spirit of the game, a sports reporter can

- Read magazine and newspaper stories about the sport and the team to understand what is trite or overdone.

- Spend time talking to coaches and players before the season starts and before game days. In a more relaxed setting, the reporter will find out what kind of a game the coach expects and what parts of the game his or her team is working on during four-hour practices.

- Know that sports are not only play-by-play recaps and statistics; sports stories are about people.

- Understand that sports stories should ask *why*. Why was the team more motivated in the second half? Why has the softball team started hitting home runs in the last three games?

- Look beyond the action on the field for stories. See the stories of relationships off the field that lead to results on the field.

- Understand that playing and winning are not the only stories. A lacrosse team that hopes to win its first game in two years can be a fascinating story of perseverance.

- See that sports has become more than the game. In professional newspapers, as players' unions wage contract battles, business writing finds its way into the sports section. In high school newspapers, as football players face pressures of using performance-enhancing drugs and dealing with college recruiters, hard newswriting finds its way among the game stories.

A good sports reporter must be a student of the game. A reporter must

- Know sports well: rules, strategy, team and player records and the like. Become as well-informed as possible by reading up on the sport, including rule-books, and talking to coaches, players and managers. Don't rely on your prior knowledge.

- Follow team and participatory sports during practice. It is not enough to secure information secondhand from coaches, players or spectators.

- Work at detecting the strengths and weaknesses of a team or an individual.

- Know coaches and players as well as possible and interview them.

- Refrain from attending games or meets as a cheering spectator. The writer has the responsibility of interpreting difficult plays and decisions to fans too excited to notice exactly what happens.

- Observe accurately.

- Be able to take notes quickly without losing the sequence of play.

- Be fair and unbiased, even though you have a favorite team or individual.

- Support all opinions with facts. Although a sportswriter has more freedom than any other news writer, he or she must not make comments without supporting them, even in byline stories.

- Be informal and as original as possible.

WRITING THE SPORTS STORY

Developing a clear focus is important in writing a good sports story. Sometimes the focus is assigned by the editor and sometimes the writer develops the idea in his or her own. Either way, the focus must be specific. Too many editors say, "Go write a story about lacrosse." Instead, the idea should be based on specific research. The lacrosse team's 10-game winning streak and the pressure it faces from entering the playoffs undefeated

will make for a much more motivated writer because he or she has a clear focus.

Later in this chapter, we cover five different sports story types. Within each type, there are examples of story ideas – not just general story topics. But in each of the five types of sports stories, the use of statistics and sports terminology is unique and a constant writing consideration. Both deserve some special discussion.

THE DIFFERENCE BETWEEN SPORTS SLANG AND SPORTS LANGUAGE

The drama of sports should speak for itself. Slang terms, hyperbole and forced language only distract from the event being reported. Instead of writing "The 145-pound blazer rumbled through the giant gridders of the goal line for sweet six," simply focus on a good factual description: "Senior running back Robert Belsher leapt over from the one-yard line for the game-tying touchdown."

So how does a sports reporter know the difference between sports jargon and standard specialized language of the sport? The sports stylebook of the University of Missouri's teaching newspaper, the *Columbia Missourian*, offers this advice.

- If a word or phrase is so obviously silly that nobody would say it, don't write it. Nobody says "grid mentor" when he or she actually means "football coach" or "cage tiff" when he or she means "basketball game."

- Try for interesting or colorful angles in your leads. But do not cram too many images into one lead or story. It can make things confusing for your readers. Adjectives and adverbs crowd stories and leads. Stick to good verbs and genuine description where possible. Use slang sparingly.

- A sportswriter should use the specialized writing of the sport that the average reader understands without getting too technical. You're not expected to explain what a jumper is in basketball but you might want a simpler explanation for "swing backside on a low post pick."

Sports Clichés

This list is just the beginning of trite quotes and phrases that a sports reporter should avoid using. Just because a coach or player said these things does not mean you have to use them.

- "We have to play as a team."

- "We have a lot of potential."

- "I think we're going all the way to state."

- "We're going to have to take it one game at a time."

- "We've got our backs against the wall."

- "The best defense is a good offense."

- "It's a rebuilding year for us."

- "These guys played with a lot of heart."

- "We need to get back on track."

- "The ball just didn't bounce our way tonight."

Developing a Sports Story with Statistics

Sports are about people; statistics and records are just measures of people. Still, statistics are an important way to develop a sports story – just don't get carried away.

Rather than say the running back "had a good day," show the reader that he "ran for a season-high 220 yards and two touchdowns." The reader now understands how good the player's performance was. The sportswriter needs to know that numbers are relative, meaning the writer often needs to put the statistics in perspective. If the goalie had 28 saves, an average reader may not know how good that is. The writer may then have to tell the reader that her save total is the second-highest total in the district.

Perspective is also important in discussing the team's record. If a team's 10–2 for the season, the reader needs to know that the two losses came to the third- and fourth-ranked teams in the state.

When using sports stars, also

- Avoid long lists of scores. More than three numbers in a sentence or a paragraph is typically too many.

- Choose only those stats that warrant highlighting or that develop the focus of your story. Use other relevant statistics in an accompanying sidebar, agate or sports briefs section.

- Double-check accuracy. See that scores add up. Question numbers that don't sound logical or reasonable.

- Gather statistics from old newspaper archives and yearbooks. Some coaches keep files on school records or old scorebooks.

Game Story Reporting

Whether looking for a feature angle or deciding the information in a straight news story, consider this list for information to focus on or include

- Significance of the event. For example, is the league title at stake?
- Probable lineups and comments on changes in lineups
- Records of the teams or individual competitors during the current season
- Analysis of comparative scoring records of teams
- Tradition and rivalry. How do the teams stand in won/lost figures in the series? Here is where the use of a graphic would be desirable.
- Weather conditions. How will possible changes affect the outcome?
- Systems of play or strategies used by teams or individuals
- Condition of players, physical and mental
- District, state or national rankings
- Individual angles, such as star players
- Coaches' statements
- Who is favored and the odds, if available
- Other specifics: crowd, cheering-section antics, new uniforms, appearance or condition of playing field

Blocking for running back Alex Carroll (#34) [10], offensive lineman Chris Olson (#70) [11] suffers a broken ankle as the Scots coasted to a victory over Forney. Olson was named Offensive Player of the Week and will be out the remainder of the season.

Division I holds stiff opponents

Football to open versus Texas High in first round

Mason **GILMORE**
sports editor ▶

It may be the best first round match up in Texas. That's what fans, critics and coaches are calling the initial round game against Texarkana Texas High at 8pm tonight at Tyler Rose Stadium. Unfortunately for the Scots, the road to state does not get any easier.

Despite moving up to the Big School Division I bracket with its one fewer game, the Scots' schedule is among the most difficult in the playoffs.

Texas High (8-2, 5-0) was considered the favorite to win it all last year before being tripped up by Division I cham-

pion North Crowley. Texarkana capped off an undefeated 12-AAAA record with a 35-20 win over Mount Pleasant. Despite graduating several top recruits, Texas High returns a solid core and a stingy defense led by DE Chris Brown [12], and linebacker Dustin Earnest [11]. Earnest successfully replaced the highly recruited Chris Collins [12] who was dismissed from the team for off field behavior.

Offensively, the Texans feature a passing attack led by quarterback Ryan Mallett [10] and receivers Marquan Matlock [11] and Curtis Sanders [12]. Texas High brings an athletic squad whose speed could give the Scots trouble.

If HP gets past the Texans, it would face the winner of the Hillcrest-McKinney contest. Hillcrest (7-2, 4-1) heads into tonight's contest from a tough 21-6 loss to Lin-

coln for the 10-AAAA title and features a balanced offense propelled by running backs Izale Williams [12] and Tommy Bryant, who have rushed for a combined 2022 yards.

McKinney (8-2, 6-1) emerges from a big 30-8 win at Lake Dallas last week. Its only losses were to playoff bound Wylie and undefeated Hebron.

McKinney's offense spotlights several effective running backs including Chris Wimbish and a strong defense led by senior defensive tackles Lorenzo Jones and Luke Swadley.

An anticipated third round match up could pit the Scots against an Ennis team seeking revenge for Scots ending the

Gold at end of tough road

▶ continued from page 21

Lion's season last year.

Ennis (8-2, 4-1) dropped a heartbreaking 30-26 loss to Corsicana and has not shown the same offensive fire power of previous squads. Key returnees include running back Mark Malone [11], wide receiver Andrew Novack [11] and a pack defensive starters who have anchored one of the toughest groups in the area.

However, the road to a rematch is not a lock, as Ennis will open against DISD powerhouse Kimball (7-3, 5-0) tonight at Sprague.

Kimball opened the season 1-3, but the Knights bounced back with a dominant 14-0 win over Denison and have not been approached other than a 7-0 victory over Seagoville.

Kimball's offense is led by Sunset transfer running back Phillip Tanner [11], who has rushed for 1062 yards and 12 TDs. Defensively, the Knights have possibly the best 11 in the Metroplex if not in Texas. Led by defensive tackle and highly recruited Demarcus Granger [12], Kimball's defense has posted six shutouts, including four in a row.

With such a formidable schedule, the Scots will need to peak at the right time and carry that success towards their first state championship since 1957.

The Scots ride an eight-game winning streak following the season's most decisive victories, 42-7 over Forney. A

struggling passing game found its mark, as quarterback Matthew Stafford [11] threw for (249) yards. On Senior night, the coaches were able to play nearly all seniors in what was a successful and confidence building game.

Missing from the Highland Park lineup will be offensive linemen Chris Olson [11] who broke his ankle in the Forney game. Olson had surgery Monday and will miss the remainder of the season. James Miers [11] fills in for Olson at right tackle while Seth Graham [11] will replace Miers at left guard.

The Scots will begin their playoff run tonight at 8.

Linebacker Wade "The Cat" Prospere [11] returns an interception 15 yds. for a touchdown in the 3rd quarter of the Forney game. Prospere filled in for injured linebacker John Callahan [11].

Fig. 7.1. Advance story. *The Bagpipe*, Highland Park High School, Dallas, Texas.

- Package statistics not used in a story. Sidebars and separate coverage are discussed later.

TYPES OF SPORTS STORIES

ADVANCE STORY

"How do you think the team is going to do tonight?"

The girls' soccer team could be 0–11 or playing for the school's first state championship ever, and people

would ask the same question. This kind of public curiosity helps explain why there are 10 hours of pregame coverage for the Super Bowl.

The advance story satisfies public curiosity and gives insight into the upcoming game, providing as many specifics as possible (Fig. 7.1). It should always answer the five *W*'s and *H*.

The high school advance story can also mirror professional sports journalism where the advance story is often told within a feature story. The advance feature story chooses one specific aspect of the upcoming game to highlight. The story is told through strong quotes, description and anecdotes. For example, the advance story may be about the possibility of a coach getting his 300th win. Another advance story may focus on how the team will replace three injured star players. The game's significance and key matchups can be primary feature focus. In a feature format, the basic five W's and H will appear in the wrap or nut graph of the story that comes right after the lead.

Because of infrequent publication schedules and early deadlines, the advance story provides certain challenges for school newspapers. When story ideas are being passed out, the sports editor or writer must think ahead to the date of publication and have a sense of how critical the game will be and how to cover it.

Games played after the deadline date but before the publication date can often change the meaning of the game that is the subject of the advance story. In this case, the sports reporter should inform the readers of the impact last week's game could have on tonight's game.

Interviewing for the advance story may require coaches and players from competing teams to look ahead to a game in three weeks. Coaches may be reluctant to think ahead of the next night's game. Clarifying the release date of the story may help calm fears that players will overlook their present opponent.

TREND STORY

In the month since the last issue came out, the football team has lost 66–0, 74–28 and – in the home-coming game – 49–0. For three weeks, the area daily newspaper has run scores, and in the halls students have talked about the disappointment.

To relive every single scoring play of each of those games in the next issue would be repetitive, if not downright torturous. A trend story is not a rehash of the plays from each game. Instead a trend story covers the highlighted trends in the course of a team's play since the last issue (Fig. 7.2).

In a trend story the big question high school sports reporters may ask is what's gone on over the last month and why?

Fig. 7.2. Trend story. *Little Hawk*, City High School, Iowa City, Iowa.

A season to smile about

Talented volleyball team is poised to take state

The members of the CHS volleyball team sure smile a lot as they play against Fort Madison. They smile during the time-outs, smile as they effortlessly keep the ball alive, and smile as they spike the ball brutally into the poor defenders. They even smile when their opponents finally score a side out.

Maybe the Little Hawks were just a little too relaxed during their regional final; one player used the word "poopy" to describe their performance. But that's what happens when you just happen to be the best team in the state. And the best volleyball team in CHS history.

They have a lot to smile about. It's been a dream season, starting last year when the seven juniors led the team to its first state tournament appearance in 21 years, placing 3rd overall. In fact it's been a dream season ever since the girls, now all seniors, started their careers in the South East Junior High gym, having undefeated records even that early. This year, they have a 41-1-1 record going into the state tournament.

There are many reasons why this team is successful. The five years the girls have played together, from summer through winter, is part of the explanation. The team is so well melded that the girls don't have to communicate much on the court—although they do—because they know where everyone is going to be.

> "We didn't feel that it was fair to say any one of us was more of a leader. We all lead at different times and in different ways."
> *Karla Hirokawa '99*

Ingredients for success

All the girls are varsity letter winners in other sports, but they keep coming back to play volleyball. Even track superstar Teesa Price, who is used to the individual spotlight in track and originally wanted to play football in junior high, can fit into the mold easily. She said, "In track you get more personal recognition, but I like volleyball because not just one player can win the game."

Or even two players. Stacy Moss and Kelli Chesnut, at first glance, are the obvious choices as team captains. They both have the most experience and they make a dynamic duo; Moss is the best setter in the state, and Chesnut holds the school career record for kills. However, the seniors decided to break tradition thi year by not choosing two captains, but instead, naming themselves all as captains. The girls are all on such an even level, both in terms of friendship and experience, that it would be awkward if only two were named as leaders. "We didn't feel that it was fair to say any one of us was more of a leader," Karla Hirokawa said. "We all lead at different times and in different ways."

"There's no hostility on the team," Chesnut claims. "People are like, 'Oh man, after all these seasons aren't you ready to kill each other?' And I think, 'Not really.' " Chesnut's words are hard to believe when watching some of the games in practice that can consist of the girls violently smacking serves at each other or pushing their teammates over in order to win. Protests of "you cheated! You cheated!" are frequent among the competitive group. For most of the practice, though, the players tend to smile and laugh a lot for members of a team that's supposed to be feeling the pressure of being the top-ranked team.

But that's the plan of the new head coach, Diane Delozier. After coach Bond Shymansky left abruptly, Delozier had to make a decision within days. She had been set on coaching freshmen like she did last year, but decided to take charge of the varsity squad. "I've always been on the outside as an assistant coach," she said. "I saw it as a challenge and a way of growing." Her 10 years of experience as a gym teacher show as she devises new games and activities, like step aerobics, to keep her team's interest and competitiveness alive.

For a player like Stacy Moss who has been doing drills for almost a decade, Delozier's creativity is a blessing. There were times at summer camps that Moss's fingers would be bleeding from setting up so many balls, but she would still continue to set the next day with sore fingers. Her persistence has paid off. Volleyball is not the most graceful of sports, especially when players have to perform awkward moves to save a sloppy pass, but Moss makes the Little Hawk offense look smooth with her precise passing, earning her the title of best setter in the state for two years.

Winning attitude

Delozier will not only be remembered as the coach that led the volleyball team to its best season, but maybe also as the nicest coach in history. During the nail-biting play-off match against West High, her calm and supportive manner helped the nervous City players as they struggled through the emotional game. "Even if we're playing badly, she never gets mad at us. She always stays positive and we respond to positive reinforcement better," Megan Recker said.

The most negative comment Delozier made that had to do with the West game was during the next day as the girls and coaches pored over congratulation cards and newspaper articles. She was upset that an article portrayed her as boasting by omitting all the praise she had for West High. "My players are supposed to be humble," she complained.

Despite its lofty perch, the team knows

photo by Britta Schnoor

humility. Recker, for instance, played on the "B2" team in junior high before moving her way up to becoming the best server in the City High record books. Emily Rowat, in particular, is used to being in the shadow of her teammates, despite playing a solid game all season long. In the low points of the West game, her steadiness never wavered and she received much of the praise after the game. But she still doesn't mind being out of the spotlight. "I like not having to worry," she said. "I just like to play my best, but I appreciate it if maybe people come up to me and say 'Wow, you did a really good job last night.'"

Poised for victory

It's the Friday after the victory against Fort Madison, and a week before state. The Little Hawks took it easy for a couple of days, but today it's time to get back on track: conditioning, drilling, and scrimmaging are on the agenda. The players play brilliantly, maybe even better than at their blow-out of Fort Madison. Passersby regularly pause in awe when Tanya Hammes goes up to the net to smash a spike. Standing a head or three above the rest of her teammates, Hammes has the most impressive physical presence. It doesn't require much of a jump for her to send a thundering kill down and to get the crowd roaring "Big T." Her height is even more emphasized when the team's shortest player, Karla Hirokawa, hi-fives Hammes to sub in for her. If Moss and Chesnut are the perfect match, then Hirokawa and Hammes are the odd couple. Hirokawa doesn't receive as many booming cheers as Hammes does, but she can silence an oppos-

ing crowd just the same when she dives and saves a seemingly lost ball. She doesn't mind playing behind the big hitters on her team. "You get to do the fun stuff like diving," she said jokingly. "I'm close to the ground so it doesn't hurt me as much."

Stacy Moss isn't practicing because of a slight back injury, but she uses this as a chance to tell stories about the team, like the time when Recker gave Price a literally real "sponge" cake. Or when Shymansky made the girls run so hard they cried. She rolls around red-faced and laughing, barely able to tell of the junior high days, when the girls covered their faces with their hands to avoid getting hit by the ball and merely fell to their knees when diving. It's difficult to believe her stories, watching the players scrimmage against each other. They can hit tremendous spikes and long dives with ease, and they never cower from the ball.

Practice ends with a session of visualization. The girls sit down on the mats of the musty wrestling room, the walls of which are adorned with slogans like "Train like a madman." Right now, though, the lights are shut off and the girls are told to close their eyes and inhale deeply. Delozier tells them to imagine the Friday of the state tournament. They see themselves stepping off of the bus and entering the arena. They imagine hearing the wild fans and seeing the opposing team warm up. They see themselves perform every move and hit perfectly and confidently, and see the final game score: 3-1, City High. "OK, come back to reality," she says as the players open their eyes dreamily. "No," she quickly corrects herself. "That was reality."

by Dan Nguyen

> **Good luck at State!**
>
> The Volleyball team will be leaving at 9 a.m. today for the tournament at the Five Seasons Center in Cedar Rapids. The first match will be against Oskaloosa at 1 p.m.

Excelling in all sports

This year's volleyball team holds many school records in many sports:

Teesa Price
4 sport letter winner
Track: 4x100 (48.83s), 4x400 (1:43.46), long jump (17'10.5), 100 hurdles (14.10), 400 low hurdles (1:03.05)

Megan Recker
Volleyball: season serving percentage (.98)

Emily Rowat
Tennis: Best singles record in the state of Iowa

Tanya Hammes
Basketball: Game, season, and career record in blocks

Kelli Chesnut
Volleyball: Season kill rating: .416
Track: 4x400

Karla Hirokawa
Softball: Total hits in a season: 73

Stacy Moss
Golf: Best district (1st) and regional place (2nd)
Hole in ones (1)
Volleyball: School record: Game, season, career number of sets.

compiled by Dan Nguyen

In the football season mentioned above, interviews with players and coaches may be highlighted in a story on the verbal abuse the players are taking for their lack of offense. You may talk to defense players who are angry because they have spent three-fourths of the game on the field. Anecdotes of players being booed by band members may be part of the story. Talking to coaches about how dejected they have become after the seven turnovers in the last three games allows you to work in statistics and show just how bad the situation has become.

Because high school newspapers rarely come out weekly or even bi-weekly, the trend story has become the primary sports coverage as the alternative to the game story (see below). Rather than include a list of the team wins of the last 10 basketball games since issue 6 was published, the story may look at the team's increasing use of the three-pointer to win six of the last seven games.

The trend story, along with the sports feature (discussed later), is the preferred format for a yearbook story.

The trend story covers a highlighted trend of a team since the time of the last publication. Even professional newspapers, which face competing television coverage including several all-sports networks, are moving away from straight game summary stories in their next-day coverage and toward more analysis and players' stories.

Covering a high school game two weeks after it has happened is like getting Tickle Me Elmo the

Fig. 7.2. *(continued)*

Christmas after it was hot. By the time you get it, it is nice, but you've seen it, your friends have all talked about it and everyone has moved on to other things. In some student newspapers, by the time the newspaper story comes out on the football team's 66–7 romp, it's baseball season.

Add information on the upcoming game to the trend story – including the impact the last month's games could have on the next game – and the advance/trend story is born (Fig. 7.3). If the girls' team is playing for the state championship the day after the publication comes out, the audience will want to learn about how it won the last five playoff matches, but readers may want to know first what to expect in the next day's title matches.

Soccer teams face Martin tonight

By Jennifer DeMent and Melora Coughran

Panther Prints staff

Tonight's varsity boys soccer game between the Panthers and Arlington Martin could be for the district championship.

Though it will only be the second district game, the two teams are expected to battle it out for the title.

"Arlington Martin will be the team to beat," coach Bill Manning said.

So far, Martin's record is 7 wins, no ties, and only 2 losses. Duncanville's record is 6 wins, 2 losses.

One of the Panthers' losses was to number one Coppell last week. Senior Kenny Boutsabouabane was lost for the game after getting a red card in the 3-2 win over Lake Highlands.

On Jan. 22, the boys defeated Jesuit 1-0 in the championship of the Kickoff Classic.

Great saves were made by Justin Daughtery and Grant Carson during both halves, but especially near the end when it was most crucial to keep Jesuit in a shut out.

Coach Manning believes that having a larger number of seniors on the team gives the Panthers a one up over Martin.

"We're deeper on the bench," coach Manning said. "We've got 18 seniors this season, the most number of seniors I've ever had."

To keep up their record, the boys continue to practice passing, shooting and other vital skills well into the season. The boys are optimistic about the season ahead.

"We've got a really good team, and when we work together we'll accomplish what we set out to do," senior Martin Perez said.

Coach Manning says the boys are well prepared for the teams they will be facing and they are looking forward to the game against Martin to see how well they do.

"This is the best group of players I have ever had in 28 years," Manning said.

The Lady Panthers also face their toughest opponent, Arlington Martin, tonight at home in their second district game.

Head coach Bryan Beck is looking forward to a win that will set a successful tone for the rest of the season.

"I expect a shutout and to come home in the running for district champions," coach Beck said.

The girls' defense went into their first district game against Arlington Bowie Wednesday having forced four shutouts in eight games.

"Our defense is real strong," coach Beck said. "But we have depth at every position."

The girls finished non-district play with a 4-4 record, including victories against Flower Mound, Midlothian, Mesquite Horn, and a smashing 13-0 win over Lancaster.

Although disappointed by their 0-3 record at last weekend's tournament, the girls showed a good performance

Aeron Brown photo

Offense

In the Kickoff Classic, sophomore Whitney Bowen keeps the ball away from a North Crowley player.

against such highly ranked teams as Plano West (3-2-0) and Ursuline (12-2-0).

"We had probably the toughest tournament last weekend," coach Beck said.

The five freshmen, five sophomore, four juniors and three seniors are led by captains Mayra Torres and junior Tiffany Cantu.

"The girls get along really well, I think we have great chemistry between the kids," coach Beck said.

Fig. 7.3. Advance and trend combination story. *Panther Prints*, Duncanville High School, Duncanville, Texas.

- Include the information on the coming event as the first part of the story and the information on the past event as the last part of the story.

- Devote more space to the coming event than to the past event, for future news is usually more interesting to readers than news of past events.

- Condense into the space available as many of the highlights of the past event as you can.

- Follow the advance story tips when writing about the upcoming game; then use the trend notes to cover the earlier games.

- Do not include a running or chronological account. That structure is suitable only for newspapers that can be more timely than most school newspapers can be or for the very special event in which there would be interest despite the late follow-up.

SPORTS NEWS STORY

Sports are a business at the professional level and have become so at the collegiate level. While some may see the high school level as unspoiled territory, issues have crept into the secondary sports scene.

Student athletes face questions surrounding recruiter tactics, NCAA eligibility, performance-enhancing drug use and sports funding. These issues have taken newspaper sports coverage outside the realm of sports as "just a game." In Figure 7.4, a sports reporter shows good news value judgment when four football players were taken to the hospital with head injuries. The reporter looked beyond the game, taking a closer look at health risks.

Fig. 7.4. Sports news story. *Chronicle,* Harvard–Westlake High School, North Hollywood, Calif.

The sports news story follows the inverted pyramid style and the other suggestions in Chapter 2 on newswriting. Make sure to consider balance, objectivity and libel and ethics in writing sports news as you would for other newswriting.

GAME STORY

Only when the high school publication gets a very late deadline on a significant game or event is the game story used. The game story offers the significant details, game summary and highlights, and player and coach analysis on a timely basis (Fig. 7.5). But the game story is not a play-by-play recap. Anyone covering a high school game will most likely have to keep game statistics. Coaches may provide stats but not quickly enough for

deadline purposes. Anyone having to write a game story needs to understand the sport well enough to keep statistics. For example, if a quarterback is sacked for a 10-yard loss, the yards are deducted from rushing yards even though he was trying to pass.

A good sports reporter writing a game story will look for key statistics, trends or moments to weave the story around. A key statistic is often a poignant fact in the lead. A senior's three-run homer that changed the momentum and started a 10-run inning may be a worthy moment to be the primary story focus.

The story is typically written in inverted pyramid structure. The lead can follow the variety of leads offered in Chapter 3 and does not have to be a summary lead. If the sportswriter chooses a nonsummary style lead, then the team names, score and primary significance of the game should come in the wrap graph. In whatever form, game story leads should begin with something significant about the game or match.

> Despite slogging through mud and puddles of water, which added precious seconds to times and made the course slick, the cross country team's overall performances Oct. 16 produced the best City League finish in 15 years.

Lisa Burgess
Paladin
Kapaun Mt. Carmel High School
Wichita, Kan.

> The 1999 state wrestling tournament was coming to a close, but Kapaun Mt. Carmel fans and wrestlers were not ready to leave. Junior Ryan Frazier swung coach Tim Dryden around on the mat, freshman Dough Hoover held up three fingers for the fans to see and the KMC audience was still on its feet chanting "Frazier, Frazier." The Crusaders had just gained its third state champion of the night.
>
> In state competition Feb. 26–27 at the Kansas Coliseum all eight wrestlers made it to the second day; three advanced to the finals.

Elaine Meyer
Paladin
Kapaun Mt. Carmel High School
Wichita, Kan.

Billo succeeds in racing debut, Blunt takes sixth after collapsing

by Jamie Albertine

In his first organized race ever, senior Andrew Billo won the Maryland State Mountain Biking Championship at Greenbriar State Park in the junior beginner race class division April 25.

Billo toured the 13-mile course, which consisted of two 6.5-mile laps, in 1:45:00 to take first in his division. His time put him 10 minutes behind the fastest racer of the day and placed him fifth overall out of 100 racers.

"It was a very technical course," Billo said. "The trails were very rocky and steep, but I had a strong showing for my first race."

Billo said he has been training since the beginning of February, biking for an hour-and-a-half to two hours on area streets everyday. "I usually try to work some big hills into my routine, traveling down Massachusetts Avenue to the National Cathedral and back, which has four or five really tough hills along the way," he said.

Senior Bertrand Blunt competed in the sport junior class of the same race; however, after riding in second for 17.5 miles of the 18-mile race, and with only a quarter of a mile of uphill climb left, he collapsed on the side of the trail. He got back up 15 minutes later and went on to finish sixth.

"I bonked, which basically means you're doing fine and then all of the sudden you can't ride and you can't move," Blunt said. "It was almost as though I was beyond exhaustion."

Blunt, a veteran to the sport, attributed his exhaustion to lack of physical preparation. "I had just finished training with the crew team and I hadn't been riding much, so I think that I just wasn't in good shape to race."

Billo and Blunt will both continue to train for upcoming competitions in the Subaru Atlantic Mountain Biking Series' eight-race spring schedule. They will go on to compete in the "Mother's Day Mauler" at Patapsco Valley State Park May 9 and in the "Crack the Nut Race" held at Walnut Creek Park in Charlottesville, Virginia May 16.

Fig. 7.5. Game story. *Black and White*, Walt Whitman High School, Bethesda, Md.

Since the game story is not a play-by-play rehash, the story does not have to be organized chronologically. Give the reader interesting and game-changing moments first. Weave in postgame quotes from players and coaches. The quotes can give the reader insight into a second-half strategy or a record-breaking day. Then move on to less important moments or points.

Possible information for a game story:

- Significance of the outcome. Was a championship at stake? Do the standings of the teams change?

- Spectacular plays. Tell about the last-minute fumble, the triple that won the game or the jumper from mid-court.

- Comparison of the teams. How did their weights and heights compare? In what part of the game did the winners excel? What were the losers' weaknesses? Make sure to support analysis with facts or coach and player quotes.

- Individual performances. Who were the game's top performers and how good were their performances? Did the pitcher throw 92-mile-per-hour fastballs and give up only one hit, or did the right halfback run for 230 yards and score on four runs of more than 30 yards?

- Weather conditions. Did mud, sunshine, heat, cold or wind make a difference?

SPORTS FEATURE STORY

The head basketball coach who coaches his three nephews and the volleyball player who plays despite the challenge of a prosthetic leg are both good sports feature story subjects. The sports feature is a story behind or beyond the game. Based primarily on human interest and oddity, the sports feature idea comes from being aware of the stories on and off the field (Fig. 7.6).

Senior **Saul Helgeson** looks on during the CHS-BHS football game. Century won, 10-7, upsetting the top-ranked Demons, "I was a little surprised at just how well we played," said Helgeson, who injured his knee the week before in the St. Mary's loss.

ROSIE PFENNING/star

The sad story of King Saul

Mike Mullen
century star reporter

BRIDGET FEIST/spirit

You'd expect him to be more sad. You'd expect to look into Saul Helgeson's deep-set brown eyes and see the extreme pain of a kid who's lost his dream. You'd expect him to talk less and blink more when the subject turned to football.

But he didn't.

You see, the saddest part about Saul's injury isn't the deep effect it had on him. It's that he's been here before.

"Everyone thinks I'm taking this too lightly, but I'm not. I guess I just got used to it," said Helgeson.

Last year, Saul was to be starting tailback on a talented varsity squad. During two-a-days in the weeks leading up to the season, Helgeson tore his Achilles tendon. He never played a down.

With Saul out, the team suffered infinitely, finishing 1-8. Players felt they were the laughing stock of the school. Their own newspaper ridiculed them. And Saul could do nothing but watch.

Last year's teams played uninspired. They underachieved and at times seemed downright apathetic. That's why this year meant so much to Saul.

He was more than ready for it. In their third game, he spun, juked, and slashed his way to 227 yards, including breathtaking second-quarter runs of 61 and 62 yards. Century won in a 32-0 blowout. It looked like Minot brought

their JV team.

Saul threatened Century's single-game rushing record, but neither he nor coach Ron Wingenbach realized it. Saul came out early, already feeling sore, he and Wingenbach agreeing to play it safe. When informed after the game how close he had come, Saul jokingly said he'd break the record next game.

"If I got another chance, I would've broken it," Saul says now.

This win put the team at 3-0, with huge wins over Minot and Fargo South. No one was laughing now.

On the sixth play of the

next game, St. Mary's quarterback Kyle Webber optioned right and turned upfield. Saul closed quickly to make the tackle and, not surprisingly, other defenders were upon Webber early. Saul saw him stumble, then go down. He tried to avoid contact, but his knee collided with the QB's helmet at an awkward angle. Helgeson didn't know it yet, but something was wrong.

"There was no popping noise or anything," he said. "But when I went to get up, I just couldn't stand."

Teammates helped Saul off the field. Coach Wingenbach hoped for the best, but he knew this was serious.

"If Saul could've walked off the field, he would have," Wingenbach said. "When I saw him half-walking off the field with two guys helping, I knew it was bad."

The Saints scored early with the wind at their back, and Century never posed a serious threat to come back. Players looked around for someone else to step up. In this game, no one did. Century lost 17-6. It is, to date, St. Mary's only conference win, and Century's only loss.

On the sidelines, a doctor examining Saul's knee said he had probably torn his MCL, but an MRI would be necessary to determine if he'd torn his ACL. The test results would mean the difference between four to six weeks and four to six months. Coach Wingenbach hoped for the best, but he knew this was serious.

Century's next game was the big one—a Friday night date with top-ranked Bismarck High. Their junior running back, Weston Dressler, had been racking up yards and making as many headlines as Saul. In a perfect world, this would've been the showdown that allowed one of them to step forward as the state's premiere tailback. But at 6:00 p.m., while Dressler put on his pads and uniform, Saul hobbled into the bowl on crutches.

Surprising everyone, Century dominated from the opening kickoff to the final whistle. The 10-7 score was no indication of how close the game actually was. The Patriots had pulled off a huge upset of their cross-town rival.

Once more, Saul Helgeson, the best player in the stadium, looked on from the sidelines.

MORE NEXT page

Saul's sad story

< FROM PREVIOUS PAGE

On the sidelines, Saul was vocal and positive. This didn't look like someone who'd just been hit with bad news, as Saul had. Earlier that day, tests had shown that he tore both his ACL and MCL. He would undergo surgery the following Friday, and begin rehabilitation in two months if things went well. His high school football career was over. No shot at BHS. No homecoming game.

As could be expected, everyone had something to say to Saul. Family, friends, coaches, and teachers all contacted him to find out how he was feeling, and offer words of advice.

"Nothing really stood out, though," Saul said. "Everyone ended up just kind of saying the same thing."

Coach Wingenbach knew he could do little to help the situation.

"I told Saul that it isn't fair," he said. "I just feel so sorry for him. There really isn't much you can say about it."

And there really does seem to be something blatantly unfair about it all. This is Grisham with writer's block. This is Jay-Z with a stutter. Saul Helgeson should not be on crutches.

"These are the same ones from last year," he says, motioning to the crutches. "I've put a lot of use into these things." He pauses, and then: ". . .been on them too much."

The post-surgery outlook seems hopeful at the moment. Saul hopes to start working out on the knee soon. It may be healed in time for him to join the basketball team mid-season as he did after last year's injury.

"We're looking at him returning in February or March," says Wingenbach. "It would be really tough for him to join up with the team then, simply because of the conditioning and shooting touch he would lack. But he may prove us all wrong, because he did

last year."

Beyond that, Saul plans on working hard throughout the off-season. He talks about playing football on the collegiate level, which, although it may seem like a long shot for someone who played 3 games in two years, is certainly not out of reach.

"I wouldn't say that I'm injury prone," Saul said. "I guess I've just been unlucky. If any coach looks at my work ethic, they will be at least give me a chance."

Wingenbach agrees.

"He came back from what would be a career-ending injury his junior year, and played very well in the first three games this year," he said. "He may not see the scholarship money that he should, though."

For three weekends, Saul was a high school football phenomenon. And now, he may have to walk on at an in-state college and impress everyone all over again. For now though, his role is restricted to observer and supporter of the current team.

And it's turning out to be quite a team.

A 13-7 win over Williston has placed them in a tie for first place in the West region. Coach Wingenbach says that, although they lost Saul, their outlook has not changed.

"We still want to play in November. We've still got 79 other guys, but now, we're a team without a superstar," he said. "We're just average guys, but in the context of a team, we're pretty good."

'Pretty good' may turn out to be an understatement. But now Wingenbach and Saul are left to think about what might have been.

"Once in a while in a coach's meeting we'll catch ourselves saying, 'Man, if only we had Saul.'"

Fig. 7.6. Sports feature story. *The Star*, Bismarck Century High School, Bismarck, N.D.

For example, in science class, football players discuss wanting to make a big hit to earn the "black mask" award. A good sports reporter might find an interesting story in the mask and what players are doing to get it or a story on incentives coaches use. In the cafeteria, soccer players mention how great it will be to see the coach get her 200th win. A story on the coach and her career highlights may be timely for the next issue. While newspaper sports features do not have to be timely, running them while the sport is in-season will make for higher reader interest. If the story is tied to a news peg, such as the expectation of the coach's 200th win, that fact should be in the wrap graph.

The types of sports features are as varied as the types of feature stories discussed in Chapter 6.

Some examples of sports feature stories that have appeared in high school publications include

- A player profile on a 6-foot 8-inch basketball forward who, despite having played the game for only four years, has been named to the All-State team and is being recruited by Division I colleges

- A human interest feature story on the increase of female weightlifters who are trying to stay in shape and prepare for their track events

- A news-feature story on the increasing number of students who are paying to have personal trainers for advice, motivation and health information

- A human interest feature story on a school's and area's top golfer who, after seeing his game break down in his last two tournaments, walked away from the game

- A human interest feature story on a group of students who coach Little League teams. The story covers why these student coaches are working with younger kids and how the coaches' advice is helping players on and off the field.

The organization of the sports feature story is as varied as that of other feature stories; however, the inverted pyramid form is rarely used. Just like other strong feature stories, the sports feature is told through strong use of quotes, observations and details.

Refer to Chapter 6 for tips on feature writing.

Strong reporting is critical in sportswriting. In Figure 7.7, the reporters interviewed college coaches, parents, athletes and counselors for an insightful look at college recruiting.

FEATURE LEADS FOR SPORTS STORIES

If you're not writing the straight-news game story lead, a variety of feature lead types as discussed in Chapter 3 can be used. Read and assess the following high school sports leads.

> Pointing to the slender substitute teacher standing awkwardly among a group of teenagers, physical education instructor Linda Wolf asks one of her students . . . "Do you think you could beat him at hoops?"

Packaged Coverage

Complete coverage of all sports and all levels – varsity, JV and freshmen – should be the goal of each publication. In a newspaper, sports briefs or tidbit sections can help cover all the teams without long stories with long lists. The packaged coverage can include game scores with highlighted player performances, district standings, key matchups and area or state rankings, among many things (Fig. 7.8). The creation of this type of coverage can be fun and varied. A list of scores from the last 20 years may accompany a preview story about a rival school. A graphic showing the team's game-winning scoring play can give the sports junkie something fun to study. Using a type size that is smaller than the body copy for the lists of scores or district standings can help save space and help the page editor pack more into the section. In the yearbook, the scoreboard should serve as a history of the year's game scores. Packaging all-district team members, statistical leaders and quotes with the scoreboard can give the reader even more of the year's highlights.

Fig. 7.7. Sports feature story. *The Spark*, Lakota East High School, Liberty Township, Ohio.

The student cautiously eyes his 6'4" opponent. Upon seeing the patches of white hair fringing his face, he states in a clear, confident voice, "Yeah, like this old man could beat me."

The odd pair steps onto the basketball court, the giant towering over the dwarf. The boy tries dribbling around his opponent's long legs, but to no avail. Finally, the man's arms reach out and snatch the ball. In one fluid movement, the man turns and shoots. Swish. "Give me the ball," he says as he returns to the top of the key. The boy, momentarily taken aback, plans to steal the ball back. However, instead of dribbling, the man simply jumps and cocks his arms, aiming the ball for the basket. Swish. "Give me the ball," he says again, the first sign of a grin cracking his face. The boy never gets the ball back. The old man wins, ten to nothing. Wolf forgot to warn the boy that Sam Jones, his substitute teacher, is a basketball legend.

Jennifer Song
Silver Chips
Montgomery Blair High School
Silver Spring, Md.

If there's one man who knows how to dodge an oncoming tree at 40 mph, it's Peter Durham. If there's one man who knows the pain of an all-too-firm bicycle seat, it's Peter Durham. If there's one man who knows his bike's body better than his girlfriend's, it's Peter Durham.

Michael Jordan
Bagpipe
Highland Park High School
Dallas, Texas

Designing a Sports Briefs Package

Since more sports news occurs than can be covered with full stories, a box of news briefs and statistics can greatly expand a newspaper's coverage. When packaging sports briefs keep these tips in mind:

Create a set style. Save time by designing the package once and using variations of the layout for the rest of the year.

Space is the enemy. Avoid wasteful elements, like bullets and extra white space. Most often type effects, like bold and italic, can replace these.

Mix up the sports. If not every sport can be covered, keep a good mix of freshman, JV, Varsity, Men's and Women's news bites.

Use agate. Agate type is small text used for stats and standings. By shrinking a sans serif to as small as 6–7 points and expanding the horizontal width to 110 percent, the paper can save a lot of space. An example:

JOHNSON 6–12, 2 HRs, 8 RBIs, 6 RUNs

Set features. Come up with 8–15 different pre-designed features and mix and match them each publication.
Some ideas include:
Player of the month, top performers, division standings, quote box, injury report, team updates, interesting numbers, marquee matchups, next week's big game, strategy highlights.

The FranklinTimes   **SPORTS**   Page 11

Busted and Broken
Injuries cut through Tiger defense, special teams

by Joe Leporis

After closing last year's season 4-2 in district and unable to reach the playoffs, Hillcrest is ranked 19th in *The Dallas Morning News* area poll one spot in front of South Oak Cliff.

Team members prepared over the summer by lifting weights and playing 7 On 7 in hopes of being better prepared for district.

Even after losing graduating seniors running back Terrace Watkins and defensive lineman David Sullivan both varsity coaches and players feel that this year they will have a strong defense. Defensive and special teams drills such as fumble recoveries and strip drills are being practiced to increase the number of turnovers.

After starting quarterback Dupree Scovell was injured, sophomore Ryan Gilbert took Scovell's spot. Gilbert led the team to a 4-4 record and the coaching staff is confident that Gilbert will be more successful this year, Johnson said.

Junior Sterling Storey is going to be vital to special teams because he is handling kickoffs, field goals and punts. Storey was 10 for 10 of extra points last year and practiced over the summer by kicking 60 to 70 balls a day and by playing soccer.

"Sterling is definitely one of the best kickers in Dallas," Coach Johnson said. "He practiced with a bag of balls over the summer, stayed in shape by playing soccer, and hit the weights."

The Panthers are going to play in a blitz style defense with five linemen and two linebackers. Coach Johnson said that the attack style defense puts more pressure on the secondary, but thinks that the rush can pressure the quarterback.

THE TICKER

THEY SAID IT

"Teams get more excited when they play us. You always have to dogfight."
- Senior Gino DiGuardi, captain of the Men's Soccer team, on the amount of the tough games the team has played this season.

"We should have scored even more points."
- Sophomore quarterback Antwaan Robinson, after JV Football's 42-14 win over Central High.

"We just couldn't match their intensity in the first half. It didn't matter what coach said in the locker room, we were going to lose."
- Senior guard Lauren Adams, after the Varsity Women's Basketball team lost to Canisius North.

PLAYER OF THE MONTH

Joseph Johnson
Running Back
Freshman Football

Even after losing graduating seniors running back Terrace Watkins and defensive lineman David Sullivan both varsity coaches and players feel that this year they will have a strong defense. Defensive and special teams drills such as fumble recoveries and strip drills are being practiced to increase the number of turnovers.
After starting quarterback Dupree Scovell was injured, sophomore Ryan Gilbert took Scovell's spot. Gilbert led the team to a 4-4 record .

BEST LINE:
October 24 at Jefferson
23 rushes, 140 yards, 2 TDs

Gilbert led the team to a 4-4 record and the coaching staff is confident that Gilbert.
photo by Jon Ulster

OTHER TOP PERFORMERS

Alicia Smith-Wagner
Junior, Midfield, Women's Lacrosse
vs Newton, October 12
5 goals, 5 assists

Ben Morales
Sophomore, Center, JV Men's Basketball
vs Jefferson, October 16
23 points, 18 rebounds, 6 blocks, 2 steals

Kristi Sanderson
First team, Women's Golf
DrPepper Tournament, October 14-15
Course record 16 under par

INJURY REPORT

Freshman Tom Sanderson
Guard, Freshman Basketball
torn ACL, out for season

Junior Susan Tedsci
Pole Vault, Women's Track and Field
sprained ankle, out for district meet

TEAM UPDATES

JV Football
After giving up 3 punt returns for touchdowns in the first 4 games, the team will shake up its special teams unit. Younger players will more starts.

JV Mens Basketball
The team is off to its best start ever, winning 3 of 4. Coach Stulten Smith hopes to continue that success into district play, which starts in less than a week.

JV Womens Basketball
When the Varsity squad graduated 7 seniors last year, the JV knew they were going to have a shortage of players. "We've had to give them all our players," Coach Jim said.

BY THE NUMBERS

6 Number of offensive rebounds for the Varsity Mens Basketball team Oct 12 vs Jefferson

30 Wins by the Freshman Football team over the last 3 years

114 Number of goals allowed by the Women's Lacrosse team in 10 games

SPOTLIGHT GAME

Mens Lacrosse at Evansville
5:45 pm, Tuesday at Wilkie Stadium

With both teams tied for second going to into the last game of the season, the winner will make the playoffs and the loser will go home.
"We're going to have to do something we've had trouble doing all year, knock some guys out," head coach Will Penn said.

DISTRICT STANDINGS

VARSITY FOOTBALL		FRESHMAN FOOTBALL		JV MENS BASKETBALL		VARSITY WOMENS BASKETBALL		MENS LACROSSE		MENS SWIMMING/DVNG		MENS TRACK&FIELD	
JEFFERSON	13-0	JEFFERSON	13-0	JEFFERSON	13-0	JEFFERSON	13-0	JEFFERSON	13-0	JEFFERSON	13-0	JEFFERSON	13-0
NEWTON	11-2	NEWTON	11-2	NEWTON	11-2	NEWTON	11-2	NEWTON	11-2	NEWTON	11-2	NEWTON	11-2
FRANKLIN	8-3	FRANKLIN	8-3	FRANKLIN	8-3	FRANKLIN	8-3	FRANKLIN	8-3	FRANKLIN	8-3	FRANKLIN	8-3
MISS COM.	3-9	MISS COM.	3-9	MISS COM.	3-9	MISS COV.	3-9	MISS COM.	3-9	MISS COM.	3-9	MISS COM.	3-9
ROOSEVELT	9-3	ROOSEVELT	9-3	ROOSEVELT	9-3	ROOSEVELT	9-3	ROOSEVELT	9-3	ROOSEVELT	9-3	ROOSEVELT	9-3
EVANSVILLE	7-5	EVANSVILLE	7-5	EVANSVILLE	7-5	EVANSVILLE	7-5	EVANSVILLE	7-5	EVANSVILLE	7-5	EVANSVILLE	7-5
NORTH	1-8	NORTH	1-8	NORTH	1-8	NORTH	1-8	NORTH	1-8	NORTH	1-8	NORTH	1-8

JUNIOR VARSITY FOOTBALL		VARSITY MENS BASKETBALL		FRESHMAN MENS BASKETBALL		JV WOMENS BASKETBALL		WOMENS LACROSSE		WOMENS SWIMMING/DVNG		WOMENS TRACK&FIELD	
NORTH	13-0	NORTH	13-0	NORTH	13-0	NORTH	13-0	NORTH	13-0	JEFFERSON	13-0	JEFFERSON	13-0
FRANKLIN	10-2	FRANKLIN	10-2	FRANKLIN	10-2	FRANKLIN	10-2	FRANKLIN	10-2	NEWTON	11-2	NEWTON	11-2
ROOSEVELT	9-3	ROOSEVELT	9-3	ROOSEVELT	9-3	ROOSEVELT	9-3	ROOSEVELT	9-3	FRANKLIN	8-3	FRANKLIN	8-3
JEFFERSON	5-4	JEFFERSON	5-4	JEFFERSON	5-4	JEFFERSON	5-4	JEFFERSON	5-4	MISS COM.	3-9	MISS COM.	3-9
MISS COM.	2-7	MISS COM.	2-7	MISS COM.	2-7	MISS COM.	2-7	MISS COM.	2-7	ROOSEVELT	9-3	ROOSEVELT	9-3
EVANSVILLE	2-8	EVANSVILLE	2-8	EVANSVILLE	2-8	EVANSVILLE	2-8	EVANSVILLE	2-8	EVANSVILLE	7-5	EVANSVILLE	7-5
NEWTON	0-11	NEWTON	0-11	NEWTON	0-11	NEWTON	0-11	NEWTON	0-11	NORTH	1-8	NORTH	1-8

Fig. 7.8. Sports package design. *Franklin Times,* Louisburg, N.C.

The men's swim team came home from Raleigh with their second state championship trophy, no hair and something unexpected – a nasty virus.

Monday was supposed to be a day of sharing the excitement of their victory with their peers, but only two or three shaved heads were to be seen in the halls that day. Eleven of the 16 swimmers from both the men's and women's teams who qualified for state were at home sick.

Irina Kuznetsov
Wingspan
West Henderson High School
Hendersonville, N.C.

AMBITION: SUCCESS:

CENTRAL HOCKEY'S WORK ETHIC?

(A) Triumph

(B) Victory

(C) State Contender

(D) All of the above.

The correct answer is D. It does not take an English major to figure out that hard work results in success. This year, Central's hard work is paying off.

Sam Zvibleman
Parkway Central Corral
Parkway Central High School
Chesterfield, Mo.

As the varsity football locker room clears after practice, senior Eric Parks see his helmet next to the three index cards taped to the back of his locker. The first card reads, "first team All-State kicker and punter," and, "All-American selection." The second card reads, "straight As" and "be a respected member by classmates."

The last card, filled with scriptures from the Bible, seems to stand out from the rest in his mind. It reads: "I can do all things through Jesus Christ who gives me strength." Philippians 4:13. It is these scriptures and goals that guide Parks and allow his faith to carry over into all aspects of his life.

Ranked as the second best kicker in the state in a coaches' poll, Parks has received over 100 recruiting letters before his senior year. He now receives two to three letters a day from top programs at universities such as Nebraska, Illinois and Iowa State. Through all his achievements, Parks has always looked back to the Lord for spiritual guidance.

Brendan Fitzgibbons
Hillcrest Hurricane
Hillcrest High School
Dallas, Texas

As you can see in these leads, good reporting and storytelling is at the heart of every sports story. The lessons in the chapters on news and feature writing apply in sportswriting. This chapter covers the differences that come with covering sports. Review Chapters 1–4 and 6 to improve your sportswriting.

Many young sports fans see being a high school sports reporter as an ideal spot on the publication staff. While the young sports fan's command of the sport is helpful, becoming a good sports reporter requires work to get beyond the clichés of the game to the drama and storytelling inherent in sports.

EXERCISES

1. From daily newspapers or sports magazines, clip and mount 10 examples of good sports story leads.
   Make note of what information the writer used in the lead. Was it a particular play? A particular trend? An anecdote? Or something else? Why do you think the writer chose that focus for the lead? Was the lead written in straight news or feature style? Why did the writer choose that style?

2. Watch one of your favorite professional sports teams over a two-week period. Make note of the team trends you could cover.

3. Make a list of 10 cliché quotes or phrases from your high school or daily publication.

4. Clip, mount and label 10 descriptive sports quotes from your school or daily newspaper or a sports magazine. Explain why the quotes are good ones.

5. Clip, mount and label 10 examples of sports statistics that were used in stories. For each, explain why you think the writer chose the statistic he or she used in the story.

6. Write an advance story from the following information. Your story will run the day before the game.

   The Bristol High School Bandits are playing the Ten Mile Creek High School Bullfrogs in a boys' basketball game.

The game will be for the regional championship. Your school is Bristol. Bristol is 23–8 so far. Ten Mile Creek is 26–1. The teams have played each other two times this season. Ten Mile Creek is the defending state champion.

Ten Mile Creek's only loss was to the Hawthorne Bearcats, 88–86. Bristol beat the Hawthorne Bearcats 64–58.

Key players for the Bristol Bandits

Clayton Hunter – position: point guard; statistical averages: 14 points per game average, 8 assists per game average; height: 5 feet 10 inches.

Johnny Miller – position: center; statistical averages: 22 points per game (best in the district), 12 rebounds per game; height: 6 feet 7 inches.

Donald Lampier – position: forward; statistical averages: 10 points per game, 9 rebounds per game; height: 6 feet 3 inches

Key players for Ten Mile Creek Bullfrogs

Geoff Mitchell – position: forward; statistical averages: 16 points per game, 10 rebounds per game; height: 6 feet 6 inches.

James Robertson – position: center; statistical averages: 28 points per game (second best in the state), 12 rebounds per game; height: 6 feet 10 inches.

Game 1: Finals of the Spring Creek Tournament, score 85–83

Highlights: Bullfrogs' Robertson scores 35, including the last 8 points of the game. Robertson hits game-winning shot with two seconds left. Bandits' Miller scores 15 points and has 5 shots blocked. Bandits' leading scorer is Hunter with 30, including 6 three-pointers.

Game 2: Finals of the Lake Bardwell Tournament, score 72–70

Highlights: Bullfrogs' Robertson scores 24 including the game-winning shot with

five seconds left. Robertson also blocks 6 shots – all of them Miller's. Bandits' Miller scores 8 points. Bandits' leading scorer is Hunter with 23, including 4 three-pointers.

Coaches' quotes

Bandits' head coach Buck Cargal (lifetime coaching record 299–71)

"We just have to go out and play much harder. We've been really close in two big tournaments, but this one's bigger. This could be Bristol's best chance to win a state title, and as you've seen, we're just a bucket or two away from that. We must get Robertson in foul trouble or keep him from getting second shots. You thought Godzilla was big, You thought King Kong was tough. I mean I saw *Halloween* when I was 10, and nothing is scarier than this kid on the court. He has dominated our team in both of the past two games. We will double-team to see if the rest of their team can beat us. I told our kids 'Robertson will not keep us from winning a state championship.' I'm expecting Hunter to have another big game. Hunter's on such a streak now. I'm giving him the green light in this game. He may shoot 20 three-pointers this game.

"This game would mean a lot to me. Not just because it would mean our first trip to the state tournament but it could be my 300th win. I can't think of any better way to hit 300 than to beat last year's state champion."

Bullfrogs' head coach Mike Keeney (lifetime coaching record 112–30)

"We just have to go give it 110 percent. Bristol has a good team. They've pushed us to the limit every time we've played this year. We better show up to play. It's not going to be a cake walk."

Keeney on Robertson: "He's the most dominating kid I've ever coached. He's such a quick jumper. And when you're already 6–10, it makes him a force that can control a game. He's clearly headed to a Division I school. He has been sick with the flu all week though. We hope he's well and ready to go at game time. If I have to rest him for the first half, I'll do it. We need a healthy Robertson on the floor."

Player interviews

Clayton Hunter

"I'm pumped for the game. We just know we can win tonight. We've been so close both times. Coach has said he wants me to take the game over. I felt really good after we beat Hawthorne. Ten Mile couldn't beat them. Our losses to Ten Mile were earlier in the year. I've been shooting a lot better since then. And Johnny (Miller) has been working on making the other guy foul him. I really want to give coach his 300th win too. He takes us home. He spends his whole summer opening the gym for us. The guy deserves it."

Johnny Miller

"Nah, I ain't scared of him (Robertson). The first two times we played them, I was going up too slow. I'm much better now. I get my shot off quicker now, and I have better fakes. He'll foul out this time, and then he won't be around to make those game-winning shots. Clayton will be doing that.

"We'll be hyped for coach to get his 300th (win). Both of my brothers played for him, and they told me 'you better win this one for coach.' I want to see coach get his state championship ring, too."

Additional information

Bandits' team scoring average: 80.0 points; opponent's scoring average: 54.1 points.

Bullfrogs' team scoring average: 78.0 points; opponent's scoring average: 55.0 points.

State rankings: Bullfrogs – number 1; Bandits – number 10. The Bandits are 0–6 in the last three years against the Bullfrogs.

7. Write a yearbook sports story from the following information. The story can be a trend story with a feature angle.

You are from Hazard Hill High School. The team mascot is the Lions. The girls' fast pitch softball team finished 19–10 for the year. It was 10–4 and finished third in the district. The team went 7–0 in the second half of district, beating every team in the district. The team opened the district schedule losing its first three games. The third place finish was the team's best ever. The team earned its first playoff berth. It lost 12–6 in bi-district to the Paradise Cougars. The team lost three starters but returned seven for the next year.

Key players: Hazard Hill finished the year with three first-team All-District players, which included freshman pitcher Jennifer Dusenberry, junior catcher Katie Mitchell and senior first baseman Karen Greening.

Dusenberry was also named Newcomer of the Year. Dusenberry pitched every game. She's 4 feet 11 inches and 100 pounds. She throws 58 miles per hour. She played for the Amateur Athletic Union team last year, and the team went to the state championship. Dusenberry struck out 10 batters in the district finale against the Tucker High School Mustangs.

Mitchell averages throwing out three people per game. She has a batting average of .376. In the district finale against Tucker High School, she threw out one base runner in the 3rd inning when the Lions led 2–1. In the top of the 7th inning, she hit a home run, giving the team a 3–2 lead. Then in the bottom half of the 7th and final inning, she threw out another base runner at second and blocked the plate getting the final out. The Lions won 3–2. The win meant the Lions would go to the playoffs.

Greening finished with a .340 batting average. A team captain, she hit three game-winning home runs in the first three games of the team's district win streak.

Player and coach quotes

Head coach James Rogers

On Dusenberry: "She's so tiny you would think a big gust of wind would blow her into the outfield. And off the field she's a clown. Those two different kinds of rainbow socks she wears are her trademark. Plus she loves to talk. You can put her in the corner, and she'll talk to the wall. But that's what the other players came to like about her. On the field, though, she takes care of business. She hasn't played long enough to be flashy and flamboyant yet. She doesn't pump her fist when she strikes out someone. She's all business. She's in control. She tells everyone where to line up. If she's going to throw a fastball, she'll move the second baseman to the left and the shortstop to the right because she knows the ball will come directly to them.

"The first game she had to prove herself. We had an honorable mention all-district pitcher coming back. The girls came to me and said, 'Why is this kid up here? Why is she on varsity?' Then she struck out 10 batters, and they finally realized she belonged."

On Mitchell: "She single-handedly got us into the playoffs. What an incredible game. She's the real leader of the team. She helped make Dusenberry a part of the team when others didn't want to give her a chance. She makes plays that you don't think she can make. She seems to have a knack for knowing when runners are going to go. Then if

they're trying to score, she will not give up the plate."

On the win streak: "After a poor district start, we couldn't go anywhere but up. We played good defense. We stopped making mental errors. In the first half we were throwing the ball to the wrong base, and we would step off the base before the ball even got there. We went back and started working in practice. Everyone got 100 grounders a day. Getting you used to doing the same thing over and over makes you comfortable in the game. When the ball's coming at you during the game, you've seen that over and over so you just do it naturally.

"It got to where me and my family would eat, sleep and drink softball. I'd wake up, get a cup of coffee and read the paper to see how the other teams did the night before. By the week of bi-district, my wife would have to leave me messages on my cell phone just to reach me."

Jennifer Dusenberry

On the playoff week: "Parents brought us balloons. People were telling us how good we were. It was cool. Then, the day of the game, we were scared. No one was saying anything. We didn't understand how much attention we were going to get. We thought we were really focused on the game, but we were really worried about what color of socks we were going to wear, how our hair was going to look."

On her play: "No one liked me at first. After I did pretty well my first game out, they started to let me be a part of the team. Karen invited me to eat breakfast with the team. After that we all got along. I'd try to do crazy stuff just to make them laugh. We had a good time. Once we knew we could have a good time and work hard in practice, we started winning."

Katie Mitchell

"Duse made the difference for us. She's a lot of fun to have on the team. She's crazy. She'll braid her hair in little knots, wear different colors of eye shadow just to get people to laugh at practice. Then when she's on the mound, she just wants to win.

"I'll never forget that game against Tucker. I just knew I had to play my best if we were going to win. When that girl came barreling down the line, I kept telling myself, 'this is for the playoffs, this is for the playoffs.' I was looking around for someone to hug after the umpire called the girl out."

Karen Greening

"I got so tired of taking ground balls at practice, but coach said it would pay off. By the time we played Tucker, we knew we weren't going to make the same stupid mistakes that cost us the first game against them. Coach just wouldn't quit on us. You can tell he loves the game. His whole family loves the game. His son would go with him to scout. He'd sit there with his crayons and chart the hitters. His wife would bake us cookies and send them to us during the winning streak. They'd have little messages on them. One would say 'Work Hard in Practice.' Another would say 'We're Thinking about You' and 'Good Luck Tonight.' "

Additional information

Tucker High School was the district champion. Two hundred people showed at the bi-district game. At most district games about 40 people showed up. The Paradise Cougars lost the next week in area competition. They finished the season 25–6.

Writing Editorials and Opinion Columns

Your community is about to hold a special election on funding an addition to your school. The proposed new construction will add more classrooms to relieve over-crowding and new athletic facilities for the expanding sports program. Voters will decide if they want to raise their taxes to pay for the addition. As the editor of your school newspaper, you think the addition is needed and hope the voters pass the tax increase. You assign a news story about the election and one about the architect's plans for the addition. To be fair and as objective as you can be since not everyone supports the tax increase, you realize that these news stories will need to present both sides of the story – those who support the plan and those who don't. But what else can you do?

To influence the voters to support the tax increase, you can use the power of the press in another way. The news stories will present the facts and sample the opinions of those who support and oppose the plan. This is an example of how the press uses its power, its ability to inform the public. Another power the press has is to persuade the public to accept something new or a change in something that already exists. The opportunities for the press to use the power of persuasion are plentiful, but nowhere do they become more evident than on the paper's editorial or opinion pages.

The editor who backs the tax increase and supports the expansion of the school's facilities can write an editorial or an opinion column and maybe persuade others that they too should support the plan. The right words in a carefully con-structed argument can change the world – or, as in this case, help decide an election. Having this power, and recognizing the corresponding responsibility to use it wisely, is why so many journalists love their work.

Editorials are the voice of the newspaper at large and are not signed even though they are usually written by one person. Editorial writers use the first-person plural pronoun, the *we* voice. An opinion column is signed and obviously represents the thoughts of one person. Opinion columnists use the first-person singular pro-noun, the *I* voice. The journalistic "license" to use the *I* and *we* pronouns, restricted to editorials and other forms of opinion writing when they refer to the writer, brings a certain authority to the piece. To the reader, these two pronouns signal a change from fact-based reporting to opinion writing. By using the *we* in editorials and the *I* in opinion columns, the writers are putting the credibility of the paper and their personal reputations on the line.

High school newspapers and other school media that publish student staff opinions should never underestimate the potential they have to influence their audi-ence. For the newspaper staff, this means that topics should be chosen carefully. Historically, editorial and opinion pages aren't widely read unless the topics are highly controversial. That fact challenges the paper's editor: Since not all topics that

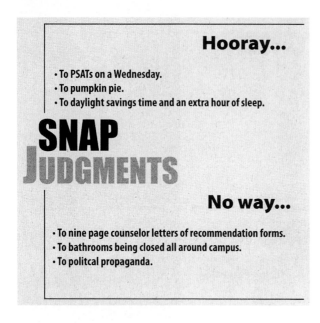

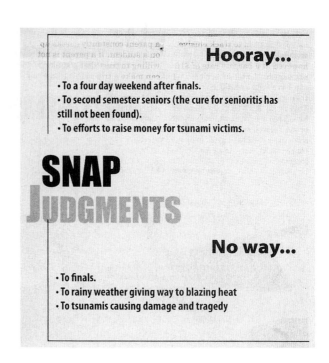

Fig. 8.1. "Snap Judgments" (editorial shorts) demonstrate that opinion can be expressed effectively in just a few words. *The Falconer*, Torrey Pines High School, San Diego, Calif.

deserve editorial page coverage are controversial, all content needs to attract, with good writing and enticing headlines, readers who usually spend little time with this section of the newspaper (Figs. 8.1 and 8.2).

To start, editorial writers should look at what will be reported on page 1 and the other news, feature and sports pages of the same issue of the paper. If the editors used good news judgment in selecting stories for these pages, then the topics covered are fresh, relevant and of interest to a sizable number of readers. Some of these topics may be judged important enough to comment on by the editorial writers and columnists. These stories will include opinions of experts and those associated with the events or issues covered, but the reporters' opinions are not included. But on the editorial page the journalist's opinions about these news, feature and sports stories can be published.

Sometimes the topics for opinion columns and editorials are not directly related to other content in the same paper, especially if the paper publishes more than one editorial in each issue. Regardless, the topic should still be of interest to students who are the paper's target audience. Topics worthy of editorial comment are not restricted to school-originated events. Some editorial topics in school papers in recent years that did not have a news or feature story tie-in elsewhere in the paper

included these: prayer in public schools; weapons in schools; dress codes; drinking alcohol and driving; wars in the Balkans; presidential elections; community volunteer service; and hate crimes.

Editorial writers and opinion columnists who write about far-reaching or global events and issues should localize their commentary in some way, bring it home to the readers and make the readers care. To editorially support a drive to end famine in Africa is commendable, but to link it to malnutrition and poverty in the United States and suggest ways students can donate time and money to end both is better.

Because editorials are the voice of the paper and are unsigned, even though they are usually written by one person, the opinions expressed in them represent the majority of those student staff members designated as the editorial board. An editorial board discusses the topic, arrives at some majority agreement and then presents one or more arguments in favor of the position it is taking. For the high school paper, those students who are editors usually make up the editorial board.

Opinions expressed by columnists usually don't undergo the same discussion and consensus process as do staff editorials. This does not mean that a signed opinion column is not edited for style, content and legal factors such as potential libel.

TYPES OF EDITORIALS

The voice of the school newspaper is heard on the editorial and op-ed (opposite the editorial) pages. Staff editorials, unsigned, are traditionally the most prominent opinion pieces in the paper. These editorials can be written for different reasons, such as to interpret the significance of an event (the news), to criticize something that has happened, to commend someone or some group for some achievement, or to advocate change and persuade readers that the paper's viewpoint is worthwhile. Some of these editorial types, especially ones that criticize or identify a problem, will also propose one or more solutions. Knowledge of all types is important for editorial writers. The power of the press, as expressed through the editorial, can be used to commend as well as criticize. With this power comes the need to use it responsibly for the good of the community the paper serves.

Advocacy Editorial

Editorials that interpret, explain, persuade and advocate change will usually be tied to a significant news, news-feature or sports story found within the same issue of the paper. The editorial will tell the reader why whatever happened is important. It can also explain the significance of an idea or condition. In some cases, it defines terms and issues, identifies persons and factors and provides background such as historical, cultural, geographical and pre-existing conditions, among others. The writer's attempt to persuade the reader to accept a certain interpretation or conclusion may be overt or subtle.

The editorial that interprets, explains or persuades can also examine the motives of persons related to the issue or event discussed or speculate on the consequences of various courses of action.

Through this interpretation of the news or explanation of an idea or condition, the staff is persuading the reader to agree with the staff's conclusions. The editorial can promote or advocate change. The facts are presented clearly, and the reasoning will seem logical to the reader if the editorial succeeds in its purpose. The editorial may also offer solutions and recommend a course of action. However, the overall tone of the editorial is not negative, nor is it a point-by-point criticism.

Fig. 8.2. Diverse opinions, often on controversial subjects, are handled on this editorial page with the "Viewpoint" column. *Wingspan*, West Henderson High School, Hendersonville, N.C.

Editorials that interpret, explain and persuade are called advocacy editorials.

Here is an example of a straightforward advocacy editorial.

Longer lunch period a gift for students, staff

The quarter-long trial period of the new 45 minute lunch will be up for review in April by the administration, who will determine whether to continue this schedule for the fourth quarter.

The proposal was originally made by members of the Student Senate, and was later passed by student, staff and faculty vote.

By adding the five minutes subtracted from morning break to the lunch period on block days, the schedule has given all students a gift. Obviously, students now have more time to eat their lunches. But this extension does more. It allows students to relax and take a real break between their morning and afternoon classes.

Additionally, staff and faculty members benefit from the longer lunches, as they are under the same, often stressful, bell schedule of the students. Like students, they can utilize the extra time to eat their lunches and complete errands during lunch.

The Student Senate made a positive and reasonable request with their proposal. No instruction time is lost with the longer lunches, and students and staff are given more time to eat and gear up for their afternoon classes. The administration should vote in favor of keeping the 45 minute lunch this April.

Tamalpais News
Tamalpais High School
Mill Valley, Calif.

In the above example, the facts are presented, an assessment of the change is made, and a course of action

– advocating continuation of the longer lunch period – is recommended. The editorial attempts to persuade readers that the longer lunch period is a success.

In the following advocacy editorial, the staff explains a proposed program and recommends its adoption. The storytelling opening, an attempt to humanize the topic, is often a successful way to persuade readers that they have a stake in the outcome.

Service learning worthwhile project

The old man's face peeps out from surrounding layers of warm winter clothes. He slowly lifts his paper plate and humbly looks up. "More potatoes?" a smiling teenager asks.

His face breaks into a wrinkled, toothless grin. The volunteer piles on the steaming mashed potatoes, and the old man walks back to a table.

At first, the teenager was skeptical about serving at the shelter, but when he walked through the doorway, he realized this was where he needed to be. The 50 poor or homeless people who passed through his line and took seconds and even thirds of mashed potatoes made an impact on him as he realized he wasn't just giving out food; he was giving acceptance and an optimism that had been absent from their lives.

"There's nothing to do in Hendersonville!" is a common cry, but a new program that is in the works will provide meaningful activities for students. The program will also give students an opportunity to change the perception that young people are slackers. A local group is currently designing a service learning program to be offered in area schools.

Some students fear this new program could be a way to force students to volunteer. For instance, at Chapel Hill High School students must do 40 hours of community service to graduate.

But that's not what the local service learning program is about. It will give teenagers a chance to be involved and learn from their experiences, and it will be totally voluntary.

While service learning will not be required, teachers, principals and parents should definitely encourage participation. Being unselfish is not always easy, and stepping outside one's comfort zone may sometimes be required, but in the long run, service learning can teach lessons no current classes teach.

West students should not ignore the coming opportunities to learn by serving.

Wingspan
West Henderson High School
Hendersonville, N.C.

The following advocacy editorial is an example of how a major news story is interpreted in an editorial. In a persuasive argument, the staff likely hopes readers will agree with its position.

Mourning Columbine: Strong must lead in fight for understanding

We can blame it on the guns, their parents or their music. It could have been the movies, the internet, the video games or maybe even their mental health. However, no matter who we blame, what happened at Columbine High School in Littleton, CO, was more than a human tragedy. It was a wake-up call.

By the time April 20, 1999, was over, two students – Dylan Klebold and Eric Harris – part of a group called the Trench Coat Mafia, had killed 13 people in that quiet Denver suburb just before turning the guns on themselves. We were all in shock. How could two children do this?

Fig. 8.3. An eye-catching illustration draws readers to the staff editorial. Reader input is evident with the "Q & A" photo poll at the bottom of the page. *Blue & Gold*, Center High School, Antelope, Calif.

New security policies and procedures have been established at WHS and suddenly schools all over the country are being evacuated, locked down and closed as a result of this incident. This case has begun to be less of a tragedy and more of an epidemic. Similar incidents are going on everyday, and we don't have to go to Colorado to find them, not to a high school. Right here in Wooster, Melrose, Wayne and Layton Elementaries have all had student threats. Safety in schools is suddenly being questioned like never before.

Following the shooting, President Clinton proposed legislation that would require instant background checks for the purchase of explosives, hold parents criminally liable when their guns are used by juveniles in a crime and raise the minimum age for purchasing a handgun from 18 to 21. Critics of gun control, though, say our society is to blame for crimes like school violence, not guns.

Yet finger pointing won't cure this issue. Taking every weapon and restricting the media won't do the job either. It is up to us as human beings to take the initial step. It is up to us to put an end to the root of the violence: intolerance and prejudice. We must not be scared and judgmental but competent and accepting.

It is time for the strong to lead instead of the weak. We must take hate into our own hands instead of waiting for the law to stop it.

Jocks don't need to live in fear and trench coat wearers don't need to live in isolation and ridicule. We're all people and we all have needs. Human contact and love are necessary for a desirable existence, for we must give love in order to receive it.

If we turn our backs now, if we don't individually start to stand up for humanity, the momentum of these catastrophes will continue.

As long as the hate flows freely so will the violence.

Blade
Wooster High School
Wooster, Ohio

In the following editorial, interpretation of the news (why is this important?) is an indirect advocacy of proposed state legislation relevant to students.

HD scholarships

FREE CASH. It caught your eye, didn't it? If State Sen. Greg Server gets his way, high school students might find themselves with some of that free money for college.

Under Senate Bill 0022, students graduating from a public or private high school in Indiana with an Honors Diploma would qualify for a scholarship award in the amount of 50 percent of the educational costs at public universities in Indiana.

What does it mean? The long-established Academic Honors Diploma would serve a purpose beyond an HD denotation on a graduate's diploma. With an Honors Diploma in hand, a student could expect to receive a scholarship equal to half of the educational costs at any public university in Indiana, a reward for four years of diligent work.

Students who meet certain financial requirements may apply for a full scholarship under current standards upon completing an HD. Under Sen. Server's current proposal, however, students would be eligible for a scholarship regardless of financial conditions.

Counselor Martha Street believes that such a program as proposed by SB0022 would "definitely" encourage students to pursue an Honors Diploma. "This would be a wonderful opportunity to help deserving and hard-working students," she said. However, Street suggests that a program might be more accepted by the general public if students were required to work at least two years in Indiana after completing a degree.

Sen. Server's proposal would not only restore the Honors Diploma to its once-sought-after glory, but it would compel students to pursue their academic work more fervently. Instead of merely offering students an "HD" at the end of a diploma, it would offer diligent students a tangible benefit at the end of their high school career.

Optimist
Bloomington High School
Bloomington, Ind.

In this brief advocacy editorial, the staff makes two recommendations following an athlete's death.

On life

No one at the Lawrence North basketball game could have known what would happen that night when John Stewart collapsed and died. In the wake of this tragedy, lessons are to be learned.

Life is fragile. A visibly strong athlete with a bright future seems safe from death. However, through Stewart we are reminded that we are not guaranteed tomorrow. The great philosopher Seneca said, "Our care should be not so much to live as to live well." Make your days count.

Secondly, we should always remember that tragedy must result in change. As more information becomes available in the next few months, it will be necessary for us to draw informed conclusions concerning the current physical examination system for sports. John Stewart's death must not be remembered only as a tragedy but as a milestone for change.

Optimist
Bloomington High School
Bloomington, Ind.

Advocacy editorials must be reasonable to be effective. Overstating a point, preaching or scolding can turn readers away.

PROBLEM-SOLUTION EDITORIAL

The problem-solution editorial is another type commonly found in newspapers. Sometimes called an "editorial of criticism," this type of editorial is used when the staff wants to call attention to a problem or wishes to criticize someone's actions. Because of the need for the paper to act responsibly, facts need to be presented to back up the criticism or to explain the causes of the problem, and solutions must be offered. This three-step process is similar to the scientific method of discovery: statement of the problem, presentation of evidence and conclusion with potential solutions.

Criticism should be handled carefully. In an editorial, it's fair to criticize a person's actions if they have some impact on others; it's unfair to criticize a person's physical characteristics or purely private actions. Readers will discount allegations that aren't substantiated with proof or evidence. Because they are expressing an opinion, editorial writers have a little more freedom than news writers regarding libel. However, name-calling and offensive language will also harm the effectiveness of an editorial and the credibility of the paper. Lies and fabrications are unethical.

In the problem-solution editorial or editorial of criticism, the persuasiveness of the problem, the quality of the evidence and the practicality of the solutions will affect its success with readers. Staffs should select problems to write about that are being talked about by a sizable number of students, and ones that offer the potential for real solutions. For example, a common problem in some schools is the lack of school spirit, but it is hardly worthwhile to write about it unless the newspaper staff has some real, workable solutions to offer.

In the following problem-solution editorial, a common school problem, student parking, is addressed by the staff.

Safety of students' cars should be an issue: Cars should be more closely monitored to prevent random vandalism

It all comes down to one question: Why must we pay $5 for a parking spot when we can't be assured that our cars are safe?

Recently, in the Live Oak parking lot, there have been multiple acts of random vandalism. Cars have been keyed, things stolen and antennas destroyed; not to mention the damage on Half Road, the only alternative parking place. All this has happened while we have two very capable and attentive yard monitors, who simply have too much area to watch at once.

This year the ASB, which has always collected $45 for senior spaces, started charging $5 to park in the parking lot for the rest of the school. The money collected goes primarily to paying for the plastic decal that hangs on the rear view mirror and the rest is saved for school activities sponsored by ASB.

We would be better off using this money to fix the lighting in the parking lot, or hiring a third yard monitor to watch the parking lot or even begin fixing the overhangs. A few individuals have proven that we need to worry about vandalism at our school and that we need to do something about it.

For those of us who drive and park in the parking lot, this is a serious concern and not to be taken lightly. While sitting in class, our last worry should be about whether or not our cars are safe.

Car damage, no matter how slight, is expensive. We, as students, need to respect each other's property and each other.

Only through mutual respect and thinking about our actions will we achieve the level of tolerance and acceptance that we want and need at Live Oak.

Oak Leaf
Live Oak High School
Morgan Hill, Calif.

In the above editorial, the problem, vandalism of student cars, is clearly stated, and several solutions are offered by the staff.

The criticism given in the following problem-solution editorial is muted, illustrating the need to avoid preaching or severe scolding in an attempt to change behavior or someone's attitude.

Students need to do their part

The season of perpetual hope is nearing once again, bringing with it a flood of opportunities for giving and kindness.

Before Thanksgiving break, Food for Families had boxes set up in the halls. With the recent devastation of Hurricane Mitch, donations of food, clothing and money were taken for the victims of that disaster. And boxes are being set up for donations to Samaritan's Purse, an organization that provides a brighter Christmas for needy kids around the world.

That's all well and good, but these efforts will come to little without the support and help of the student body. For whatever reason, Uni's response has traditionally been a bit tepid.

Maybe this year it will change. Food for Families was an enormous success, and the Gargoyle hopes that present and future efforts at giving become as established as that one.

It's cheesy, yes, but give a little.

No, give a lot.

Clean out your pantry, donate your clothes, and give money to charitable organizations.

Give of your time. Free time is in short supply among Uni students so it's important to make time.

Christmas is now the holiday of getting, despite what we'd like to believe in America. Let's return to it to where the focus belongs: on giving to others.

Gargoyle
University High School
Urbana, Ill.

Here is another example of a problem-solution editorial, one that criticizes the school's strict adherence to policy. The primary subject, the reversal of the school board's decision not to allow a student to participate in graduation ceremonies despite his inability to complete his studies due to an illness, was reported extensively on the front page of the same issue of the paper in which this editorial was published.

District lets Schmidt walk for graduation

Schmidt walks.

It was at first a rallying cry, a demand by the student body for Cameron Schmidt to participate in graduation. After a student protest and media blitz, the Deer Valley School District Governing Board took a vote, and it became a statement of fact. Schmidt walks.

"Rocket Boy," David Silverstein, is returning to Desert Sky Middle School on April 26, after a vote in a closed-door session on Tuesday. He was suspended after school officials discovered a homemade rocket in his locker. The rocket, which the district considered a firearm, fell under DVUSD's zero-tolerance policy.

Tuesday night, the Governing Board buckled under pressure from students and national media, taking two votes, relenting two times. The hard line was sacrificed, but they did the right thing. The decisions were in the best interests of both the students and the district – a win–win situation for all parties. We hope that in the future, it will not take NASA astronauts and *The Today Show* for school officials to make such judgments.

These two events reflect a disturbing attitude in education. The Deer Valley District has shown a dedication to the letter of the law, the policy by which we are governed. This attitude starts at the top. The Superintendent, Dr. Gerald Cuendet, stated that policy was law in this district. It is an outlook common in district officials, administrators, and some teachers.

The job of a school district, the education of students, requires that students come first in all decisions. Educators are here to educate, and students are here to learn. Each should do this to the best of their ability, and the school district should facilitate, not disrupt, this process. When considering tough issues and making hard judgments in the future, the district must keep this in mind. Their first priority must always be people, not policy.

Ridge Review
Mountain Ridge High School
Glendale, Ariz.

COMMENDATION EDITORIAL

Commendation editorials are an important option for editorial writers. In most communities, including the school, a newspaper has status and is a power center. Because of its position, the school paper observes what is going on in the school and in the other power centers. When a person or a group does something extraordinary, the paper notices and may report that achievement in a news, feature or sports story. But it also has another choice; the paper can praise the person or group directly in an editorial. This elevates the person or group to a special level of notoriety.

Typically, these commendation editorials praise or pay tribute to someone or an organization that was performed successfully beyond the norm. Topics can include, among others, the retirement of a teacher or administrator; a state sports championship for a team or a state title for an individual athlete; the death of a student, teacher or administrator who was an inspiration to others; a successful end to a charity drive or fund-raiser; the addition of new sports to the athletic program; and student community volunteer work.

If the paper publishes more than one staff editorial in each issue, it may be that one could be an editorial of commendation. If the paper publishes only one staff editorial in each issue, the decision to write an editorial of commendation should be carefully considered, and the person or group praised should be especially deserving. Persons and groups can also be commended in opinion columns.

In the commendation editorial, the reasons for the praise should be clearly stated and the impact of the achievement on others should also be included. These editorials are not usually long unless the person has achieved much or the impact is varied and complex.

An organization and a person are both praised in this commendation editorial. Why they deserve this praise and the impact of the changes they made are clearly presented.

Getting and spending: Customers profit from store's improvement in efficiency, variety

The past months have seen significant changes in the student store, all to the benefit of the students.

Most important was the addition of the barcode scanner. This makes store operation quicker and easier. Workers are no longer required to use the tedious numbering system that was previously in place, and can simply scan the item. This reduces the number of workers necessary in the store at any given time and speeds the line.

Another time-saving change is the elimination of cash. Now, instead of receiving change, students will receive credit in their store accounts, even if they don't have a standard charge account. Students will then be able to buy until the money in their account is gone.

In addition, Treasurer Cody Truscott ('00) has expanded the product line and is confident the store is well stocked enough that it will not run out of products again. The student store has made progress toward providing healthy food for students. After Spring Break, the store will begin selling fresh bagels.

We praise Truscoff for improving this student service, and thank the Student Council for appropriating the hundreds of dollars necessary for the repairs. Their

progress is encouraging, and the Student Council should continue improving its most prominent student service.

Academy Times
Charles Wright Academy
Tacoma, Wash.

In this commendation editorial, the school's administration is praised for changing a policy. The editorial also explains and interprets the news behind the commendation.

Prudent change in graduation time: Religious conflict averted through change in the ceremony's time

By changing the time of the graduation ceremony from 7:30 p.m. to 8:30 p.m., the administration has clearly made the prudent and correct decision.

The decision will enable students, who otherwise would have found it impossible to attend the ceremony due to religious commitments, to be present.

This year, Central was unable to reserve its commencement on a Sunday evening. Instead, it was planned for a Saturday evening, a day that presents religious conflicts for various students.

In delaying the commencement, the administration gives all students – regardless of their religious faiths – an opportunity to participate in the memorable ceremony.

The other alternatives for the administration are limited to changing the ceremony's location and day. Both of these options are costly, impractical and unrealistic. Thus, delaying the ceremony one hour is fair and accommodating.

As principal Bill Meyer points out in a recent letter addressed to the seniors' parents, the change in time may actually help those students who want to spend more time with their families before the ceremony. Perhaps this later starting time may become a new tradition at Central.

The fact that the problem was solved immediately points to a healthy educational environment. Central's diverse student population differs from most schools in the St. Louis area. It is not likely that these other schools would have made similar accommodations. Hence, Central students gain a unique lesson in tolerance and understanding.

The way in which the administration handled the potential problem deserves commendation. They conferred with parents, teachers and students. STUCO members, who were also included in the dialogue, offered reasonable solutions to the problem. This exemplary determination to solve the problem on everyone's behalf serves as a model on solving similar school-related issues.

Parkway Central Corral
Parkway Central High School
St. Louis, Mo.

BRIEF EDITORIAL COMMENT

Brevity has its merits, and one- or two-paragraph editorials can be effective. They are mostly useful if only one point is made and little evidence or background information needs to be given. Sometimes these editorials have standing column heads, such as "Ten Second Editorials," but they are unsigned as are longer, fully developed editorials.

Here is an example of a brief editorial comment in two paragraphs:

Seniors urged to celebrate graduation in safe manner

It seems that every year around this time the news is filled with tragedies of graduating seniors getting killed due to alcohol related incidents.

The Demon Dispatch implores the members of the class of '99 not to become

another statistic. Though graduation is a special moment in every teen's life, drinking is not the way to celebrate. There are plenty of ways to celebrate without endangering your life or the lives of others.

Demon Dispatch
Greenway High School
Phoenix, Ariz.

EDITORIAL SHORT

Another type of editorial, especially popular in the student press, is the editorial short or quip. It is distinguished by its length and organization. As its name indicates, it is brief, from one word to one or a few sentences. Usually, editorial shorts or quips are grouped together as a list under a standing column heading and include commendations and negative criticism.

Editorial shorts or quips are also random comments: One commendation or criticism does not necessarily relate to any other one on the list. Student papers sometimes label their shorts as "thumbs up, thumbs down," "cheers and jeers" or "rants and raves," or they apply a letter grade to each to indicate pleasure or displeasure. Many of these brief comments are not specific to school, but they are of interest to students. Sometimes they are humorous or note the changes in styles and popular culture.

EDITORIAL CARTOON

Perhaps the most succinct form for an editorial is the editorial cartoon. In a few words or a sentence or two if the cartoon is a strip rather than a single frame, the editorial cartoonist can do what the editorial writer does – commend, criticize, interpret, persuade and entertain. Coupled with distinctive art, usually a line drawing, the cartoon is a favorite form of commentary for readers.

Cartoons can stand alone, unrelated to other topics on the editorial page, or they can be directly tied to a print editorial. By a distinctive drawing style and a voice, an artist should develop an opinion that comes through both in the words and in the drawing itself. Because an editorial cartoon is opinion and the artist often uses caricature (exaggerated features), the artist

The Kernal

Tagging: crime not art

If you take a close look around East High's campus, you'll notice that there are patches of discolored paint pretty much everywhere inside and out of the school, even on trees, all in an effort to cover up tagging.

Tagging has been and continues to be a serious problem on campus. If this form of expression needs to be displayed by people, perhaps they should get used to painting their own personal property. Teens who don't have anything to paint should stick to their notebooks rather than buildings. East High security is cracking down.

Tagging anywhere is not a good choice. It is a crime and is unappealing to the eye. Those who tag should realize that even though they're having fun, they're destroying private and public property, and eventually somebody will have to fix it.

There are forms of tagging that can be considered artistic. These artists have found a way to express themselves in a legal, artistic manner by painting murals or developing graphic art skills.

Unfortunately, not all of the people that choose to tag decide to become actual artists; they eventually become pursued criminals.

In an effort to crack down on graffiti, the administration has been recording all tagging done on campus and familiarizing themselves with each and every crew.

Every crew has their own name and their own style of tagging, which makes it easier for administration or police to identify them.

So, why tag when you know you're going to get caught?

Some people do it for the adrenaline rush, but that's what rollercoasters and scary movies are for. If you want to try something extreme, why not try mountain climbing, skydiving, or bungee jumping? Either way, you are risking your life.

In a gang or crew, tagging becomes more offensive to other groups, and just like in any action movie you will end up with a rival. But life isn't a movie, guns are real, and people won't get into a rut trying to fly their super aircraft to destroy you with a laser beam.

Tagging: it's just not smart.

STAFF EDITORIAL

Letter To The Editor

Funding not put to good use

DEAR KERNAL,

It's great that we've got signs taped to our crumbling walls stating that this school site facility is clean, safe, and maintained in good repair, but it's a false advertisement. The ceilings in some places are stained because of water damage.

Desks are constantly falling apart because they are not "maintained in good repair." Walls have holes in them. Black widows hide in corners of almost every hallway. Disease-infested rats die in the attic, and the stench is unbearable for weeks. Roaches crawl over our shoes to find food. Safe? Disgusting.

Bathrooms have lacked soap for days, almost weeks. We lack paper towels to dry our hands with when we use the cold water and no soap. We have to use toilet seat covers to dry our hands with, if there are any. Some of the stall doors lack locks.

We have no privacy when we are using the restroom. We have to have someone hold the door closed. If not that then we have to be really talented to keep it shut. The trash bins that the girls use to put their used supplies in are always overflowing.

I find it humorous that the school has enough money to build a new field house, a new awning in the quad, update the cafeteria, and add red, blue, and gray tiles to the top of our bathroom walls, yet we do not have enough money to fix our walls, buy new books, fix the desks that pinch our skin, get rid of the rat, roach, and black widow infestation, and buy simple things like soap and locks that cost $3 for our privacy when we use the restroom.

If we actually had soap to wash our hands with, maybe there would not be as many sick students as school, which leads to the student being absent, which leads to the school losing money.

Submitted by senior Ande Castaneda

I Like Toast

For breakfast what I love the most
Is a buttered piece of crunchy toast
Fresh from the toaster, nice and warm,
To feed me in the early morn'.
I'll take it with me on the go
Or sit and eat it nice and slow.
By itself or with some bacon,
With toast you'll never be mistaken.
Forget the Cheerios and the Corn Flakes
A piece of toast is all it takes
To make your breakfast better than most
All you simply need is toast!

By Rebecca J. Levy, freshman

What do you think?

Submit letters to the editor and original work to room 218 or e-mail EBKernal@yahoo.com

Note: All letters subject to editing for grammar, punctuation, and spelling

THE KERNAL

Editor-in-Chief
Joel R. Paramo

Managing Editor
Melanie M. Moyes

Design Editor
Leticia Gamez

News Editor
Daniel Munn

Features Editor
Travis L. Mattias

Focus Editor
Maria Krauter

Entertainment Editor
Rebecca M. Landucci

Sports Editor
Jordan S. Henry

Copy Editor
Michelle Maldonado
Assistant: Nicole Fimbres

Page Copy Editor
Katie Walker

Staff Photographers
Samantha Canez, Julie Pinales, Melanie Moyes, Maria Krauter, Daniel Munn, Joel Paramo

Staff Illustrators
Leticia Gamez, Joel Paramo, Arturo Bocanegra

Business Manager
Danessa Jimenez

Finance Manager
Xochitl Ramos

Ad Manager
Emy Wu

Promotion Manager
Arturo Bocanegra

Distribution Manager
Julie Pinales

Exchange Paper Manager
Carly Rozell

Reporters:
Molly Devers, Byanka Cortez, Sarah Galindo, Nicole Garza, Tim Gragg, Kegan Henry, Nina Krauter, Janet Mize, Cady Queen, Robert Rodriguez, Jazmine Ross,

Adviser
Randy Hamm

The Kernal is a monthly publication of the journalism class of East Bakersfield High School. *The Kernal* is an open forum for students, faculty, and alumni of East High.

The opinions and views expressed in this newspaper are the sole responsibility of the staff and do not reflect the views of either EBHS or the Kern High School District.

Fig. 8.4. Graphics and art transform this editorial page into a lively showcase for opinion content. Note the invitation to readers to submit their viewpoints. *The Kernal*, East Bakersfield High School, Bakersfield, Calif.

has some freedom in creating something that may be humorous, satirical, ironic and even stinging. However, the art should not ridicule in an unjustifiably mean-spirited or hateful way. When a caricature is created, the exaggeration of someone should be in good taste and not unduly note someone's physical abnormality.

If editorial cartoon captions or conversation "bubbles" are hand-lettered, they should be legible. Art should be carefully drawn so the reader can quickly grasp the intended message. (See Figs. 8.4 and 8.5.)

WRITING THE EDITORIAL

For an editorial, the writer should select a topic that is tied to some story that will be published in the same issue of the paper in which the editorial will appear or has some merit and the potential for high reader interest. A local angle, even on a national or international situation, or on a widespread belief, is important to the success of the editorial. Readers will connect more quickly and in greater numbers if they see immediately that the topic has some relevance for them.

Before the editorial's opening is written, the writer should phrase the main point of the editorial in one or two sentences. By doing this, the writer will likely find it easier to keep the focus of the editorial on target. This will also help unify the editorial.

The topic needs to be thought through carefully, especially if the focus of the editorial is to negatively criticize a condition or an idea. The writer needs to fully understand the topic.

Since an editorial requires the presentation of some facts, some evidence, the writer needs to do research. Data should be gathered, and opinions should be found and considered. An internet search can provide data and expert opinions, but the internet is not fully reliable. A second source should always be checked to provide verification. *Fact checking for accuracy is as important for editorials as it is for news stories.* Since brief or medium-length editorials are more likely to get read and influence readers, the writer will have to ultimately be selective in the evidence that is presented. Finding local data and local opinions to help support or to refute an argument is also important, and this type of evidence may be preferable to national data and experts who live far beyond the school. An internet search and in-person or phone contact to gather information and opinions are both recommended.

Ideally, an editorial board, made up of the editors and assistant editors of the paper, will review the topic, consider the evidence and agree on a position taken. The writing is traditionally done by one person. Since many editorials argue a point, it is important for the board and writer to weigh all possible counterarguments; this will help the writer to select the best evidence to include in defense of the position the paper will take in the editorial.

Fig. 8.5. Student editorial cartoon. Alison Wong, cartoonist, *Parkway Central Corral*, Parkway Central High School, Chesterfield, Mo.

If the editorial board members are divided on an editorial stand – no unanimity – the results of a board vote – in favor, not in favor – can accompany the editorial. Other options, especially for highly controversial topics, include inviting someone with an opposing viewpoint who is not a member of the paper's staff to write a guest editorial. Someone on the staff who has an opposing viewpoint could write a signed opinion column on the topic.

Most editorials are divided into three parts: (1) the introduction, (2) the body or evidence and (3) the conclusion. The opening tells the reader what the staff believes; the body tells the reader why the staff has this belief or opinion; the conclusion tells the reader what the staff thinks should be done based on the evidence presented, or it summarizes the situation without providing any solutions.

Although any type of lead presented in this textbook for writing news, feature or sports stories can be used for an editorial if it suits the topic, the exact type may depend upon the purpose of the editorial. In addition to an attractive headline, the opening sentence should also stimulate or pique reader interest.

Since the lead is the introduction, the first or second sentence should also state briefly the situation that prompted the editorial to be written. For example, a commendation editorial praising the accomplishments of a retiring drama coach could open with: "'The play's the thing,' and it has remained so for both William Shakespeare and Betty Johnson, MHS drama coach who is retiring in June after 30 years and 60 productions on the MHS stage." This opening sentence includes an often-quoted line from Shakespeare's "Hamlet" and the reason for the editorial, the retirement of a long-term teacher.

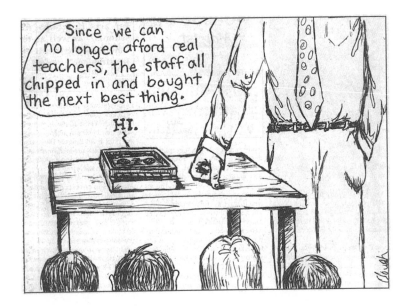

Fig. 8.6. Student editorial cartoon. Michael Clough, cartoonist, *Blade*, Wooster High School, Wooster, Ohio.

The body of the editorial is developed by presenting the facts that support the opinion or stand taken in the introduction or opening. The body can also include the opinions of experts and others who support the position taken by the newspaper staff or who refute the opinions of others on the topic. This is done clearly and concisely. Writers need to select the best facts and opinions that support the position. Too many facts and opinions will result in an overly long editorial and diminish the editorial's effectiveness.

Good, precise facts are essential in an editorial. Generalizations and clichés weaken the argument. Tell the reader where the facts come from if this seems important. Examples and comparisons and contrasts may also strengthen the supporting evidence. Sources and authorities quoted should be of the highest quality and level of expertise possible. For example, it is better to cite the U.S. Department of Education as a source for statistics on high school graduation rates rather than an article in *Time* magazine. For an editorial about teens and sexually transmitted diseases, it would be better to cite the opinions of a doctor than a receptionist in a clinic that specializes in this area of public health. Documentation of statistics and facts is important for the credibility and strength of the editorial.

The conclusion of the editorial should include one or more of these: a summary of the situation; suggestions or recommendations to solve the problem addressed or change the minds of those who have opposite viewpoints; or a new but related question or provocative statement for the reader to think about. Sometimes, an editorial can be effective if it only poses questions and doesn't provide any answers; the editorial writer wants the reader to do some soul-searching or arrive at his or her own conclusions or answers. The conclusion can also bring the reader back to the opening through repetition of key words or by fulfilling the reader's expectations raised in the opening. If a question is posed in the introduction, then the conclusion would logically provide the answer.

Whether the conclusion offers a solution, summarizes the main idea or poses more questions, it should have punch and leave the reader with something worth remembering. It can be thought provoking, challenging, affirming, clever or alarming. In the example of the commendation editorial that used a popular line from "Hamlet" to begin, another quote from Shakespeare could be used to conclude: "'All the world's a stage' for Mrs. Johnson, and her many fans will be waiting at the stage door after the final curtain call for the spring play to get her autograph this time. She's the real star of MHS theater." The quote used in this conclusion is from Shakespeare's "As You Like It."

WRITING THE OPINION COLUMN

The editorial and the opinion column have one major similarity: They are both opinion or subjective analysis. They have some important differences.

Opinion columns are signed and are the opinions (using the first-person pronoun *I*) of one person, unless the columnist chooses to include the opinions of others. Editorials are unsigned and are the opinions of the staff as a whole, even though they are written by one person. Opinion columns are less formal than most editorials; columnists have more freedom and usually more space to present their ideas.

Columns often are structured the same way as an editorial, beginning with an introduction, followed by the body and ending with a conclusion. The storytelling or chronological method of development can also be used. Rarely would the inverted pyramid style of development – most to least important information – be chosen by the writer.

Columnists often develop a style and a voice or select topics to write about that are consistently one type. Some always select topics that can be written about humorously. Others always write about money or travel or sports. Some write about what is often called "the human condition," the triumphs and tragedies of human life. Some always champion the underdogs in society, those less fortunate than most people. There are columnists who write above the average reader's vocabulary and intellect, appealing to highly educated readers. Some write only about the English language and how we use or abuse it. There are countless possibilities for each columnist to "own" a unique or nearly so subject.

Many columnists develop a unique opening or closing line or a word or phrase that is always included. This helps distinguish the columnist from others who may be writing about similar topics and becomes a sort of trademark or signature style. High school columnists can do the same thing with their column writing. It works when it is unique and consistently used.

A column is also identified with a consistently used title, often set in a typeface and with graphics that are the same as those for other regular columns in the paper. These are sometimes called "standing heads," since they are in every issue of the paper and never change. The columnist's byline is prominently featured, and sometimes a mug shot (small face shot) of the writer is included. Column titles may or may not be indicative of the column's usual content. Titles are usually brief, and many use clever wordplay. For example, "Jock Talk" could be a sports column, since "jock" is a slang term for athlete. Or, "B-sides" could be a title for a column on alternative music: A "B" side is a slang term for the old 45 rpm record, which had two sides. The "A" side was the hit single, and the "B" side was the usually seldom-played opposite or flip side.

The following opinion column ties into a major national story about the murder of a Wyoming college student who was gay. It is an example of how a columnist can express personal opinions that may or may not be shared by others on the newspaper staff. Opinion columns are one person's voice, not the voice of the paper (the editorial is the group's voice). The columnist also cites credible and appropriate sources for some of her statistics.

Message results from Shepard's death

An unopened letter sits on my desk. I can't send it but I can't throw it away. I remember vividly the day I decided to write it. I sat at the kitchen table on a cold Thursday morning eating my breakfast and scanning the paper.

Checklist for Editorials

- Are the form and style appropriate to the content and purpose?
- Does it have a purpose and accomplish that purpose?
- Does it make the reader think?
- Is the writing clear, vigorous, direct and simple?
- Are conversational words used?
- Is the argument logical?
- Is the evidence clear and the best available to support the position taken?
- Are enough facts given?
- Does it sound sincere?
- Does it get to the main point quickly?
- Does it make points without preaching or talking down to the reader?
- Is the opening sentence interesting enough to attract readers?
- Are the paragraphs short?
- Is the editorial overwritten and too long?
- Does the topic relate to the school or to student interests?
- Will the headline attract readers?
- Is it written in the first person plural?
- Is the topic connected to a story published in the same issue?
- Does the position taken represent the majority of the paper's editors?
- Is it unsigned?

Before anything else on the front page, his image first caught my eye. He was beautiful, with dirty blond hair, piercing blue eyes and a youthful easy smile. I remember the wave of shock that overcame me as I read the headline: "Police arrest four in beating of gay student."

As I read the article, I became nauseous as images of his smashed-in head and his scarred and bleeding body flashed through my mind. He was hung crucifixion-style on the fence post where he was left to die – a display to the whole world of the overwhelming hate two men felt toward homosexuals. This beautiful, promising young man was on the verge of death because of someone else's hate.

That night I wrote him a letter. I told him to remember that the whole world was not like those two men who beat him. I said that I held him in esteem for his courage to be openly gay. I told him he was constantly in my prayers and my thoughts.

I wanted him to not give up hope; I wanted him to live.

Right before I went outside to put the letter in the mailbox that Monday morning, I heard the news on the radio. I was too late. Matthew Shepard, the beautiful boy with the dirty blond hard, piercing eyes and the easy smile had died the night before. I remember the tears of grief that I fought back that morning and during school. When I got home I cried bitterly.

I felt like I should have done something to prevent what happened. I couldn't understand how people's hate could drive them to kill. Few events in the past have affected me so strongly.

I've heard it said "Hate is a strong word," but that adage contains more truth than most people realize. Hate is the strongest emotion. It's an emotion that doesn't have to be triggered by something large because it gains momentum quickly. This emotion knocks away all morals, reason and control and can push someone so far that he would even hurt or kill for hate.

There were 7,947 hate crimes committed in the United States in 1995, according to an FBI report, and 1,016 of those incidents were based on sexual orientation. According to an Amnesty International public statement on Matthew Shepard's death, while violent crime in the United States in general has gone down, hate crimes are on the increase.

How can someone hate a group of people or person he does not know or has never even met? Sadly, hate is usually directed at people who are different from others. Whether it be a person's personality, clothes, race, religion or sexual orientation, the reason for the hatred all boils down to the fact that a person is different. Ignorance, also, causes hate. Often, when people are not familiar with others, they may not understand the other's ways. People generally fear what they do not understand and therefore hide this fear with hate.

If one were to ask those who hate homosexuals if they have homosexual friends or relatives on which to base their opinion, most would probably answer "no." Instead, many use stereotypes to justify why they hate certain people because inside they really don't know why.

The last reason why someone hates another person is rarely ever admitted but often true. Many choose to hate so that they may hide that they are surprisingly similar to the person they are hating. This hatred occurs because they fear being ostracized and, therefore, choose to hide under a shield of hate.

Why hate? It takes so much effort and energy and certainly doesn't accomplish anything positive. Hate may hurt the person at which it's aimed but in turn shows one's lack of knowledge, lack of respect and lack of confidence.

The sad fact is that our community and school are not immune to the hate that brought about Matthew Shepard's murder.

I become distraught when I walk down the steps of B building and see that someone has "I hate gays" written across his backpack. I look sadly at the words of hate angrily etched onto bathroom stalls, school walls and desk tops. I cringe at the constant animosity among the varied groups of students in our school.

Hate is hate. Insulting words have the same impact as the butt of a gun smashing in someone's head.

The letter I wrote to Matthew remains on my desk as a constant reminder of how far hate can go. Often, I pick the letter up and think about Matthew. I'm certain that he's in a better place now, but I feel guilty for not being able to prevent his death.

If only I could have been his friend. If only I could change people's minds. If only people didn't hate.

Clare Jellick
Lion's Roar
Gahanna Lincoln High School
Gahanna, Ohio

EXERCISES

1. Bring copies of your city paper to class and read the editorials. Are the topics related to news stories on page 1 or an inside news page? Classify the editorials according to type: advocacy, problem-solution or commendation.

2. List five groups or persons in your school who should be praised for some special achievement. Select one and write a short 200-word commendation editorial.

3. List five concerns students have today about their lives. For example, students may be concerned about lack of privacy or violence in schools. Select one and write a short 250-word advocacy editorial.

4. List five problems in your school. The problems could be with the schedule, the building, the curriculum and the athletic program, among other possibilities. Select one and write a short 250-word problem-solution editorial.

5. You are invited to be an opinion columnist for your school paper. You are asked to write about life as a teenager – a wide-open field. Select a name for your column. List five topics you would like to write about. For example, you might like to comment on dating, your siblings or getting your driver's license. Select one topic and write your first column. Keep the length to about 350 words. Since this is a signed opinion column, you will write in the first person.

6. With your school, community and peers in mind, write a list of 10 editorial shorts. Half of your list should be commendations ("thumbs up"), and half should be negative criticism ("thumbs down").

7. In small groups, form editorial boards. As a group, list three topics worthy of an editorial in your school paper. Discuss the topic and determine if you can agree on the paper's official position on the topic. Someone in the group should write a summary statement (one or several sentences that states the situation and the paper's decision). When the class convenes as a whole, each group should share the results of its editorial board meeting.

8. Bring copies of a current issue of the local newspaper to class. Select a story, column or editorial that you read that you would like either to question or to comment on positively or negatively. Write a short (about 150-words) letter to the editor of the paper. (Most papers publish letters from readers.) Send it and then watch to see if it is published.

In-depth Reporting

Schoolwide cheating is rampant in some communities. School districts try to decide how to solve problems with inequitable school and learning situations. School boards constantly debate how to spend tax dollars. Violence in school is a new national dialogue. Charter schools are beginning to affect public school enrollments and funding dollars. States try to connect school funding and performance. Students are required to pass exit exams to earn diplomas in some states.

As school communities grow more complex, opportunities for in-depth reporting present challenges for scholastic journalists in reporting for both the newspaper and yearbook.

In-depth reporting is needed when complex issues or situations are being discussed and written about. Coverage of in-depth topics may require a greater commitment of resources – both staff members and time – as well as a greater need for understanding of all sides of the issue. Teams of reporters, photographers and editors may need to be assembled to properly cover complex topics of concern to the publication's readership. Those teams may be gathering information over a course of time before they ever come together to actually write and report a story.

In-depth reporting may take many forms. It may be a single page of coverage in the newspaper, or it may be a series of articles published over a period of time. It might be published on the double truck – the center spread of the publication, where the pages are actually printed on one sheet of paper. The double truck allows different opportunities for layout. Since the pages are a single sheet of paper, headlines and visuals can be brought across the two pages to unify them. Two pages of content can also appear on facing pages without actually appearing on the double truck. Or an in-depth story may appear as a "package" of content, taking up a majority of space on a page in a specialized presentation.

In the yearbook, in-depth reporting can also take many forms. The opportunity to cover topics of significant reader interest will not only broaden the depth of the yearbook's reporting but will allow the publication to occasionally break the pace of presentation. Breaking this pace will offer opportunities for different kinds of content.

TOPICS FOR IN-DEPTH COVERAGE

Controversial, sensitive topics such as drug and alcohol abuse, sexuality and school violence have been used as topics for in-depth coverage. While these topics are relevant to teenage audiences, reporters and editors need to make sure their decisions on covering in-depth topics are appropriate for their school communities. Coverage of sensitive topics should be discussed carefully among staff members, and decisions about how these topics can be covered should be carefully decided. In some cases, neutral reporting methods may offer more sensitive ways of topic coverage. For instance, rather than using first-person accounts of student drug use or sexuality, interviews with professionals will provide less controversial, though maybe not as interesting, ways of covering the issue. Student journalists must make sure they cover topics responsibly.

Schools continue to face the same difficulties as the community in general. However, students need to look specifically at the concerns of their individual readers as possible topics for in-depth coverage. Following the beat system already in place on most publications staffs, student journalists can start to look for areas of concern.

SCHOOL BOARDS

What the school board or the school's governing body decides affects every student at the school. Is the school considering changing graduation requirements, changing the length of the school day or year, requiring students to wear uniforms, allocating money for new facilities, debating whether to hold a bond election or tax levy for a special project? All of these topics would be of concern to student readers. Someone from the student newspaper staff should attend all school board meetings.

Beyond the local school board, the state's educational governing body will also make decisions that affect schools in your state. Many of these decisions are studied for months in advance. Monitoring the decision-making process will offer opportunities to share possible changes with readers and report their initial reactions before the changes are made. National educational trends and decisions may also be important in your school community.

ATHLETICS

Athletic programs in schools are rich areas for in-depth reporting. How does the athletic department monitor use of illegal substances such as growth hormones and steroids among athletes? Does the school have an athlete who is being heavily recruited by colleges or professional programs? Who decides how much funding is provided for sports in the school, and is it equitable among major/minor sports and men's/women's sports? Do programs share equal facilities for equal amounts of time? Is the school changing scheduling of teams and opponents that could affect competition or travel time? Be sure reporters are talking frequently to coaches and athletic directors in the school.

CURRICULAR AREAS

Maintaining contact with the heads of curricular programs and development, school department heads and others who make decisions about academics will enable student journalists to monitor changes in curriculum that will affect students and the programs in which they participate. Other areas of curricular concern include elimination of programs, reduction of teachers and consolidation of school resources such as counseling and advising programs. Teacher concerns such as students buying essays on the internet or rampant cheating in the school could also be examined. Do students sign an honor code? Is it uniformly enforced among students and athletes?

What about computer resources in the school? Are filters used to censor student browsing? Are books censored from the library? Do local citizens with extreme viewpoints show up at textbook adoption time?

EXTRACURRICULAR AREAS

Changes in clubs and organizations and student activities will affect every student who participates in them. Some schools have cut funding of club activities; others have restricted student field trips and activities because of funding cuts. Schools are constantly debating whether or not religious clubs can meet or activities can be held during the school day or in school facilities. Prayer before school activities continues to be a national and local issue.

BEYOND THE SCHOOL

Community changes that affect the school should also be examined. Is the school's neighborhood changing in ways that would affect the school? Is the school located on a major street that might be dangerous to cross? Are the lights and turning lanes adequate for the numbers of cars that use them? Has the school started safety measures such as installing radar detectors or locking all entrances except the main one during the school day? The school's effect on the neighborhood should also be considered. Do students gather in stores and fast-food restaurants close to the school? Do these businesses ever restrict the number of students who can be in the store at one time? Have the businesses been in touch with the school about their concerns?

LOCALIZING NATIONAL TRENDS

Obviously, the last few years have been volatile for many schools. Changing times and trends are ripe for in-depth coverage. Offering students the opportunity to voice their concerns about these changes is a valid use of space. Publications can also offer readers forums for discussion of issues as complex as voting rights, drug and alcohol use and abuse, teen pregnancy, body piercing, stress, college acceptance and juggling the stress of school, jobs and financial commitments (see Fig. 9.1).

The key to good coverage is localizing the issues – reporting them from your readers' point of view. Stories with a local angle will always be of more interest to the readers of a particular publication. Quotes from local sources will help place the story in context for the publication's readers. Discussing the relevance of the topic to the readers will also be important in helping them place it in context.

Local professional sources can also be interviewed and used as sources to help put the topic in perspective in your local community. This is a far more relevant way of reporting than reporting information obtained from the internet that has no local connection to the school or community. For instance, in a story on teens being paid to rat out other teens to prevent teen drinking and alcoholic parties reported in the *Central Times*, Naperville Central High School, Naperville, Illinois, December 19, 2003, the reporter interviewed the state crime commission's executive director. The state crime commission co-sponsors Operation Payback, a program in Illinois in conjunction with Mothers Against Drunk Driving.

In-depth reporting should also pique readers' interests about issues that will help them understand the diversity of students in the school, with topics ranging from racial differences and sexual preferences to students who categorize themselves as alternative in the school.

Basically, good journalists listen. They observe. They hear. They bring these observations into the publications arena by discussing them at staff meetings where the exchange of information will help the staff decide how to cover them.

Fig. 9.1. An entire page devoted to the topic of sex shows a mature discussion of a controversial topic. In addition to defining popular slang terms connected with sex by using students' quotes, the coverage includes an overview of teen hook ups and a focused sidebar on the consequences of teen sex resulting in a pregnancy for one couple. The color illustration and feature headline at the top of the coverage help draw the reader into the package. *Tide Lines*, Pottsville Area High School, Pottsville, Pa.

Fig. 9.2(a)–(c). A controversial decision to hire an outside company to initiate a gang intervention program at the school was the subject of continuing in-depth coverage in the *Eagle Eye*. The newspaper conducted an investigation of the project's success at other schools after the school district agreed to pay $65,000 to project organizers for a needs assessment. That coverage was published in a special insert and won a national student journalism award. The project organizers publicly criticized the newspaper's coverage. *Eagle Eye*, DeSoto High School, DeSoto, Texas.

GETTING STARTED

Unlike traditional story reporting, in-depth will usually require far more time. Much of that time will be spent doing research in different forms, from talking to fellow students and teachers to learning and reading on the internet or in the school or local library. Often, in-depth reporters won't even be able to start interviewing until they've done a fair amount of research so they learn and understand the topics they're writing about. If the topic is one being localized for the school publication, reading national reports will give the reporters access to information that will help form questions and lead the reporters to logical sources and resources. Reporters should be careful to only use this backgrounding information for research and to avoid repeating quotes that have already appeared in print in professional publications, even if attributed to those publications.

Once the basic research has been done, the reporters or teams can begin to understand what kind of space commitment they will need for their in-depth report. Making that decision before the research has been done may only ensure that the story isn't given enough space or is given too much space in the publication. If reporters, editors and photographers are working together, the entire team needs to sit down together to talk through the research and reporting and to decide just how much space will be needed to present the information.

Regardless of the space allocation, the publication should help the reader understand the significance of the information through its placement and layout in the publication. Identifying the story as a special report, in-depth report or other such label will help focus attention on the importance of the information (Fig. 9.3). Starting the story on the front page and continuing it inside the publication is another way of alerting the reader to the special content. This coverage is known as "jump coverage" since it jumps from one page to another. Many yearbooks have begun using jump coverage for serious issue reporting.

FULL-PAGE COVERAGE

In the newspaper, a full page of coverage may be all that's necessary to adequately cover a topic. Even with a full page, the reporter should be discussing the story's angles with a photographer or visual thinker so the story can be visually interesting as well as adequately reported. Well-written, detailed headlines will help the reader understand the importance of this story. Visuals will offer another layer of information that can attract the interest of the reader. With a long article, the layout should also offer some visual text relief such as text heads or drop caps at natural junctures in the story. Or pull quotes from the story can be extracted and used in the layout.

DOUBLE TRUCKS

If the story demands more space, the natural space to consider is the double truck – the center spread, as it is often-times referred to (Fig. 9.4). The newspaper will always have two facing pages printed on one sheet of paper that offer options for layout and presentation. Multiple visuals can be used.

Fig. 9.2(b).

Information can be presented in a variety of story-telling forms to amplify the main story. This information offers the reader an opportunity to learn something presented in a different way, possibly a more visual way, than the main story. Because readers are attracted to information in different ways, these smaller, different story forms may pull the reader into the main text (see Chap. 20).

BEYOND THE DOUBLE TRUCK

When coverage demands more space, reporters should consider series reporting: stories broken into parts and presented over the course of several issues. The challenge in series reporting is to make sure the information lends itself to a series of stories and to make sure the information is logically presented in the series. Complex topics such as cheating or a series of changes planned for the school's curriculum would work for a series of reports. A visual device such as a logo helps readers identify with the story as it appears in each issue. A series would be less effective in a publication printed monthly or less frequently. Even in a bimonthly or trimonthly publication, the series should recap the previous reports before presenting the new information so the reader remembers the context of the previous report.

SPECIAL ISSUES

In the case of a story with a strong timeliness factor, such as a tragedy or breaking news event, the staff might consider publishing a special section or a special edition if an event occurs between the publication's publishing deadlines. Marshaling the staff's resources, editors may be able to quickly bring together necessary writers and visual reporters to report and photograph the event. Cooperative publishing efforts between different schools are another possibility if events occur in school districts with multiple campuses. If the staff doesn't have the resources to obtain pictures or other visuals, obtaining copies from local media such as community newspapers is another possibility.

Fig. 9.2(c).

THE YEARBOOK

Yearbook staffs should not overlook the in-depth form for coverage either. In-depth coverage helps change the pacing of storytelling in the yearbook, offering staffs the possibility for longer stories and different reporting. Covering significant or complex issues that have occurred during the year can amplify coverage in other parts of the book. Sports sections can tackle the same kinds of issues as the newspaper or can give special coverage to teams that have won championships. Academic coverage offers possibilities for discussion of curricular changes or changes in policy and procedure. Coverage of issues that help date the year add dimension to student life sections. Many schools have been experimenting with magazine format reporting, using topic-oriented coverage for issues such as pressure, achievement or stress. Focusing on personal profiles of interesting or accomplished students is another way to add some dimension to the coverage. Significant school events during the year that attract large numbers of students are other possibilities for in-depth coverage.

WRITING THE IN-DEPTH STORY

Rarely will traditional news story forms work successfully for the in-depth report. Reporters will need to build the story around the information and the significance of the information that has been gathered. The depth of the information gathered will make the task of organizing the information more important. Talking through the story with the other team members, other reporters or editors will help the process of writing. Writing an in-depth story will be more similar to writing a long feature story: The lead needs to grab the reader's attention and make the story's importance clear from the outset.

Note the way this lead begins on a story titled "After accident, family mourns death of son":

> When Tom Clough walked off the St. Agnes altar on March 26, doing his best impression of an athlete pounding his fist against his heart twice and then pointing into the sky, he was sending his final farewell to his son, Jake, at his funeral.
>
> Freshman John "Jake" O'Conner Clough, 15, died March 22

Fig. 9.3. Broadening students' awareness of other cultures and traditions, the *A Blast* took an in-depth look at the Hindu religion as the Hindu students in their school were celebrating the Festival of Lights in their culture. The coverage included information to help students understand the religion. The coverage focused on Hindu students in words and pictures. The *A-Blast*, Annandale High School, Annandale, Va.

Fig. 9.4. Double trucks, the center pages of the newspaper, are perfect spots for in-depth coverage. Because the pages are printed on one piece of paper, content can span the pages creating a strong presentation. This look at students' unhealthy habits ranges from a story on the problems of a fast-food diet, to a serious look at teen drinking from the female perspective. Large, colorful pictures help guide the reader through the content and balance the weight of the story. Smaller text heads help provide summaries for the long text. *Silver Chips,* Montgomery Blair High School, Silver Spring, Md.

at Children's Mercy Hospital. Though the autopsy is not yet finalized, the initial autopsy shows that he died due to infiltration of the feeding tube into his abdominal cavity. The food and medicine that was supposed to go to his stomach was being flushed through the body cavity.

His funeral ended three and a half weeks of ups and downs in the hospital following a bike accident in late February. The family had his body cremated and will send his ashes to the family's condo in Florida, where they vacationed every summer.

Peter Goehausen
The Harbinger
Shawnee Mission East High School
Prairie Village, Kan.

Would you continue reading this story? Probably. If you knew this student. Even if you didn't. The lead is compelling and creates a strong interest in reading more.

Here's another one on a story about students who suffer from seizures:

> Students in their seventh hour classes crowded about the front of their classrooms, some attempting to sneak out into the hall, through the doors and out of school. The minutes passed, 2:38, 2:39, and then the announcement bell sounded.
>
> Uh, yes. Teachers and students, if you would please disregard the bells, disregard the bells please. Remain in your classrooms and wait until we come on again to release you. Thank you, please disregard the bells, disregard . . . 2:40 and no one leaves the classrooms.
>
> In this semester alone, there have been two East students that have suffered seizures during school, leading to these time-freezing announcements. The school's protocol when dealing with seizures is to limit chaos, resulting in lock-downs until an ambulance arrives or the victim is relocated to the nurse's office. The effect on the school is brief. Though seventh hour lockdowns may make students five minutes late to track, the one who has just undergone the seizure has to worry about it happening again. They have to worry about it for the rest of their life.
>
> Amanda Allison
> *The Harbinger*
> Shawnee Mission East High School
> Prairie Village, Kan.

Because reporters will gather information for in-depth reports over a period of time, the deadline pressure of a normal story won't usually apply. This will give the reporters more flexibility in polishing the writing. In addition to an interesting lead, in-depth reporters should make sure they have interesting anecdotes and illustrations, effective transitions, tighter writing and stronger emphasis on the relevance of the topic or event to the reader. A good editor can make a big difference in improving the writing of in-depth reports to make sure the story's organization is clear and logical.

Here's more of the story from Peter Goehausen. Note the reporting he has done to weave a story for the reader of Jake's life and struggle to recover:

> "He was a very lovable guy," his uncle John O'Connor, who was the family spokesman, said. "His presence will be missed."
>
> The family plans on putting together a bike ride in Jake's name, with the proceeds going to the Brain Injury Association of Kansas.
>
> Those who knew Jake described him as being a very affectionate, family-oriented person who would never miss an opportunity to spend time with his family. His hobbies included golfing with his dad, exploring the creek behind his house and their annual trip to Florida.
>
> **Coming to East**
>
> Jake came to East from St. Agnes Catholic School where he went for seventh and eighth grade. Before St. Agnes, he went to Westwood View and Highlands elementary.
>
> "Jake's mom went to East," O'Connor said, "and that was his first choice because he knew a lot of kids there."
>
> After three months at East, a new opportunity arose for Jake: joining the bike club.
>
> "Jake was a very eager, excited rider," Mr. Brewster said, "and his parents were very excited for him to participate in an organized sport."
>
> Jake was new to competitive cycling, but he did ride his bike around his neighborhood. During Jake's three-month participation in the bike club, he participated in all of the rides offered. He had not yet ridden competitively.
>
> **The Accident**
>
> On Feb. 24, Jake was doing what his bike coach, Brewster, told him to do and getting in some extra miles on his bike. He rode the mile and half long ride by

himself to his cousin Lucy's house to gossip with her, something he would often do.

When Jake was on his way home he rode through a blind corner and ran a stop sign at the corner of 64th and Granada, the *Kansas City Star* reported.

Jake ran into the side of a truck coming from the stop side and landed on the street. Had he not been wearing a helmet, the doctors said, the accident would have immediately killed him.

"They (Cloughs) were just in a moment of shock when they were informed about him," O'Connor said. "It is almost unexplainable."

Jake was then rushed to KU Medical Center where he was in a coma. He was diagnosed with serious head injuries, a collapsed lung, a broken collarbone, and a separated shoulder. The next 72 hours were the most crucial for Jake and his family.

"Once they stabilized Jake," O'Connor said, "the doctors gave us a good prognosis (that he would recover)."

Wakeup Wednesday

Once the good prognosis was out, all the family could do was watch and wait for Jake to awake out of his semi-induced coma, he was unconscious but also medicated.

On March 2, the doctors came into Jake's room in the morning trying to get him to regain consciousness. Jake wouldn't budge. After the doctors left the room, Mrs. Clough looked up at Jake and she saw his brown open eyes glancing around the room. Six days after the accident Jake was finally out of his coma.

"When she (Mrs. Clough) saw Jake open his eyes," Jake's aunt Mary O'Connor said, "she immediately said 'Hi!' and told the doctors about it."

He opened his eyes several times on what the family called "Wakeup Wednesday." Jake was still unclear of his surroundings and unable to speak, but he was awake.

Family Sleepover

As the family often did on weekends in their living room, they had a family slumber party. For the first time in over two and a half weeks they were able to sleep under one roof, at the hospital.

"It was so wonderful to have our family back together again," Mrs. Clough wrote in an online CarePage, that gave updates of Jake's condition, "even though it was challenging with 3 of us on a twin size sofa bed."

Since "Wakeup Wednesday" Jake had started to regain his senses. Though he wasn't able to speak or move his left side then, he was able to count to five, and gave a thumbs-up sign and one-armed hugs.

Happy Birthday

On March 18, Jake turned 15. Also on his birthday, he made a step toward recovery when he was transferred to Children's Mercy to begin his rehabilitation. After Jake was transferred over in an ambulance, his grandparents, aunts, uncles and cousins all came to his room to celebrate his 15th birthday. Since the beginning of his rehabilitation, one of the family's goals was for him to be able to eat birthday cake, and Jake was able to.

After doing preliminary observations on March 18, the doctors and nurses were very optimistic about Jake's recovery.

"He was very determined," Mrs. Clough wrote. "It makes us laugh for thinking he wasn't motivated before this. We now know he was just saving his determination."

New Place

After spending the weekend after his birthday in constant rehabilitation, the doctors were hopeful that he would be able to be out of the hospital in six weeks.

On Monday afternoon, however, Jake's condition began to worsen when the medicine and food from his tube began to pour into his abdominal cavity, according to his family. The hospital could not give any information. And after fighting to save his life, Jake passed away early Tuesday morning.

The family's wish is that whenever anyone sets out to ride their bike, they will always remember to wear their helmet.

"Jake will never be gone," St. Agnes priest Father Don Cullen said at his funeral. "His home will just be in a new place."

Another important consideration is keeping multiple sources straight in the reporting. Readers need to keep straight the names and identities of the sources quoted in the story. Information can become difficult to understand if the readers can't follow the source of the quoted material or remember who that source is.

Fig. 9.5(a). The beginning of the war in Iraq in 2004 provided this yearbook staff with an opportunity to localize its coverage in the yearbook by inviting a group of students to participate in a focus group where they discussed their feelings and attitudes about the war. The students listed the names of the participants and then used their initials next to their responses about various questions asked during the focus group. Local coverage is always preferred in student publications. *Etruscan*, Glenbrook South High School, Glenview, Ill.

Fig. 9.5(b). When a student athlete from the competing school broke his fourth vertebra in a football playoff game against Austin Westlake High School, the Westlake community came to the player's aid with fund-raisers to support his medical bills. On this spread, the yearbook staff covered the extensive efforts made by its community and included a picture of the injured player. The staff also included a copy of a letter written by the player's family to the local newspaper, thanking the school community for its support. *The Chaparral*, Westlake High School, Westlake, Texas.

In this multisource story on the realignment of their school district for academic and athletic competition, the author had to deal with multiple sources, both teachers and students. Notice how she kept the sources straight by providing attribution to preface many of the quotes. Note also how many people were interviewed for this story.

Highland Park will remain in Class 4A for at least the next two years after falling just four students short of meeting the adjusted 1,925 minimum enrollment for Class 5A. While classification has not changed, HP will moved from district 22-AAAA to 11-AAAA, altering the competition in both athletic and academic arenas.

"Every two years UIL realigns districts in order to keep competition among different schools equitable," UIL Athletics Coordinator Rachel Seewald said. "They also look to reduce travel time so schools aren't traveling inaccessible amounts."

When realigning districts, Seewald said UIL takes about 1,280 enrollment numbers from schools in Texas and, in accordance with rules and regulations set up by the UIL consulate, establishes cutoffs for each conference.

◀ Recruitment tables set up during lunch periods in the high school provided teens with one opportunity to collect information and even sign up for different branches of the military. Gunnery Sergeant Phillips hands out pamphlets for the Marine Corps.

▶ While serving their country in Iraq, hometown friends and PAHS graduates John W. Ruch Jr. and Anthony Buehler meet up with each other in Baghdad.

Recruitment tables set up during lunch periods in the high school provided teens with one opportunity to collect information and even sign up for different branches of the military. — Raymond Panchari • junior

"I think it's awesome that our troops have finally captured Iraq's evil tyrant."

Flipping through the channels, every other station trumpeted the message of Sadaam Hussein's capture. Newscasts updated war efforts in Iraq and portrayed the image of a run-down tyrant.

"I am in favor of our troops in Iraq. We need to start cracking down on terrorists and take the chances to take down dictators. I am very glad that finally something was done about Sadaam and his ways. The torture he puts thousands of civilians through is terrible and hopefully justice will put him through just a taste of the anguish and mental torment," junior Charles Bobinis said.

War hit home for many individuals in the area as they were forced to bid farewell to family and friends setting out to protect the home front.

For faculty member Mr. John Ruch Sr., the reality of saying "goodbye" to a family member going to Iraq came all too quickly when his son, First Lieutenant John W. Ruch Jr., a 1997 graduate, was sent to Iraq in March, 2003.

"A military officer is an honorable profession. As a member of the U.S. military, I know that I am helping to make a difference in the world, especially now. It is an unbelievable feeling knowing that you are directly con-

tributing to helping destroy terrorism and the threats to our freedom," graduate John W. Ruch Jr. said.

Mr. Ruch exchanges e-mails with his son two or three times a week and they talk on the phone once a month.

"He called on one of the reporter's satellite phones. It sounded like he was on a cell phone and there was a slight delay. The conversation lasted about 15 minutes and we talked about how he was doing and what was going on here at home. It was great to hear his voice," Mr. John W. Ruch Sr. said.

While in Iraq, soldiers were often forced to work with people they had never even met before.

John W. Ruch Jr. was fortunate enough to meet up with one familiar face while in Baghdad, Captain Anthony Buehler, a 1995 graduate.

"I was sent to Baghdad International Airport, which is 1st Armored Division's Headquarters, to pick up Class IV supplies (sand bags, HESCO baskets, barb wire, wood, etc.) and I was to link up with Captain Buehler. It never

occurred to me until I pulled into the Division Engineers' Headquarters, where Tony is the supply officer, that this Captain may be Tony Buehler. Sure enough, it was and we were both surprised to see each other," John W. Ruch Jr. said.

"I am always concerned about John, that is something that's there all the time. But he's a professional soldier and that's his job," John W. Ruch Sr. said.

Men and women; young and old; black and white; people from different paths of life – strangers brought together through tragedy to triumph over terrorism.

"Knowing that I am helping to protect the United States and also my family and friends is why I decided to devote my life to the military," 1997 graduate John W. Ruch Jr. said.

"We NEED to start CRACKING down on terrorists,"

*Editors Note :These statistics are from a random survey taken of 100 Pottsville Area High School students.

Doing their part
to stop terro

◀◀ **64%** Percentage of students against the reinstatement of the draft.

GRADUATES IN IRAQ
LIFE MAGAZINE
PAGE CREDITS — COPY: Samantha Blum. DESIGN: Brianna DelValle. PHOTOS: Kayla Fehr, John W. Ruch Sr.

"Basically UIL just sits down, looks at enrollment numbers and establishes cutoffs without knowing what school is what," Seewald said.

The sparse amount of schools in West Texas pose the most difficult problem for UIL. Currently, about 50 percent of the land mass in Texas is contained in Region 1, or West Texas, while the other 50 percent covers Regions II–IV. This leads to difficult travel times, particularly for West Texas schools, which are sometimes 200 miles apart.

For HP, travel to Forney and Terrell, both averaging half an hour away, could lead to more missed class time, particularly for freshman and junior varsity teams who compete earlier in the day. Now with only five district opponents versus previous six, HP must schedule one more non-district football opponent, which could lead to added travel time.

Julia Foran [11] said that while extended travel time is unfortunate, it will, however, provide an opportunity for the volleyball team to better prepare.

"Longer traveling time allows us more time for mental imagery on the bus and hopefully more team bonding," Foran said.

Fig. 9.6(a). When a teacher in the school had a son sent to Iraq, the Pottsville Area High School yearbook staff conducted a survey of students about the possibility of reinstituting the draft. In addition to covering the teacher's son (a graduate of the school), the yearbook staff interviewed the teacher about his son's experiences and printed a picture of the son with another of the school's grads, also serving in Iraq. The recruitment of students by the military during lunch at the school was also pictured. *Hi-S-Potts*, Pottsville Area High School, Pottsville, Pa.

Fig. 9.6(b). Tackling a difficult subject such as divorce provided this yearbook staff with in-depth coverage that helped tackle a serious subject in a serious way. In addition to picturing students whose parents had divorced (using pictures provided by the students) the spread also printed statistics credited to DivorceMagazine.com. *Legend*, William R. Boone High School, Orlando, Fla.

According to One Act Director J.E. Masters, the biggest event to happen to this area is the realignment of DISD districts into 10 and 13, which increases the chances that they do not eliminate each other too early.

"Instead of aligning the Dallas districts into District 9 and 10 or 13 and 14, they've split the Dallas district so they won't have to play each other until regional semifinals," Masters said.

Current HP 4A opponents Mesquite Horn, Pearce and Richardson will move up to 5A. Joining HP in the shift from 12-AAAA to 11-AAA are Mesquite Poteet, West Mesquite, and Wylie.

New members include Forney, which will move up from 3A, and Terrell, which HP has played in both non-district and post-season contests. This places HP in a six-member district, while the old 12-AAAA district had seven teams.

"I think it's going to be a tough district there next year and because of that we'll have to prepare harder," said varsity football player Matthew Stafford [10]. "We'll have to make sure we're focused game day and throughout practice."

In particular, Stafford predicts that learning the strengths and weaknesses of new opponents Forney and Terrell will be time-consuming.

"I think we swap film with other coaches so that shouldn't be too much of a problem," Stafford said. "But it will be a definite challenge dealing with new game plans of teams."

As the largest 4A school in the state, the football team will now qualify for the Big School Category, eliminating one play-off game. According to assistant football coach Rex Norris, the football team's guaranteed Big School standing gives it an important advantage.

"In previous years it was guess and check because there were teams bigger than us and teams smaller than us," Norris said. "Before playoffs, we had to look at both small and big schools for preparation."

As a Big School competitor, HP will also play a new round of opponents in playoffs.

"I think our team is looking forward to playing people we've never played before in the Big School competition," Stafford said. "In previous years, we've always played Small School. This will be a new challenge."

Fig. 9.7. Covering academic issues is important to any school publication. Policies in academic curriculum are a good place to start exploring the possibility of in-depth coverage. One of these policies, a growing trend in many school districts, allows students to take Advanced Placement courses though they may not have achieved a passing grade on a qualifying test for the course. The process, called an override, is controversial because it puts students in danger of failing a course they are unprepared to take. In this in-depth look at the policy, the writer interviewed students, teachers and parents of students who had gotten into AP courses through overrides. *Spark,* Lakota East High School, Liberty Township, Ohio.

A potential move to 5A would make HP one of the smallest schools in class 5A. According to estimates from the Registrar's office, HP will graduate 460 this year, and currently enrolls 489 juniors, 457 sophomores and 496 freshmen. These counts could rise with a large incoming 8th grade count and potentially push HP over the 1,925-student cutoff for 5A in two years.

Even though enrollment will increase by 2006, HP is not guaranteed a place in 5A because UIL adjusts minimums every t rs. According to *The Dallas Morning News*, minimum enrollment for 5A grew from 1,865 in 2000–2002 to 1,910 in 2002–2004 and 1,925 for 2004–2006.

"I think the [football coaches] were upset that we did not move up to 5A this year," varsity football player Hunter Pond [11] said. "I think they wanted a bigger challenge [as] it's more fun to compete in 5A. But, [they] are content with 4A because it's still a big challenge."

Other sports, however, have been relieved by the prospect of less competition within the district next year. According to a survey given February 20 by *The Bagpipe*, 67 percent of students favor staying in 4A while 33 percent favor moving to 5A.

"[District realignment] would be horrible for swimming because the times at 5A are so freakishly faster," varsity swim captain Bryan Jester [12] said. "Even the guys at Pearce, our main competitor, will probably not do as well next year."

Furthermore, Jester views the district's staying in class 4A as an opportunity for more athletes to participate in competition.

"Because Pearce is moving up to 5A, more people will get a chance to swim and perhaps make it to regionals," Jester said.

While varsity volleyball player Audra Janak [11] agreed that the loss of rival Pearce will make competition easier next year, it might also have some negative effects.

"We've never really had that much competition within our district," Janak said. "Pearce was our only big competitor and unless one of the new teams fills that void, we really won't have someone to get excited about playing."

Teammates Ashley Edwards [10] also foresees some negative effects from loss of early competition, affecting team readiness later on in the season.

"[Next year] when we will play easier teams at district," Edwards said. "But when we go to playoffs we will have to play at a much higher lever, which might be kind of a shock."

Varsity basketball players Matthew Fritts [11] said games against Pearce will not be the same outside of the district.

"We will still play Pearce in a non-district game, but it's not going to be the same," Fritts said. "It will diminish our rivalry against them and take away the fun competition."

While some athletic teams remain divided over whether district realignment would be an advantage or disadvantage for their team, others such as wrestling, cross country and track, who will not feel direct competition consequences from district realignment, remain calm.

"We've always wrestled 1A to 5A, and we're used to that," wrestling captain Keegan Mueller [12] said. "The district doesn't change for us. Even Forney and Terrell, the two new schools coming in, don't have wrestling teams."

Since cross country and track enter meets at 5A, they, too, will not be directly affected by district realignment. According to Masters, One Act will also not be as affected by district realignment.

"No matter who One Act competes against, in reality we're only competing against ourselves," Masters said.

Whether or not HP will move up in future years, competition in both 4A and 5A remains solid.

"It might be a bigger accomplishment to win a state championship at 5A than 4A," tennis captain Tomnny Collins [12] said. "But whether you win a state championship at 4A or 5A, it's still winning a state championship, and that's something you're going to remember for the rest of your life."

Mallory Biegler
The Bagpipe
Highland Park High School
Dallas, Texas

Another possible in-depth story idea comes as a follow-up to this story in the next year. An analysis of how the district realignment did impact both athletics and academics would make a great in-depth story. By then, the impact of the 8th grade class on the school's total enrollment would also be known, adding to the importance of the follow-up story.

ANONYMOUS SOURCES

When reporting controversial or sensitive topics, students may request that reporters not use their real names. Using them may prevent the student from agreeing to be interviewed for the story. Using a real name or closely identifying circumstances of a student's particular situation could cause embarrassment and ridicule. Reporters should be sensitive to the need to protect identity when the story is sensitive or controversial, but the publication should have a policy in place for dealing with anonymous sources. (See Chapter 22 for more information on this topic.) In the following story on drugs, the newspaper chose to change students' names to avoid problems when the story was published. Asterisks by the names indicated a name change.

All hell was breaking loose in *Brian's apartment. It was the day of DHS senior *Josh's eighteenth birthday. He and

*Mike, also a senior, had left Josh's parents' house to find a "real" party, leaving Josh's mom with a black forest cake to eat herself. They had made their way to the small, private party at Brian's apartment. Upon arriving they had taken three hits of acid each. Instead of seven people in the two-room, 680 sq.ft. apartment, there were now nine – and anyone else who wanted to wish Josh a happy birthday would be arriving soon.

Heather Bell
Update
Herbert Henry Dow High School
Midland, Mich.

LAYERING INFORMATION

Beginning with the headline, readers should understand the story's intent: where the story is heading and what its details will provide. The story's lead should be interesting and relevant to the reader. Visuals, whether photographic or illustrative, should add to the information provided in the story. Alternative story forms such as sidebars, infographics, factoids, quote boxes or question/answer formats should amplify the information in the story form, rather than repeating information in the story itself. Complicated statistics or numerical information should be extracted from the story and presented in alternative story format, where this information will be more easily understood by the readers.

THE NEED FOR ACCURACY

In-depth reporting often involves complicated and complex information. It may require the journalist to find meaning in numbers, to examine public records or to edit a lot of information that may have occurred over a course of time. Working with a good editor will ensure that information is logical and clearly and accurately presented. Numbers and dates should be checked and rechecked for accuracy of information. Complex quotes should be simplified so they are easy to understand. Running quotes – those that are too long to contain in one paragraph – should be an option. Running quotes don't use closing quotation marks until the end of the quote. Each new paragraph of quoted material begins with opening quotation marks.

In-depth reports are among the most important forms of reporting for student publications. Not only do they provide important information but they provide context and texture for the events that occur during the year.

EXERCISES

1. Make a list of possible topics for in-depth coverage in your newspaper or yearbook. Divide your list into beat areas that are currently used by student reporters or beats that could be used to generate topics. Or use the examples of possible beats discussed in this chapter, beginning with school boards.

2. During class changes, during lunch periods and using time before, during and after school for a complete week, make a list of topics that students are talking about with each other. Write down all topics, including those that would not, at first, appear to be subjects for stories in the school paper. Bring the lists back to class the next week and make lists from everyone's lists. What topics appear most often on the lists? What topics have you already covered? What topics should be further discussed?

3. Using professional newspapers or magazines, find examples of three in-depth stories. Find one that begins on the front page (or cover) and continues somewhere else. Find one story that only takes up one page (or spread). Find one story that includes one form of visual storytelling (see Chap. 20). Analyze the stories and answer the following questions:

   (a) What is the news value of this story?

   (b) How many sources were used in the story?

   (c) What background information appears?

   (d) What anecdotes and personal information are included?

   (e) Are the sources kept separate and logically referred to?

4. Using one of the in-depth story ideas generated in exercise 2, brainstorm for a possible headline idea and for visuals to accompany the story.

5. Using one of the in-depth story ideas generated in exercise 2, begin backgrounding the story by doing some research on the topic. Begin by consulting resources available in your library or through the internet. Prepare a list of information resources for the topic. Next, make a list of possible local sources; use the local phone book or other local resources. Prepare a list of questions you would ask of your local resources.

6. Using an in-depth story published in your school newspaper or yearbook, or in an exchange publication, find an example of an in-depth story or account. Analyze it by answering these questions:

   (a) Is the topic relevant to the school, and is that relevance clear?

   (b) Has the story been localized?

   (c) Does the story contain difficult statistical or numerical information that needs to be extracted from the text?

   (d) How many sources were quoted? Is the source information clear and relevant?

   (e) Does the story contain effective anecdotal evidence?

   (f) Do you lose interest in the topic? If so, at what point and why?

   (g) Does the story answer all your reader questions? If not, which questions still need to be answered?

7. Read a week's worth of copies of your local community newspaper for possible in-depth coverage ideas or go online and read five different online newspapers from different locations.
   Compile a list of 10 story ideas that could be localized and used in the school newspaper. Compile a list of sources and resources.

8. Invite a couple of members of the school board and your principal to class to discuss possible changes or issues being discussed by your school board, your district and the state's educational governing body. Have an informal discussion with the school officials about coverage of these and other topics. Discuss coverage of controversial topics that affect your school or that students are talking about that you would like to see covered. What suggestions do the school officials have for covering sensitive or controversial topics?

9. Read the following story in which the student's identity was protected (see *). Do you think it was necessary for the writer to omit the identity? Are there clues provided that would make the student's identity obvious to a student reader? Is this an instance where it is appropriate to change the identity of students?

Effects of drinking and driving spill over into adulthood: A night like any other turned into a nightmare for two teens

The sirens flashed and the ambulance came to a deadly halt. The street lights cast an eerie glow on the pavement and a young boy's body lay twisted at the curb. Shards of glass glistened and alcohol laced his breath. It could have been anyone, but on this night, it was him. It was him, and he was only 16.

"We'd done it a hundred times before but just didn't think about it. Someone tried to stop us, but we were like, whatever. We'd seen it on TV, but when you're 16, you think 'It could never happen to me.' That's the world's biggest cliché," Jeff* said.

The night ended with a bad accident and a dead friend. No one knew who was driving, and at that point no one cared.

They were just two average high school boys. Both did relatively well in school, played sports and liked girls. On the weekends, they partied.

He'd only had a few drinks and although no one was supposed to leave, both Jeff and his friend thought they could handle it. "We all put our keys in the hat, but it wasn't like we'd never done it before," he said.

Despite attempts to stop them, the two got into the silver-gray car and rolled out of the driveway. Neither was sure who should drive or which route to take. It didn't matter why they left. As they headed down the main roads and veered onto the side streets, Jeff and his friend began to take driving less seriously. In a split second the car had struck the curb, rolled viciously, and Jeff's friend lay silent, just outside his reach.

"I wish I would've known that could have happened," he said. "We just wondered where we could find our next buyer – no second thoughts."

In a single night, it was over, but the pain followed Jeff into the upcoming week and still remains with him to this day.

"The whole time they said, 'Oh no, he's going to be all right,' but they lied to me. I knew they were lying," Jeff said. "The entire time I didn't care about me. I was scared and wanted things to be okay."

Only a few hours after reaching the hospital, Jeff's friend was pronounced dead. "I knew it before they told me," he said.

The days that followed were riddled with guilt, fear and worry. How could anything like this happen to someone so young, so innocent, and with so much potential?

At school, some people were dealing well with it while others found it difficult to grieve and even harder to cope. The hallways echoed mourning and Jeff felt sick.

"Some people were like 'What the hell is wrong with you? How could you let this happen?'" Jeff said. "And others tried to tell me it wasn't my fault. But if it wasn't my fault, whose fault was it?"

The emotional wounds were still fresh and Jeff had to face his friend's parents before he could heal.

"The hardest thing I had to do in my whole life was to tell his parents I was driving the car," he said. "They told me they were glad I told them and they were glad it wasn't me."

Though the days at school were extremely difficult to deal with, nothing could compare to the funeral Jeff had to face only a few days after the accident.

"I remember going in there to see him. That was the worst part by far. When you see the person in there and they're dead," Jeff said. "I remember the smell – I'll never forget the way he looked. Seeing him there, dead, was the worst part. You could tell there was a lot of make-up; it didn't look like him."

With the accident behind him, Jeff never did forget. "I never tried to," he said.

For years he didn't drink and was even paranoid when his parents had a glass of wine with dinner. "I've never driven drunk since," he said. "I hang out with some of the same people and they haven't learned anything from it.

"When it's not you, they still think, 'It'll never happen to me,'" he pauses. "And like I said, that's the biggest cliché ever."

Update
Herbert Henry Dow High School
Midland, Mich.

Covering Entertainment

Spending the evening parked on the couch watching two World Wrestling Entertainment featured stars duke it out in what many people could only describe as "acting" might not appeal to everyone. But whether students spend their money on the latest CD by their favorite artist, the newest action movie on DVD or a decent meal to impress a new date, students like to be entertained. New forms of entertainment aimed at young viewers, such as many of the programs on the CW network, continue to evolve.

Students spend their free time and weekends listening to music, going to movies, renting videos, watching television, attending plays, reading, eating out and participating in a wide array of activities that draw their interests. These activities, more than anything else that goes on in school, bond students to each other through shared interests. School publications can hardly afford to ignore entertainment if they want their coverage to appeal to student readers. Entertainment can be broadly interpreted to include everything from seasonal coverage of events such as Halloween haunted houses to coverage of the fall television lineup.

Entertainment reporting can also include coverage of lifestyle topics such as fashion and health and fitness, particularly if the publication doesn't offer a section tailored to student interests outside of school. As in other forms of reporting, entertainment writers need to make sure they are backing up their opinions with specific facts and examples.

Good entertainment sections seek to offer a broad range of entertainment coverage. Students should consider the varied forms of entertainment available to them when deciding on content and coverage. These include movies, music (live and recorded), plays and performances, television, books, restaurants, videos, games, museum exhibits and web sites. Beyond these forms, subcategories of genres exist. For instance, music falls into categories as broad as country to heavy metal. A good entertainment section seeks to cover all interests, not just those of the writers on the staff. Inviting voices into the newspaper's coverage from outside the staff will help diversify this coverage.

Entertainment in school publications takes four primary forms:

- Advance stories – those that appear in the publication before an event occurs. These stories help create interest in upcoming events and provide students with information about attending the event, purchasing tickets and what to anticipate from the event.

- Reviews – student critiques of entertainment in which student writers offer their opinions about events that have already occurred or about new releases or issues.

- Columns – personal, on-going articles that provide information about various entertainment topics, usually about narrowly focused topics.

- Features – stories whose focus is built around particular topics or events with entertainment angles.

issue 1

Four fresh shows this fall

New shows are coming, and here's a taste of some of the goods the networks hope you watch | Evan Favreau

a&e 15

CSI: NY

Helpful Equation: *CSI: Crime Scene Investigation* + *CSI: Miami* x skyscrapers = *CSI: NY*

When: Wednesday, Sept 22 at 9 p.m. on CBS
Who is recognizable: Gary Sinise (Forrest Gump, Ransom)
Who isn't: Melina Kanakaredes, Carmine Giovinazzo, Vanessa Ferlito
What it is: There obviously isn't enough *CSI* on television, so CBS has felt the need to fill that gaping hole with *CSI: NY.* Following the extreme success of the previous shows, this New York version features your standard list of characters. Led by an obsessed crime scene investigator who thinks everything is connected (Sinise) and his equally dedicated partner (Kanakaredes), the group consists of a good-looking investigator, a reclusive coroner and a hard-hitting detective. But the crimes make the show, and *NY* should continue in the *CSI* fashion of fascinating investigating.

CRIME SCENE INVESTIGATORS: Gary Sinise and Melina Kanakaredes star as partners in CSI: NY.

Other New Shows:

LAX	NBC	Sept 13 at 9 p.m.
Boston Legal	ABC	Oct 3 at 9 p.m.
Dr. Vegas	CBS	Sept 24 at 9 p.m.
The Mountain	WB	Sept 22 at 8 p.m.
Drew Carey's Green Screen Show	WB	Thursdays in Oct at 7: 30 p.m.
Second Time Around	UPN	Mondays at 8:30 p.m.
Veronica Mars	UPN	Tuesdays at 8 p.m.

Lost

Helpful Equation: *King Kong* + *Jurassic Park* + *Cast Away* = *Lost*

When: Wednesday, Sept 22 at 7 p.m. on ABC
Who is recognizable: Matthew Fox (*Party of Five*)
Who isn't: Everyone else in this ensemble cast
What it is: From J.J. Abrams, creator of *Alias,* comes a new series about people abandoned on a deserted island. This story has been told before, from *Gilligan's Island* to *Cast Away.* But this show promises something different. For starters, after a plane crashes there are many survivors. 48 of them to be exact, and they all come from a large variety of professions and social classes. These differences, combined with the harsh reality of being abandoned, are sure to make people clash. With these many survivors, the ensemble cast is large and features a variety of fairly unknown actors. Though not all survivors are depicted in detail, every single survivor is a character portrayed by an actor, and could play into the overall story. But the show will feature more than social clashes and survival; it is established in the first episode that there is something else on the island.

Already Premiered:

Father of the Pride	NBC	Tuesdays at 8 p.m.
Hawaii	NBC	Wednesdays at 7 p.m.
North Shore	FOX	Mondays at 7 p.m.

The Next Great Champ

Helpful Equation: *American Idol* x *Rocky* - Mr. T = *The Next Great Champ*

When: Tonight at 8 p.m. on FOX
Who is recognizable: boxing champion Oscar De La Hoya
Who isn't: The 12 aspiring boxers
What it is: Everyone thought that reality television had addressed everything possible. Well, everyone was wrong. FOX is bringing us reality boxing in the form of *The Next Great Champ,* hosted by Oscar De La Hoya. Twelve wannabe boxers will fight each other literally, in order to win a contract with De La Hoya's promotion company and a possible title shot. In a bit of a twist, each contender will be joined by someone from their personal life, in an attempt to up the ante on the personal tension and struggle. But if this show doesn't please the boxing community, they can always try NBC's own boxing show, *The Contender,* with Sugar Ray Leonard and Rocky himself, Sylvester Stallone.

Joey

Helpful Equation: *Friends* x Joey Tribbiani - everyone else = *Joey*

When: Thursday, Sept 9 at 7 p.m. on NBC
Who is recognizable: Matt LeBlanc (*Friends*)
Who isn't: Paulo Costanzo, Drea de Matteo
What it is: Friends may never end, but the show certainly did. NBC had a hard time parting with his nephew and sister. popular series, so enter *Joey,* the spin-off with that not-so-smart guy everybody loves to love, but nothing else has followed him, as Joey Tribbiani (LeBlanc) has moved to Los Angeles to pursue his acting career. He joins his sister and moves in with his 20-year-old nephew, who is a genius and a literal rocket scientist. Dumb guy living with smart guy, hilarity ensues. At least that's what NBC is hoping for.

ALL IN THE FAMILY: Joey Tribbiani with his nephew and sister.

Sept. 7, 2004

Fig. 10.1. An advance story about the fall television season features a look at four new shows of interest to students. In addition to the six capsule summaries, the page features a list of other new shows and a list of shows that have already premiered at the time the advance story was prepared. *The Harbinger,* Shawnee Mission East High School, Prairie Village, Kan.

WRITING THE ADVANCE STORY

When events are occurring in your community or in nearby communities that appeal to students in the school, they can be covered in advance of the actual performance (Fig. 10.1). When possible, editors should assign these stories to students who are interested in the particular artists or events; these students will create stronger stories because of their greater understanding.

Advance stories about musical performances should mention new information such as the release of a new CD or hit single that often provides the basis for such events. Describing past performances will give the readers a basis for comparison between the new and previous performances.

Writers should be careful not to draw information from professional publications when writing advance stories. Writers should not quote professional publications that have had opportunities to interview the artist or the performance. Instead, the writer should concentrate on interviewing students who have seen the performer previously or who are fans of the performer and can talk with an informed voice about new releases and likely highlights of the upcoming event.

Providing extra information, such as the dates, times and locations of the performance, the cost of tickets and the availability of tickets will be useful to student readers. In suburban areas or outlying locations, maps to the performance venue can also be helpful to students interested in attending the event, particularly when held in downtown locations in large cities.

Students should be industrious in seeking to obtain copies of publicity pictures to use with the advance stories. Students can use file photos of a previous performance or could contact a local record store to get press kits or publicity photos. The internet can also be a source for students seeking to contact record labels. It also is becoming more common for performers to "go live" in online chat rooms to answer fans' questions. Many performers are using the internet to get in touch with their fans and create stronger interest in their latest releases. Snippets of songs from new albums are often available through audio clips on the internet.

Often, reporters can obtain and use CD-ROM publicity information provided by the promoters' or performers' labels or movie distributors. These CDs often provide downloadable digital images and other useful publicity information. Information about television seasons and new shows is constantly available on the networks' web sites.

In large cities, it wouldn't be possible to write advance stories about every upcoming event. Editors should seek diverse coverage appealing to a wide range of student interests. Coverage can be supplemented with the publication of an ongoing calendar of listings. Publications with web sites can maintain updated calendar listings on the sites, encouraging students to visit the sites to update their knowledge of upcoming events.

WRITING THE REVIEW

Have you ever read a review and become furious over the narrow-minded point of view expressed by the writer? Few publications offer students the opportunity to read a review of something written from their point of view. Student publications can provide that voice. Not only can reviews be written by members of the publication staff but staffs should seek to include diverse points of view through the inclusion of reviews written by student readers, particularly those who are interested in a particular area of entertainment. Reaching out to students who are known for their musical knowledge or their dramatic knowledge can provide publications with strong, diverse coverage and thoughtful, informed points of view (Fig. 10.2).

Newspapers that publish infrequently must pay particular attention to how they review entertainment. Writing reviews of performances that are still fresh in the students' minds and still present in their conversations will prove to be far more effective than covering events long after they've occurred. If it isn't possible to review the entertainment in a timely manner, it may be worth using only a picture from the event with a well-written caption or using a quote collection featuring a series of short quotes from a variety of people on the highlights or

Fig. 10.2. Just in time for Halloween, the staff of the *Update*'s Pulse section reviewed seven potential rentals to set the mood for party throwers and goers. Complete with pictures of the movie covers, the quick-read reviews are written by three reviewers and end with icons rating the potential "scare" factor of each of the movies. The "bleeding" headline and background art add to the overall theme of the presentation. *Update*, H.H. Dow High School, Midland, Mich.

disappointments of the event. Publications with web sites can offer student-written reviews of concerts and other performances as soon as they are written. This frees the pages of the printed paper to stay more current and timely.

Reviews of some forms of entertainment, such as CD and video releases, books, restaurants, web sites, games and museums or galleries have longer timeliness factors.

Good reviews recap basic information such as the date and location of the event and give the reader a sense of the event from the beginning paragraph. Was it fabulous? Was it a disappointment? Was the performer in rare or weak form? Reviews maintain reader interest by supporting information that is specific and detailed. Were particular songs included that might be indicative of a performer's range? Was something omitted that left the people in attendance feeling disappointed?

Reviewers should provide information about the show, as well as the performer. How did the supporting performers do? What about the staging? The quality of the sound might also be a factor in the show's evaluation.

Giving the reader a sense of the crowd size, the size of the arena or venue and the weather conditions – particularly if the event is staged at an outdoor arena – can also provide relevant information.

When reviewing dramatic productions, books and movies, writers should give the reader a sense of the plot but should be careful to avoid giving away endings, surprises or developments that could spoil the performance for the reader.

In all cases, opinions should be backed by relevant examples. Writers shouldn't be timid about being critical if they feel the performance warrants a negative review. But the writer must also make sure the examples support and justify the opinion of the performance.

In the case of certain kinds of reviews such as book, CD, video and web site, quick reviews of several diverse kinds can interest a greater number of student readers. This is another area where student opinion can be brought into the newspaper. Students frequently ask their friends' opinions about good books, videos and CDs. Reviewers should establish a simple, but relevant, rating system for various entertainment forms, similar to the ubiquitous thumbs up and down from movie reviewers Roger Ebert and the late Gene Siskel. *Vanity Fair* magazine always includes a quick-read survey of

three to four well-known celebrities, asking them, "What book is on your nightstand?" or "What CD are you listening to?"

At certain times of the year, homecoming, school-wide special dances or prom time, publications could provide reviews of restaurants that students might want to frequent for a special occasion. Letting the reader know the range of entrées, the price range of the food, the ambience and other relevant information about the dining experience (are reservations needed? how about extra money for valet parking?) can be useful and informative. Occasional reviews of new restaurants in town or in nearby communities can expand students' knowledge of opportunities close-by.

Reviews of cultural venues specific to communities near the school or those that students would drive to visit on weekends also are effective and provide a service to the newspaper's student readers.

An excellent way to review the fall television season is through polls or surveys asking a wide variety of students for projected hits or misses of the season. Asking questions such as what someone likes about a show and who his or her favorite character is and why and providing information about the show's airtime and channel can give students information they will use.

Many students play hand-held or computer video games. Reviews of new games and options will attract the interest of these players (Fig. 10.3).

At night, at home, many students spend their free time surfing the Web. A computer surfer in the school might be a good voice to add to the entertainment page or section. He or she could offer students a review of popular sites and navigation tools. These sites could help students plan spring break vacations, access information for term papers or learn about colleges and programs they offer.

Students publishing in communities with museums can provide information about exhibits of local talent, traveling exhibits or special performances hosted by the museum. Touring shows and performers will be of interest to many students. Many of these performances are tied to holidays. A touring company might be performing *The Nutcracker* at Christmas time.

WRITING THE COLUMN

Just as editors with thoughtful comments add significantly to the editorial page, entertainment columnists can expand the voice of the entertainment page or

Playing your cards right

Las Vegas and balding middle-aged men: in the past, gambling was a social activity that was always associated with things of the aforementioned nature. Today, however, it has turned into a teen trend that has been popularized among many Hinsdale Central students. "I think the majority of all

Recently gambling has become a popular form of entertainment for Central teens. Is it a healthy social activity or has it gone too far?

trantstafford

teen boys have played poker for money," said John Smith*, sophomore, who is an avid gambler. "It's a fun way to spend a Saturday night."

Although gambling may be an enjoyable activity for teens, many parents have started to speak out against it. At New Trier High School, numerous complaints were made against playing cards, and they were banned from the school. The parents felt that their children were being taken advantage of by other students and that they were losing significant amounts of money.

Contrary to the harsh rules against gambling at New Trier, there is no rule against gambling in the student handbook at Hinsdale Central. "I don't think there should be any rule against card-playing," said Pam Kalafut, Activities Director at

*To protect the identity of those quoted in the story, all the names followed by an asterisk have been changed.

14 ▪ devils'advocate ▪ jan'05

Hinsdale Central. "I don't believe in rules for everything, and I think it is up to the teacher in each class to do as they see fit," Mrs. Kalafut said.

She thinks that New Trier went too far when making rules on gambling, even though she understands where the concerned parents were coming from. "I don't think cards are evil," she said.

Bob Smith*, John's father, agrees with Kalafut. "The kids shouldn't spend so much money, but I think gambling overall is okay," he said. Gambling is something that he has seen go on with kids for a very long time and does not see it fading any time soon.

Although Mr. Smith believes that gambling is okay as a social activity, he does believe it should be banned from school. "There should be no card playing or gambling in school. New Trier was justified in banning cards because a school should solely be a place

for education," Mr. Smith said. "It is not appropriate to play cards at work, and school is like a workplace for teenagers."

His son, John, also believes that gambling is not appropriate in school. "I wouldn't want students [gambling] in school because it's just not the time nor the place to play cards."

John thinks that there is nothing wrong with gambling if everyone involved understands the rules and the bets remain small. "Gambling is a good form of entertainment. My friends and I only play for five dollars, so I don't see the harm in that," John said.

There are some teens, however, that can get addicted to gambling. Steve Robins*, senior, has seen this happen on many occasions. "I have seen tons of kids lose ridiculous amounts of money and they just keep playing," Robins said. "They just don't know when to stop."

Mr. Smith also commented on this tendency. "Some kids will

jan'05 ▪ devils'advocate ▪ 15

Preoccupation
People with gambling problems spend a substantial amount of time thinking about strategy, including the next time they will gamble, or how to obtain money to use on gambling.

Borrowing to pay for losses
Problem gamblers may spend so much money on gambling that they do not have the money to pay for necessities.

"Chasing" losses
Gamblers with problems often feels that they need to win back past money they have lost. This often leads to a feeling of entrapment.

Are you addicted to gambling?
Although it may seem extreme for a high school student, gambling can become an addictive habit, and here are some of the warning signs.

Gambling to escape negative emotions
People with gambling addictions rely on gambling to lift their spirits until it becomes the only thing capable of making them feel good.

Lying to conceal gambling
Addicts try to minimize or cover up gambling with dishonesty.

Inability to stop or control gambling
Addicts may attempt to quit but might be unable to give up their games. They are unable to stick to a spending limit as well.

information courtesy of www.lifespan.org
compiled by Cara Fahey

get addicted just like adults, and then lose too much money," he said. "That shouldn't happen, and we can prevent it by putting a limit on the amount of money that children can spend."

In cases similar to John's there are limits put on the amount of money spent; however, there are some students who participate in games with little or no control over the money the players choose to bet. George Wilson*, senior, plays four times a week and has seen kids lose as much as $600 in one night of card playing. "If [some teens] lose money they will keep on trying to play to get it back, and then lose more," Wilson said. "If they have the money to lose, it is their money so they can gamble it."

There are those who simply play for fun and others who play for financial gain.

"I play about once every two

weeks and even more during the summer," John said. "I love playing cards because of the complex strategies and the adrenaline rush I get from playing and betting. It's fun when you win money, but it's also fun even if you don't."

Other teenage gamblers play for the money. "It is a quick way to win some extra cash," Wilson said. "And I usually only spend 20 to 50 dollars and have made as much as $200 in one night."

Mr. Smith did not introduce his children to the idea of playing card games for money, but he does advise them on the game. "I encouraged them not to overspend and to have fun and I taught them how to play the game better, but I wasn't a big advocate of gambling," Smith said.

With ESPN's recent presentation of the World Series of Poker, and the Travel

Channel's Poker Tour, more and more teens across the country are watching the game on television and are starting to try playing poker at home and with their friends.

"Everyone watches it on ESPN and, then, [they] go out and play it," Robins said. "It is like the new fad. Texas Hold'em has become especially popular due to professional play and TV coverage. In a recent poll by the National Gambling Impact Study Commission, 52 percent of teens ages 13 to17 approved of gambling and playing cards, and 72 percent of teenagers said they had played in the last year alone, despite the fact that it is illegal to gamble under the age of 18. "So many people have been playing cards since they were kids, so I don't feel like I am doing something illegal [when I gamble]," Robins said.

Kalafut also gambled as a

teenager. "I came from a big gambling family and they got me into poker," Kalafut said.

Mr. Smith plays around four times a week with friends and on partypoker.com, a web site used by many players from across America. The site offers several different card games and poker with real and fake money, but is easily accessible to under-age gamblers. "I've tried online gambling, and it is pretty similar to playing with your friends, and being 18 I can legally do that," Wilson said.

When it comes to teens and gambling, there is only one sure bet. As expressed by Mr. Smith, "Kids have been gambling a long time, and that's the way it's going to stay." ▪

contributing reporters: Libby Doyle, Taylor Marten, and Tiffany Tang

16 ▪ devils'advocate ▪ jan'05

Fig. 10.3. Popular teen activities often mimic popular culture. The interest in poker, made popular by cable television shows featuring celebrities playing the game, has spawned interest in private poker games. In this entertainment feature, the staff of the *Devils' Advocate* not only took a look at the increased popularity of playing poker, but also at the implications of gambling involved in private parties. A sidebar chart provides information about gambling addictions. *Devils' Advocate*, Hinsdale Central High School, Hinsdale, Ill.

CULTURE Corner

Rock Without Rules
Indie Brings Rampant Experimentation to the Music Scene

by Rahul D'Sa
'05

"Indie, or independent, rock was born out of the ashes of traditional alternative music. Indie rock was as much a response to mainstream alternative as it was a continuation of it."

Kurt Cobain descended into the dimly lit basement of his Aunt Mari Earl during his Christmas vacation in 1982. He emerged a few hours later with "Organized Confusion," his first homemade demo record, created with little more than one electric guitar, a borrowed bass, an empty suitcase, wooden spoons, and a raspy tenor voice. Five years later, Cobain formed Nirvana, a group that would slowly rise to prominence in the underground music scene. As their fan base spread, Nirvana grew into one of the leading bands in alternative rock, a catchall category for bands that didn't fit into any conventional genres.

Finally, in 1990, after much encouragement from Sonic Youth and the Smashing Pumpkins, David Geffen of Geffen Records signed a record deal with Nirvana, resulting in the band's first major label album, *Nevermind*. The impact on alternative rock was unprecedented. Record sales reached new heights; thousands of new fans attended concerts; and "Smells Like Teen Spirit," the lead single of the album, was played over and over again on MTV. Ironically, alternative music had become mainstream.

Indie, or independent, rock was born out of the ashes of traditional alternative music. Indie rock was as much a response to mainstream alternative as it was a continuation of it. At its most fundamental level, "indie" is simply another umbrella term for bands that are on small, independent record labels or groups that aren't signed onto labels at all. Covering categories from Britpop to lo-fi to alternative remnants, the numerous indie groups on the current music scene are tied together by little more than their connection to underground music.

A major part of indie rock's appeal, however, is precisely this disunity. With no corporate restrictions, general ideologies, or desires to conform to popular standards, indie is rock without rules. The result: rampant experimentation. For example, Sonic Youth, an experimental rock band that has towered over the indie scene for almost twenty years, frequently use a variety of tunings for their guitars and sometimes even apply screwdrivers under the strings to achieve microtonal drone sounds.

The trend of experimentation prevails in modern indie music as well. Mogwai, a British rock band formed in 1995, abandons lyrical narratives altogether and instead focuses on ambient instrumental pieces. Unlike most popular music, Mogwai's songs deal exclusively with creating a definitive mood through their synthesized recordings and deep guitar feedback. On their latest CD, *Happy Songs for Happy People*, Mogwai repeats simple melodies over and over again, each time adding a new varia-

tion, harmony, or countermelody, slowly increasing the complexity of the track. Their meticulous work with harmony and dynamics makes for a musical experience of a much higher quality than the radio typically offers.

Another band known for continually breaking away from musical orthodoxy is Modest Mouse, an indie rock trio from Washington. Led by Isaac Brock, they juxtapose nonstandard lyrics and minimalist acoustics with jarring guitar solos and loud bass lines for shockingly refreshing results. In 1998, they released their breakthrough record, *The Lonesome, Crowded West*, which received much critical acclaim from alternative media sources. In 2000, they released their first album with a major record label: *The Moon and Antarctica*. To the surprise of those who claimed it would be the death of one of indie rock's most prominent bands, Modest Mouse managed to maintain their distinctive sound while polishing the rough edges off their sound. After the success of that CD, Modest Mouse returned to the studio; and their newest album, *Good News for People That Like Bad News*, will be released in April of this year.

But not all of indie rock is avant-garde and new wave. Belle and Sebastian, a lesser-known Scottish pop band, masterfully create upbeat, fast-paced, sunny songs reminiscent of 60's classics. Their recently released album, *Dear Catastrophe Waitress*, showcases a collection of their invariably energetic tunes. Additionally, bands like The Decemberists and Bright Eyes have a unique acoustic-folk sound that appeals to a wide variety of listeners. *Five Songs*, the Decemberists' debut LP, contains many indie classics, including "Shiny"; and their latest release, *Her Majesty, the Decemberists*, only continues their trend of high-energy tracks and free-flowing lyrics.

A new band to burst onto the indie rock scene is the electropop duo The Postal Service. Formed by Ben Gibbard from Death Cab for Cutie and Jeff Tamborello of Dntel, the group combines mechanical techno backing tracks with energized lyrics and pop-like hooks on their first LP, *Give Up*. Matt LeMay of Pitchfork Media commented, "As an avid listener of indie rock, I'm confident that The Postal Service will be the next big thing. And, as we can see from their first album, they have a whole lot of potential."

And all these bands barely scratch the surface of the indie world. There are a host of other bands, CDs, and concerts hidden in studios, music stores, and smaller locales throughout the country. And every day, as a new group assembles in a basement or garage, another potential indie phenomenon is born. ✦

6

Tarmac • April 2004

Fig. 10.4. Students with particular interests in entertainment often use their knowledge to write intelligent and thoughtful columns. These columns can broaden the range of coverage in entertainment sections and pages. This column provides students with a thorough background in "indie" rock while updating readers on new bands and releases. *Tarmac*, Chaminade High School, Mineola, N.Y.

section. Columnists should be chosen for their thought-provoking commentary on a wide range of entertainment issues and topics.

Columnists should avoid the pitfall of using column space for reviewing and critiquing entertainment unless that is the designated purpose for the column and only if additional, shorter reviews are provided from other student voices.

Columnists should make sure to use fresh, original material, taking advantage of the fact that their voices are unique. Quotes and information should not be borrowed from published sources or taken from the internet without permission of the site manager. As in other forms of information, columnists should make sure to substantiate their opinions with strong, supporting statements (Fig. 10.4).

Students with strong interests in narrow entertainment forms may be too limited for column writing. In that case, the staff should consider using a variety of columnists who could alternate writing the column. These alternating columnists could also write about a variety of entertainment forms. Opening up the column space to a guest columnist from outside the newspaper's staff could also add to the diversity of entertainment coverage. The occasional use of two columnists with opposing points of view could broaden the coverage.

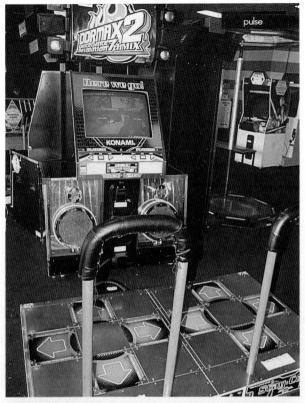

Fig. 10.5. Capitalizing on the popularity of what began as an arcade game, *Devils' Advocate* entertainment writers localized the story by showing how students in their school were playing versions of the game on Playstations at houses on the weekends, and how the game had been used as a fundraiser by the Key Club. *Devils' Advocate*, Hinsdale Central High School, Hinsdale, Ill.

Fig. 10.6. A good entertainment page provides a broad range of information to its student readers. Leading with a story comparing MP3 players, the staff of the *A-Blast* also includes two CD reviews and a TV show review on its page. Adding to the usefulness for the reader, the page utilizes small, boxed icons which identify the cultural form reviewed and which succinctly summarize the reviewers' opinions ending with a letter grade. Adding to the diverse page, horoscopes appear along the right side of the page. *A-Blast*, Annandale High School, Annandale, Va.

WRITING THE FEATURE

As with other kinds of feature stories, the entertainment page or section offers writers opportunities to enrich the newspaper's coverage with stories of interest to a wide range of readers.

Student writers should brainstorm with fellow staff members as well as with non-staff members from throughout the school to originate fresh coverage (Figs. 10.5 and 10.6).

A drive-in theater, a popular hangout, an unusual restaurant, the history of the oldest movie theater in town or a behind-the-scenes look at a dramatic production can all provide interesting feature coverage.

Feature coverage does not have to be limited to traditional writing. Photographers can team up with writers to tell stories visually: to show performers studying their lines, building the sets, sewing costumes and learning choreography, for instance. These pictures might be a more interesting feature approach to a behind-the-scenes look at a dramatic production. The writer could add a short, well-written story to the mix to provide the details.

Expanding traditional definitions of entertainment coverage, writers should think about adding coverage of other forms of entertainment such as health and fitness training. Some of this coverage could be used in the sports section, but if that section is already taxed for space, consider the broad appeal of its addition to entertainment. After all, entertainment is what students choose to do to amuse themselves in their spare time. What students do for entertainment will continue to evolve. Entertainment writers should be looking out for ways in which they can expand their traditional coverage and tap in to emerging student interests. If students are spending their evenings in the living room watching the World Wrestling Entertainment on TV and then spending $50 on a ticket to see a live version of the show when it passes through town, the newspaper should be tapping into that interest. The more diverse the coverage, the better.

EXERCISES

1. Read a professional review in a popular cultural publication such as *Entertainment Weekly*, *Premiere*, *TV Guide* or *Rolling Stone*. Make note of the reviewer's use of opinions backed up by examples. Underline each opinion and its supporting example in the review. Next, note how the review begins. What other details are provided by the publication to help the reader learn more about the entertainment form being reviewed? For instance, is there an overall rating, a separate listing of a cast, a list of songs from an album or a plot summary? Are these extra details helpful to the reader?

2. Attend a local production of a play or dance group, the opening of a museum exhibit or a live concert performance. Write a review of the production. Make sure to obtain a copy of the program, if there is one, to provide you with correct spellings of names. Determine what supplemental information could be provided visually with the story. Make sure to back up your opinions with examples.

3. Gather a sampling of opinions from at least 10 students on several TV shows that they enjoy. Edit the survey information to reflect the most interesting information you obtained. How could this information be presented in the entertainment section of the newspaper? Draw a pencil sketch of how you would use the information.

4. Generate a list of entertainment story ideas using internet resources, local magazines, newspapers and calendars. Make a list for seasonal coverage, community coverage and coverage of cultural entertainment trends such as the World Wrestling Entertainment or teen television programs. How could these be covered in the newspaper?

5. Prepare an advance story for an upcoming entertainment event coming to your town. Do research by reading about the event on the internet or by reading previously written articles about the performers. Localize your story by talking to students in your school who will be attending the event. Prepare a list of questions you could ask them to help you include relevant information in your advance story. Should you supplement the advance story with an additional story containing information such as the time, date, ticket price, location and location details of the upcoming event? How could you present that?

6. Write a column about an entertainment issue about which you are concerned. Begin by doing some research about your topic as background for the writing. Interview other students in your school to get their opinions. Since you're writing a column, you can use the first-person form of writing.

7. Read this restaurant review by Laura Flamm from the *Devils' Advocate*, Hinsdale Central High School, Hinsdale, Ill.

A new twist on an old tradition

Finding a traditional Chicago pizza place – complete with dark booths and a host from the old country who doesn't take names – can be difficult in a world full of generic pizza franchises. But an excellent traditional Chicago pizza place that doesn't have a traditional pizza on the menu?

Yes, it's true. Located in the basement of an old Victorian house rumored to be a lookout post during the 1929 St. Valentine's Day Massacre, The Chicago Pizza and Oven Grinder Co. has seen plenty of business since its opening in 1972.

Though the menu is limited, the originality and quality of the food make up for any lack of variety. The baked-to-order half or one-pound pizza pot pies and calzone-like Oven Grinders follow the Mediterranean bread appetizer well without any drastic belt loosening. Throw in some tortoni for dessert, and you're set. Though this pizza place is pretty easy on the pockets (a typical meal runs anywhere from 10 to 20 dollars), watch out, young credit card-wielding patrons; this place takes only cash.

In a world of warmed over Domino's from the cafe, the Chicago Pizza and Oven Grinder Co. gives Grandma's homemade pizza pie a run for its money.

Chicago Pizza and Oven Grinder Co. 2121 North Clark Street (three blocks south of Fullerton), Chicago 773.248.2570

Open: Monday–Thursday (4 p.m.–11 p.m.), Friday (4 p.m.–12 a.m.), Saturday (12 p.m.–12 a.m.), Sunday (12 p.m.–11 p.m.).

Directions:

Take Interstate 290 (Eisenhower) to Lake Shore Drive, follow north to Fullerton exit, turn left onto Fullerton and follow west to the intersection of Clark and Fullerton, turn left onto Clark.

Now answer these questions:

(a) Underline the passages in which the writer describes the atmosphere of the restaurant.

(b) Did she like the restaurant's food? List specific ways in which she justified her opinion of the food in the review.

(c) Did she leave anything out of the review that would have helped you decide whether or not to eat at this restaurant?

(d) What are her criticisms of the restaurant?

(e) How do you think this restaurant review serves the needs of her suburban Chicago's high school reading audience?

Yearbook Reporting and Writing

Elvis, Andy Warhol, the Statue of Liberty, Disneyland, Cheerios and the high school yearbook are all icons of American culture.

As an icon, a revered symbol, the high school yearbook enjoys a status that exceeds that of almost any other memento of the teenage years for many. Sophisticated or not, it is eagerly anticipated before publication and cherished afterward. It has enjoyed this status for more than 100 years.

With such an endearing history, it's no surprise that the production of a yearbook is often serious business, requiring specialized training in many areas, including reporting, writing and editing. Even though the photograph remains the most enjoyed and important piece of a yearbook, the accompanying text – photo captions, stories and headlines – is a significant contributor to the effectiveness of the yearbook as a memory or history book.

THE MISSION OF THE YEARBOOK

Clear and simple, the yearbook's mission is to report the events and issues of the day and the persons involved in them. It shares most of the goals of a school newspaper, and many of the skills needed for success in one are as important for success in the other.

Reporting in a yearbook is done through words, photograph and story-related art. Since the book is published annually, the scope of its coverage extends for one 12-month period, beginning with the events that occurred and issues that were discussed since the last volume of the yearbook.

Although most of the book reports events that occurred on campus or at a school-sanctioned or -directed event off campus, some non-school-related events, issues and activities involving students are included in the yearbook. Some nonstudent and nonschool stories, such as condensed coverage of major world news, may be included to broaden the usefulness of the book as a more complete history of one year.

To be fair and inclusive, all student population groups – racial, ethnic, religious, cultural, economic, sexual orientation – are represented in the pictorial and editorial coverage. This pluralistic or multicultural approach is a conscious part of the book's balanced coverage plan. Photographer, and reporters make a special effort to include students outside of their own group of friends.

Each story that is reported in the book, in words and pictures, is accurate, fair and honest. Successes and failures are reported, even though the overall tone of the book is usually upbeat. Minority viewpoints are included, and topics of concern to teenagers, even if controversial, are presented in a fair, mature and tasteful way.

Like the school newspaper and magazine, the yearbook is free of libel and observes the restrictions placed on it by law and media ethics. In an attempt to be humorous, some yearbooks have published captions, photos and other content that were false, were not in good taste and even damaged a person's good name and reputation. This type of seemingly harmless but potentially harmful work is prohibited in a book that follows the standards of good journalism. A yearbook is more permanent than a newspaper, magazine or web site, and errors and libel published in a yearbook are more difficult and costly to correct.

COVERAGE PLANNING FOR EACH SECTION

Coverage – the picture and word stories – within the book's major sections reflects both traditions and new events, issues and personalities. The traditional sections – student life, academics, clubs and organizations, sports and portraits – can be presented with fresh angles. Other sections, including magazines-within-the-book, advertisements, student art and literary work, among others, can supplement the core sections.

Even the core or traditional sections can be defined in other ways as content is shuffled to present the overall story of the year in a different order or format. As long as the reader is not confused or hampered when he or she is reading the book after publication, creative ways to organize content can be successful. Some books have successfully organized content seasonally, month-by-month and even day-by-day. Others have organized it thematically, such as students at work, students at play and students after-hours.

Theme Development

One option for the yearbook is to select and develop a word theme, a single word, phrase or sentence that serves as a hook for story and design continuity throughout the book. The word theme can be topical and linked to stories reported in the opening, closing and other sections of the yearbook (Fig. 11.1).

A word theme tied to specific events or issues related to the school community or to teenagers in general is often more effective than one that has no relevance to students or is hackneyed. Before a word theme is finalized, the yearbook staff should ask this question: Will this theme be as clever, exciting or fresh when the book is finally published as it seems now as the book is being planned? Some word themes, like product advertising slogans, become tired clichés within months if they are overly used and too popular.

If the word theme isn't obvious or is complex, its meaning or the reason why it was selected should be explained briefly near or in the opening of the book.

In addition to introducing a word theme on the book's cover and developing it initially in the opening, it can reappear on divider spreads and, occasionally, within sections before it is concluded in the brief closing section. Even the endsheets, which hold the book's cover onto the pages, can include some theme development. The words themselves can also be altered to add variety and relate more specifically to a section.

Word themes are not mandatory for a book to be a successful history of the year. Themes can unify coverage and help the book's marketing plan, but continuity can also be achieved in other ways, including through design. A mix of a design motif, such as a logo, and a subtle, sparingly used word theme can be a successful compromise between an extensively developed wood theme and a book with none at all.

The Student Life Section

Often a catch-all section, the student life portion of the yearbook contains coverage of social activities and the discussion of issues of concern to teenagers (Fig. 11.2). In addition, this section may include local, state, national and international news.

Events are reported and issues presented because they are newsworthy or have substantial human interest appeal and may be a significant part of the school's traditions.

These events, both social and academic, such as prom, homecoming, plays and musicals, concerts and graduation, that are tradition-based are usually reported in this section of the book. Although they are likely to be included every year, an angle is presented in both the editorial and pictorial coverage that is specific and newsworthy or emotionally involving.

Breaking news (coverage of events that are not yearly school traditions such as a visit to the school by a dignitary, the opening of a new addition to the school and unusual weather that disrupts the school) is often placed in this section of the book.

Summer and vacation activities, after-school work and leisure time recreation such as hobbies, dating and

Everything you ever wanted to know...

Without fail, the arrival of 9:30 a.m. brought the "Ding!" of the speaker system and the morning announcements: the daily distribution of information—club parties, parking problems, Panther praises—kept Northerners involved, aware and up to date. And as usual, there was plenty to talk about.

Kent Mathers and Ray Bohannon won the title of the state's top administrators, while Donna Hansen and Trish Winnard earned National Teacher Certification. SUN hit it big with an unopposed bid for OASC State Secretary, and the yearbook took top honors at OIPA with the best book in the state. Five Merit Semi-Finalists and four Drama All-Staters added accolades.

The hype and headlines blared loud and clear, but the what about the *rest of the story. . . ?* (CONTINUED NEXT PAGE)

scream too Excited enthusiasm pumps up the crowd at the home football game against Lawton Sept. 25. Sophomores Crystal Kadron and Lindsay Guttery, freshman Casey White and sophomore Abbie Broughton scream Panther pride from the stands. "The best part of the game is the crowd," Broughton said. "Sometimes it's kind of mellow if we're losing, but everyone cheers and has a blast when the team's winning." Off a big win over sister school Putnam City, the varsity faced a crushing 32-0 loss to Lawton's Wolverines. PHOTO BY CASSIE GILL

Senior Khoa Lam lets loose with a bingo.
Junior Tracey Ashcraft gets helping hands.
Seniors Casey Hiss and Mathan Parasuram act out.
(PHOTOS BY CASSIE GILL, MICHAEL DOWNES, JUSTIN GLASSON)

travel are also found in the student life section. To present an accurate and complete picture of teenagers today, coverage of off-campus, nonschool activities involving students is important.

In addition to events and activities coverage, issues important to teenagers are reported in several forms in this section. Social issues, such as sexuality, religion, drug and alcohol use and personal safety and violence, and academic concerns, such as study habits, cheating and college entrance exams, are the sources of some of the topical stories reported in student life.

Humorous features on a wide range of topics, from April Fools' Day pranks to first dates and summary reports on significant local and international news, usually with a local or school tie-in, round out the student life sections in many books. Humor should not contain any libel or innuendo that may conflict with community standards of acceptability. Reporting student reaction to world and national events is preferred to secondhand summaries of the events with no local angle.

If books from different schools are compared, differences in school traditions and the racial, ethnic and religious makeup of the student population will result in content differences within the student life sections. As the student life section is planned, the special observances and activities of the school's minority groups should be included. Even in non-minority-related stories, photographers and writers should put minority faces in candids and their opinions in word stories throughout the book.

The catch-all nature of the student life section gives editors the freedom to add some new stories each year. Even though the coverage of annual events dominates this section, the first-time story will likely be popular with students and help mark the book as a unique edition.

Fig. 11.1. "Et cetera" is the word theme for this book, and on its opening spread, it promises readers, with a bold headline, that the book includes "Everything you ever wanted to know." A word theme can be used to unify or link content throughout the book. *Panther Tracks*, Putnam City North High School, Oklahoma City, Okla.

Fig. 11.2. Homecoming, a traditional student activity, is often reported in the student life section of a yearbook. *Trail*, Overland High School, Aurora, Colo.

THE ACADEMICS OR LEARNING SECTION

Learning takes places both within the classroom and in more informal settings in the school, home and other places. The academics or learning section of the yearbook presents an opportunity to present both classroom and nonclassroom education. How extensive this coverage will be will depend upon the size of the book and the extent of the school's curriculum (Fig. 11.3).

Each academic department and course considered for coverage should be examined for news value. The traditional news values – consequence, timeliness, proximity, prominence, human interest – should be considered when coverage is planned and content is judged. This question is central to editorial and pictorial coverage: What's new this year? Focusing on the answer to that question and examining its news values will help ensure fresh reporting and prevent nonspecific content with little potential reader interest.

Another approach to coverage in this section can be tried if after careful research little is found of hard news value or little has changed from the past year. The human interest angle can be pursued. The editorial content can be interview-driven, with emphasis on issues or personalities. Those enrolled in a class and those teaching it can be the focus of the story rather than what's new in the course content or how it is being taught.

not quite the real thing Costumes adorn John Reis and Todd Pinley, juniors, as they act out divorce court in English teacher Connie Copley's second hour American Lit. II class. The class read *Ethan Frome*, and then role-played a divorce between Ethan and Zeena. They selected their clothes from a trunk Copley kept in the back of her room.
PHOTO BY KATIE WIND

going back to nature Tree images appear on sophomore Kelly Watters' paper as she draws them, Oct. 7, outside during art teacher Nancy Grimes' Basic Art class. Grimes asked the students to draw a nature scene outside the building. "I liked the project, but it was kind of hard to stare and concentrate on a tree bark for an hour," Watters said.
PHOTO BY LISA SCHRAMBER

the man in the mirror His reflection helps Brandon Spivey, sophomore, in the drawing of his self-portrait, Oct. 14, in art teacher Nancy Grimes' fourth hour Basic Art class. Grimes had the students study their features in the mirror before drawing themselves. The self-portraits were a week-long project for the class.
PHOTO BY JOHN PELRAN

burning away the calories In order to determine the number of calories her of calories in a plain peanut, Evan Gorman, junior, and David Godfrey, sophomore, execute the Emergency Food Calorie Lab, Oct. 5, in science teacher John Mackin's second hour Traditional Chemistry class. Mackin asked the students to imagine they were flying high above the Andes Mountains when their plane lost power. They suddenly found themselves plummeting to the ground. They saw three bags, each with 50 pounds of peanuts, cheetos, or mini marshmallows. Not knowing how long they would be stuck in the mountains, they had to choose one of the bags—the one they thought would sustain them the longest in the months or weeks to follow. Each student had to burn a cheeto, a marshmallow and a peanut to determine the amount of heat each one produced. They lit the food with matches, and held the food on a paper clip under a soda can filled with water. After burning the three types of food, the students found the peanut would have been the best choice to make because of its high calorie content.
PHOTO BY KATIE WIND

Off Again then On Again

computer malfunctions cause class disruption, frustration when computer game freezes

"I hate computers!" Alison Streb, junior, screamed in business teacher Leslie Calvert's third hour Computer Applications class, Oct. 21. "Oh no, oh no, this can't be happening to me."

Classmates, who were learning how to use borders in Microsoft Word,

turned to Streb as she pushed her chair away from the computer in anger.

"Mrs. Calvert, I had a winning game," Streb said. "What am I going to do? Andrew (Koebbe, senior), can you help me? My computer is broken!"

Koebbe turned to help her.

"No, do not turn it (the computer) off," Streb said. "Can't you fix it without turning it off? I was right in the middle of a game!"

"There is no way I can fix it without turning it off," Koebbe said. "It's frozen."

"Well, at least let me stare at my computer screen for a while," Streb said. "I need to reflect on my success before you touch it."

After studying her screen, Streb turned to Koebbe and said, "Okay, you can turn it off." As Koebbe turned off the screen, others went on with their work.

Streb turned the computer back on and started again. Koebbe and Streb then finished their assignment and began playing games on their computers.

going the distance One ruler is not long enough to measure the distance for Anne Shea and Trent Smith, freshmen, when they figure out how far a car traveled, Oct. 5, during science teacher Ron Zapf's second hour Physical Life Science class. "The lab was really fun to perform," Smith said. "We measured how far the car would go with various lengths of elastic."
PHOTO BY KATIE WIND

fly like an EAGLETON

FORMER SENATOR SPEAKS TO STUDENTS ABOUT IMPEACHMENT

As a loud voice boomed over the intercom, Thomas Eagleton, former U.S. Senator, stopped talking in mid-sentence and said, "I've never been this close to God."

Lecture Hall A exploded with laughter. Principal Franklin McCallie was the voice on the loud speaker, introducing Eagleton to the school.

Eighty students sat in the Lecture Hall, Oct. 22, to hear Eagleton talk about the impeachment process.

"At first I thought it was going to be really boring, because I'm not really into the government or anything," Molly Holekamp, junior, said, " but it turned out that he was a really good speaker."

He told the group if Congress impeached Clinton and Vice President Gore that Newt Gingrich would be President. "If that happened," he said, "I would move to Australia."

"It was very interesting," Bret Gracey, junior, said. "Eagleton also told us he didn't think Clinton would be impeached. It was really neat to hear an opinion from someone who has been involved in the government."

If all subjects are not covered in separate stories, ways to combine coverage can be tried. For example, all core curriculum courses for a grade level could be reported as one story. Or all courses that involve laboratory work or focus on workplace skills could be combined. All courses that include computer use could be linked. Another way to condense coverage of formal classroom courses would be to select, for coverage, one class for each hour or time period of a school day.

Learning that takes place outside the formal classroom has a place in the yearbook. Within the school itself, students studying alone or in groups in media centers, in libraries, in lounges, in cafeterias, or on outdoor lawns and patios can be the focus of a story. Tutoring and mentoring activities and students who take classes at colleges or other schools to supplement their regular high school courses can be covered in this section.

Feature stories with an academic angle can be included in this section too. Some suggested topics are student study habits, using the computer and the internet to learn, career and life skills learned from various classes, studying for exams, preparing for college entrance exams and standardized tests, favorite books read for class, favorite science lab experiments and recollections of learning in junior high and elementary school. Some books have randomly selected one student from each grade level and reported his or her class-hour by class-hour day, including lunch, with pictures and text story.

Fig. 11.3. In a book that reported the events of the year month-by-month, several newsworthy happenings inside the classroom during October were covered on this spread in the academics section. *Pioneer*, Kirkwood High School, Kirkwood, Mo.

SWEETSOUNDS

By Russell Graney and Kelly Haupt

The delicately balanced harmonies of violins, violas, celli and basses could be heard outside the door to Room 401, the rehearsal room for the middle school orchestras. The advanced orchestra,

Orchestra members perform a combination of modern, classical music at concerts, competitions.

directed by Ms. Dow, provided an opportunity for experienced musicians to become competent in the performance of both classical and modern music. Mr. Knudson, the beginning orchestra conductor, worked to make younger musicians comfortable with their first encounter in orchestra. Asked why she chose the viola, beginning orchestra member seventh grader Dana Jones explained,"All my life I've been like my sisters, so I was happy to find that I could play something other than the cello and violin." Practicing at home was stressed and weekly record sheets showed how much time students had spent.

Some of the music played this year included selections from *The Lion King*, Dvorak's *Symphony #8* and the *Concerto* Dvorak's *Symphony #8* and the *Concerto Grosso*, featuring eighth grade soloists Won Jun Lee, Russell Graney and Michael Sullivan.

The orchestras presented three concerts this year in December, March and May. They also took part in two competitions. The District Festival in March included local schools, and the *Music in the Parks* festival in May involved middle schools from the entire Mid-Atlantic region. Following the May competition, students enjoyed the rest of the day at Busch Gardens in Williamsburg.

1. Elyse Morel (7) whose violinist grandmother got her started, plays at the winter concert. 2. Perfecting their style, violinists rehearse during class. 3. Soloist Won Jun Lee(8) entertains the audience with *Concerto Grosso*. 4. Concentrating on his music, bass player Sean Freeman (8) sight reads a new piece. 5. Jina Kim (8) rehearses with her cello. 6. Symphonetta cellist Cassie Johnson (8) practices her scales. 7. Orchestra concert performances were important for bass players Steven Petty (7) and James Hirsch (8).

Sarah Rich • *8*

"I got started playing violin because my dad and older brother played before me. Also, you can be concert master if you play violin."

Jeannie Rose • *8*

"I enjoy playing theme songs from movies because the audience seems to enjoy them more."

88 Orchestra | Organizations

Orchestra | Organizations 89

Fig. 11.4. Action candids and a feature story comprise the coverage of the school's orchestra on this spread in the clubs and organizations section. *Sentry*, Robinson Middle School, Fairfax, Va.

Some books include teacher and staff portraits within this section; however, a section with just teacher and staff photos is not a true academics section. Others include these faculty mug shots in a schoolwide portrait section.

The Clubs and Organizations Section

The clubs and organizations section traditionally has two purposes: to document through group photos those involved in the activity and to report on the activities sponsored or undertaken by the group (Fig. 11.4). If space allows, each school-sanctioned group is covered on a separate page or spread in the book. If space limits this, coverage of groups can be combined on a single page or spread, if possible, by similar goals or activities. For example, all groups that do volunteer work in the community, all groups that perform for the public, or all groups that perform music could be clustered together.

Group photos with identification of those pictured, though important, should not dominate or represent the only presence of the group in the yearbook. Care should be taken to produce a photo with face sizes large enough so that each member can be recognized. Usually, group photos should be cropped to remove anything below the shoulders and above the tops of the heads. Large groups can be divided into two or more segments to ensure sufficient face size and recognition.

As is the case with other sections, news values are considered for the editorial and candid photo content that accompany the group photos on these pages. Reporters should ask: What's new this year? Even if the club sponsors the same events every year, there are new participants and, perhaps, new results. Candid photo content needs the same approach as copy to stimulate reader interest. Even if the space allocated to a club is less than one page, a minipackage of a group photo, one candid and captions and a brief story could be effectively integrated into a multigroup page or spread.

A feature rather than a news approach can be taken for editorial coverage. Club participants' involvement, including their reactions to club activities or goals, can become the coverage focus. Other feature approaches could be used: exploring the group's history, reporting the benefits or drawbacks of membership, focusing on post-high school, college, career or life links, and writing about time and financial commitments made by members. A single theme, perhaps linked to the book's word theme, could run throughout the section, unifying all copy for clubs. However, reporters should guard against formula writing – text that has the same type of lead and story development from page to page with only the names, dates and other specifics changing.

Some books place all group photos for organizations and sports in a separate section or in the book's index. Some books integrate the clubs section with the academics section; in many cases, the clubs have an academic tie-in. If a book has a section exclusively for group photos, some graphic or minifeature running throughout this section will unify it and add more reader interest.

As in other sections in a yearbook, even well-written copy can be monotonous if the same approach is used repeatedly within a section and throughout the entire book. A mix of news-features and human interest feature copy may prevent this from occurring.

THE SPORTS SECTION

Yearbook journalists often find the sports section to be the easiest to apply news values to content. The most obvious news value is conflict, with prominence also

being likely. Largely, this section is a review of specific athletic accomplishments by team. Each contest has all or most of the characteristics that make it newsworthy (Fig. 11.5).

One of the first decisions made by a yearbook sports editor or reporter is which contests to cover and which ones to ignore or list in a summary, composite scoreboard. Space limitations usually prohibit the reporting of all contests for any team sport. The reporter weighs the importance of each contest when selecting the ones to write about.

After the reporter selects the most significant contests, they are ranked from most to least important; the season wrap-up story will open most often with the highlights of the most important contest, a summary of the season's record or the exceptional accomplishments of one or more team members. Further story development will likely include summaries of the contests judged as less important than the "big game."

Assessments about the successes, shortcomings or failures of the team should be sought by the reporter from key team members, coaches and fans and then reported with attributions within the story. The reporter should avoid the temptation to comment on the quality of the team's performance.

Usually, an end-of-season wrap-up story that is presented chronologically fails to capture the most significant highlights or interesting facts in its opening paragraphs; reporters should avoid the chronological summary, except as a follow-up to the opening paragraphs and initial story development that present the season's most important achievements.

The sports reporter may choose to write something other than a season wrap-up story for any or all teams. If a complete season's scoreboard is published in the book, there may be no compelling need to reiterate this information. A feature story on some aspect of the team would be an appropriate substitute. Some possibilities include a comparison of the team's record for the past 10 seasons, coaching strategies, training procedures, rivalries, player superstitions, what it's like behind-the-scenes during a game, and player statistics or end-of-season awards.

In addition to either the season summary or other feature story and a season scoreboard, editorial coverage can be augmented with other text sidebars. These are shorter than the main story and can be stand-alone quotes from players, coaches or fans, individual player statistics, a brief history of the sport, an explanation

Fig. 11.5. Word reporting is segmented into six stories in addition to complete captions on this sports spread. In addition to the main story, there are four first-person shorts (two from athletes, one from a coach and one from a fan) and one brief summary under "What we saw." *Aerie*, Lancaster High School, Lancaster, Calif.

of rules, an athlete's diet or training schedule, collegiate or professional sports highlights (to make the book more of a comprehensive history of the year) or other information of interest to readers.

Photo coverage in the sports section usually includes a team group shot and candids of the team in action. It is often desirable to link the main story lead to one or more of the candid photos. Behind-the-scenes candids and a limited number of mug shots can supplement the game candids and group photo.

Some yearbooks have expanded coverage in the sports section to include personal, nonteam student sports and recreation, as well as athletic-related issues and controversies of general interest. Examples of nonteam or nonschool sports that could be reported include snowboarding, in-line skating, rodeo, cycling, climbing, hiking, weight lifting and surfing. General interest, sports-related stories could include college scholarships for athletes, the Olympics, use of supplements for muscle growth, sports injuries, eligibility requirements and sports heroes.

To a certain extent, tradition plays a role in how much space is given to each sport. Sometimes this has been seen as unfair by some readers or some athletes who think their sport deserves as much or equal coverage. It is important to provide sufficient space to girls' as well as boys' teams and to include recreational sports that are popular with a minority population group within the school, but fan interest should be considered too. The sports editor must balance the need to be fair with the realities of spectator or reader interest and real news values.

THE PORTRAIT SECTION

Since one of the book's purposes is to document those persons who were enrolled in the school for a specific time, the book's portrait section is especially important. For many years, books have done that and more, expanding coverage within the portrait section to include many human interest feature stories and other information (Figs. 11.6 and 11.7).

Portraits should be uniform in size within a class or division, but uniformity in poses, dress or background is optional. Since this may be the only picture of a student in the book, it is important to spell the person's name correctly and get the best possible reproduction of the photo from the camera stage to the final printing.

If a person is not pictured, do not substitute an empty space or cartoon character with any words such as "camera shy." Simply list all those not pictured in an alphabetized list at the end of the portraits for that class or division.

In addition to formal names adjacent to the portraits, some books list school activities and other data such as a brief motto. Variations in the amount of extra copy accompanying a name may disrupt the layout. An alternative is to place these activities in a separate addendum at the end of the portraits or near the close of the book. If mottoes, prophecies or other material is included, the editors should review them carefully for libel or derogatory or unsuitable words. The editor, adviser and school may all be legally responsible for everything that is published in the book, including content submitted by those pictured but not on the yearbook staff.

It is now common to include short features and candid photos on portrait pages. Usually, these features are pertinent to the class or grade level in which they appear. One popular feature is a brief personality profile or a story focusing on one aspect of a person's life such as a hobby or unusual accomplishment. Some features are on student nonschool interests such as music, movies, cars, aspirations for the future, foods and restaurants, after-school jobs and opinions on national politics and concerns "in the news." Sometimes, these features focus on students who excel academically, such as the top 10 students. No topic is potentially off limits for reporters assigned to the portrait section. Sometimes the book's theme can suggest a series of topics for features in this section.

Candid photography in the portrait section should be varied. Since the portraits (face shots) dominate the pages, it is advisable not to use too many close-ups of faces

Fig. 11.6. Most student portrait sections include profiles on selected students. This page of a two-page spread also has a short-answer poll, "Who is your hero?" at the bottom of the page. *Pilot*, Redondo Union High School, Redondo Beach, Calif.

Uniting the past and present

Redondo High unites a father and son through common experiences

Redondo alumnus George Irwin enjoys being able to share similar high school experiences with his son. "I love spending time with my son and teaching him how to surf," Irwin said.

Senior Ashton Irwin's eyes widened as he gazed upon El Porto's shore, decorated with anxious surfers perched on their boards, waiting for the perfect wave. The skies were gray and overcast; he heard the calls of sea gulls over the crashing and ebbing of waves. His father's eight-foot Beaker surfboard dived into freezing salt water. Irwin's new Body Glove wet suit, given to him by his dad, Class of 1964 alumnus, provided little protection against the shocking chill of the water. Ashton's focus was not on the sudden numbing of his finger tips and toes, but on the perfect wave that would enable him to become "just like dad."

Irwin's experiences surfing alongside his father have inspired him to follow in his father's footsteps. George Irwin, Ashton's father, admits to the similar personality traits between the two. Both love the thrill of learning a new trick in the water and both love to work hard on the things they love. This similar work ethic brings the two closer even during the good and bad times.

"My dad grew up with the Beach Boys during the sixties, and I wanted to be apart of that surfing culture," said Irwin. The similar high school experiences and interests have helped to develop a stronger bond between father and son. "Surfing definitely brought me and my dad closer" said Irwin. Since Irwin's first surfing lesson with his father, the two have developed both a "close buddy" father and son relationship that continues to get stronger.

~Corinna Miller

Spending time at the beach is one of senior Ashton Irwin and his father's favorite past times. "I want to be like my dad, so of course I like hanging out with him," Irwin said.

Fig. 11.7. Portrait section human interest features often spotlight students for their achievements and special interests. *Pilot,* Redondo Union High School, Redondo Beach, Calif.

as candids. Graphics can be used to enhance the design and to carry bits of editorial content and even the theme throughout the section.

THE SPECIAL SECTION AND SPECIAL CONTENT

Some stories don't seem to fit into any section, and some, including those once-in-a-lifetime ones, are just so important that they deserve a special section of their own. The school celebrated its centennial, the principal of 25 years retired, a graduate was elected the state's governor, a hurricane closed school for a week and damaged the building or the girls' basketball team won the state championship. These are the kind of "big" stories that likely don't happen each year. When they do occur, an editor needs to decide where to place them in the book (Fig. 11.8).

A traditional section can be expanded to accommodate the special story, or a new, usually smaller section can be created. The new section, since it is unexpected and not found in last year's book, will get more attention and will be considered by many to be important. Its placement within the book is another consideration. Placed near the opening, its importance is stressed. However, a story on a major event that occurs without much advance warning – hurricane or tornado destruction – will have to be placed, depending upon the publishing deadline, wherever it will fit since much of the book may have already been completed.

Some special sections are published every year. Reporting local, state, national and international news and sports and entertainment highlights as a series of stories gathered into one section is a popular option. Some preprinted inserts of this kind are available from yearbook publishers. Often, this section takes on a newsmagazine look, with art and photos accompanying the stories. Nonlocal photos can be purchased from photo service bureaus such as Worldwide Photos of the Associated Press in New York City. A local newspaper may allow the yearbook staff to print some of its pictures; credit should be given to outside photo sources in the form of a credit line next to each photo. As much as possible, these stories should be localized with student and community tie-ins.

Although yearbooks rarely publish long, in-depth reports, some books break with this tradition. In addition to their traditional coverage, they focus on one topic, often a teen or community concern, and report it on several consecutive spreads. Usually with more text than photos or graphics, these multisourced stories are often

placed in the student life section. If they extend beyond three or so spreads, they could be a distinct section. For example, racial, ethnic or religious prejudice or dating and sexuality could be the subject.

Multispread stories are not restricted to coverage of controversial or sensitive topics. Lighter topics – teen fashion trends, cultural festivals, homecomings – can be developed into longer stories that extend for two, three or more spreads. Occasionally extending a story beyond the norm (one spread) creates an unexpected and usually pleasing surprise for the reader.

Yearbooks can also showcase student creative writing and reproduce student artwork. A section with poems, essays, short stories and other literary forms and reproductions of paintings, drawings and other fine art can add the visual spark to the text. The result is a literary magazine within the context of the yearbook.

A humor section and an occasional humorous story in other sections are also options. A humor story requires special editing to remove any libel or offensive content. Light, human interest topics are best suited for humorous treatment. Some are the best Halloween ghost stories, April Fools' Day jokes, embarrassing things that happened on dates and the best student excuses to teachers for late assignments. Instead of humor presented in prose form, a comic strip could be created just for the yearbook and run as a mini comic book.

Student and faculty deaths can also be covered in the yearbook. The preferred form is the brief, newspaper-style obituary. The obituary should give the basic facts – birth and death dates, full name, survivors, major life achievements – and can also

Fig. 11.8. Major unexpected events that happened during the school year need to find a place in the yearbook. Editors need a flexible page-plan to allow for these occurrences. *Aerie*, Oak Hall School, Gainesville, Fla.

Feature Story Ideas for the Yearbook

- Popular destinations for spring break
- College visits
- Names students give their cars
- Sports heroes
- Unusual study places
- Preparing for SAT/ACT tests
- Buying a prom dress
- Favorite internet websites
- First dates, first kiss
- Extracurricular activities of your teachers when they were in high school
- How many Jessicas, how many Michaels? How many students in your school share the same first (or last) name?
- One book students would bring with them to a deserted island
- Favorite music to study by
- Caffeine addicts
- A day in the life of a straight "A" student
- Athletes on the sidelines due to injuries
- In 10 years, what job will you have?
- Banned book week
- Diversity of languages spoken by students
- Home schooling
- Buying your first car
- Students as community volunteers
- The body-obsessed teen
- Legal rights of 18-year-old students
- Violence in America – students' views
- What "Sesame Street" taught seniors
- Catalog and internet shopping for clothes
- Favorite electronics
- Time crunches: study, work, recreation
- Backpacking, hiking getaways
- Discovering your family tree
- Olympic dreams of your school's athletes
- Local bands, local music scene
- Classes then and now, what was taught at your school 50 years ago compared with what is taught today

include comments from those closest to the deceased, such as friends, teachers and parents. The cause of death is desirable but not required. A photo should accompany the text. An obituary in this form is appropriate and dignifies the person's life and death. It is preferred to a tribute; a tribute could accompany the obituary as a separate story. The appropriate place to put an obituary is at the close of the portrait section.

Another option for marking the death of a student or faculty member is to print his or her name and dates of birth and death under a heading "Died This Year." This would be printed following the portraits for the relevant class or the faculty section, adjacent to the list of those not pictured. A yearbook staff should adopt a policy for reporting deaths so when one happens it is easier to respond to student, faculty and parent requests.

FACT GATHERING AND REPORTING

To effectively capture and summarize an event in pictures and words requires advance planning by a team of yearbook journalists, including editors, reporters, photographers and artists. Working at times together and other times independently, each of these students contributes visual and verbal pieces for what will eventually become a complete story.

At the beginning of the school year, the editor plans a ladder diagram, a page-by-page delineation of the book's contents. Some pages may be set aside for unanticipated stories or "breaking news." The creation of the ladder is the first step in reporting the year's stories. Almost every story gets a name, one or a few words to identify the page's or spread's contents.

After the ladder is completed, individual story assignments are made by the editor. With a team approach, the editor discusses the assignment and the possible photo, text, art and graphics for the story with the adviser and with the reporter, photographer and layout designer who will work on the story. This prereporting stage suggests coverage angles for the reporter and photographer to pursue. Some flexibility should be allowed, for the reporter and photographer may find other newsworthy angles equally or more important during the fact-gathering and photo-shooting stages of the story development. The editor and adviser can also suggest specific interview sources and other resources, which may be especially important for inexperienced reporters and photographers.

As the story is developed by the reporter and photographer, a layout designer and artist can do preliminary design work for the story spread. Usually, the design coordinates with other stories within the same section of the book. Completed graphics and other art, and the final layout or complete pagination of the spread's contents, is not done until all the visual and word page elements are completed, including the final editing. This two-stage layout design process allows for some possible changes in content between the time the story is assigned and when it is fully completed.

The team approach is collapsible if the staff is small or organized in a different way with one person completely responsible for the reporting, writing, photography, graphics, layout design and pagination. In that case, a team may still be formed with the addition of the editor and the adviser as consultants and, in the case of the editor, the person who checks the story before it is published.

Ideally, the story is developed in advance of the event, is reported and photographed as the event occurs and is finished within a week or so after the event. This allows for easy fact checking, identifying persons in photos and soliciting comments from those involved in the event while it is still fresh in their minds. Reporting done long after an event will likely suffer from lack of specific and colorful commentary and possibly no candid photos.

Reporters can conduct interviews in person, over the telephone or through computer email. Questions should be prepared in advance, but there should be some flexibility to pursue unexpected angles that arise during the interview or for spontaneous follow-up questions.

Background information and other facts previously published can be gotten from the school's newspaper; previous yearbooks; statistics available in the school's athletic, activities and administrative offices; and the school's library. A keyword search on the internet may also yield some useful information. For nonschool stories, the fact gathering may expand to community resource centers. For example, for a student life story on teen volunteer work in the community, potential sources for interviews and records are local hospitals, churches, senior citizen centers, hospices, the United Way and various charities.

The photographer should plan how the story will be told in pictures before the event or photo shoot takes place. The reporter needs to convey to the photographer what kind of pictures are desired, including specific content, sizes (verticals and horizontals) and angles (close-up to long distance or wide angle). Who is involved in the event and what is occurring should be fully understood in advance so the most relevant action and persons are shot.

For most photo stories, a range of close-up to long distance shots and vertical and horizontal shapes should be taken. The long distance shot sets the stage and provides an overview of the scene; a medium shot focuses on the action and identifies those involved; a close-up shows the emotional impact on one or more participants. Then the reporter and layout designer will have a good variety of pictures to consider as they build the layout during the editing and pagination stages. Being able to select from this variety will likely create a photo-word story with more visual impact than one with more limited photo images, such as all horizontal close-ups.

Photographers are also helped by seeing a preliminary layout for the story so they have some idea as to how their photos will be used.

A staff artist or visual reporter may join the story team at either the prereporting stage or as the story is edited and the layout is being drawn. The story may be enhanced with the addition of an information graphic – a chart, graph, diagram, map or fact box – which is another way to report the story. These are called "information graphics" or, abbreviated, "infographics" or "infographs." In some ways, they are like other special effects, and they should be used infrequently.

Since the yearbook is more permanent than a newspaper or magazine, and is published only once a year, fact checking, verification of spelling, especially of names, and editing for libel or unsuitable content is vital at all stages, including the final proof from the printer.

WRITING THE WORD STORY

Once the facts and comments have been gathered and the reporter has the photos that were taken of the events, the word story can be written. Seeing the photos that will be used for the story will help the reporter write a story that links directly at

- Extreme sports
- Origins of your school's name
- Most often broken school rules
- Training as a distance runner
- Shoe, footwear trends
- Most influential person in students' lives
- Defining popularity
- On the job, students at work
- What do students fear?
- Teacher of the year: Who would you name?
- The book that changed your life
- Five characteristics of highly successful students
- Dinner from a vending machine
- Dating dos and don'ts
- What you can do (and can't) during the short break between classes

least one or more of the photos with the word story. For example, on the same spread, a photo of the winning goal in the state soccer championship match can be linked directly to the main word story that leads with a replay of the scoring of that goal. Not all photos on the spread have to be directly linked or referred to in the text; stand-alone photos with fully developed captions are acceptable.

Upon examination of the information and opinions recorded during the fact-gathering stage, the reporter decides if a news or a feature method of story and lead development will be used. Sometimes this decision is made by an editor who wants a particular style used for all stories within a section.

If a news approach is taken, the writer evaluates the information and ranks it from most important to least important – in other words, the inverted pyramid form of story development is used. Opinions, both direct and indirect quotes, are used to qualify facts. Often, the news summary lead is selected to begin the story, with some or all of the *what, who, where, when, why* and *how* answered in the opening paragraph. The writer may also choose a news-feature lead for a news-style story. The news-feature lead often focuses on the most unusual of the *what, who, where, when, why* and *how* in the first sentence and opening paragraph.

The *when* element, the timeliness aspect, is not as significant in a yearbook as it is in a news story in a newspaper. There rarely are advance stories in a yearbook, and it is assumed by the readers that the events covered in the book happened this year (although beginning a story with "This year . . ." is considered a weak and avoidable opener).

The *what, who, why* and *how* answers usually make much better lead paragraphs and opening sentences. They are more consequential and have more human interest value.

All opinion in the story is attributed to someone. Direct quotes are included only if the comments or facts are unusual or colorful. Indirect quotes (paraphrases with no quotation marks) are used frequently. The writer's opinions are left out of the story. For example, if a reporter wrote, "The homecoming game win was the biggest victory of the season," it would be bad journalism because the adjective "biggest" expresses an opinion. To use "biggest" properly in the sentence, it has to be attributed to someone other than the reporter. As a direct quote with attribution, it would be better to write: "The homecoming game win was the biggest

victory of the season," said football captain Jeff Stone. Or as an indirect quote: According to football captain Jeff Stone, the homecoming win was the biggest victory of the season.

Even if the inverted pyramid style is used, which allows for deleting the final paragraph if space is tight, the last paragraph in a yearbook story deserves as much creative attention as the opening one. If the yearbook story needs to be shorter, it should be trimmed in other ways or places.

If a feature story or infographic is the style used, the reporter examines the information and opinions for human interest appeal (Fig. 11.9). What potential emotional impact could any of the facts or opinions have on readers? The facts or opinions with the strongest potential to raise the curiosity of the reader and elicit a response – happiness, sadness, humor, shock, amazement, disbelief – could become the story's lead. A clever play on words; allusions to commonly known literary or artistic works, films or songs; and other devices used in storytelling can be effective openings for a yearbook feature. Storytelling is somewhat the opposite of the inverted pyramid; the highest point of interest – the climax – is not in the opening or, usually, the immediate follow-up paragraph of the storytelling form of writing.

Space limitations in a yearbook and the form itself usually mean the feature story will be narrowly focused on one or a few facts and opinions. Feature writers sometimes report only what some have called a "slice of life," a limited but interesting or newsworthy piece of someone's life. The scope of the yearbook feature is smaller than that of the yearbook news story or news-feature. For example, a feature story about a teacher who is retiring could focus on her recollections of her favorite or most troublesome former students. A feature for a homecoming story could be a behind-the-scenes look at the building of one parade float.

Leads for features are often more creative or unusual than ones for yearbook news stories, which often use a summary opener. All the lead variations found in Chapters 3–7 in this book will be useful for yearbook feature writers.

Since the yearbook largely focuses on people and their activities, the feature form is especially suitable for personality sketches and descriptions of the sights, sounds, smells and human emotional responses of an event. Also popular is the "you are there" story, with the writer putting the reader into the situation through the mind and body of one actual participant. A story

Fig. 11.9. Feature writing, with a human interest angle, is the most common form for text stories in a yearbook. This word and photo story is about the first day of school for some students. *Decamhian*, Del Campo High School, Fair Oaks, Calif.

about a driver's education, behind-the-wheel class, focusing on one student driver, is an example of this form.

Following the opening paragraph, the feature is developed with more facts and often many direct and indirect quotes from the person profiled or from a small number of persons whose opinions add color and interest to the story.

The closing paragraph deserves almost as much creative attention as the opening. The reporter may save an especially interesting quote, fact or statistic to use here, one that may help sum up the main focus of the story or refer back to the lead.

Students like to see themselves and their friends in photos, and they like to read what their friends and others had to say about an event or issue reported in the yearbook. To satisfy this natural reader curiosity and to report a story with more depth and accuracy, the reporter should include student sources and quote students directly and indirectly in most feature, news and news-feature stories. Readers are curious about what others think and have done. If they see names in a story, they are more likely to read it.

In addition to citing names and including comments from those interviewed, the story will likely be more interesting if as many specific details are included as possible. Include exact statistics and facts, rather than generalities and vague estimates. For example, a homecoming football game story could open: "A chilly north wind and a kick-off temperature of 45 degrees didn't stop nearly 2,000

Central fans from giving their undefeated Cardinals a standing ovation as they entered Brown Stadium for the 40th homecoming football game." The same lead, without most of the details, could read: "A sell-out crowd gave the football team a standing ovation as it entered the stadium for the home-coming game." The former has more color, has more details and would likely be more interesting to readers; the latter is acceptable, but not as good as the former.

To achieve uniformity, consistency and professionalism, yearbook reporters use accepted journalism style when they write. The Associated Press publishes a style manual that is commonly used and is applicable for most high school writing. This textbook has a style chapter that will be useful for yearbook writers too (Chap. 12).

Some of the common style concerns for yearbook reporters include dates and numbers, abbreviations for school group names, courtesy titles and class identifiers for students and the capitalization of courses, classes and events. If the Associated Press style manual is adopted, a supplement could be created to address some school-only needs.

Paragraphs, especially the lead or opening, are short, often one to three sentences long. However, this recommendation should not create an obvious pattern. A variety of paragraph lengths is usually desirable. Sentence lengths should also vary; the reader should not be aware of any patterns unless, for example, a staccato is created for an intentional effect. Short paragraphs and simple sentences encourage readership.

Word choices are important if writers want readers to start and finish their writing. Reporters should select specific nouns and lively, active verbs when writing the story. Generally, for news, news-feature and feature stories, the use of adverbs and adjectives is usually restricted to the indirect and direct quotes from sources cited in the copy. However, other writing forms – storytelling or first-person accounts, for example – are less restrictive.

Reporters should verify the spelling of all names. The permanency of the yearbook and its status as likely the only published history of one year in the life of a school and its students and staff make the need to be accurate one of the most important concerns for all reporters and editors. Spell checkers in software programs should not be relied upon as the only verification for accurate spelling. Unless the spell checker has a customized dictionary, it can't verify most proper nouns. Checking the accuracy of dates, statistics and any unusual information is also important. A yearbook is a record, and all facts and figures should be correct. A reporter can double-check notes as the first draft is written. An editor should also verify important statistics and facts during the editing process.

Careful editing will also include an evaluation of the flow or development of the story. The transitions from paragraph to paragraph should be smooth. With the exception of the question and answer, or Q&A, format story form, the reporter's questions should not be included as transitions. The interviewees' responses and simple transitional words such as "according to" and simple attributions such as "said" are preferred; writers should avoid the awkward and space-wasting use of phrases such as, "When asked what she thought of . . ."

OTHER WAYS TO WRITE THE STORY

Text copy, whether it is the only story on the spread or is made up of two or more stories, including sidebars, can take forms other than the prose form of news, news-features and features. Deviations from these traditional and popular journalistic forms may be desirable occasionally to break what could be a monotonous flow or to fit information that could be better reported in another form (Fig. 11.10).

The short story or storytelling form may be appropriate for certain topics. Similar to children's stories or short stories read in literature classes, the opening of this journalistic writing form includes some set-the-scene description, the presentation of the principal persons and the introduction of some conflict that needs to be resolved. The body of the story tells the reader how the persons involved in the situation go about resolving the conflict. The story's ending is the solution to the conflict and how it affects the persons involved. With this form, the suspense builds to a high point of interest near the end of the story.

Many think the storytelling form of writing is how persons naturally relate incidents to each other. This form could be effective for reporting an especially significant athletic contest or relating a specific science class experiment and its results, among other possibilities.

The question and answer interview format, or Q&A, with a brief lead that introduces the interviewee and summarizes the reason why the person is being interviewed, is another alternate text form. It can be used for long interviews with newsmakers such as the school's principal or a star athlete who holds several school records in a particular sport. The long, full-story Q&A should be used only sparingly so it doesn't lose its uniqueness. The short-form Q&A, made up of (1) one to only a handful of questions and responses from one person or (2) one question and responses from several persons, can be a useful and frequently used sidebar in any section of the book. For example, in the sports section, the short-form Q&A sidebar could be an interview with a team's captain or senior athletes who lettered in the sport. The shorter Q&A can even be used on every spread.

Dialogue or a playlike dramatization could be a suitable way to present a word story on a variety of topics in any section of the book, especially a section on student life. The dialogue could be fictitious for a story about dating, with the story labeled as fiction. Or a real situation, such as a report on the first day of school, could be dramatized with real dialogue and real "stage" directions.

In theme copy and sidebars in any section, the first-person diary or journal story form can be an effective form for many topics. This form can be an appealing contrast to the third-person, objective form of the news, news-feature or feature story. A participant in an event can provide a compelling, personal and often emotional "insider" account that can reveal more than an interview with a reporter.

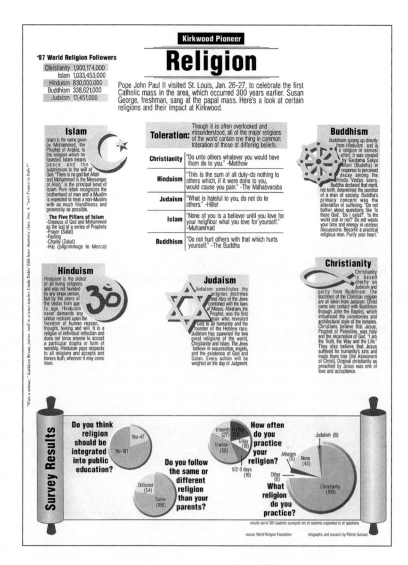

Fig. 11.10. The word story in a yearbook often takes a form other than prose. Here's an example of a large amount of information delivered efficiently to readers through a full-page information graphic. *Pioneer,* Kirkwood High School, Kirkwood, Mo.

Though rare, information presented as a poem, song (complete with music), crossword puzzle, cryptogram, essay or form more commonly associated with other print media can provide a unique and successful surprise element to the yearbook. These forms may not be suitable for news with a serious edge.

Although more commonly found in newspapers, the information graphic is another alternate way to present a story in a stand-alone or supporting way in a yearbook. The information graphic, or infographic, the shortened term, is the incorporation of one or more illustrations, photos, graphics or some other form of art with words and/or figures to report specific, often narrowly focused, information. These elements are tightly organized to form a self-contained message. This process – creating the information graphic – is often called "visual reporting" and is the product of reporters and artists working together.

Information graphics can take many forms. Some are bar graphs, pie charts, timelines, summary boxes, diagrams and lists. Some of these are more appropriate for newspapers than yearbooks. Scoreboards in the sports section are the most common information graphic in yearbooks. In addition to a listing of the results of a season's contests, they can also include small photos, art, brief quotes and a list of record holders for the season. All of these elements are organized into a "box" or self-defined rectangle. The scoreboard serves as a quick reference for the reader.

Another popular information graphic is the list. The results of student surveys, such as most popular movies or television shows of the year, are organized into a list. The list can be graphically enhanced with art and display type to create an attractive page element. Diagrams, such as an architect's blueprint of the school, and timelines, such as one that traces the history of the school for an anniversary book, are also appropriate for the yearbook. Bar graphs and pie charts, without any art, are not recommended for yearbooks since they lack visual interest.

Schools with large populations of students who speak a language in addition to English may want to publish some copy in other languages. This could be especially suitable for stories and events involving a large number of English-as-a-second-language students. For example, coverage of students celebrating Mexican Independence Day could be printed in Spanish and, if space permits, with an accompanying English translation. Publishing an entire yearbook as a split run, each edition of the same volume in a different language, though ambitious, could positively affect sales and the status of the yearbook, especially among communities without the yearbook as a tradition.

As is true with visual special effects, overuse of any nonprose way of writing the word stories of the year can greatly diminish their appeal. An occasional first-person account or Q&A will likely add the variety that readers enjoy.

CHECKLIST FOR THE YEARBOOK REPORTER

- Brainstorm for story development ideas with other staff members.

- To coordinate and exploit all possible visual and verbal elements of all major stories, work as a team with a photographer, page designer and, possibly, an artist.

- Working with a photographer, plan each photo shoot to get a full range of shots, from close-ups to long shots, verticals to horizontals.

- Interview more people for a story than you think you'll need; select the best responses far the word story.

- Tell some aspect of the story with a brief sidebar, an information graphic or an alternate story form. Readers may prefer several short word stories on a spread rather than one long story.

- Choose the best journalistic story form for the content – news, news-feature or feature. Or use the story-telling method of development.

- Write a lead that grabs the readers' attention; develop the story to hold their attention; end the story with some sparkle, something memorable.

- Link the main word story with at least one photo on the spread, preferably the dominant photo (the largest photo).

- Double-check the spellings of all names and proper nouns.

- Review your word story and accompanying photos for positive multiculturalism. Be an inclusive yearbook so all the school's population groups are represented.

EXERCISES

1. Find out the racial, ethnic and, if possible, religious composition of your school. List each group as a separate heading. Now list events and issues important to each group, such as special celebrations. Finally, prepare a list of yearbook stories that report some or all of these events and issues. Some events and issues could be combined into composite stories representing all or several groups.

2. List five events, such as the school's musical, that your yearbook covers every year. Under each, list five new angles to report that don't duplicate reporting done in the most recent yearbook.

3. Develop a five or more point checklist for photographers who will cover a sports event for your yearbook. What should they shoot? Should they shoot the spectators?

4. Select one aspect about teens and driving such as moving violations, arrests for intoxication, insurance rates or motor vehicle deaths and find some statistics about it. How can you use this information in a story in your yearbook?

5. Write a first-person journal account as a student focusing on one of these events: class picture day, any Friday, the opening day of the school year, the day of a final exam or the day when classes were canceled due to bad weather.

Using Journalism Style

When writing a story for your school newspaper, yearbook or magazine, would you write *Nov. 22, Nov. 22nd, November twenty-second* or *November 22? Number 10* or *number ten? Twenty-fifth* or *25th? Marathon County, Marathon county* or *Marathon Co.? Well known* or *well-known? U.S. Army, United States Army, Army of the United States* or *army of the United States? Atlanta, Georgia, Atlanta, Ga.,* or *Atlanta, GA?*

The English language permits so many variations that a stylebook, or manual, is necessary to provide consistency. Otherwise, for example, one story might have *Jan. 13, 2007* and another *January 13, 2007.*

Either AP (Associated Press) or *The New York Times* style is appropriate for student publications, although some adjustments may be made. Students will then, as career preparation, learn style that is practiced in the professional workplace. Many commercial newspapers depart occasionally from AP style to suit local readers' preferences. The style sheet in this chapter offers some variations on AP style suitable for student publications.

Some suggested primary style considerations follow.

NAMES AND IDENTIFICATION

The first time a person is named in a story, his or her complete first and last name along with some identifier should be used.

Faculty members are identified by position or subject taught, whichever is appropriate for the particular story. Titles can also indicate job, rank or profession (for example, coach, principal, superintendent, nurse, counselor, athletic director, English teacher). Short titles precede names: "English teacher Laura Pearson" or "basketball coach James Rogers." Longer titles usually follow: "Mrs. Wendy Smith, chair of the Language Department," or "Marci Rosmarin, School Centered Education committee chairperson."

Students are identified by class, year of graduation or some other method appropriate to the school (senior Sarah Kagan; Ian McFarland, '08; Bryan Dykman, 4).

In some stories students may be identified in other ways. For example, an editor-in-chief of the paper may be identified by that title if it is appropriate to the story. In sports stories players are identified by the positions they play or hold (Colin Allred, linebacker; Captain Morgan White). Do not make up titles by mere description, such as "harpsichordist Becky Lucas." Alumni are identified by year of graduation (Margie Pak, '90). Only one identifier is needed on first reference. Do not overdo identifiers, such as "senior forward and team captain Karen Greening." The other relevant identifiers can be used in subsequent references.

A student publication may choose to make no distinction between name references for adults and students, or it may choose to differentiate. Today, major newspapers differ on the use of courtesy titles for women and men (Mr., Mrs., Miss and Ms.). Some papers use no courtesy titles, some only for women and some to indicate a married couple. These titles are rarely used in sports coverage. If courtesy titles are used for adult women in your publication, request from each adult woman her preference for *Ms., Miss* or *Mrs.* and abide by it. If no preference is sought, use only *Ms.* or *Mrs.* For adult men, use *Mr.* Whether courtesy titles are used is not as important as is a consistent plan for all stories, all year. When courtesy titles are used, they typically appear on second and subsequent references.

The second and every other time the adult is mentioned in the story, use the courtesy title and the last name, or just the last name. For example, the first reference would be "math instructor Jennifer Dusenberry," and the second reference would be "Ms. Dusenberry," or "Dusenberry." If there would be no confusion, the proper name can be alternated with the job title to give more variety. For example, for second and further references, the story could read, "the math instructor said' and then, later, "Ms. Dusenberry said." The job title with the last name may also be used for the second and further references.

A choice exists for the second and any further times the person is mentioned in the story. Some student publications use only the last name in these succeeding references; others just the first name. The former follows most professional style manuals. Either is acceptable, as long as a consistent plan is adopted and followed for every story, all year. If a story mentions many persons, it may be less confusing to follow a policy of using only last names in second and further references.

Accuracy of name spellings should be a priority. Remember, what you think is spelled "John" could be spelled "Jon," "Jonn" or "Jean." If the adult uses only a first initial and a full middle name, then respect that preference. Do not use only a first name initial and a last name. Husbands and wives should be referred to by name (Mr. and Mrs. Jeff Mays or Jeff and Shonda Mays, *not* Mr. Jeff Mays and wife).

CAPITALIZATION

Capitalization rules are pretty standard among publication style guides.

Always capitalize the following:

- All proper nouns and proper adjectives (Joyce, Shakespearean, Antarctica)

- All titles when they precede names (Principal Vickie Richie, Queen Elizabeth)

- First and all words in titles of books, periodicals, speeches, plays, songs, except for articles, prepositions and conjunctions (*A Tale of Two Cities, Sports Illustrated*, "Free Speech, Its Problems," *Friends*, "Rudolph, the Red-Nosed Reindeer," *Man against the Sea*)

- Holidays and special school events (Thanksgiving, New Year's Day, Homecoming, Senior Day, Spring Swing)

- Sections of the country (the West, the Atlantic States)

- Names of nationalities and races (Indian, German, Ethiopian – also see later discussion for identification of minority groups)

- College degrees when abbreviated (B.A., M.A., Ph.D.)

- Names of clubs, buildings, departments, schools, colleges (Spanish Club, Beardsley Gymnasium [or Gym], English Department, Ferris High School, Cornell College)

- Names of streets (Fifth Street, Oak Avenue, Park Boulevard)

- Geographical names (Hudson River, Lake Tanganyika, Rock of Gibraltar)

- Names of classes only when the term *class* is used and the reference is to a particular class in the school (Freshman Class, Sophomore Class, *but* freshmen, seniors)

- Names of specific courses (American Literature I, *but* the field of American literature; History II, *but* the study of history; Journalism III, *but* journalism as a career)

- Names of languages (English, French, Korean)

- Names of athletic teams (Yellowjackets, Bullfrogs, Green Wave, Blue Blazers)

- Words or abbreviations, such as *No., Fig.* and *Chapter*, when followed by a number, title or name (No. 10, Fig. 4, Chapter 6)

- All other words traditionally capitalized, such as noun references to the deity of all monotheistic religions (God, the Father, Allah), political parties and the like. Consult an English handbook when in doubt.

Do not capitalize the following:

- Titles when they follow names (Seth Levy, assistant principal; Ryan McGlothlin, director of athletics; Daniel Villarreal, chairperson of the Social Studies Department; Angela Yeung, editor-in-chief of the *Evanstonian*)

- Names of school subjects, unless they are languages or specific courses (He is taking Spanish, American History I, Physics M. and Art IV. He hopes to study chemistry and journalism next year.)

- Directions, unless they mean a geographic place (He lives on the south side of the street. She moved to the South.)

- Parts of time (a.m., p.m., o'clock)

- Seasons of the year, except when personified (fall, winter, but Old Man Winter)

- Names of rooms, offices, buildings, unless they have an official proper name (room 159, the journalism room, the guidance office, the fieldhouse, the library, but Ragland Reading Room, Beardsley Gym)

- The subject of a debate, except the first word (Resolved: That free enterprise is basic to this American way of life)

- Committees (entertainment committee, refreshment committee)

- Descriptive or occupational words used as "titles" (pitcher Roy Halladay, actress Halle Berry)

- Title modifiers such as *former* and *the late* (the late John Lennon, former President Clinton)

- College degrees when spelled out (bachelor of arts, master of science, doctor of philosophy)

ABBREVIATIONS

Normally most publications avoid all but standard, commonly understood abbreviations of accepted titles, but here are the usual "rules."

Abbreviate

- Names that are well-known as abbreviations (YMCA, PTA, AIDS, UN, NASA, NATO). Note: Write such abbreviations without periods and without spaces.

- Titles when they precede last names (Dr. Garcia; Rev. Kelly, *but* the Reverend Lynn Kelly; Mr. and Mrs.; all military titles, such as Pvt. and Lt.)

- Names of states when they follow the name of a city, except very short or one-syllable names, such as *Iowa, Ohio, Utah, Maine* (Madison, Wis.; Buffalo, N.Y.; *but* Des Moines, Iowa)

- Names of months when followed by a date, except very short months, such as April, May, June, July (Nov. 19, 2009; Oct. 7, 2008; but June 14, 2007)

- College degree (B.A., M.A., Ph.D., Ed.D., D.D., LL.D.)

Do not abbreviate

- Names of streets (Eastwood Avenue, Central Street)

- Titles following a name (Susan Ginsburg, professor of history)

- Days of the week

- States when used without a city

- *Percent* (the symbol % should be used only in tabular material or in headlines when used with a figure)

- Positions when not used as titles (secretary, treasurer, president)

- *Department* (English Department)

- *Christmas* (not Xmas)

- The year, except when used to identify students or alumni (2007; Libby Nelson, '04)

- *United States* as a noun; it can be abbreviated as an adjective (in the United States, but U.S. history)

NUMBERS

Spell out all approximate numbers and numerals up to and including nine except for dates, scores, addresses, ages, time and money (about 2,000 are expected; Sept. 4, 2008; Ames, 14, West Des Moines, 7; 7 Wilson Avenue; 5 cents; 3 years old).

Do not begin a sentence with a number in figures; if a sentence must start with a number, it should be spelled out. (Twenty-five students will . . . ; or About 25 students will . . . ; *not* 25 students will . . .)

Spell out ordinal numbers (sixty-sixth).

Do not use *d*, *rd*, *st* or *th* in writing dates (May 29, 2006; *not* May 29th, 2006).

When two numbers are used together, avoid confusion by spelling out the first, whether the number is above or below *nine* (fourteen 4-year-old children, *not* 14 4-year-old children).

In a list containing numbers below and above *nine*, use figures for all. (Those on the committee include 5 from GAA, 11 from the Student Council, 3 from the French Club and 14 from the hall monitors.)

For sums of money less than one dollar, use figures and the word *cents* (10 cents, *not* $.10; 5 cents, *not* 5 cts.).

Do not use ciphers when giving the exact hour or an even number of dollars (4 p.m., *not* 4:00 p.m.; $5, *not* $5.00).

Do not use the date when an event occurs within or close to the week of publication (Friday, next Friday, last Tuesday, tonight, yesterday).

For numbers of four or more digits, except serial numbers – house, telephone, pages, years – use a comma (4,945; 469,958,000).

PUNCTUATION

No style manual includes all the rules for the use of all punctuation marks. Any good English text will do that. A style manual should, however, include any deviations from standard English style. A few special uses are common in newswriting, and they should be included in a style sheet.

The Comma and the Semicolon

Do not include a comma before the *and* in a simple series. (Those on the committee are Susan Clarke, Paul Block and Dale Jackson.)

Do not use a comma between a man's name and *Jr.* or *Sr.* (Fred Black Jr.).

Use commas and semicolons in lists of names and identifying terms. (The committee consists of Gerry Brown, chairman; Shawn Jourdain, vice-chairman; and Cam Carhart, secretary-treasurer.)

Use a semicolon between the main items in a series when commas occur within the series.

Use a comma in a compound sentence before the conjunction. (The Key Club led the school in the aluminum can drive, and the Chess Club nearly tied.) When the coordinating conjunction is not present, use a semi-

colon. (The Key Club won; the Chess Club came in second.) When the coordinating conjunction is present, use a semicolon if there is extensive punctuation in one or more of the clauses. (The Key Club, with 27 juniors and seniors, led the school in the aluminum recycling drive; but the Chess Club, with five sophomore members, nearly tied.) If the clauses are both short, either the comma or the conjunction might be dropped. (The Key Club won and the Chess Club lost. The Key Club won, the Chess Club lost.)

The Colon

Omit the colon in a list following a *be* verb, such as *are* or *were*. (Those elected were Stefanie Boyar, Suresh Vasan and Bryan Parker.)

Use the colon to cite time in a track event (3:05.2).

Quotation Marks

A period or a comma at the end of a quotation is always put inside the quotes. (We have just read "The Lottery.")

A question mark or an exclamation mark goes inside the quotation marks only if it belongs to the material quoted. (Have you read "The Lottery"? She asked, "Have you finished the story?")

A semicolon or a colon always goes outside the quotation marks. (Incomplete homework assignments may be a symptom of academic "burn-out"; it is a sign of more serious problems.)

Use quotation marks around the titles of one-act plays, computer games, TV shows, speeches, poems, short stories, songs and articles within publications ("The Telephone Only Rings Twice," "Friends," "Birches," "The Outcasts of Poker Flat," "Tenderly"). In addition, Associated Press style uses quotation marks for book, play, works of art and album titles; however, italics are an acceptable style chosen by some publications for these composition titles. Some publications choose to follow a literary rule to italicize *wholes* but to put *parts* in quotation marks. By this rule, album titles would be in italics and the song titles would be in quotes. Establish a style and be consistent.

Do not put quotation marks around familiar nicknames; ordinarily only use nicknames in sports stories (Babe Ruth, Magic Johnson). But unfamiliar nicknames should be quoted (Don "Duffer" Stevens).

Do not put quotation marks around slang expressions (to do so implies an apology for using them).

Do not put quotation marks around names of animals or characters in books or plays.

The Apostrophe

Ordinarily form the possessive of all singular nouns by adding the apostrophe and *s* (the boy's book, the fox's den). If the singular noun ends in *s*, add the apostrophe and *s* (hostess's address) unless the next word begins with *s* (hostess' seat). Because stylebooks vary, it is correct to have only the apostrophe after a singular proper noun ending in *s* or to add an apostrophe and *s* (Charles' hat, Charles's hat). Consistency requires you choose a stylebook and follow it every time.

Form the possessive of a plural word ending in *s* by adding only an apostrophe (the boys' books, the girls' uniforms).

Form the possessive of a plural word not ending in *s* by adding an apostrophe and *s* (men's league, children's party).

Use an apostrophe in abbreviations of classes or years (Amanda Allison, '06; Class of '07).

Use an apostrophe followed by *s* to form the plurals of single letters and numbers and of symbols (A's and B's, size 7's, How many *c*'s in recommend?). The apostrophe is not, however, used for plurals of numbers or multiletter combinations (1990s, ABCs). Stylebooks vary on the use of the apostrophe for plurals when there is internal punctuation in a multiletter combination. Note: The plural *s* added to italic letters (or titles) is in roman type (three *Newsweek*s).

Use the apostrophe, not opening single quotation marks, to indicate omission of letters (wash 'n' wear, *not* wash 'n wear or wash n' wear).

Omit the apostrophe in names of organizations when the possessive case is implied and in certain geographic designations (Citizens League, Actors Equity Association, Pikes Peak).

The Hyphen

Use a hyphen in compound numbers and fractions (forty-eight, three-fourths). Remember a hyphen joins, so no spaces are used before and after a hyphen.

Use a hyphen with compound adjectives of two or more words (note-taking skills, grade-point average, front page story, out-of-state student, all-state diver). Note: A hyphen is not used after an adverb ending in *ly* (tightly laced shoes). The hyphen is frequently omitted when two words are joined to function as a noun; see a

dictionary for current spellings, since form changes (makeup *not* make-up; layout *not* lay-out).

Use a hyphen when combining numbers and measurements to make an adjective (Jones is a 210-pound tackle; Johnson is the 6-foot-8-inch center).

The dash is used to separate or create a longer pause when a comma will not suffice. A dash is visually longer than a hyphen. A space is used before and after the dash.

ITALICS

Italicize

- Some publications use italics for names of books, long musical selections, plays and record albums and may use italics for names of newspapers, magazines and boats or ships. However, widely used AP style puts the names of books, long musical selections, plays and record albums in quotes and capitalizes the names of newspapers, magazines and boats and ships without any quotes or italics.

- Words from other languages that have not become an accepted part of English (The meal was prepared *à la française*; Geoffrey's goal is to graduate *cum laude*.)

- A letter of the alphabet or a word used specifically as a word (The word *letter* has two *t*'s in it.)

- An editor's note to a story

- A word to be emphasized (He repeated he had *never* been a candidate.)

Use italics for emphasis with caution. A reader ignores overused italics.

SPELLING

Since a number of words have several correct spellings, a style manual should include the preferred forms of those appearing most frequently in news stories. For other words, consult a standard dictionary to determine the preferred form, which should be used consistently.

Following is a list of words that frequently appear in school news stories and are often misspelled. Make your own additional list.

EXAMPLE 12.1

absence
a cappella
adviser
advisory
algebra
all right
alumna (f.s.)
alumnae (f.pl.)
alumni (m.pl.)
alumnus (m.s.)
apparatus
arithmetic
assembly
association
athlete
athletics
attendance
audience
auditorium

backfield
baseball
baseman
basketball
believe
biology
bookkeeping
business

cafeteria
calendar
captain
chaperon
cheerleader
chemistry
choir
chorus
classmate
college
commencement
commercial
committee
council (student)
counselor
criticism

curriculum
custodian

defense
drama

eligible
embarrass
emphasize
English
existence
experiment

faculty
familiar
February
field house
finally
football
foreign
foreword (in a book)
forty (but fourth)
forward (on a team)
fullback

geometry
German
government
graduation
grammar
guard
guidance
gymnasium

halfback
handball
heavyweight
high jump
hockey
homecoming
homeroom

incidentally
initiation
intramural
its (possessive), it's (it is)

laboratory
league
lettermen
library
lightweight
lineup (noun), line up (verb)
literature
long jump
lose vs. loose
lunchroom

mathematics
misspell

necessary (but unnecessary)

occasion
occurred
occurrence
offense
opponent

permissible
phase
physics
planning
poll vs. pole
practice
preparation
principal (of your school)
privilege
professor
psychology

quarterback
quartet
questionnaire

receive
recommend
referee
registrar
rhythm
role vs. roll
runner-up

schedule
secretary
semester
semifinal
senior
separate
sergeant
shining
shortstop
shot put (but shot-putter)
similar
society
sophomore
Spanish
speech
sponsor
stopping
studying
superintendent

tackle
teenager
textbook
theater
their vs. there
thorough
tomorrow
tonight
touchdown
treasurer
tryout (noun), try out (verb)
typewriting

unanimous
university
until
upperclassman

volleyball

weather
Wednesday
weekend
weird
whether vs. weather
writing
written

SCREENING SEXIST EXPRESSIONS

What we say and write about men and women often reveals attitudes toward sex roles that many persons find objectionable. Language does affect values, especially when we are speaking of persons who belong to groups other than our own. In general, our goal should be to avoid the use of words and phrases that directly or indirectly suggest limited opportunity for members of any group, whether by sex, race, ethnic description or religion.

Gender-free terms should replace sex-designating terms. Change

- *Mailman* to *mail carrier*

- *Fireman* to *fire fighter*

- *Policeman* or *policewoman* to *law enforcement official* or *police officer*

- *Newsman* or *newswoman* to *reporter*

- *Actor* and *actress* to (only) *actor*

- *Chairman* to *chairperson* or *chair*

Job designations by gender should not be mentioned unless pertinent to the story. They imply that the occupations are inappropriate for the individual holding them. Change

- *Male nurse* to *nurse*

- *Woman* or *lady lawyer* to *lawyer*

MARITAL STATUS, APPEARANCE, SEXUAL STEREOTYPES

The appearance of a woman (or man) should not be described unless the description is essential for the story. A girl-watching or male-watching tone – using words or phrases such as *buxom*, *blonde* or *big hunk* – should be avoided. Clichés and jokes at women's or men's expense such as *woman driver* or *dumb jock* should also be deleted.

PROBLEM WORDS

For greater accuracy and less damage to sensitive value systems, find substitutes for problem words. Change

- *A member of the Christian right* to *religious conservative* or *religious activist*

- *Forefathers* to *ancestors*, *forerunners* or *forebears*

- *Man-hours* to *work hours*, *staff time*

- *Common man* to *the average person*, *the ordinary citizen*

- *Lady* (unless that connotation is appropriate) to *woman*

- *Man-made* to *manufactured*, *produced*

- *Coed* (as a noun) to *student* (logically, the term *coed* refers to any student at a coeducational college or university)

- A reference to a man or a woman to *feminist* only if he or she identifies himself or herself as one

- *Muslim terrorist* to a more specific political group if the person(s) is a member of a group that is involved in terrorism

RACE OR ETHNIC LANGUAGE

Identifying someone as a member of a minority group is done only when it is essential to the reader's full understanding of the story. The decision to use racial, ethnic, religious or sexual orientation labels should be made only after careful consideration for their news value.

Minority groups of all kinds deserve to be identified, if there is a need to use such identification in the story, with labels acceptable to them and conforming to what is advocated by official groups representative of these minorities.

Racial, ethnic, religious or sexual orientation stereotypes, like male–female ones, should be eliminated from all writing, art and photography. Some of this bias is subtle and unintentional. For example, if you are doing a story about unmarried teenage mothers, it would be wrong to cover, in words and photos, only those of certain racial or ethnic groups, since being unmarried and pregnant crosses all racial, ethnic and economic boundaries.

A good reporter needs to understand that some words are used within the community, but once someone outside the community uses the words, they carry derogatory meanings. Other words such as *barrio* started as neutral descriptions but over time have suggested derogatory stereotypes and should be avoided.

Labels popular and acceptable in the past may not be acceptable today. For example, the term *Negro* was acceptable for media use in the 1960s, but today *black* is used, and *African-American is* now preferred by many. If a reporter has doubts, a comprehensive, up-to-date style manual should be consulted. When race or ethnicity is relevant, a good reporter may ask what label is preferable.

Acceptable labels for some of the major minority groups in the United States include

- *Asian-American*

- *African-American or black*

- *Native American or American Indian*

- *Hispanic, Latino/Latina, Chicano/Chicana* – although any one of these is considered derogatory in certain regions of the United States

- *Native Alaskan*

- *Pacific Islander*

- *Gay* (male), *lesbian* (female), *homosexual*

Some of the subgroups within a large minority group prefer to be identified by more specific labels such as *Chinese-American, Cuban-American* or an exact

Indian tribal name (which may not be the commonly accepted tribal name imposed by traders and settlers). The best advice is to be current and specific.

Some minority groups have media membership organizations, such as the following. Students and teachers can write to these organizations to request information on programs, learning materials or scholarships.

Asian American Journalists Association, 1182 Market Street, Suite 320, San Francisco, CA 94102. Tel: (415) 346-2051; email: national@aaja.org.

National Association of Black Journalists, 8701-A Adelphi Road, Adelphi, MD 20783-1716. Tel. (301) 445-7100; email: nabj@nabj.org.

National Association of Hispanic Journalists, 1000 National Press Building, 529 14 Street NW, Washington, DC 20045-2001. Tel: (202) 662-7145; email: nahj@nahj.org.

National Lesbian and Gay Journalists Association, 1420 K Street NW, Suite 910, Washington, DC 20005. Tel: (202) 588-9888; email: nlgja@aol.com.

Native American Journalists Association, 555 Dakota Street, Al Neuharth Media Center, Vermillion, SD 57069. Tel: (605) 677-5282; email: info@naja.com.

The Center for Integration and Improvement website at ciij.org can be helpful in dealing with racial and ethnic language.

Editing Copy: Coaching Writers

Publication writing, at its best, is a story torn and pasted inside a locker door, a dog-eared page of a yearbook, the topic of a cafeteria conversation over pizza and corn.

Writing is putting words on a page that people use, quote and remember. A writer and a copy editor working together can make that happen. To produce stories that readers want and need to read, the copy editor must discuss the story with the writer at many stages of the writing process. The copy editor works with the writer to improve writing. A good copy editor may not be the best writer on a staff but is someone who understands what makes good writing.

Copyediting used to mean capitalizing "Dallas Cowboys" and taking a comma out of "lions, tigers, and bears." Oh my, how copyediting has changed. Copyediting now encompasses a practice called *coaching writing*, which means discussing the story during the writing process. Correcting spelling, grammar and style errors is still a very important part of copyediting. Today a copy editor also coaches writers by asking the right questions and discussing the content, structure and flow of a story.

THE COACHING WRITING PROCESS

Understanding the coaching part of copyediting will give the copy editor something to say to a first-year staff writer or an experienced sports editor asking for writing advice. Discussion can happen just outside the lockers during a passing period. The copy editor can ask the questions in a five-minute phone conversation. And the intense writing discussions can come in a secluded area of the hallway outside the staff room during class. Taking copyediting beyond proofing for spelling and punctuation errors is critical to improving writing.

One of the keys to good copyediting is to know what questions to ask the writer. Coaching questions should come from the editor who sees the story from the reader's perspective. The questioning process should help the writer develop a sense of the story's purpose and focus.

"What did you learn about this story?"

"What part of the interview or observation did you have a reaction to?"

Questions such as these should be aimed to help the writer talk out the story. By answering these questions, the writer can discover what is new or interesting.

The questions can be organized so that the copy editor asks them in three basic stages: the planning stage, the collecting stage and the writing stage.

PLANNING STAGE

"So what's the reader going to want to know?"

"What are you, the reporter, going to need to know before you interview? What will help you make sure you understand what's being said in the interview?"

"What do you think the reader is going to find interesting in this story?"

The purpose of coaching questions in the planning stage is to help the writer hone the questions or focus before the interview. The questions also ask the writer to think about what sort of background he or she needs to do before starting to collect the information through interviews. When talking through the planning stage, the reporter should develop an outline of the information needed.

COLLECTING STAGE

"What did you see when you went to play practice?"

"What details do you remember from the ballerina's room? What do those details say about her?"

"What do you think your best quote is?"

Questions in the collection stage should help the writer sort through the images and information gathered from interviews and observation. The copy editor will also help the writer see what information is needed through reinterviewing or reobservation. During this stage, the copy editor may help the writer find a lead or the first quote.

WRITING STAGE

"So what do you think this story is about?"

"What do you think is going to be complicated about this story? What do you think is going to be hard for the reader to understand?"

"What surprised you in what people said when you interviewed them?"

The questions in the writing stage should be aimed to help the writer sort through the research and interviews. The writer should be trying to decide which are the best quotes to use verbatim or word-for-word. The questions can help the writer to decide what parts are complicated enough to require careful wording or step-by-step treatment.

In any of the three stages, the copy editor's role is also to give the reporter something to build on and to get the writer excited about the story.

"I liked that quote that you had from Coach Dupree. That could go high in the story."

"I think the teacher who survived her bout with cancer and then wanted to tutor Josh, who was facing brain cancer, is a great anecdote that could be your lead."

Identifying the strongest parts of their research is crucial to helping writers improve each draft.

But now the deadline is approaching. The copy editor has talked the writer through the eighth draft. Time is a factor, and final changes have to be made. As the deadline approaches, the role of the copy editor starts to evolve from that of writing coach to fixer.

RESOURCES NEEDED TO COPYEDIT

A good copy editor will want to have quick access to the numerous resources.

- A journalism stylebook, such as the one from the Associated Press or *The New York Times*, as well as a school style sheet.

- A dictionary and thesaurus, even though both may be built into the word-processing program. A complete, unabridged dictionary on CD-ROM will be useful. Some word-processing programs have dictionaries and thesauri as well as spelling checkers. The checker should be customized to include style points, frequently used names and other words common to high school events and teen issues.

- A school directory that lists all students, faculty and staff so the reporter and editor can verify the spelling of names and, for faculty and staff, titles. This information may be available electronically in some schools through the registrar or data clerk.

- Local business and residential telephone books to verify the spelling of names and to check addresses.

- An almanac and biographical dictionary, useful for verifying facts and the names and accomplishments of well-known persons who may be cited in stories.

- A grammar handbook with a quick reference section, helpful for both reporters and editors. The copy editor may want to prepare a list of the most common grammatical errors to post for all reporters.

- Back issues of the school newspaper and recent school yearbooks and magazines to verify information in story updates and for ongoing coverage.

Hunkered down in the middle of these resources, the copy editor can begin the final edit. To evaluate the story, the copy editor breaks it down into parts.

THE LEAD

- In a straight news lead, is the most important and timely information there?

- Could the lead be shortened and remain clear?

- In a feature lead, does the anecdote, image or statement fit the tone and focus of the story?

- Are all the facts correct?

The lead makes a difference in whether students actually read the stories. The lead is that crucial to the story and therefore something very precious and personal to writers. If the writer's lead is saved, he or she will promise to clean the copy editor's room for 20 years. If the lead is shredded, it may be another year before the copy editor reviews the same person's writing again.

In some professional publications, a copy editor on deadline is asked to discuss the lead with the writer before making any changes, while edits later in the story can be made without consulting the writer.

BODY ORGANIZATION AND FLOW

While most beginning writers would like a formula here, there isn't one.

But a copy editor can certainly start with these questions:

- Are there unanswered questions?

- Did you organize the parts of the story so that they make sense?

- Did you read the story aloud to make sure the story flows?

In their book *Coaching Writers*, Roy Peter Clark and Don Fry list these among their tips for copy editors to give writers:

- Ask what the reader needs to know and in what order.

- Arrange the material into a narrative with a beginning, a middle and an end.

- Write a series of subheads for the sections by visualizing what the story will look like.

- List the players and their motives.

- Type two screensful quickly without worrying about sentences or sense, then print it, underline important things and rearrange them into an outline. Then kill the two screensful.

- Arrange materials into scenes, chapters or both.

REPORTING

FACT CHECK

The copy editor should be a master of detail and, if necessary, challenge every fact, every name and every word.

- Eliminate doubtful facts.

- Check facts against each other to ensure consistency.

- Confirm facts and verify names.

- Check figures, especially to see that totals tally.

- Be especially careful of dates and times. Check every date, month and day with the calendar.

The copy editor should read to see whether all important information is given. If not, he or she should insert the needed facts or return the story to the reporter. The copy editor should not guess at facts or information but should double-check facts before automatically changing them.

The copy editor should make sure the writer has used the right source for the right information. If a science teacher says three teachers are retiring, the copy editor should have the writer double-check the information by interviewing the principal.

Journalists should typically avoid encyclopedias, weekly newsmagazines, books and newspapers as firsthand research. The writer should use these sources as background, then go straight to people for interviews.

For depth in the story, the copy editor should ask the reporter to consider these as possible sources:

- Students

- Student polls

- Teachers

- Parents

- Alumni

- District statistics

- Doctors/psychologists

- Regional education administrations

- Municipal/county statistics

- Professional sources

- Building or local administrators

- Area college professors

- Teens at other schools

- School organizations or clubs

- Book authors

- Advocate organizations, such as Mothers Against Drunk Driving or the National Rifle Association

CLARITY AND CONCISENESS

Once the copy has been corrected for reporting errors, the copy editor makes sure each sentence and paragraph is clear, active and strong. If the copy editor has to stop to say, "Huh? I don't get that" or "Wait, I need to reread that sentence," the writing may not be clear. If the copy editor says, "I really want to stop reading now," then the writing may not be concise. Odds are that the writer needs help reorganizing paragraphs or recasting sentences.

The copy editor can put the following list next to the piece to be copyedited and go to work.

- If any paragraphs need to be rearranged, do so.

- If paragraphs are repetitive, combine them or delete one.

- If paragraphs are too long, divide them.

- If the copy has long lists of names, put them into a sidebar or replace them by summarizing the contents.

- Emphasize an important idea by placing it at the beginning of a sentence.

- Tighten the writing by eliminating unnecessary words, phrases and clauses and by combining related expressions.

- Simplify complicated sentences.

- Energize sentences by changing passive voice verbs to active voice (occasionally, of course, the passive voice may be desirable). In the following sentence an active-voice verb is better.

> **The Wampus Cats played a strong defensive game. (Not: A strong defensive game was played by the Wampus Cats.)**

In the next sentence a passive-voice verb is better because it features the subject.

> **Ryan Coleman was reelected Student Council president. (Not: The student body reelected Ryan Coleman Student Council president.)**

- Eliminate trite expressions.

- Strive for sentence variety.

- Improve diction by using specific and exact words: *quibble* is different from *argue* or *debate*; *nice* is general for *affable*, *kind*, *pleasant* or *desirable*; *candid* is a synonym for *frank*, *impartial*, *open*, *sincere*, *straightforward*, *truthful* and *unprejudiced*, but with its own special meaning; *tree* is general, while *pine*, *oak* and *elm* are specific.

- Eliminate editorial comment unless the story is the type in which it is permitted, that is, a column, an editorial or a review.

DETAILS

While a copy editor may correct spelling, style and grammar mistakes along the way, the possibility is always there that those errors will be made again in the correction process. One last read to polish the story is necessary. The credibility of the writer and the publication depend on it. The reader who sees three spelling errors in one paragraph will doubt the accuracy of the reporting in the rest of the story.

In the last read-through of a story, the copy editor should:

- Correct misspellings. Use but don't depend on a spell checker. For example, the computer still doesn't suggest "they're" when the writer incorrectly used "there."

- Correct errors in grammar and usage.

- Correct errors in style.

- Adjust stories to prescribed length:

    – cut paragraphs

    – eliminate unimportant sentences or paragraphs

    – combine two sentences, making one sentence a subordinate clause or phrase in the other

    – change clauses to phrases and phrases to well-chosen words

    – use a single vivid verb or noun in place of a less specific verb or noun plus modifiers

COACHING WRITING CONTINUES

The copy editor's job should not end even after spelling errors are corrected and the story is published. Set aside a few minutes to discuss the story with the writer without the pressures of a deadline.

"How did you feel about the story?"

"What, if given time, would you have done to improve the piece?"

"What other interviews did you still need?"

An after-publication discussion should be aimed to evaluate the story and to learn lessons from the process. The copy editor can commend a strong lead, correct habitual problems or reinforce some practices that the writer can use to improve the next story.

Making the point that the writer has a good eye for details, needs to do more interviews or needs to double-check facts can only improve the quality of the publication and the writer as the year goes on.

While a younger writer must be open to this discussion or criticism, both writer and copy editor must set aside egos and focus on improving the product. Writing tends to be a very personal endeavor, so any critical analysis of that work may make the writer want to do a Jackie Chan move on the copy editor.

Remembering that both the writer and copy editor are there to give the reader a clear, interesting story should help to eliminate any tension or any need for a trip to the emergency room.

Maintaining a civil tone eases the pain of critical analysis. The copy editor who barks out, "this stinks" or "what nose-pickin' moron wrote this," will not get the writer's respect or attention. The copy editor could easily begin with, "How can I help you on that story?" or "I think that's a great story you have this deadline. Let's talk about it."

While a copy editor's name may not appear at the top of the story, the lack of such recognition does not reduce the copy editor's worth.

A good copy editor understands that his or her goal is not only to improve the piece on the computer but also to improve the writer's skills.

A dedicated copy editor takes pride in the basketball player who actually stops in the gym to read this month's issue. He or she enjoys the progress of the entertainment writer who can now understand how to organize feature stories.

Skills of a Copy Editor

- Have a broad knowledge; stories in all fields will pass the copydesk:

    1. Be acquainted with all important events and trends.
    2. Know your own publication and its policies.
    3. Be alert to the times.
    4. Know books, plays, magazines and reviews, legal and governmental structure and procedures.
    5. Know names, localities, political and other social relationships.
    6. Know geography, history and human nature.
    7. Know your own school and community.

- Be able to write standard English and to edit it into poorly written stories:

    1. Be skillful in handling sentences and paragraphs.
    2. Have a strong command of words.
    3. Be able to make all writing concise.
    4. Be able to edit copy consistently according to the stylebook.

- Be able to distinguish editorializing from a sound inference based on fact. Edit out all editorializing. The following is not editorializing since the first phrase is followed by fact:

    "Maine will meet its toughest opponent of the season Tuesday when the undefeated Arlington Heights Yellowjackets invade Memorial Stadium."

- Have what may be called a "bifocal" mind, one that shifts instantly from meticulous examination of details to the overall story.
- Recognize effective, even dramatic writing.
- Have a creative imagination; be able to see a good story in a poor one and to shape it by good editing.
- Exercise great care and patience.
- Understand reference sources and be able to consult them quickly and easily.

	HOW THEY ARE USED	WHAT THEY MEAN	HOW TYPE IS SET
TYPE SIZE and STYLE	Lansing, mich.--	Capitalize.	LANSING, Mich.—
	College Herald	Small caps.	COLLEGE HERALD
	the Senator from Ohio	Change to lower case.	the senator from Ohio
	By Alvin Jones	Bold face.	**By Alvin Jones**
	Saturday Evening Post	Italicize.	*Saturday Evening Post*
PUNCTUATION and SPELLING	The Spy	Emphasize quotes.	"The Spy"
	Northwestern U.	Emphasize periods.	Northwestern U.
	said, "I must . . .	Emphasize comma.	said, "I must . . .
	Johnsons	Emphasize apostrophe.	Johnsons'
	picnicing	Insert letter or word.	picnicking
	theatre	Transpose letters.	theater
	Henry Cook, principal	Transpose words.	Principal Henry Cook
	days	Delete letter.	day
	judgement	Delete letter and bridge over.	judgment
	all right	Insert space.	all right
	those	Close up space.	those
	Geo. Brown	Spell out.	George Brown
	100 or more	Spell out.	one hundred or more
	Doctor S. E. Smith	Abbreviate.	Dr. S. E. Smith
	Six North Street	Use numerals.	6 North Street
	Marion Smythe	Spell as written.	Marion Smythe
POSITION	Madison, Wis.--	Indent for paragraph.	Madison, Wis.—
	today. Tomorrow he	New paragraph.	today. Tomorrow he
	considered serious. Visitors are not	No paragraph. Run in with preceding matter.	considered serious. Visitors are not
	But he called last night and said that he	No paragraph.	But he called last night and said that he
	]Jones To Conduct[or ⟨Jones To Conduct⟩	Center subheads.	**Jones To Conduct**
MISCELLANEOUS	He was ~~not unmindful~~	Bridge over material omitted.	He was mindful
	one ~~student~~ came	Kill corrections.	one student came
	or more	Story unfinished.	
	30 or #	End of story.	————————

Fig. 13.1. Copy editing symbols.

COPY EDITING ON A COMPUTER

On-screen story editing is practiced by most collegiate and professional publications and is becoming increasingly popular among high school publication staffs. For those staffs who find copyediting on paper to be a more thorough process for catching errors, Figure 13.1 presents a set of copy-editing symbols to use. Copy editors who do all copyediting on screen should develop a set way to differentiate between editing comments and actual text. Publication staffs use all caps, outline text, underlined text, strikethrough letters or italics to identify all copy-editing comments. Some word-processing programs have nonprinting text commands to use.

Management of edited story drafts must be handled carefully. A disorganized staff might find an early draft full of spelling errors and copy-editing comments published in the newspaper or yearbook. The organization system that the publication staff chooses may depend on the copy-editing system and computer system in place.

At Carmel High School, the *HiLite* staff submits all copy electronically, preferably by email. The reporter saves the copy under his or her name, a slug and the issue date, such as Willis/farmingclub/8-17. The copy goes to the copy editor who edits it and adds his or her title to the file name so it becomes Willis/farmingclub/8-17/copyed. From there, the story goes to the assigning editor and then to the editor-in-chief, with each person making edits and adding to the file name. The final version then gets saved to the server in the "copy to place" folder. Page designers use only the final draft in that file to design the page.

COMMON EDITING MISTAKES

- Using synonyms for *said*. Don't worry about the overuse of the word *said*. The word is neutral enough not to cause problems. Don't force words such as "he smiled" or "she chuckled" as attributions when it is physically hard to chuckle a quote.

- Using the school initials. Most students do not have to run back to the lobby to check the seal on the floor to remind themselves where they go to school. Initials in a school publication are a redundancy unless the story is making a comparison with other high schools.

- Inconsistent use of style rules. Do not use *May 29* in one story and *May 29th* in another. Know the publication style rules and stick to them.

- Improper use of *it's*. *It's* should be used where the words *it is* will work. *Its* is used to show possession.

- Including "when asked" to set up quotes. The reader assumes that direct quotes are results of questions from a reporter, so omit the phrase. "When asked" can be correctly used if there's a need for clarity. One case may be in a speech story where the reporter is including quotes from a post-speech interview.

- Combining several quotes in the same paragraph. When the speaker changes topics, a new paragraph is recommended. The new paragraph helps the reader understand the change in focus. Shorter paragraphs make readability easier from a design standpoint.

- Misuse of the word *stated*. The word should be used only when the quote is from a written or prepared text. The word *stated* should not be used to attribute spoken words.

- Name misspellings. Never assume you know how to spell a person's name. *John Smith* could be spelled *Jon Smithe* or *Jonn Smythe*. Do not even assume the name in the school records is correct. The reporter should ask the person to spell his or her name.

EXERCISES

1. One of the first steps in learning how to edit copy is to study and learn the most common principles of the style manual. Consistency in style is often the difference between an excellent and a potentially excellent newspaper.

   Study your style manual, or if you do not have one, use Chapter 12 as your guide. Rewrite each of the following exercises on a separate sheet of paper. Some of the cases may not be covered in your style manual. They are included here to promote class discussion and an eventual consensus. If your newspaper does not have an official style manual, these exercises may be used as the basis for forming one. You may occasionally need to consult your dictionary or other style manuals to settle a problem.

   (Note: Consider the first time you see a name to be the first reference. If the same person appears in later sentences, copy edit as though the references are the second and subsequent references.)

Names and Capitalization

1. Ferris high school basketball players worked out for three hours Friday.

2. The Itasca Wampus Cats defeated the Bonham purple warriors 10–1 at Friday's baseball game.

3. The freshman service club is collecting toys for families who lost their homes in the floods.

4. Senior Seth Levy did not want to take a History class, even though it was required.

5. Jeannie Elliott scored two goals in her first soccer game.

6. Mrs. Whitney Bodine started her lesson by singing the National Anthem.

7. The children loved Mrs. Whitney Bodine because her teaching style was a little unorthodox.

8. The birds often nest in the roof of the gym during the Fall.

9. First baseman Jason King hit two home runs off Starting Pitcher Johnny Seale.

10. King spent the next three games on the bench of tovar memorial ballpark.

11. Amanda Webb '08 is recovering from a broken leg suffered during a rodeo accident.

12. More than 200 students showed up for the class party at bardwell lake.

13. New students are expected to enroll in at least one class of german or spanish.

Abbreviations

14. Teachers received a 1% pay raise even though they asked for a 10 percent increase.

15. The play is scheduled for February 15.

16. Academic Decathlon members will travel to Okla. for their retreat.

17. Dallas Cowboys running back Tony Dorsett holds the National Football League record for the longest run.

18. Wed. was the first day students were allowed to return to school after the accident.

19. The district added eight more portables along Lampier St.

20. The SCE ruled that teachers would have to remove all tatoos.

21. Speech teacher Rebecca Bennett is in her fourth year as the head of the Fine Arts Dept.

22. Two 15-year-old hunters rescued a baby deer in the hills of Asheville, North Carolina.

23. Six members of the state championship team signed letters with N.C.A.A. Division I schools.

24. Monday was the last time the boy was late to Doctor Olivia Belsher's class.

25. The Downhill Ski Club will meet at 5 p.m., November 23, in the library.

Numbers

26. Calculus teacher Gregg Fleisher started class at 7:00 a.m.

27. The gymnast fell off the balance beam in her 1st attempt.

28. The next game is May 29th.

29. The boy's father sold the car to his youngest son for one hundred dollars.

30. The Panthers won the area soccer championship two–one.

31. Senior goalie Susan Killough made 4 saves in the 6–1 bidistrict win.

32. The drill team will meet at freshman Tricia Hughes' home at fourteen Churchill Road.

33. Pianist Pam Murdock, seventeen, will perform a medley of Peter Frampton songs at 6 p.m., Monday, in the concert hall.

34. Wide receiver Colin Fitzgibbons caught touchdown passes of five, 10, fifty-five and 33 yards.

35. Admission to the concert is fifteen dollars.

36. The boy moved to Boston from a town with a population of one thousand five hundred people.

37. More than twenty-five students were home with food poisoning.

38. Junior Caryn Statman couldn't stand another day with 20 5-year-olds.

Punctuation and Italics

39. Freshman Adrienne Lee could not believe that her mom packed her bananas, apples, and oranges for lunch.

40. In Friday's choir concert, soprano Amy Cunningham sang <u>I Love a Parade</u>.

41. "Why do I have to go to the Coldplay concert with you", Cunningham said.

42. Leon Solimani, a 224 – pound linebacker, joined the team after the second game.

43. Sophomore Sarah Strauss' goal is to appear on the cover of Rolling Stone.

44. Senior class president Bryan Parker admitted to getting five Cs and two Bs on his report card.

45. The workshop's steering committee included: Mike McLean, secretary, Mary Pulliam, president, Chris Modrow, historian, and Randy Vonderheid, treasurer.

46. The Class of 82 will have their 20-year reunion this year.

47. Sophomore Duane Yee played the lead role in the school's presentation of <u>Hamlet</u> Tuesday night.

48. I absolutely love the dog "Astro" in the cartoon The Jetsons.

49. President Tanner Bodine, Jr. will speak to the Sketch Comedy Club on Jan. 15.

50. Freshman James The Real Deal Ragland will start at center in the opening game of the playoffs.

2. We learn to recognize printed words in much the same way that we learn to recognize persons we know. Their overall appearances seem to be enough to give us quick identification.

Psychologists call the total appearance of an object its configuration or the sum of its parts. We can hardly take the time to spell out every word we see in reading copy. We learn to depend on configuration or total form in examining for correctness. We therefore should challenge any word form that raises the slightest suspicion that it is mispelled.

Did you catch it? "Mispelled" is misspelled! This is a troublesome word that should always be examined. Other spelling demons are listed below.

Number a paper from 1 to 50. Let your hunches guide you and rewrite those words you believe are misspelled. Mark OK if the word is spelled correctly. (If a space is left blank, you are charged with an error.) If you sense a word is incorrectly spelled, you may add one-half point to your total score, even though you haven't spelled it correctly.

Hint: More than half the words are misspelled.

1. recieve
2. alright
3. sophomore
4. berserk
5. habatat
6. misjudgement
7. lieutenant
8. restraunt
9. accomodate
10. fourty
11. repremand
12. sabotage
13. seperate
14. protocol
15. larceny
16. ilegal
17. occured
18. sponsor

19. elegible

20. corupt

21. corparate

22. excell

23. succeding

24. commit

25. facsimile

26. penicillin

27. paralel

28. elipse

29. embezzlement

30. incidious

31. patronage

32. athlete

33. decathlon

34. potpurri

35. nourish

36. concensus

37. liason

38. libary

39. Febuary

40. lisence

41. municipal

42. legistlature

43. indictment

44. peeve

45. hary-kary

46. fallible

47. questionnaire

48. misspell

49. oponent

50. integral

3. An Associated Press Managing Editors committee created a list of the 50 most common errors in newspaper writing. Examples of these errors appear in the following sentences. Correct the following errors in word usage, spelling and grammar.

1. The parents served refreshment afterwards.

2. The funeral service was held in the First United Methodist Church.

3. Even though the senior had less errors on the test, he made a better grade than his brother.

4. More than half of the town went to church on Easter Sunday.

5. The game will start at 8 p.m. tonight.

6. The principal agreed to drop the policy prohibiting people from wearing hats in the building and the increase of the number of minutes between class periods.

7. In the summer months, more than half of the senior class was employed.

8. I'll never be able to tell who's dog this is without an identification tag.

9. The sprinter won the race after alluding the former state champion.

10. The committee, composed of three juniors, five seniors and five teachers . . .

11. Junior Hili Banjo headed up the fashion show.

12. I implied that the speaker was talking about the principal when saying "He was wrong."

13. The team must improve it's rebounding to win this year.

14. Freshman Aaron Ofseyer decided to become a meteorologist rather than a Jewish rabbi.

15. Economics teacher Suresh Vasan closed down his car business to become a teacher.

4. Cut unnecessary words. *Dallas Morning News* writing coach and assistant managing editor Paula LaRocque lists the following phrases as examples of wordiness in newswriting. Your job is to make them more concise. Cut the extra words or replace the phrase with one word that's more precise.

1. make use of
2. true fact
3. personal friendship
4. conduct an investigation into
5. on the occasion that
6. large in size
7. 12 noon
8. set a new record
9. a distance of 35 miles
10. in the vicinity of
11. crisis situation
12. in the event that
13. a number of
14. the reason is because
15. consensus of opinion

5. Edit the following story written for a daily newspaper. Using all you've learned in this chapter and Chapter 12, correct all errors.

Sweet Water, Tex – National guard troops patroled yesterday against looter after-tornados carved a 2-mile long, half-mile-wide swath through this east Texas town, killing 1 person, injuring some one-hundred others; and leaving 1500 persons homeless.

Ranging up to $20 million, dollars, officials said the destruction toll could have been worse. They marvelled at the fact that only one person was a fataality.

"After i saw the extent of the damage, I thought we'd have many more inujries and certainly more deaths," said Sweetwater mayor David Maddox. "It was luck. It was a miracle."

As national guardsman patroled the streets to watch for looting, volunteers and salvation army workers served over 2,000 meals to person left homeless by the disaster, said Mitchell Anderson, Public Relations Director for the Salvation Armys' Texas division.

"Sweetwater is still in a mess. People are cleaning up but it will be a long time", said Mitchell. "People are sifting through the debris by hand. Thats all that is left from some of these trailur homes".

The U. Weather Bureau said 2 tornadoes smashed into the sothern part of the city of 12,00 early Saturday after merging in the air.

Mayor Rick Rhodes estimated property damages at between $15 and $20 million and sid that about 100 persons were injured and some 1500 left homeless.

Police Chief Jim Kelley said clean up efforts were progresing. "We're getting a lot of volunteer types," he said. "Their swooping in there, and they're helping."

Governor George Bush visited the city yesterday and talked with residents's of the Sun Village Housing Project, a Federally subsidized development for senior citizens which was hard hit. The storms only fatallity ws a 87-year-old man who lived there.

One resident, Gadys lane, stood looking through what used to be a side wall of her house asd Bush spoke.

"It was just like I was in a vacum," said Mrs. Lane. I was down on my knees begging the lord to take care of me. I didn't care about the house.

"The only thing I can say is tough times never last, but though people do, and we've got a lot off toughj people around here," said Bush.

6. The following sentences contain errors in fact, structure and style. Using copy-editing symbols, correct spelling, grammar, punctuation, redundancies and sexist expressions.

1. Mary has studyied filing, bookeeping, and word processing.

2. Exhausted after the days work, it was difficult for Joan to enjoy the concert.

3. Bridgetown's 46 policemen in January, February and March, in 27,647 man-hours of work drove 117,786 miles – more than four trips around the earth, or 22,000 miles farther than the maximum distance from the earth to the sun.

4. The students were given the basic fundamentals of the course.

5. The sponsers were elated over the finantial outcome which netted a little over one hundred and fifty dollars.

6. Cattle graze on ranges in the district, and farmers grow cotton, vegetables and citrus fruits, including grapes.

7. 15 girls from each school will be at the Central high school which will make 150 girls.

8. After working day and night for the past monthes the 82 piece Central band, under the direction of L. Irving Cradley are ready to do their best to win the district title at Dacon tomorrow night.

9. My turn finally came to bowl.

10. She had neither completed her English nor her Spanish.

11. Plagiarism is where you take the work of another and pass it off as your own.

12. He was a member of the committee in charge of the making of the student directory.

13. He hoped to get the true facts of the problem.

14. Coach Joe Voegle, of Spalding Institute, is the director of the clinic and hopes to have a prominent referee to be appointed by the local refferee's association, appear at one of the sessons to explain the new rules and their affect on the game.

15. In describing his earliest beginnings he said he had grown up as a child.

16. Arriving late at night, all the lights in the house were out.

17. The teacher asked for a brief synopsis of the book.

18. Housewives are feeling the pinch of inflation.

19. Jim is a person of strong will and who always gets his own way.

20. The team had won two straight in a row.

21. Those elected were Jack Swanson, President, Mary Clements, vice President, and Dale Cook, Secretary treasurer.

22. The cleaning women were already in the building when we left.

23. After his death he received the award posthumously.

24. A rattlesnake bite, followed by a series of homemade anecdotes, sent an Almont man to the hospital yesterday.

7. The next two stories are rough drafts turned in to you, the copy editor. Using the coaching writing tips in this chapter, write out a number of questions to ask the writer to help improve the story. What points would you make to the writer to improve the story for the next draft? What good information does the writer have here? What information does the writer need to go back and get before writing a second draft?

Story 1

Marcus Goree isn't your average basketball player. He's 6–8. And he's one of the best in the area.

Many other players on the team have been playing since they were little. Goree's only been playing for four years.

Originally, Goree wanted to play football. It wasn't until coach Gail Dupree asked him to play basketball that he decided to play.

Dupree said that Goree didn't look a basketball player. Besides being tall, he said he was skinny and pretty clumsy at first.

"Goree was like the Scarecrow in the Wizard of Oz," Coach Dupree said. "He had a great work ethic, but he had no self-esteem. The only thing I did that year was fix his self-esteem. Even his teammates would tell him he was sorry. All I did was tell he was the man."

But Dupree worked very hard with Gorree for the next two years.

"Marcus is a coach's dream," Coach Dupree said. "Some players come in and think they know everything so you can't coach them. Goree know nothing so all he wanted to do was to be coached."

Goree improved and was a leader on the team his junior year. His scoring has improved as well. Enough now that colleges are recruiting him. He attended all the camps he could this last summer. He goes to scouting combines where scouts have been impressed by his ability to dunk.

He's being recruited hard by a lot of schools including University of Southern California, Texas, Baylor and New Mexico. Some scouts have even come to his house. But Goree still has to improve on his SAT score before he can be eligible for a scholarship. He says he's not worried.

Neither is coach Dupree.

"I feel real happy for Marcus," Coach Dupree said. "He came so far in four years. It makes me feel good to watch him play. He overcame a lot to get where his is now. In four more years, who knows where he'll be."

Story 2

Sophomore Warren Oakes thinks he's tough. Every time he walks in the gym for P.E. class, he flexes his arm at Coach Duff, and that's why she calls him Muscles. But today when he flexed his arm, she did not give him her usual reply.

"You forgot to say 'Hi Muscles.' Remember that's my name Coach Duff," sophomore Warren Oakes says as he flexes

his arm and gives her a tough look. "Are our friends coming today?" he asks, referring to the three students from the E.D. Walker unit who join them to form the seven-person adaptive P.E. class.

As he continues to tell a joke about Bill Clinton, the gym door opens and in comes the trio wearing sneakers, shorts and smiles – the usual attire for this P.E. class.

The adaptive P.E. class was designed to provide special education students, especially the three who transferred from E.D. Walker special education high school, with a sheltered class to develop their skills and coordination. But unlike the other P.E. classes, they do not run long distances or do any strenuous exercises. Instead they play simple games and warm up with easy exercises.

"There's no hostility, no meanness, no rudeness," P.E. coach Kathleen Duff said. "In here it is such a warm and loving environment. The kids are so sweet."

When Coach Duff agreed to teach the new class, she had no idea how many would be in the class or what disabilities they would have. When only two showed up on the first day, she worried she wasn't going to have enough for a game of four-square. But a few more showed up in the next week, so she didn't have to throw the towel in. Now her dilemma lies in creating games that everyone can understand and enjoy.

"I just try to incorporate activities where everyone feels success at their own level, while still feeling comfortable, and also at a level where everyone feels challenged," Coach Duff said.

These activities include modified versions of softball and bowling, which are both sports that can appeal to a wide range of disabilities. A special ramp was also transferred from E.D. Walker so that 20-year-old Kelly Newsom, who is autistic, can push the ball from waist-level and knock down pins like everyone else.

Even though dart-throwing and bowling are geared toward the individual level, they are seldom done alone. Someone is always there shouting "Way to go" to someone else.

During a routine 15-minute walk last week, Newsom lost interest and started walking towards the side of the gym. Just as she was about to sit down on the gym floor, Oakes turned around and said something motivational to her to get her back into the group. Newsom smiled, grabbed his hand and restarted her laps.

When freshman Rosa Lopez refused to participate in darts, Oakes told her to wake up and get up there and take her turn. When she did, she ended up with the highest score and a high five from Coach Duff and Oakes.

But sometimes it takes longer to get it right. Senior Jose Garcia swung at the plastic softball a whole lot more than once before smacking a home run into the back wall. It took Oakes three or four tries before he could get a dart to stick in the board. But they never give up and Coach Duff never stops prodding them. As soon as she said, "Come on Muscles, let's see what you can do," he stuck one on the outside of the dart board.

"A lot of coaches say if we don't do very well then they don't like it," Oakes said. "But if we mess up in class then Coach Duff always say at least we try. I think she's got a real heart for helping people."

Last year Oakes felt left out in his P.E. class because it was so big. He felt naglected by his coach and often refused to dress out. The reason for this was never clear, but now he suits out everyday, so he is obviously more comfortable.

During the last half of fourth period, the P.E. class moves to room 131 to watch TV or spend time talking to Coach Duff. Oakes tells her about his life and about his activities outside of school.

"We talk about anything from his interests to our shared interest of jazz music to daily happenings and concerns about school," Coach Duff said.

Writing Headlines

Chapter

14

Next time the school newspaper goes out, sit and watch your readers. It's not quite MTV entertainment, but you will learn something. The majority of readers are scanners. Watch as their eyes dart from side to side, from headline to headline or photo to photo as if they were watching a tennis match. Readers will scan the page looking for that one key word or phrase that touches a part of their lives or that's clever enough to make them laugh. Then they'll stop and begin to read.

This observation exercise will reveal how important headline writing is. The headline, or the large type on top of a story, is what catches the readers' attention. A vague, poorly written headline sends readers off to the horoscopes, and the writer's hard work is dismissed. A well-written headline entices readers to read the lead, and you are one step closer to the goal of getting people to read a story.

The headline is important because

- It names or summarizes the important facts of the story. The headline makes it simple for readers to glance quickly through the newspaper, yearbook or magazine to select which stories to read.

- It communicates the mood of the story. The headline gives readers a sense of the story's tone. A feature story's light tone can be conveyed through a play on words. A news or a news-feature story would have a headline with a straight-forward informative voice.

- It signals the relative importance of the story. The headline's role in helping readers decide which story is more important is discussed in Chapter 16. The general rule is that the larger the type, the more important the story.

TEASER AND TELLER HEADLINES

Copy editors refer to headline content as either a "teaser" or "teller." The teller headline gains the reader's attention by clearly and concisely summarizing the story. The voice of the teller is typically straight-forward. Teller headlines are most often designed using one or two standard typefaces.

The teaser headline attracts by arousing curiosity or by entertaining readers. A play on words such as "Try-athlete" may intrigue readers enough to pause at the story. But to make sure readers take the next step to read the lead, the teaser should always be accompanied with a teller headline as a secondary headline. In this case, the teller "Sophomore hopes to finish first triathlon after five attempts" helps to clarify the story. The teaser headline is typically connected to a feature story or any story that is not a straight news story.

In many magazines, newspaper feature packages and yearbooks, designers make creative use of type on the teaser headline. The typefaces often mirror the content of the story in an attempt to entertain visually. Designer headlines are discussed later in this chapter and in Chapter 16, the design chapter.

GETTING THE WORDS TO FIT ON THE PAGE

Headlines have to fit into a specific space on the page. That's one of the greatest challenges in headline writing. The larger the typeface size, the fewer the words that can fit into the space. How to determine the number of letters or words that can fit has changed over the years.

Computers with page design, word-processing or paint and draw software allow the headline writer to see instantly if the headline fits. In any system, if the headline doesn't fit, the editor adds or subtracts information or looks for shorter or longer words to say the same thing. The rewriting process is the same when manually counting headlines; however, the process can be slower.

Computers have allowed the writer to change the type size or the letter spacing in small amounts to make the headline fit. But that doesn't mean headline writers should scrunch their cherished words so that they are unreadable or shrink the size so they are hardly bigger than body type. The minimum and maximum sizes of headlines are discussed later in the design chapters.

For the purpose of explaining how to make headlines fit, the count assigned to each letter, space and punctuation mark will be one unit. Note below how the system works. Also notice how each line is counted separately and there are no spaces counted at the end of the lines.[1]

1 1 1 1 1 1 1 1 1 1 1 1 1 1 1 1 1 1 1 1 1 1 1 1 1 = 26 count

Senior gains new identity,

1 1 1 1 1 1 1 1 1 1 1 1 1 1 1 1 1 1 1 1 1 1 1 1 1 1 1 1 1 1 = 30 count

access to liquor in 45 minutes

KINDS OF HEADLINES

While teller/teaser labels for headlines refer to content, headlines are also identified by appearance – certain kinds of headlines have certain content qualities.

A one-line headline is basically a single, unbroken sentence. Typically, the one-line headline is a teller.[2]

FBI mounts manhunt for '72 grad

A two-line headline is one sentence broken into two lines.[3] Each line is counted separately. A gap of white space is unsightly at the end of one line of a two-line headline.

Halloween flooding devastates residents

A three-line headline is one sentence broken into three lines. Typically these are teller headlines. Remember that each line counts separately.[4]

Irish dancers
win first place
at talent show

A deck is a secondary headline that is positioned under the main headline and is typically a teller.[5] The deck can go under another teller headline. The deck always adds information and is helpful in explaining complicated stories.

Cancelled permit
foils annual parade

■ Tailgate party to replace Homecoming tradition

The hammer is a short phrase or even a single word that is set in a point size much larger than the headline underneath.[6]

STUCK
Juniors denied off-campus;
lunch lines longer than ever

A tripod is a combination of a large word or phrase followed by a two-line headline set in type half the size.

Both lines of the second part nearly equal the height of the larger, opening words, as in this headline.[7]

Meriting recognition: 12 seniors selected as high achievers on PSAT test

The jump headline accompanies the part of a story that continues on a different page.[8] Many jump headlines may be written as another headline for the story – usually as a one-line headline. However, some publications opt for using only key words, such as in the following jump headline for a story about a foundation's evaluation of a school.

REPORT CARD   Continued from front page

Designer headlines, used primarily for newspaper features and in yearbooks and magazines, establish the mood through choice of type. They are also created by adding graphics or manipulating type size. Readability of type should still be a consideration in creating a designer headline. Well-written designer headlines that use type to match the content or message can be extremely effective (Figs. 14.1–14.5).

WRITING A TELLER

Even though the headline has the fewest words of any element in a newspaper or yearbook, it often requires as much thought and care as the story and other elements on a page. While headlines typically are created on deadline, the writer should put maximum effort into creating good ones. If the story was written by someone else, read through the entire story to understand the content. Mentally, or on the computer screen or paper, summarize the most important information in the story in one brief sentence. Try it again, this time trimming even more words. Rewrite, using synonyms or reconstructing the sentence, until the headline fits the space, tone and content of the story.

The headline should follow these guidelines:

- Be accurate, above all. Specific facts in the headline should be completely supported in the story.

- Be informative. Try to answer as many questions as a news lead does.

- Be fair. If the story covers two sides of an issue, try to reflect the differences in the headline. Do not editorialize directly or indirectly unless the headline is for an opinion story such as a review or editorial. The headline should give the same impression as the body of the story.

- Do not put anything in the headline that is not in the story.

Fig. 14.1. *Update*, Herbert Henry Dow High School, Midland, Mich.

HEADLINE CONSTRUCTION RULES

Headline-writing rules are continually changing among professional newspapers and magazines. *The New York Times*, for example, now uses articles such as *a, and* and *the* more often than it used to. The use of past tense verbs is more accepted to make sure the headline is clear. Still most publications adhere to the following guidelines:

- Avoid padding. *A, and, the, their, his* or *her* should not be used in hard news headlines. Notice the deletion of the word in brackets in the following headline.

  Director calls [the] possibility of drug testing athletes 'highly unlikely'

  However, use of *the* in the following headline is necessary to keep the headline from sounding awkward.[9]

Rollin' dough

District to gain
funds from ads
on buses

Fig. 14.2. *Panther Prints*, Duncanville High School, Duncanville, Texas

  All in the family

  Students suffer when mothers battle disease

- Use active verbs in tellers.

  Sick and tired

  Rare disease drains senior's energy, health

- Omit forms of the verb *to be*, if possible. Notice the correct deletions of the words in brackets.

  Senior party preparations [are] underway as graduation nears[10]

  Flu bug attacks students; many absences [are] reported[11]

- Opt for the active voice over the passive voice whenever possible. The first headline shows the correct use of the active voice; the second the correct use of the passive voice.

  Debate team ranks first in district, state contests

  Five '97 graduates given top awards at commencement

- Use the present tense to describe past events. This use is known as the historical present.

  Council approves $1 million renovation project

- The past tense is showing up in more publications, especially when it enhances clarity. In the following

Fig. 14.3. *Stinger,*
Irmo High School,
Columbia, S.C.

Dallas Morning News headline, past tense is used because the killers were dead by the time the story ran.

Pair made video before Littleton killings

• Use the infinitive form of the verb for future events. Any other tense would only confuse the reader.

Crawl-space renovation to begin within month

• Do not separate the following items from one line to the next. Avoid these breaks:

1. Preposition and its object

AP Art students pressured to finish portfolios, pass exam

Pat Garrison's game is getting better and better all because he has *a head for golf*

Garrison shoots for the Green!!!

Fig. 14.4. *Green Raider,* Ridley High School, Folsom, Pa.

2. Parts of the same verb

> **Science club president to promote plastic recycling**

3. Parts of names that belong together

> **Senior waits 10 hours for Star Wars premiere in pouring rain**

4. Abbreviations

> **Alum wins NC AA top honor**

5. Noun and its adjacent adjective

> **HHS Band involves feeder-school bands to boost future participation**

6. Compound words

> **Texas tourist jumps under subway to save toddler**

VIOLENCE
coming closer to home
Abuse leaves terror in path of destruction

Fig. 14.5. *Peninsula Outlook*, Peninsula High School, Gig Harbor, Wash.

- Don't repeat words in the headline.

  Test scores fall

  Students' test results fall for third consecutive year

- Generally use numerals, although numbers through nine may be spelled out.

  Tennis team dominates: Eight head to leagues after an almost flawless season[12]

  Senior class collects 123 pints in blood drive[13]

- "Down style," or capitalizing only the first word of a headline and all proper nouns, has become the preferred style of most publications.[14]

  Irmo experiences two fires in two days

- Instead of general words, as in the first headline, opt for specific words that fit the same space. The second headline has been written with stronger, more precise language.[15]

  New bill requires increased language requirement

  State may require two years of high school Spanish

- Punctuate headlines correctly; omit periods.

  1. Commas are often used to replace *and*. In all other cases, standard English usage rules that apply for commas apply in headlines.[16]

     Yellow Ribbon Week reminds friends, family to listen

  2. Use the semicolon to attach two related thoughts.

     Tornado destroys field house; clean-up to take three weeks

  3. Use single quotation marks rather than double.

     **Putting 'the boot' down
     Delinquent parking tickets prompt school officials to purchase new tool**

- Do not use obscure or unnecessary abbreviations.

> *Wrong:* **New FHS principal changes discipline plan**
> *Right:* **New principal changes discipline plan**

- Never abbreviate a day of the week.

- Never use a day of the week and date together.

- Do not abbreviate months except when a numeral follows (Jan. 27).

- Write nothing in the headline that isn't in the story. If you know something interesting or important has been omitted, insert it in the story.

- Do not use names unless the persons are commonly known. Use a synonym that would be more meaningful.

- Avoid placing headlines and nonrelated pictures near each other, especially when an unexpected connection may be perceived.

FEATURE HEADLINES

Entertainment is the goal when writing the teaser headline. *Dallas Morning News* editor/writer Nancy Kruh discusses the process for writing a feature headline and offers tips.

> With feature journalism now a staple in every section of the daily newspaper, copy editors are being called upon increasingly to write headlines that sell a story with word play, as well as information.
>
> Crafting a feature headline that's entertaining, compelling and sophisticated requires all of a copy editor's creative skills. The best editors tend to look upon the challenge almost as a word game: How can you make a headline fun – and make it fit the space? The deftest headlines are a delight with or without the story: "She stole his heart, so the police had to write her a ticket," "If all goes as planned, it's an accident," "Hundreds of mouses flock to cat's Web page," "It's picture day at school, so make it a snap."
>
> Becoming an accomplished feature-headline writer takes practice but also requires an avid attentiveness to language and popular culture. You simply can't write wonderfully inventive headlines such as "Nobody troubles the nose I've seen" – as *Dallas Morning News* copy editor Steve Steinberg did for a column about the perils of an oversized nose – without knowing the old expression "Nobody knows the trouble I've seen." Imagine trying to write a feature headline about, say, "Star Wars" without knowing about The Force or R2D2.
>
> Besides wracking your brain for idioms associated with the main themes of your story, you also can rely on a dictionary, which often includes common expressions in its definitions. (For example, here's some of what *Webster's New World Dictionary* offers for "heart": "eat one's heart out," "after one's own heart," "break one's heart," "take to heart," "do one's heart good." There also are all these related words: "heartache," "heart attack," "heartbeat" and "heartburn.") Many other reference works besides the dictionary have compiled slang expressions and idioms; check your local library or bookstore for those.
>
> Once you've gathered a few catch phrases, it's time to get your wheels turning. Here, for example, is how Carolyn Poh, another accomplished *Dallas News* copy editor, brainstormed a headline for a feature about the coffee-table books on sale for Christmas. First, she gathered words associated with "books" and "coffee," such as "tome," "binder," "pages," "chapter," "slick," "cream," "sugar," "beans," "grind" and "stir." Then she free-associated her way to these four clever headlines: "Best of tomes, worst of tomes" (a play off Charles Dickens' "best of times, worst of times"), "Binders keepers," "In the slick of things" and "Cream of the coffee table." The latter

was the one ultimately selected for publication.

Here are a few guidelines that can help you get inspired when you're assigned to write a feature headline (examples have all been written by *Dallas News* copy editors):

1. Freshen a cliché by exploiting its literal meaning. For instance, "A chip off the old block" is a flat and trite headline if the accompanying story is about sons who have taken up their fathers' professions. But the same headline is fun and inventive if the fathers happen to be carpenters. Here are other examples: "Kids' tastes get a bit hard to swallow," "Women's soccer team has the world at its feet," "Bartending couple endured two rounds of love on the rocks," "Toilet-seat debate has ups and downs."

2. Turn an idiomatic expression into a catchy headline by switching words: "Sculptor has stones of heart," "You've lain in your bed – now make it."

3. Alter spelling, but not pronunciation: "Cat gives paws to writing career."

4. Alter (very slightly) spelling and pronunciation: "The musician with sax appeal," "Mooch obliged: Author relies on fans' hospitality for national book tour," "Fame thrower."

5. Use a word with two meanings (but only if both meanings are appropriate): "He has few reservations about hotels," "The business of having a baby is all in the delivery," "She has never been hooked by the lure of fishing."

6. Use rhyming words or alliterations: "Saucy Aussie," "Noodling with doodling," "Star-studded dud," "Rough-neck romance," "Intricate intrigue hits home."

7. Change a word in a well-known phrase: "Self-adhesive stamps: If you can't lick 'em, buy 'em," "They're only young twice."

8. Employ evocative and subject-appropriate language: "Tale of American West shoots for suspense," "The forceful return: 'Star Wars' blasts into theaters again."

9. Use opposites, such as "up, down" or "rich, poor": "Hard times bring out a light touch," "Novel makes short work of long life."

10. Have your own say. A direct comment to the story or its subject, particularly in the upper line of a deck, can be quite an eye-catcher: "Beat it, kid: Not everyone likes 'Little Drummer Boy,'" "Give 'em yell, mom: Dallas Cowboys cheerleader is 37, married and has four kids," "It's Ms. Cinderella to you, bub: New play toughens a traditional heroine."

A few final thoughts: Word-play headlines have become so popular, editors occasionally stretch puns beyond the bounds of reasonable taste, inviting groans from readers. You'll have to decide for yourself where you draw the line, but here are a few excesses you can use as benchmarks: "Allergies must have a wheezin'," "There's a lot of finny business going on here," "She's Hillary-ous," "With cows, it's always one thing or an udder."

It's also wise to avoid certain idioms and headline tricks that have become hackneyed over the years. These include playing off the subject's name, "Tom is Cruising to another hit movie"; using parentheses, "Naughty but (n)ice cream"; and employing any of these clichés: "Yes, Virginia, there is a Santa Claus," "A sign of the times," and "Tis the season." Relying on these crutches is not just unimaginative. It's lazy.

Some examples of quality feature headlines from high school publications include

- A sports story about two girls trying out for the school's wrestling team

  Wrestling with change[17]

- An entertainment story about the drama club's twisted production of "Alice in Wonderland," where Alice is in an insane asylum

  Alice in . . . La La Land[18]

- A sports story about a St. Louis Cardinals record-setting home run season

  One dinger with extra distance, please . . . Big mac super sizes the homer record

- A health story about the increased uses and effects of caffeine

  Buzzing about caffeine
  Wonder drug helps
  many students make it
  through school day[19]

- A story about an alumni Trey Dyson, who had an extraordinary college freshman season

  Slicin' & Dyson

  SV alumnus tears through opposition, named Rookie of the Fall at USC

- A news-feature about the campaign of a mother whose son was killed in a drunk-driving accident

  A drunk driver shattered the lives of a local family. Now in memory of her son, Sue Anderson gives Lakota students . . .
  A crash course

- A news-feature about social committee preparations for the WPA dance.

  Making themes come true
  Student Council Social Committee
  Head creates decorations for WPA[20]

- A story about the problems homeowners in the community have had with students' reckless behavior

  Neighbor Hoods
  U-Highers' reputation in community
  could use some holiday giftwrap[21]

NOTES

1. *Lowell*, Lowell High School, San Francisco, Calif.

2. *Redwood Bark*, Redwood High School, Larkspur, Calif.

3. *Paladin*, Kapaun Mt. Carmel High School, Wichita, Kan.

4. *Lance*, Robert E. Lee High School, Springfield, Va.

5. *Edition*, Anderson High School, Austin, Texas.

6. *Maroon*, Stephen F. Austin High School, Austin, Texas.

7. *Panther Prints*, Duncanville High School, Duncanville, Texas.

8. *Axe*, South Eugene High School, Eugene, Ore.

9. *Central Times*, Naperville Central High School, Naperville, Ill.

10. *Apple Leaf*, Wenatchee High School, Wenatchee, Wash.

11. *Apple Leaf*, Wenatchee High School, Wenatchee, Wash.

12. *Trapeze*, Oak Park and River Forest High School, Oak Park, Ill.

13. *Peninsula Outlook*, Peninsula High School, Gig Harbor, Wash.

14. *Stinger*, Irmo High School, Columbia, S.C.

15. *Stampede*, Burges High School, El Paso, Texas.

16. *Panther Prints*, Duncanville High School, Duncanville, Texas.

17. *Hy News*, Belleville Township High School, Belleville, Ill.

18. *Academy Times*, Charles Wright Academy, Tacoma, Wash.

19. *Tide Lines*, Pottsville Area High School, Pottsville, Pa.

20. *Mission*, Shawnee Mission North High School, Overland Park, Kan.

21. *U-High Midway*, University High School, Chicago, Ill.

22. *Hillcrest Hurricane*, Hillcrest High School, Dallas, Texas.

23. *Hillcrest Hurricane*, Hillcrest High School, Dallas, Texas.

EXERCISES

1. Clip and mount five tellers and five teasers from your area daily newspaper. Explain the difference.

2. Clip and mount five headlines from your area daily newspaper and rank them for quality. Explain why each grabbed your attention and why.

3. On a separate sheet of paper grade each of the following headlines (a) to (j) on how well it

exemplifies the principles of good headline writing. Justify your grade.

(a) A news-feature about what people can do when they turn 18[22]

Opportunities increase as students reach 18

(b) An informative feature story about how to pack for holiday trips[23]

Packing tips for perfectly wrinkle-free holiday vacations

(c) A story about protesting an assembly film

Commotion is caused by picture

(d) A straight news story about a faculty retirement

Murdock leaves Central faculty; successor named

(e) A football game story

Team excels in 42–7 win

(f) A new story about a new musical

"Leader of the pack" is named musical

(g) A news-feature on a new program requiring truants to clean up the school

**Cleaning up their acts
New custodian enforces community service**

(h) A feature story about keeping New Year's resolutions

Resolving problems

(i) A feature story about a special education physical education class

**Something special in the air

P.E. class encourages students to learn skills in positive atmosphere**

(j) A news story about an upcoming state poetry contest

Roper to compete for first state title

4. For the following story write a two-line headline with each line counting no fewer than 17 and no more than 23.

A Lakota freshman school student has been charged with illegal possession of a deadly weapon after the student was allegedly found with a BB gun in his locker on April 22.

Along with the legal charges, the student has also received a ten-day suspension and a recommendation for expulsion for his illicit activities.

The weapon was found after a school administrator received an anonymous tip that there was a student at the school who claimed to have a gun.

According to Assistant Principal Lee Corder, after the administration called the police a brief investigation of the student was held and the BB gun was found.

Corder feels that the situation was dealt with efficiently.

"I think that it [the investigation] created very little disturbance in the building," said Corder. "It was handled quickly and responsibly without incident."

Lakota freshman Andrea Piri said she was amazed that something like this could happen.

"I was surprised that anybody would bring a BB gun to school. It's obvious that they'd be caught," said Piri.

Lee Delaveris
Lakota Spark
Lakota East High School
Liberty Township, Ohio

5. Write a one-line main headline counting between 16 and 22 and a one-line secondary headline counting between 26 and 32.

"To bee or not to bee." That is the question concerning maintenance personnel who have to deal with the campus bee problem.

The typical lunch has been drastically changed for those students who eat outside, because of the bee swarms around trash cans. Lunch-goers move from table to table and girls scream at the top of their lungs, when pestered by a bee swarm.

"I just sit there and hope the bees leave me alone," senior Bruce Nguyen said.

"We are doing as much as humanly possible to get rid of the bees at this point," plant manager Connie White said. "You're messing with the forces of nature when you leave out food. Students can help by putting trash in its proper place."

Assistant principal Quinn Kellis also emphasized the need for a clean campus. "The problem we have is we can't spray insecticides while students are on campus. So we've been using traps and mild soap that's diluted to kill the bees," Kellis said. "The best solution is to keep the area clean."

Though the hive has been located, everyone still needs to do their part, White said. Once a month the kitchen cafeteria area is sprayed by an exterminating firm, but that doesn't stop them from coming back.

Patty Barney
Ridge Review
Mountain Ridge High School
Glendale, Ariz.

6. Write a one-line main headline counting between 13 and 20 and a two-line headline with each line counting between 22 and 29.

After two years of discussion, the banning of book bags will become a school policy effective at the beginning of the school year.

There are several reasons that the administration thinks this is a good idea.

"They block hallways, doors and classroom aisles. If we needed to evacuate the school properly, the book bags would be in the way. Fire prevention officer (Dean E. Spitler) did an inspection and recommended that we get rid of them. To continue having book bags would be going against a professional opinion," Principal Dr. Kathleen Crates said.

Another reason backpacks are a problem is that they enable students to bring unnecessary items into the building.

"They allow students to carry in things that aren't healthy in the learning environment. From pop bottles to weapons, they can carry it in without anyone knowing that they have it. They add to the congestion in the halls and are also clinically proven to be bad for students' backs," Crates said.

Hidden objects in book bags are also a concern to Junior Principal Patrick Hickey.

"From the standpoint of security, book bags give students a way to bring contraband into the school. There are hundreds of book bags laying around unattended, and no one questions whose book bags they are. Students could easily leave a book bag that is dangerous laying around in the cafeteria or music wing.

"When purses are left laying around, people bring them down to the office right away. No one would think twice about taking a book bag down to the office," Hickey said.

While administrators think eliminating book bags will increase security, some students are opposed to the whole idea.

"Book bags are supposedly a fire hazard, but I don't understand how a pile of books that could get scattered on the floor is any better than books inside of something. We could find an alternate solution to the problem, like using book bag racks in the classrooms," Junior Amy Chester said.

Yet there are also students who don't really care about the new book bag policy.

"It's not like people are going to have to go to their lockers every period, you take two books and go to your classes and switch books later. There is a big enough place to put them under your desk where they won't be in the way. There are ways to get around without a book bag, but no one wants to work with the system," Sophomore Mike LaRocco said.

Kristin Cramer
Blue & Gold
Findlay High School
Findlay, Ohio

7. Write a one-line headline counting between 26 and 32.

With a high voltage smile, Kevin Dixon, Summit's junior and high school science teacher, carefully places 12 ocean blue marbles on the wooden game board.

"Blue marbles represent the electrons, red marbles represent the protons, and the yellow ones represent the neutrons," he says.

Instead of drawing how the atomic structure of the carbon atom looks on the chalkboard, Mr. Dixon uses a new game to give a better feel of how atoms are made.

He also uses the other new "toys" he received this past summer, including plastic maps of the human body and frog.

A grant of $7,500 approved by operations manager Fred Dallas and general manager Larry Lenzi of Multifoods Distribution Systems of Dallas, paid for the Summit's new dry laboratory.

"No water, no specimens, or no chemicals. Everything is a model," said Mr. Dixon in describing a dry lab.

In addition to the new game, Mr. Dixon received CD-ROMs that have computerized versions of earth worms, frogs, fetal pigs and even the human body; new National Geographic videos; and plastic maps of the human body.

"The kids up here learn better from tactile styles, meaning they work better with their hands," explains Randy Cothran, the alternative school's principal.

The new dry science laboratory was designed specifically for this purpose. The CD-ROMs that use computer animated versions of the frog will help the students see how the insides of the frog, or whatever model being used, looks like instead of using live frogs.

"Anything on computer is tactile; anything you can touch is tactile. It helps the students learn better," Mr. Dixon said.

When students use the new program, an animated scalpel appears on the computer screen and a student can start to dissect the computerized specimen with a click of a mouse.

Although the students have not been introduced to the science laboratory yet, Mr. Dixon anticipates it to be a successful learning tool, and most of all, fun for the students.

"The lab will be open to any students at the Summit," he said.

Mr. Dixon and Mr. Cothran stress that the students learn much better with their hands, rather than reading it out of a textbook.

Trisha Nemec
Panther Prints
Duncanville High School
Duncanville, Texas

8. Write a one-line headline counting between 26 and 32.

Vandals, allegedly TPHS students, broke into Del Mar Pines Elementary School damaging or stealing $7,000–8,000 worth of equipment Nov. 5th.

There is a $1,000 reward for information about the break-in, which is technically considered a "commercial burglary." The incident occurred between 8 p.m. and 1:25 a.m. The vandals stole two TVs, three VCRs, three boom boxes and one laptop computer. They also destroyed one computer and one boom box. Three windows were broken in the process and several doors were forced open. All four buildings of the school were broken into, with damage being done to the majority of the rooms.

"Everything seems to be pointing to students of TPHS. The police say this because there was a pep rally at a high school Thursday night and the elementary school is located very close to it. It was obviously done by high school age kids," Marci McCord, administrator at Del Mar Pines, said.

No school was held on Friday due to the destructive vandalism. This caused some problems for busy parents who had to deal with their children not being in school for a day. A school-wide security system is going to be installed at the approximate cost of $5,000 to prevent further problems involving burglary.

"Most kids at TPHS are really good. They help us out a lot here. A few bad apples ruin it for everybody. We shouldn't be too judgmental about these," McCord said.

Detective Lew Johns is in charge of the case. Police suspect multiple vandals who were of high school age based on the kind of damage done. Fingerprints were collected at the scene of the crime, and have been analyzed although information from the fingerprints has not been released. There is at least one suspect currently.

Del Mar Pines officials ask that anyone who has information regarding the break-in call either Del Mar Pines at 481-5615. Detective Johns at 552-1700, or 235-TIPS.

Brett Howell
Falconer
Torrey Pines High School
San Diego, Calif.

9. Choose a feature story from a newspaper or magazine. Write six different teasers for the story. Keep them short. Be creative.

Understanding Typography and Production

Helvetica, Fenice, Times Roman, Hobo, Zapf Chancery, New Baskerville, Stone. New names for school mascots?

Students who learn to love typography instantly recognize these names as particular styles of typeface design, and those that get hooked by the type bug can even point out the distinctions of the individual letter forms. Typeaholics learn to love and appreciate the eccentricities and quirks of letter forms and exploit their principles in well-designed type displays.

Because the page designer can be the best friend or worst enemy of the writer, good designers understand and appreciate the value of carefully chosen type. They understand how the space between the letters – kerning – and the space between the lines of type – leading – can add to that readability.

With the advent of desktop-publishing software, student designers literally have at their fingertips the power to transport their readers through visual/verbal displays of their word content. They can add to the feeling a reader has for a page design or topic.

Although the vast majority of schools are now using computers and desktop-publishing programs for production of pages in a process known as *computer pagination*, other schools with limited access to computers rely on traditional methods of type preparation, primarily on services that provide desktop publishing.

With the proliferation of desktop-publishing software, many companies have begun selling typefaces. Type CDs can be ordered through numerous vendors, and typefaces can be bought and downloaded to the computer directly off the CD by simply calling in a credit card number. Many typefaces are offered for free over the internet. Some of these typefaces will display correctly on a computer screen display but will not print correctly. It's best to buy typefaces from companies that specialize in selling type.

TYPE TERMS

Defining terms that relate to typography will help the designer in choosing and understanding type.

- *Typeface or font*: a range of type in all the characters in one size and weight.

- *Type family*: a range of text in weights (i.e., light, bold, heavy, extra bold) and postures (i.e., italic, bold italic) for a particular typeface. Some typefaces are versatile, offering as many as 10 or 11 variations of structure within the same type family. Other typefaces might offer only one variation of the face.

- *Leading*: the space between the lines of type. Body text is traditionally set with 2 points of leading (the size of the type plus 2 extra points of leading; i.e., 9 point type/11 point leading). Solid leading means the type size is equal to the leading value (i.e., 9 point type/9 point leading), which could cause ascender and descender letters to merge if they align in the text.

- *Body text*: generally between 9 and 12 picas, the size in which traditional text stories appear on the page.

- *Bullets*: typographic or graphic devices used to mark entry into paragraphs or text passages. Bullets can be dots, squares, checks or symbols and can be used in color to create repetition.

- *Display type*: type sizes 14 points and above used to display information such as headlines, secondary or deck headlines and other graphic information.

- *Drop caps*: letters set in larger sizes at the beginning of text or throughout the text, directing the reader's eye to the beginning of stories. These letters usually "drop" into the first few lines of text. Hence, the name. In addition to drop caps, letters can "rise above" the other lines of text, can be set to the side of the text or can be printed beneath the text in a color or shade of color.

- *Agate type*: the smallest point size type a publication uses. Agate type is traditionally used for setting sports scores and classified ads in newspapers. The size might range between 5 and 6 points.

- *Alignment*: the method used for starting and ending lines of type. Left aligned means the type starts on a common left margin but features uneven arrangement on the right. Right-aligned features type with a common right arrangement, but a ragged left alignment. Centered type is type set to the middle of an alignment.

Justified type lines up on both the left and right edges. Force justified is a computer alignment that will add space between letters or words of type to cause them to fill up a line of space. This pattern creates awkward "rivers of white space," which inhibit readability.

- *Points*: a unit of measurement in type. There are 12 points in 1 pica. Type that is 1 inch in height is 72 points tall.

- *Pica*: a unit of measurement in type. There are 6 picas in an inch.

- *Baseline*: the line upon which all the letters sit.

- *Descenders*: letters that fall below the baseline and include the letters *g, j, p, q* and *y*.

- *Ascenders*: letters that rise above the baseline and include the letters *b, d, f, h, k, l* and *t*.

- *C/lc*: refers to the use of capitals and lowercase letters in design.

- *Down style*: the practice of capitalizing only the first letter of a headline and proper nouns that occur after the first letter. The style is easily read because it mimics sentence style.

- *Small caps*: refers to the use of letters that are the height of lowercase letters but have the posture of capital letters.

- *X-height*: refers to the height of the lowercase letters in proportion to the capital letters. Typefaces with large x-heights are more visible on the printed page, especially in small sizes.

CATEGORIES, OR RACES, OF TYPE

Although type could be classified in numerous categories according to its historical origin, placing type in six simpler categories makes it easier to use and reference.

SERIFS

Serif types, by tradition the easiest typefaces to read, are marked by the finishing strokes or touches on the ends of the stems. These finishing touches were indicative of particular styles as designed by their original designers. Serif typefaces have been the preferred choice for text for centuries. Because of this tradition of readability, serif typefaces remain popular for text type. The serifs often help the reader connect the letters visually (Fig. 15.1).

Most designers place serif types into subcategories based on the time period in which they were designed. For example, old style serifs, among the first serif

Fig. 15.1. *The Bruin* of McMinnville High School in Oregon, creates a striking front page through strong use of photography and typography in its broadsheet format. Starting with a front page profile on a student who moved out of his parents' house, the rest of the front page moves the reader into three other front page stories. The paper's designers help the reader distinguish between front page features and news through the changes in type. The front page package uses a distinctive, special typeface and is contained in a black box. The paper's primary news story on a new club promoting tolerance is typographically different from the smaller news stories at the bottom of the page. A combination of deck heads amplifies each headline and provides additional information to help readers into the stories. Story references run across the flag at the top of the page and a column of short items runs along the left side of the page. *The Bruin*, McMinnville High School, McMinnville, Ore.

typefaces, are noted for consistent contrast, sloped or rounded strokes and slanted and curved serifs. The rounded letters will also exhibit an angled tilt in the swelling. The tops of the ascenders will have a distinctly oblique serif. The serifs angle out from the stem and end in a bracketed serif.

The transitional serifs exhibit more contrast between thick and thin strokes, show almost no tilting in the angle of the swells of the rounded letters, are slightly less oblique at the tops of the ascenders and often have squared off serifs rather than rounded ones.

The modern serifs have a pronounced difference between the thickest and thinnest strokes, have completely vertical stress, feature serifs that are squared off and have unbracketed serifs.

SANS SERIFS

Sans, a word originating from French for *without*, indicates typefaces whose strokes do not end in serifs. Known as being geometric, precise and monotonal, sans serif typefaces are great for creating contrast between body type and other kinds of information, and in organizing information. Many typeface designers rely on sans serif typefaces for headlines, secondary headlines and text heads (small heads within the text). Additionally, sans serif typefaces are great choices for information used in

alternative story displays. They create contrast with the main story and are easy to read in smaller amounts of information.

SQUARE OR SLAB SERIFS

Square or slab serif typefaces end in precise, blocky or straight-line serifs. Although difficult to use in text type because of the wide nature of the letters, slab serifs suggest a certain ruggedness and stability. They can work for display type and for contrast between different kinds of information displayed (Fig. 15.2).

SCRIPTS OR CURSIVES

Typefaces that resemble connected or disconnected handwriting, scripts or cursives suggest a certain informality and can work effectively in certain kinds of advertising or in displaying specific kinds of information (Fig. 15.3). Their low readability and low contrast make them difficult to work with for headlines or other strong visual hierarchy displays.

BLACK LETTER

Most commonly referred to as Old English, black letter types are often associated with the nameplates of newspapers such as *The New York Times*. Of Germanic origin, these typefaces have extremely low readability, especially when used in all-cap lettering.

Fig. 15.2. In contrast to the serif typeface used in most body text, many newspapers choose to use sans serif typefaces – those without serifs – on headlines for strong contrast. Bold, condensed sans serif typefaces are particularly strong in contrast and help focus the reader to the beginning of each story on the page. On this front page, the staff has also created strong eye movement through the use of the blue cover used first on the sans serif typeface in the flag, then repeated along the left column in the index. Finally, a light tint of the blue appears behind the listing of solo and ensemble winners at the bottom of the page. An additional repeated typographic element appears in the two versions of sans serif type used in the nameplate. The two extremes – thick or heavy and thin – help to keep the two words in their flag separate though the words are touching. Note the repeat of that technique in the headline on the band feature photo. *Viking Vanguard*, Puyallup High School, Puyallup, Wash.

Black letter typefaces are often used for engraved invitations and to invoke certain moods at Halloween and other holidays. Few scholastic publications have use for any black letter typefaces.

NOVELTY

Types that can't be simply categorized into these other classifications often are labeled as novelty or miscellaneous typefaces. Exhibiting some "extra" quality, they are designed to display characteristics of their names or quirky characteristics that cause them to attract attention (Fig. 15.4). Novelty typefaces should not be used for text display and should be limited to display type. Too often, designers rely on novelty typefaces to do the job of good design. A well-written and clever headline in a standard typeface can be far more effective than a poorly written one displayed in a novelty typeface.

CHOOSING TYPE

Page designers are better off choosing serif and sans serif for most of their type design. Within these categories, bolder variations of serifs and sans serifs work best for display type such as in headline displays. Book or roman weights work best for copy display. An occasional use of a script or novelty typeface for a logo or for the theme statement might be effective in conveying the content of the message and in creating contrast with the other type choices.

With the advent of desktop publishing, a vast array of typefaces has been made commercially available. Some of these typefaces are quite visually effective, with smoothed edges that will print and read well. Others are produced by cheaper methods and could cause problems for printers when they use digital file format or when they download fonts to their systems. It's best to check with your printer when making typeface choices. Remember, too, that if your printer does not own the typeface choices you use in your designs, you will need to provide a downloadable file of that type to the printer in order for the type to print correctly in the finished design.

Fig. 15.3. Script typefaces, often resembling someone's personal handwriting, are friendly and personal. In this question and answer story format with an English teacher, the use signals to the reader that this content is different from a traditional story, delving into her personal life and religious background. The contrast between the bold serif type on the questions and the roman weight on the answers also helps the readers jump into each question and answer. The white space separating the individual questions and answers also provides good readability for this package. Finally, the informal picture adds to the package of information that invites the reader in for a closer look. *Crossfire,* Crossroads School, Santa Monica, Calif.

Fig. 15.4. Double trucks – subjects receiving two pages of coverage in the center of the newspaper – often present subjects that may lend themselves to the use of novelty or special typefaces not used on news or other traditional pages. In this double truck coverage on "Fighting the Flu," the designer has used a strong visual dominant cutout image to anchor the novelty headline and to provide some quick facts from a survey with students. The truck's main story also keys into a relevant news story relating to a cold remedy that is also a main ingredient in the making of the drug metamphetamine. The quick poll of students detailing what they do when home with a cold provides a good sidebar to the main story. The remedies sidebars across the bottom of the page provide quick-read information with cutouts of the various remedies. Color has been used effectively throughout this truck's coverage, inside the main headline and across the sidebars on remedies. The whole package of information is interesting to read and visually interesting to look at. *Bagpipe*, Highland Park High School, Dallas, Texas.

Designers need to consider several factors of type selection that affect readability and legibility (Fig. 15.5).

- *The X-height of the type.* Typefaces with large X-heights often have large, open counters in their letters and will print visibly and easily on the page. These typefaces are known as "big on the body." Some old style serifs have smaller X-heights, have smaller counters and eyes (the inside of the lowercase letter e) and need increased size on the page to encourage readability.

Fig. 15.5. The editorial page of the newspaper is one in which a distinctive look should be achieved. Readers need to be able to differentiate the persuasive content of this page from the more objective content offered in other sections of the paper. *The Battery's* editorial page features two editorials side-by-side, both set in larger type in wider widths than the other page material. The larger type helps balance the wider lines of the text set at 26.5 picas. The page's bold sans serif headlines provide clear entry into each column. The vertical layout of the editor's column along the right side of the page is balanced by the horizontal layout of the rest of the page. Finally, a well-organized masthead contains both the staff listings and the editorial policies of the paper in a succinct boxed area. *The Battery*, Abilene High School, Abilene, Texas.

- *The width of the text line.* Very narrow lines of text and very wide lines create difficult reading patterns. When designers set type in widths as narrow as 5 picas, they should choose typefaces that are slightly condensed and should avoid justified lines of type. Type set in wide lines, generally wider than 20 picas, will be more difficult for the reader's eye to follow.

- *The alignment pattern.* While it's generally accepted that justified type alignment and left-aligned type are the easiest reading patterns, some designers choose centered type for headline display and right-aligned for captions placed to the left of a picture.

- *The typeface itself.* Novelty typefaces are often difficult to read and to discern in print. The characteristics that give them novelty classification can make them hard to read. They should be avoided for long text displays.

- *The posture of the type.* Italic type and type set in bold weights generally create slower, denser reading patterns for the reader's eye. Use these postures in moderation.

Fig. 15.6. Many newspapers have pages in which smaller stories appear to help break up the pacing of the content. On this page called "Mixed, the section about life," each headline is designed with attention toward an individual contrast that helps separate the "blurbs" from each other. Various forms of contrast have been used to create these headlines, including mixing sizes, typefaces, positions and color. Note that the individual headlines are designed as strong units of type which bind them strongly to each blurb. *The Harbinger*, Shawnee Mission East High School, Prairie Village, Kan.

- *The color of the type.* Type in color can also slow readability. Color works best when used in limited amounts of type, such as headline displays, bullets, drop caps, headers and pull quotes.

- *The leading.* A current typographic trend shows designers using increased leading measures. On a computer, auto leading is usually activated. Auto leading will add a percentage of the point size of the active font's character to the leading value. Setting your own leading values gives you control over how far apart the lines of your text appear. For instance, type set in all caps is harder and slower to read. A designer can counteract that readability by setting the leading value at a higher percentage so the lines appear to be farther apart. The extra white space will "air out" the type, making it less dense. Designers should become accustomed to setting pure leading values rather than letting desktop-publishing programs make leading choices for them. Most desktop-publishing software programs also allow designers to change the auto leading value in a preferences file.

- *The kerning.* The space between letters and numbers can aid readability. In setting headlines in display type sizes, desktop-publishing programs' preset leading values will create typographic spacing problems. Numbers, for instance, will usually print too far apart. Other letter combinations can be tightened to eliminate uneven white space. Setting kerning values should be done individually between letter pairs in combination with the kerning control in the program. Kerning is difficult to see correctly on the computer screen. It isn't until the designer prints out a copy of the page that he or she can see typographic gaps in kerning. The object of correct kerning is to make it invisible and consistent.

Some layout software programs offer predetermined "tracking" values that can be used in place of individually kerning letters. These values often range from loose to very tight. Unfortunately, they don't take into consideration individual kerning problems and should not be used to replace good individual letter kerning.

TYPE CONTRAST AND CREATIVITY

One of the most interesting and rewarding areas of type design is choosing and designing type for visual creativity. Many combinations of type can be created that display a sense of the spirit of the design.

A headline should serve as a unit of information on a page. Designers can create contrast through combinations of type categories, by emphasizing words in the type display, by using color and by changing the positioning of the type display (Fig. 15.6).

Creating emphasis words in headlines can be done through size, through type posture and through color. Emphasis words should be carefully chosen so they work effectively with the story's content. In emphasis headlines, subordinate words such as articles and prepositional phrases can be lightened through weight, posture and size.

Color can bring the reader to a particular part of a headline. Repeating that color for text heads or story subheads can exploit the principle of grouping. Our eye tends to group things by shape and color (Fig. 15.7).

Headlines can be woven together in interesting arrangements and patterns. Headlines whose baselines have been rotated 90 degrees will effectively display information in bolder typefaces and when only a limited number of words is rotated. Desktop-publishing

Fig. 15.7. Strong use of type and color can help organize information in a page design. The combination of typefaces used in this headline attracts particular attention to the word *happening* which also appears in the warm red color, moving it forward on the page. Its size and color give it dominance in contrast in the headline. The color combination from the headline has been repeated vertically down the page for the circular dates used next to each event. The repetition of the blue from the main headline has been repeated in each event headline, further serving to connect the information. The staff's limiting of color use to display or headline type is logical and maintains strong readability for the individual stories which appear in traditional black on white. Reversing body type or using body type in color serve to make the type seem harder to read. *Bagpipe*, Highland Park High School, Dallas, Texas.

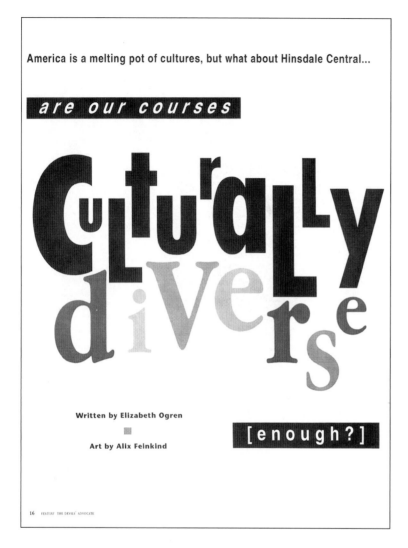

America is a melting pot of cultures, but what about Hinsdale Central...

are our courses

CuLtuRaLLy diVerse

[enough?]

Written by Elizabeth Ogren

Art by Alix Feinkind

16   FEATURE THE DEVILS' ADVOCATE

software makes it easy for designers to set type on skews, to baseline shift selected letters of type and to set type into shapes (Fig. 15.8).

In using any of these methods of contrast, the designer must consider readability as the most important factor.

Type wraps or run-arounds are created when the designer interjects a visual, a logo or an illustration into the type display and causes the type to contour to the shape of the visual. Often, the pictures are used as cutouts, where their backgrounds have been removed leaving only a shaped image. Because these shaped images are "active" visually, designers should limit their use. Designers seeking type run-arounds should make sure the lines of type created by the run-around are readable, that hyphenation isn't excessive and that the reader isn't being asked to make awkward jumps around the visual. Using justified alignment on the text display will usually be more effective when type runs around an image, particularly one with four sides (Fig. 15.9).

Desktop-publishing software also makes it easy for designers to create type picture boxes in which the letters can be filled with color or pictures. Doing so requires pretty bold type displays and recognizable images or effective use of color.

Fig. 15.8. Skewing the baselines (the lines upon which type normally sit) creates a typographic headline that again visualizes the verbal message, diversity. Mixing capitals and lowercase letters reinforces the effect. *Devils' Advocate*, Hinsdale Central High School, Hinsdale, Ill.

TYPE CONSISTENCY

Creating style templates for the various type patterns in a publication will create consistency and ensure that the publication doesn't have a scattered, eclectic look on every page. It will ultimately save the designers a lot of time when importing text from word-processing software programs used by different staff members.

In a desktop-publishing software program, style sheets can be defined for each individual type area on the page. These could include the text type, headline type, secondary headline type, caption type, folio type and any other design styles being used by a particular page or section of the publication. Style sheets offer designers the opportunity to choose typeface styles, sizes, leading values, kerning values, indents, colors, drop caps, rule lines and many other type specifications. The style can also be defined by clicking in a type display and setting that up as a style sheet. Once set and saved in a template mode, the styles will open when a designer opens the template and begins designing a page for that template. Style sheets save designers enormous amounts of time checking consistency from page to page.

Fig. 15.9. When type contours to an image, the designer must pay particular attention to how the type reads. When wrapping text around images, designers should make sure the widths of columns aren't compromised by the wrapping. In this design, the contouring of the type to the curved shape of the surfboard works well to maintain readable line widths for the text. Leaving hyphenation turned on ensures that the lines will set effectively, preventing holes of white space appearing between words. The image used inside the main headline adds to the visual interest of the page. Sidebars add interest to the page through their design and use of type. *The Tower, Grosse Pointe South High School, Grosse Point Farms, Mich.*

Elements that should be consistent throughout a publication include the body text, the folios, standing heads, the nameplate, section headers, pull quote designs, captions and secondary or deck heads. The use of special, stylized headlines set in typefaces that are not consistently used throughout the publication will often be by designer choice. These heads, referred to as "art heads," shouldn't overwhelm page content or interfere with readability.

Observe good professional newspapers such as the *Boston Globe*, *Chicago Tribune*, *Minneapolis Star-Tribune* or any good local newspaper to see how creative and attractive headlines can be designed using a limited number of typefaces consistently throughout the newspaper. These publications create attention-getting headline display on feature pages through creative headline content and strong, creative arrangements of type.

When placing text type on a page, designers should ensure that baselines align in columns of type that fall beside each other. Most desktop-publishing software programs enable designers to control the baseline alignment within a text box. Text shapes tend to appear in modules, or four-sided design shapes, although other patterns can be used.

Captions should be placed under or next to pictures, preferably in a point size or two smaller than the text size used on the page. Using bolder weights, italic posture or condensed type variations allow captions to contrast with body text and be seen more easily in the design.

Visual hierarchy in design ensures that a reader processes information in a logical and coherent way. Designers should choose sizes, weights and postures of type to draw the reader into the largest type display first and should then subordinate the type sizes and weights for information in a logical way. Text heads, pull quotes and secondary or deck headlines should appear in type sizes that are larger than text size but smaller than headline size, and in a typeface whose weight provides contrast to the body text.

Large passages of body text should not appear in italic or bold. Designers should seek to use the "book" or roman (text) weight versions of the type for ease of readability.

Captions and page folios should be smaller in the visual hierarchy. The smallest size type used on the page might very well be for picture credits giving credit to the photographers who shot the images. These picture credits often appear in type as small as 6 or 7 points.

Placement of elements on a page or spread is another factor in hierarchy. Elements placed in prominent page positions, known as the visual entry points, should be larger and more prominent. As the reader's eye moves toward the bottom of the page, typographic display (usually headlines) will become smaller. This story placement is also determined by the news value of the content (Fig. 15.10). See Chapter 1 for more on news values.

PRODUCTION

With the advent of desktop-publishing software, most designers have taken over primary responsibility for the pre-press production of their publications. Files may be sent directly to printers as pdf files, portable document format, which will imbed the images and the typefaces used in the designs. Some staffs still print out their pages on high quality printers with resolutions of 600 dpi or above and provide the camera-ready pages to the printer to be converted into film for plating.

Schools using laser printers will find improved reproduction of type and image. Laser printers create characters and images by drawing them through a computer language, such as Adobe's PostScript or OpenType or through TrueType, on a metal drum with a laser beam. The image becomes visible by electrostatically attracting dry ink power – toner – to the image. The toner binds to the paper by heat and pressure. Laser printing is similar to the process of photocopying.

Some schools use ink jet or dot matrix printers for output. These methods are lower quality than PostScript and are generally not acceptable for student publications.

When taking electronic files to a printer or service bureau, the designer must make sure to include all file formats, scans and typefaces that will be used in the production of the pages. Most desktop-publishing software programs have the capability to "collect for output," so they can gather the files they will need to ensure correct printing or will warn the designers of missing file information. Designers can often access utility checks to see if any files are missing that would cause the information to print incorrectly.

Schools can also purchase tabloid printers capable of outputting pages at 11 × 17 inches or larger and provide those printouts to the printer for reproduction.

Fig. 15.10. Helping readers through the content of pages is a strong function of headline size and design. In this front page, a strong front page package is designed for maximum visual hierarchy by the reader, providing a clear entry point into the page. The headline features negative leading and overlapping letters in a strong all-capital type arrangement that cleverly leads the reader to a story about school rivalries. The package utilizes a sans serif typeface picked up in various accessories on the page including the deck heads and pull quote. The headline at the bottom of the page in traditional serif type provides a strong second entry point without competing with the primary package. Along the right, a series of teasers to inside content provide visual interest and help bring the color down the page from the newspaper's flag atop the page. Captions in bold italic type provide contrast to the serif of the body text. *The Update*, H.H. Dow High School, Midland, Mich.

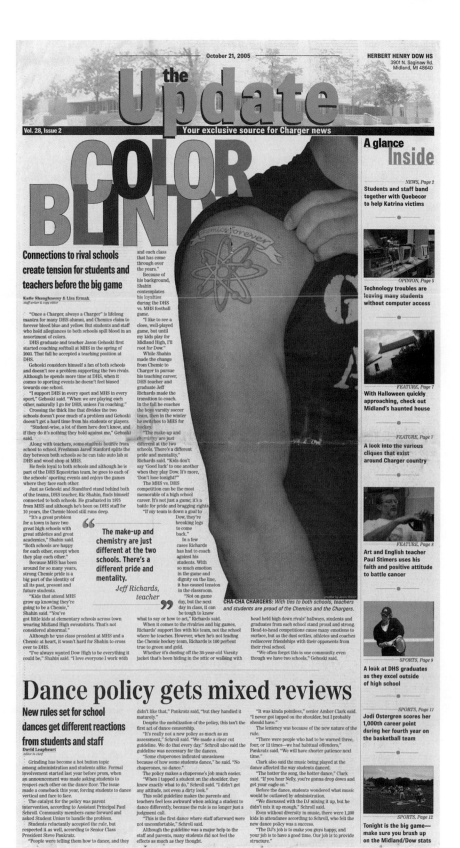

Best-selling and Favorite Typefaces

According to the Adobe Company, the best-selling Adobe typefaces in the world are:

- Adobe Caslon Regular
- Minion Regular
- Tekton Volume
- Adobe Garamond Volume
- Trajan Volume
- Warnock Pro Regular
- Adobe Jenson Pro Regular
- Lithos Pro Regular
- Myriad Pro Regular
- Nueva Regular

The Font Bureau's best-selling typefaces:

- Interstate Regular
- Sloop Script One
- Agency Regular
- Agenda Medium
- Bodega Sans Medium
- Magneto Bold
- Grotesque One One Bureau
- Empire Regular
- Californian Roman FB

FontHaus's best-selling typefaces:

- Carpenter
- Ovidius Script eFamily
- Sitcom
- Amethyst Script, PN
- FH Sans eFamily
- Caslon Antique Roman
- Bank Gothic eFamily
- Heatwave
- Erazure
- Fleche Regular

International Typeface Corporation's best-selling typefaces:

- ITC Officina Sans Volume
- ITC Franklin Gothic Volume
- ITC Conduit Complete Family Package
- ITC Garamond Book
- ITC Bodoni Six Volume
- ITC Stone Sans Volume
- ITC Berkeley Old Style Volume
- ITC Grimshaw Hand
- ITC Officina Serif Volume
- ITC Avant Garde Gothic Condensed Volume

PRINTING

Most printing today is done by the offset lithography method, based on the principle that oil and water do not mix. The offset method is printing from a smooth plate surface onto which the image has been "burned," or exposed through a large camera. The areas to be printed are treated so ink (oil-based) from the printing rollers adheres to them, while the remaining surface is treated with water rollers that reject the oily ink. The inked image is then transferred – offset – to a rubber roller surface, called a "blanket," that prints the image on the paper.

In order for photographs to be reproduced through offset printing, either they must be scanned directly into the desktop-publishing program and produced as output or the originals must be screened by the printer and stripped into the pages where holes created by black or red windows on the layouts will provide clear areas on the negatives.

Offset lithography for newspaper printing is primarily done by web presses, presses that print from continuously fed rolls of paper. Presses are also being perfected that print both sides of the paper at the same time, making the printing process fast. Most web presses are limited in the kinds of paper they are able to print, so papers with higher pulp content, such as newsprint, are ideally suited for web presses. With improved presses, printers can use higher grades of paper, allowing many publications to be printed on paper that is "whiter" and heavier than newsprint.

A popular variation of offset printing is a flexographic press used primarily in newspaper and paperback book publishing. An inexpensive and simple method of printing on a web-fed press, flexographic printing uses rubber plates and water- or solvent-based inks in a two-roller system. The process is considered more environmentally friendly since soy-based or vegetable inks can be used in combination with recycled paper stocks.

Yearbooks and magazines are also printed primarily through the offset method, but often on sheet-fed rather than web presses. Sheet-fed presses take single sheets of paper into the press at a time and can print both sides at once. The single sheets are large, allowing for the printing of several pages on each side of the form. Each side of the paper is known as a flat and might consist of four or eight pages. The two sides are called "signatures." A signature is then folded and trimmed to allow for normal reading. A printer determines how many forms are required to produce the book's or magazine's total page run.

Because the pages on a signature must be arranged in what is known as "printer spreads," pages that will print across from each other, printers often use "imposition software" on the electronic files provided by the school. Designers find it easier to design in "reader spreads," the configurations of pages that face each other when reading.

Books and magazines require binding, a method of holding together the printed pages. Magazines are usually bound by saddle-stitching, a method of placing staples in the center of the magazine directly in the gutter. Magazines can also be "perfect bound," where strips of glue applied along a flat gutter hold pages together. "Side-stitching" is used to refer to staples placed not in the gutter but slightly away from the gutter.

These binding methods have a definite effect on page margins and gutter margins. Magazines printed and saddle-stitched will open completely flat, allowing designers to take information closer to or across the gutter without a problem. Other binding methods, including mechanical or wire binding, side-stitching and perfect binding require larger gutter margins because the pages don't lay completely flat. In newspaper printing, only the middle pages of the paper will actually be printed on the same sheet of paper. This "double truck," as it's referred to in newspaper design, offers an excellent opportunity for staffs to design areas that go across the page.

Yearbooks are bound by collecting and sewing together the various forms or signatures by a process known as "Smythe-sewing." Binders use big machines that look like sewing machines to stitch a heavy-weight thread across the forms. Then a wide gauze strip is glued to the sewn pages and attached to a hard-back cover that has been rounded and backed to allow the book's multiple pages to lay open for reading. The gauze is covered on the inside by end sheets or end papers, often incorporating a design or color. Small, decorative "headbands" are finishing touches at the top and bottom of the sewn forms that cover up the binding.

Before offset became the primary printing form, other methods were more popular and are still used by some printers. These forms include letterpress and gravure printing.

Letterpress, the standard before offset, is printing from a raised surface. Type characters are cut into metal. Before metal type was invented in 1450 by Johann Gutenberg, they were cut into wood.

Gravure printing uses a raised or sunken surface into which the image has been etched. Gravure printing is excellent for high-quality reproduction, especially of photographic images, and is used in book publishing, in textile printing and by magazines such as *National Geographic*.

With improvements in desktop publishing and laser printing, many schools produce their pages directly from laser printer output, either photocopied or mimeographed, often in school print shops. Improvements in photocopiers now allow for quality photoreproduction and can be used effectively in small schools without incurring printing charges for short runs where a limited number of final copies is needed.

The use of color in printing is referred to as either "spot color," the use of a single color, or "four-color," the use of full color. Color adds significantly to the overall cost of the printing. The use of very specific color shades or tones can be chosen from patented inking processes manufactured by companies such as the Pantone Matching System, the most common method used in printing in the United States. These colors could actually incur "five-color printing," adding to the color cost. Four-color printing simply means the paper has to pass through four individual color inking presses that contain cyan (blue), magenta (red), yellow and black inks in order to reproduce as full color. Five-color requires the page to pass through an additional color press to apply a special colored ink (Fig. 15.11).

With color becoming more of a standard in printing, fully digital presses are being developed that allow for faster and less expensive use of color. Already, many yearbook staffs have produced full-color volumes. It's also common to see color throughout a high school newspaper. In order to reproduce color photographs in a newspaper, magazine or yearbook, the pictures must be "separated" into the four-color negatives needed to produce the color image. This can add significant costs to the printing job. With digital submission, the cost is minimized since the images print out digitally. Many yearbook publishers require four-color photos be submitted in the actual size they will appear in the book. If they are not, the staff could incur additional costs.

In high-quality printing, especially in which color is used, designers will be able to check proofs of their color before the job is actually printed. Low-end proofs, often "bluelines" or brownlines because of the color they appear in proof form, allow staffs to check photographic and type positioning and to check for errors in the copy. High-end color proofs are provided by different processes when required for color proofing and matching. Making corrections to either proof form will incur additional charges. Proofreading should be done as completely as possible before proofing occurs.

Printing is one area of technology that will continue to evolve. Already, printing press manufacturers are developing four-color, high-speed presses that will enable a digital file to go directly from the printer's front end, connected directly to a PostScript computer, immediately to the plating process, the last step before actual printing. Low-end printing processes, such as photocopying, also continue to evolve, making short-run printing possible from the local photocopying facility for almost immediate distribution.

Fig. 15.11. The use of full color in printing is becoming more common in high school newspapers due to changes in printing technology and cost. Keeping color from overwhelming the design becomes an important consideration in using color. In this front page, four-color photographs have been used, including the cutout image at the right side of the page. The page also takes advantage of the use of spot color, in this case red, to move the reader's eye from top to bottom and to create color unity in the design. Designers must make sure that color doesn't overwhelm the content of the news. *The A-Blast*, Annandale High School, Annandale, Va.

EXERCISES

1. Find examples of each of the six main categories or races of type, including serif, sans serif, square or slab serif, scripts or cursives, novelty and black letter. Cut out an example of each from a newspaper or magazine and label it. Discuss the use of the typeface within the context of the publication.

2. Using newspapers from out of town or from another state, find five examples of logos used in advertising for local businesses, products and services. Try to find an example of a logo for a local restaurant, a service, a children's store, a clothing store and a motel/hotel. Cut out each logo and paste it on a sheet of paper. In groups of three, exchange your lists and discuss your impressions of the businesses or services based on the logos. How would you dress to go to the restaurant? Is the children's store exclusive or mainstream? Who would the consumers be for the clothing store?

3. From newspapers or magazines clip five examples of type that fit the criteria for being readable and legible. List the factors that make the type examples readable and legible.

4. Visit the websites of these type houses (companies that make and sell typefaces for use in computer applications):

> Adobe Type: www.studio.adobe.com/us/type/main.jsp
> International Typeface Corporation: www.itcfonts.com
> FontHaus: www.fonthaus.com
> 2Rebels: www.2Rebels.com
> Lucas Fonts: www.lucasfonts.com
> Émigré: www.emigre.com

At each site, browse through the offerings including free font offerings and articles about typefaces and designers. Compare the type offerings and the prices for purchasing various typefaces and type packages.

From the different sites, identify a typeface that would be readable for body text and one that would not. Support the reasons for your choices.

Choose a typeface that would work for a headline on the following topics:

> Beauty
> Sports
> Homecoming
> Stress
> Graduation

5. Find examples of type that use the following techniques for creating contrast: a headline in which a word or two is emphasized through size variation; a headline in which color has been used to create contrast; a headline with an interesting arrangement and positioning of words; type that has been set on a skew or where the baseline is shifted from a normal position; and a type run-around or wraparound. If you have access to a computer and design software, using these samples create your own headlines in the same styles.

6. Using a local newspaper, examine the front page and an inside page and discuss the paper's use of visual hierarchy. If you have access to a pica ruler, measure the point size of the headlines on the front page and write the size next to each headline. Discuss the newspaper's consistency in use of body text, secondary or deck heads, bylines, headlines and captions. Next, look at the way in which the stories appear on the page. Draw boxes around each story unit (it may include a related picture) and see how many fall into modules of four sides. Look for consistency with the placement of text baselines in related columns of text.

7. If you have a local print shop or newspaper in your town, arrange a visit to the print shop or invite a printer to talk to the class, bringing examples of the different printing steps. Observe the printing method being used by the printer and have the technicians explain the different printing steps from start to finish. Ask questions about any process or procedure you don't understand.

8. Get copies of a newsmagazine such as *Time*, *Newsweek* or *U.S. News and World Report*. Open

the cover and find the staples used in the binding. This process is called "saddle-stitching." Open to the center of the publication and see how easily the pages lie open. Look at pages facing each other at the back of the magazine where elements are printed across the two pages. Observe whether they line up correctly. Next, get a copy of *National Geographic*, a magazine that is side-stitched. Open the cover and find the staples. Open to the center of the publication and see how flat the pages lie open.

Look at two pages printed across from each other at the back of the magazine where the elements have been printed across the two pages. Do they line up? Get a copy of the school's yearbook. Look at the end sheets at the front and back of the publication. Notice how the end sheets are holding the printed pages into the cover. Examine the spine and see how flexible it is in allowing the book to lie open. Look into the spine at the top or bottom of the book and see if the binding is finished with headbands.

Newspaper Design and Layout

Just as drivers need a road map when going on a long trip, readers need guidance in making sense of the information presented to them in a newspaper. If no attention is given to the way the newspaper is visually presented to the reader, few readers would be interested in reading the content of a typical edition. Layout designers are integral partners to writers, editors and photographers. Good writing deserves to be read. Good photographs should be viewed. It's the job of the designer, sometimes referred to as the "presentation director" at professional newspapers, to make sure the reader stays interested despite distractions and shortened attention spans.

Typically, high school newspapers appear in one of three sizes: newsmagazines, traditionally 8.5 × 11 inches; tabloid size, traditionally 11 × 17 inches; and broadsheets, traditionally 12.5 × 21.5 inches. While the professional press grapples with converting news size to tabloids or to scaled down broadsheets of 12 × 18.5 inches, some scholastic publications may also be affected, especially if the local newspaper prints them.

The layout designer can employ the principles of good design to maintain effective visual hierarchy and attractively designed pages (Figs. 16.1–16.3).

ELEMENTS OF DESIGN

Designers begin by considering the elements they will work with on the page. Text, including headlines, captions and stories, will create gray masses of weight on the page. Because text can "gray out" in long columns, creating long masses of text that can discourage readability, designers should pay attention to visual devices that will help break up the text and offer options for readability. Elements such as drop cap letters – large initial cap letters starting paragraphs – or text heads – small headlines placed within the story that help to create transitions at natural junctures – work well as visual breaks (Fig. 16.4).

Pictures, both black-and-white and color, as well as visual illustrations and drawings will create the weight of black on the page and in design. These denser visual areas need to be balanced with both the text weight and the space not used on the page, known as "white space."

White space, which makes up about 50 percent of all pages, creates the weight of white on the page and in the design. White space refers to both the space not used by the designer to create separations and alleys between text, as well as spaces left horizontally between the lines of the text, between the decks of the headlines and between the various elements of design. White space is an effective device for moving the reader from one element to another on the page. Surrounding a larger story with a bit of extra white space will dually serve to draw the reader to that element while creating separation between it and other page elements (Fig. 16.5).

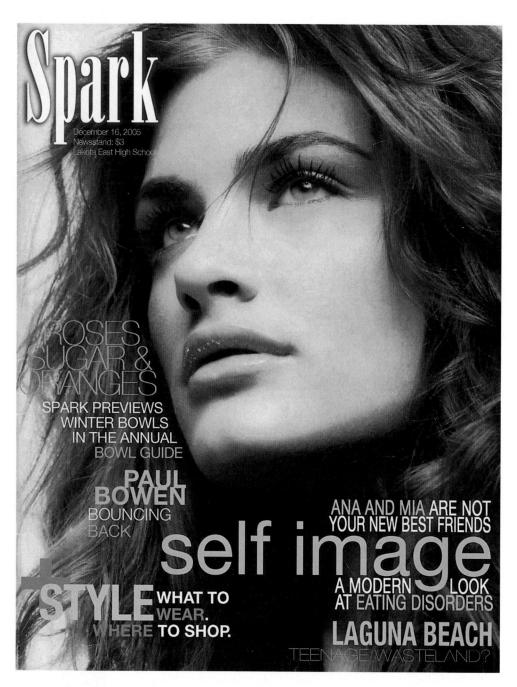

Fig. 16.1. Newsmagazines are increasingly popular formats for high school publications. Most newsmagazines employ a traditional "magazine" cover format, featuring a large image that "teases" their primary editorial content. Compelling photographs and illustrations allow designers to create a strong visual approach. Employing cover lines or additional teasers in type help editors promote content from within. *Spark*, the newsmagazine of Lakota East High School in Ohio, also uses color in its cover to give the publication the look of a professional magazine, a publication familiar to students. This image featured a centerpiece story on self-image. *Spark*, Lakota East High School, Lakota, Ohio.

Fig. 16.2. In a tabloid format, visual hierarchy and page architecture become important components. A primary story package features a combination of elements including the beginning of the story on abstinence, a feature headline and deck head, each adding information for the reader's understanding of the story. Visually, the package includes a graphic plus two photos, with the bottom being a strong dominant entry point. Two additional "news" stories and visual teasers or promos across the top of the flag add to the mix on the page. The vertical story on staggering school start times on the left helps break up the horizontal blocks of the other two front page stories. A gray screen behind this story sets it apart from the other information, but helps to give it important emphasis on the page. Additionally, the spot color, or single color, used in the newspaper's flag has been repeated in a chart accompanying the bottom story on a drug investigation in the school. The repetition of the color helps the reader connect the top to the bottom of the page. *Stampede*, W.H. Burges High School, El Paso, Texas.

Learning to balance the three elements and weights of design will ultimately allow the designer to create interesting, reader-friendly pages that will effectively showcase both text and visuals and create clear reading patterns for the reader.

PRINCIPLES OF GOOD DESIGN

Balance: Balance in design simply means that the page is visually and evenly weighted. It doesn't mean that everything appears the same size, but it does refer to

The Squall

May 20, 2005 — Dexter High School — Volume XVI, Issue 9 — 2200 N. Parker Road Dexter, MI 48130

"The seniors are done. Go out and have fun. Run in the sun with a hot dog bun."

Playin' hard: The womens soccer team is on their way to the top pg. 11

Scandal: Junior Spencer Ryan hacks his way to a 10 day suspension. pg.7

Battle for time: Battle of the Bands rescheduled for May 26 pg.6

Little becomes permanent high school principal

Student is Young Citizen of the Year finalist

Senior pranks tollerated until laws are broken

Early college application has benefits

U of M: Walking through campus, senior Whitney Holmes explores her future school. "I applied as soon as you could," Holmes said. "I didn't want to have to worry about where I was going to college and go through the whole waiting process."

Community members questions district's honesty

Fig. 16.3. In a broadsheet format, designers can maximize the packaging of content and pay particular attention to photo size. In *The Squall,* a minimum amount of space is used in the design for the flag and promos, allowing the maximum amount of space for the design. A package on early college application uses an image that becomes the central focal point of the page, combined with a story and a quick-read sidebar/quote combination. The page features four other stories, all of which are contained on this page without jumping content to an inside page. Tight editing allows stories to be contained on pages. Strong, bold sans serif type is used consistently, but varies in size, to allow the designers to create visual hierarchy. Small, tightly cropped pictures, primarily headshots, are used appropriately with the other stories. Only the bottom page story adds a picture to the coverage. White space is effectively used in this design, which utilizes a narrow background grid structure, allowing space to emerge, isolate and draw the eye in to the elements presented in the narrow grids. Note also the use of repetition from the red used in the flag to the bylines. *The Squall,* Dexter High School, Dexter, Mich.

Fig. 16.4. Visual entry points connect readers to content, especially in the design of broadsheet newspapers. Effective use of blue and yellow spot colors helps draw the eye from the top of the page to the bottom. A package of information utilizes an interesting collage image: a quote/head shot, a By the Numbers sidebar and an additional picture. The second story adds a sidebar summary and picture. Both stories begin with drop cap letters, an additional reader entry point, and deck, or subheads, providing additional information. Promos line the right side of the page in a size large enough to make them visible for the reader, followed by a news fact and corrections. The page space is effectively balanced and provides strong hierarchy for the eye. *HiLite*, Carmel High School, Carmel, Ind.

FRIDAY
november 12, 2004
vol. 51, no. 2

theremarker

newspaper of st. mark's school of texas

dallas, texas

REMEMBERING A SON, A FRIEND

from heartbreak, a purpose

'We are really hoping that Gordie's death will be the straw that broke the camel's back and that we can make this a national thrust.'
- *Leslie Lanahan*

FOREVER MISSED - Objects from Gordie Bailey's life are scattered around his parents' home. Despite his many talents, including sports, acting and playing the guitar, his mother will always remember the sense of humor and engaging personality of her son, who had just begun his college career at the University of Colorado at Boulder.

A grieving COMMUNITY

Headmaster affirms school's resolve. Page 7.

Max Downing '04 remembers his friend. Page 7.

The best way to honor Gordie Bailey. Commentary, Page 14.

Information on alcohol education can be found at Bailey's website – www.thegordiefoundation.org.

She heard the phone ring.
She was shocked by the unexpected voice that began to speak.
"I made the lacrosse team."
He was on his own. Gordie Bailey, former Marksman and freshman at the University of Colorado at Boulder, was finally a college man. No rules to follow. No parents to worry about. But he still took time to call his mom.
"Do you have the schedule yet?" Leslie Lanahan asked, eager to see her son in uniform.
"No. But I'll get you one as soon as I can."

That was the last conversation the mother and son would ever have.
That very night was the night he was waiting for - the night of the Chi Psi mountain ritual.
It was the night Bailey and his fraternity brothers would bond.
The night he would get his Chi Psi pin.
The upperclassmen marched the pledges up the Colorado mountainside. Confused. Blind-folded.
Unsure of what would transpire in the

Boulder wilderness, Bailey's knees shook with each step he took.
After waiting idly atop the mountain for 30 minutes, Bailey and the pledges took off their blindfolds to find no upperclassmen in sight.
Hearing them from a distance, the pledges ran across the mountain and met their brothers in front of a bonfire lined with ten bottles filled with whiskey and wine.

CONTINUED, PAGE 7

Story by **Frankie Shulkin,** EDITOR IN CHIEF and **Alex Mann,** MANAGING EDITOR, NEWS

DAVIS HALL Time to move on

Long-time faculty resident already feeling the loss of his 'home'

by Jon Goulding
FEATURES EDITOR

The room is cozy but not crowded. Books overflow the shelves while clippings and posters are tacked all over the walls. A filing cabinet rests just inside with a chair in front of it, for visitors. A bit further into the office are the basic necessities: a chair, a table, a computer.
Behind the chair is a view from which he can watch the center of the school ticking timelessly along. He loves that view and will miss it. The room is not disorganized, but holds that slight disorder characteristic of anything well lived-in.
What makes a home? Is it the place where a person spends the most time? A place associated with growth

and companionship? A place for which someone's heart will sink when left for the last time?
By every definition, Davis Hall is Larry Cavitt's home.
"I think the hardest thing will be to watch it get torn down," Cavitt said.
Davis Hall will definitely be torn down. The uncertainty up in the air on whether to renovate the building or level it has hit the floor.
Since its re-opening in 1946 after a fire that left only the brick skeleton standing, Davis Hall has been remodeled and renovated at other times.
It has seen just under 60 classes graduate - in recent years just outside its north windows which front the Ida M. and Cecil H. Green Commencement Theater.
It is not a perfect structure, and

Cavitt himself points out the leaks in the windows and the temperature troubles. But those are small inconveniences. "It's home, and so, no matter what its flaws are, there's a part of you that hates to see it go, and that's the way I feel about this building," he said.
Over his 36-year tenure, Cavitt has lived in six Davis Hall offices. He has lived in the same number of personal residences. But while moving from house to house has taken him down many roads and across many neighborhoods, moving from one office to another has always been a simple trip down or across a hall since he moved into Davis Hall in 1970.
"I've been in this professional home longer than in any other home I've ever been in," Cavitt said. "It does

CONTINUED, PAGE 2

Board sets 'solid plan' for moving forward

• Board of Trustees members voted last spring to do away with Davis Hall rather than renovate the oldest and most iconic building on campus after studying the issue in depth. Members have established a solid plan for campus growth.
• The school has hired the Blanchard Group of Richmond, VA, to produce a master plan for the school. Blanchard team members will formulate their plan by January.
• It is not known where the new building will be or when it will be built. The Blanchard Group's study will make recommendations based on interviews of administrators and department chairs.
• The school remains firm in its commitment to keep the memory of Davis Hall alive for future Marksmen. A "fitting remembrance" for both Davis Hall and the Davis family is planned for the new building, according to board action.

Fig. 16.5. White space is one of the best ways for designers to isolate content and help the reader see special content. The front page story detailing the death of a former student from a fraternity-hazing incident is packaged with photos showing parts of his life from photographs in his parents' home. The narrow columns of white space appearing on the left and right sides of the package help isolate this story from other front page content. *The Remarker*, St. Mark's School of Texas, Dallas, Texas.

Fig. 16.6. Strong visual hierarchy, consistent typography and dominant picture use are the hallmarks of these pages. The newspaper's flag and section flags appear in the same typeface and green color. The front page features a balanced layout and strong, serif typography in different sizes, to create visual hierarchy. The section openers (entertainment and sports) repeat the strong typography, each offering the reader entry into two main stories and a variety of short news briefs packaged across the bottoms of the pages. Designers have balanced visual use on each page, and have used devices such as pull quotes, deck heads and a front page chart to break up the text and add visual interest to the content. *The Bagpipe*, Highland Park High School, Dallas, Texas.

creating design that prevents the look of any design elements becoming distracting. If all the pictures are placed at the top of the page, the page will look top-heavy. The same problem will occur if all the pictures appear on the left or right side of the page. A large visual at the top of the page (creating a dense black weight on the page) needs to be balanced with something visual at the bottom.

Rhythm: Rhythm often refers to the visual flow of the page: good typography that coordinates well together, for instance, or a range of headline sizes that work well together for the size of the page being designed.

Unity: The pages must create unity throughout the publication so there's a sense of repetition in the use of elements that the reader grows familiar with during the reading process. Using a particular style of type and design for the nameplate and for elements that appear consistently throughout the newspaper, often referred to as "standing heads," is a good way to create unity. Using the same size and typeface for most stories or using the same type family for headlines will also give

the publication a unified look. The need for unity doesn't mean the designer can't deviate from the newspaper's typeface styles for a feature story or for an in-depth piece. Doing so helps to draw the reader's attention to something of special content in the newspaper. However, using different typefaces for every story in the newspaper will confuse unity, creating disparate and confusing messages for readers (Fig. 16.6).

Scale: Depending on the size of the publication, the designer must start with a series of vertical spaces dividing the page. These vertical spaces, called "columns" or "grids," help guide the reader in placing stories in the design. In addition to vertical columns, some designers will use an intricate series of horizontal columns to maintain alignment across pages and spreads so that lines of type within stories will also align. The grid or column method should create an appropriate and readable width for lines of type and layout of stories.

Proportion: Proportion must be considered by the designer. Maintaining proportional differences of 1:3

Fig. 16.7. Using packaging, this page builds the dominant use of space around a feature on the Live Strong bracelet/movement featuring a large illustration holding the headline. The yellow in the headline recreates the bracelet and connects the two visually. In addition to a major feature story on the bracelets, the story localizes the fight against cancer through a feature on a local student raising money by participating in a bike ride, and a quick facts factoid. The package is nicely balanced by a homecoming story running horizontally across the bottom of the page and a teaser column along the left. The use of hairline thin rule lines help divide each story into its own module on the page and provides an anchor for the "cutout" arm. Without the line, the arm would appear to be floating on the page. *Update,* Midland High High School, Midland, Mich.

creates asymmetrical designs that are far more visually interesting than symmetrical ones. For instance, when using a visual in design, the proportion of the largest visual on the page should often be two to three times larger than any other visual. Similarly, larger, more important stories should take up more space on the page than smaller, less important stories (Fig. 16.7).

Visual hierarchy: One of the designer's most important considerations, visual hierarchy is used to help the reader understand the significance of the information's importance. Stories with greater news values should appear at the top of the page with larger headlines. As the reader's eyes progress from the top of the page to the bottom, the headlines will be smaller in size to indicate a less important news value. This pattern of visual hierarchy is maintained on every page to help readers process information and edit the content they will read (Fig. 16.8).

INFORMATION PACKAGING

Another important consideration for designers is "packaging" the available information for the reader. Sometimes, a designer only has a single story without visuals. Working with an editor, a designer might be able to extract some of the information from the story and present it in a separate story placed adjacent to the primary story. Or, working with a photographer or an illustrator, the designer might be able to have a combination of photographic and text elements in which to present a single story. This combination might give the readers greater interest in the information. A reader might look at the shorter story presentation, find something of interest and begin reading the primary story. Or something in the visual or in the caption for the visual might give the reader a reason to read the primary story (Fig. 16.9).

Because of readers' splintered interests and attention spans, information packaging is becoming a more important consideration in layout and design. Packaged stories generally are given prominent page display and visual hierarchy, often focusing the reader's attention to that content first when looking at the page. Because of this, designers often surround a package with a bit more white space to further draw the reader to the content.

Packaging information requires the designer consider various approaches to layout. These include visual through photographs or illustrations or typographic through dominant headline displays. Working with pho-

tographers and illustrators, designers can come up with effective ways of displaying visual content. (Also see Chap. 20.)

GRIDS AND COLUMNS

As mentioned before, designers begin working on pages by dividing the space into a number of vertical and/or horizontal spaces depending on the size of the publication. Traditionally, newsmagazines often work with fewer vertical grids or columns, while larger formats such as broadsheets offer more options for dividing the page space (Fig. 16.10). In recent years, professional newspaper designers have begun using 12-column grids for broadsheets. Smaller publications, such as the newsmagazine, will rarely divide space into more than five to seven grids or columns. To do so would create awkward column widths.

Multiple-grid formats offer designers wide choices in creating layouts for stories. Readability of column widths must be considered when deciding how wide to make columns of type, but combining these columns and creating wider columns generally makes for ease of readability. The more narrow grids can be used for detail elements such as captions, drop cap letters or nut graph deck heads. Placing text in narrow grids, as narrow as 5 to 7 picas, generally produces low readability. When using narrow columns for text, designers should consider using condensed typefaces and unjustified alignment patterns so the text doesn't appear with frequent hyphens or large holes of white space between words (Fig. 16.11). (See Chap. 15 for more information.)

MARGINS AND SPACE

External margins are white space borders surrounding the page on all four sides. Necessary in newspaper printing because the presses cannot print to the edge of the page, margins also provide balance to the page and create alignments for the text, causing the readers' eyes to return to natural points on the page. Generally, margins can be as narrow as a quarter of an inch or can be a bit wider depending on the publication's page size.

Internal margins, the spaces between the columns vertically and horizontally, should be consistent and even for pages to look balanced and well proportioned. Although exceptions are sometimes made, vertical internal margins tend to be about 1 pica wide. This space allows designers to place text columns beside each other

Fig. 16.8. Editorial and opinion pages have a tendency to "gray out" if careful attention is not given to providing some visual relief. This opinion page effectively provides a wider grid for the staff editorials anchoring the left side of the page with a reduced sized flag appearing above them. The presence of the flag helps to make it clear to readers that these are the staff editorials. An editorial cartoon appears beneath the staff editorials. The staff has also chosen to illustrate two of the letters to the editors. A packaged opinion poll anchors the bottom of the page on the right, providing a concise and visually interesting use of space and content. The staff masthead anchors the bottom of the page horizontally. *The Southerner*, Henry W. Grady High School, Atlanta, Ga.

Fig. 16.9. Sports content is usually relegated to pages within newspapers. When content and circumstances warrant it, this content is sometimes given more prominent display. When the girls placed second in the state swim meet, the editors of *The Bruin* decided to package the story and place it on the front page. A great reaction picture, showcasing the girls' reaction to seeing their winning time in a relay, is paired with a shot showing a touching moment of encouragement between the coach and a swimmer before she competed. The entire package was placed just beneath the newspaper's flag and features a headline appearing at the top of the package, a common packaging device that helps to alert the reader to the content's importance. The front page then continues with traditional news content and a digest along the left grid. Note the use of extra white space, referred to as "rails" or narrow grids, which helps separate the package from the rest of the traditional news content. *The Bruin*, McMinnville High School, McMinnville, Ore.

Girls cut it close

Grizzlies claim second place at State Swim Meet

Story by **Drew Hunt** — Photos By **Ross Sherwood**

Receival of Gates foundation grant almost certain

Sophomore prank entertains few, annoys many

Back | Forward | Stop | Refresh | Home

Address: | www.selfimageonlinecommunities.com | > go

double-clicking on danger

story • caitlyn zachry   photo • pohul khera
art • lauren woodrick and ashley stewart

the night of the new moon.
    1:47 a.m.
    Pentagram, candles, incense, food – "good" food and "bad" food. Food to be saved and savored later, and food to be destroyed.
    These are the makings of the Summoning of Anamadim, or of "Ana," the goddess of starvation, the champion of restriction.
    The Summoning of Anamadim, a ritual which can be found on Ana's Underground Grotto, includes food sacrifices and is completed only at 1:47 a.m. on the night of a new moon. The ritual's purpose is to summon Anamadim, the goddess of starvation, in order to increase success in restriction. Psychologist Dr. Susan Mendelsohn describes anorexics as having "ritualistic behaviors, and a very irrational thought process." She is concerned that actions such as the Summoning of Anamadim increase anorexics' ritualistic tendencies.
    "[The Summoning of Anamadim] is exacerbating their already ritualistic ways of behavior, and telling them that it's okay," says Mendelsohn.
    Ana's Underground Grotto provides tips, quotes, and "philosophy" to anorexics in addition to the "Ritual." The Grotto refers to anorexia as "a lifestyle and a choice, not an illness or disorder."
    "If you regard 'ana' as a disease rather than a lifestyle or choice, and especially if you see yourself as the victim of an eating disorder, in need of recovery, seeking recovery, or having recovered, it is strongly suggested that you leave this site immediately," reads the "Background/Philosophy" section of the Grotto.
    The Grotto, a strictly pro-ana (anorexia) website, has a counterpart, Project Shapeshift, that consists mostly of forums. Throughout the winter holidays, many of the some 6,950 members of the pro-ana and pro-mia (bulimia) website are pairing up with "buddies," who serve to motivate each other

in dieting endeavors. During October some members of Project Shapeshift participated in Octoberfast, a group/partner fast that endures for at least one week.
    According to Mendelsohn, websites like the Grotto and Project Shapeshift serve only to perpetuate anorexia and bulimia. Mendelsohn, who specializes in eating disorder patients, has been in private practice since 1991, and is familiar with pro-ana and pro-mia sites because "some [of her] patients used to visit them."
    "They [pro-ana and pro-mia websites] should be banned, because [eating disorders] become a game," says Mendelsohn. "People are constantly trying to outdo each other in how sick they can get."
    Like most pro-ana or pro-mia websites, the Grotto sports a disclaimer warning potential viewers to refrain from entering the site. The Grotto describes the site as "a loaded psychological gun" and says that it will not be responsible if you choose to play with the said gun. But, according to Mendelsohn, people with eating disorders will enter these sites "no matter what the disclaimers say."
    "People can put as many disclaimers as they want," says Mendelsohn. "They are just not taking responsibility for feeding all of this information to sick people."
    However, a greater concern for Mendelsohn is the misinformation found on sites like the Grotto. According to Mendelsohn, the people who write statements like "you can live indefinitely without food as long as you have water" (the Grotto) are in "major denial."
    "[Those running pro-ana/pro-mia websites] think it's fine because they don't have enough nourishment for their brain to function," says Mendelsohn, implying that their judgement is impaired due to their own anorexic status. "And, they're on an endorphin high because of fasting."
    Despite the fact that Lakota East junior Martina Bell admits the information posted on pro-ana sites "might be fabricated

Fig. 16.10. Newsmagazines generally use standard magazine structure of three or four grids or columns on each page. Within that structure, designers can choose to vary the grids by combining them into wider grids and then creating rails of white space around them. In this design, the designer has used visual devices to make the page represent a web page, the subject of the content. By using wider grids and rails of white space on the left page, the designer helps attract interest to the beginning of the text. The facing page employs the traditional three-column grid, reserving the right grid for a sidebar separated visually from the main text by a headline and a gray box fill behind the text. *Spark*, Lakota East High School, Liberty Township, Ohio.

a little bit," she admits to looking at them sometimes.

"[The best advice I've gotten from a pro-ana site is to] drink liquids with no calories, so you're not hungry," says Bell.

Bell has had four pro-ana themed Xanga.com blogs, all of which she has deleted, the most recent one because her mom found it. According to Bell, pro-ana Xangas are most useful to keep track of calories, food intake, and goal and current weights.

"[My Xanga] was kind-of a way to just vent," says East junior Eileen Heaney, who kept a pro-ana Xanga for a couple of months. "I just don't like to keep journals under my pillow."

Heaney, who stopped using her Xanga because she lost interest, says that she still uses random MySpace and Xanga websites to help her lose weight. Even though she admits that these websites are "exaggerated," she still looks to them for advice.

52% of East girls

22% of East boys

have seen Xanga or Myspace websites that display "thinspiration" pictures

taken from a survey of 161 Lakota East females

taken from a survey of 143 Lakota East males

According to Aftab, the main problem that WiredSafety faces is that "a lot of sites that promote dangerous behavior, like bulimia and cutting, are not illegal in the United States." Aftab says that most of the issues WiredSafety faces in having dangerous websites removed arise from smaller networks.

"All of the big networks like Yahoo and MSN are very responsive to our concerns," says Aftab. "The problem is some of these sites are hosted by smaller networks that don't know who we are and don't care."

Anorexics.net, hosted by a "personal server," is described by its creator, whose forum name is Baby Fat, as a "support" website. However, it contains a "photo vault" in which girls pose with hip and pelvic bones protruding, their entire spines visible, and ribs exposed clearly enough to be counted through the skin. Also mixed throughout the "photo vault" are photos of

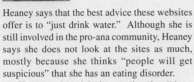

It's disgusting, it's sad, it's pitiful.

Heaney says that the best advice these websites offer is to "just drink water." Although she is still involved in the pro-ana community, Heaney says she does not look at the sites as much, mostly because she thinks "people will get suspicious" that she has an eating disorder.

However, Mendelsohn worries that "these sites will kill [viewers]," comparing them to "websites on how to make a bomb."

"It's disgusting, it's sad, it's pitiful," says Mendelsohn. "The people visiting [these sites] need to get professional help as soon as possible."

However, there are fewer pro-ana websites now because Internet safety groups alerted website hosts to this dangerous behavior.

WiredSafety, the largest and oldest Internet safety group, is one of these such groups.

Parry Aftab, cofounder of WiredSafety, says "it is not so much shutting down these sites. It is teaching kids responsible behavior."

WiredSafety, a worldwide charity that has been run by volunteers since 1995, works mostly to notify website hosts, such as Yahoo and MSN, of terms of service violations (which can include pro-ana sites). They also want to educate parents and help them with Internet supervision.

Heaney thinks that the "crackdown" on pro-ana websites was unfair because it disconnected anorexics from their so-called family.

"It shouldn't be [legal]," says Bell. "It's not like anorexics are the KKK."

celebrities, including Kate Moss, and a picture of a girl leaning over a toilet, with her finger shoved into her throat. However, Baby Fat maintains that the photos of "obese" and "emaciated" people are provided to "show the devastating effects of having an eating disorder."

"This site is not a recovery site. It is also not a 'pro-anorexia' site. It is a community of friendly people who share a commonality and need support," reads Anorexics.net's homepage.

However, Heaney uses Anorexics.net for "thinspiration," or pictures of lean people, which are used to "inspire" weight loss. Mendelsohn, who has only visited a pro-ana site on two occasions, believes that the creators of pro-ana websites, "like cult leaders" attract people with "low self-esteem, and no sense of self."

But, according to Mendelsohn, the main hindrance to recovery in anorexics is an unwillingness to recover. Mendelsohn, who says she still sometimes has anorexic thoughts, describes anorexics as "the toughest."

"When they don't want to get better, they won't," says Mendelsohn.

According to Bell and Heaney, the members of pro-ana websites most often do not want to get better. In fact, some websites even host "challenges" to see who can lose the most weight within a given time period, such as a week.

"It's like, 'Let's see who can be the best anorexic of the week,'" says Bell in disgust. "It's not a sport." ✱

connecting to the clientele

sidebar • ashley hall

Dr. Susan Mendolsohn has two Masters degrees, a doctorate and 14 years of counseling experience. But no job.

At least, she does not consider it a job. It's a passion, a mission, a duty.

Mendelsohn is a psychologist who specializes in eating disorders, a combination she has found to be rare, especially in the Cincinnati area. She suffered from anorexia and bulimia herself in her teens and twenties. Her experiences with her own parents not acknowledging her sickness, which many parents do, and her misery in college caused by her eating disorder, help her understand what her patients are going through.

"I really do empathize with these patients," she says. "I really, really understand their psyches. I relate very well to them. My personality, my training and my personal experience all are what are making me so very successful."

Mendelsohn is the psychological consultant for eDiets.com, has been featured in numerous newspapers, magazines and shows, including *The Wall Street Journal* and *Glamour*, and was named the 2004 Businesswoman of the Year in Ohio by the National Republican Congressional Committee (NRCC).

Despite her accomplishments, Mendelsohn is still driven to educate people about eating disorders and their dangers, and treating those already suffering from them. She is trying to become known for helping males with eating disorders.

"The boys are suffering way more in silence and dying in silence," she says. "I really, really wish to God that I could educate a whole world all at once. Just knowing that I can help people help themselves makes me go to bed at night very, very happy."

Mendelsohn says that treating anorexic patients is difficult because of the nature of the illness, and believes this could be why there are not many doctors who work with these patients.

"Anorexics do not believe that they have a problem. The bulimics are much easier to treat than anorexics," she says. "It's hard to find people who specialize in eating disorders, and it's very difficult to find psychiatrists or medical doctors that will specialize, I think because of the liability [of working with these patients]. So many of them are going to die, and then we get sued."

Despite the stress and risk involved with treating these patients, Mendelsohn continues to follow her passion because she recognizes the rarity of those in her field of specialty and personal experience with eating disorders.

"I'm thankful that this has happened to me, because it has made me better at what I do," she says. "Eating disorders are very serious. They're killing all generations of people." ✱

GREAT expectations

Senior Parris Cooper expresses her free spirit by fighting for future dreams of going to culinary school. Despite her father's disapproval, Cooper takes road less traveled.

All of her life, senior Parris Cooper's father had told her he wanted her to go to a 4-year university. Ever since she was a child, she was aware of his goals for her. When she told her father she wanted to talk, her stomach was in knots and she couldn't keep her nervousness from showing. She was a sophomore about to knock down 15 years of dreams her father held for her. She calmly explained that she didn't want to go to a 4-year school at all. Instead, she wanted to take culinary arts classes at a vocational school.

"He really wants me to go to a university like (University of California,) Davis or (Sacramento) State, but I know what I'm interested in," Parris Cooper said. "I really want to do culinary arts. I don't want to take 4 years to find out what I want to do at a university. I've already decided."

Cedric Cooper, Parris Cooper's father, was taken aback by her decision, not completely believing her at first. He questioned her motives, thinking it was simply a phase. His goals for his daughter had been at the front of his mind for 15 years and it seemed that they had been destroyed in a single moment. His only remaining hope was that she would change her mind and see the safety of a 4-year college where one can make mistakes and try different subjects. He felt that at a university, she could get a better education.

"If I didn't know what I wanted to do, I would agree with my dad," Parris Cooper said. "I would go to a 4-year school and try different things. But because I do know what I want, I'm going to stick with it. I think he means well, as far as wanting me to go to a 4-year school and I respect that a lot, but it's not what I want to do."

Parris Cooper hopes to attend the Institute of Technology for 7 months to take courses in the Culinary Division of the school. She took the placement exam for the school this year and passed, meaning she can attend the school next fall if she chooses. She had also applied to American River College because it offers culinary arts courses, but preferred the Institute of Technology because the courses are only 7 months long, as opposed to 2 years at ARC.

Parris Cooper's college choices are somewhat limited by her monetary resources. Because her father is not financially capable of supporting her through college, she will be working while attending classes.

"It doesn't really matter to me what job I have to do to work my way through college," Parris Cooper said, "but if I could work at a restaurant, it would be wonderful because then I'd be doing culinary arts at school and still doing that at work."

Perhaps as a result of his own current economic situation, Cedric Cooper has concerns that his daughter might not be able to support herself on paychecks coming from a career in culinary arts, a factor in his desire for her to attend a 4-year university. Conversely, the fact that Parris Cooper will be paying for much of her education may have contributed to her desire to go to a cheaper vocational school.

"I think the fact that she will be working through college played a part in her decision of schools," Cedric Cooper said. "I think it definitely was a factor."

Parris Cooper agreed that money was a factor in both her and her father's opinions on colleges and careers.

"One of the biggest things is that he wants me to make a lot of money," Parris Cooper said. "With culinary arts, first starting out, I wouldn't be making a lot. But as an end result, I'd be a lot happier. I love to cook for people and I love to see the smile on their faces when they have a good meal, versus counting cash."

Her passion for cooking and her insistence that she knows what she wants has started to sway her father's feelings on her future in the past 2 years. Her passion for culinary arts stems both from her father and her mother, who, although divorced, both contributed to shaping her interests.

"I was in the Navy, so I'm always hoping that one of my children will join the Armed Services as well," Cedric Cooper said. "So I told her there are cooks in the Navy too."

While Parris Cooper's mother is fond of cooking and passed that interest to her daughter, Cedric Cooper was once in the Navy and has tried to pass that passion to his children as well. Unfortunately for him, Parris Cooper's mother has been more successful. Parris Cooper attributes her goals to her admiration of her mother's cooking, rather than a desire to join the Navy.

"My mom is where my real passion for cooking came from," Parris Cooper said. "She can cook just about anything she puts her mind to, from Italian to Thai."

While her mother immediately supported her goals, Parris Cooper's father has been slower to come around to his daughter someday becoming a master chef.

"At first, I wanted her to do something different (than what she decided to do), but that's what she chose and I support her," Cedric Cooper said. "As a parent, you always hope your children will do things you want them to do, but children are people and they are allowed to make their own decisions, and I accept that. She's a big girl."

"I'm going to stick with what I want to do with my life, but I hope that my dad is happy because I'm happy with what I'm doing," Parris Cooper said. "I think now he realizes that this isn't just a futile dream I have, that this is a reality. He's a lot more supportive now. My dad really believes in me and he believes I can (become a chef)."

"I see a bright, very successful future for her," Cedric Cooper said. "I'm happy with that. She enjoys (cooking) and that's why I think she will be successful in it."

And if she isn't, she does have a back-up plan. If becoming a chef is impossible, she intends to go into massage therapy, another career that does not require a degree from a 4-year university.

However, as it is an even lower-paying career than those in culinary arts, Parris and Cedric Cooper should both be glad for the bond of understanding they have formed.

—Erin Harris

B&G Graphic by Katie Clark

Fig. 16.11. When text wraps around (or contours) to illustrations, logos or pull quotes, designers must pay careful attention to the readability of the text. Designers should avoid creating awkward jumps across an illustration, confusing patterns of readability, and extremely short or long line lengths. Gaping holes of white space within the lines of text will also create distractions in the readability. Additionally, text wrapped to a shape or to a picture needs a clear separation of space from the visual. On this page, a contour illustration has effectively been wrapped into the text without creating problems of readability at the top of the page. At the bottom of the page, the photo is allowed to wrap into the text column on the left side, but the designer has made sure the text appears separated from the visual and maintains readability. *Blue & Gold*, Center High School, Antelope, Calif.

without the lines of text becoming confused with those appearing next to them. Horizontally, the designer should also maintain a consistency in space separation. To help the reader differentiate between unrelated content, 2 picas of horizontal separation are suggested. When a publication's layout creates large areas of unplanned white space the layout can distract the reader's eyes from the content and concentrate his or her "eyeflow" in these large white holes. Therefore, the designer must plan carefully to ensure that separations, both vertical and horizontal, are consistent throughout the publication (Fig. 16.12).

MODULAR DESIGN

If you were to go back and study design from the 1950s and earlier, you would find designers creating story layouts that generally weren't easy to follow. Columns of type might extend vertically down a page several inches and in the next column extend down the page by a greater or lesser number of inches. This design pattern, often referred to as "dog leg design," for its resemblance to a dog's leg, has been abandoned in recent years in favor of easier readability patterns.

Today, designers primarily use modular design. Modular design involves placing information in vertical or horizontal shapes of four sides. Although designers can't always make design modular, especially on pages where ads of different sizes are placed, the fewer deviations from even text columns, the easier it will be for the reader to follow the flow of the story. Packages of content can also follow modular design principles, with all elements lined up within four sides (Fig. 16.13).

PREPARING FOR DESIGN

The process of designing first involves sketching a preliminary plan for the page, often referred to as a "page dummy." These page dummies, usually drawn in reduced size, allow the designer to consider the options for placing elements on the page before actually sitting down at the computer to formally arrange the elements. Dummies should reflect the external page margins and the grid or column method and should show the internal margins. Along the page horizontally, inches will be scaled down to reflect the depth that stories will take on the page. Preparing pencil dummies allows the designer to experiment with placement of elements and to determine whether designs will reflect solid design principles

in completed layouts. Moving elements around on the dummies will offer designers options for story placement as well as visual size and placement.

Because dummies are a designer's sketch pad, a common method of indicating elements is used. Headlines might be represented by a series of X's on the design with a suggestion indicated for the actual size and typeface. Stories will be indicated by arrows drawn vertically down columns indicating both the width and the length of the assigned story. Pictures and visuals will be represented by large boxes with an X drawn in them. Designers can write in a short description of the picture assigned to that spot.

Dummies are often drawn well in advance of the completion of stories and the completion of photographic assignments. When stories are edited and visuals are complete, designers should re-evaluate the dummies to make sure the designs reflect the edited stories and the strength of the visuals. If story length or picture quality has changed, designers should reflect these changes by drawing new dummies. For instance, if a photographer's best image is a vertical, but the dummy predicted a horizontal dominant image, the designer should redraw a new dummy utilizing the strength of the actual photograph rather than the planned photo.

Although editors often give writers suggested story lengths when making story assignments, story lengths can change during the reporting process. If a story becomes longer or shorter than the assigned length, designers will also need to make changes to their dummies.

Good designers will become adept at designing pages. Page dummies should be easily changeable to reflect the importance of stories and the value of visual strengths. Throughout the process, the designer must remain flexible and sensitive to changing news value and story-telling potential. Never should visuals be forced into positions that compromise their potential. Never should a story be edited just to fit a space on a dummy. Rather, designers should work from the strength of the reporting, editing and photography when laying out the pages. This process will guarantee the most successful method of bringing information to the reader.

After page dummies have been adjusted and redrawn, designers should take them to the computer for completion of the pages. Templates reflecting the margins and column grids of the page can be stored in the computer with typographic style sheets, organized type libraries that will facilitate consistency throughout the publication, and libraries containing logos, standing

Fig. 16.12. Consistent internal margins help separate and organize newspaper content. When creating grids in layout software, designers should set baseline grids equal to the type's leading value in the preferences function and then make sure to allow type to snap and lock to grids. This page from *The Squall* is inviting to read with consistent internal spacing both vertically between columns and horizontally between story content. Additionally, a narrow vertical grid of 6 picas has been created to allow for flexibility in content. Note the use of deck heads top and bottom in 6-pica widths marked by black boxes as visual entry points. Additionally, the designer allowed white space into the design creating a more interesting layout. The use of the page's primary package in the center of the page also provides strong visual interest and helps to balance the page top and bottom. The strong bold weight of the sans serif typeface in the headline further guides the reader down the page. *The Squall*, Dexter High School, Dexter, Mich.

Fig. 16.13. Modular newspaper design, in which all content appears in four-sided boxes, or modules, does not mean the page will be uniform. The key is making each module a different size and shape to allow for balance and contrast. Four modules appear on this page of election coverage, each with its own shape and size. The largest module is placed at the top of the page with a headline horizontally centered into the illustrations on the right side of the module. A full-page vertical module on the right provides strong contrast to the other modules. Appropriate red and blue color has been used repeatedly in each module to connect and unify the content. Each module is easily seen and separated by the use of rule lines and white space. Each module also features a variety of visual entry points breaking up text and allowing a variety of jumping in points for quick reads. *Stampede*, Burges High School, El Paso, Texas.

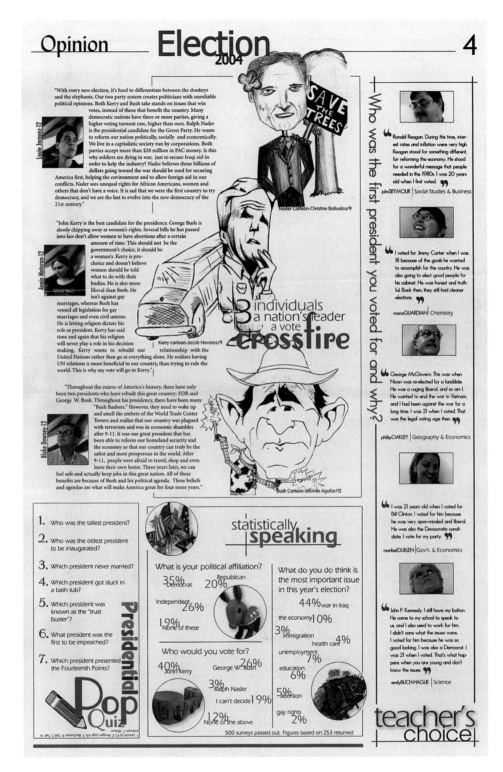

heads and other visual devices that might be useful. Stories written by individual writers and edited on-screen can be imported through word-processing programs into the templates and flowed into the design. Staffs using page layout and design software will find endless opportunities for creating interesting designs. Large initial letters dropped into the text, text heads breaking up the text and other graphic devices for text relief are easily created through layout and design programs.

Photographs taken with digital cameras can be downloaded directly into the computer and imported into picture spots on layouts. Or, pictures taken with cameras using film can be scanned on flatbed or negative scanners and imported into picture spaces on layouts. Care should be taken when cropping to ensure that picture content is not distorted or stretched. Locking proportions or checking to make sure the x/y scaling coordinates maintain the same percentages will prevent pictures from being stretched. Importing the pictures directly into the layouts helps designers see how the pictures will be cropped and helps them evaluate the page's balance by seeing the actual density of the text, visuals and white space.

SPECIAL CONSIDERATIONS FOR DESIGN

FRONT PAGE

A front page is the window to the publication. It is the reader's first impression of that issue, and it should look different each issue (Fig. 16.14). Some elements should maintain consistency, including the design of the newspaper's nameplate and the design of other elements such as teasers that attract readers to inside content and index information that points readers to the rest of the publication. Many newspapers have begun using color on their front pages, either in the nameplate information or more extensively in color photographs.

Front page content should offer information that readers will find interesting and relevant. Old news, or news that readers will already be aware of, will rarely provide interesting front-page content for readers with access to multiple forms of information. Many publications package a front page "feature" story rather than trying to print news. Because many publications publish infrequently, a feature story, in-depth story or similar content will give the designer many options.

Front pages can often contrast longer stories with shorter news briefs, teasers to inside content and digests (short bursts of content). Visual entry points result when readers have multiple starting points on a page. Optional starting points attract different kinds of readers – those who are scanners as well as traditional readers.

Something of visual interest should appear high on the page, preferably above the fold. In newsmagazines, a photograph with a cover teaser to inside content might be the only content on the front page. Regardless of the visual used, designers should vary its size and placement in subsequent issues to avoid predictable layout patterns.

Typography used in nameplates should be functional, clean and simple rather than heavily ornamental or over-designed. The nameplate should establish the newspaper's identity without competing with the content of the front page. The typeface should be readable and distinctive. Because the typeface in the nameplate should be repeated for section headers and standing headlines elsewhere in the publication, it should work well in smaller sizes. The nameplate should also include the date of issue, the volume and issue number in Arabic, rather than in roman, numerals and the name of the school.

As the reader turns the pages, each page should include a page folio – information placed at the top or bottom of the page that includes the page number on the outside of the page, the name of the publication and the date of the publication.

INSIDE PAGES

Items such as columns, news briefs, section heads and other content that appears in each issue can be visually designed to repeat the typeface in the nameplate, as well as the style or arrangement of type in the nameplate. Inside pages can repeat the name of the newspaper as it appears on the front page. This repetition gives the publication a unified appearance (Fig. 16.15).

Designers can employ different grids or column methods in different sections of the paper. Using varying column widths offers visual variety and creates distinctive content areas for the reader. Sections of the paper can start on single right pages to create reader awareness of content change when it isn't possible to print separate sections.

Throughout the newspaper, designers will need to deal with placement of ads. Ad space should be designed so it leaves modules of space for content rather than awkward, uneven spaces. Some publications, especially newsmagazines, place several ads on single pages,

Fig. 16.14. Front page content should appear different in each issue of the newspaper. While some consistency will be maintained through use of the nameplate and typography, readers should expect to be surprised by the front page. *The Harbinger*'s front page in a short tabloid design (13 inches vertically instead of the standard 17 inches) surprises its readers with each issue. In this front page, a serious news story about protests against the banning of gay marriage at the Topeka state capitol, the design is treated more conventionally using a longer text story and dominant and secondary art. In the other issue (see p. 262), a more visual approach has been created on a feature story about healthy food choices in school vending machines. The designer's use of a vending machine background covering the entire page creates interesting art that works visually with the headline. The text has been placed on a translucent background to allow for readability. While the story gets started in this box, the content jumps to an inside page where it finishes the text. *The Harbinger*, Shawnee Mission East High School, Prairie Village, Kan.

allowing ad content to be separated from editorial content (Chap. 21). The only pages on which ads shouldn't appear are the editorial or opinion pages. In most newspapers, ads traditionally don't appear on the front page or section fronts inside the paper. Many European professional newspapers are now placing advertising on their front pages, primarily in narrow horizontal banners across the bottoms of the pages.

Designers should also design facing pages as single visual units to prevent problems in the design. Placing banner headlines across the tops of two facing pages will create off-balanced designs and could confuse the reader. Visuals shouldn't appear directly across from each other in the design, or facing pages will appear off-balanced.

FEATURE PAGES

Feature page design is the heart and soul of the designer's work. Creating strong visual/verbal connections through well-designed illustrations or excellent photographs combined with strong, detail-oriented headlines gives designers endless opportunities for creating interesting visual units. Surrounding these feature packages with a

continued on page 3

Fig. 16.14. (continued)

bit of extra white space brings the reader to the story content and helps separate it from the rest of the page's content. Designers should seize the opportunity to be creative, clever and fun when the content dictates. When serious or complex content is being used, the designer needs to make sure the design reflects the more serious tone of the content. Color should also be used appropriately on feature pages.

Feature pages offer designers the opportunity to be a bit more experimental with typeface choices. Many newspapers change typefaces for feature presentations to help the reader understand the change in content (Fig. 16.16). Typefaces with visual connections to the story content can be effective, or the newspaper can choose a different but consistent typeface for feature content throughout the publication. For instance, many professional newspapers switch to strong sans serif typefaces for feature stories despite using a serif type for headlines on other news stories. The arrangement of type and the positioning of the type in relationship to the story can also be more creative. White space can be more generously used on feature pages to isolate and separate the content of the stories from other page content. The leading of the type in the story might be expanded to indicate its special content.

EDITORIAL PAGES

Because editorial pages should reflect the opinions of the newspaper's staff as well as other contributors, and therefore should mark the change in voice that editorial pages represent in the newspaper, the staff should design these pages distinctively. Editorials should be clearly labeled as such. The headline should clearly state the staff's editorial position. Using a different column grid will also help differentiate the editorial content. Many staff editorials appear in consistent positions and in wider column grids on the editorial page (Fig. 16.18).

Fig. 16.15. Headers and standing heads, used repeatedly throughout a publication, provide strong direction for readers accustomed to the design. In this paper, the inside folios appear at the top of the page in black boxes 3.5 picas wide. The type is reversed, or white, inside the boxes, and contains the page number, date of the issue and the section of news. The page is anchored at the bottom with ads. On the arts page, the beginning page of the arts section contained within the paper rather than as a separate section, the use of a wider box of 5 picas holds the section header. A shorter black box groups the page number, publication name and issue date information into a separate box next to the standing head. Note how the repetition of the black reverse boxes in thinner widths (2 picas for artlines and 1.5 picas for quotables) repeats the look of the standing heads, but is appropriately scaled down for the content on the page. Because this is a section front, ads have been kept out of the design. *The ReMarker*, St. Mark's School of Texas, Dallas, Texas.

Fig. 16.15. *(continued)*

arts

A few 'odd' things dotting local arts scene as fall turns to winter

Local fine arts paid off big at the Oct. 5 senior auction.

The St. Mark's Upper School Chorus and Orchestra rocked the competition, except for the faculty-hosted dinner. Liz Trice played dirty.

In reality though, everyone was a winner, "everyone" being the Senior Class. And the winners being fine arts people. That doesn't make sense.

Which brings us straight to Homecoming. People are still talking about the groundbreaking event, which included a live band, a chocolate fountain, and the thrill of possibly being crushed by an airplane. Congratulations to Drew Lassiter, the 2004 Homecoming King. We wish you a long and prosperous reign.

By the time you read this, the first coffeehouse of the year will have already occurred, but we are still quivering with breathless excitement. It was a spectacle of music, dance, improvisation and free admission.

Hot on the heels of coffeehouse will come six performances by two separate casts of Andrew Lloyd Webber's *The Odd Couple*. The play will be performed in the center of the black box with the audience on all sides, creating a more realistic atmosphere. And Adam says that the play is actually by Neil Simon, but I'm not sure if I believe him.

We highly recommend that everyone see both the male and female versions of the show, as they will be quite different. The female version, for example, has nearly double the number of X-chromosomes, while the male version puts more emphasis on the Y-chromosomes.

Tryouts for the winter musical, *Taming of the Fiddler*, will follow in the wake of all of these dazzling performances. And what a wake it will be. Imagine a flock of doves made of pure artistic genius floating gently on a wind made of subtlety and craft, and you will get an idea of the nature of this wake.

Regardless of the magnitude of the aforementioned wake, we encourage everyone to audition for *Fiddler on the Roof*, which is the musical's actual name. I don't know what Nathaniel was talking about. Supposedly, this show has numerous male roles, and pretty much every guy who tries out will probably get a part.

If you're still not convinced, we suggest that you take to heart this unverified generalization: being in the musical makes you more attractive to the opposite sex. Remember, the newspaper can't print it if it's not true.

On that note, we leave you to your studies and revels. Remember, as you part, this newly-coined cliché: open yourself to art, and art will open itself to you. Adieu.

what's inside the LAVA LAMP?

nathaniel **BILHARTZ** & adam **BLACK**

'The female version of *The Odd Couple* has nearly double the number of X-chromosomes, while the male version puts more emphasis on the Y-chromosomes.'

Making the most of his professional debut in Plano Repertory Theatre's production of *Camelot*, sophomore John Aldous takes advantage of this 'first chance'

a life in the spotlight

by Philip Woram
ARTS EDITOR

Chance.

That's what it all comes down to. It's the chance to become what we want; to fulfill our dreams and ambitions. It's by chance that we come across an experience that makes us realize our passion. And for sophomore John Aldous, sometimes, it's that one chance to make it all happen.

For actors like Aldous it's chances that make all the difference. Like the chance to be cast in "Camelot", a serious professional play. The beginning of every career starts with an opportunity. And as his first professional production, "Camelot" is the beginning of the long road to becoming a full time actor.

But this opportunity, like all of his others, began with waiting. Waiting for that phone call after the

student PROFESSIONAL

Catch fellow professional student actor sophomore Anthony Schoeffler in Dallas Children's Theatre's production of *The Best Christmas Pageant Ever*, Dec. 3-19 at the El Centro College Theatre. Visit www.dct.org for more information.

audition, a time when actors are tortured by nervousness and anticipation. "I had thought that it went well, but wasn't expecting a call. A month went by, and I thought, well, at least I got more audition experience," Aldous said.

The first time Aldous had to wait for such a call was when he first got started in acting. As a sixth grader at Highland Park Middle School, he decided to try out for the school musical "The Lion the Witch and the Wardrobe".

It began with a middle school play, a chance for Aldous to earn extra credit. He had never been involved in plays or acting before but this was an opportunity he could do.

What Aldous couldn't do was foresee the impact this play would have on him. "I got cast in a bit role, and instantly got submerged into the world of theatre. It fascinated me," he said. "I don't know what it was about becoming a totally different person for the time that you are on stage. I auditioned for more roles

UNDER THE STAGE LIGHTS - Sophomore John Aldous pauses on the set of his first professional stage production, Camelot, at Plano Repertory Theatre's Courtyard Theatre. The production, which ran for three weeks, closed Sunday.

at HPMS, and from then on out was a lead for every play and musical until I 'graduated' from HPMS."

This spawned a passion for Aldous. He began taking acting lessons with Lynn Ambrose, a premier

actress in the Dallas theatre community. And, by chance, she happened to be doing a production of the musical "Peter Pan". "I got cast as Captain Hook. As they did more youth productions at Trinity River Arts Center, I eagerly auditioned for them," Aldous said.

The speed of his career took off, being cast as lead in plays all over Dallas as well as Atlanta. But with this came sacrifice.

"The hard thing about theatre is that it consumes your life. I didn't go to St. Mark's homecoming because I had a performance that night. However, it is what I love doing," said Aldous.

But more than homecoming and not playing sports, the sacrifices of an actor can be overwhelming. "I have thought long and hard over whether or not I want to go into theatre as a career. I know that it's hard to make a living when starting out," said Aldous.

For Aldous, though, sacrifices make the artist. In Steven Sondheim's *Sunday in the Park With George*, the title character's

'I do want to be a true artist when I am older, despite the sacrifices on the way.'
— Sophomore John Aldous

getting STARTED

Aldous isn't the only Marksman to act professionally. Here are some professional theatres where other aspiring student actors can get a foothold in the acting world:
- Plano Repertory Theatre
- Dallas Children's Theatre
- Classical Acting Company
- Garland Civic Theatre

concessions inspire and teach him important lessons on his path to virtuosity.

"He has, as true artists do, brought a little light into the world through his own personal sacrifice. And this made me realize that, I do want to be a true artist when I am older, despite the sacrifices on the way," Aldous said.

"Not many people would be willing to do that and devote their life to their art, but perhaps that is why true artists are so incredibly rare," he said.

---

artsline

Changes made to Coffeehouse

Several things were new or different at the first Coffeehouse of the fall. Most notably, perhaps, was the change in seating. Because this weekend's performances of *The Odd Couple* will be done in a theatre-in-the-round style, seating for Coffeehouse, too, was done in a round arrangement.

Unlike last year, when student equipment was used for all of the sound, the Black Box's mixing board and speaker were utilized for the acoustic acts. Stage lights on the "performance platform" helped to focus audience attention on the acts. Selling concessions was another major departure from Coffeehouse tradition.

Got a tip for us?

The ReMarker welcomes contributions for arts items, quotes and photographs for "Artsline." Send your suggestions to:

remarker@smtexas.org

with the subject "Artsline." While we welcome all suggestions, we cannot guarantee their publication, dependent upon space considerations and appropriateness of the suggested subject area.

Band, Orchestra winter concerts to be held in December

The semi-annual band and orchestra concerts are to be held later this season. The band concert will be Dec. 3 in the Decherd Performance Hall, at 7:30 p.m.

The following week, on Dec. 10, orchestra members will offer their concert at 7:30 p.m., also in Decherd Hall.

Following each performance there will be a reception in the Robert Earl Cullum Commons area.

As in all concerts, performances are free and open to the public.

quotables

"We have to dance!"

— *Senior Jonathan Lind, improvising changes to a scene in a rehearsal for The Odd Couple.*

Fig. 16.16. Special feature content or themed content deserves special design attention in the newspaper. *The Spark* staff devoted 12 pages of its newsmagazine to in-depth coverage of reading. Introducing the section, the designers created a background of a book to place text explaining the reason for the coverage. Each subsequent spread was treated as a chapter of this book and focused content on topics introduced on the cover. The visual of an open book was repeated on both outside edges of the spread. Additional visual highlights include the decorated drop caps mimicking classic literature and the repetition of pull quotes packaged with a photograph of books. Each spread's left page features a consistent visual look with a visual and explanatory headline. Copy end symbols mark the end of each story and sidebar throughout the section. *The Spark*, Lakota East High School, Liberty Township, Ohio.

The Reading Issue

Written and Illustrated by the SPARK staff

As the results from the Gates-MicGinitie Assessment Test of 365 Lakota Freshmen show that one in five current sophomores cannot read at grade level, the SPARK examines issues surrounding reading:

❖ According to the Literacy Network of Greater Cincinnati, approximately 200,000 adults in the Greater Cincinnati area are functionally illiterate.

❖ Since 1998, the Middletown Public Library's circulation of book has decreased by more than 23,000, while the media circulation has increased by almost 78,000.

❖ According to the Spark survey, technology -- cellphones, television, instant-messaging,video-games, and the Internet -- has provided kids an alternative to reading.

Editorial pages will make extensive use of standing heads in a consistent design for the newspaper's columnists. Columns often feature small face shots of the writers.

Visuals on the editorial pages will be primarily editorial cartoons. Cartoons should be used to help break up the text. Other options include photo polls where several people are asked the same question and their responses are edited to reflect the most interesting comments. Photo polls can picture small, tightly edited head shots of people whose responses are printed. The backgrounds and head sizes in these pictures should also be consistent.

Letters to the editor or to the newspaper's web site from readers will often appear on these pages.

The newspaper's masthead and its staff listing should also appear on the editorial page. The listing may include only the major editors of the paper or everyone on the staff. The masthead should appear in a consistent place on the page. Many staffs also choose to include their editorial and advertising policy in agate-size type as part of the masthead.

The primary concern on the editorial page is preventing the pages from appearing too dense with text or from "graying out." Designers should seek to keep the pages interesting and visually appealing.

Fig. 16.16. *(continued)*

❖ READING ❖

A PEDAGOGICAL VIEW

*Teachers at Lakota East discuss
their views on reading.*

Chapter 6

Story by Lisa J. Baldwin ♦ Photos by Amanda Evans

ith the recent light brought to the awareness of kids' reading, teachers at Lakota East discussed and debated reading issues in focus groups facilitated by the SPARK. According to Bobbi Hume, who has been teaching English for 19 years, there have always been the students who may not be reading at grade level, who do not read the assigned novels, and who do not do all that they are supposed to do. But over the years, with the discussions of her students, she has begun to notice something else: more and more kids each year *dislike* reading.

Hume recalled when she first started teaching that it wasn't uncommon for almost every kid in the room to be carrying around a book, whatever was popular. She chuckled at the thought of the "horrible" V.C. Andrews, the rage. She also remembers when students finished reading the novels, they would discuss the books and were eager to read more. "Kids were actually reading in their free time," the former AP English teacher said. "And I just don't see that now. Not only do they not read, but my kids tell me that they do not like to read. They do not enjoy it; they don't see any value in it."

Lisa Schmaltz agrees as even in high school there were books that she didn't like to read that "I was forced to read that I didn't read," says Schmaltz. "However, I was reading two or three other books independently aside from that." So while she "faked" her way out of *A Tree Grows in Brooklyn*, Schmaltz was reading something else. For her, it was the idea of assigned reading.

"I think we tend to want to see that this is some brand new societal problem and I don't really think it is. There are readers and there are people who don't read. And that is the way it has always been. And who am I to pass judgement because I find value in it," says Becky Richards, also an English teacher at East.

And while the exact reason as to why students do not like to read is unknown, teachers have noticed that often students are predisposed against reading when they enter the English classrooms.

"Kids carry reading baggage with them," says English teacher Darren McGarvey, who finds that as juniors enter his class they are passive readers. "And we talk about that in the beginning of the year through a survey of assessment. You've got the majority of kids saying that they hate to read. And they bring that in with them from somewhere." McGarvey doesn't know where that comes from, but he sees that more and more kids are shutting out reading, saying that they hate it.

" I think we tend to want to see that this is some brand new societal problem and I don't really think it is. "

Richards adamantly continues with McGarvey's idea, by saying that the same students that claim they hate reading will eventually admit that they have never read an entire book in their English careers.

"I find this mind boggling, how they can hate it yet they never even read it," says Richards.

Larry Meibers, a math teacher at East who is known to read many books, feels that perhaps there is a dislike for reading because of students' comprehension level. For example, he says that if kids in the lower level math have trouble reading, then they

RK November 17, 2003 PACKAGE

DOUBLE TRUCKS/CENTER SPREADS

The middle two pages of the paper are printed on one sheet of paper, offering the designer endless possibilities for treating the space as one design unit. Large headlines can be placed across the gutter, the fold between the two pages, and visuals can be used in even larger sizes.

Double-truck coverage should be built around large and significant visual display. Visual–verbal connections should be strong and should attract the reader to the information presented in the design. A strong visual used significantly large in the design will usually be more effective than a variety of smaller visuals. Using a flexible grid or column method offers possibilities for changing the width of text in different parts of the

Fig. 16.16. (continued)

READING

he founded Thornapple in 1997, he believed that the unusual combination book and wine store would thrive in West Chester.

"Books and wine go together," he says. "When I look at the people who read, demographics show that they are the kind of people who like to surf the Web, who like fine dining and reading and wine."

Anagnostou says he also paid close attention to the school districts, carrying the summer reading lists in addition to everything else. At one point, he says, he carried nearly 1000 different titles.

But the heyday of Thornapple's book sales ended January 1. Anagnostou decided to stop selling books and gradually begin removing them, acknowledging his inability to fight competition from larger businesses. A Barnes & Noble is slated to be built further down Cincinnati-Dayton Road, touting all of the advantages of a major chain. So-called "big box" stores are able to purchase books in mass quantities, then sell them to customers for what Anagnostou calls "a ridiculously low price."

"I honestly can't compete," he says. "Everybody loves David and Goliath stories, but for the most part they are kind of rare. Goliath nailed 100 guys before David got him."

Earl Johnson, manager of the Little Professor located near Thornapple Wine Shop, is planning to weather the storm. But though Little Professor is a franchise and not an independent store, the competition from larger chains has impacted it.

"Naturally we would expect sales to go right along with the general population growth, but big box stores at best case limit growth," says Johnson.

Johnson adds that larger chains have a track record of moving into areas that already have successful independents, because a flourishing market indicates high demand from the reading population.

As Anagnostou sees it, the tactic is simply part of the nature of business.

"It's always been their *modus operandi*," he says. "It's a fact of life. I'm sad about not selling books, but I've seen it happen so often before."

To avoid the formation of monopolies, large chains are carefully monitored. When Barnes & Noble, the largest book retailer in the United States, moved to acquire Ingram Book Company in 1998, an antitrust lawsuit successfully stopped the merger in order to protect independent bookstores.

But large chains nevertheless continue to dominate the book market, says the 2002 *Consumer Research Study of Book Purchasing*, with 41 percent of all teenage book sales occurring in large chains. Independents accounted for only 17 percent of book sales, while used book stores composed only four percent. In addition, seven percent were sold on the Internet, an alternative market that is expected to double over the next five years.

Regardless, Anagnostou still prefers the freedom and fulfillment of an independent store. He has lived the corporate life working for a division of Electronic Data Systems, and he says that he is thoroughly disillusioned with that way of life.

"I was kind of discouraged by the whole corporate culture so I decided to take the plunge," he says. "I mean, look at corporate life these days. I cannot imagine all of their stresses, deadlines, and worries."

Anagnostou favors Thornapple because it not only deals with the economy's marketplace, but also keeps people involved in what he calls the "marketplace of ideas."

"People need to allow themselves to get in and think about news," he says. "Be creative. Be daring. Think for yourself."

Anagnostou's wife Julie, who co-owns Thornapple with him, also prefers the independent life. She works as a pharmacy technician for Anthem in addition to running Thornapple, noting that Thornapple has an entirely different, relaxed atmosphere.

"When you're independent, you're your own boss," she says. "You really get to know the people you service, whereas in big chains you do not have that personal relationship."

Johnson also emphasizes the relaxed ambience of smaller bookstores, adding that Thornapple and Little Professor share the advantage of convenience.

But Debbie Horman, Community Relations Manager for Barnes & Noble, refutes criticisms of impersonal big box stores. She says employees are thoroughly trained to match the knowledge and personality of smaller store workers, and adds that she finds her work environment pleasing rather than stressful.

"I've always wanted to work in a bookstore," she says, "because I've always loved books. This is a way of indulging that love."

Horman adds that an important aspect of Barnes & Noble is the atmosphere, which she describes as "friendly and homey." Barnes & Noble, in addition to Border's and other large retailers, offers plush couches where customers can linger, nap, and read. Many locations also offer coffee shops or cafes, where Horman observes groups of students congregating daily.

"You can always tell when it's close to finals," she jokes. "The cafes are packed."

Thornapple Books and Wine was too small for a café or a cozy couch, but for Anagnostou it was enough to contain a limitless passion for books.

Even as he resignedly discusses the nature of business, he strays on to the topic of books, gradually working up a speech about becoming a fearless reader.

"People need to allow themselves to be challenged," he says, emphatically spelling it out on the table with his hands. "They need to be *fearless* readers."

Though Anagnostou may have lost the battle to sell books, he has not lost the passion to read and to share them.

"I love books," he says eagerly. "They influence and excite."

And for an instant, the look in Anagnostou's eyes is reminiscent of a dauntless third-grade boy's, captured in a moment of triumph and freedom on a cherished library card. ●

double-truck presentation to create contrast and relieve the reader's eyes. Each part of the package should add to the overall presentation of information. Visual forms should provide contrast with strictly verbal forms in offering information to the reader. White space should also be a consideration. Filling up all corners of the page from top to bottom, left to right, will result in pages that look static and cluttered. Using extra white space around the visual or around the headline display will help provide balance on the page (Fig. 16.18).

SPORTS PAGES

Sports page designs will often utilize larger, action-packed pictures of teams in competitive situations on the field or court. Sports pages can also utilize sports briefs columns providing capsulized summaries of teams' seasons as they progress. Features focusing on sports personalities, issues or controversies can enliven the sports pages, providing interesting and diverse coverage.

PENCIL this in

by Andrew Hamilton and Veronika Joy

FORT WORTH STOCK YARDS

A look down the Stock Yards strip shows what was once the centerpoint for Fort Worth's agricultural industry.

Stock Yard Trip
November 16

Kent Messer's AP Human Geography class will visit the Fort Worth Stock Yards next Tuesday. The purpose of the trip is to help students better their knowledge of the Von Thunan Model that deals with agriculture, land use and urban development.

"One of my goals is to take a field trip once a semester," Messer said. "Fort Worth and the Stock Yards are perfect locations as a whole to conduct a field trip on our current unit."

The Stock Yards has been revived in the last 20 years as a memorial to the former epicenter for buying, selling and trading livestock. Cattle trading today is limited at the Stock Yards; the location serves as monument to a once thriving Fort Worth industry.

"The field trip to Fort Worth is a real life scenario for the concepts we are currently learning in class," Hunter Pond [12] said.

Only students enrolled in the two Human Geography AP periods this semester are allowed to go.

Classic Series
November 18-21

This year's Classic Series will present William Shakespeare's *A Midsummer Night's Dream* Nov. 18-21 in the Large Auditorium.

Open auditions were held in September. About 85 students in all grades vied for 42 slots reading excerpts from the play.

"Although I've auditioned for the Classic Series for the past four years, I still got nervous," Elizabeth Hill [12] said, who plays the part of Hippolyta.

Unlike previous years' productions, *Midsummer* has more female roles, director J. E. Masters said. "It was [also] time for a comedy," he said.

This is the high school's third time to perform the 16th century play. The story follows four young lovers' adventures through an enchanted forest. The plot thickens as fairies interfere with the mortal world.

With the final casting done, costume, lighting and set preparation are underway. A moss-covered tree will loom over the stage, standing 20' tall on a 40X40' base. Designer Kimi Brown [11] got the idea in last spring's Tech Theater class.

"[Initially], I allowed my imagination to run free and tried to devise a vision truly unique," Brown said.

Tickets are $5 and can only be purchased in the Box Office one hour prior to performances. Subject to change depending on football playoffs, performances are scheduled at 7pm Thursday and Friday and at 2pm Saturday and Sunday.

School Shorts

Next Tuesday, **Nov. 16** is the **last day** 2nd period classes can **donate to** the **Canned Food Drive**. The Community Service Council encourages each student to bring 20 cans.

Student Council would like to clarify that the **final Club Day** of this semester will be **Nov. 17**.

The **final Lunch On the Lawn** of this semester will be held **Dec. 8** during regular lunch periods in the Cafeteria. Featured patrons include Amore, Peggy Sue BBQ and Wild About Harry's. In addition, Jamba Juice will be present during 5th and 6th periods to make up for running out at the last Lunch.

NHS Tapping
November

With applications in consideration since, Oct. 25, junior and senior NHS wannabes must now wait for the annual tapping ceremony. As in previous years, the exact tapping date will be a surprise.

The tapping process involves existing NHS members who go to new members' classes and announce names. Those admitted receive a candle and may then go to the Cafeteria for a congratulatory reception.

"The whole process of applying to NHS puts a lot of pressure on [students]," applicant Lawson Hopkins [11] said. "But if you get in, it is so rewarding and such an honor."

The tapping date is a mystery, adding to the application suspense.

"This year, there are around 200 applicants both seniors and juniors," co-sponsor Janis Knott said.

The actual induction of new NHS members is not until December 1, but applicants should be ready for the tapping any day now.

Mock Trial
November 22-23

The judge, attorneys, defendants and jury members are ready. Nov. 22-23, from 8am to 2pm, Jay Harris' Business Law classes will try a civil case determining liability in an electrocution case. Unlike previous mock trials, this one names three defendants: the power company, school district and home owner.

Harris chose the roles his students will portray through an application process.

"The trial is not scripted," Harris said. "The kids have to choose the direction of the trial, opening and closing statements and their own questions; they have to think for themselves."

Harris is concerned that students understand courtroom and legal procedure. He selects actual cases from Minnesota courts but never researches the verdict.

"[Last year's mock trial] was one of the best experiences I've had in high school," said former attorney Gibbons Addison [12], who hopes to pursue a career in law. "The intensity was on a level unprecedented. I enjoy the thrill of a trial."

The trial will take place in the Large Auditorium. There is a professional look to the set, complete with laptops for student use and visuals during trial.

Parents and students are welcome during the day. A replay of the trial will air on Channel 16.

Angel Drive
November 29 - December 7

As the gifting season approaches, so does the annual Angel Drive. Hosted by the Community Service Council (CSC), this effort allows students a chance to share the holiday spirit with children less fortunate.

"It's important because we're so accustomed to receiving so many gifts during the holiday season [yet] just this one gift to these kids means all the world," CSC Co-president Abby Baer [12] said.

The drive will be set up in the Cafeteria during lunch periods and in the CSC Room, G-128.

Cut-out paper angels will have written instructions for either a boy or a girl: the age and possible gift ideas for that person. The average gift costs $15–$25; possible gifts range from basic necessities like socks and school supplies to Legos and Barbies.

The gifts will be distributed to kids at Captain Hope's Kids, a shelter for homeless children, and Sensor for Protective Services, a shelter where the majority of children were removed from abusive homes.

For the past five years, the CSC goal was to donate at least 200 gifts. Last year they received 100–150 gifts.

"This really makes a difference, and everyone gets involved," CSC Co-president Melissa Melcher [12] said.

The Angel Drive starts Nov. 29 and continues through Dec. 7.

During a Monday rehearsal for *A Midsummer Night's Dream,* Jessica Nanney [12], who plays fairy queen Titania, readies for the last act. "Having a lead is a big deal," Nanney said. "At times it can get overwhelming, and it takes a lot of commitment, but it's a good character for me to play."

Fig. 16.17. Covering club and academic news is important in any newspaper. Making sure it is timely and designed in an interesting way is primary to its readability. This page of news briefs and club happenings appears on the first news page of the *Bagpipe*. Each brief is packaged with a visual, either an illustration or a photograph, to add interest. The date in the month when the event occurs is grouped with the headline in an italic variation of the headline typeface. *Bagpipe*, Highland Park High School, Dallas, Texas.

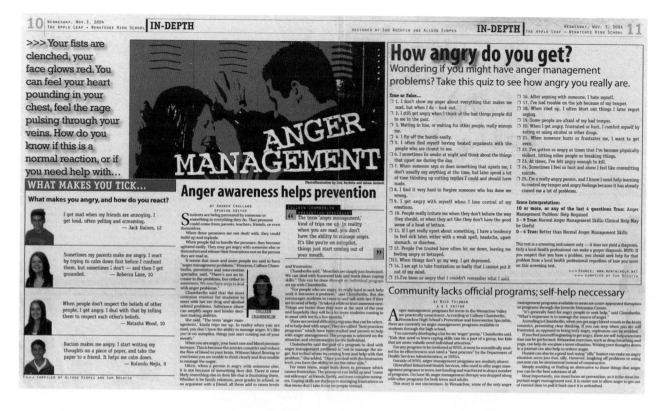

Fig. 16.18. Double trucks, the center pages of the newspaper, allow for multiple design options and content coverage. Because the content is printed on one sheet of paper, designers can ignore the gutter and reconfigure the design, taking content across the page. Often used for in-depth coverage, double trucks need to maintain strong visual anchors and a variety of content to keep readers interested. This in-depth look at anger management packages a strong headline and photo illustration together with an explanatory deck head. Each module on the page offers a different focus and presentation including a column by a prevention specialist, a quiz, a student poll and a news story on community programs. Red color has been used effectively here to help unify the individual components in the design without overdoing it. *Apple Leaf*, Wenatchee High School, Wenatchee, Wash.

PICTURE USE

Pictures are strong reader entry points, and because they are important in design, photographs deserve special attention. Pictures in strong vertical or horizontal shapes are far more interesting than square shapes. People in photographs should be large enough so their heads are at least the size of a nickel. Static pictures of people posing for the camera are not as interesting as pictures showing people in natural situations (Fig. 16.20). (Also see Chap. 20.)

Pictures shouldn't be an afterthought in design, confined to small spaces in the corners of pages or layouts. Rather, designers should seek to design from the strength of good photographs, using them in significant sizes and in interesting positions. Careful attention to cropping will make strong pictures even stronger and more visually interesting.

Well-written, detailed captions will add to the appeal of good pictures. Some readers will only read the picture caption without ever reading the story that accompanies it. Thin, hairline or 1 point rule lines placed around pictures in the design will help give them definition on the pages.

SPECIAL CONSIDERATIONS FOR USING COLOR

SPOT COLOR

Just as in professional newspapers, color is becoming more common in school newspapers. Spot color – the

Fig. 16.19. Content should dictate design. Pages should offer fresh looks and interesting approaches when appropriate. Topics such as fashion trends should be handled differently from year to year. Taking an interesting and fresh look at the fashion trends in their school, the staff of *The Star* newspaper did a question/answer quick-read with a variety of students, including those with alternative styles and a teacher. Featuring real people in their dress of choice makes the coverage interesting. Two fashion letters to the artists, a fun addition to the content, and a top ten poll of fashion cool things in the school supplement the design. Cutout pictures emerging from the question/answer boxes add visual interest and energy to the presentation, balanced by the dominant size of the model in the middle. *Star*, Century High School, Bismarck, N.D.

use of a single color in design – is a less expensive way of using color than four-color. Four-color, called that because it is made from the four process colors, magenta or red, cyan or blue, yellow and black, requires the page to be run through four different presses, each applying one of the colors (Fig. 16.21).

Newspaper printers may offer the staff spot color called "run of the press" (ROP) at an even cheaper price. ROP color simply means the printer will use color already on the press, with the staff taking advantage of that color. Unfortunately, the color used will not be the staff's decision, often resulting in weak, less effective use of color. For instance, if the printer is already printing a publication with yellow spot color ink and uses it in your publication for the nameplate or for display type, the weak color may not be strong enough to lead the reader's eyes to the type displays that you've designated as color in your design.

When used effectively, spot color can create unity through the publication. Warm, strong colors such as red are better spot color choices for visual signals such as headlines and standing headlines. Cool colors, such as green and blue, will be less active and weaker as visual signals. Lighter percentages of warm colors work well to display content in "screened boxes," when the designer is seeking to separate the content and draw the reader's eyes to it.

Designers should be careful to avoid overusing color, particularly spot color, by using it for every headline in the publication, page or spread. Inappropriate use

Fig. 16.20. Packaged content usually requires the use of more than one picture or illustration. Offering the reader a variety of visuals adds content and interest to the coverage. Packages of two to three pictures offer designers the option of adding to the information readers are given, visually and verbally. In a front page story on a group of students who traveled to Spain during the winter break, the *Pilot's Log* staff was able to include a picture of the group and a variety of the sights they saw on their trip. *Pilot's Log,* Hasbrouck Heights High School, Hasbrouck Heights, N.J.

ISSUE III SPRING 2005

"The Voice of the Students"

HASBROUCK HEIGHTS

pilot's log

A TOWN CALLED CORONA
It started as a farming community, but the advent of the airplane changed all that. By the 1940s, Heights was a booming town.
Pages 8-9

SPRING SEASON OPENS
Baseball, softball, track, golf and tennis all are in the swing of things as they kick off the 2005 spring season.
Pages 15-16

HASBROUCK HEIGHTS HIGH SCHOOL   HASBROUCK HEIGHTS, N.J. 07604

Students take trip of a lifetime to Spain

Historic sights, local cuisine and lots of fun were all part of itinerary

AMANDA KISTNER

On Feb. 27th, 16 students, four teachers and three parents emerged from their flight from Spain, sleep deprived, hungry, but most off all, thrilled with the week they had just experienced.

Eleven days prior to their return to America, the students of Carmen Carr's Spanish IV and AP classes left for their own "Eurotrip."

"I was nervous, yet excited for the adventure I was about to embark on," Andrea Algauer, junior, said.

The students landed six hours later in Madrid, Spain, but not before boarding their connecting flight in Amsterdam.

During their stay, the group visited Madrid, Cordoba, Sevilla, Granada, Valencia, Barcelona and Costa del Sol. They experienced first hand what they had studied in school. In addition to exploring the many wonderful architectural details displayed in buildings and monuments, they were exposed to hundreds of years of history.

"The best part of Spain was the history that everything contained. The streets and the people were so different from what I had been used to," Rosa Paredes, senior, said.

While the trip was a very educational experience, the group found ways to enjoy the trip beyond the tours. They received a lot of free time during the day when they were able to wander around and, of course, shop.

"My favorite city was Torremolinos because there was a really long road that was packed with shops and places to eat, and at the end of the road was the beach. It was beautiful!" Jaclyn Hohnecker, senior, said.

They also attended some shows, including gypsies performing the Flamengo in an actual cave.

However, there were some down sides to the trip. Due to a rigorous schedule during the day and limited funds, the students found it

difficult to experience the Spanish night life that they so enthusiastically looked forward to.

"When we got back from the tours, we were all so tired. Most of the time I just wanted to relax, but I am glad

Photos by Vanessa Santana

Winter Break meant flying to Spain for sixteen students and their teachers. Shopping in Barcelona, seeing the Lizard of Gaudi in Barcelona or looking at the city from the top of the La Giralda in Granada were all part of the trip to Spain. "I loved it all," Vanessa Santana said. "It was so different from America that we didn't mind exploring so many different cities in so short a time period. I was tired, yet it was all worth it."

that we did as much as we did," Bijal Shah, junior, said.

Most of the students agree with Stefan Dombrowsky, senior.

"This trip is something that could never be compared to another trip

in school. In many ways, it was terrific. However, I will never go on another trip with a tour group again," Dombrowsky said as he smiled broadly.

It has been nearly 12 years since Carr had taken a group to Spain. She

> "We saw amazing sights that you would never see here--palaces that were thousands of years old, the third largest cathedral in the world, Christopher Columbus' tomb, the cathedral that allegedly held the Holy Grail and much more."
>
> MARLENA GIL, SENIOR

decided that this year would be a good time to go because her students are well-mannered and responsible. Moreover, they were very persistent about going. However, she had her own secretive reasons for going-- to practice their Spanish.

"It was an experience filled with growth and confidence building. The students found that they were able to communicate on their own in Spanish. They were even able to bargain at stores and markets. I was proud that they were able to accept another culture and feel comfortable. They have matured a lot over the years," Carr said.

Some students became so comfortable, they found it tough to let go.

"Even after we returned home, I still found myself speaking Spanish," Juliana Jackson, senior said.

What's Inside

- 2 -
Junior Formal
Dancing and having fun is what the Junior Formal is all about. The students dropped the books and had a special night for everyone to remember.

- 3 -
Teterboro Plane Crash
The recent Teterboro Airport plane accidents raise many questions and leave neighboring towns and citizens wondering if they are safe.

- 4 -
Tsunami Relief
District wide fund-raiser had students rolling, counting and donating pennies to help support the Tsunami Relief efforts. It was more than just pennies. Each penny represented a life lost.

-12-
5K Run Set to Go
Dedicated to the memory of three teachers, this annual event helps students on the road to college by providing scholarships.

of color in headlines can affect the reader's perception of the story's content and news value. Body text in color will slow the reader down in processing the information and could discourage readability.

Some colors simply do not work well for color use. Colors such as yellow are difficult to read and will create weaker, less visible content. The most agreeable combination for text is black on white. Reverse type, white on black, slows down the reader and creates dense type areas in the newspaper.

FOUR-COLOR

Four-color is expensive to produce and, because of the way a newspaper is printed, can only be used on certain pages without incurring additional costs. Color photographs must be separated into the four process colors before they can be reproduced in the newspaper unless they are submitted as digital files electronically. Separating traditional color prints into the four process colors is expensive and time-consuming. The cheap quality of newsprint results in high color saturation, and the off-white color of the newsprint results in colors that won't reproduce as vividly or accurately. But with almost all professional publications using color consistently, many high school publications are using color in every issue, even if just for color photographs. Advertisers requesting color for ads can sometimes help bear the cost of color used elsewhere in the newspaper, but news content and value should always be appropriate when designing with color.

PACING THE PUBLICATION

When decisions are made about content, designers should work closely with reporters and editors to make suggestions for effective visual presentation. Teams of writers, editors, photographers and designers working together can improve the story-telling process for the reader.

Deciding on the most effective way of telling stories means the publication will vary its content and create flexible and varied story-telling forms (Fig. 16.19). When reporting events that have already occurred, teams should look for ways to make

Fig. 16.21. Four-color is becoming a standard printing choice for many newspapers. With color, designers have more options including taking color from a dominant picture or illustration and using it to connect to the verbal content. This front page features a compelling image of students using body paint to promote school spirit, but in a way not permitted by their school. The designer took the blue color and integrated it into the headline using a painting effect in the type. Two additional colors are used in the headline to create contrast with the blue. Many schools use four-color only on the front and back pages as a way to use color economically. Since these pages are really one printing surface, it cuts down on the costs. *The Harbinger*, Shawnee Mission East High School, Prairie Village, Kan.

the information fresh and interesting. A picture page with a succinctly written story and detailed captions may provide all the information necessary and be far more interesting than a traditional prose presentation reporting primarily old news. Or, in a story about the costs of athletic programs, a good infographic showing how much money is spent on an athletic uniform from jerseys to shoes might be a more interesting way of telling that story without any traditional text accompanying the infographic.

Creating teams in the student newsroom will improve discussions of content and storytelling and will ensure that pages don't slip into predictable story counts or layout designs from issue to issue or page to page within the same issue. Involving different kinds of storytellers, from writers and editors to photographers and illustrators, in decision making will ensure that all options are considered. Individuals will feel more empowered in the process, and no one's strength will become an afterthought in reporting. (Also see Chap. 20.)

KEEP IN MIND

- Mixing alignments can create visual contrast and draw the reader's attention to particular stories. A primary story in left-aligned type will create contrast and comparison for that story in relation to others on the page or spread.

- Headlines need a strong visual voice. Using bold, sans serif typefaces will help organize the headline information and create strong reader entry points into story beginnings.

- Reverse type and screened type can slow down the readability of stories. The use of such devices should be limited.

- Boxing or framing elements should be done only when the content dictates its use. Boxing an element brings the reader's attention to the story's content in a stronger way. Try to avoid boxing more than one story on a page, or the reader will see a conflicing and confused visual hierarchy.

- Generally, column widths of 10 to 20 picas are preferred for ease of readability.

- Captions are most effective when placed underneath the pictures they describe. Using a contrasting typeface for the caption helps to create contrast with body type.

- Packaging summary stories such as news briefs and clubs' briefs into well-written, tightly edited reports will result in higher readability than a series of stories separately placed on a page.

- Every page needs a dominant visual entry point placed prominently on the page, preferably near the top.

- Using screens of color or black for placement behind text slows down the reader's eyes and should be used sparingly. Screens should be kept to lighter percentages, such as 20 to 30 percent. Coarse screens with visible dots per inch will also create reading static. Designers using laser printers should increase the dots or lines per inch in the printing command to keep dot patterns light and less distracting.

- After completing designs, print them and hang them on a wall. View them at arm's length, as readers will do. Evaluate their effectiveness using the design principles. Make sure the design creates clear and logical reading patterns and makes best use of available design elements.

EXERCISES

1. Take an issue of the local or community newspaper and evaluate its use of the design principles, including balance, rhythm, unity, scale, proportion and visual hierarchy.

2. Using a local or community newspaper, find an example of packaged content, including a single picture and story; two or more pictures and story; and two or more story forms and illustration. Examine each package and notice how the reader's eyes are brought into the package. Notice what visual design devices were used by the designer in creating separation between the packaged content and the rest of the page's content.

3. Using a copy of a local newspaper, indicate the front page's margins by drawing lines around them. Using a different color pen, indicate the width of the paper's grids or columns. Measure the widths using a pica ruler and mark the width of the columns on the page. Measure the width of the internal margins and mark it on the page. Measure

between unrelated content areas and note the width of the newspaper's horizontal internal margins by marking it between each story. Draw boxes around each individual story package and note whether the design is laid out in modular design units. Do the same with an inside page with ads placed on the page.

4. Using a copy of your school's newspaper and a dummy sheet, draw a pencil dummy for one of the paper's pages. Make sure to indicate accurately the length of stories and the height of headline displays. In each picture space indicate the width and height of the picture and include a one- or two-word "slug," or summary, of what the picture will be. Compare your dummy to the actual page, checking for accuracy.

5. Using a dummy sheet, draw a design for a sports or news page for the next issue of your school newspaper. Begin by deciding what content should be on the page. Then indicate in the dummy the amount of space each content area should have. If you have access to a computer and to a layout software program, transfer your design onto a page template.

6. Look through several copies of exchange newspapers from other schools. Find examples of pages that are well designed. Write a short paragraph explaining what makes the pages successful and attractive. Find examples of pages that are poorly designed. Write a short paragraph explaining what makes these pages less successful in design.

7. Find examples of pages in professional or school newspapers that use strong vertical and horizontal photographs. Analyze each picture's use in the paper: How is the picture's size and content used in the design? Does the picture's caption add to the information obtained from reading the story? Is the picture strong enough to serve as a visual entry point for the reader?

8. Using a copy of your school newspaper, circle every entry point on the page.

9. Find an example of a double truck in your school newspaper or in an exchange newspaper from another school. Answer these questions: Is there a central visual entry point? Is it typographic, illustrative, photographic or a combination? Is the page well balanced? Is the text material sufficiently divided so it maintains interest without "graying out"? Is the content deserving of the space and effort needed to tell the story?

10. Find a page in a newspaper or in your school newspaper that uses only spot color. Is the color used effectively? Does it make visual connections in its repeated use? Is the color distracting from the content of the page?

Next, find a page in a newspaper or in your school newspaper that uses four-color. Is the color used effectively? Is the color used in more than just photographs on the page? Where else has it been used? Is the color creating distractions or adding to the appeal of the design?

Next, compare both color pages to a black-and-white page. Which do you prefer? Why?

11. Find a page in a newspaper that uses stories laid out in varied column widths. Measure the widths of the columns with a pica ruler and write their widths on the page. Are the narrowest and widest widths between the recommended 10 to 20 picas? Are the widths readable and attractive in the design? Do they help provide contrast in the content?

Yearbook Page Layout

Small groups of students gather together in hallways and outside areas around the school carefully turning each page of a freshly printed book. Stopping to admire themselves or their friends, they erupt in spontaneous laughter as they relive memories of the school year. It must be yearbook delivery day, that special day in the late spring, summer or fall when yearbook staffs deliver their much anticipated and prized volumes.

A historical record of the year, a yearbook seeks to capture coherently the sights, sounds and memories of the school year in a volume that fairly represents the students in the school and their diverse interests.

Yearbook design has undergone revolutionary change in the last decade, primarily due to the integration of desktop publishing. The changes have occurred in every area of design, from the way yearbooks tell stories to the integration of visuals on spreads. Gone are many of the rules that made yearbook design formulaic and static (Fig. 17.1).

Even with relaxed rules, the principles of good design remain intact: quality photographs that capture the moments involved in high school activities, well-written copy that serves the historic function for its student readers, complete caption information and informative and well-designed headline displays.

Even the organization of the book has been an area for experimentation by yearbook staffs. Many have moved away from clichéd, catch-phrase themes to graphic or single-word unifiers. Staffs have experimented with the traditional section organization to organizing and reorganizing content in as few as three sections. In response to yearbook innovation, many state and national judging associations have relaxed rules to allow for experimentation.

Using the theme "Three Times Over," the *Deka* staff of Huntington North High School divided the book into three sections: "Pleasure," "Power" and "Prosperity." Each of the three sections accommodated two of the book's traditional sections. Other sections have experimented with dividing the book by senses: sight, smell, touch.

No matter how the yearbook is organized or unified by its designers, it's important to understand the elements that lead to successful and attractive page designs.

SPEAKING THE LANGUAGE

Defining terms yearbook designers need to know will help you understand how to get started with page design (Fig. 17.2).

- *Body copy*: the text that verbally tells the story on the page. Stories can also appear in alternative forms that could include sidebars, infographics, question and answer formats, first-person accounts, bio boxes, charts and diagrams, pull quotes and factoids. Often, alternative forms of copy are used to supplement traditional text stories. Several forms can appear on a single spread to amplify the overall story being told.

Fig. 17.1. In order to appeal to more student readers and show more people in the book, many yearbook staffs have begun using pictures in smaller sizes, but increasing the number of pictures on the spread. In this design, the designer has created several content areas on an academics spread organized by months. The spread features a dominant image, appearing twice as large as any other stand-alone image. The spread's contemporary design offers nine different "modules" of content, each presented in a different visual/verbal way. Note the variety of visual entry points for the reader's eyes and the number of students pictured on the spread's content. *Tonitrus*, Rocklin High School, Rocklin, Calif.

- *Bleeds*: photographs that cover page gutters or that cover external margins and align with page edges.

- *Captions, or cutlines*: the information describing picture content that should be included for most pictures. Complete captions identify the principal people pictured (full name and grade in school), state what they are doing (in present tense) and can add detail, background or results (can be written in past tense). Captions often use quotes from the key pictured people as second or third sentences.

- *Divider pages*: a single page or spread that uses a distinctive design and introduces the beginning of another part of the book. Traditionally, sections of a yearbook include theme, student life or activities, academics, sports, ads, index, clubs and organizations and the people section.

- *Drop caps*: oversized introductory initial letters that drop into the first few lines of the story to visually mark and lead readers into the beginning of the text. The typography in the drop cap should match the largest or boldest type in the headline for strong visual repetition. Additionally, other forms of capped letters include rising caps, oversized letters that sit on the first baseline of text and rise into white space above the text, and side caps. Side caps appear in narrow margins to the left of the beginning of the text.

- *External margins*: the white space on all four sides of a layout used to showcase the content.

Fig. 17.2. Page elements found in yearbook spreads are identified in this example: (A) graphics; (B) bleed; (C) headline; (D) body copy; (E) gutter; (F) folio; (G) internal margin; (H) caption; (I) external margin. *Hornet*, Bryant High School, Bryant, Ark.

- *Folios and page numbers*: page numbers should go to the outside edges of the pages, but folios can be expanded to include information such as specific page content and section content.

- *Graphics*: the use of lines, borders, screens, colors, textures, illustrations or particular styles that create visual continuity when used consistently in design.

- *Grids or columns*: a series of equal or unequal design spaces created between the margins to guide placement of content.

- *Gutter margin*: the area of space between the pages. Gutter space should be taken into consideration when a photo bleeds or goes across the gutter.

- *Headlines*: Each introductory page needs a headline to draw the reader into the page content. Headlines are often combinations of primary headlines, those that are largest in the design and often created as a design unit, and secondary headlines. Secondary headlines should amplify and expand the reader's knowledge of the page content by adding details through specific facts and information. Secondary headlines are often referred to as deck heads.

- *Internal margins*: margins between columns or grids that separate content.

- *Spread*: two facing pages. Yearbook designers usually design spreads instead of individual pages.

"It's a rush to **perform.**
Sometimes it can be **overwhelming,** but you have to take
all the **energy** the crowd directs toward you and put it into your performance.
But the best thing
– where the **action** really is –
is afterward, when people come up and say,
'Dude, I love the **music!**'
and I say, 'I do too!'
and then we just hug."
- *senior Jack O'Brien*

"While preparing for both **Midwest Clinic** and the
Rose Bowl Parade was a lot of hard work and **pressure,**
both **experiences**
turned out to be well worth every **second** we put
into them."
- *junior Annie Scofield*

Action

Pressure

Performing with his band, All Due Respect, senior Jack O'Brien screams into the microphone at the
Battle of the Bands on Jan. 11, a fundraiser sponsored by the *Featherduster* and TEC. All Due Respect
was one of seven bands selected through a tryout process to perform at the annual event
and went on to place second in the competition.

Drum majors junior Annie Scofield, senior Mark Godard and junior Tiffany Yeh lead the marching
band in line around the track at Chaparral Stadium before the season opener
against Westwood on Sept. 6. The band practiced almost daily before school and during zero hour in
the stadium to prepare for halftime performances and the Tournament of Roses Parade appearance.

Opening
4

Opening
5

Fig. 17.3. Generous use of white space in the design offers a balanced layout, particularly when large, dominant images are featured. Generous white space can also be used to create distinction for pages such as opening sections which should appear visually different from the rest of the design. In the opening section of this yearbook, designers chose compelling dominant images, displayed them large, but surrounded by lots of white space. The designers added quotes from each primary person in the photograph above the image. Beneath each photo, a full caption with a catchline was provided. *El Paisano,* Westlake High School, Austin, Texas.

- *Spread unity*: elements that connect two facing pages so they are visually perceived as one design unit. These can include pictures bleeding across the gutter, graphic devices such as lines or background textures, or headlines that span the pages.

- *Theme*: a verbal statement that is used and repeated in key elements of the book to unify its design. Often called a "catchphrase," it is chosen by the staff because it relates to something about the school or about the year. The traditional areas in which themes appear include the cover, the endsheets (front and back), the opening pages, the divider pages and the closing. Theme design can also be integrated into sections of the book through special features or through "minithemes" that play off the theme phrase.

In recent years, many staffs have experimented with using devices other than traditional catchphrases to unify the book. These devices can include graphics, colors, logos or combinations of these.

- *Visual hierarchy*: a clear sense of size, proportion, scale and content that leads the reader through the design in a coherent way. Readers' eyes should be moved through the content, often following a Z reading pattern.

- *Visual continuity*: design factors that keep a section of the book coherent and unified. These factors can include graphics, particular typefaces and grid or column structures.

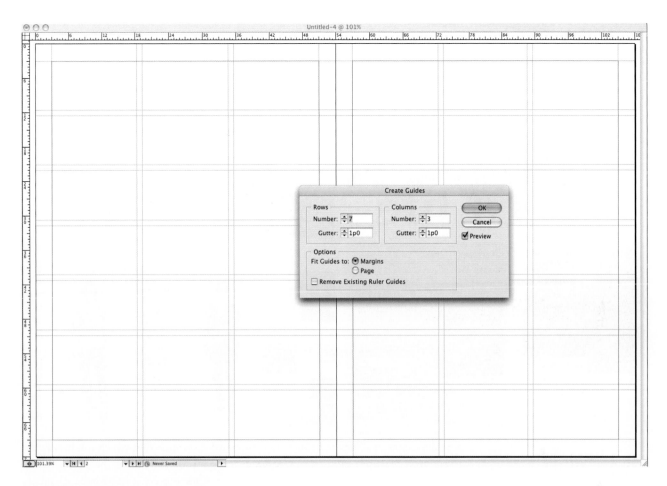

GETTING READY TO DESIGN

A yearbook designer begins with a page area set to the size of the finished book. This size ranges from 7.75 × 10.5 inches to 8.5 × 11 inches to 9 × 12 inches. While it's traditional for the yearbook to be printed as a vertical book, some staffs have even experimented with the standard sizes by turning the books horizontally and having the books bound on the narrow side.

Once the designer knows the book's trim size, margins are created on the page. Progressive margins – those narrowest at the gutter and widest on the bottom margin – are traditional in magazine and yearbook design. Margins allow pages to maintain white space to frame content in a consistent manner throughout the book and allow for placement of page folios. Folios traditionally appear in the bottom margin but could appear in other locations (Fig. 17.6).

The designer then decides on a grid or column structure to provide a skeletal structure for placing content. Generally, a designer should stop an element on every margin at least one time on a spread to define it or make it visible in the skeletal page structure. Stopping content between the margin and the outside edge of the page will be confusing to the reader because it will blur the margin's structure. In this case, the designer should bleed the content, but primarily if it's pictorial. Bleeding copy can be a problem for the printer and for the reader, since some of the verbal content could be compromised when the book is bound. Most schools are

Fig. 17.4(a). In desktop-publishing software, designers can specify the number of columns (the vertical grids dividing the pages) and rows (the horizontal columns dividing the pages). By using these divisions, designers can create organized and logical layouts using traditional designs or modules. Modular design has become a recent yearbook design trend in which content is divided into modules of varying shapes and sizes on the spread. Varying the content in the modules creates interest and pacing.

Fig. 17.4(b). Starting with a series of narrow rows and columns helps designers create modular designs. This spread has been created in eight modules. Note how each module's presentation varies both in copy and picture presentation. Each module is a four-sided shape, varying between horizontal and vertical presentations. Contemporary topics include coverage of fashion and costs of cruising, both of which provide historical context. Additionally, extra internal space has been used to help separate modules, but within modules thinner spaces are used for related content. *Tonitrus*, Rocklin High School, Rocklin, Calif.

now designing in software programs such as Adobe's InDesign which might include customized features from the publishing company or printer of the book. These customized features allow student designers to work more easily with the elements of the yearbook's design. They also enable the designers to specify margins, grids or columns and rows. Rows differ from grids or columns because they create horizontal guidelines, another option for designers to use to align elements across pages and through sections of the book.

Not all designers use strict column grids or structures in design. Some choose to create free-form designs in which pictures and other page elements are placed without regard to staying within grids or columns. While this can be a successful design strategy when used by experienced designers, most beginning designers find it easier to design within a grid page structure (Fig. 17.5).

Many magazines use three- or four-column designs as standard structures throughout their publications. Yearbook designers often find greater freedom by experimenting with a series of narrower grids, often as narrow as 4 or 5 picas wide. Using a more narrow grid pattern allows a yearbook designer to combine columns and internal margins to create a variety of content widths. Options for using narrower column grids appear primarily in elements used for display and could include:

- *Visual/verbal separators:* use of a column as an isolation element

- *Display space:* use of a column to create stronger display area for a typographic element or a picture element

- *Alternative copy space:* use of a column for a different form of content for contrast (Fig. 17.6)

High school, the crossroad of our lives, occurs not in days, not in hours, but in sheer seconds. In the quickening clatter of footsteps, in the pierce of every bell, in the nonsense of giggling gossip, the precious seconds tick, quickly, continuously. For four years we search, frantically, for who we are, for what we will become. And just as we begin to grasp the reality of the world around us, our time has ended. We gather the memories of the past four years, wistfully taking them in, realizing that our moments of high school will soon blur into the rest of our lives. Yet, somehow, these memories — prom, homecoming, state championships — remain more prevalent than any other moment in time. After college, after careers, after kids . . . high school lives on. For in something so fleeting, so intricate, we see a glimpse of reality, of the truth that is within us all.

Jacqueline Wilber
Class of 2003

life's a *blur*

Fig. 17.5. Breaking away from traditional gridded design is often appropriate for dramatic use of pictures and for special content in the yearbook. This photo, shot using a slow shutter speed, effectively captures visually what the headline conveys verbally, and makes a strong connection for the reader. Copy is placed just at the hand's grip, effectively leading the reader to the beginning sentence. Varying structure and breaking away from traditional design allows for reader surprises with content, and helps to provide pacing for the yearbook. *Legacy*, Roosevelt High School, Sioux Falls, S.D.

In recent years, student designers have created section templates for yearbook design. A section template is essentially like creating a style sheet for the design of an individual section of the book and can include a basic column structure, a headline style, an alternative copy style and a format for the layout. The styles can be saved as templates in a desktop-publishing program and can be opened by individual designers.

In addition to saving the skeletal page structure, a page designer can create a type template so text brought in from a word-processing program can be "styled" to the typeface choices, sizes and alignments for that section for uniformity. These are referred to as style sheets and can be defined for both copy styles and paragraph styles. Additionally, layout software programs enable designers to create "libraries," electronic storage areas for visual or typographic devices.

Section templates can save a lot of time for individual designers but can also result in a heavily stylized section that compromises picture quality and creates visual redundancy, or visual uniformity, when the reader looks at the book. Therefore, designers should be careful to keep the templates flexible. Designers should be able to base their picture placement decisions on the content of the pictures to be used on the spreads, rather than making those decisions by conforming to a predetermined picture size or shape.

An additional consideration for yearbook designers should be content in design. Yearbook staffs have to sit down and decide how they want to tell stories to their

Fig. 17.6. Narrow grids or columns – as narrow as 3 to 4 picas wide – offer the designer many options for column multiples for pictures and verbal content. Many yearbooks moving to modular design start with narrow column skeletal structures which give them multiple options to create the modules. When using narrow grids as a structure, designers must realize that any single grid is probably too narrow for copy and will need to combine at least two grids for comfortable reading. This yearbook design features several modules covering trends. Note the horizontal black module providing a strong break in the design. *Tom Tom*, Danville Community High School, Danville, Ind.

readers in terms of page allocation and story-telling forms. Pacing is an important consideration in design because it allows the designer flexibility when designing content. For instance, big events during the school year might need more than one spread in the book. An example might be homecoming, the prom, a big school celebration or a winning sports season. In those cases, the best way to tell the story might be on two to three carefully planned layouts that continue the coverage just as a magazine might do. This coverage is often referred to as "jump" coverage since the coverage jumps from spread to spread (Fig. 17.7).

Other topics, such as modes of transportation, might be better covered through a single page of coverage or through a traditional double-page spread. Many schools give clubs single pages of coverage. Tackling a serious issue that is relevant to the school or a big celebration such as an anniversary might call for a special section of coverage of many spreads. Designers need flexibility in covering topics so the stories can be fully covered.

Content can also be organized around general topics such as stress. Individual stories on a spread could include different methods for dealing with stress, what causes stress, relaxation techniques or a poll indicating most stressful times of the day or year (Fig. 17.8).

Yearbook designers also have to be aware of story-telling forms. Let's take the modes of transportation idea. Having photographers take pictures of cars in the parking lot is not the way to tell this story. Good pictures need people in them.

We trudge off to the halls of Casa Roble every day, driven by some mysterious force. Our parents want to see the 4.0 GPA. Our administration demands a next generation of thinkers. Our teachers think we need to know where the graph crosses the X-axis. Those are their reasons. Reasons that are valid, but not ours. We come in search of something else, something unique, something we can only find here. We care little for the computer applications, verb conjugations, and senior projects of their school. We seek the hidden communities and inner-workings that beat in harmony with our hearts. In the following section, *Rampages* offers a series of stories that detail the everyday lives and events that illustrate the essence of high school life. The following pieces are meant to look into emotions in a manner that any student can relate to, and paint portraits of our school that anyone can recognize. It is important to note that all of the photos in this section are completely independent of the stories, so as you read this section (or just look at the pictures), don't go thinking Billy Bob from the picture in the upper right is "guy with spiky hair" in the story below. Now, that said, the question we want to ask here isn't "Am I just a school?" but, "Am I just school?"

by Michael Catinari

UNDER THE SURFACE
OBSERVING THE WORLDS OF STUDENT LIFE

Although most see high school as a place of learning, it is also a place of feeling. We not only sharpen our minds but shape our souls as well.

44 student life

Enraged by the sliding of his drums, Kyle Crosier winces as he strives to complete the set at Casapolooza on September 17. The event featured two campus bands, Trapped In Suburbia and Victoria Secret Police. "That night I was upset because my drums were slipping. That is why I looked especially angry," said Crosier. Photo by Crystal Arroues

Doing a series of individual vignettes of student drivers and their unusual cars with bio boxes of relevant questions (such as where the student got the car, how much it costs to maintain and the most unusual element of the car) might make that topic one worth covering. Having the photographers shoot the pictures in interesting settings where simple backgrounds could be used to display the cars would also make the pictures more interesting than those shot in crowded, busy school parking lots.

Every event that happens during the year should be considered for its storytelling potential before any attempt is made to design a spread. Content in the book should also evolve from year to year. Cultural trends mark change. Several years ago, yearbook staffs started covering trends such as students using ATM machines and students surfing the internet. Now both of those topics are rather dated. A careful evaluation of the book's content needs should be made by the entire staff at the beginning of the year. Flexibility should also be built into this system so the staff can appropriately cover unforeseen events as they occur during the year.

DESIGNING THE PAGES

A designer needs to have all the component parts before beginning design. Carefully edited pictures that show varied content, different people, strong compositional

Fig. 17.7. Using the concept of a special magazine inside the yearbook that relates to the book's theme "Influences," this special jump section continues on for several spreads. The section is held together visually through similar design styles. The section offers well-written commentary on a variety of lifestyle issues, most of which are written in the first person. The use of the nouns across the top of each spread, with one word in black and the others in gray, indicates the focus of that spread's attention. *Rampages,* Casa Roble High School, Orangevale, Calif.

Fig. 17.7. (continued)

styles and combinations of both vertical and horizontal forms will help the designer in creating an appealing design. The designer could work from the section template with the typographic styles also defined and saved as part of the template.

Once the page content has been decided, the photographs taken for that content should be gathered, and decisions should be made about their use. These decisions should include the following:

- Choose the dominant image. The dominant image should be the most compelling photographic choice. Close-ups, emotion-filled shots, strong angles and interesting content will always draw a reader's attention. Isolate the picture from among your choices that does this best (Fig. 17.9). The editing process is one that works best when done in partnership with a photographer. See Chapter 20 for more information on choosing and editing pictures.

- Edit your supporting images. Eliminate pictures that show the same or similar content, pictures that show the same person more than once and pictures with weak quality such as those that are out of focus or that have backgrounds that interfere with the subject matter. Decide how many images you want to place on the spread, that is, how many you need to tell the story. Additional editing considerations are using pictures with the same number of people in them or with only one person in them and using too many pictures shot from the same camera angle or with the same lens. A good story needs close-ups, detail shots, wide angles, medium shots and a variety of telephotos.

- Look for strong horizontals and verticals. Horizontals and verticals are the most interesting visual forms. Avoid square-shaped pictures.

- On the computer open the section template and begin designing by first placing the picture that has been chosen as the dominant image. In traditional design, a dominant would be used on the page that would be two to three times larger than any other supporting picture. Recent trends indicate that staffs are using dominant pictures in smaller size ratios to allow for the integration of more images on the page.

  Preferably, the picture's focus should face toward the gutter rather than off the page, keeping "eyeflow" on the page. Some designers are allowed to ask the photographer or the publisher to merely "flop" or "flip" the negative if the picture isn't facing into the page. Doing so is an ethical compromise. It's better for the designer to use the natural direction of the image. Another content consideration should be whether the picture bleeds across the gutter. The designer must be sure that important content, such as faces, won't be printed in the gutter, where they will be trapped in the binding and impossible to see.

- As each picture is positioned in the layout, the designer should plan for the placement of the caption for the picture. Readers prefer captions placed adjacent to the pictures they describe. Move 1 pica (the internal gutter) away from the picture and indicate where the caption will be, type the caption in on the computer or import it from the word-processing file.

Fig. 17.8. Combining clubs coverage through common themes and ties, yearbook staffs avoid problems with redundant copy and pictures. Combining coverage of three clubs into one spread, this staff created content modules that featured coverage of the clubs in a variety of ways. A main copy block ties the clubs together based on their making a difference in the school. Using a horizontal module of quotes and head shots gives the staff an opportunity to increase the number of students pictured in the book. A module called "The Big Event" features an accomplishment of each of the clubs. The coverage also includes a first-person feature and candid photographs with extended captions. *Silhouette*, Plainfield High School, Plainfield, Ind.

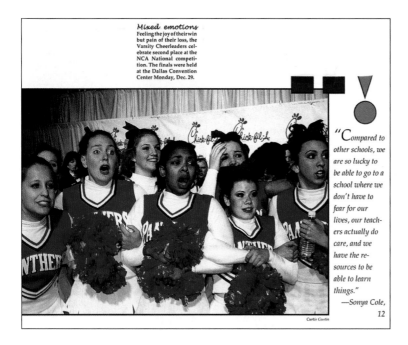

Mixed emotions
Feeling the joy of their win but pain of their loss, the Varsity Cheerleaders celebrate second place at the NCA National competition. The finals were held at the Dallas Convention Center Monday, Dec. 29.

"Compared to other schools, we are so lucky to be able to go to a school where we don't have to fear for our lives, our teachers actually do care, and we have the resources to be able to learn things."
—Sonya Cole, 12

Curtis Gustin

Fig. 17.9. Dominant images should be chosen for their potential story-telling content and their ability to stop and focus the reader's attention on the spread's content. Emotion, such as that showing on the faces of these cheerleaders who just won second place in a competition, holds the reader's attention and freezes the moment for the yearbook reader. *Panther*, Duncanville High School, Duncanville, Texas.

Two captions can be stacked 1 pica apart, but when three captions are stacked together, the reader will have a harder time figuring out the coordination of the captions with the pictures. Designers should also avoid placing captions directly on top of pictures. Unless there is a consistent, even tonal area for placement, the type could become unreadable. Also, the content of the picture can be compromised when the caption is placed on top of it.

Captions should conform to column widths and should be consistent in column widths on the spread. An exception might be a caption appearing in a single column on a narrow column structure.

In yearbook design, another device a designer can use to create section style is a caption lead-in, a specifically designed style of typography that provides information for the caption and helps direct the reader visually to each of the captions (Fig. 17.10).

Yearbook designers should also keep in mind that type spanning across the gutter will be a problem due to the book's binding. Words could become trapped in the gutter and become unreadable. Designers who want a headline to move across the gutter should probably design the headline so the words stop at the gutter margin on the left page and start again at the gutter margin on the right page. Using heads bleeding across the gutter requires careful attention to writing. Text and captions should never be placed in the gutter.

- When placing the next image, the designer should make sure it is placed apart from the dominant image by only 1 pica, generally the size of the internal margins. Stay on the column guides and use a combination of columns that allows the photograph to be showcased effectively without compromising its content. Continue to use strong vertical and horizontal crops.

- Continue to place the pictures in the layout until a pleasing arrangement has been created. The designer should also place the body text from the word-processing program and make sure that the line lengths are readable and that the story is laid out in a module, a shape with only four sides. Copy in multicolumn grid formats should use a combination of columns that allows for ease of readability, generally widths between 10 and 20 picas.

Positioning the headline in the layout will be an important decision. While it is traditional for headlines to be placed adjacent to their stories, a headline can appear next to the text, underneath it, jutting into it or dropping into it in a "well" arrangement. If a nontraditional headline placement is chosen, the designer should take advantage of a typographic device such as a strong drop cap in the dominant

Fig. 17.10. Visual unifiers such as color, and graphic devices such as lines, can provide strong continuity across a spread and through a section of the yearbook. Using the color green, a dominant color featured in several of the photographs, this staff created visual unity through both color and graphics. The headline appears in green and green outlines. Green is featured in all the rule line graphics and is lightened to a percentage in a sidebar and in the scorecard headline. Using the greater than symbol (>) as a visual entry point unites factoids in the copy block and points to wins in the scorecard. Green vertical lines appear on the right sides of captions. Finally, exaggerated quote marks note a student's quote, also appearing in a lightened percentage of the green color. *Hornet*, Bryant High School, Bryant, Ark.

headline style to focus the reader's attention to the beginning of the story.

As the designer works, attention should be given to placing white space so it appears toward the outside edges of the layout, rather than trapped between page elements. Grouping pictures together and placing captions in outlying areas creates strong page eyeflow.

Many schools now shoot pictures on digital cameras and scan images after film is developed. The value is that the images can be viewed on the computer screen in their actual locations and sizes. Designers can make sure faces are not trapped in the gutter, that pictures are cropped effectively and that content works well together on the spread.

SPECIAL CONSIDERATIONS

- Portrait pages require designers to work with large blocks of student portraits, usually shot by a studio photographer hired by the school district. These pictures are generally arranged as a single vertical or horizontal block on each page, with narrow rule lines placed between the photos for separation. Place name blocks to the outside edges of the pictures in first name/last name arrangement (Fig. 17.11).

Even if these portraits are shot by different photographers in the school's community, it is important for the yearbook staff to work with the photographers to

Fig. 17.11. Portrait pages are best arranged when the panels of pictures appear in rectangular shapes on the spreads. Head sizes and backgrounds should be consistent. Name blocks should appear to the outside edges of the panels aligned next to each panel in normal first name/last name arrangement. In senior sections, placing the students' activities with their names adds interest. Adding features and sidebars to panel pages offers design opportunities, especially when the portraits are printed in color. Moving features from left to right spreads will vary the interest points on the spreads. *Excalibur*, Crown Point High School, Crown Point, Ind.

keep the head sizes in the pictures a consistent size. Differing head sizes on the pages will create distracting images.

- In sports and clubs sections, group shots should be laid out as horizontals and should be cropped tightly so no extraneous visual information appears with the group. Careful coordination between the group shot photographer and the page designers is required to ensure the group shot shapes will work on the layouts. If the photographer arranges the group in a strong vertical design, the designer will have to accommodate that shape on the layout, which could pose problems. In an attempt to make the pictures larger to show the individual faces of the club or sport members, many staffs have moved the group shots to separate sections of nothing but group shots. Published in special inserts or sections at the ends of sports and club sections, these allow readers to thumb through "albums" of images looking for their friends. Regardless of where in the book they are placed, the heads of the people in group shots need to be at least the size of a dime so they will be visible.

- The design of theme pages, section dividers and other thematic elements will need special attention. Readers need to know they are looking at special content. Designers should pay attention to consistencies in graphics that will help the readers visually "group" or connect these elements when they come to them in the book. Creating a strong graphic style in the opening and closing section, and adapting elements of that style to the dividers, will reinforce this design for readers. The use of color, larger pictures, logos and specially designed text will help readers connect these elements. Designers also might use wider text displays, increased leading or similar typographic devices (Fig. 17.12).

Copy in theme pages needs to be unique, specific and interesting.

Many schools using catchphrase themes will break the theme down into "mini-themes" and incorporate these phrases into copy or special features in individual sections of the book. This helps re-inforce the theme idea through the entire book.

- Designers who use photos cut into shapes that follow the contour of the actual photo content should keep in mind that those shapes are strong attention-getters since they are active shapes. They usually will provide visual entry and dominant attention on the page. Designers should simplify the rest of the design to prevent competing visual elements. Also, photo cutouts need to be anchored on the page or attached to something visually. One way to anchor these pictures is to add shadows in an image editing or page design software program.

- Pay attention to the design of the ad section. Display ads from local businesses need to be visually different. Avoid using the same typeface in each ad. Make sure each ad has a strong visual or a strong type message. Column methods may be used for the ads that correspond to the ad's price. For instance, many staffs now sell their ad sections by dividing page space into a series of blocks. Many books offer as many as 9 to 12 blocks of space on a page. Advertisers can then purchase a multiple of blocks for their ads. Some schools offer discounts for full-page ads (Fig. 17.13).

The use of senior ads, friend ads and club ads has enabled many staffs to eliminate the outside sale of ad space. These ads can be sold in standard sizes by dividing pages into module shapes and selling blocks or combinations of blocks. In the smaller block sizes, the yearbook staff might want to create a standard design style, enabling the parent to add an individualized message or picture.

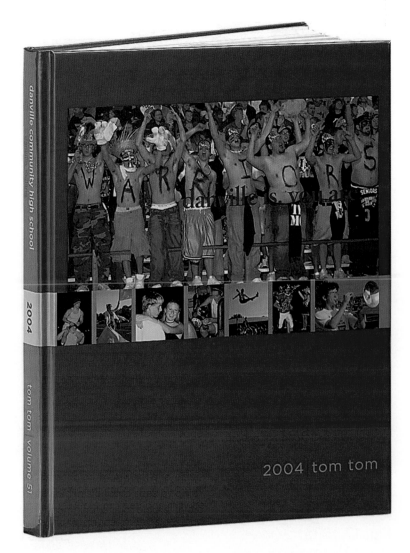

Fig. 17.12(a). Using the theme "danville is, you are," the *Tom Tom* begins its theme presentation on a cover filled with pictures of students that wraps around onto the back. Note the introduction of a burgundy color and the shape of the strip of pictures wrapping around the book. The theme reinforces the fact that each student in the school has unique qualities which make the school also unique.

danville is. you are.

7 | traditions

33 | priorities

49 | involvement

109 | details

71 | relationships

Like no other. 1. Supporting the varsity football team against Crawfordsville, sophomore Allie Bertalot, freshman John Harvey and sophomores Tiffany Baldwin and Sarah Adolf sit in the Mob section on Aug. 30. 2. In Mrs. Michelle Clark's physics class, junior Matt MacPherson demonstrates his roller coaster project on Oct. 23. 3. At soccer practice on Aug. 22. senior Drew Brokamp waits to subbed back into the drill. 4. Competing in a hot dog eating contest during Spirit Week, junior Shea Pierce feeds junior Andrew Pierson at the prep session on Sept. 26. 5. On the sidelines due to injury, freshman Kayln Donahue watches the girls' JV soccer team practice.

danville community high school
100 warrior way
danville, indiana 46122
317.745.6431 | phone
317.745.3908 | fax
www.danville.k12.in.us
student enrollment | 641

2004 tom tom | volume 51

Fig. 17.12(b). On the title page, the first page of the book, visual devices introduced on the coverage reappear for the reader. The theme statement continues and the horizontal shape in burgundy provides a ground for the pictures, each containing people from different sections of the book along with page references and section titles. Note the book is divided not into traditional sections, but into five sections: traditions, priorities, involvement, details and relationships.

Ad sections are excellent places to include features that help students remember the cost of different items during their school year or for community-related features. In all cases, careful attention should be given to designing interesting ad sections.

• Another section that can be used to amplify the book's theme development is the index. Every person pictured in the book should be listed in one complete alphabetical index. The index is also an excellent place to list the book's advertisers, clubs, sports and activities as they appear throughout the book. The index should be designed with a column structure in place. Typographic devices such as dot leaders can be used between the name and the page numbers to lead the reader's eye across the listings.

Many schools enliven these pages by including candid pictures with captions or by including an alphabetical section of club and sport group shots throughout the index. Making the group shots large enough for each individual face to be the approximate size of a dime is a good rule of thumb for group shot size.

• Schools whose yearbooks publish in the spring encounter early spring deadlines preventing coverage of the complete school year. Many of these schools choose to publish a small special insert, usually given to a printer in the local community who can produce the work in a short amount of time. These special inserts cover the activities of the school that occur after the book has been sent to the yearbook publisher. In addition to giving the staff continued design work throughout the semester, the special spring magazines make the yearbook a more complete book. Many staffs continue using their section design templates and theme styles in these inserts. Incorporation of the section can be accomplished through a special glue strip on the insert. The student can then decide where in the book to place the insert.

Many yearbook publishers also sell special entertainment and news event sections that can be purchased and placed in each book to add to the coverage of the year.

CD, DVD AND INTERACTIVE COVERAGE

With the growing increase in personal computers, many schools expand the coverage of the yearbook by producing DVD additions to the printed book. The value

Fig. 17.12(c). The opening section continues the visual strategy: the burgundy horizontal bar, a series of small pictures each containing people doing a variety of activities, a lower case headline using the same typography as in the theme statement and the use of condensed sans serif type for the text and captions. The staff has added reader value to the spread through a series of quotes from students, each relating to a unique quality in the school.

of these productions comes in their ability to include movies and sound as natural adjuncts to the printed content of the book. Eventually, staffs can be creative in designing content for these sections, which could include the entire portrait section of the book, for instance. Rollovers could include students' names, participation in school activities or awards won during the year, or where they're headed after high school.

Senior ads could eventually include the parent's voice actually congratulating or reading a message to the senior student.

Club and sports group shots are another natural fit for the DVD yearbook. Students too often complain about the small size of the pictures used in the printed book. Displaying the pictures on a computer or television screen enables students to see the pictures in larger sizes and to view the individual faces in the groups. Again, content could be added in rollovers.

DVDs can also include more audio-visually oriented events of the school year – the sounds of the homecoming royalty being announced at the game with footage from that event, the school fight song played by the band at a pep assembly or an entire special event such as a talent show – offering many choices that are limited in the printed book and that offer value to the printed book in terms of its historical value to the students.

Companies have emerged to offer the special production services of the DVD to the yearbook staff. Many of the companies offer training and lend equipment for producing the content. They then offer training in editing and production of the

Fig. 17.12(d). A divider spread for the traditions section contains elements of the theme design to create visual cohesion for the book's structure. One large horizontal image is introduced, but reinforced by the pattern of smaller, clustered pictures running across the bottom. The burgundy horizontal bar has been replaced with adjectives that describe who the students are in the pictures beneath. The use of condensed, sans serif type is repeated. A short index of content within the section appears on the right to reinforce the reader's understanding of a non-traditionally named section.

actual DVD. Some schools sell these products separately from the book, although most schools package the product with the actual printed book as a supplement.

THE USE OF COLOR

Color has become the standard in yearbooks as it is in many other facets of design. Yearbook publishers already offer full-color books, and many schools have taken opportunities to print these products. Most yearbook photographers now shoot digitally where formats are shot in color and later converted to grayscale if the images are not reproduced in color.

Color can add significantly to the impact of the book, displaying the beautiful blue skies, fall colors, winter snows and spring flowers that students experience during the year.

Using color effectively in design requires attention to detail. Display type used for headlines and secondary headlines works well in color, but smaller type displays such as copy and captions rarely read effectively in color. Colored text type tends to slow down the reader, discouraging readability.

Warm colors always come forward in design. Designers looking for color connections through photographs can often pull color, or repeat strong color, from a dominant image and create a strong connection between the photograph and the page content. This color repetition will often create a connection visually for the reader of the page (Fig. 17.14).

talkative artistic fun complicated playful diverse preoccupied irreplaceable loud simple irreplaceable nervous overworked accepting confident traditional impatient innovative uncertain athletic bold chaotic determined stressed encouraging curious brash rebellious edgy undefined ritualistic crowded passionate exhausted forgiving unique competitive brave intimidating busy colorful spirited **danville is. you are.**

Fig. 17.12(e). Endsheet design repeats the theme color, but features adjectives describing the students in the school, featured in large type. *Tom Tom*, Danville Community High School, Danville, Ind.

Too much color, or overuse of color, can also create confusion in design. When color is overused, the reader is overwhelmed by the color and distracted from the content. Color used effectively can create connections. Pull warm colors – red, oranges, yellows – to the forefront and let cool colors – greens, blues – recede.

Attention should be paid to color values when choosing colors. Some colors are hard to work with on white backgrounds, particularly some shades of red, yellow and green. Color contrasts need to be strong and effective. Textured backgrounds with color can also add clutter to the page and distract from the content.

EXERCISES

1. Using the layout software provided by the school's yearbook printer, design a layout in standard three- or four-column layout. Start by linking to pictures that have been shot by yearbook photographers that could actually be used in the design. Import text from a word-processing file or by using the software's text placeholder function. Create style sheets for the copy. Write a headline and a deck or secondary headline for the content. Proof the layout before printing. Hang up your layout and get a classmate to critique its strengths and weaknesses according to the following parameters:

   (a) Did you maintain consistent internal margins with only 1 pica of space separating content?

   (b) Are there white space holes that distract the eye?

   (c) Is the dominant image large enough to serve as a central entry point to the design?

   (d) Are the supporting pictures of varied shape, size and content?

   (e) Is the design visually attractive?

2. Brainstorm for at least five different techniques that could be used to create a theme or graphic device that would work for your school's yearbook for this year. Begin by making a list of interesting facts about the year at your school. From that list, generate ideas for each fact. Share the list with classmates and get their opinions on visual and verbal ways in which your ideas could be expressed.

3. Using the yearbook from your school or exchange copies of yearbooks, look at the theme or graphic unity of the book. In small discussion groups, critique it using these questions:

   (a) Is the theme or graphic unity clearly understandable to the reader?

   (b) Is it presented in a contemporary and interesting way on the cover?

   (c) Is the theme or graphic unity included on the endsheets (unless they are white)?

   (d) Is the theme or graphic unity clearly developed in both the opening and closing pages of the book?

   (e) How do the divider pages continue the theme or graphic unity?

   (f) Do you think the staff was successful in developing the theme or unity throughout the book? In what other ways was the staff able to reinforce the theme or graphic unity?

4. Get a copy of your state's judging standards for the yearbook. Evaluate your school's most recent yearbook using the judging standards. How well do you think your school's yearbook fulfilled the standards? What are its strengths; its weaknesses? How could these weaknesses be improved?

Fig. 17.13. Ad sections have expanded beyond community ads to include senior (grad) ads, friend ads, club ads and relevant features. Even traditional community ads will be more interesting if they feature names of students who work at the business or who are related to the business. In this lively ad spread, a variety of ad sizes is used, all featuring pictures. The staff uses a consistent identifying name running vertically starting at the top right-hand side. Content in senior ads is often left to the buyer, although the staff can offer standard designs to choose from, or can offer to help design the ad. This staff has included "index card" features (top right-hand corner) on students throughout the section to add interest. Note the information in the feature is presented in a question/answer format for quick reading. *So Anyway*, Bay High School, Bay Village, Ohio.

5. Create a graphics file by cutting up magazines or newspapers and looking for 10 examples of the following visual treatments:

   (a) Headlines with secondary or deck headlines

   (b) Use of color in design

   (c) Caption starters

   (d) Graphics such as use of color, lines, screens and textures

   (e) Sidebars or supplementary copy treatments

   Cut out each example, paste it on paper and write a short explanation of why you think the example works successfully and how it could be adapted for a section of a yearbook.

6. Choose a section of the yearbook and develop a design strategy for the section using the graphics file you created in exercise 5. Create both a visual and a verbal strategy for the section. Make a list of the typefaces you would choose for the body text, captions, folios and other verbal treatments you

Fig. 17.14. Many yearbooks are becoming completely four-color books, using color throughout the book rather than limited to certain sections. When four-color printing is used, designers must ensure that color doesn't overwhelm the content or take away from the photographic presentation. On this spread on the prom in the student life section, the designer matched the green color of the dress in the dominant picture and picked that color up as an accent color to unify the spread. Placing the headline in green logically leads the reader from the picture to the copy. The green color is also used to visually separate a module of quotes on the right-hand side. Additionally, this staff's theme employed a series of color bars which reappear in the horizontal module across the bottom of the spread. Individual colors from the color graphic are used in the grouped caption block to note the beginnings of captions, and in the quote collection module on the left-hand side of the page. While the page is colorful and lively, the color is effectively used. *Saga*, Loudon Valley High School, Purcellville, Va.

have designed. Specify point sizes, leading values and typefaces for each verbal area on the spread. Using your design strategy, paste up a sample of your design using material from magazines. Evaluate the spread's design strategy by presenting it to your classmates and having them critique its strengths and weaknesses.

7. Using picture magazines such as *Sports Illustrated* or *National Geographic*, cut out three layouts that you think are successful and write a critique of the strengths by answering these questions:

   (a) Does the use of pictures tell a complete story?

   (b) How does each picture contribute to the strengths of the visual presentation?

   (c) Does the verbal content complement the visual content?

8. Divide into teams of three to five students with each team taking a different section of the yearbook. Evaluate the content in the section in the last three copies of the school's yearbook. Has the content evolved or has it remained consistent? What evidence

of cultural trend coverage is in the section? Does the section tell stories in different ways? Is any special section coverage included? Could any special content have been included? Is the design different in each of the three volumes?

9. Look through a collection of magazines and newspapers and compile a list of catchphrases that appear in ads, in headlines or in other content areas. Without choosing a particular product's advertising slogan or using material that would be too closely identified with a product, which phrases could be used as themes? Would any of these catchphrases be workable in your school's yearbook? Next, look through a book of idioms, or commonly used expressions. Write down expressions that would be relevant to your school this year.

10. Look through galleries of award-winning yearbooks at the website for the National Scholastic Press Association by visiting its website: www.studentpress.org/nspa/index.html. Look for the link to the Best of the High School Press. View selections from different winners in the yearbook categories. Choose several that you find visually appealing and justify your reasons for your selections.

Newsmagazines, Special Sections, Inserts and Supplements

NEWSMAGAZINES

A student dies in a drunk-driving accident, three weeks before the next newspaper comes out. The student's death, the fourth such death in this community in the last two years, resulted from an alcohol-related incident. Clearly it is a story that warrants coverage. A lack of timeliness doesn't allow for the standard straight news story. An $8^{1}/_{2} \times 11$ or letter-size newsmagazine won't allow for the page 1 in-depth story most broadsheet newspapers run.

The student newsmagazine was born of a situation like this one. The student newsmagazine, a print hybrid of a newspaper and a feature magazine, began and grew in popularity in the 1970s. It has maintained its position, second to traditional school newspapers, throughout succeeding decades. In the introductory situation, a newsmagazine could cover a wide range of stories. The impact the student's death had on the parents and friends could be one news-feature. The publication could report on the community meetings to solve the problem of underage drinking. The alternatives to drinking could be an informative sidebar.

Professional weekly newsmagazines such as *Time* and *Newsweek* obviously cannot compete with the timeliness of the radio, TV or even daily newspapers, so they found a niche market in providing the public with more depth and even analysis of the week's news. Student newsmagazines have not moved as much into the area of news analysis. In fact, high school newspapers and newsmagazines have more similarities than differences. The cover, design and coverage are the three primary aspects that distinguish the newsmagazine.

COVER

One of the most distinctive characteristics of the newsmagazine is its cover or page 1. In contrast to newspapers, which usually display three or more stories on page 1, a newsmagazine displays one story as its primary or only focal point. The publication's size, which is typically tabloid or an $8^{1}/_{2} \times 11$, dictates such treatment because three or more stories would give the cover a crammed appearance. The cover may be a photograph or some art or the start of a story. The cover space may be shared with brief teaser headlines about other stories inside the publication. Often, the cover story jumps inside for continued special display, sometimes in the centerfold. This introduction and development of the cover story and the focus of the story as a news-feature are two of the most significant distinguishing characteristics of a newsmagazine.

The story that's featured on the cover should have substantial reader appeal, one that has facts that may not be known to most readers. It should be carefully and accurately reported and well written and edited. It should contain much original source reporting and be worthwhile. The *Kirkwood Call* cover highlights 23 pages on desegregation, affirmative action, racism and successful minorities (Fig. 18.1). Not every cover story has to be a serious, earth-shaking investigative piece. However, most should report either a significant academic-related concern, such as the impact of the school budget or changes in class scheduling, or a school tie-in to a topic of interest to high school students, such as physical fitness or diets. Traditional school activity stories, such as homecoming or the school play, can be featured on the cover, but a special effort should be made to provide a fresh angle to these stories.

With only the nameplate and teasers occupying space, the cover is a blank canvas for the designer. Start a story there, use a strong photo or piece of art alone with a headline or package any combination. Make sure all the pieces are good. After all, the cover is the reader's first impression.

The photo or art should have a strong center of interest that appeals to students. Visuals should be cropped to maximize the impact of the center of interest and should be technically flawless with proper contrast (Fig. 18.2). If artwork is used, it should reproduce with sufficient contrast and tonal quality. Whether you use art or a photo, you'll need a teaser and a teller headline to go with it. An action photo with people will also require a caption, which can appear on page 1 or inside the cover page. The story that starts on the cover can

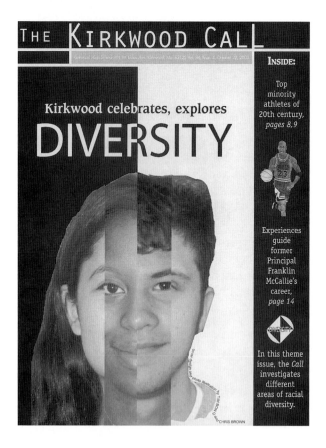

Fig. 18.1. Cover from the newsmagazine *The Kirkwood Call*, Kirkwood High School, Kirkwood, Mo.

Fig. 18.2. Cover from the newsmagazine *Spark*, Lakota East High School, Liberty Township, Ohio.

jump inside to the centerfold or to another prominent inside page position (Fig. 18.3).

Many newsmagazines split their cover space between a cover story or stand-alone photo/art and a series of teaser headlines or refers (referring to inside content). These brief headlines can be lively, startling and captivating, noting a story or other element and enticing the reader to look inside the publication. Artwork, small photos and graphics can be used in conjunction with these headlines to heighten interest.

The nameplate and accompanying essential information – the name of the school, the city and state, the date of issue, and the volume and issue numbers – should be included on the cover, usually at the top or the top half of the page. The typeface and design should be readable, professional-looking, contemporary and suitable for the contents. Inside section folios and other design elements can be designed in the same style and with the same typeface as that used on the nameplate.

DESIGN

The size of the newsmagazine often dictates the inside page design and organization. Much of the publication is organized into departments or sections and displayed as a unit. For example, all the news summaries are placed on one page or into one designated portion of a page, collected under a standing head. The departments and sections are labeled with content headings, such as sports, news, in-depth and entertainment. The smaller-size page doesn't often allow for more than one package of briefs or a story and sidebars. The newsmagazine in Figure 18.4 used multiple pages to cover the personal and medical side of Parkinson's disease. Four pages allowed the designer room to use dominant sans serif type and photos, bold and repeating graphic shapes to create a reader-friendly unified package.

The general appearance takes on a magazine look once the cover story and the departmentalized inside content is placed (Fig. 18.5). Design unity is achieved in some basic ways through selection and careful use of text and display type; through use of grid and columns; through similar design for page, section and regular column headings; and through special art and graphics that embellish everything from page folios to text initial letters and backgrounds. Much like a well-designed newspaper, the successful newsmagazine is designed as a package.

Ads are placed at the bottom of inside pages, excluding the cover, centerfold and editorial and op-ed pages. Occasionally, ads are grouped on one page and given a department heading and graphics to conform to the other sections and departments.

Fig. 18.3. *Hillcrest Hurricane*, Hillcrest High School, Dallas, Texas.

Fig. 18.4. *Mission*, Shawnee Mission North High School, Overland Park, Kan.

It is unwise to have two facing pages with only ads because readers are more likely to skip over them.

Design continuity is usually maintained in regularly published sections, such as sports or features, through uniform grid and column structure; text and display type size and face variations; and the design of standing heads, folios and graphics. The front page of these inside sections often carries a version of the newsmagazine's nameplate, customized to indicate the specific content within the section.

COVERAGE

Infrequent publication of a newspaper due to budgetary, time or staffing constraints has led some schools to adopt the newsmagazine in place of a regular newspaper. However, factors other than frequency of publication may cause a staff to change its format from a newspaper to a newsmagazine. One is the desire for a change. If a change is made, editors should draw up a plan to ensure that the readers are still given all the information they need as students. For example, an investigative cover story on teenage alcohol abuse is fine, as long as the results of the debate tournament are also printed somewhere in the newsmagazine.

Monthly newsmagazines, or those published less frequently, have to focus substantially on the advance story to retain the credibility, vitality and timeliness necessary for a news medium. By "featurizing" most news and focusing on angles

Fig. 18.4. (continued)

other than immediacy, the newsmagazine that is typically published monthly has minimized the timeliness dilemma.

The primary focus of a newsmagazine is on feature material or news-features that de-emphasize immediacy or timeliness – the *when* angle – in favor of such other news elements as consequence, proximity, human interest and the *why* and *how* of an event. News is largely featurized. However, a news peg is often essential to this featurization.

Newsmagazine content is similar to a newspaper's and includes news-features, news summaries, editorials, opinion columns, in-depth and investigative reports, sports and a variety of human interest and informational features. Visuals, such as photographs, illustrations, cartoons and information graphics, complete the editorial plan.

Outside of the staple of the newsmagazine – the feature – newsmagazine sections and their contents break down like this:

- The centerfold, if not used for the jump of the cover story, gets special attention. It can contain an in-depth feature with related sidebars and visuals or a photo essay. It is second only to the cover in prominence and for readership. It can showcase the best writing, photography, art and graphics.

- Editorial page and op-ed page (opposite the editorial page) content includes traditional newspaper elements: a staff editorial; opinion columns; letters to the editor; an editorial cartoon; reviews of films, theater, live and recorded music,

Photos: (top) David Heyne, (middle) Greg Back, (left)
Maria Abascal and Matt Faig, and (bottom) David Heyne.

ON THE COVER: William Ryan's photo
showcases the current poker craze at East.

Fig. 18.5. Contents page from the newsmagazine *Spark*, Lakota East High School, Liberty Township, Ohio.

television, books and other events; guest columns; interpretive and analysis pieces; and the staff masthead. Occasionally, random reader opinion on topical issues is included in a photo poll or similar device.

- News stories, including capsule summaries, gathered into a briefs column are placed on one page or more within the same section. They are not scattered throughout the publication as is sometimes done in a newspaper. Some newsmagazines will do a newspaper-style front page without the nameplate on page 3 of the newsmagazine. Thus, the newsmagazine has a magazine-style cover and a newspaper-style front page inside.

- Sports reporting is handled in much the same way as news. Results of competitions are summarized in sports packaged briefs. Advance contests are highlighted as major stories, and opinion columns and features on recreation and personal fitness are included in the overall sports budget.

- The newsmagazine can include some specialty reporting on student lifestyle interests, such as health and personal grooming, personal finance and money management, employment and continuing education opportunities, legal concerns and entertainment previews. Reporting of local crime, with student or school tie-ins, and deaths of students and faculty and staff are also common in both student newsmagazines and newspapers.

SPECIAL SECTIONS AND INSERTS

The impact of a multimillion dollar bond issue or the statistics and emotions of a basketball team's state championship run can make for special coverage through an insert, a special section or a special edition.

For sections devoted exclusively to one-time project reporting – such as an indepth story and sidebars on summer jobs or an investigative piece and sidebars on the funding of sports in the school – the layout and overall design can differ from the design of the other sections. Some elements, such as the body text, will remain constant, but a different type may be used for headlines, and different graphics and photo treatments may be included. The number of columns may also differ from that of the main publication.

Special sections can be used as seasonal or special events advertising shoppers. For example, the December holidays, prom, spring vacation travel or a new fashion season can be the focus of a four-page ad section. All ad copy could relate to the central theme or event. Related consumer stories could tie into the ads to complete the promotional package.

Major news events are often the subject of special sections. Staffs can decide to give readers more depth to major events but should be sure the coverage is warranted. In Figure 18.6, the staff of *The Lancer* developed a 12-page drinking

deep impact

BY NANCY WANG

Losing a loved one in a car accident profoundly affects everyone. The death of former TOHS student Kurt Mautner is one such example.

WHATEVER TROUBLES LIFE brought, Senior Erin Cummings knew there was one person who would listen.

"Since he was my brother's best friend, he was kind of my older brother too," Cummings said. "Anything I couldn't tell my brother, I would tell Kurt."

Then on Sunday, March 17, 2002, she suddenly found herself without her confidant.

Kurt Mautner, then a junior at TOHS, had been driving to Simi Valley that morning to go bowling with some friends. Mautner was about to change lanes when a car in his blind spot sped up. Mautner quickly swerved, overcorrected, and swerved back again, going over the shoulder and hitting a tree. Passenger Chris Chatfield survived, though with serious injury; Mautner died at the scene.

Mautner's death deeply affected the student body; he had been very involved in journalism, ASB, and the dance team.

"In a school community it affects so many people, not just the students," peer-counseling advisor and school counselor Skip Shaver said. "I don't think students realize some-times

how attached adults get. It profoundly affects us too."

The day after the accident, Mautner's friend Matt Maccarone, who had graduated the previous year, had a dirt biking accident. Just earlier that day, he had been at school with other mourning friends. Maccarone was placed into intensive care, but did not survive. He passed away on April 3, 2002.

In those few weeks, the peer-counseling room was filled with students.

"We connect old age to death. You [young people] are not supposed to die," Shaver said, explaining the shock of the tragedies. "You're at that age when you feel like nothing can happen to me, only to others."

Alumna Becky Quan felt the full impact of the two accidents; she had sat between the boys in ASB the previous year, often joking around with the two friends.

She was closer to Mautner. Just the year before they had attended a leadership conference where they learned about Every 15 Minutes and brought the idea to the school. They were in charge of organizing the event, but, according to Quan, pro-c r a s t i n a t i o n ensued and the event did nòt take place that year.

Then the accident happened.

IN MEMORY—

This plaque, dedicated to Kurt Mautner by the dance department, hangs in the Girls Activity Room

MOURNING—*The dance team performs in Kurt Mautner's memory.*

"When Kurt died, it was a wake up call that I need to grow up and I need to take care of myself," Quan said.

Safe driving became a much more important issue to her. The next year, Quan participated in the Every 15 Minutes program as one of the people who "died."

Cummings especially struggled with Mautner's death.

"The most difficult part was that whenever something really bad happened, I'd always have Kurt there to talk to about it," Cummings said.

Cummings also stopped attending church. It took six months, her brother's urging, and another car accident-related death, this time her cousin's, for her return to her faith.

"A part of you never gets over it [a friend's death]. But you still have to process it," Shaver said. "You need to get together with people and talk about the good times. You need to communicate long term."

Grieving is a slow process, but both Cummings and Quan come to terms with what happened.

"I've gone from hating the whole situation and just wishing it never happened to just accepting it," Quan said. "You have to be thankful for what you have."

The tragedy has also made Cummings appreciate those around her more.

"One of the things that hit me hard about it is that I never said goodbye," Cummings said. "I think about it now whenever I say good-bye. Whenever I get in fights with friends or whatever, I try to resolve it so nothing goes unresolved."

The tragedy has also changed their attitudes toward dangerous and careless driving.

"I yell at my friends when they speed. I hate cars. I really do," Quan said. "If people could walk everywhere that would be wonderful."

Speeding bothers Cummings just as much.

"I don't want to say something, but people like that are kind of self-ish," she said. "They don't realize their actions affect other people."

These days, Quan still keeps in touch with those she had befriended in mutual mourning. Cummings has resumed her conversation with Mautner since visiting his grave a year after his death. Now she visits it once or twice a week.

"It keeps that connection there," she said.

theLancer Special edition Thursday, December 2 2004

8

FAST FACTS

- Forty-six percent of eighth graders have tried alcohol and 20 percent of eighth graders have been drunk at least once. (Johnston, et al, 2003)

- About three in every ten Americans will be involved in an alcohol-related crash at some time in their lives. (NHTSA, 2001)

Fig. 18.6. *The Lancer,* Thousand Oaks High School, Thousand Oaks, Calif.

and driving section in connection with the school and communities' "Every Fifteen Minutes" program. The special section tackled the insurance and legal problems that come with a "Driving under the Influence" conviction. Story-telling pieces on the emotional impact that a student's death in a drunk-driving accident can have made the section personal to the reader.

Other opportunities for special sections or inserts include major sports accomplishments, student and other elections, significant academic program changes, senior graduation and all-school events such as homecoming. These one-time extras can give more students opportunities to serve as editors, as well as provide more display space for writing, photography and art. Often, these extras are keepsakes because of the event they commemorate.

Special sections or inserts may be done as stand-alone extras published outside of the regular newspaper or newsmagazine schedule. An unexpected event, such as a school sports championship, may even lead to a special, stand-alone edition (Fig. 18.7).

SUPPLEMENTS

Ambitious staffs from around the country have added magazine supplements to their newspaper. These supplements are distinct in content, design and sometimes size from the host news publication.

Supplement content varies, but it is different from the traditional mix of news, features and opinion in the host newspaper or newsmagazine. Some examples of supplements are collections of students' creative writing, personality interviews, entertainment guides and sports features. Some are produced as class projects, largely independent of the regular newspaper production staff.

Supplements are usually smaller in size than the host news publication. For example, a broadsheet newspaper may have a tabloid-size supplement, and a tabloid-size publication may have am $8^1/_2 \times 11$-inch supplement. In Figure 18.8, the *Spark*, an $8^1/_2 \times 11$-inch publication, produces a 5×7-inch College Bowl preview supplement.

Size is not the only way to distinguish a supplement from its host. The design varies. A supplement is designed as a magazine or a newsmagazine, with special cover treatment and other visual signs dictated by its unique content.

Fig. 18.7. Special section from the *Rockwood Summit Talon*, Rockwood Summit High School, Fenton, Mo.

Planning a Newsmagazine, Special Section, Insert or Supplement?

Answer these questions to create a statement of purpose for the publication.

• Why are we publishing it?
• Who will want to read it?
• Why will they want to read it?
• What will they read and see?
• What will make it unique?

Photo manipulation computer programs and computer art programs have put professional-looking design within range of many more high school publications. Design and coverage ideas come from many sources. A variety of newsstand magazines can provide both design and reporting inspiration. No design or story should be copied or plagiarized, of course, but these ideas can be altered and localized, or they may suggest new interpretations. A clip file or bulletin board for random ideas should be kept in the staff workroom. All staffers should be encouraged to bring in file ideas – a headline, a photo, an ad, a story – to build a resource center. Since newsmagazines and newspaper supplements draw on both magazines and newspapers for their format and style, clips from both are helpful.

Magazine-style newspaper supplements broaden the publishing experiences of students. Students learn both newspaper and magazine production.

Planning is critical when selecting management of the supplement or insert. The editor or top editors of the supplement or insert should be someone other than the editor of the host publication to avoid work overload. However, the editors should communicate regularly to match production schedules and to avoid duplication.

Students can get a head start on advertising supplements or inserts by planning all of them at the start of the school year. Ads may be sold in the fall and related consumer stories written during lulls in the production schedule of the host publication.

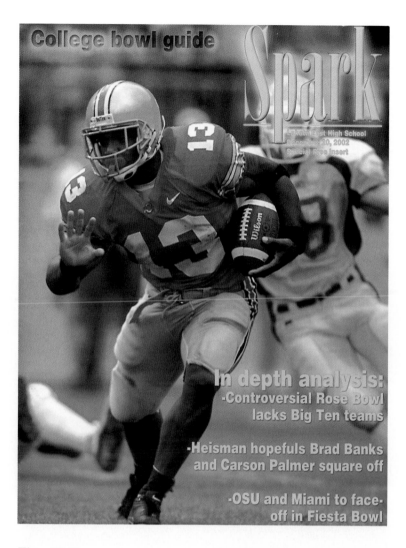

Fig. 18.8. Supplement from the *Spark*, Lakota East High School, Liberty Township, Ohio.

Special project reporting usually requires more time than most other reporting assignments. A reporting team, including a graphic designer to provide the supporting information graphics, might work one issue ahead to ensure thorough and accurate work.

EXERCISES

1. Examine copies of one or more of these national newsmagazines: *Time*, *Newsweek* and *U.S. News and World Report*. What sections or departments does each have? How is the cover story presented on the cover and then jumped inside? What news is summarized? What evidence do you see of design continuity in each publication?

Your publication planning checklist should include the following:

- Statement of goals
- Target audience
- Frequency of publication
- Content plan
- Promotion plan
- Format and design plan
- Type and printing specifications
- Content submission plan
- Staff organization plan and duties list
- Production schedule
- Budget
- Reader evaluation tool

2. Choose a topic or event from the last year that could have been a focus of a supplement for your publication. Plan the supplement. Develop at least five story ideas and three sidebars for the supplement. What photos or illustrations could you have for the supplement? What information graphics could you include?

3. Take a broadsheet publication or a tabloid currently designed in standard newspaper layout form and redesign the front page. Decide on the primary story and then sketch your design.

4. Prepare a list of topics that could be reported in depth in either a supplement or a newsmagazine cover story. List five that are school related and five that are local, state or national stories with student tie-ins.

5. Plan a supplement for your present news publication. Sell advertising to finance its production costs. Review the publication planning guidelines in this chapter as you begin your work.

Online Journalism

As computers and online services grow faster, the information superhighway has become like the German Autobahn – more of a super highway where speed and access are almost unlimited. Students cruise through information resources at school in their classrooms and at home through personal computers. Tapping the potential of this resource, student journalists can do research and interviewing for their own reporting and can offer their student readers supplemental information and additional contact with their publication outside its normal publishing schedule.

Students tapping into the potential of the internet will find unlimited information resources. Not only can students research and gather information, they can read information that has appeared in print on similar topics. They can even interview and communicate with people, organizations and governmental agencies that might have been unreachable through traditional methods such as the telephone. Using powerful search engines and limited search requests, students can conduct efficient online research to gather information on topics ranging from entertainment to serious in-depth reporting. In the professional press, computer-assisted reporting, as this process is known, has enabled stories to be written more accurately and thoroughly on a variety of subjects. Tapping into resources previously unavailable or inaccessible is now possible due to the wealth of information available through online sites.

Learning to conduct efficient online searches in computer-assisted reporting may be enhanced by consulting with librarians or media specialists, who can help student journalists to navigate complex sites and information. Consulting with economics teachers and those who teach statistics can aid students trying to make sense of complex numbers and information they have gathered from online sites.

From time to time, students may also have access to entertainment figures, political candidates, media figures and others through online services that make these personalities available to those using their services. Students can view actual scenes in places as remote as outer space, can tour museums in locations around the world and can access the resources of libraries and news-gathering organizations. Students can participate in online forums with other student journalists or can conduct online forums to gather information for future stories.

Student publications can independently or through web providers create web sites where students can access information and up-to-date reports and where students can view video and still photographs and hear audio clips. Waiting for the next issue of the school newspaper to publish a late-breaking story or announcement is a thing of the past for student journalists with online publications (Fig. 19.1).

The availability of such instantaneous and exciting resources introduces new, unique problems and situations for student journalists. Companion web publications can and should be more than mere repeats of the printed publication, but managing and updating the information may require additional resources, both

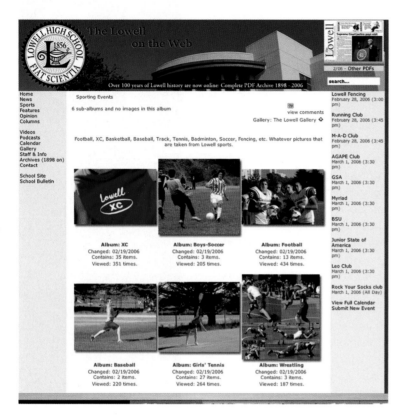

Fig. 19.1. An excellent use of a publication's website is to supplement the printed publication with additional information. In this online gallery, students can access photo galleries containing a variety of pictures. This kind of supplemental coverage offers benefits to both readers and photographers that extend the publication's value. Galleries should be kept updated to encourage visitors and to stay timely throughout the school year. *The Lowell on the Web* (www.thelowell.org), Lowell High School, San Francisco, Calif.

people and equipment, in order to do a good job. Publications may need to recruit additional staff members to manage the online publications. Those with knowledge of online software skills will be particularly valuable. Or student journalists can collaborate with students in broadcast classes to provide their readers and viewers with fresh, updated information. Publications should have a definite plan for providing content online before even beginning to experiment with such efforts. Creating an online site that is never updated or changed, especially after advertising its coming, ensures its failure.

CREATING WEB PUBLICATIONS

Many schools and school districts have already created online sites to keep parents updated and to provide information to those in their communities, particularly taxpayers. School publications can become links from these already existing school sites with the permission of the school or district. Using online web providers such as the American Society of Newspaper Editors (www.asne.org) provides student publications with opportunities for online publishing at very nominal costs. The school's parent district will often offer to host publications online, although it might have a strict policy dictating use of information on the site (Fig. 19.2). Using existing web site providers can help student publications get their sites up and running without worrying about designing the space. School sites may have censorship policies or may require information be submitted to their web masters before being placed online. Publications staffs may find those restrictions too limiting in what they are able to do with their sites.

Because internet sites are accessible to virtually anyone with a computer, some schools have created strict rules about content that can appear. For instance, some schools have prohibited pictures of students from being published online or have disallowed publishing the names of the students in pictures on the online site. Other schools require permission forms, known as "photo releases," be signed by individuals and sometimes parents of the individuals in pictures before their pictures can be placed on a web site. Online publications often must protect their First Amendment rights, just as they do in printed publications. (See Chap. 23 for more information.)

During the interviewing process, reporters may want to mention to their sources that the information they are providing may be used on a web site, just as they mention to sources that they are being interviewed for a story for the newspaper, yearbook or other publication. If the interview is being conducted online, or if information is being gathered in publication emails or polls, students should be informed of the publication's intent to use the responses in print. Student journalists should be sensitive to the way in which information obtained from online interviewing or polling can be skewed by repeated contributions from single sources. Some students may make frivolous comments or may not take the interview seriously, particularly if they can reply anonymously to the questions (Fig. 19.3).

Using information obtained from web sites requires the attribution of those sources in the story. Information used in a story appearing in a web publication should be used primarily for research and backgrounding, just as it would be if a reporter was reading a story in a printed publication. Original research is always preferred. Interviewing local sources provides information of greater value to the publication's readers. Reporters can provide web resources for readers so those seeking additional information can easily access it.

A web master, an online editor, needs skills similar to those of the student editor. The person chosen should understand news values, bring an understanding of good news judgment, be organized and exhibit leadership skills. The web master can work almost as an equal to the print publication's editor in determining how stories will appear on the web site and how the information will be different from that of the printed publication. The web master will possibly need the resources of a different group of reporters who can update printed stories and edit content that doesn't make it into the printed publication. Web writers can develop their own stories, either ones that occur between publishing deadlines or original ideas that are more appropriately presented on the web rather than through the printed publication. Reporters can work with the web staff to gather information through email forums or through responses gathered by including the publication's email address or writers' individual email addresses at the ends of stories.

Students can be encouraged to respond to information they have read in the printed publication. That response can be printed through traditional letters to the editor or can be placed on the web as a forum for discussion and dialogue. These discussions can prove valuable to the printed publication in gauging reader opinion and interest in information that could form the basis of future content.

The process of picture editing ensures that some good photographs won't be used in the printed publication. A good web photo editor will cull through the edited film, looking for additional good quality pictures to place on the web site. Many professional sites, such as those of large metropolitan newspapers, offer navigatable slide shows where additional photographs appear, often accompanied by video and audio clips. The professional press is utilizing all multimedia forms

Fig. 19.2. Online hosting is a feature of the American Society of Newspaper Editors web site (www.highschooljournalism.org) which features a section devoted to high school journalism. **(a)** On the high school journalism splash page, headers direct the user to content areas including sections for teachers and an "Ask a Pro" section featuring interviews with professional journalists.

Fig. 19.2. (continued) **(b)** At myhighschooljournalism.org, student newspapers are provided with space to post their online content for a nominal fee. **(c)** The site lists by state each high school newspaper's online link.

in providing complete storytelling to its readers. Many high schools with broadcast journalism programs will want to collaborate with their print partners to offer a full range of content. Creating similar slide shows would be a perfect opportunity for providing a greater number of pictures of students at events such as the prom or homecoming where the printed publication is limited in how many pictures will be shown. Just as in editing for print, the photo editor should make sure the content in the pictures is varied and interesting. An effort should be made to picture a diverse group of students. Technical quality must also be considered (Fig. 19.1).

Working with videographers, reporters can obtain sights and sounds reporting that can be edited and digitized into short film clips on the Web to supplement the printed information and provide additional information in ways that the printed publication cannot provide. Or the student publication can make arrangements to actually broadcast events on the web site. Recently, editors for the Carmel, Ind., *HiLite Online* simultaneously broadcast one of their school's football games on their web site.

INVOLVING THE READERS

Newspaper staffs can offer their readers access to additional content on their web sites. For instance, a student who wants to review an entertainment form may be interested in writing about it on the Web, particularly if it is timely. Many students will be interested in reading a web report about a concert that happened the previous night or a CD that was just released. Linking the reader to the band or entertainer's web site, as well as other web sites of interest to those readers, will generate more interest. This same concert review printed in a publication two to three weeks later will be old, outdated and uninteresting to student readers who are thinking ahead to the next upcoming concert.

Online publications should cause printed publications to evaluate how they tell stories and how they present information to their readers. No longer limited by long lapses between publishings, newspapers must keep content fresh and lively in both the print and online publications to maintain interest. The flexibility of using writers in different ways may give online and print publications more opportunities for feature-oriented or in-depth writing requiring longer reporting periods.

Publications can sponsor photo contests or literary writing contests in which students can submit poetry, short stories, art or photographs and have the works published periodically on the web site. If the school has a published literary magazine, this project might be sponsored cooperatively with that staff. Or teachers of creative writing classes, art and photography classes and other hands-on classes could choose student work to appear on the web site during the semester. Students whose work appears on the site could be tapped as potential staff members for either the web site or the printed publication.

ENHANCED YEARBOOK CONTENT

Yearbook staffs have endless possibilities for web content. Maintaining interest in the publication as it is created, a yearbook web master can edit content and publish it on the web site to provide previews of the printed book or to supplement its content. Showing students' pictures that have been shot from various events will make the students excited about the printed publication. The book's sales campaign can be advertised on the web site. Forms for purchasing the printed volume can be provided on the site, and options for paying for the book can be provided.

Once the yearbook staff has decided on a theme for the book, it can be shown on the web site to get the students excited about the book. If the staff doesn't keep the design of the cover a secret until the end of the year, the cover could be posted on the site. Or the staff could conduct an online vote on possible cover ideas if staff members are having a hard time deciding between several designs. Giving readers a personal stake in the outcome of the book will make them more connected to the publication throughout the year.

Yearbook staffs can provide supplemental coverage that is impossible to include in the limited space of the printed book. The possibilities here are endless but could include audio/video clips from club events and special school activities. Club group

Fig. 19.2. *(continued)*
(d) An additional feature is this National Edition, providing a summary of interesting news and links from newspapers across the country. The site is an excellent opportunity for students to compare story ideas and to see how other high schools covered stories. American Society of Newspaper Editors, Washington, D.C.

Fig. 19.3. The Carmel *HiLite Online* edition features a "Greyhound Poll" where students can vote on various issues posted to the site. Tallying the responses and keeping the winning selection up-to-date lets students see how their fellow students respond. Online polls can also be used for polls and graphs connected to published content. *The HiLite Online* (hilite@ccs.k12.in.us), Carmel High School, Carmel, Ind.

shots could be enlarged on the screen so faces could be seen more easily than in the printed book. Polls and surveys could be conducted online for inclusion in information graphics or in other reporting. Again, reporters should be sensitive to the comments made through online reporting. Minor sports and different level sports could receive expanded coverage.

On the yearbook website, as on the newspaper web site, content could be interactive. Students could submit photographs, first-person writing or artwork that the yearbook staff could edit and use.

DESIGN OF THE WEBSITE

Most publications will want to make the web site's design similar to the printed publication's. Using the printed nameplate will create a connection to the printed publication. The web site can use a series of connections to sections of the yearbook such as student life or academics. The newspaper can categorize the web stories according to news, feature, sports or other sections (Fig. 19.5). Content unique to the website should be highlighted.

Type chosen for the web site should be easily read. Readability should be a primary concern. Type in standard typefaces will process more easily and will appear more consistent regardless of the kind of computer the student reader uses. Type should be large enough in size to be visible on the screen. Designers should be aware of the need to keep line lengths short, between 10 and 20 picas for easiest readability, and attention should be given to devices such as leading, the space between the lines of type. Double-spacing between paragraphs and other design devices such as text heads within the text will aid in readability. Stories on the web may need to be edited more tightly but certainly should contain content different from that in the printed publication. The stories can provide updated information, supplemental information or reaction. Links to additional information can be created in the text.

Rather than the entire stories, headlines with summaries of stories can be provided. Interested readers can then click in to read entire text presentations. This digest service benefits readers scanning content for something of interest.

Color is another important consideration for web designers. Just as certain colors are difficult to read on the printed page, color can complicate readability on websites. Black type on white screens remains the clearest and least tiring color choice. Designers should be very careful about combining black on red or on other bright colors because the type will appear to resonate or move on the screen. Many readers will be discouraged by low readability and will stop reading. Just as the designer is the best friend to the written word in print, the same applies in online publications. Design should be secondary to readability.

Photographs should be scanned at resolutions and in compression formats that will enable easy viewing but will keep the files compact enough to open easily and quickly for the viewers. Photographs already scanned for the printed edition at higher resolutions should be reduced to the 72 dots per inch resolution needed for faster web viewing.

Links to content should be easily accessed and clearly located. Placing links in consistent typographical designs in one location on the site will help readers find them. Navigation of the site should be user-friendly. Including email addresses of the online staff and making it easy to contact the online staff will ensure reader contact. When possible, links to additional information about stories and topics can be placed at the ends of stories for readers who are interested in obtaining more information. Providing an online search engine by topic will eliminate some of the frustration of readers looking for specific content.

Video and audio clips should open easily and should be digitized in standard compression software so interested viewers will have easy access to the information. Careful attention to editing will make best use of the space and memory nececssary to include these clips on the site.

Occasional reader surprises such as contests, forums, special events and dialogues will keep readers coming back to the sites for fresh content. Contest giveaways such as free yearbooks or free newspaper subscriptions would be appropriate prizes.

Fig. 19.4. In addition to hosting an award-winning online site, the staff of the *Paly Voice* also provides blog space for its writers. Interactive content in which students are invited to contribute helps create strong interest in online sites, and keeps readers visiting for updates. *The Paly Voice* (www.voice.paly.net), Palo Alto High School, Palo Alto, Calif.

COOPERATIVE EFFORTS

As more schools develop web sites and online content, publications can create cooperative efforts with publications in their regions and states. Some states such as Texas have already established statewide efforts to share information and news reports. Linking to other publications' sites can provide student readers with other perspectives and points of view about issues of concern in their own schools. Linking to state and national press associations gives readers opportunities to compare news in their schools to that of other schools. Student writers can also access information about other schools in their state and in the nation when doing research for stories. Many newspapers include summary reports of news from other schools to keep readers informed of happenings in schools around the state and region.

Students can also arrange for joint interviews through internet providers. The subjects can respond to questions in real time. Interviewers can follow up with questions in response to comments from other interviewers or from the subject being interviewed.

Fig. 19.5. A directory of stories from the features section gives readers a headline and capsule summary of the stories plus links to the full text. Directories help readers make decisions about the content offered on sites. In addition, the left column directs readers to section headers and recent issues of the paper. The staff also provides full links to the newspaper and to links of possible interest to readers. *The Lion's Roar*, Newton South High School Newton Centre, Mass.

A different form of cooperative interviewing is video conferencing. Through school or district video-conferencing facilities, students can interview people in distant locations and can actually see and talk to them through video hook-ups on both ends of the conference. Pursuing this possibility broadens the resources available to student journalists. Video conferencing can either be one-way or two-way communication.

With all the communications possibilities available to student publications, and with more sure to come in the future, student journalists can take advantage of better research and reporting opportunities to improve their ability to tell stories, both visually and verbally.

EXERCISES

1. Visit the website of your local newspaper, if it has one, or of a larger, regional newspaper. Analyze its effectiveness by answering these questions:

(a) Is the site visually interesting and easy to read?

(b) Is color used effectively?

(c) Is the site easy to navigate; is it easy to find specific information on the site?

(d) Is it easy to contact staff members for comments or questions?

(e) Is the content different from that of the printed publication? Is it fresh and updated frequently?

(f) Are pictures used effectively on the web site?

2. Visit the Student Press website at http://studentpress.org/. Once at the site, click on "NSPA," the National Scholastic Press Association website. Then click on "Best of the High School Press Online." The site maintains links to winners of the national press association's annual contest for

newspaper websites. Visit several newspaper websites and analyze their effectiveness in design and content. Which sites are your favorites? Why?

3. Using college financial aid as a search topic, compile a list of resources that you might want to visit online to do research on this topic. Then visit some of these sources online. What sources are most valuable to you? What links did you find from your online search that proved even more valuable? How could this information be used in research for a possible story in your school newspaper? From information you obtained in your online search, compile a list of questions you might ask of a local source.

4. Using online resources, find answers to the following questions and note the websites from which you obtained the information:

   (a) How many people live in your state according to the most recent statistics?

   (b) How many people live in your county?

   (c) How many people live in your metropolitan area?

   (d) What's the average income in your state?

   (e) What's the major industry in your state?

   (f) What's the per capita growth in your state?

   (g) What's the average rainfall in your city each year?

5. If your school or student publications have an online site, evaluate its effectiveness using the criteria in exercise 1. In class, discuss the site's strengths and weaknesses.

6. On paper, outline and sketch an online site for yourself. Choose a name and design for the site. What colors would you use? How would you divide your site's content?

7. Visit the website of a metropolitan city newspaper and view an online photographic display. Are the photographs easily viewed? Do they load correctly? Do the photographs offer interesting content and information?

8. Visit the website of the Newseum, the Interactive Museum of News (www.newseum.org) and click on Today's Front Pages. Click on the websites of three of the newspapers, and compare the way the information is presented on the website compared to the printed front page. Note stories that have been updated and added since the print edition was published.

9. Invite the school's media specialist or a local media specialist to discuss online search engines and efficient online searches. Prepare a list of five general topics from five different sections of the newspaper to use as sample search topics.

Visual Storytelling: Pictures, Art and Graphics

Close your eyes. Think about a picture that has significant personal meaning to you. Recall the smallest details of its content from the expressions on the faces in the picture to the clothes the people are wearing.

Keep your eyes closed. Concentrate on a famous picture you've seen or studied but didn't witness in person. Recall the significant details of the picture's content.

Amazing, isn't it? Almost everyone can recall the content of a favorite personal image and a famous historical image just from memory. Such is the power of visual images. Details as minute as facial expressions, clothing and other circumstances of the pictures can be vividly recalled by people with such information stored deeply in the hippocampus of the brain, the brain's permanent storage area.

Just as images are important and powerful in everyday life, they are important in student publications. Readers with distracted attention spans or bombarded with information resources will edit the information they choose to read and see. Images with stopping power, those that readers find interesting and meaningful, will be viewed and often remembered.

In a student publication, images can be used for a variety of reasons: to identify, to report, to entertain, to inform and to amuse. But most importantly, pictures are an important part of the story-telling process. They shouldn't be used to fill space, to decorate pages or for other extraneous reasons. Rather, pictures and other visuals should be used because they add to the verbal reporting. They provide a different kind of interest and information to the publication, and they appeal to and attract the interest of readers in different ways.

For the yearbook and newspaper, photographers should constantly be shooting pictures in the school, in classrooms, in hallways, before school, after school, at sports events, at club meetings and at other special events. Photographers should carry cameras to class with them so the students in the school become accustomed to having their pictures taken and will react with natural expressions instead of reacting to the presence of the camera.

Experienced photographers will help younger, less experienced photographers by mentoring them through the process of shooting, especially in large gatherings where they may be intimidated by the size of the crowd or during sports events when they need guidance to cover all the parameters, from the crowds in the stands to the action on the court or field. Shooting as partners will enable the photographers to feel more comfortable and less conspicuous and will result in the photographers moving around, getting close to the subject matter.

Fig. 20.1. A good black-and-white photograph has a wide range of tones from black to white. Highlight areas, such as the sky in this picture, which often wash out in high-speed black-and-white films, should show detail and should not disappear into the page. Midtones should show range from lighter gray to darker gray. Shadows should be black. The photographer covering this cross-country event exposed her film correctly and rendered a print that will reproduce well in a student publication. Alexandra Fuller, Park City High School, Park City, Utah.

Photographs aren't the only form of visuals available to designers. Cartoons, illustrations and infographics can also provide visual interest to stories and enliven page layouts. Staffs should look beyond their own members in seeking illustrators and cartoonists to add variety to layouts.

The use of effective graphics in design also adds to attractive layouts. The use of rule lines, screens, colors and text details gives the layout designer many tools for effective design.

PHOTOGRAPHS

Photographs should be used in design both for their content – what they add to the verbal information – and for their technical strengths. Technically, a picture's strengths must be solid. Good publications staffs create acceptable parameters for technical strength and adhere to the standards throughout the publication. Selecting content, on the other hand, is more subjective. A student trained as a good picture editor can prove valuable in working with photographers and editors to select the pictures for publication that do the best job of providing meaningful content.

Technical Parameters

A good photograph has several qualities. First, it's always in focus so the important content can be seen and understood by the viewer. Second, the picture should have a range of good exposure. Areas of the picture known as the shadows are rendered in shades of black in the print. Midtones show as shades of gray. Highlights are the lightest areas of the print, but not necessarily white. Generally, the highlight areas should retain some detail (Fig. 20.1). When using more than one picture on a page, it's important that the tones in the pictures are consistent. A washed out print will lose all appeal next to a picture with good tonal control.

When taking the picture, good photographers are careful to correctly expose the film or digital image using the camera's light-metering system. In a traditional darkroom, good photographers use printing filters that help them reproduce all tones of good exposure. In the darkroom, photographers learn to use advanced printing skills that enable them to "burn in," or darken, areas that would reproduce without tone in the publication or will "dodge" areas that would reproduce too dark and with all solid tonality.

Now in the electronic darkroom, the tools of the traditional darkroom are available to photographers through programs such as Adobe's Photoshop or Photoshop Elements.

Good photographers must take the publication's printing method into consideration when preparing the print for publication. Many newspaper and yearbook printers have a difficult time reproducing black-and-white photographs in which the contrast – the range of tones – is too extreme. Prints with a little less contrast will often reproduce more effectively. Photographers must then adjust the contrast in their finished prints to ensure the tones will be reproducible.

Another important quality of a good photograph is one free from technical flaws, such as fingerprints and scratches that may have occurred during the film development or printing stages. When these scratches show up on the final print, good photographers will take time to use spot-toning fluid and fine brushes to correct these flaws. In the electronic darkroom, photographers use similar tools to perfect the image. Digital camera equipment should be kept clean and protected to ensure that similar problems do not occur electronically. Digital chips in SLR cameras attract dust through static charge and may need to be cleaned professionally from time to time. "Point and shoot" digitals are immune to this problem. Good filing systems for negatives and clean darkroom practices help eliminate these preventable flaws from occurring in film cameras.

Good electronic filing systems are particularly important to the digital photographer. A protocol needs to be established to ensure that a consistency is maintained in electronic storage of images. Consistency is also important in ensuring that every photographer is saving images with set guidelines determined by the publication's need. Adobe's Photoshop can be set to "batch" images with a sequence of actions that can be applied to each image in a file for uniformity.

Fig. 20.2. The emotion of this picture makes it one that is immediately attractive to readers. The photographer used a fast shutter speed to stop the action of this teacher during a homecoming pep rally. The clean background and repeating pom-poms add to the photo's appeal. In addition, the subject is large in the photograph, which further adds to the appeal. *Aurora*, Lee's Summit North High School, Lee's Summit, Mo.

CONTENT AND COMPOSITION

Good photographs have strong content. While evaluation of content is subjective, certain qualities are universally agreed upon.

A good picture uses good compositional techniques. Photographers can take advantage of many techniques when placing the content in their images. Using some of the traditional rules of composition will improve the content.

- *Center of interest.* The reason why the photograph was taken should be obvious to the viewer. The content should be immediately visible and strategically placed in the frame (Fig. 20.2). Beginning photographers who stand too far away from their subjects may create images in which the viewer is left to search for the photograph's meaning. Photographers who fill the frame with meaningful content will produce images of higher visual interest. With standard lenses, photographers

may need to be as close as 5 to 7 feet away from their subjects in order to fill the frame with meaningful content. Those who have longer lenses, called "telephotos" or "zooms," can bring content into their frames from a distance farther away from the subject.

- *Rule of thirds*. Photographing a subject by placing it directly in the middle of the frame usually results in a less interesting and static picture. Long a rule in art and architecture, the "golden mean points" dictate that meaningful content be placed in areas of the frame other than in the center. When looking through the viewfinder of the camera, the window that enables the photographer to see the content, the photographer can visually divide the space into thirds both vertically and horizontally. The intersections of these thirds result in the golden mean points. These points are more powerful areas for placing primary visual information in the frame. When using the rule of thirds, photographers should make sure that what is next to the subject is adding to the visual context of the photograph (Fig. 20.3).

- *Leading lines*. Lines in photographs can lead the viewer directly to the primary subject matter. These lines can be obvious, such as a road or path someone is walking on, or can be subtle, such as geometric lines repeated in a stairwell or in an architectural detail (Fig. 20.4).

Fig. 20.3. Photographers can add to a photograph's dynamic appeal by placing the subject matter at the intersection of the rule of thirds — two vertical and horizontal intersections that occur when looking through the viewfinder and dividing it into thirds. Here, the photographer had his camera held vertically and he used the bottom right intersection to place his subject matter. Note the strong balance of the Frisbee in the top left corner providing a natural frame for the subject. *Devils' Advocate*, Hinsdale Central High School, Hinsdale, Ill.

- *Framing*. Framing in a picture takes advantage of foreground or background detail to provide a partial border or frame around the subject matter (Fig. 20.5). Portrait photographers often use parts of flowers or tree branches to subtly frame the faces of their subjects to provide textural interest. Photographers shooting scenic images often place nearby trees in the foreground in the image to show distance and scale.

- *Grounds*. Though photographs compress three dimensions into two, they can still show depth and indicate spatial differences. Placing meaningful content in the

Fig. 20.4. Especially in sports, arms and legs can serve as visual leading lines that take the viewer into the action of the moment. Note how your eyes are led by the strong direction of the vertical arms and fingers in this volleyball shot. The horizontal lines of the flag in the background provide strong framework, but the shallow depth of field keeps them from becoming distracting to the action. Rob Mattson, Lamar High School, Arlington, Texas.

Fig. 20.5. In this picture story on a junior ROTC unit at the school, the photographer used the strong shape and uniform detail of the color guard members to frame the sergeant's face as he inspects the unit. The photographer used his depth of field sharply on the sergeant and allowed the color guard members to be slightly soft in focus to direct the reader more strongly to the sergeant, the subject of this picture. *Hurricane*, Hillcrest High School, Dallas, Texas.

Fig. 20.6. In this package of pictures from the school's recent homecoming, editors have selected a variety of pictures that show different aspects of the celebration. Edited down to six pictures with a paragraph of information and captions, the pictures capture the spirit of homecoming in a more interesting way than an outdated verbal story. Note the tight cropping on each picture and the strong use of story-telling images. *The ReMarker*, St. Mark's School of Texas, Dallas, Texas.

foreground, the middle ground and the background of the image will take advantage of this principle (Fig. 20.6). If the information in any of the areas is not contributing to the contextual information, the photographer can often use a technique known as shallow "depth of field" to improve it.

Depth of field refers to the range of focus from the foreground to the background in the image. Photographers control the depth of field through three factors when taking the picture: the lens used, the size of the aperture or lens opening and the distance they are from their subjects. A good photographer seeking to eliminate a distracting background could change camera position to effectively clean up the information behind the subject, preventing it from being distracting. But if changing position isn't possible to completely eliminate the distracting elements, the photographer could use shallow depth of field to make the background information less focused and less distracting. Viewers will concentrate visually on areas of sharp focus rather than areas that are out of focus in the image. When using shallow depth of field, the information in the frame isn't blurry, indicating camera movement when the picture was taken. Rather, it's soft in focus.

- *Lighting.* Interesting lighting can make a picture more appealing (Fig. 20.7). Silhouettes – images that show shape against a light background – are one example of interesting lighting. Dramatically lighted skies or interesting sunsets after storms can also create lighting that adds to a picture's appeal. Pictures shot with light coming into the camera from side angles will result in interesting "side light" that emphasizes texture and form. Outline light, strong light from behind the subject, can provide a "halo effect" in the picture, particularly effective when shooting people since the sun will be away from their faces. Pictures of people shot in bright sunlight with the sun behind the photographer will result in "flat light," or light that flattens the shadows and eliminates any detail. The photographer will also have problems with squinting subjects whose eyes may be almost shut. Shooting outdoors on overcast days will also result in flat light where no shadows or texture detail will be present.

- *Impact.* As mentioned earlier, impact is the photograph's stopping power. A viewer may be attracted to an image because of its dramatic content. Pictures of conflict often fall into this category. Dramatic images of peak action in sports have strong impact because they show viewers action that is often impossible to see on the field when the event is being viewed. Or pictures shot at peak moments may show players' bodies at diagonals to the ground, indicating the intensity of the moment. This diagonal motion is also visually interesting because it's dramatic.

Fig. 20.7. Interesting light can make an otherwise ordinary situation more interesting to look at. Schools are often built with rows of windows providing strong backlight in both classroom and hallway areas. Taking advantage of the strong backlight in this hallway, the photographer let the lighting add to the graphic appeal of the photograph through the shadows cast by the windows and by the light appearing on the students' faces. Aiming cameras at windows or into light requires special attention to exposure. Eric Diamond, Essex Junction High School, Essex Junction, Vt.

Fig. 20.8. School events often provide great opportunities for school photographers looking for good emotion and reaction shots. At a dance honoring seniors, students dancing and having fun are immediately obvious from these two images. The photographer showed the good times from this event. Shooting in gyms, cafeterias and auditoriums at night requires the use of a flash. Controlling the flash intensity is vital in making pictures that aren't washed out or overlit by the flash. *The Cardinal Voice*, Laguna Creek High School, Elk Grove, Calif.

Fig. 20.9. Anchoring the front page, this stand-alone picture dominants the design and brings the reader into the page in a strongly visual way. The photographer used a longer lens to bring the subject into the frame from a distance away. The pictured subject shows interesting emotion as she participates in a parade with other members of her school's drill team. The design of the headline above the picture helps the reader see it as a separate visual element in the design. *Panther Prints*, Duncanville High School, Duncanville, Texas.

Impact can result when strong emotion or reaction is present in a picture. High school is a ripe ground for emotion. Competitions are held for clubs and organizations. When someone is named a winner or a loser of such a competition, emotion is bound to occur. Sporting events are full of emotion, with players, fans, cheerleaders and parents all interested in the outcome. Even classrooms in the school can be arenas for emotion or reaction when a student is asked to perform a dissection in biology, present a speech or act out a literary classic with classmates (Fig. 20.8).

Impact can also result from humorous incidents. A group of cheerleaders practicing a pyramid who tumble into disarray with arms flailing and intense laughter will cause the viewer to feel the fun of the moment. A student holding a baby for the first time in a child development class will elicit viewer response if the interaction between the student and the baby is interesting. Meaningful relationships will create interesting content with impact. Schools are full of potential relationships including those of older and younger students, peers, friends, boyfriend/girlfriends, teachers and students, and athletes and coaches, to name just a few.

TELLING STORIES THROUGH PHOTOGRAPHS

Often, a well-chosen, single image will be effective in presenting information to a viewer. The single image can be used by itself as a "stand-alone" photograph, or it can accompany a story. A stand-alone image requires a complete caption to give the reader the necessary information and detail and to provide identification for the people pictured. Many newspapers use stand-alone images in a particular design style, with a small headline, or catchline, above the image and a complete caption underneath. These stand-alone photos are often set off in the design by rule lines or boxes to indicate their singular story-telling function. Stand-alone pictures can be news pictures, pictures of events or activities, or feature-oriented pictures used because of their interesting content (Fig. 20.9).

Single pictures used to accompany text should be carefully chosen. The content should amplify that of the verbal text. Designers should vary their size and placement in the design so they don't become predictable and static. The images should be cropped to strengthen content and eliminate distracting elements. The picture's size and shape should be determined by its strengths and should not be dropped into predetermined holes in the layout or compromised in content because of a predetermined picture shape on the layout.

PICTURE PACKAGES OR GROUPS

When more than a single image is needed to tell a story, a picture package or group can be used. Usually two or three images, a picture package is edited to make sure each image in the package adds to the reader's understanding of an event. Therefore, photos should contribute different information. For instance, one picture might be an overall or wide shot giving the reader a feel for the event. Another shot might be a close-up where the photographer has used a longer lens to isolate a few individuals participating in the event. An additional shot might show the outcome or result of the event or activity (Fig. 20.10).

Another type of picture group is a picture sequence. Sequences are used to show a series. A speaker with an interesting visual speaking pattern could be shown in two or three shots with different expressions and gestures. A sports sequence is appropriate to show a pivotal play or series in a game. Or a sequence could show how to do something such as how to paint a mascot on a face before a big game. How-to sequences sometimes use numbers in the captions (Fig. 20.11).

PICTURE STORIES

Picture stories are just like verbal stories except told with images rather than just with words. A picture story should have a beginning, middle and end. Subjects for picture stories are abundant in schools. Subjects should be broad enough to offer a range of picture possibilities, but narrow enough to be able to tell the story in about five to seven well-chosen pictures. Picture stories can be used on single pages or on double trucks (Fig. 20.12).

Fig. 20.10. In a multipicture package, photographers are given space to showcase work from a special week-long event in the school. Designed and placed on a gray background, the multi-picture package features a variety of moments from the event, all featuring people involved in the activities. The use of white frames and shadows around the images make them look like a scrapbook of images from the event. Each picture features a well-written caption placed next to or underneath the image, each featuring a catchline. The photos are packaged with a visually interesting headline leading the reader into the feature. *Battery*, Abilene High School, Abilene, Texas.

Fig. 20.11. A sequence of pictures is appropriate for the topic of helping a reader understand how to help a person who might be having a seizure. Note that the sequence includes both the right and wrong way to help the person, information that could be potentially life-saving to a victim. *The Harbinger,* Shawnee Mission East High School, Prairie Village, Kan.

A photographer working on a picture story needs an adequate amount of time to be able to develop the story. The time commitment involves observation and could also involve a bit of research before the photo shoot even begins. A photographer might work in conjunction with a reporter so that a verbal story can appear with the picture story to complete the presentation. Good, detailed captions should also be a part of the presentation. In a picture story, a dominant picture, at least two to three times larger than any other, should establish the event for the reader. The dominant image should be the largest in size in the layout, but it should also be the most compelling image. It doesn't necessarily have to be the beginning picture in the story.

The other pictures accompanying the dominant image should be carefully edited to make sure that each is contributing new information to the reader's understanding of the event. Careful attention should also be paid to making sure each picture is a different size and shape in the layout, with emphasis on strong verticals and horizontals. Pictures in stories should be edited so the people in the images are different sizes. The number of people pictured in each photograph should also vary (Fig. 20.13).

Picture stories should not be "how-to" edits in which the reader is shown how to do something sequentially. That is a picture sequence, not a picture story.

TRADITIONAL AND DIGITAL SHOOTING

When photographers are learning to use equipment, they may find it easier to work with simple 35 mm cameras, long a staple of the publications' world. Simple 35 mm cameras have working light meters that require the photographer to take light meter readings and change both f-stop settings and shutter speeds. Learning how to use these settings will help the photographers learn to control depth of field to eliminate a distracting background or to use a fast shutter speed to capture moving action.

More advanced photographers will feel comfortable with more advanced cameras, those with sophisticated, multimode exposure systems and automatic focusing systems. These cameras often use dedicated flashes, those that determine and set correct exposure with flash systems made for the camera. Beginning photographers using sophisticated automatic cameras may be intimidated by the equipment until they learn to work all the bells and whistles on the camera.

Fig. 20.12. A picture story is a story told in pictures, but with accompanying text. A good picture story avoids visual redundancy through careful editing that ensures each picture contributes new information to the story being told. In this picture story on the school's band taking third place in a state competition, a well-edited and effectively cropped set of images tells the story of this competition. A smaller time sequence covers the top of the page and provides another dimension of information for the reader. Strong use of shallow depth of field in the dominant image, taken with a long lens, makes the picture a great choice to lead the page. Strong emotion is shown in two of the images, contributing to the quality of the story. A strong headline in a special typeface and in a color echoing the band's achievement, accompanies the story, supplemented with a smaller deck head providing detail. Each caption is appropriately placed adjacent to each image, and each begins with a catchline. *Panther Prints*, Duncanville High School, Duncanville, Texas.

Simple and advanced 35 mm cameras enable the staff to purchase a range of lenses for shooting. In addition to traditional 50 mm lenses, which reproduce subject matter in normal view, a staff needs additional lenses so the content of photographs can vary, avoiding visual redundancy in lens use and selection.

A wide-angle lens, starting somewhere in the range of 35 mm and encompassing lenses as wide as 24 mm,

Fig. 20.13. Rather than writing about an event that occurred some time prior to the newspaper's publication date, this staff decided to tell the story through a photo essay, a collection of images from the event. The dominant image is compelling and interesting, drawing the reader into the image. A small detail shot, a close-up of a performer's hands, is placed in the headline area, which breaks the layout. Good cropping adds to the impact of this story. Note each picture tells the story of the event through the people involved, and each image contributes a different piece of information about the event's activities. A variety of shapes and sizes appear in the images. *The Harbinger*, Shawnee Mission East High School, Prairie Village, Kan.

will enable the photographer to shoot "wide shots," those that show a greater range of subject matter horizontally in the frame.

Extremely wide lenses, sometimes called "fisheye lenses," will be novelty lenses that are too limited for normal shooting. More extreme fisheye lenses produce pictures that show a 360-degree range and produce images that are completely round.

Beyond the 50 mm standard lens, photographers can benefit from a range of short telephoto and zoom lenses. Short telephotos, beginning at about 70 mm, will enable photographers to shoot portraits, for instance, without being right in the subject's face. In a classroom, a short telephoto will enable a photographer to bring action into the camera lens when he or she can't move in close to the subjects. Short telephoto lenses work well in some court shooting, such as volleyball or basketball, from certain angles on the field.

Zoom lenses incorporate a range of focal lengths in one lens. Popular with many publication staffs, zooms have some limitations. They aren't as "fast" as fixed focal length lenses, because they incorporate a range of focal lengths in one lens. A fast lens is one with a large maximum f-stop or lens aperture such as f/2 or f/2.8. Fast lenses are often important in high school shooting because the light situations in the school are often dim. Lenses with larger maximum f-stops will enable the photographer to shoot without resorting to flash or artificial light. Zoom lenses are usually heavier to hold because of the range of focal lengths incorporated into their design. This heaviness can result in camera "blur" or movement that will be visible in the picture. A staff considering a zoom lens should shop carefully for one with a minimum of limitations.

Medium telephotos provide a focal length of between 100 and 200 mm. These lenses are useful in classrooms and in many sports shooting situations, especially for court sports such as tennis, volleyball and basketball.

Long telephotos range from 300 mm lenses and longer in focal length. Few schools can afford to buy really long, "fast" telephoto lenses because they will often cost thousands of dollars. Instead, many schools opt to purchase slower lenses, those with maximum f-stops in the range of f/3.5 or f/4. These slower lenses may be adequate for the school's shooting needs, but setting cameras at high ISO settings will create greater grain in film and greater pixellation in digital formats. Other quality factors will also be lessened at high ISOs. Poorly lit football stadiums will render these lenses mostly inadequate even with fast films if the maximum shutter speed isn't fast enough to freeze the action on the field. A sports photographer will usually need to shoot at shutter speeds as fast as 1/500 of a second to stop sports action. With sophisticated cameras offering even faster shutter speeds, faster lenses become even more of an important factor in stopping action.

A better option might be for the school to occasionally rent or borrow a long telephoto lens. Many large camera stores rent equipment. Renting such a lens a couple of times during a season might be adequate. However, using a long telephoto lens for the first time will prove difficult for most photographers without any previous experience. The lenses are heavy, difficult to use and difficult to stabilize. Long telephoto lenses must also be used with a monopod, a single-legged support system that screws into a thread in the lens and provides support for it during use.

Many schools begin mentoring programs with local professional newspaper photographers and others in their communities. These professionals often shoot the school's athletic events. The mentor might be willing to occasionally let the school's photographers use the lens and might provide instruction on its use during a few minutes of a game. Many local newspaper photographers started out as high school shooters and remember the limitations of sports shooting without the right equipment.

Some photographers will buy lens doublers that will double the range of the lens. For instance, a 75 mm lens will now shoot 150 mm. Lens doublers may be a good choice, but they will reduce the maximum f-stop of the lens, and they may lead to images that aren't sharp if they aren't good optical investments.

Other options for obtaining lenses are pawnshops, garage sales or internet buying sites such as eBay.

Another necessary accessory is a flash to shoot in low-light situations. Photographers shooting with fast film in low-light situations can avoid shooting with direct flash, flash aimed directly at their subjects from camera position. Photographs shot with direct flash will have harsh, dark shadows and will often reproduce with washed out or faded highlight or bright image areas. Even with good printing in the darkroom, photographers will have a hard time eliminating these artificial effects that will be distracting when reproduced in the yearbook or newspaper.

Newer camera models often sell companion flashes called "dedicated flash systems." These sophisticated flash systems provide automatic exposure for pictures when using flash.

Flash use will be more natural when it is "bounced" off a low white ceiling or wall. Photographers using flashes with pivoting heads can aim the head at an angle so the light will hit the wall or ceiling and bounce light back to the subject. This technique requires the flash be used at a stronger intensity setting. The photographer must set the distance for the flash, adding the flash to ceiling and ceiling to subject distance to get a correct exposure. The technique also requires a ceiling no more than about 10 feet away. The bounce flash technique provides a shower of light on the subject that is very pleasing, rather than harsh. The photographer can combine bounce flash with a small white card placed on the flash head. This card will kick light back into the subject's face and eyes.

Flash can also be used off-camera in what is called "indirect flash." The photographer can throw the shadows behind the subject or out of camera range by aiming the flash out of the picture range but still illuminating the subject.

Flash may also be used outdoors in what is called the "synchro-sun" technique. This technique will help even the shadows provided by natural light or can provide stronger, more interesting light outdoors on overcast days.

Many schools have already begun buying digital cameras, which record images electronically inside the camera. These images are then downloaded directly into the computer to be placed in layouts. The advantage of digital cameras is the instantaneous image capture allowed by the cameras. They are very useful for deadline shooting, when the time required to process and print the traditional way in a darkroom would be prohibitive.

Even though many digital camera models are now competitively priced, good digital cameras offering a range of options and sophisticated shooting settings are still beyond the affordability of many schools. Many schools settle for simple digital cameras with lower resolutions and limited options. These will work effectively for the occasional deadline picture but will need to be supplemented by cameras shooting traditional film, especially for difficult shooting situations such as sports.

Simple, inexpensive Polaroid cameras are preferred by some staffs waiting for digital cameras to become more affordable. Polaroids enable the staff to quickly produce images, such as mug shots or simple event shots, for deadline needs. However, the film is expensive and will result in wasted money in the hands of an inexperienced shooter. Polaroids also have little use other than shooting head or mug shots.

Point and shoot cameras, with simple operation, will enable almost anyone on the staff to produce usable images. But the limitations in lens use will prevent these cameras from working in all shooting situations. They are excellent choices for loaning to clubs and organizations whose members may be attending a field trip or competition in a distant location that staff photographers would not be able to attend. Loaning them to chaperones or club sponsors accompanying the groups will also be a good way to get pictures that otherwise might not be available to the staff. Encouraging this cooperative camera arrangement is a good way for staffs to expand their coverage.

Similarly, a supply of single-use cameras provided to underrepresented school populations, club members attending distant events or staffers who need to shoot pictures for stories for deadline will be helpful in fulfilling the photographic needs of the newspaper or yearbook. Many schools without the benefit of separate photography staffs will find a need to supply writers with training and cameras in order to provide their own photographs.

Staffs should make sure to keep a log of where the film or cameras have been placed and to follow up with the contributors to make sure the pictures are returned to the staff. Some yearbook staffs offer training sessions for contributing photographers to teach them basic compositional skills before passing out the film or cameras. Giving printed photo credits for the contributors in the yearbook or newspaper will be an appropriate way of providing recognition for these outside staff contributors.

Occasionally, pictures can be obtained from local media outlets including community newspapers. Yearbook staffs often get a certain amount of professionally shot film as part of their yearbook portrait contract. In all cases, it is better if students take their own pictures for their own publications, but seeking the help of outsiders is sometimes necessary to ensure good coverage.

CAPTIONS AND CUTLINES

Every picture, with few exceptions, will need a caption. Captions are complete sentences that provide information and details about pictures for the reader. Complete names should always be provided. People in pictures should be named from left to right, but it isn't necessary to include "left to right" since that's a normal reading pattern. When pictures are being named in some other arrangement, such as clockwise, it might be necessary to state the naming pattern. Staffs should make sure the names in captions are spelled correctly by double-checking the names against an official list of students provided by the school's registrar or through a staff resource file. Many schools with computerized records may be willing to give the publication staff a computerized list of student names. Each year, the staff can delete the graduating seniors and add freshman and new students to the list without starting completely over. Staffs may also want to further identify students by using their year of graduation or traditional grade in school (freshman, sophomore, etc.) after their names.

Captions can start with small-sized overlines, brief summaries that provide visual entry into the caption information. These overlines, or "catchlines" as they are sometimes called, should be printed in a contrasting typeface, possibly a bold or a bold italic, in a point size one or two sizes larger than the caption type. In yearbooks, sections will often be designed to coordinate the graphics in the page headlines to the design of the overlines. Overlines are commonly used in newspapers with stand-alone photos. Often, the overline appears above the picture (Fig. 20.14).

Captions can begin with different parts of speech to avoid a redundancy in their grammatical construction. For instance, on a yearbook spread with seven pictures, if all captions begin with names or with prepositional phrases, readers will become bored with the construction. Details and specific nouns should be used to add to the reader's understanding of the story. Captions can be more than one sentence in length. Often, a second sentence is used in yearbook captions to add outcomes or results to the first sentence's description of the pictured information (Fig. 20.15).

Because captions describe what is going on when the picture was taken, the information should be in present tense, especially in the first sentence. Follow-up information may be written in past tense to indicate the passage of time.

SHARING SENTIMENTS
Junior Julie Arnold discusses her IB experience with her freshman buddy in the new IB buddy program.
photo by Lindsay Barclay

Good captions require good reporting. If photographers don't provide basic caption information for the designers, reporters should talk to the people in the pictures to find out what was going on and possibly to obtain quotes. Making up information about what was going on will usually result in inaccurate information, threatening the credibility of the staff. On the other hand, caption information should not be obvious nor should it merely repeat what the viewer can tell from looking at the picture.

In naming people pictured in group shots, the rows should be designated as "front," "second," "third" and so on until the back row. Using "first," "second," "third" without "front" and "back" is confusing. In group shots, complete names should be used in the captions. Again, it isn't necessary to tell the naming pattern unless it isn't left to right.

To add dimension to captions, quotes are often included. Reporters can ask questions of the people pictured to get their reactions to the pictured information. Quotes will often add rich texture and personal understanding to the captions.

Captions should be placed adjacent to the pictures they describe, either under the pictures or next to them. If the picture bleeds across the gutter, the caption should not bleed unless the picture is on a double truck or centerspread. In that case, the caption should be placed under the picture on the widest side, beginning on the margin of that page. In placing long captions under wide, horizontal pictures, the designer may want to break the captions into columns to keep the line lengths from being wider than comfortable reading patterns allow.

Fig. 20.14. Overlines, or catchlines, in reverse type on gray bars help provide visual entry points into the content areas. They also take advantage of the fact that most students will enter the content through the picture areas. Complete captions on each picture further draw the reader's eyes through bold identifiers prefacing the caption information. Note that the photographer's picture credits are placed at the end of the captions in a contrasting, condensed typeface. *The Edition*, Anderson High School, Austin, Texas.

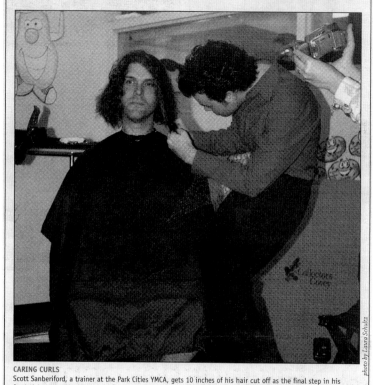

Trainer loses locks to facilitate wishes

CARING CURLS
Scott Sanberiford, a trainer at the Park Cities YMCA, gets 10 inches of his hair cut off as the final step in his fundraising campaign for the Catch-a-Dream Foundation, which gives terminally ill children a chance to enjoy the great outdoors. Sanberiford cut off one inch for every $1,000 he raised.

photo by Laura Schultz

Fig. 20.15. A complete caption identifies the subject of the photo and provides the reader with specific details about what was happening at the time the photograph was taken. As a stand-alone picture, one used without an accompanying story, the picture has been bordered with a rule line and uses a headline style that provides an entry point for the reader. *Bagpipe*, Highland Park High School, Dallas, Texas.

Some publications include the photo credit (for the person who took the picture) at the end of the caption. Others place this information at the bottom right edge or on the right side of the photograph. No matter where it appears, a picture credit is needed for each photograph. The picture credit can appear in a type size a point size or two smaller than the caption information, and it can be in a contrasting typeface, such as a condensed type.

CROPPING PHOTOGRAPHS

Cropping is both a visual and a physical process. Visually, cropping seeks to improve the content of the photograph by eliminating distracting elements or those not needed to tell the picture's story. Good cropping makes the image have more impact in the design and can correct certain photographic flaws such as scratches or the subject being too small in the picture because the photographer was too far away (Fig. 20.16).

In sports shooting, cropping can make pictures more dramatic by removing parts of the photograph not essential to the action. For instance, in upper-body sports such as volleyball and basketball, cropping out the legs of an athlete using primarily her arms can make the interaction of the arms and the ball more dramatic. In cropping sports shots, designers must also be aware that cropping out the ball or eliminating the opponents removes the visual context of the pictured action and weakens its meaning. In sports action shots, the ball should definitely be part of the image.

If pictures are submitted digitally, the images can be scanned or downloaded directly into the computer and produced or submitted electronically. These photographs will already be placed in picture positions on the pages. Designers will be able to see the effects of their cropping and picture use. Pictures imported into layout and design programs should not be stretched vertically or horizontally from their original proportions. Designers should carefully check the measurements palette when the pictures are imported to make sure the x and y scaling coordinates remain consistent.

Pictures produced and submitted to the printer as prints will often require cropping by the printer before the pictures are stripped into the layout windows. Pictures printed through traditional printing will be halftoned, reshot through a halftone camera through a fine screen, in order to allow the continuous tones of the image to be rendered through dots and reproduced in ink. Before submitting the image to the printer, the designer will need to indicate cropping on the print to allow the proportions of the image to be correctly reproduced in the desired size.

In yearbook publishing, printers often provide the staffs with cropping devices, often a pair of large L-shapes connected by a diagonal bar. The designer sets the cropper to the desired shape, positioning the square along the outer edges of the desired space on the layout and tightening the diagonal bar to hold the proportions of the space. Then the cropper is applied to the picture. As long as the bar stays in place, the two Ls can be moved to allow the proportions to stay consistent. Cropping devices have small indentations in the corners to allow the staff to place cropping marks with grease pencils without placing them directly on image areas.

PHOTO EDITING

Visual redundancy results when the same information is repeated in photographs, just as verbal redundancy results when information is repeated in print. A good picture editor working carefully with the other photographers and designers can make a big difference on a publication.

Unfortunately, many staffs give someone the title of photo editor without training that person to do the job or explaining what a photo editor does on a publication.

Photo editors should be present at all staff and planning meetings and contribute to the discussion of story development and advance planning. They should help writers develop photo assignments that will both contribute to the story development and be possible for the photographers to shoot. They should tailor assignments to the photographers, taking into consideration their individual strengths. They should discuss the assignments with the photographers and suggest possible picture angles and images and should make sure the photographers have the right equipment and supplies to adequately shoot the assignments. Photo

Fig. 20.16. Tight cropping adds to the impact of this reaction shot of a student involved in a pudding-eating contest at school. The crop also results in a strong vertical shape. Consulting with photographers on the best crops for photographs is crucial in good publications' photography. Michael LoBue, Golden West High School, Visalia, Calif.

editors should make sure photographers are provided with detailed information about the events or activities they will shoot, including the time and place they will occur and the possible use of the pictures in the publication.

Photo editors should make sure darkroom and camera supplies are frequently inventoried and should be responsible for making lists of needed supplies well in advance of the supplies running out.

After photographers shoot and process film, photo editors should individually sit down with the photographers over a light table using a loupe magnifier, a small viewing device that enlarges the negative and shows the detail. Photo editors can offer photographers advice on cropping, on improving their shooting and on technical problems such as proper exposure. As mentors, photo editors can help younger photographers improve their photographic vision and improve their abilities to contribute to the story-telling function of the publication. Occasionally, inviting in local professional photographers, perhaps those who have graduated from the school in previous years, will also help mentor and develop the vision of young photographers. These photographers can help students by explaining how to do something, such as how to correctly use a flash, or they can look at the pictures the photographers have shot and offer advice on improving the composition and content.

Using a grease pencil, a soft-leaded pencil that writes on photographic paper, the photo editor, photographer and page designer can decide which images should be enlarged from the overall shoot for use in layouts by individual staff members. The grease pencil can also indicate the proper cropping for the image as it's enlarged by the photographer.

After enlarging the images, photographers should make sure to provide complete caption information for each image. Photographers are journalists, too. During assignments, they should carry reporter's notebooks, small notebooks that slip into camera bags or pockets, in which they can record the names of the people they photograph as well as other details. When covering a game, the photographer should get a copy of rosters or programs so names can be easily matched to numbers on uniforms. Also during sporting events, photographers can occasionally shoot a frame of the scoreboard so the progression of important plays during the event can be referenced.

Last, photographers should do any retouching to correct any visual flaws in the final print. Spot toning fluids in a variety of warm and cool shades can be used with a range of fine brushes to touch up flaws in prints. A print-finishing area where an enlarging lamp is provided will help the photographers when spot toning.

Prints should be stored in files or envelopes labeled with appropriate subject matter such as "varsity football," "homecoming" or "fall play" and stored for later use by staff members when drawing layouts.

This constant processing and editing of film during the year will ensure that photographers become more competent and will help organize the photographic process so photographers don't have unrealistic amounts of work to do just at deadline time. It also ensures that good quality prints can be produced when photographers have ample time to improve print quality.

Digital picture files can be downloaded and viewed in a variety of software editing programs such as Adobe Photoshop or PhotoMechanic. As photos are viewed, they are tagged to indicate files that will be kept. Untagged files can then be eliminated in the editing process.

For the yearbook staff, this collection of edited prints shot during the year and stored in clear files should be used when designing layouts. Taking out the possible pictures and choosing the best ones will provide the strongest edit for the yearbook spreads. The editing should be a collaborative process by both designers and photographers or the photo editor. When choosing pictures for spreads, designers should make sure each picture is chosen because it contributes different information to the spread, shows different action and people and offers different sizes and shapes of images to use in the layout.

For staffs using digital cameras or scanning negatives or prints, photo editors should make sure photographers are trained to complete the digital work. A consistent, clear and easily understood method of filing the images for the layouts should be used. Consistent scanning will make a big difference in overall picture quality. Photographers should use picture-editing software to complete basic picture alterations such as burning, dodging and cropping. Backing up computer files is always a good idea, especially during deadline time. Also, original images should be carefully stored for retrieval in case images are lost or missing in the computer files or layouts. An organized system of storage and retrieval will prove invaluable in meeting deadlines and in maintaining historical files for future use. It will also ensure that negatives are properly taken care of and easy to find.

ABUSE OF IMAGES

Because photographs are so important in the design process, designers should be careful not to abuse them in their layouts. Following are some of the abusive design decisions that can weaken the impact of photographs.

- *Creating cutout shapes.* Removing the background of the photo in image alteration programs is quite quick and easy (Fig. 20.17). However, unless the picture was shot in a photo studio or planned as a cutout, removing the background by cutting it out can result in a loss of contextual information that distorts meaning. Cutout shapes are visually active and need to be grounded in design by being placed next to lines or borders or by creating a soft shadow of the image to appear with it.

- *Creating cookie-cutter shapes.* Applying shapes such as circles, triangles or ovals on pictures compromises their content in the same way as cutting out the images. Contextual information is removed or cropped. Readers have a hard time understanding the meaning of incomplete information. Pictures designed to be placed in shapes should be carefully shot by photographers in studios where the backgrounds can be controlled.

- *Mortising pictures.* Placing pictures so they overlap or touch each other can also compromise content. If the pictures have areas of dead space where they can overlap, it's generally a good indication that they need tighter cropping. Overlapping the images also creates connections between pictures where there may be no real connection.

- *Duotoning images.* Duotoned images are those in which a single color has been applied to a black-and-white image. Duotones are often effective. For instance, duotoning black-and-white images with brown ink will give them the effect of sepia-toned prints, a classic brown-toned bath applied to pictures to give them the look of antiquity. However, using garish or inappropriately bright colors on images of people will make the pictures distracting. Rather than viewing the content, viewers will try to find meaning in the colors.

- *Tilting photos.* Photos turned so they are slightly off a straight horizontal baseline will result in pictures that seem slightly playful and off-kilter. Tilting should be

Fig. 20.17. Cutout photographs with no backgrounds are best when created that way in a studio shot against a white background that can easily be removed electronically on a computer. This photo cutout works well with the story format. *Informer*, Laingsburg High School, Laingsbury, Mich.

Code of Ethics, National Press Photographers Association

The National Press Photographers Association, a professional society dedicated to the advancement of photojournalism, acknowledges concern and respect for the public's natural-law right to freedom in searching for the truth and the right to be informed truthfully and completely about public events and the world in which we live.

We believe that no report can be complete if it is not possible to enhance and clarify the meaning of words. We believe that pictures, whether used to depict news events as they actually happen, illustrate news that has happened or to help explain anything of public interest, are an indispensable means of keeping people accurately informed; that they help all people, young and old, to better understand any subject in the public domain.

Believing the foregoing, we recognize and acknowledge that photojournalists should at all times maintain the highest standards of ethical conduct in serving the public interest. To that end, the National Press Photographers Association sets forth the following Code of Ethics, which is subscribed to by all of its members:

1. The practice of photojournalism, both as a science and art, is worthy of the very best thought and effort of those who enter into it as a profession.

2. Photojournalism affords an opportunity to serve the public that is equaled by few other vocations, and all members of the profession should strive by example and influence to maintain high standards of ethical conduct free of mercenary considerations of any kind.

3. It is the individual responsibility of every photojournalist at all times to strive for pictures that report truthfully, honestly and objectively.

4. As journalists, we believe that credibility is our greatest asset. In documentary photojournalism, it is wrong to alter the content of a photograph in any way (electronically or in the darkroom) that deceives the public. We believe the guidelines for fair and accurate reporting should be the criteria for judging what may be done electronically to a photograph.

5. Business promotion in its many forms is essential, but untrue statements of any nature are not worthy of a professional photojournalist and we severely condemn any such practice.

6. It is our duty to encourage and assist all members of our profession, individually and collectively, so that the quality of photojournalism may constantly be raised to higher standards.

7. It is the duty of every photojournalist to work to preserve all freedom-of-the-press rights recognized by law and to work to protect and expand freedom of access to all sources of news and visual information.

8. Our standards of business dealings, ambitions and relations shall have in them a note of sympathy for our common humanity and shall always require us to take into consideration our highest duties as members of society. In every situation in our business life, in every responsibility that comes before us, our chief thought shall be to fulfill that responsibility and discharge that duty so that, when each of us is finished, we shall have endeavored to lift the level of human ideals and achievement higher than we found it.

9. No Code of Ethics can prejudge every situation; thus common sense and good judgment are required in applying ethical principles.

Statement on manipulation of photographs:

As journalists we believe the guiding principle of our profession is accuracy; therefore, we believe it is wrong to alter the content of a photograph in any way that deceives the public.

As photojournalists, we have the responsibility to document society and to preserve its images as a matter of historical record. It is clear that the emerging electronic technologies provide new challenges to the integrity of photographic images. This technology enables the manipulation of the content of an image in such a way that the change is virtually undetectable. In light of this, we, the National Press Photographers Association, reaffirm the basis of our ethics: Accurate representation is the benchmark of our profession.

We believe photojournalistic guidelines for fair and accurate reporting should be the criteria for judging what may be done electronically to a photograph. Altering the editorial content of a photograph, in any degree, is a breach of the ethical standards recognized by the NPPA.

applied only if it's appropriate to the content of the image. A tilt of less than 12 degrees will also maintain stronger readability for the image.

- *Creating photo patterns.* A recent trend in using pictures is positioning them in patterns with similar-sized shapes and with the images touching or separated only by thin hairline rules. A pattern needs visual contrast in tones and in content or it will be viewed as one large, continuous image.

- *Creating collages.* Blurring images together through image manipulation software can be effective if it is done for a specific purpose and its use is limited.

- *Creating postage stamp-sized images.* Especially trendy in yearbook design, the use of multiple images in small sizes needs careful attention. Pictures need to be carefully cropped and edited to make sure they will still be "readable" in such small sizes. Maintaining quality in multiple images may be difficult for some staffs.

Visual Storytelling

Decide on a visual strategy:

- *Photographic.* Use photo(s) large and dominant if photo(s) is good and would attract the reader's attention; ask the question: What photos would help tell the story? Avoid set-up, posed or clichéd shots.
- *Illustrative.* Use if the story lends itself to illustration rather than photographic treatment; keep in mind that illustrations should be really strong visually and dominant in size. Give your text to an artist so the artist can connect visually with the words in the story.
- *Typographic.* If you don't have strong photographic or illustrative material to choose from, consider using a typographic treatment, including large primary heads with detail-oriented deck heads; varied headline positions; typography that matches the mood or tone of the story; emphasis type; large initial caps; and other type-as-illustration techniques.

Decide on a verbal strategy:

- *Factoids/summary boxes.* Use if the story contains policy changes or suggests a strategic approach. Can also be used to summarize the major points made by speakers. Consider small bullets to draw in the reader's eye.
- *Profile box.* Is the story primarily about an individual or a group? If so, consider a profile box with relevant information headers in bold type. Set the profile in a typeface contrasting in weight and stroke to the primary story.
- *Harper's Index/Q&A.* Use if the story is full of facts and figures that could use simplification. Also use for elections.
- *Timelines.* Use for stories that are sequential in organization of information, that trace historical significance or that show change over a period of time.
- *Sidebars.* Use if there is an angle or dimension to the story that is particularly interesting or could use more detail. Sidebars can be written in first person to amplify a particular detail of the main story.
- *Infographics/locator maps.* Use if the story has a complex set of numerical sequencing or data that can be better understood through visual presentation. An infographic should be based on visual icons. Avoid straight pie charts and encyclopedic charts. Look to *USA Today, Time, Newsweek* and other popular publications for interesting ways to clarify information through visual means.
- *Story or paragraph captions with a picture package.* Telling part of the story through a package of two or more pictures that show different aspects of the story can be valuable. Make sure the captions add to the presentation by adding information through a few sentences or a couple of graphs of information.
- Always possible:

Callouts. Callouts are pull quotes in which interesting, relevant or colorful quotes or information is displayed in a point size larger than the body text but smaller than the headline text (preferably about 14 to 18 points), with a distinctive design strategy that the reader recognizes. If the person is particularly colorful, or the story controversial, consider a box of quoted material. This can also be used as a pro/con box to present conflicting viewpoints.

Logos. Develop a visual strategy based upon icons that immediately relate to a story, lend it a graphic strategy and visually tie together a series of stories, particularly over a course of time or in different parts of the newspaper.

Text Heads. Break up the story by inserting subheads at natural junctures in the story to help create reader "eyeflow."

Always keep in mind:

- Combining two or more of these forms may help the reader understand the story more clearly. If so, determine which are appropriate and avoid duplication of information.
- To avoid reader confusion, make sure information presented in alternative story forms looks different from the main story. Consider using a sans serif font if the story is in a serif font. Consider using a different weight of text if fonts are limited. Consider varying the line widths of alternative copy. All of these techniques will help indicate to the reader that the information is separate from the primary story.
- Make sure your visual/verbal forms are helping the reader clarify and process the information being presented. Keep your reader in mind at all times. Don't add visual/verbal forms unless they do clarify information.
- Make sure the visual/verbal storytelling forms are helping to attract the reader to the story. Remember that offering the reader a variety of visual/verbal forms may cause the reader to enter the story in a different way. Make sure the reader is getting valuable information regardless of whether he or she enters the story through the main story.
- Remember your time frame. What can realistically be produced in the amount of time you have before publication? Consider your resources. Do you have someone with the ability to produce complicated or stylistic art? Do you have time to work with a photographer to produce top quality photographs that add to the reader's understanding of the story?
- Keep the writer's angles, situations or focus in mind at all times. Connecting visuals with verbals reinforces the story and makes it more vivid for the reader. Make sure every person working with the story understands where the story is going. If it changes, or if team members discover new or interesting angles along the way, rethink the visual/verbal. Add to or adjust as necessary. Don't repeat information.

- *Flipping or flopping images.* When photographers print pictures in the darkroom, they place the negative in the enlarger so it will reproduce as it was seen in the camera. Designers sometimes create layouts in which the "eyeflow" in the picture might be facing off a page, leading the reader off the page with the eyeflow. In these cases, designers sometimes resort to flipping the image, by having the photographer or printer reverse the image's eyeflow. Doing so is considered ethically dishonest.

  If writing or numbers appear in the picture, they will be backward, immediately alerting the viewer to the picture's changed orientation. Even without numbers or words, people in the pictures will be aware of a change in details, such as a part in their hair or jewelry or watches appearing on the wrong arm or hand. Rather than flipping images, designers should work to arrange pictures so the eyeflow faces naturally toward the gutter. This is another reason for a need in flexibility when drawing dummies or layouts, particularly if it's done before the pictures have been taken and edited.

- *Creating visual clichés.* A good photographer avoids visual clichés, pictures that are common and often overused. In sports, clichés result when photographers shoot predictable images. For instance, in basketball the cliché shot is the one of the player shooting the ball in the basket. Because high school photographers rarely have the restrictions on shooting positions that college and professional sports enforce, they should move around the court and field when shooting. Moving out of the end zone when shooting basketball will enable photographers to try different shots such as defensive moves rather than always shooting the offensive action.

  Taking pictures of teachers standing at the blackboard or administrators talking on the phone results in clichés that are often posed because the person being shot thinks the photographer wants the photograph to appear that way.

- *Creating highly stylized images.* Particularly on yearbook staffs, designers draw layouts before the pictures have been taken. Planning for a highly stylized form of picture use, such as overlapping large image areas, extreme shapes or sizes or other stylized devices, can create compromises in image quality and content. Designers intent on creating such styles should con-

sult carefully with photographers and photo editors to see if these styles will be possible and to make sure the photographers are looking for images that will accommodate the designers' needs, if possible.

Image Alteration

With the growth in image-altering software programs, it is now easier than ever to manipulate images by combining parts of them, by moving objects around in the images or by editing out parts of the images and replacing them with other images. To do so may be unethical and could cause legal problems for the staff.

Photographers must protect the truth and accuracy of their images, just as writers must check the accuracy of their reporting. In news and feature pictures, readers expect the content to be accurately represented. Altering news and feature images should not be allowed in a publication. Allowances are made for alterations that could be made in a traditional darkroom: burning, dodging, adjusting contrast and cropping.

However, in the last few years, artistic uses of altered images have been extensively used for illustrative purposes. As long as the photographer is altering only his or her own images, and not combining them with others without permission, these illustrative uses of photo manipulation could be considered like any other illustration. They should be labeled as photo illustrations or photo enhancements, rather than with traditional photo credits, to help the reader understand that they are illustrative, not accurate portrayals of news or feature events (Fig. 20.18).

Not all readers will understand the differences between the labeling of pictures as traditional photo credits or as photo illustrations and photo enhancements. It is important for students to understand the need to protect the readers' belief that what they see in a picture really happened.

The National Press Photographers Association, the association to which most professional photojournalists belong, adopted a code of ethics when image manipulation software problems were emerging in the professional world. This code of ethics is one that student photojournalists should seek to understand and use (see "Code of Ethics," p. 336).

ART AND ILLUSTRATIONS

In addition to pictures, illustrations can be effective visuals in publications. Illustrations should be used

PHOTO COLLAGE BY RYAN NAGATA

Football players brave scorching heat for the chance to play.

Making the Cut

by Evan Parker

IT's 110 DEGREES OUTSIDE at Pacific University in Stockton, California. Here, the San Francisco Forty-niners are running drills. It's summer training, tryouts, hell month, whatever you want to call it.

The players use every bit of energy to show the coaches that they can play good football, that they can play Forty-niners football. Some players want to play for the Forty-niners so badly that they run themselves into the ground. Some players get so dehydrated that they are on IVs in between plays; some just give up and go home. Some run 'til they puke, and a few 'til they end up in the hospital.

Defensive Linebacker Curtis Easson says, "People only see the stuff on Sunday, the games. What they don't know is how hard we work outside of the games. Sometimes we can work 12 hour days during the week. You have to work extremely hard to get to this point, but it is worth it."

"...The level of competition in sports is so high today that it seems like nothing less than perfect performance is acceptable..."

At the end of the day, the Forty-niners sit in their air-conditioned dorm rooms, but they can't move; they can't even think. They don't want to think because the only thing on their mind is the heat, the running, the sweating, and tomorrow's practice. They want to go home to their pools, their margarita machines, and their toddlers.

Some players go home with serious injuries. Some ailments are due to hot weather and some result from athletes pushing beyond what their bodies can handle to play pro football.

But these injuries aren't just limited to professional sports; this August two high school football players in the Midwest died from the heat at their training camp. For what? "Even though it is really hot, I love playing the game so much that it doesn't bother me. I am willing to take that risk to play this game," said Harvard-Westlake football player Andrew Beckett, who has been practicing in temperatures in the 100's.

In the past few years, we have lost many young athletes to drugs, ailments, injuries, and now the weather. But in order to keep sports exciting, the athletes have to be so much better, faster, and stronger than the average human. The level of athleticism and competition in sports is so high today that it seems like nothing less than perfect performance is acceptable.

To succeed at any level, athletes have to pay a price. That price can be paid by giving up their afternoons for practice or by putting on pads and gear and running around under the blazing sun. Some pay the price with hard work and dedication, and sadly, some end up paying the price with their lives. The irony is, without that kind of dedication and desire, sports wouldn't be half as exciting.

Fig. 20.18. This photo illustration, electronically manipulated to make it look like the football player is on fire, works well with the story about what it takes to be a professional athlete. The photo credit indicates that the picture is a collage rather than an actual image. *Crossfire*, Crossroads School, Santa Monica, Calif.

when designers are seeking to show something different from what a photograph will show or when a photograph is inappropriate or impossible to get. Using a variety of illustrative forms will also provide reader surprise and keep the visual content fresh and interesting. Illustrations in a range of styles – from cartoons to artistic renderings – can effectively coordinate with story content (Fig. 20.19).

Illustrations don't have to be created solely by staff members. Just as professional publications do, staffs can seek outside artists of different talents and styles to add dimension to visual presentations. Allowing the illustrator to read the story or text will result in illustrations that tell stronger visual stories. Combined with strong headline presentations, these illustrations can be refreshing and fun.

Illustrative style possibilities are endless. Creative photographers with access to studio lighting and supplies can create interesting photo illustrations. Collages, three-dimensional art, watercolors, pen and ink drawings, caricatures – all could effectively showcase verbal content. Communicating needs with art teachers and outstanding art students with interesting styles will provide other opportunities for visual presentation.

Good artwork should be detailed and provide dimension. Single-dimension artwork is often flat and uninteresting. Artists should make sure to be inclusive in representing school populations.

INFORMATION GRAPHICS

An additional form of visual presentation is information graphics, information presented in visual ways. Information graphics utilize visuals as ways of breaking down complex information and making it understandable to readers. Information graphics can appear in a variety of forms, including pie charts, graphs, bar charts, locator maps, diagrams and sequence maps (Fig. 20.20). Good information graphics can be designed with the help of statistical charting software programs for better accuracy in representing the information. Sources of information used in the graphics should be provided to

Fig. 20.19(a). Taking advantage of artistically talented students in the school, publication staffs can add to their visual variety by occasionally using good artwork. This magazine, appearing as a supplement to the normal broadsheet newspaper, features the strong use of art introducing the story on women, math and science and was drawn by a student in the school. *Acumen* (a supplement to the *HiLite*), Carmel High School, Carmel, Ind.
(b). Combining type and image creates a really strong portrait of a student who became the subject of a question and answer feature. Because of his academic aptitude, the student's picture was combined with mathematical images circling his head to give the reader an immediate visual clue about why he was chosen for this large feature. *HiLite*, Carmel High School, Carmel, Ind.

help the reader understand the accuracy of the information presented. Or, if using the results of a student poll, the size of the sample providing the information should be presented at the end of the information graphic.

Information graphics should be used to help readers process and understand complex information, especially numbers, trends and statistics. They can also help readers understand how something happens or where it happened and who the key players were.

Staff artists are logical resources for information graphics, or if the school offers a class in computer graphics, students can be recruited to help create information graphics.

Accuracy is crucial in presenting information visually just as it is in presenting information verbally. Numbers, representations of numbers and comparisons should be checked for understandability, accuracy and clarity.

Fig. 20.20. Instead of a traditional prose story on the new design of the $20 bill, the staff of the *Hillcrest Hurricane* created an information graphic in which it presented information in a visual, rather than a verbal, way. Note the numbered pullout points illustrating new features of the bill. The bottom of the information graphic adds two additional pieces of information to the reader's understanding of the topic. *Hillcrest Hurricane*, Hillcrest High School, Dallas, Texas.

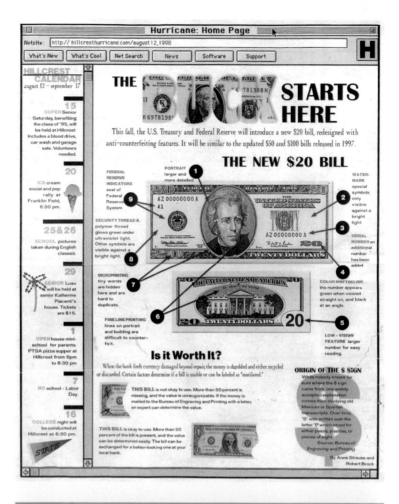

Fig. 20.21. In this newspaper's contents listing, shades of gray and black are effectively used to separate content areas for the reader. Reverse type and gray type in appropriate sizes provide good contrast. The leading and point size of the type lead to readability even though the type is used in nontraditional color. Screens of black are perceived as color tones by readers. *Hillcrest Hurricane*, Hillcrest High School, Dallas, Texas.

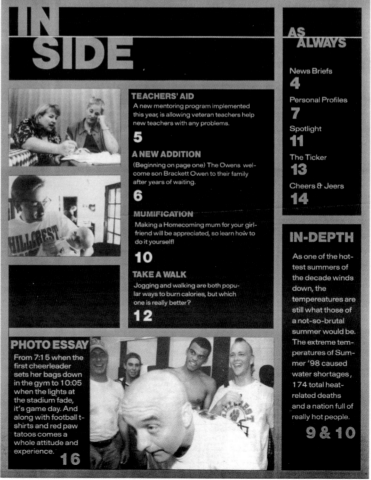

OTHER GRAPHIC FORMS

In addition to creating visual interest through photographs and illustrations, designers have other graphic tools to create visual interest. These include the use of rule lines, boxes, screens of color, isolation elements and text display elements.

Rule lines can be used singly or in several variations of widths combined together. Rule lines can separate, connect, frame or box content. Rule lines are sometimes used to create visual connections between separate pages when they are designed as a single visual unit.

Designers can use screens, shades of solid color, to isolate and separate content, to connect visual elements and to bring the reader's eyes to a particular area of the page (Fig. 20.21).

Isolation elements, primarily created through increased white space, can isolate and separate visual from verbal or move the reader's eyes from one page area to another.

Designers have a wealth of text display choices for creating interesting graphic areas on pages. Headline designs, arranged as strong visual units on the page, can utilize size and shade changes as well as changes in typography to create interesting displays. (See Chaps. 14 and 15.)

The use of drop caps, large initial letters beginning paragraphs, or text heads throughout the story will add contrast and break up large passages of gray text. Pull quotes can be lifted from the text and placed in display-size type to draw interest to the text. Designers can use other devices such as white space between story transitions or between natural junctures in the story to vary the density of the text.

Graphics work best when they work somewhat invisibly. Overdone graphics that draw attention to the graphics and distract the reader from the overall page content should be avoided. The ultimate goal of good visual communications is to contribute to the storytelling process.

EXERCISES

1. Using magazines or newspapers, cut out examples of photographs that exhibit these rules of composition: impact, center of interest, shallow depth of field, rule of thirds, interesting lighting, action and emotion. Label each photograph and tell what its compositional appeals are.

2. Develop a set of parameters for the quality of images that should be used in a publication. Consider these factors: Will or should the staff use pictures that are out of focus; that show the backs or tops or people's heads; that are scratched or marred by poor practices; that are of the same people; that are flipped or flopped; that are of staff members' friends? Justify your reason for each decision.

3. Using a supply of old pictures from the yearbook or newspaper staff, find a picture that would be a good stand-alone shot. Design a style for how the picture could be used in the newspaper. Write a catchline and caption for the picture.

4. Using some archived picture files, open pictures in a photo imaging software program such as Adobe Photoshop. Locate the cropping tool and practice cropping the pictures using the tool. Use a variety of crops to determine which crop works most effectively. The software will allow you to save versions of your crops for comparison or will enable you to undo as you work.

5. Import a picture into a layout on a school computer using the publication's layout program and scanning equipment. Practice cropping the picture electronically.

6. Cut out five examples of information graphics from professional publications. Find examples of a pie chart, a bar chart, a diagram, a locator map and a chart. Examine the content and determine whether the forms have been used effectively.

7. Find examples of these abusive picture techniques: a cutout image, an image cut into a cookie-cutter shape, a mortice, a photo pattern, a photo cliché and a collage. Paste each example to a sheet of paper and write an explanation of how each was used in print. Was it effective in its presentation?

8. Using these five topics visualize picture stories that could be developed for each of the topics: the prom,

graduation, homecoming, a field trip and a debate tournament. Make lists of possible pictures that could be taken and indicate what kind of lens might be appropriate for each picture. Go through your list and add compositional qualities that would improve the pictures.

9. Using a digital camera, photograph an event or activity in your school. Download the pictures onto the computer and edit them using the computer software program your school uses. Write captions for each of the images and design a picture package using the images. Make sure one of the pictures appears in a dominant shape and size in the package.

10. Cut out five different pages from professional publications in which artwork or illustrations have been used instead of pictures. Paste each to a sheet of paper and explain its effectiveness in visualizing the story it illustrates. Underline passages in the story that relate directly to elements of the art or illustration. Explain how it utilizes detail and color. What style is used in the art?

11. Cut out examples of layouts that have rule lines; color used to separate and isolate content; headline units using color, contrast or visual detail; white space used for visual or verbal separation; and pull quotes and text heads in a story. Paste each example to a sheet of paper and label each with its graphic use. Evaluate the effectiveness of each graphic use.

Advertising in Newspapers and Yearbooks

It's a favorite American teen pastime – spending money – someone's, anyone's.

There's Heidi, who just had to spend her $340 check from flipping burgers at the Dairy Mart. Then there's Ryan, who would whine until his mother bought "the right brand" of cereal. Teens are spending more money today than ever before. Teenage Research Unlimited Inc. found that teens represented a buying power of $169 billion in 2004. The increase in teen buying power in the late 1990s made student publications a viable advertising medium for businesses.

Look around and take notice of all the ways businesses focus their advertising on teens. Soft drink companies vie for exclusive school vending contracts. Broadcasting companies provide televisions in exchange for showing advertising along with newscasts in classrooms. Companies buy advertising space on school buses. School newspapers and yearbooks offer advertisers a direct link to America's 30 million-plus teenagers.

The communication link creates a beneficial relationship for everyone involved. The four major roles advertising plays for publications, businesses and readers are:

1. *To provide income for the publication*

   Nearly all media – newspapers, magazines, internet, radio and television – derive most of their income from advertising. School publications with little school funding find advertising a necessity. Even those publications with school district funding may find advertising a great way to raise money for buying additional computer or camera equipment.

2. *To perform a service for businesses*

   Because the school newspaper and yearbook communicate with teens in a limited geographic area, businesses can reach a specific audience with focused messages about products and services. Clearly, as shown in the introduction, teens provide a market that businesses want to reach. With daily newspaper readership shrinking among teens, the school's newspapers, yearbooks and web sites are effective ways for businesses to reach a younger audience. Advertising can create brand or business name recognition, sell products or services or help hire employees.

3. *To perform a service for readers by making them aware of products and services*

   Students are always searching for new restaurants, weekend jobs or the latest sales on athletic shoes. Advertising can make students aware of all of these things. Advertising can help students earn money and then help them spend it wisely. Informing students about services such as an SAT prep class or a driving school will help meet student needs.

4. *To build a bond between the business community and the student body*

Even though scholastic publication advertising is not a donation, ads in a high school newspaper or yearbook are still signs of local support. Building a bond and respect between the student body and businesses strengthens the sense of community. When a pharmacy buys a full-page yearbook ad, parents and students shop there, in part, to show their appreciation for the business's investment in the student endeavor. The community, as a whole, is stronger for such an exchange.

CREATING AN ADVERTISING PROGRAM

Advertising can be a vibrant, fun part of the scholastic journalism program. From the preparation stages to the sales visits to the design and placement, each stage of creating an advertisement is creative and interactive. The many possible career choices in the field of advertising are explored in Chapter 24.

PREPARATION

An informed salesperson is a successful salesperson. The advertising salesperson must fully understand information about the school, the publication and the business. The advertising director should collect and organize such information to arm and train advertising salespeople so they can bring the three together.

One of the first steps is understanding the market or, in this case, the student audience. The best salesperson knows who makes up the audience, their buying power and their habits. Students spend large amounts of money. Sometimes it's their money. Sometimes it's their parents' money. Conduct your own market survey, and you may be surprised by how much students spend, what they spend it on and where they spend it. Lakota East High School found that seniors spend an average of more than $130 a month. Multiply the individual spending profiles times the more than 1,500 students at Lakota East, and you will see that the *Spark* reaches an audience with sizable spending power.

A few questions you can include in your own student survey are:

- How much do you have to spend in one week?
- How much do you spend for clothes each school year?
- In what stores do you buy these clothes?
- What do you do for entertainment each week?
- How much do you spend on this entertainment each week? How much for movies? Concerts? Video games? Videos? Other activities?
- How much do you spend per week on food? Outside the school cafeteria, where do you buy this food?
- How much do you spend on school supplies each week? Where do you buy them?
- How much do you spend on transportation? Do you own a car?
- Which stores do you buy from the most? Why?
- Which stores do you buy from the least? Why?

Keep the survey short to encourage students to complete the form. A one-page questionnaire with ranges of answers to circle may help. In addition to knowing the buying power and habits of the readers, a good salesperson needs to know how many people are in the school and where they are from.

The advertising staff should take all this information and incorporate it into a set of professional-looking sales aids. The sales aids can include a rate card, a flyer and sales charts or graphs.

Although it can be many sizes or shapes, the rate card, typically, is a small brochure containing all the basic information about advertising in the publication, the publication itself and the market. The rate card should be a well-designed brochure that answers most of the advertiser's questions (Fig. 21.1).

The card could include some of the following information:

- publication dates
- deadline dates for space reservation and copy
- basic publication information such as address, phone number, fax number and email address

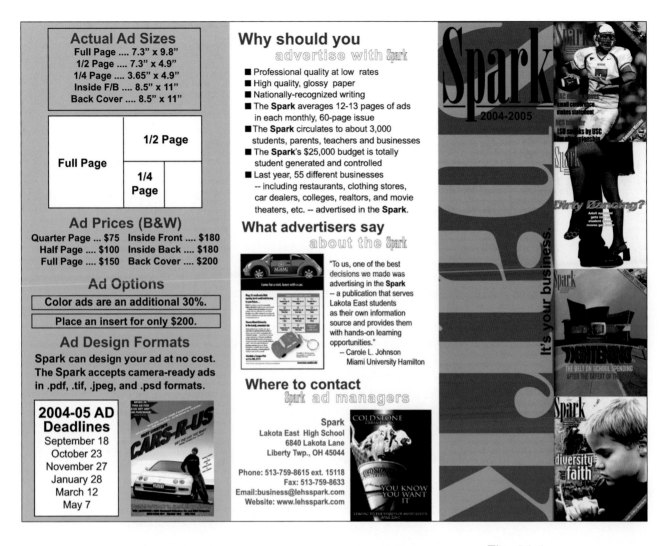

- reasons to buy an ad in the publication

- readership information, such as number of readers, buying power and habits

- policies on what ads you will and won't accept

- billing and payment policies, such as discounts, acceptance of checks and billing dates

- design information, such as a requirement that logos must be on a white background

- additional costs, such as charging for taking photographs for the ad

Don't overwhelm the advertiser with information. Make the rate card easy to read and use.

The sales graphs and charts can be as varied as the publication's sales needs. For example, compare the percentage of students who read your publication with the percentage who read the closest major daily. Display all the tuxedo rental businesses

CARMEL	Art Bortolini • 506-1030 • abortolini@hilite.org
HIGH SCHOOL	Jon Campbell • 575-9276 • jcampbell@hilite.org
HiLite	Stacie Feldwisch • 848-2821 • sfeldwisch@hiite.org
AD SALES STAFF	Nichole Freije • 848-1789 • nfreije@hilite.org
520 East Main Street	Chase Graverson • 844-3240 • cgraverson@hilite.org
Carmel, Indiana 46032-2299	Dave Hoffman • 843-1980 • dhoffman@hilite.org
(317) 846-7721, Ext. 1143	Quinn Shepherd • 844-2408 • qshepherd@hilite.org
Fax: (317) 571-4066	Jon Titus • 571-9744 • jtitus@hilite.org
Web: www.hilite.org	Jake Wilson • 844-5437 • jwilson@hilite.org

Fig. 21.2. Advertising staff business card. *HiLite*, Carmel High School, Carmel, Ind.

that have advertised in your publication as a way to encourage other formal wear businesses to do the same. List the dates of upcoming dances and special events along with survey information about the amount of money students spend getting ready for the big occasions. These flyers can be quick reference material for a salesperson.

Every salesperson should also be armed with staff business cards and contracts. The Carmel High School *HiLite* staff is able to get all of the advertising staff on one card (Fig. 21.2).

A professional packet of material, typically uniform in design, serves several purposes. The packet gives the salesperson something to work from during a sales call. If the businessperson is busy or uninterested, the salesperson can leave the packet for later reference. The business owner may come back to the packet and will have the prices and phone number handy when he's ready to call and purchase an ad. In any case, a professional packet can help refute what has been the age-old adult opinion that all teens are lazy or unprofessional.

The salesperson may also have billing forms, proofing forms and an assortment of sales and thank you letters (Fig. 21.3). The additional forms can help establish a trust and bond between the business and the salesperson, increasing the likelihood that the business owner will buy again.

PUBLICATION KNOWLEDGE

A good salesperson should not have to refer to the packet for basic information such as advertising rates and deadline dates. The numbers should be as familiar to the salesperson as his or her birthdate. The salesperson needs to know the number of subscribers to the newspaper or the number of yearbooks sold, the number of students in each class (freshman to senior) and the percentage of boys and girls.

A basic understanding of the publication can dispel the myth that you are some kid out begging for money and enhance your image as a professional.

ADVERTISING POLICY

A written advertising policy will help salespeople deal with questions that arise.

The policy may deal with ad sales for political campaigns, health centers where pregnancy tests or abortions are performed or businesses that get a majority of their income from liquor sales. In one case, a pizza place that students frequent has a logo with the words "Friends of wine and beer." Does your policy prohibit the running of the ad? Do you ask for a different logo? Ask to crop that portion out?

Does the ad have to sell a product or service? What happens if a person buying space in the newspaper of a high school with a large Jewish population wants to run an ad claiming the Holocaust never happened? Do you accept congratulations ads? Do you accept political ads?

What about sex-related advertising? Does your yearbook run an ad for a store that sells condoms? Do you advertise R-rated movies? What about a tanning salon ad with a photo of a woman in a revealing swimsuit?

The advertising policy may also deal with minimum advertising sizes. A 1 × 1-inch or a 1 × 2-inch ad is often not large enough to adequately advertise a product or service.

Some schools also have policies on what can be included in senior yearbook ads. Senior wills-type messages with inside jokes are a libel and ethics concern for some publications.

Business Knowledge

The salesperson must observe and understand the business he or she is trying to sell an ad to. Know that a sporting goods store has new school team T-shirts to sell. Know that students are into buying crushed fruit drinks. Information such as what products or services students buy from the area clothing stores, movie theaters and video stores will make you a valuable ally for the business owner.

Discover answers to questions about each business:

- Who is the store manager?

- Who is the person who handles the business's advertising?

- What products or services does this business have of interest to your readers?

- What medium does the owner prefer advertising in? What sizes of ads does this business buy regularly? What is the business trying the hardest to sell?

- What upcoming events are there that the business would be interested in advertising for?

Putting the Salesperson at Ease

Knowing who to talk to and what to talk to them about will put the advertising salesperson at ease.

Taking all this information and combining it into a smooth sales approach can still be difficult. Practice helps. Organize an ad meeting in the summer. Invite a professional salesperson to discuss tips for selling ads. Role-play typical ad sales calls to practice the approach. The more times a person talks through a sales approach the more at ease he or she will feel.

CARMEL HIGH SCHOOL FAX COVER SHEET

520 East Main Street • Carmel, Indiana 46032-2299

Phone (317) 846-7721, Extension 1143 • Fax (317) 571-4066

Jake Wilson, HiLite advertising manager • jwilson@hilite.org or hilite@ccs.k12.in.us

Page 1 of _____-page fax to 571-4066

To: **Jake Wilson** (c/o Tony Willis)
Carmel High School HiLite

Fr: _____ (name)

_____ (business advertised)

Re: Ad proof response

Da: _____

I have reviewed my ad which will run in the _____ issue of the Carmel High School student newspaper, the HiLite and I am returning it with this cover sheet as follows:

❏ It has no corrections or changes and may be printed as is.

❏ I have described below any changes, deletions or additions that need to be made:

_____

_____

_____

_____

❏ On the ad that accompanies this cover sheet, I have clearly marked changes, deletions or additions that need to be made.

Signature: _____

I wish to receive a second proof after these corrections are made: ❏ YES ❏ NO

THANK YOU FOR YOUR ASSISTANCE. WE APPRECIATE YOUR BUSINESS.

Fig. 21.3. Proofing form. *HiLite,* Carmel High School, Carmel, Ind.

Ad Script -- A typical day on the job

*(The setting is Papa John's Pizza. Phil is a **SPARK** ad salesman. His job is to make money. This could be the middle, end or beginning of the year. Regardless, Phil does not return without a filled out ad contract for fear of bodily harm from the hands of Amy Silver or Catherine Matacic. The time is 4 p.m. The salesman is dressed professionally. He is calm, cool, and collected. He has some background on the business: their competitors, previous advertisements with SPARK, their competitors advertisements in SPARK, and their prime target audience. Phil is just being himself and flashing them a handsome smile. Advertisers like to be secure with and trust the people they send their checks to. That trust and security hinges on the moment he walks in their store. Phil must make a good first impression.)*

Phil: Hi! May I speak with the manager?
Papa John's Delivery Boy: He isn't in right now.
Phil: Well, may I speak with the assistant manager?
Papa John's Delivery Boy: Hold on one second. *(Delivery boy goes and fetches the assistant manager, who is on the telephone. Phil has to wait a couple of minutes. John Deluca approaches the counter.)*
John: Hi! How may I help you?
Phil: My name is Phil Tork, and I'm from Lakota East High School's nationally acclaimed student newsmagazine **SPARK**. I've come here to tell you about a great opportunity your company has been missing out on. That opportunity is the local teenage, pizza hungry market. The easiest way to hit them and their parents is through their school. **SPARK** distributes to over 1,000 students, parents, teachers, and community members. We are one of the largest high school publications in the state and have been in operation for over five years. We would like you to consider advertising with our paper. Here is a copy of our ad information, publication dates, ad sizes and also a placement sheet. We do inserts and would gladly print out coupons with your ad. Coupons are a really good idea because those indicate to you whether the ad is working and whether you are satisfied with the job we are doing. Here is a list of other companies in the area who have advertised with us. I'm pretty sure Pizza Hut and Dominoes are on the list. Our space fills up pretty quick. So are you interested?
John: Do I have to give you the money now? *(Looks unsure about what he is getting into.)*
Phil: You can but you don't have to. After each publication is distributed, we will send you a bill through the mail. If we make any mistakes on your ad, we will gladly give you a free ad in our next issue. If you buy more than one ad a year, we can easily change the ad to say something else, but you would need to send us the new information.
John: Okay. I'll purchase a quarter page for the October, December and May issues. *(Phil fills out the required spaces on the placement sheet, informs John of the total price and writes down the company's name, address, and telephone number.)*
Phil: We have the technology to do camera-ready ads. Do you have any material that you would like to see placed in the ad, such as your logo or coupons? *(John hands him what he wants on the ad.)* Would you like us to design the coupons for you?
John: Sure.
Phil: What would you like them to say? How about ... *(The lights and sound fade out on the scene. Phil has just received a lot of stringbook points toward his quarter grade and a lot of gratitude from the business department. And all it took was to become a salesman for a day.)*

NOTE: NOT ALL ASSISTANT MANAGERS OR MANAGERS ARE AUTHORIZED TO PURCHASE ADS. IF THEY CAN'T, ASK WHO TO TALK TO, OR WHEN THE OWNER WILL BE IN, THEN STOP BACK ON THAT DATE. DON'T GET FRUSTRATED IF YOU DON'T SUCCEED IN EVERY STORE YOU WALK INTO. JOANN TIEMANN TWO YEARS AGO WENT TO OVER 12 STORES IN ONE DAY AND ONLY TWO STORES BOUGHT ADS.

Fig. 21.4. Ad script. *Spark*, Lakota East High School, Liberty Township, Ohio.

The role-playing should be realistic. More experienced salespeople will know the scenarios that you may face in the sales call. Some examples are

- The business owner who doesn't have time

- The owner who doesn't advertise in high school publications

- The manager who uses the "I already donated money to the band" excuse

Then be creative. Will the owner question the image of your school? Will the owner be abrupt and angry because she had to fire an employee that morning? Will the owner agree to buy an ad only if you also pass out flyers for him? The more situations you face in role-playing, the more comfortable you'll be in dealing with situations as they arise in real sales calls.

Before going out to sell, salespeople should have a specific territory to cover. The territories can be organized regionally. A salesperson may feel more at ease if covering an area in his or her neighborhood with businesses he or she frequents. Establishing a rapport between the salesperson and the business is important in a successful sales call. Another way to learn the sales call is to go with a more experienced salesperson.

THE SALES CALL

There's one sure way to fail in a sales call. Walk into a business and mumble, "Do you want to buy an ad?" You'll get the easy response. "No." You do not need to fail. Give the business owner a reason to buy. A salesperson should know that because businesses differ, the reasons they would want to purchase ads vary. The salesperson must communicate the information that fits the needs of the particular customer and the special type of store. An advertiser convinced of the value of advertising in the school publication can be spoken to differently from one who is skeptical. A new business owner may need information about your school's location and size as well as the total buying power of your readers. A previous advertiser may need a reminder that prom is only four weeks away.

A salesperson may have made contact with the business owner before making the sales call. Some publication staffs call and make appointments to come by. If you are not comfortable with the business to begin with, a face-to-face call to set up an appointment

may be better. While the visit could be time-consuming, considering many managers or business owners may not be in or available, making the appointment face-to-face will go further in establishing a rapport with the business owner. A long-time Dallas newspaper advertising salesperson said that the business owner must like you as much as the publication to want to buy an ad.

A salesperson armed with all the knowledge and sales aids mentioned earlier will be more at ease in the presentation. Remember that the salesperson is a skilled individual who helps the business owners communicate better with students through a school publication. As discussed in the opening, the creation and sale of advertising is a professional service.

Some considerations in making the sales call:

- Dress in appropriate clothing.

- Begin with a reason the business owner would want to advertise.

- Know all the reasons why a business owner should advertise in the school yearbook or newspaper.

- Try to determine all possible objections a business owner might raise and plan valid rebuttals.

- Remind advertisers that the most effective ads are not one-time propositions. A salesperson should emphasize that regular advertising builds an image in the minds of readers that brings product and store recognition. A store running an ad only once has a poor chance of leaving a lasting impression. After all, consider the number of McDonald's ads you've seen since you were born.

- Go armed with a predesigned ad for the business. The time you take to develop a concept and design an ad will show the business owner that you care about his or her business. Even if the sales call does not end in a sale, the salesperson has been successful in building the respect of the business owner.

- Keep notes to analyze the results of successful or unsuccessful sales presentations with businesses. A file on a business will help the salesperson keep up with the account. For example, too often a business owner may say, "I really want to advertise before prom." A good note taker will write down the owner's comment and return six weeks before prom.

- Understand that many chain businesses look to corporate offices to purchase advertising. Some publication

(a)

(b)

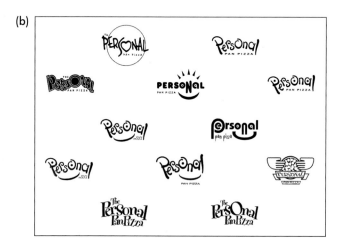

(c)

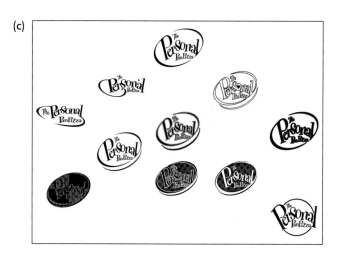

Fig. 21.5. **(a)** Ad designs often begin as quick, rough sketches. **(b)** To develop a quality design, brainstorm a lot of possibilities. Notice here how many different logo designs the agency developed for this lively Pizza Hut campaign. **(c)** After settling on a look, the ad designer can still make subtle changes to it. **(d)–(f)** The finished product is a varied display of media and conceptual development. Notice in (e) and (f) the clever play of the idea of a "personal" pizza. *Pizza Hut, the Pizza Hut logo and Personal Pan Pizza are trademarks of Pizza Hut, Inc., and are used with permission.*

salespeople have been successful by persistently calling corporate offices to make the sale. A publication can join certain agencies that sell advertising to corporations on behalf of a large group of school publications, primarily newspapers. In other cases, salespeople have encouraged local managers of chain businesses to use community relations funds to buy advertising for their products or services or for hiring purposes.

- Tactful persistence pays off. Most sales are made after at least five calls. Rapport and respect take time. Coming back to the business owner to show new designs or to see if he or she needs anything will often pay off eventually. Patience and persistence are key.

TELEPHONE SALES

In some schools where administrations are concerned with the liability of allowing students to leave campus to sell ads, a phone campaign may be a necessity. A good written phone script may help. However, the script should not sound as if it is being read. The sales tips above typically apply. A face-to-face meeting after school or on a weekend prior to a cold call is preferable and will help establish a rapport with the business owner. A telephone call may also suffice on a follow-up call when the salesperson has already made the sale and is trying to extend it for another issue.

CREATING AN ADVERTISEMENT

Research estimates in the late 1990s show people will see an average of more than 1,600 advertising images a day. Incredible, isn't it. Faced with advertising images on billboards, book covers, web sites and T-shirts, among many others, the reader will not give much notice to a business card thrown onto the page. The quality of the ad concept and design is critical.

Advertising must have a message that sells name recognition, connects a feeling to the product or informs the reader about benefits of the product or service. One ad sells the cool, go-all-out image of a brand athletic shoe. Another ad convinces a student that if he wants to impress his date, he'll buy roses from the florist at the corner. A third ad sells the 15 percent discount on burger and fries students will get when they show their school ID at the neighborhood burger restaurant.

DEFINE THE MESSAGE

Often the advertiser knows what aspect of the business he or she wants to advertise. Whether the advertiser suggests some copy or the advertising salesperson develops the message, make sure the point is simple. The message can be as specific as "Rent your tux for homecoming from us" or as abstract as "the Pizza Shack sells fun." Both are simple, clear messages that must be visually and verbally communicated in an interesting way. The message should clearly define what makes the particular business advertising different from all other businesses of the same type.

In the book *Hey Whipple, Squeeze This: A Guide to Creating Great Ads*, Luke Sullivan explains what a good ad must accomplish:

> It's as if you're riding down an elevator with your customer. You're going down only 15 floors. So you have only a few seconds to tell him one thing about your product. One thing. And you have to tell it to him in such an interesting way that he thinks about the promise you've made as he leaves the building, waits for the light, and crosses the street. You have to come up with some little thing that sticks in the customer's mind.[1]

Sullivan provides a wealth of suggestions for delivering the message creatively through a print ad. Here are a few of his suggestions:

---

1. *Hey Mr. Whipple, Squeeze This: A Guide to Creating Great Ads*, Luke Sullivan, Copyright © (1998 John Wiley & Sons, Inc., New York, N.Y.). Reprinted by permission of John Wiley & Sons, Inc.

(d)

(e)

(f)

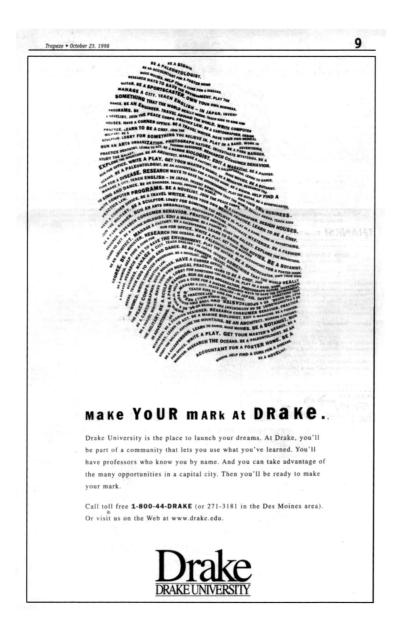

Fig. 21.6. Advertisement. Drake University, Des Moines, Iowa.

- Find the central truth about your whole product category. The central *human* truth. Hair coloring isn't about looking younger. It's about self-esteem. Cameras aren't about pictures. They're about stopping time and holding life as the sands run out.

- Focus first on the substance of what you want to say. Remember styles change; typefaces and design and art directions, they all change. Fads come and go. But people are always people. They want to look better, to make more money; they want to feel better, to be healthy. They want security, attention and achievement.

- Ask yourself what would make you want to buy the product.

- Get to know your client's business as well as you can.

- First, say it straight. Then say it great. To get the words flowing, sometimes it helps to simply write out what you want to say. Make it memorable, different or new later. First just say it.

  Try this. Begin your headline with: "This is an ad about . . ." And then keep writing.

  Whatever you do, just start writing.

- Remember notebook paper is not made solely for recording gems of transcendent perfection. A sheet of paper costs about one squillionth of a cent. It isn't a museum frame. It's a workbench. Write. Keep writing. Don't stop.

- Think of the strategy statement as a lump of clay. You've got to sculpt it into something interesting to look at. So begin by taking the strategy and saying it some other way, any way. Say it faster. Say it in English. Then in slang. Shorten it. Punch it up. Try anything that will change the strategy statement from something you'd overhear in an elevator at a sales convention to a message you'd see spray painted on an alley wall.

- Try writing down words from the product's category. You're selling outboard engines? Start a list on the side of the page: Fish, Water, Pelicans, Flotsam, Jetsam, Atlantic, Titanic, Ishmael.

  What do these words make you think of? Pick up two of them and put them together like Tinkertoys. You have to start somewhere. Sure it sounds stupid. The whole creative process is stupid.

- Allow your partner to come up with terrible ideas; just say "that's interesting," scribble it down and move on.

- Don't look for what's wrong with a new idea; look for what's right.

- Stare at a picture that has the emotion of the ad you want to do.

- Cover the wall with ideas. Don't settle on the first passable idea that comes along.

- Quick sketches of your ideas are all you need during the creative process. Just put the concept on the paper and continue moving forward.

- Get it on paper quickly and furiously. Be hot. Let it pour out. Don't edit when you're coming up with ads.

  Then later, be ruthless. Cut everything that is not A-plus work.

THE STEPS IN CREATING THE ADVERTISEMENT

Taking the ideas from the brainstorming process to the computer screen is the next step. The design breaks down into four elements: illustration, headline, body copy and logo. Each of the elements should work together to communicate the clear message that was developed in the steps above. In Figure 21.6, the Drake University ad creates the simple idea of "make your mark at Drake." That mark visually is a fingerprint. Look closer to see that the mark Drake wants you to make is by writing a play, designing homes and helping find a cure for a disease. All the elements work together to deliver their message that Drake University will help you be somebody.

The illustration, a photo or artwork, is usually the dominant feature of the ad. In the visual hierarchy, discussed in Chapter 15, the illustration is typically more prominent than the other elements. The advertising art director wants to demonstrate the product, service or business, the feeling or the benefit. People are visual. Good dominant visuals, placed in the optical center, grab the reader's attention. In Figure 21.7, good-looking flowers for homecoming is the important message. The illustration makes that message clear with a tightly cropped strong visual of tulips.

The headline is rarely used as the dominant visual element in an ad. However, the headline is still critical in whether the advertisement effectively communicates its message. The ad's headline should give the benefit of the product or business and

Fig. 21.7. Advertisement. *HiLite*, Carmel High School, Carmel, Ind.

Two Types of Advertising

Display Advertising

Display advertising is exactly what its name suggests – advertising that displays, through type and illustrations, the product or service a merchant wants to sell. Well-designed display ads have type appropriate to the product or service and effective illustrations and borders. Such ads help to make news pages attractive and direct readers' attention to the ads.

Classified Advertising

Classified advertising is also exactly what its name suggests – advertising in the section of a paper that classifies products and services under appropriate headings: "Jobs Wanted," "Used Books" and services available primarily for teenagers. Few school papers have classified ad columns, yet a classified ad column is just as appropriate as it is for a large city daily. Such a column could be a source of revenue and perform a real service to readers. Personal ads in newspapers are discouraged because they can create ethical and in some cases legal problems. Make sure all ads sell a service that is legal.

complement the illustration. In Figure 21.7 the headline targets the teen market with the store's primary sales message that it will make sure your flowers will look good for homecoming. In this ad's case, as it should be in all well-designed ads, the type selection helps create a feeling for the business or product. The script type adds to the elegant feeling the art director wanted to create. Type contrast or art, as discussed in Chapter 15, can also be considered. A well-written headline, created in a clean and easy to read serif or sans serif type, is preferable to illegible novelty type. Ad headlines should also be short and punchy. A secondary headline in many retail ads, or ads that advertise a specific store, may be the store name. Often, however, an advertiser has a logo that you will use. But once again, rarely is the name of the store the dominant headline. In Figure 21.8, the student designer asked the advertiser if he could redesign this tailor's ad so that the ad actually sold an emotional impression along with name recognition. What the designer developed was an ad where the stock photo image (which the student got the business owner to purchase) and the font choices created a stylish feel.

The *U-High Midway* newspaper takes a light approach to creating a connection between the business and the teen market. In Figures 21.9 and 21.10, the Chicago school publication uses student models and entertaining copy that plays off popular TV shows to attract readers.

The copy is the written text of the ad. The copy reinforces the message communicated in the headline and illustration. The text should be specific and vivid, helping to sell the product or service by personalizing the benefits of the product. In the Drake University ad (Fig. 21.6), the headline states you can make your mark at Drake. The copy lists the specific ways this can be achieved (for example, by being part of a community where you can use what you learn and by having the personal attention of professors).

If the ad is a retail ad, which advertises a specific business, the copy will usually include the basic information of address, phone number and store hours. The local retail ad is also more likely to include prices for specific products. Try to limit the copy. Keep it short and snappy. In the visual hierarchy of the design, the body copy typically is secondary. The designer should choose much smaller type sizes and weights. Clean, easy to read serif and sans serif types are preferable.

The logo is the trademark of the company. Typically company-provided, the logo is given larger display than the body copy, but not usually larger than the headline and illustration, which are being used to sell the product or the service.

Make sure that the logo is on a white or light background if you have to scan or reproduce it. A logo on dark-colored paper will muddy and become unreadable in the reproduction.

As already mentioned, the illustration is usually the dominant element in the design. The reader's eyes are attracted by the illustration, and from there the eyes must make a clear and logical movement through the ad. The eye movement is called "gaze motion." The reader's eyes move left to right, but a dominant football player on the right side of the ad looking to his left into the headline will surely take the reader's eyes to the headline. Use visual hierarchy to move the reader's eyes through each element of an ad. A larger headline under a dominant illustration will be a logical gaze motion. The last thing the reader should see is the logo. The concept works like hearing a song the moment before you get out of your car in the morning. The last song you hear sticks in your mind throughout the day. The art director hopes the same thing happens with the last visual element you see – the logo. Then advertising works like going to a party where you do not know anyone but one person. In a crowded room, you seek out the person you know to talk to. You're comfortable with the person you're familiar with. Logo or name recognition creates such familiarity. An advertiser wants a reader zipping along a row of restaurants to stop at the one the reader recognizes from an ad.

White space is also a consideration in ad design. White space can help to frame and give emphasis to elements. Elements should not be crammed into a space. Avoid the use of decorative dingbats and big, overwhelming borders. A simple one-point rule often suffices. Let the four elements defined earlier – illustration, headline, body copy and logo – attract the reader's attention.

SOME OTHER CONSIDERATIONS IN AD DESIGN

- Do not put coupons on back to back pages in the newspaper.

- Once you've completed an ad design, try it out on some friends. Let them look at the ad and see if they get the desired message. Ask them what message they got from the ad to see if it matches the desired one. If an ad takes explanation, it fails.

- After the ad is designed, the process is not over. Providing the business owner with an ad to proof or proofing the ad yourself is critical to doing good business. Make sure the ad contains an updated coupon date, correct address, fax and phone information and a cleanly reproduced logo.

- Once the advertisement runs, the advertising salesperson should deliver a copy of the newspaper or the yearbook page to first-time advertisers to encourage repeat business. A tear sheet or copy of the reproduced ad serves as proof of the business's purchase.

- Make sure all billing is prompt.

- A satisfied advertiser is a repeat advertiser.

Fig. 21.8. Advertisement. *Harbinger*, Shawnee Mission East High School, Prairie Village, Kan.

Fig. 21.9. Advertisement. *U-High Midway*, University High School, Chicago, Ill.

EXERCISES

1. Evaluate the ads in Figures 21.11–21.13. Do they really sell a service or a product? Is the concept creative? Are they effectively designed? If not, how might they have been improved? Is the copy effective? If not, why not? In your discussion use all the principles you studied in this chapter.

2. Write a carefully composed critique of an ad from a recent issue of your school publication. Discuss the kind of advertising it represents, the layout, the copy and the placement on the page. Is the advertising professional? Is the business getting its money's worth? Redesign the ad, if necessary.

3. Choose three of your favorite TV commercials. Explain what product benefit each ad is trying to communicate and how the ad communicates the message. Decide which ad is the most creative and explain why.

Fig. 21.10. Advertisement. *U-High Midway*, University High School, Chicago, Ill.

4. Conduct a market survey of the purchasing power and buying power of your student body. In small groups, discuss what areas you need to survey in order to collect information that would help an advertising salesperson. Distribute the poll through homeroom classes or during an activity period.

5. Make a list of possible advertisers for your school publication.

6. Select a product or service that you know well and believe would be appropriate for an ad in your school publication. In small groups, discuss what the possible message or benefit for the product or service would be. What makes it better than other products or services similar to it? Design an ad for it with the message you selected in mind.

7. From daily newspapers or magazines, clip, mount and label three ads that you think are especially effective in layout. Beneath each discuss the reasons for its effectiveness. If you have an overhead projector, plan to show the class your best ad.

8. Select five area businesses and decide what information an advertising salesperson would need to know about the businesses to sell them an ad. Vary the business types.

Fig. 21.11. *Hillcrest Hurricane*, Hillcrest High School, Dallas, Texas.

Fig. 21.12. *Hillcrest Hurricane*, Hillcrest High School, Dallas, Texas.

Fig. 21.13. *Hillcrest Hurricane*, Hillcrest High School, Dallas, Texas.

9. Label the prices of 10 ads in your yearbook and newspaper to prepare for a sales call. Use removable self-adhesive notes if necessary. Are there extra costs for photography? Are there discounts?

10. Prepare a sales pitch for the following businesses. Role-play in front of the class with another class member playing the business owner. Have the class discuss the demonstration.

   (a) A flower shop that you hope will buy an ad in the issue before homecoming;

   (b) a new sporting goods store;

   (c) a new multiscreen theater that is trying to hire employees;

   (d) a restaurant that specializes in 20 types of burgers.

Ethics for Student Journalists

Whether their work is published on paper, published online on the web or broadcast on radio or television, journalists are legally restricted and morally guided by some specific laws and guidelines and some general underlying principles. Some of these rules and principles are called "ethics." Laws and ethics are what a journalist calls upon to help answer sometimes troublesome questions (can a reporter tape a phone conversation? accept a free concert ticket?) about news gathering, reporting, writing and editing.

WHAT ARE ETHICS?

Learning the difference between good and bad conduct is a measure of maturity in a society. As children mature into adolescence and then adulthood, they ideally acquire standards or codes of conduct that are based on moral judgments. These are called personal ethics.

Personal ethics, the standards one lives by to do the right thing in everyday life, are often derived from the examples set by the home, school, church, peers and government and are desirable if one is to live happily in a morally good society.

Personal ethics tell someone that murder is generally bad and wrong and that sharing food with someone who is poor and hungry is generally good and right.

In addition to personal ethics, many professions, including medicine, law and journalism, have special ethics for members of those professions to follow. For journalists, these ethics guide them in the pursuit of truth in the news-gathering process. Organized into a code or set of guidelines, journalism ethics reflect journalism's mission in society, personal morality and some media laws.

THE FIRST AMENDMENT, MEDIA LAW AND ETHICS

The First Amendment to the U.S. Constitution is the basis for the laws and codes that guide journalists in the United States in their work. It provides the freedom journalists need to gather information (including from the government) that may be newsworthy.

Although the free press part of the First Amendment is one of the most important safeguards in the Bill of Rights, it is a general statement. Since the Bill of Rights was ratified in 1791, federal courts, the U.S. Supreme Court, Congress and state governments and courts have elaborated on what a free press means, including at the high school level.

Through the years, these court decisions and laws have created legal guidelines for journalists to follow as they gather and report news. Some of these laws tell journalists if how they get information is illegal – for example, tape recording a telephone conversation without the other person's knowledge is illegal in certain states. Other laws, such as those on libel, deal with the publication of information that is not true.

However, laws are not enough to guide a journalist on the job. Personal and professional ethics answer many of the questions regarding news gathering that laws don't answer. Journalism membership associations, such as the Society of Professional Journalists, and individual media companies, such as the *Washington Post* newspaper, have written codes of ethics for their members and employees. The codes are revised occasionally to meet the ever-changing job of gathering the news for publication.

School media – newspapers, yearbooks, magazines, broadcasts and online web sites – are affected by many of the same laws that guide the nonstudent media; the U.S. Supreme Court further limited the First Amendment press rights of public school students in 1988. (See Chap. 23.)

Like their nonstudent counterparts, school news media often supplement legal guidelines with additional standards of practice. Whether compliance is voluntary or mandatory, codes of ethics for journalists have these additional benefits:

- They help establish a sense of professionalism among all who work for one news organization or belong to the same association, and among journalists at large.

- Adherence to codes helps establish credibility with readers and viewers; the public is confident it can believe what it reads, hears and sees.

- Codes provide a uniform measure for dealing with news-gathering problems. Journalists bring diverse training and personal values to their work. Codes alleviate the potential for problems that could be caused by uneven training and different values.

JOURNALISM NEEDS AN ETHICS CODE

Although the American public hasn't always held journalism and journalists in high esteem, journalism is a reputable and respected profession and is the only one specifically mentioned for protection in the First Amendment. Because of its importance in an open society with a freely elected democratic form of government, journalism needs to be governed by a code of ethics.

Journalism serves many useful and vital functions in a democratic society:

- Journalism informs the public about facts and events that are important to it.

- Journalism ensures the free flow of information that is important to the birth and continuation of a democracy.

- Journalism provides a forum for diverse viewpoints.

- Journalism serves as a watchdog of government and other institutions to alert the public about wrongdoing.

- Journalism advocates changes in the public's interest.

- Journalism pursues the truth with unwavering commitment.

To meet these responsibilities and fulfill its mission, journalism needs an ethics code that allows for self-evaluation and results in public confidence in the accuracy and fairness of the work being done.

INDIVIDUAL JOURNALISTS NEED AN ETHICS CODE

An ethics code will only be effective if the journalists who work at the newspaper or other medium that has a code know it and use it to do their work. Each journalist, no matter the significance of the job being done, has a stake in the credibility of the publication with the public.

To meet the demands of the job and to live up to the standards society and journalism itself have set for those who work in the profession, these goals are important to achieve:

- A journalist can be trusted to be accurate, honest and independent and to keep promises.

- A journalist is respectful and is sensitive to community standards and taste.

- A journalist has a high regard for personal privacy.

- A journalist treats persons with courtesy and compassion.

- A journalist is fair and impartial.

- A journalist is concerned about completeness and the context of facts and opinions used in stories.

- A journalist acknowledges and corrects errors.

- A journalist listens to the questions and complaints from the public.

- A journalist strives for excellence in all aspects of work.

- A journalist considers the public interest in decision making.

If a journalist follows these guidelines, then the highest ethical standards are being observed and the credibility of the work will be unquestioned.

ETHICS IN ACTION: NEWS GATHERING

Few would argue with the merits of these lofty ideals, but how they apply to real, on-the-job reporting and editing, including in a high school newsroom, is sometimes confusing or overlooked.

Journalism ethics govern the process of reporting and publishing, from the first inkling or idea, through the information-gathering stage, to the writing and editing steps and, finally, to the finished, published work. This is valid for print, broadcast and internet-based publishing.

The reasons why a story is reported and how the information for that story is obtained are often as important to a journalist as what the story finally becomes once it is published. Ethics enter into these stages of the reporting process.

In the planning or prereporting stage of a story, the reporter – sometimes with the guidance of an editor or, in a school newsroom, a faculty adviser – analyzes the potential for the story. Questions such as these come to mind: How newsworthy is the story? What does the public need to know? Who will the story affect? What will the effect be? Some of these questions aren't answered until after all the information is gathered. One or more angles of the story are selected to investigate, and sources are considered for the necessary information to develop the story. At this stage, the reporter considers the fairness and relevance of the angle or angles chosen and the qualifications and reliability of the sources selected for the interviews and other fact-finding.

Also at this stage, the reporter's own stake in the story is considered. The reporter removes him- or herself from the story if he or she is personally involved in it in a way that could lead to a conflict of interest accusation from readers or if the reporter has some significant bias regarding the topic. For example, a student reporter who is a member of a student government body and a reporter for the school paper should not report on student government activities in which he actively participates. If he did, readers might think the story was not objective.

If the story lacks news or human interest values, its publication may be considered an example of distortion of the subject's importance, bias toward a special interest group or propaganda. If the sources aren't seen as reliable by the public or they aren't the most knowledgeable, the credibility of the story, the reporter and the publication will suffer.

Conflict stories with differing opinions are often troublesome for reporters. With these often complex, multisource, conflicting opinion stories, the reporter should carefully present all of the information, double-check facts for accuracy and include the opinions of those involved, especially those who have a minority or opposing view. The result will then likely be a story that is considered by most readers or viewers to be fair. For example, gun control is a controversial issue in many places, and proponents and opponents have strong opinions. A reporter who covers this topic should accurately report the positions on both sides of the issue. However, not all topics deserve equal coverage of opposing views. Some stories, such as the Holocaust, don't usually need the kind of opposing viewpoint balance that is required in other stories.

During the fact-finding or reporting stage of the story, the reporter also calls upon personal and professional ethics for guidance. The reporter asks several questions: Has enough information been gathered for the reader to clearly and fully understand the story? Depending upon the complexity and depth of the story, do the points of view represent different ages, races, sexes or ethnic or other groups? And, as was done in the reporting stage, the reporter again assesses the quality and validity of the sources: Are the "expert" persons and records the best and most reliable available?

Whether in person or on the phone, during interviews the reporter clearly informs the interviewee that the information being sought may be published. If the reporter is seeking off-the-record information for background and not for publication or quoting directly or indirectly in a story, that is also made clear to the interviewee.

Quoting a source accurately is vital to a reporter's and the publication's credibility. Use of a recorder or good notetaking is important for all interviews. As a matter of good ethics, the interviewee should be told that a recording is being made. It is also illegal to tape-record phone conversations in some states. The appropriate time to clarify information or check the completeness of a quote from a source is during the interview or during a follow-up phone call or second in-person interview. Beginning reporters, especially, will want to verify quotes and facts before ending an interview. It is unprofessional and it hurts the credibility of the paper for a reporter to give a source a completed copy of the story before it is published.

It is unethical and likely illegal for a reporter to steal or knowingly receive stolen information for a story. Although there may be some exceptions to this with consideration for the life or death importance to the public of the story, it is rarely justifiable. Within a school, taking records from the school's office without permission is stealing.

Use of the internet by reporters to gather information raises some ethical concerns. Because of the ease of creating and widely disseminating information on the internet, the accuracy of some of it could be doubted. Internet sources may not be as reliable as other sources. The person or agency sponsoring the web site may be a factor regarding its reliability. The accuracy of information obtained on the internet should be verified through other sources if possible. Reporters who gather information from internet bulletin boards or chat rooms should identify themselves as reporters and tell those involved that what they are writing may be published. A reporter who monitors chat rooms and bulletin boards or subscribes to listservs only for background information and not to quote someone as a source for a specific story does not have to identify himself or herself as a reporter. Persons who participate in an internet chat room, bulletin board or listserv don't automatically think they may be the source for a published story, so reporters should respect this privacy.

ETHICS IN ACTION: WRITING AND EDITING

During the writing stage, ethics again play a role as the reporter turns recordings, notes and drafts into a polished story ready for publication.

The reporter writes a lead that doesn't distort any information or slant the story in a deceptive way. If a narrative or story-telling lead and method of story development is used, the reporter should avoid embellishing the facts just to tell a more exciting story. If the inverted pyramid form is used, the reporter should consider the order in which the facts are presented, from most important to least important with regard to what the reader needs to know rather than what the reporter personally thinks is interesting. Overemphasizing or overwriting any one of the *what*, *who*, *where*, *when*, *why* and *how* of a story can distort the facts.

All facts and statistics and the spelling of names are verified. This complies with one of the reporter's most important goals, accuracy. Incorrect information and errors in spelling, especially in a person's name or other proper nouns, negatively affect the publication's credibility with its audience.

Direct and indirect quotes are reviewed for accuracy too. Are the quotes fair and used in the context of the questions asked during the interview? The reporter takes great care to accurately and fairly represent the words of the person being quoted.

As the story is developed, the reporter is mindful of the divergent viewpoints encountered in the fact-finding stage and incorporates them into the story. If a divergent view is not newsworthy – it may be old, too bigoted, false – then balance just for the sake of balance may be unnecessary. The reporter and editor judge each story individually for balance.

Upon examining a final draft or during the editing stage, if there is any question that some readers may think the story unfair because of a perceived lack of balance or a missing fact, the reporter may want to reopen the fact-finding stage and interview one more person or search for information in one more source. This may be especially important if the topic is somehow controversial. The reporter may be unaware of the need to revise the story until after it is written and given to someone else for editing.

Finally, and most important, the reporter examines those who have a stake in the publication of the story. Will anyone be hurt or helped by the story? If someone will be hurt, can the reporter defend the harm as justifiable or deserving? Does the good outweigh the harm? Sometimes it is wise for the reporter to put him- or herself in the place of the person who may be harmed to resolve any questions as to whether or not publication is justifiable.

The reporter also realizes that sometimes doing the right thing will not please everyone and someone may be harmed. The result of this kind of prepublication analysis may mean that the story will be changed to maximize the good effects and minimize the harmful ones. The final test is: Are the reporter's personal ethics satisfied?

QUESTIONS AFTER PUBLICATION

After a story is published, the reporter or editor may be called upon by readers to explain some aspect of it or defend its publication entirely. In advance of this potential questioning, the reporter should be able to stand by his or her story as true and newsworthy.

Depending upon the importance of the story, a follow-up may be planned to report the criticism or explore new angles suggested by a reader.

If an error is found in the story, a correction should be published in the next edition. If a clearer explanation of some facts in the original story is warranted, even though no errors were found, then a clarification should be published. Both corrections and clarifications should be published in a prominent but appropriate place, though usually not on page 1. Often they are published on the editorial page.

To possibly improve a publication's credibility with the public and to provide readers with a regular outlet to air their complaints about the publication, a reader advocate can be appointed. The advocate would be a student who is knowledgeable about how a news medium functions but is not on the editorial or business staff. The reader advocate is a neutral party who investigates reader complaints and issues brief reports that will be published in a subsequent edition.

An alternative to a reader advocate is a publications advisory board composed of students and nonstudents (teachers, parents) who convene only to mediate staff disputes or to review reader complaints and issue explanations or make recommendations for change. An advisory board does not serve as a censor for any prior review function.

A MODEL ETHICS CODE FOR HIGH SCHOOL JOURNALISTS

In addition to the personal ethics and obligation to fairness and accuracy a reporter brings to a story, other, very specific rules and guidelines have been created by news mediums and professional journalism groups for journalists to follow. Most nonstudent news mediums adopt a formal code of ethics. Student journalists may do the same, including acceptance of codes by such groups as the Society of Professional Journalists. However, students are likely to need some guidelines and rules specific to student media as well.

Student journalists may want to incorporate some or all of these rules and guidelines, organized alphabetically here, into their own code of ethics:

Acceptance of free tickets, gifts, meals, transportation and other amenities is questionable. Generally, gifts from news sources and vendors should not be accepted. However, token gifts such as pens, notepads, T-shirts and the like may be accepted if there is no indication that the gifts are being offered in return for some influence regarding the content or operations of the publication. Some say the dollar value of acceptable gifts shouldn't exceed $5. If money is available for tickets, a sports reporter or arts critic should not accept free tickets to an event he or she is assigned to cover. The same is true for transportation to an event and free meals. From a practical standpoint, most school publications don't have budgets to cover these expenses. In that case, acceptance of free admission is okay, but the reporter should be reminded that there is no obligation to do a more positive story because of the free admission.

Advertisers should not receive special treatment or undue favorable comment with regard to editorial content.

Anonymous sources should be used sparingly if at all. The credibility of a story suffers if information is not attributed directly to someone. However, anonymous sources may be used if the editor considers the information to be important enough. If possible, the information offered by an anonymous source should be verified with another source, even if the second one is also anonymous. In the published story, the unnamed source will be more credible if he or she is linked even generally to some agency or institution; the need for anonymity should be carefully preserved by not being too specific. If the editor is unsure about the reliability of the information or source, it is wise to hold or kill the story. (See *Confidentiality*.)

Clarifications – further explanation or additional facts that may make some information clearer to the reader – may be published if the story is significant. They can be placed adjacent to *corrections*.

Confidentiality should not be promised to a source by a reporter without the permission of the editor and after consultation with the publication's adviser. Granting and preserving the confidentiality of a source is often difficult for a nonstudent journalist and nearly impossible for a student journalist. Generally, confidentiality should only be promised to a source if there is real danger that serious physical, emotional or financial harm will come to the source if his or her name is revealed. Some states legally honor the confidentiality bond between a source and a journalist. In some cases reporters who refuse to reveal a source's name can be jailed or fined. Most likely, secondary school student journalists are not covered by any state shield laws, which may protect nonstudent journalists. Consequently, students could be compelled to reveal a source's identity.

Conflict of interest can negatively affect the credibility of the reporter and the publication. To avoid a conflict of interest, a reporter should not be assigned to cover a story in which he or she has any substantial involvement. An editor should decide what degree of involvement would disqualify a reporter from a story. A reporter is obligated to tell the editor about any memberships or participation in any activities that may be a reason to disqualify him or her from a story. For example, a reporter who is a student government member should not report student government activities. This policy helps ensure a certain amount of objectivity that is important to the publication's independence.

Corrections are published in the next edition of the publication in a prominent and consistent position. Errors are never knowingly published. Corrections for yearbook errors can be published as an insert and distributed separately.

Crime news gets special care from reporters and editors. Care should be taken to protect the rights of those charged with but not convicted of a crime. The person charged is the "suspect" or the "alleged . . ." The reporter must know the state laws regarding the identification of those persons under 18 years who are charged or convicted of a crime. Criminal cases are a matter of public record, and the records, unless otherwise dictated by a court, are open to student reporters.

Crime victims usually receive special care from journalists. Reporting the names and addresses of crime victims may be governed by state laws. Students who write crime beat stories need to know the laws that affect coverage of sexual abuse crimes such as rape and incest. Generally, victims of sexual abuse are not identified. However, some journalists and legal officials now advocate the identification of these victims. If law permits, this may be negotiated between the victim and the editor. Also, the victim of nonsexual crime may be identified; the publication has some responsibility to give some protection to the victim, such as publishing an inexact address. A question the reporter asks him- or herself is "What harm will result if the victim is identified?" With the exception of major crimes, an arrested person is not named until charges are filed.

Electronically altered photos (using a scanner, software and a computer to change the content of photos in any way other than improving contrast or removing flaws such as dust or scratches) are prohibited in most instances, and always for news or news-feature photos. Readers, including those for news-oriented web sites, expect the photo they see published to be the exact image of what existed when the photo was shot. Slight cosmetic changes, whether done on a computer or in a traditional darkroom, are acceptable. Photos for certain kinds of human interest feature stories, such as fashion coverage, can be altered electronically – objects can be added, removed or reshaped, for example. Highly fanciful photo images, clearly done with the assistance of a computer, can also be published since the reader will easily detect that reality has been tampered with. Photos for all hard news stories, including sports, which are nonfeatures, should not be given a fanciful, computer-altered interpretation.

Fabrication (creating a person, a situation, a dialogue, statistics or any pivotal or incidental information and passing it as real) is prohibited in most instances and almost always in news stories. If anything fictitious is included in a story, it should be clearly stated that the person, situation or whatever is fiction. Generally, columnists have more freedom to create characters and situations, and readers usually realize the intent.

False identity, concealed recording devices, stolen documents and *eavesdropping* are methods of gathering news that are ethically questionable or illegal for all journalists. In the normal course of gathering news, no journalists should misrepresent him- or herself. In extraordinary circumstances when information can not be gotten any other way and the nature of the information is seen as extremely important to the well-being of readers, an editor, upon consultation with an adviser, may give permission for a student journalist to go undercover and to misrepresent him- or herself. Care should be taken to avoid harmful situations. A journalist should not steal or knowingly accept stolen materials. Only under extraordinary circumstances should a reporter record an interview or speech without the permission of the speaker or interviewee. However, permission is unnecessary when the interview or speech is routine and frequent and the recording is openly done. Permission is assumed. For example, a reporter may record the weekly press briefing by the mayor without requesting permission each time. Tape-recording a telephone conversation without the agreement of the other party is illegal in at least 10 states. The obvious placement of a tape or other voice recorder in full view of the interviewee may be sufficient, but a polite request will usually lead to permission granted. Committing an illegal act such as entering a locked, private building without permission to record a source is prohibited. Entering a person's computer email files without permission is also prohibited. Eavesdropping to gather news is often unethical, even if legal entry is made, because it presumes that the reporter has not properly identified him- or herself.

Identification of a person as a member of any group (racial, ethnic, religious, sexual-orientation, economic, social or other) should be limited to those instances when that membership is essential to the reader's complete understanding of the story. Labels of any kind should be used carefully to avoid negative stereotyping. If a group label is used, the reporter should use the one accepted by journalists and acceptable to the person being so identified. For more information on this, refer to Chapter 12.

Journalists should neither directly assist nor hamper *law enforcement* officials with their work. Traditionally, the press is a watchdog of government and law enforcement, and it must remain independent to preserve this function. Some states provide better protection for journalists than others, and sometimes journalists are jailed for refusing to cooperate with police investigations and court proceedings for not submitting notes and photographs to the police or the courts. Laws protecting journalists and their materials are called "shield laws." However, law enforcement agencies and government have an obligation to give public information to the press.

Membership on multiple staffs may be a problem for student journalist. If a journalist is on the staff of more than one medium, that journalist should not cover the same beats if the two or more mediums are competitive and have a similar frequency of publication. Print and online publications are often competitive. The school newspaper and yearbook would not generally be competing mediums in this case. This prevents the dilemma as to which medium gets the story first.

Negative stereotyping (generalizations in stories and photos that may unjustly and negatively stereotype a population group) should be a factor for consideration as stories are edited and photos selected for publication. All aspects of reporting, from the selection of interviewees and research statistics to the content of photos, should be examined for fairness. Population groups subject to this problem are often racial, religious, sexual-orientation or ethnic minorities. For example, a story about unwed, school-age mothers should not be limited to one race or economic group, and a story about openly gay teens should not automatically include comments from nongays who disagree with homosexuality on religious grounds. In these two instances, negative stereotypes could be that only minority girls have children outside of marriage and that being gay is immoral.

News and commentary should be easily distinguishable. News and news-feature stories that include analysis should be labeled as "analysis." Opinion columns, including reviews, should be identified as opinion or commentary in some consistent way.

Ownership of work produced belongs to the publication regardless of whether the staff member is paid or not. An editor or adviser may authorize reproduction of the work in a form other than its originally intended form. The act of voluntarily joining a staff indicates acceptance of this policy.

Reporting personal details about a public person's life is an ethics consideration for a reporter and editor when the public person is associated with a newsworthy event or issue. For the sake of high school media, public persons include the school's administrators, teachers, school board members and those students who are acknowledged leaders such as a class president or the star of the school's basketball team. (See Chap. 23 for a more thorough presentation of public figures and privacy.) Public figures, including those private persons suddenly thrust into the public spotlight by an unexpected event, are open to more media scrutiny of their private lives than a private person. The journalist takes great care to report only those facts about a public person's private life that are newsworthy and relevant to the reasons why the person is a public figure. Although public figures, especially elected officials and those who are employed by public institutions, have an obligation to talk with the press, a journalist should not overly badger a public figure for an interview or photo. Repeated polite requests and reminders of the public's right to know will usually be successful.

Photo illustration and posed photos are acceptable; group poses don't need any special notice, but if action is recreated for the sake of a photo, the accompanying caption should mention that the scene was recreated.

Photos of victims of accidents, crimes and natural disasters should be monitored carefully by the editor. They have a tremendous impact on the reader. The victim's privacy may conflict with the public's right to know. It's not always easy to draw a line between sensationalism and reality and good and bad taste. Care should be taken to maintain the dignity of the persons in the photo. Why the reader should see the photo should be considered carefully before it is published.

Plagiarism (taking someone's words, art and other original work and passing it off as one's own) is prohibited and may be illegal if the source of the work is copyrighted or otherwise legally protected. For the purpose of journalism, plagiarism is further defined as word-for-word duplication of another's writing, whether it is printed on paper or electronically on the internet. It also refers to duplication of broadcasts on radio or television. Facts taken from a published source should be attributed to the source and independently verified if possible. Paraphrasing published information is acceptable, but copying the original writer's unique phrases is unacceptable. For a story, a direct quote from a live person is preferable and may have more credibility than a direct or indirect quote from another newspaper, magazine, book, web site or other published source.

Profane or vulgar words are a part of everyday conversation, right or wrong, but generally they are not used in student news media. Profane or vulgar words are not in themselves legally obscene. Use of them in student media is rare and is limited to those cases when they are judged by an editor to be essential to the full understanding of a key aspect of a story or central to a person's style of speech. The age range of the readers is a factor to be considered; use should be prohibited for publications serving readers under 14 years. Profane and vulgar words should not be used to sensationalize a story or to shock readers. For example, a story about the sale of illegal drugs, to be authentic, could include conversation and words that may be profane or vulgar

if the reporter and editor consider these words to be pivotal in the recreation of the drug sale. A story about someone saying profane or vulgar words and then being reprimanded in some way for doing so may also be a case when the words themselves are pivotal to the story. Sometimes using ellipses in place of the words draws more attention than the word itself; however, this may be an acceptable compromise. Community standards also are a factor to consider.

Sexist labels and descriptions should be eliminated from writing and replaced with neutral words. For example, the use of "ladies" to distinguish a boy's sport from a girl's should be reviewed for possible sexism and lack of parallelism; if "ladies' basketball," then it follows that "gentlemen's basketball" would be parallel. If "boys" is used, then "girls" is the preferred opposite.

Sexually explicit words that refer to body parts and functions, not vulgar or profane, should be used for accuracy and understanding in all stories about health and sexuality. Vulgar street language should not be used in place of medically acceptable terms. For example, a story about AIDS may need to include terms that have sexual overtones to make the story factually accurate and truthful.

EXERCISES

1. As a reporter for the school paper, you are assigned to cover the Student Council. You are not an elected or appointed member of the council. Should you vote in the all-school Student Council elections?

2. You are a reporter for the school newspaper. Later, you also join the school's drama club and the Young Republicans. You do not cover the activities of either of these two groups for the paper. You are asked to act in the school play and to be the vice president of the Young Republicans. Should you accept these offers and still remain on the newspaper staff?

3. The principal of your school is arrested for driving while intoxicated. Should you report the arrest in your school newspaper? The Student Council president of your school, an 18-year-old, is arrested for driving while intoxicated. Should you report the arrest in the school newspaper?

4. Two of your faculty members die in a two-week period. One dies of a heart attack and the other dies of AIDS. Should you report the causes of death in your paper?

5. As the movie reviewer for your paper, you are invited to a free screening of a new film. At the screening, the film's distributor is giving everyone a complimentary T-shirt and the soundtrack compact disk. Should you accept the invitation to the film and the accompanying promotional merchandise?

6. Planned Parenthood asks to buy ad space in your newspaper. Should you accept the ad?

7. You are the editor of your school yearbook. During the school year there is a shooting on school grounds, and three students are killed. Your student photographer has pictures of the bodies, each covered with a blanket, lying where they were shot. You report the shooting in your yearbook. Do you publish the pictures of the bodies?

8. As the newspaper editor, you hear that students under the legal drinking age are buying alcohol regularly at a local liquor store. Should you assign an underage reporter to attempt to buy liquor at the store and then write about the results of your "sting"?

9. As a reporter for the student life section of your yearbook, you decide to interview several lesbian and gay students at your school for a story about sexual orientation. You promise these students that their real names will not be used. Should you have made that promise?

10. For a story about unmarried teen mothers, you photograph a group of five teen mothers, three black and two Mexican Americans, with their babies. The mothers agree to be photographed and identified in your story and the photo caption. Your school has a minority population of 5 percent black and 25 percent Mexican American. Are there any ethical concerns for you, the reporter-photographer, regarding this story?

Student Press Law

When the authors of the U.S. Constitution and Bill of Rights were pondering the protection of individual freedoms, were free expression rights for young students debated? Did they think the student press should be uncensored? No opinions on this were recorded; it is unlikely that the subject was ever considered, although the first student newspaper in the United States, *Student Gazette*, was published in 1777 at the William Penn Charter School in Philadelphia.

Nonetheless, student journalists in the United States have some of the same free expression rights given to other journalists in the First Amendment to the U.S. Constitution. Through the years since the final ratification of the Bill of Rights, which includes the First Amendment, on Dec. 15, 1791, legislators, judges and others have defined this right in more detail. They have created laws that now govern all journalists.

What students publish in their print newspapers, yearbooks and magazines, broadcast on radio and television and post online on the internet is guided by state and federal court decisions and state and federal laws adopted since the First Amendment was accepted. These court decisions and laws affect official, school-sponsored student media. In some cases, they also affect personal media, communication that is published off-campus and not sponsored or sanctioned by a school.

However, not all student media are subject to all or the same laws. Whether the student media are published in a public or private school and where that school is located can affect the application of these laws. Media published by students off-campus and with no school support are not usually affected by some of the laws that govern media published in a public or private school.

WHERE YOU PUBLISH MAKES A DIFFERENCE

How a public school differs from a private school in some basic ways is an essential consideration for the study of the First Amendment and its application to student journalists who attend these schools and publish their student media.

- A public school is funded primarily with money from local, state and federal governments.

- A private school is funded primarily with money from individuals and nongovernmental bodies.

- Public schools must conform to government laws because they are funded with money from governments that enact these laws.

- Private schools must conform to only some government laws because they are funded mostly or wholly with nongovernmental money.

- One law that private schools do not have to enforce is to allow free expression to those who attend a private school.

- In public schools in all states and in the District of Columbia, students have limited free expression rights.

- By enrolling in a private school in all states, except California, and in the District of Columbia, students voluntarily relinquish their constitutionally protected but limited right to free expression.

- In California, students enrolled in private schools have had limited free expression rights since 1992. In that year, California passed what is known as the Leonard Law, Education Code section 94367, named after the law's primary sponsor, Senator Bill Leonard. The law prohibits private schools in California from punishing students because of "speech or other communication" that would be protected by the First Amendment if engaged in outside the high school or college campus.

- Private schools in other states and the District of Columbia may voluntarily allow free expression.

Since some private schools allow their students the same limited free expression rights as public schools, regardless of their location, the information in this chapter will be relevant and useful to all student journalists. Some laws, such as those on copyright and libel, do not distinguish between public and private school media and are applicable to both.

Some laws regarding free expression rights apply only to student journalists in specific states. So where you publish may be a factor too.

WHAT THE FIRST AMENDMENT SAYS

Constitutional scholars say that free expression rights were so important to those who founded the United States that these rights were listed for protection in the opening statement of the Bill of Rights. The denial of free expression was one reason the colonists rebelled against British rule.

This statement of free expression, the First Amendment, states: "Congress shall make no law respecting an establishment of religion, or prohibiting the free exercise thereof; or abridging the freedom of speech, or of the press, or the right of the people peaceably to assemble, and to petition the government for a redress of grievances."

Freedom to publish information and opinion was considered so important by James Madison, and others who wrote the Constitution, and George Mason, whose writing in Virginia help inspire the Bill of Rights, that the press was named as the only specific occupation receiving this special, protected status.

But this status enjoyed by the press was not to remain unlimited for long. During the more than 210 years since the adoption of the First Amendment, courts and legislative bodies have curbed press freedom. Despite these limits, even extending to high school media, the essence of the right granted in the First Amendment to the press remains a guiding principle in our society.

THE COURT SYSTEM DEFINES FREE EXPRESSION FOR JOURNALISTS

Those who granted the press in the United States its freedom also provided a constitutional mechanism for those who disagreed with the press to challenge its information-gathering methods and what it published. That mechanism is the federal court system. A state court system exists for each state and functions in a somewhat similar way to the federal court system.

If someone thinks what is published in the press is unlawful, or if someone thinks there is unlawful interference with the publication of something, that person may petition the court system to find out if the action is constitutional and legal. Public school media and public school officials, as agents of the government, must abide by the Constitution and the decisions of the courts.

The federal court system, which has decided most of the important cases in student press law, is organized in this way:

- The federal courts are divided into trial and appeals courts.

- Federal trial courts are called "district courts."

- Appeals from district courts are taken to one of 13 circuit courts (such as the U.S. Court of Appeals for the First Circuit).

- Appeals from the circuit courts are taken to the U.S. Supreme Court.

- Rulings (decisions) from one circuit court do not apply to other geographic circuit court jurisdictions.

- Rulings (decisions) by a circuit court do apply to all the district courts under its geographic jurisdiction. When lower courts must abide by rulings of a higher court, the lower courts are *following precedent*; the higher courts have *set precedent*.

A hypothetical censorship situation involving a high school student can illustrate how the federal court system works.

A public high school student in Illinois was suspended from school for distributing an alternative student newspaper, one not sanctioned by the school, on campus before the school day began. The suspended student sued the school in federal trial court for denial of his First Amendment rights. The court found that the student was denied his First Amendment rights. The school then appealed the decision to the U.S. Court of Appeals for the Seventh District (Illinois is in the seventh district). The appeals court reversed the lower court's decision and said that the school had not violated the student's First Amendment rights. The student then appealed the appeals court decision to the U.S. Supreme Court. The U.S. Supreme Court agreed to hear the appeal and decided in favor of the student. The Supreme Court's decision then became the law for all the states, setting aside the decision made by the appeals court.

If, in this hypothetical case, the U.S. Court of Appeals for the Seventh District had affirmed or agreed with the first court's decision and no further appeals were made, then this decision would become the law for those states within the seventh district, including Indiana, Wisconsin and Illinois.

Laws and actions by government, including public schools, can be challenged through the federal courts. These court decisions help interpret and form the ever-evolving body of law in the United States.

SUPREME COURT DECISIONS AND STUDENT MEDIA

With the growth and maturity of student media in the 20th and 21st centuries, disputes over content, editorial control and circulation have led some student journalists, teacher-advisers and school officials and the public into federal courts to air a grievance. Federal courts at all levels – district, circuit and the highest court, the Supreme Court – have decided cases pertaining to free expression for public school students. Many of the precedent-setting decisions have been made by the circuit court.

The U.S. Supreme Court has decided three cases directly relating to high school student expression, verbal (written and oral) and symbolic: *Tinker* (1969), *Bethel* (1986) and *Hazelwood* (1988). The *Hazelwood* case was the first one directly regarding student media, but the majority opinion by the justices mentioned other forms of student expression. Two of these three cases, *Tinker* and *Hazelwood*, have affected student media more directly than the *Bethel* case.

In deciding the *Hazelwood* (Missouri) *School District v. Kuhlmeier* case in 1988, the Supreme Court, in a majority opinion, said public school officials could censor student expression in a nonforum, school-sponsored activity, such as a student newspaper, yearbook, magazine or broadcast. To censor, the school official must present a reasonable educational justification. The Hazelwood East High School principal censored stories on teenage pregnancy and the effects of family divorce on children.

In the *Bethel* (Texas) *School District v. Fraser* case in 1986, the Supreme Court said that the First Amendment does not prohibit school officials from determining what speech in the classroom or in school assembly is inappropriate and allows school officials to discipline students for vulgar or otherwise offensive speech. The case was the result of the punishment of a student by school officials for using vulgar references and innuendoes during a school assembly.

In 1969 the Supreme Court acknowledged that high school students have First Amendment rights in its *Tinker v. Des Monies* (Iowa) *Independent Community School District* decision. The court said a student's free speech rights are protected as long as that speech does not disrupt the work of the school or the rights of other students. The school officials had punished students for wearing black armbands during school to protest the Vietnam War.

Along with some decisions made by lower courts, the *Tinker* and *Hazelwood* cases now form the basis of student press law and guidelines for public, and in some cases private, high school media.

The 1988 *Hazelwood* decision did not overrule the 1969 *Tinker* decision, but it did narrow its application in significant ways.

TINKER AND ITS LEGACY

For almost 20 years, the *Tinker* decision and some other significant lower-court cases helped high school student journalism develop a legal framework to operate under and encouraged professional standards. In 1988 the Supreme Court's *Hazelwood* ruling significantly altered that legal framework. Though its impact is diminished,

Tinker remains a basis for much of the student press law followed today, and many legal experts consider it to be the most important First Amendment case for students.

The *Tinker* case, however, didn't begin as a student media confrontation. It began when three students, one in junior high and two in high school, despite a ban by school officials, wore black armbands to school to protest the Vietnam War. Suspended from school for this action, they sued the school district, claiming a violation of their free expression rights under the First Amendment. They lost in the lower courts but won in the Supreme Court. The decision expanded free expression rights.

- The justices said that students and teachers do not lose their rights of free expression once they enter the schoolhouse door.

- Free speech by students in school is protected as long as it does not cause a "substantial disruption or a material interference with school activities."

- Students have a right to voice unpopular opinions.

- The decision applies to both junior and senior high schools.

Although *Tinker* was about symbolic speech (wearing an armband), it soon was applied to other forms of speech, including student media. The sweeping statements made by the justices in the majority opinion became the basis for a series of lower-court decisions that favored free expression for students. These lower-court decisions had limited application because of the courts' geographic structure.

LOWER COURTS APPLY *TINKER* STANDARD

One of the first lower-court applications of *Tinker* to student media was made in 1970 in *Scoville v. Joliet* (Illinois) *Township High School District Board of Education*. The Seventh Circuit Court of Appeals said that two students could not be punished for distributing an underground (alternative) paper on school grounds despite content in the paper "urging students not to accept, for delivery to parents, any propaganda issued by the school and to destroy it if accepted."

The school claimed that this statement could bring about disruption of the school. The court said that no disruption actually occurred, so the students could not be punished. The threat of disruption was not sufficient reason to deny free expression; in this case, the expression was in the form of distribution of a non-school-sponsored student newspaper.

In another post-*Tinker*, pre-*Hazelwood* decision that expanded student free expression rights – *Fujishima v. Chicago* (Illinois) *Board of Education*, 1972 – the Seventh Circuit Court of Appeals said that a principal may not review a publication prior to distribution. A school rule requiring prior approval by the principal was ruled as unconstitutional. The publication was non-school-sponsored.

Another important lower-court decision before *Hazelwood* affirmed the concept of a student publication being a public forum. In *Gambino v. Fairfax County* (Virginia) *School Board* (1977), the Circuit Court of Appeals for the Fourth District said that once a school newspaper is established as a "public forum," it cannot be censored even though the school financially supports it and the students receive academic credit. The court defined "public forum" as a publication that (1) consists of published news, student editorials and letters to the editor and (2) is distributed outside the journalism classroom.

Building upon the *Tinker* and these and other lower-court decisions, many student publications and school districts adopted three guidelines that included the central *Tinker* provision on disruption and two other areas of unprotected speech.

- Students will not publish any material that could substantially disrupt the school routine.

- Students will not publish anything that is obscene.

- Students will not publish anything that is libelous.

Under the protective blanket of the *Tinker* decision, student media at many schools have freely reported a range of topics, including school budgets, teacher contract disputes, teenage sexuality and child abuse, without prior review or censorship of any kind.

THE *HAZELWOOD* DECISION AND ITS IMPLICATIONS

Unlike *Tinker*, which was broadly about free expression and the expansion of First Amendment rights to students, the *Hazelwood* decision directly targeted school media and who controlled their content, and it limited the First Amendment rights of students.

Student journalists at Hazelwood East High School in suburban St. Louis, Mo., had written articles about a variety of topics of concern to teenagers for publication in their school newspaper. When the paper was returned from the printer, one page was missing, which included an article on teenage pregnancy and one on the effect of divorce on families. Exercising prior review, the school's principal ordered the two stories to be removed before publication. It was customary at the school for the adviser to submit the paper before publication to the principal for his approval.

The three Hazelwood East students who wrote the censored articles decided to sue the school for violating their First Amendment right of free expression. The school's principal said he censored the articles because he thought the topics were inappropriate for a high school publication and that the students interviewed in the story about teenage pregnancy, who were not named, could be identified by the readers. This happened in the spring of 1983.

In 1985, a federal district court in Missouri agreed with the principal and said that the censorship was acceptable. The court said that the newspaper was a part of the school's curriculum and not a forum. This was a significant reversal of a trend, since *Tinker*, of federal court decisions generally extending free expression rights to student journalists. But the three students appealed the decision to the next highest court.

More than three years since the censorship occurred, the Circuit Court of Appeals for the Eighth District, in July 1986, reversed the lower court's decision and found that the students' First Amendment rights had been violated by the school. The court said that although the newspaper was produced by a class, it was a forum for student expression and could not be censored.

Yet the saga was not over. Unhappy with the decision, the school district had one appeal left, to the U.S. Supreme Court. In October 1987, the Supreme Court justices heard arguments from the lawyers representing the students and the school. About three months later, Jan. 13, 1988, the Supreme Court issued its decision.

By a five to three vote, the justices found in favor of the Hazelwood School District. This far-reaching decision brought these changes:

- The Supreme Court gave school officials the right to censor student media under certain circumstances.

- Although the *Hazelwood* case was especially about a student newspaper, the decision affects all high school media, including yearbooks, magazines, radio and television broadcasts and video.

- There are two crucial aspects to the decision: (1) the definition of a school newspaper as a public forum and (2) the justification for the censorship by the school official.

- The Supreme Court decided that the Hazelwood East paper was not a public forum and therefore not protected by the *Tinker* decision.

- In calling the Hazelwood paper school sponsored and not a public forum, the court gave three criteria to determine if a school publication is school sponsored: (1) Is the work supervised by a faculty member? (2) Is the publication designed to impart particular skills or knowledge to student participants or audiences? (3) Does the publication use the school's name or resources?

- If the answer is yes to any of these questions, then the publication is considered school sponsored and may not be protected under the First Amendment and *Tinker* guidelines. Clearly, the public forum notion was narrowly defined, if not severely impeded, by the Supreme Court.

- Whether a school publication is produced as a credit-bearing class, or an extracurricular activity, does not matter in the public forum consideration under *Hazelwood*.

- The Supreme Court said that the Hazelwood East High School adviser acted as the final authority in almost every aspect of the production, including content. There was no written policy stating that the paper was a forum. These two points led the court to decide that the Hazelwood paper was not a public forum.

- Censorship may not be allowed under the *Hazelwood* guidelines if the student publication is a public forum. One of the strongest determining factors is an official policy statement by the school designating the publication as a public forum and giving student editors final authority on content. In these cases the broader *Tinker* guidelines apply.

- Although censorship by school officials was permitted by the court with the *Hazelwood* decision, it is not required. School officials may choose not to exercise this right.

- Although prior review of a school-sponsored publication by the school administration is permitted without written guidelines under the *Hazelwood* decision, it undermines the authority of the editor and publication adviser. Prior review threatens a publication's credibility as a reliable news source, its ability to serve as a watchdog of those in charge of the school and its overall independence. Even though it is permitted, authorities such as the Student Press Law Center say it is unwise to exercise it.

- If a school official decides to censor student media, the official must be able to prove that the censorship "reasonably relates to legitimate pedagogical (educational) concerns."

- The school official who censors student media has the burden of demonstrating that the standards set by the Supreme Court under *Hazelwood* have been met.

- The Supreme Court gave some examples of content that could be censored: (1) material that is ungrammatical, poorly written, inadequately researched, biased or prejudiced, vulgar or profane, or unsuitable for immature audiences; (2) topics such as "the existence of Santa Claus in an elementary school setting, the particulars of teenage sexual activity in a high school setting, speech that might reasonably be perceived to advocate drug or alcohol use, irresponsible sex, or conduct otherwise inconsistent with the shared values of a civilized social order"; and (3) material that would "associate the school with anything other than neutrality on matters of political controversy."

- The Supreme Court also said that a school official may review nonforum, school-sponsored publications before they are printed.

Although the *Hazelwood* decision substantially limited the free expression rights of student journalists at many public high schools and narrowed the application of *Tinker*, the *Tinker* decision is still law for those student publications that are officially designated by school officials as public forums and those alternative, nonschool student publications, print and online.

POST-*HAZELWOOD* COURT DECISIONS

Since the Supreme Court's *Hazelwood* decision in 1988, several lower federal courts and state courts have decided cases that affect high school media in certain states and, to some extent, curbed the reach of the 1988 landmark case.

The first post-*Hazelwood* decision came quickly. In the same year as the Supreme Court's decision, the Ninth Circuit Court ruled, in *Burch v. Barker*, that a school policy requiring students to submit a non-school-sponsored publication to school officials for review prior to distribution was unconstitutional.

Although this decision was made in 1988, it originated in 1983. Five students from Lindbergh High School (Renton, Wash.) were reprimanded by school officials for distributing an alternative publication at a class picnic. The students sued, claiming the school violated their First Amendment rights. Nearly four years later, in 1987, a federal district court in Washington ruled in favor of the school officials.

The students appealed the decision, and the higher court reversed the lower court's decision and found in favor of the students.

The *Burch v. Barker* decision, a victory for independent, non-school-sponsored media, applies to all public schools within the Ninth District, including Alaska, Arizona, California, Hawaii, Montana, Nevada, Oregon and Washington.

In 1989, two federal courts told two high schools to what extent they could apply the *Hazelwood* decision. A Connecticut court ruled, in *Lodestar v. Board of Education*, that a school could not censor a student literary magazine because the magazine had a history of independence and was not primarily a school activity designed by school officials. In neighboring New York state, another court said, in *Romano v. Harrington*, that a paper produced after school hours and not in a credit-bearing class had more freedom to comment editorially than a paper produced during school hours in a credit-bearing class. The New York school had fired its newspaper adviser after the paper published an editorial disapproving of the then-proposed national holiday commemorating the birth of the Rev. Martin Luther King Jr. The adviser sued, claiming a violation of First Amendment rights.

In a case that originated in 1989 but wasn't decided finally until 1994, *Desilets v. Clearview Regional Board of Education*, the New Jersey Supreme Court affirmed a junior high school reporter's right to publish a review of two R-rated movies.

Reporter Drien Desilets wrote reviews of *Mississippi Burning* and *Rainman* for his junior high paper, *Pioneer Press*. In his articles, he recommended the movies, but he didn't include any dialogue or profanities from the movies. The school's principal, exercising prior review before publication, deleted the reviews from the paper and said he objected to the subject matter of the films, not the content of the reviews. Later, a lawyer arguing in court for the school district said the reviews violated the district's policies against material "believed to constitute a danger to student health."

In ruling in favor of the student, the highest state court in New Jersey said, "the R-rated movie reviews in this case do not appear to raise educational concerns that call for the kinds of editorial control exemplified by the (U.S.) Supreme Court in Hazelwood."

While Drien Desilets was fighting for his free expression rights, students at a public school in Massachusetts became involved with a would-be advertiser in a content dispute that would lead to a Supreme Court ruling four years later.

In 1994, Douglas Yeo, a community activist in Lexington, sued the Lexington School Board after student editors of the Lexington High School newspaper and yearbook refused to publish his paid advertisement encouraging sexual abstinence. The school had enacted a condom distribution policy in 1992, and Yeo had tried to place the ad since then. The students said it was their policy to not run ads of a political nature. The school allowed the students to make content decisions regarding their publications, including the placement of paid advertising.

Yeo said his First Amendment right of free expression and his Fourteenth Amendment right to equal protection had been violated by the refusal to run the ad. Yeo claimed that the paper and yearbook are government publications because they are published at a government-supported public school.

The school and students won the first round in the district court, which said that not the school but the students, who are not considered agents of the state, were responsible for the paper's content and could refuse to publish an ad. Yeo appealed the decision to the First District Court of Appeals.

The First District Court reversed the lower court's decision and found that the two student publications were government publications and the student journalists were state actors. It based its decision, in part, on the fact that both publications carried the name of the school. Yeo won this time, but his victory proved to be temporary.

Backed by support from the National School Board Association, the Student Press Law Center and others, the school's attorneys asked for and were granted a rehearing of the case by the appeals court. The court also withdrew its decision. Following the rehearing, the appeals court justices said that students were not agents of the state after all because decisions made by the students are not attributable to the school. "As a matter of law," said the justices, "we see no legal duty here on the part of school administrators to control the content of the editorial judgments of student editors of publications."

Yeo then asked the U.S. Supreme Court to review the First District's decision. In fall 1998, the Supreme Court declined this request. The decision by the First District justices stands as law. Student journalists at Lexington High School and at public schools in the First District now have the freedom to establish their own advertising policies, refusing those they find objectionable.

In 2004, a former high school journalist from Michigan won a censorship case in a U.S. District Court; the decision also curbed the reach of the *Hazelwood* decision for some students.

Utica (Mich.) High School reporter and editor Katy Dean wrote a story in 2002 for the school's newspaper about the claim of a Utica resident that fumes from idling school buses contributed to his lung cancer. A school administrator ordered her story to be removed from the paper before it was published. Dean protested at this form of censorship and eventually sued the school district for loss of her free expression rights. Two years later, she won her case. The court ruled that Dean's story should be published in the school paper and an acknowledgment by the school's administration that the story was unfairly censored should accompany it.

The judge in the Dean case said that the Utica paper was a limited public forum and that management of the paper lies in the students' hands. He further said the censorship was "indefensible."

The decisions in the Dean and Yeo cases show that the *Hazelwood* standards don't thwart free expression rights everywhere and in all situations.

PUBLISHING ON THE INTERNET

Law governing what is published on the internet is evolving almost as rapidly as the technology used in this form of communication. Publishing on the internet is, in some ways, no different than publishing through more long-established means, especially print. Generally, laws that apply to student journalists who publish print newspapers, yearbooks and magazines apply to those who publish online versions of these same publications or new ones that don't exist first in print. As is the case with print media, where and when an online "publication" is produced does make a difference regarding the application of some of these laws. Even the reporting and information-gathering process, if the internet is involved, may also be governed by certain laws.

If the online publication is produced at a public school during school hours with the school's computers, and it is entered onto the school's server as its host web site, then it is generally governed by the *Hazelwood* standards and subsequent lower-court decisions. The question regarding whether the online web site is a public forum may be a determining factor in the extent of the application of *Hazelwood* standards. If a site is established as an open forum through a written policy by school officials, then content is controlled by the students. If there is no history of the web site being an open forum, then it is subject to potential prior review and censorship by school officials.

Regardless of the status of the web site as an open forum, libel, privacy, obscenity and copyright laws apply to the work that is posted online. Regarding these four areas of press law, online writing, art, photography, sound and video should be treated as if they were printed. For now, libel laws that apply to publishing something in print will apply to something that is published on the internet on a web site or posted as a public email message. Students should be aware that the act of publishing on the internet can be as simple as clicking the "send" button on a computer monitor screen. Even though the school may be the internet provider, it is the students who are legally responsible for the published internet work if the school does not involve itself in the editorial process.

Web sites and email may or may not be a reliable, accurate source of information for a story. A second online or "human," in-person contact may be necessary to check facts. Letters to the editor arriving by email should be verified with a follow-up phone call because

the paper is legally responsible for whatever it publishes, even a nonstaff person's writing.

Reporters who seek opinions and information for stories from others in internet chat rooms and through email should identify themselves as journalists and tell those whom they talk with that their responses may be published. This is good ethics and protects the sources' right to privacy.

Facts and opinions taken from the internet and used in a story should be attributed to the internet source just as facts and opinions from in-person interviews and other traditional sources are attributed by the reporter.

Some schools have restricted school-sponsored online publications in various ways that are different from restrictions placed on print media at the same school. These restrictions have included the removal of last names from persons mentioned in all stories and the prohibition of photos of students who could be identified. The most common reason given for these restrictions is to protect the students from nonschool predators; the distribution of print publications is more restricted. Opponents of these restrictions say that the elimination of last names and photos strips the online publication of much of its news value.

Using the internet at school to gather information for print and online stories is also subject to emerging legal restrictions. In an attempt to limit access to web sites that contain material that some find objectionable, some schools have placed filtering software on their computers to block a student from reaching the objectionable sites. Critics of this say that the filtering often blocks students from legitimate educational sites that may contain some of the same words or phrases used in the objectionable sites but the words are used in a much different context. A student reporter, for example, who may be researching on the internet a story about breast cancer may be blocked by a filtering system from access to all sites that contain the word "breast."

Federal, state and local governments have also dealt with internet content and access. The federal government enacted laws that attempted to control access to web sites, particularly in public schools and libraries, considered objectionable to minors due to the sites' explicit sexual nature. It also enacted laws that punish those who knowingly provide objectionable material to minors over the internet. Opponents of these laws claim that the internet is protected by the First Amendment and that its global scope makes it difficult to control. So far, courts have said governments must not restrict the content on the internet, but that could change.

Since laws that govern media differ from country to country, which country's laws apply when the information is on the global internet? That question remains to be answered. There are troublesome issues, such as who can be sued for libel if someone from one country claims she was defamed by someone from another country in an online chat room? Is the internet provider, the host of the chat room, liable and the "publisher" in this case? Do the libel laws of the country where the libelous remark was read apply, or where the libelous remark was typed on a keyboard and sent out onto the internet? Courts around the world will likely wrestle with these problems for years.

OTHER WAYS TO EXTEND FREE EXPRESSION RIGHTS TO STUDENTS

Even though the *Hazelwood* decision hampered the free expression of public school students, there are ways other than the federal court system to protect student First Amendment rights. Laws and educational codes at the state level can lessen or nullify the effects of *Hazelwood*.

California's Education Code Section 48907 is an example of state-level legal protection for students. It reads:

> Students of the public schools shall have the right to exercise freedom of speech and of the press including, but not limited to, the use of bulletin boards, the distribution of printed material or petitions, the wearing of buttons, badges, and other insignia, and the right of expression in official publications, whether or not such publications or other means of expression are supported financially by the school or by the use of school facilities, except that expression shall be prohibited which is obscene, libelous, or slanderous. Also prohibited shall be material which so incites students as to create a clear and present danger of the commission of unlawful acts on school premises or the violation of lawful school regulations or the substantial disruption of the orderly operation of the school.

Passed in 1976, the California code is similar to the standards of student press conduct following the *Tinker* Supreme Court decision. Despite the subsequent *Hazelwood* decision in 1988, the code remains in effect.

Massachusetts became the first state since *Hazelwood* to pass a law protecting "the rights of students to freedom of expression in the public schools as long as it does not cause any disruption or disorder." The law also protects school officials from civil or criminal action for any statement made or published by students. The law, Sections 82 and 86 of Chapter 71 of the General Laws of Massachusetts, was enacted in 1988.

In the Massachusetts law, it is important to note the protection given to school officials. Some school officials in other states support editorial control of student media by a school official as protection against libel and other claims made against the publication or the school. However, legal experts, including those at the Student Press Law Center, say that if school officials do not control the editorial content of the student publication, then it is unlikely they or the school could be sued successfully for libel or other illegal content.

Since 1989, Arkansas, Colorado, Iowa and Kansas have passed laws protecting student expression similar to the ones in California and Massachusetts. First Amendment advocates in other states have attempted to get their state governments to follow suit, but so far they haven't been successful.

Some school districts have adopted policy guidelines giving First Amendment rights to students under their jurisdiction. In Dade County, Fla., the public schools have a policy that follows the *Tinker* guidelines. It prohibits three unprotected areas of speech: (1) libel, (2) obscenity and (3) expression that causes substantial disruption. Despite some challenges, the Dade officials have reaffirmed these guidelines since the 1988 *Hazelwood* decision.

The Student Press Law Center has written standard policy guidelines and model legislation. Student journalists and advisers in school districts with no student media policy guidelines may want to work with their school administrators to adopt the Student Press Law Center's guidelines for student media.

UNPROTECTED EXPRESSION: LIBEL AND OBSCENITY

Even if there had never been the *Tinker* and *Hazelwood* Supreme Court decisions, there are some things all

How to Protect Yourself from a Potential Libel Claim

- Know your sources. Are they trustworthy?
- Don't publish information from a source who won't reveal his or her name even to you, the reporter.
- If you think the information from the source is controversial or may be doubted by others, ask the source if the information is true.
- Carefully separate fact from opinion. Don't report allegations as facts and attribute all opinion.
- Take good notes. Don't rely on memory.
- If the source has documents regarding the subject, ask to see them and then compare them to what the source said in the interview.
- Review complex and potentially troublesome stories with editors.
- Verify information with a second source (or more) for complex stories.
- If you have any doubts about the truthfulness of a statement, particularly one that may be derogatory about another person, don't publish it.
- Avoid personal "attack" stories. Deal with criticism of someone's performance as part of a story that deals with the underlying issue.
- Publish corrections and retractions if you find out after publication that something you wrote is not true.
- Once a story is published, answer all complaints politely and as soon as possible.
- Know the law.
- Ask your publication's adviser for advice.

journalists, including students, cannot publish. These fall into the broad category of unprotected speech and include libel and obscenity. A third, as defined by the *Tinker* decision and pertaining to public school students, is any expression that substantially disrupts the order of the school.

Libel is printed communication – words, photographs or artwork – that exposes a person to shame, public hatred, ridicule or disgrace, damaging a person's reputation in the community or injuring the person's livelihood. For libel to occur, four conditions must exist:

- The communication was published, in that it was given to at least a third party.
- The person(s) supposedly libeled can be identified.
- Injury or damage to reputation has occurred.
- The publisher (editor, writer, photographer, artist) knew the communication was erroneous and was negligent.

Provable truth is the best and only absolute defense against libel. Even if damage has occurred, if the communication is provably true, no libel would exist. Believing something is true without evidence is insufficient.

A publication, print or online, is legally responsible for any libelous communication it publishes, even in third-party letters to the editor, advertisements and quotes from sources.

Privilege is a second defense against libel. Reporters can publish fair and accurate accounts of official proceedings, such as school board meetings and court proceedings, and reports, such as court records, without being overly concerned about libel. Although accuracy is always expected, the reporter does not have to verify the accuracy in such proceedings and reports.

For example, if at a school board meeting that is open to the public a teacher is accused of falsifying credentials, the accusation can be published even if later the accusation is proved incorrect. For fairness and as a matter of good journalism ethics, the publication would be obliged to print the correction or an updated story.

A third defense against libel is the *public official, public figure* rule. If a person is designated as a public official or public figure, actual malice in publishing a story would have to be proved. The person bringing the legal action against a reporter, for example, would have to prove that the false and damaging statement was published with knowledge that the statement was false or with reckless disregard as to whether it was false or not.

Distinguishing between public and private officials and figures is an important factor in determining a defense against a libel claim. A *public official* is a person who has or appears to have a substantial responsibility for or control over the conduct of government affairs. Public school principals, superintendents and school board members are public officials. In some jurisdictions, teachers are public officials.

Public figures are those persons who voluntarily thrust themselves into the public limelight due to personal achievement or who have attempted to influence the resolution of a public controversy. A public figure is, for example, a student who voluntarily runs for student government office or a student's parent who circulates a petition to ban certain books from the school library.

It is not easy to determine the status of a person as a public figure. Likewise, it is difficult for the plaintiff (the complaining party) in a libel case to prove actual malice by the reporter.

A fourth defense against a libel suit is the *fair comment* rule. A reporter and others in journalism are allowed to express an opinion about a matter of public interest. Some examples of this are reviews of movies, television, music, plays, concerts, restaurants, athletic contests and the performance in office of elected officials. For a journalist to successfully use fair comment as a defense, there must be real public interest in the matter, and it must be an opinion, not an allegation of fact. Also, the opinion must be based on certain facts that must be stated. Satire generally is not libelous providing it is clear to the audience that it is a satire and should not be understood as serious fact.

Although no cases have been fully prosecuted in the courts in the United States, students under the age of 18 may be sued for libel. The reporter, photographer or artist may be sued, as well as the editor for approving the work. The school may or may not be held accountable, depending on state laws.

Essentially, obscenity is hardcore pornography, and it arouses sexual feelings through its explicit and graphic depiction of sexual activity. However, the courts have said that vulgarities, four-letter profanities and material that is offensive or in poor taste are not legally obscene. The Supreme Court also said that material that is not obscene for adults could be obscene for those under 18 years old, but it still must meet the 1973 standards (content must not be libelous or obscene or cause significant disruption in the school).

As defined by the Supreme Court's *Tinker* decision, the third area of unprotected speech for high school students is any material that would substantially disrupt regular school activities. The Supreme Court said a threat or potential disruption is not a sufficient reason to censor a publication. The burden is on the school official to prove substantial disruption.

For high school journalists, the material in question should be considered within the context of the story. For example, a story about sexually transmitted diseases may need to include description and words of a sexual nature. This type of story requires explicit, clinically acceptable language that some may consider offensive or inappropriate for a teenage audience. However, these words and descriptions would not be considered obscene by the Supreme Court's standards.

Although vulgarities and profanities are not obscene, most journalists refrain from using them in their work unless they are intrinsic to the accuracy and completeness of the story. Although these words may be a part of everyday conversation, they are seldom used in published journalism.

COPYRIGHT AND STUDENT JOURNALISM

Journalists, including those who work in art and design, can look at copyright law in two ways: It protects their original work from unauthorized use by others, and it reminds them as they are creating their work that they cannot use work done by someone else without permission from the creator. Although this is simply stated, in practice it may not seem this obvious or easy to follow.

All material is automatically copyrighted once it is produced, even without a formal registration of the copyright. A copyright can be indicated in these ways: ©, *copr.* or the complete word *copyright* plus the name of the copyright holder and the year the work was first published.

How to Protect Yourself from a Potential Obscenity Claim

Obscenity is another type of unprotected speech in the United States. Obscenity was defined by the U.S. Supreme Court in *Miller v. State of California* in 1973. To be legally obscene, material must meet all three of these criteria:

- Whether the average person applying contemporary community standards would find that the work, taken as a whole, appeals to the prurient interest
- Whether the work depicts or describes in a potentially offensive way sexual conduct as defined by state law
- Whether the work, taken as a whole, lacks serious literary, artistic, political or scientific value

Almost all creative works can be copyrighted, including newspapers, yearbooks, magazines, photographs, ads, plays, CD-ROMs and sound recordings. News or facts cannot be copyrighted, but the collection of those facts into a news story can be copyrighted.

To register a copyright in the United States, a form can be requested from Information and Publications Section LM-455, Copyright Office, Library of Congress, Washington, D.C. 20599. Or a copyright can be registered online at http://lcweb.loc.gov/copyright/. The cost to register a copyright in 2000 was $30.

No copyrighted material may be reprinted or republished in a nonprint form without the approval of the copyright holder unless it is done under the "fair use" exception granted by law. Part of a copyrighted work may be reproduced without permission under the "fair use" law if:

- The use is for a nonprofit, educational purpose.

- It doesn't affect the potential sales market of the original work.

- It doesn't reproduce a substantial portion of the work (regardless of the length of the work).

Writers can use excerpts from books, magazines, plays, music or similar works to review the works or to use as supporting material in an opinion column, editorial or story. As a matter of ethics, the author or creator should be cited.

Work found on internet web sites is protected by copyright laws. Art, video, photographs and music have the same copyright protection as stories, and journalists should respect the creator's ownership. Artwork and photographs shouldn't be copied from other published sources and used in yearbooks or other student media without the permission of the copyright holder.

Unless a specific contract exists between the creator of the work and an employer, and unless the creator is a paid employee, the employer owns the copyright for the work. In some circumstances, especially in a freelance or school setting, the creator gives the employer one-time use of the work but retains ownership.

PRIVACY RIGHTS AND JOURNALISTS

Journalists are sometimes torn between what they see as the public's right to know and an individual's right to protect his or her privacy. This conflict isn't inherent in every news story, but when it does become a problem, there are some ethical standards and laws that guide journalists and those under scrutiny.

States have laws respecting the right of privacy for all persons. The right to be left alone is not, however, absolute. Public figures – a president, film actor, musician, superintendent of schools, school principal – have a limited right to privacy. A private person who is thrust into the spotlight because of involvement in a newsworthy event may also lose the right to privacy.

One form of invasion of privacy is intrusion into a person's solitude or into his or her private area activities. Intrusion can be the use of sound recorders, cameras and other physical news-gathering devices.

A second form of invasion of privacy is the publication of private facts about a person that would be offensive to a reasonable person and of no legitimate concern of the public. Publishing private and sensational information about a person's health, sexual activity or economic condition is an example of this form of invasion.

Reporting news events that occur in public is not an invasion of privacy. Information from public records, such as birth and death certificates, police reports and judicial proceedings, may be used by reporters. However, the newsworthiness of facts about a private person should be judged in these ways:

- The social value of the information.

- How deeply the facts intrude into the person's private activities.

- The extent to which the person voluntarily assumed a position of public notice.

The passage of time may also affect the newsworthiness of a fact. If private and sensational facts about a formerly public figure who is now a private person are reported, an invasion of privacy claim may be justifiable.

The third type of invasion of privacy is the publication of information about a person that is false or places the person in a *false light* (the person would be regarded incorrectly by the public). The information must be highly offensive to a reasonable person and published with knowledge or a reckless disregard of whether the facts are false or would put the person in a false light. An example of this type of invasion of privacy would be the inclusion of such information in a photo caption that accompanies a photo of a person, thus making something untrue appear to be true.

The last type of invasion of privacy is *misappropriation*, which is the use of a person's name, likeness or endorsement without the person's consent – often to sell a product. Student journalists are encouraged to get the written consent of any person whose name or likeness appears in an ad. If the person is a minor, parental consent may be necessary, depending on state law.

ACCESS TO PUBLIC MEETINGS AND PUBLIC RECORDS

Records of official government proceedings on the local, state and federal levels are important information sources for reporters. Every state, the District of Columbia and the federal government have *freedom of information laws*, allowing all citizens access to a vast amount of information. Individual state laws vary, and there are some restrictions on just exactly what information can be made public.

Information in all sorts of forms – paper, computer files and video- and audiotape – is accessible according to these state and federal laws. Access to these records may not be automatic and instantaneous, due to variations in the laws. In many cases, a reporter has to apply to the agency in writing to receive the information.

Unfortunately for reporters, the states and the federal government do not maintain a central location or one controlling agency for all government records. Each agency maintains its own, so a reporter must learn what agency has what kinds of information. On the local level, the location of records is fairly obvious. Minutes of a school board meeting are kept at the school board office. Records of police arrests are kept at the police department or county courthouse.

The process is more complicated on the state and federal levels. Beginning reporters must learn how the state and federal governments operate in order to submit requests for information to the correct agency.

Reporters usually have to pay for copies of these records. Some states and the federal government may waive these fees if the reporter's work will benefit the public. The reporter has to request the fee waivers.

Governments at all levels place some restrictions on the kinds of information that can be made public. These restrictions are exemptions in the freedom of information laws. Restricted information includes some medical, personnel and law enforcement files; student school records; and library circulation records. On the federal level, exemptions for national security reasons are noteworthy. Exemptions vary by state.

Reporters must learn the freedom of information laws in each state in which they work, as well as those of the federal government.

Student reporters should ask their state's attorney general's office for clarification on the use of state freedom of information laws by those under 18 years of age.

If a reporter has difficulty obtaining information despite the freedom of information laws, other legal and more direct means sometimes are available, including in-person and telephone interviews with those involved in the government proceeding.

Open meetings laws (sometimes called *sunshine laws*) are related to freedom of information laws. All states, the District of Columbia and the federal government have these laws. In general, open meetings laws require certain government agencies to open their meetings to the public. Reporters who cover government proceedings in person rely on these open meetings laws to allow them to gather information.

States and the federal government place some restrictions on public access to meetings, but a closed meeting that excludes reporters is the exception. The underlying idea is that government should operate in the sunshine (thus the term *sunshine laws*).

Some examples of *closed* or *secret meetings* (also called *executive sessions*) include personnel actions, such as hiring and firing employees; legal discussions with attorneys about impending actions; and labor union negotiations. For example, a reporter may not be allowed to be present when a teacher union negotiates with the school board for a new contract. Government agencies are usually required to announce meetings and agendas in advance, even for emergency sessions. Thus a reporter can anticipate news coverage.

Student reporters should consider school board, city council and other local government meetings as good opportunities to cover news events firsthand. The open meetings laws give them access to these proceedings. If possible, student reporters covering government groups for the first time should call officials of the groups in advance to introduce themselves and to get any agendas and other instructions available to the media. Press credentials may also be required.

WHERE TO GET LEGAL ADVICE

For legal advice, often at no cost, student journalists and advisers can turn to various local, state and national organizations. One of these groups, the Student Press Law Center (SPLC), is the only national organization serving exclusively as an advocate of student First Amendment, free expression rights.

The SPLC answers questions about the laws governing student media, ethics and concerns about publication policies. With its staff lawyers or through its legal referral network of lawyers who donate their time to students and teachers throughout the United States, the SPLC also gives legal advice on censorship and other First Amendment issues. (The address for the SPLC is included in this book's "Professional and Student Organizations" – see p. 395.)

State civil liberties unions may be contacted for support in First Amendment controversies. Their local addresses can be found in the phone book or with the help of a librarian in smaller cities or rural areas. These state groups and their national parent group, the American Civil Liberties Union, also have sites on the internet's World Wide Web.

Many large commercial newspapers maintain legal counsel who specialize in press law. A reporter or editor of such a paper may be contacted for help.

Colleges and universities with journalism programs often have a professor who specializes in press law. That person could be a source of help with media-related law questions and First Amendment issues.

CASES CITED IN THIS CHAPTER

Bethel School District v. Fraser, U.S. Supreme Court, 1986.

Burch v. Barker, U.S. Court of Appeals for the Ninth Circuit, 1988.

Dean v. Utica Community Schools, U.S. District Court, Mich., 2004.

Desilets v. Clearview Regional Board of Education, New Jersey Supreme Court, 647, A.2d. 150 (NJ, 1994).

Fujishima v. Chicago Board of Education, U.S. Court of Appeals for the Seventh Circuit, 1972.

Gambino v. Fairfax County School Board, U.S. Court of Appeals for the Fourth Circuit, 1977.

Hazelwood School District v. Kuhlmeier, U.S. Supreme Court, 1988.

Lodestar v. Board of Education, U.S. District Court, Conn., 1989.

Romano v. Harrington, ED-NY, 1989.

Scoville v. Joliet Township High School District Board of Education, U.S. Court of Appeals for the Seventh District, 1970.

Tinker v. Des Moines Independent Community School District, U.S. Supreme Court, 1969.

Yeo v. Town of Lexington, U.S. Court of Appeals for the First Circuit, 1997.

EXERCISES

1. What are the Freedom of Information (FOI) laws in your state? Consult your librarian or do an internet search. There may be a Freedom of Information Commission in your state. Your state attorney general's office may also help. The Society of Professional Journalists also maintains a database on all state FOI laws. How would you use the law to help you get information about someone arrested in your city for a drunk-driving accident or to find out all the bidders and their bids for the purchase of new school vans for your school district?

2. Has anyone in your state within the last 10 years filed a libel suit against the media? Report the specifics and the resolution of up to three instances. Consult your librarian or a lawyer or do an internet search. Briefly discuss if your student publication could be sued for libel and what you would do to resolve the conflict.

3. Name the justices on the U.S. Supreme Court. Did any members of the present court vote on the *Hazelwood* case in 1988? If any did, how did they vote? Who selects the justices, and how long do they serve on the court?

4. As a class, discuss this question: Under what circumstances could a private person become a public figure with regard to libel laws and privacy concerns? Is the daughter of a U.S. president a

public figure? Is your school's football coach a public figure? Is a person who is wounded in a robbery a public figure?

5. If a juvenile in your school is charged with a crime, can your student newspaper print the name of that student? Discuss the legal and ethical issues involved.

6. Can you reprint in your yearbook or newspaper a Jim Davis "Garfield" comic strip? Can you use the "Garfield" character as a stand-alone figure?

7. As a class project, conduct a First Amendment petition drive. Reprint the First Amendment with the heading "Ballot Initiative" on it and ask a random mix of persons in a public area, such as in front of a shopping mall, if they support the statement and would sign your petition to get it on the ballot in the next general election. Keep track of those who read it but decline to sign the petition or say they don't support it. Discuss the implications of your findings.

Careers in Media

Few high school athletes will ever play professional sports. Few high school band members will ever appear on stage at Carnegie Hall later in life. Few high school drama students will ever appear on Broadway stages. But student journalists can not only earn money for their work in high school and in college but can pursue many opportunities for careers after high school.

In addition to learning tangible skills that can be used later in life, high school journalists also develop strong skills in critical thinking, logic and organization and interviewing. According to research that appeared in a 1994 study of high school journalists entitled *Journalism Kids Do Better*, authors Jack Dvorak, Larry Lain and Tom Dickson found proof that journalism skills pay off for students. Among the study's findings: Journalism kids do better in 10 of 12 major academic areas; journalism kids write better in 17 of 20 comparisons of collegiate writing; journalism kids value high school journalism more highly than required English courses in fulfilling major language arts competencies; and finally, journalism kids are "doers" in schools. They are more involved in cocurricular and community activities.

Students who become editors and managers of their publications develop critical leadership and people skills that will definitely help them later in life. High school publications provide a strong sense of accomplishment for the individuals working on them since they are seen by a large community of people in and outside the school. With the growth of online publications, that audience continues to grow. Student journalists can win individual and staff awards for their work and can even earn college scholarships. Once in college, former high school journalists can use their portfolios of work to get paid positions on college publications even if they aren't pursuing journalism as a career.

The skills learned on high school publications will prove valuable in other ways. Desktop-publishing skills will help students produce more polished presentations for class work. Photographic skills will improve even family snapshots. Advertising skills will arm students with persuasive arguments and marketing skills. Writers will be able to research, write coherent and well-organized papers and quickly compose their thoughts. Designers will be desirable volunteers for school or community organizations in need of brochures or flyers for projects.

In addition to working for school publications, many students seize opportunities to expand their portfolios by contributing to community newspapers, teen sections and school public relations offices.

In the last few years, many professional newspapers have started teen sections and have begun training programs or internship programs for students who are interested in journalism careers (Fig. 24.1). Although few pay the student writers who become correspondents for these sections, student journalists can improve their skills and build their portfolios with contributions to these sections. The sections are published frequently, often weekly. Students can usually find time to work on both the teen sections and their own student publications if they have good organizational skills.

Fig. 24.1. The *Chicago Tribune* publishes "Red Eye," a special tabloid edition each weekday aimed at younger readers, many of whom are reading the paper while commuting to work on public transportation. In addition to providing traditional news and sports coverage, the publication includes entertainment news and calendars of events of interest to its young audience. *Chicago Tribune* Publishing Company, Chicago, Ill.

Teen section reporting often gives students opportunities to report and photograph events of broad interest. The newspaper may even send the student reporters and photographers to professional events, giving them opportunities to write stories and use photographs in both the teen section and their own publication. Another advantage of working on community publications is they allow students to interact with professionals. Not only will students improve their journalism skills by working with professionals but they will also get the chance to ask questions about careers in media and find out the paths these professionals took to get their media jobs.

Small- or medium-size community newspapers often hire students as "stringers," particularly in sports departments. Stringers are writers or photographers who periodically contribute stories or photographs to a publication. Stringing for a newspaper during high school can result in forming relationships that could lead to paid internships during summers away from college or during holiday periods or to permanent positions after college.

Many students choose to work for more than one student publication during high school to expand their skills. Writing for both the yearbook and the newspaper, or photographing for both publications, gives students the chance to have more of their work published and to hone their skills. Or students may prefer to contribute different skills to separate publications, broadening their abilities and giving them an opportunity to see where their interests develop.

Almost all school districts have public relations offices and other publications' offices. For instance, the athletic director's office may be in charge of publishing a football program or other sports publications. The school's public relations director may publish a newsletter mailed to parents or may maintain a web site for the school district. Or, each high school's principal may publish periodic information sent to parents. These publications provide opportunities for students who can often earn internship or local credit. If credit isn't possible, students can still gain published examples for their portfolios.

AFTER HIGH SCHOOL

Countless opportunities abound for working on college publications. Yearbooks, magazines, newspapers, online publications, college and department publications offices – all will provide students with opportunities to pursue their interests in media careers. Many college publications offer paid positions on their staffs or provide a certain amount of money per article or photograph used in the publications. Working on college publications offers opportunities to cover interesting speakers, well-known entertainers, competitive sporting events and breaking news.

Majoring in journalism or media-related careers will provide students with the training they need to prepare for professional jobs. Large colleges of communications or journalism schools will enable students to choose between different areas of communications as majors. Within these majors, specific career skills are available. For instance, in some schools advertising majors can choose between tracks in creative advertising or advertising management. Advertising management jobs prepare students for careers as account managers or media buyers. Creative advertising skills will prepare students for jobs as creative directors or art directors.

Working on college publications is rarely required, even when a student is majoring in communications. Students who choose to supplement their classroom education with hands-on work on college publications will find more opportunities for summer internships and job positions after college. College publications also provide leadership training in staff management. Membership in college press associations provides opportunities for winning awards and recognition and sometimes cash prizes. These associations also host annual national conventions where students can expand their knowledge and create liaisons with professionals.

Student chapters of professional press associations create connections with professionals and offer interesting discussions of topics journalists face in the real world such as ethics and job hunting. They can also offer opportunities for internships and awards. The National Press Photographers Association offers a student competition called College Photographer of the Year. The winner of the competition receives an internship and prizes. The William Randolph Hearst student competition offers students in accredited journalism schools a wide range of contests from writing to photography categories that provide cash prizes and recognition for winners. The Society of Professional Journalists recognizes outstanding student chapters and college publications.

Students preparing for careers in media need good portfolios of published work to show prospective employers for internships and jobs after college. The portfolio can be compiled of work published in college publications, as well as work published during intern-

ships or other professional opportunities. Almost all media organizations offer formalized internship programs in various areas from advertising and editing to photography. Competitive internship programs have early deadlines, usually near the end of the fall semester, for students to complete the application process. College students often do two or more internships during college, some for college credit or for pay. Colleges often require students to obtain junior standing in school before completing an internship for credit. This ensures the students will have taken the basic courses in their field of study so they will be prepared for the work they will be asked to do in the internship. Starting out at smaller media organizations is a good way to get an initial internship. Many students complete a second internship at medium- to large-sized media organizations.

As newsrooms seek to diversify their staffs and do a better job of representing the voices of their diverse communities, they provide many opportunities for minority students interested in media careers. The Poynter Institute for Media Studies in St. Petersburg, Fla., offers several competitive minority programs, including one in design. Syracuse University in conjunction with the Newhouse Foundation offers a minority fellowship for graduate study in newspapers for students interested in journalism careers who haven't majored in communications in undergraduate programs. The fellowship includes a full-tuition scholarship, an internship at the Syracuse newspapers, a stipend and the possibility of a job at a Newhouse newspaper after graduation. The Dow Jones Newspaper Fund offers a summer internship program for minority students. Minority students have their own professional organizations and national conventions where recruiting is a primary concern.

Students can also obtain yearly updated internship information from professional organizations such as the Society for News Design and the National Press Photographers Association.

AFTER COLLEGE

Students who have had a good internship and have built competitive portfolios during college will find endless opportunities for entry-level jobs after college graduation. Even without an undergraduate communications degree, a competitive portfolio and internship experience will help students obtain jobs in media. With the growth of media forms, students can look in many areas of communications to find job opportunities.

Fig. 24.2. Cover of *Newspaper Career Guide.* The Newspaper Association of America publishes a yearly guide to newspaper careers. It can be obtained for free from the association. The guide contains information that helps students sort their skills and interests into career areas available in newspaper. Reprinted with permission of the Newspaper Association of America.

ADVERTISING

Jobs in advertising range from sales and account management to media buying. They also include creative areas such as art direction and copy writing. Media buyers, account managers and ad salespeople work with the advertising accounts. Creative jobs involve creating concepts and campaigns for advertising clients and may encompass both print and broadcast work. Many advertising agencies employ people in related agency endeavors such as public relations and logo design.

Those interested in advertising can also find opportunities within media organizations such as newspapers and magazines and within the parent companies of media operations. Many newspapers and magazines are owned by large media conglomerates, companies that could own a variety of media forms.

PUBLIC RELATIONS

A growth area in communications, public relations departments are a part of almost every corporate agency, including health care systems, professional sports teams and major entertainment businesses. Smaller companies may hire public relations agencies, often called "full-service agencies," for their capability at handling everything from crisis communications to public relations campaigns.

Public relations agencies hire designers to create logos, brochures, flyers, pamphlets, annual reports, campaigns and any other communication such as a corporate newsletter distributed to company employees or customers. Public relations departments and agencies hire good writers capable of writing press releases that will be sent to media outlets to inform them about developments within a company or organization. Freelance photographers are often employed to shoot photographs for annual reports or to produce photographs of personnel who have been hired or promoted. Basic photographic skills can be quite helpful to people working in public relations departments within companies. Often, the company will not be able to hire a freelance photographer to shoot pictures of every corporate event that the office may want to include in company newsletters. Digital cameras can prove quite helpful in giving public relations professionals access to photographs for various needs.

NEWSPAPERS

Of course, newspapers need good writers and editors. But newspapers hire people with many other skills. Newspapers need people with wide-ranging visual skills – those who can create interesting page layouts, coherent and useful information graphics and compelling photographs and those who can do so under deadline pressure (Fig. 24.2).

Newspapers hire good designers who can create interesting page designs on a daily basis. Presentation directors are often the managers or overseers of newspaper design departments. They work with illustrators, graphic artists and other designers.

With the growth in newspaper online sites, entire areas of newspaper newsrooms have expanded to encompass people who keep the newspapers' websites updated throughout the day and night. Websites often employ their own staffs of writers, photographers, designers and producers. Individuals with multiple skills will be valuable assets to web site managers.

Many newspapers are members of larger media organizations, offering opportunities for journalists to produce work that is seen by a larger audience.

Small newspapers often hire students who have some photographic knowledge. With limited photographic personnel, small newspapers need writers who can occasionally take their own photographs. Knowledge of basic camera operation and compositional skills will prove helpful to young journalists seeking entry-level jobs.

Writers or students trained in information-gathering and researching skills can find interesting jobs in newspaper research libraries. With the growth in computer-assisted reporting, newspapers need people who can conduct information research and who can make sense of the information they find. They often work hand-in-hand with reporters as stories are developed.

WEB AND MULTIMEDIA DESIGN

The growth in the internet has created an entirely new area of communications growth. Companies specializing in creating and maintaining web sites for corporate clients hire people with media skills. Some of these same companies are involved in other multimedia forms such as producing DVDs.

Web design companies often create web sites for corporate clients and may continue to maintain the sites by periodically updating the information on them. Or they create the websites and turn them over to the companies, often providing training to the site producers.

Web designers are also involved in creating web advertising or can work for advertising agencies in creating web advertising.

Multimedia designers work on projects such as books, magazines, catalogs and promotions. They can work for multimedia production companies, be employed by individual media companies or freelance for a variety of clients.

MAGAZINES

Although many magazines hire freelance writers with established reputations for feature-length articles, a staff of writers, designers and managers is in place to handle the day-to-day operations of the magazine's production. Magazines hire good editors and fact checkers, those whose responsibility it is to check the accuracy of the information in the stories before they go to print.

Magazine designers are often known as art directors. They are responsible for the design of the feature-length articles, as well as the overall design of the publication. From time to time, the publication's design might need to be updated, a process known as a redesign. Redesigns are often done by staff designers, although occasionally outside design consultants are hired to work with the magazine's staff.

PHOTOGRAPHY

In addition to photojournalism, a career practiced by photographers who work for newspapers and some magazines, photographers can study advertising or illustration photography. Advertising photographers are hired by companies who need product advertising or by advertising agencies in producing ads or campaigns for clients. The creative vision and skills of advertising photographers help them secure clients. Illustration photographers are hired primarily to illustrate feature-length articles.

Many photographers prefer documentary photography, a form of storytelling used by magazines such as *National Geographic*. Documentary photographers are concerned with in-depth photography, and their vision can take them all over the world to document conflict, people, strife and accomplishment. These photographers work primarily as freelancers and can spend many years building their reputations before being hired by top professional magazines. Many photojournalists grow interested in working on long-range projects and initiate or accept documentary projects either as freelance work or for the publications for which they photograph.

Most publications also hire picture editors, those whose responsibility it is to manage the operation of the photographic operations on their publications. Picture editors rarely shoot. They spend their time making

NEWS   ENTERTAINMENT   LIFESTYLES   SPORTS   MONEY & GADGETS   DISPATCHES   Search   GO   ADVANCED SEARCH

tfp ONLINE.com | asap

An Online Division of the Chattanooga Times Free Press

wn   *Ap* Commander Still Eyes Iraq Troop Reduction   *Ap* French Quarter Cathedral Holds Sunday Mass   *Ap* Inspections at Northwe

Reggaeton A Sound is Born

A musical multimedia presentation from asap, produced by JAIME HOLGUIN, photographed by BERNADETTE TUAZON and designed by SHAZNA NESSA, with interviews by VANESSA PETIT.

PHOTO ILLUSTRATION/ J. MYINT

Exclusive Features

Supreme Court: 2035
Looking Way Ahead Who will fill the robes in 30 years?

Raising Eyebrows
Levy Petting How Eugene Levy made my heart go pitty pat.

It's My Country Too
Muslim in America Add "sexy" and "funny" to "misunderstood."

Fig. 24.3. Premiering in September 2005, "asap" is a new, online service provided to member newspapers by the Associated Press. The site features coverage of lifestyles, money and gadgets and dispatches in addition to traditional news coverage. Associated Press, New York, N.Y.

assignments, editing film with photographers and advising the publications about how the photographs should be used. Most picture editors are former photographers who have worked their way into management positions. Beyond picture editing, newspapers hire managers for picture departments and to oversee the newspaper's visual direction. These editors are often given the titles of assistant managing editor or managing editor.

WIRE SERVICES

Wire services are agencies that provide information to various publications from across the world. Publications pay subscriber services to receive data feeds from wire services. Set up in bureaus in worldwide locations, wire services provide stories, photographs and graphics. The Associated Press, Agence France-Presse, Reuters and Getty are among the largest of the world's wire services. Wire services also provide content that can be used at members' online sites.

Just as on a newspaper staff, the agencies hire writers, editors, photographers and managers to service each bureau and to provide coverage of events happening in their locations.

Because many publications are now owned by large media companies, these conglomerates offer their own network services of reporters, designers, photographers and artists who produce material that can be used by member publications.

BROADCASTING

In addition to hiring staffers who can write, produce, photograph, edit and anchor, radio and TV operations need designers for producing on-air graphics. Students with good design skills and knowledge of standard software packages can transfer their skills to broadcast editing equipment to produce graphics for story content and to produce story promotions graphics for use during ratings periods.

Some TV networks have their own online website staffs, as well as staffs who produce promotional DVDs for new and special programming throughout the year. These promotions require writers, producers, photographers and editors.

FREELANCING

Freelancers can work for several publications and can be hired by different companies and organizations. Because they work for themselves, rather than for an organization, they have to be good financial managers, schedulers and promoters, or they have to hire people to do these jobs for them. They can pick and choose from among the jobs they are offered. Freelancers rely on their reputations to get work, or they hire reps to show their portfolios and help them get hired for various jobs.

Freelancers must maintain their own equipment, such as computers and cameras, and be responsible for their own transportation. They often have to plan for retirement, maintain health plans and pay taxes throughout the year.

Freelancing work for multimedia companies and web production companies is in demand, with designers often moving from project to project, working for different companies for various periods of time.

OTHER OPPORTUNITIES

In addition to the growth in multimedia and traditional media forms, other career opportunities are abundant for people with media experience. Book publishers, most primarily located in New York City, hire copy editors and designers to work in their publishing operations.

Companies that publish catalogues need to employ people who photograph, write copy and design the publications or online sites. E-commerce, selling directly online, is now an accepted and growing form of doing business for many companies.

Beyond the professional world, students who have journalism experience may want to use their skills in public service opportunities. Journalists can perform public service work that helps special interest groups or philanthropic causes.

Journalism skills will be even more valuable as communications tools continue to evolve and change. Wireless, broadband technology will increase forms of communications and create new ones. Computer technology continues to evolve. Media forms will converge and overlap. Students with broad skills and knowledge will be highly competitive in the job market.

Another media buzzword, "convergence," means many traditional media forms will evolve and blend, requiring employees with wide-ranging skills in a variety of different media areas.

Regardless of the form messages take, individuals with media skills will find they are valued in a job market where information is instantaneously reported and received.

EXERCISES

1. Plan a journalism career day or week for your class. Divide the class into various groups based on media forms. Have each group contact professional organizations to obtain speakers. Each group should plan and coordinate the speaker's appearance in the class. Groups should prepare the class for the visits by providing brief biographical information about the speakers in advance. This information can be obtained from each speaker. Students should be encouraged to generate questions for each speaker. If possible, videotape the speakers for later use.

2. Look through the *Newspaper Career Guide* for ideas for careers. Make a list of your interests and strengths in journalism. How could these interests be tailored to specific media careers?

3. If your local newspaper publishes a youth page or section, contact that section's editor and invite the editor to speak to your class. Find out how students from your school can get their work published or how they can become contributing editors for the section. Discuss story planning and ideas. Where do the newspaper's stories originate? How could these ideas be used by your newspaper or yearbook staff?

4. Invite a group of staff members from a local college newspaper, online publication or yearbook to speak to the class about getting jobs on college publications. If possible, arrange a follow-up visit to the college publication's offices for a tour. If your community does not have a college, invite a group of the school's alumni now working on college publications to the school during a college vacation or break period. Ask them to bring copies of their published work to discuss with the class.

5. In groups of three to four students, plan newsletters for various community or volunteer groups such as the local zoo or the Humane Society or for your school if the school doesn't already publish a newsletter. Identify a need to be served by this publication in advance of planning it by contacting the organization about its communications needs. In each group, discuss the needed content and draw a sketch showing a possible design for the newsletter, including a nameplate. Discuss and present each newsletter in the class.

Professional and Student Organizations

American Copy Editors Society
  3 Healy Street
  Huntington, NY 11743
  ph: (800) 393-7681
  email: administrator@copydesk.org

American Press Institute
  11690 Sunrise Valley Drive
  Reston, VA 20191
  ph: (703) 620-3611
  fax: (703) 620-5814
  email: info@americanpressinstitute.org

American Society of Magazine Editors
  810 7th Avenue, 24th Floor
  New York, NY 10019
  ph: (212) 872-3700
  fax: (212) 906-0128
  email: asme@magazine.org

American Society of Newspaper Editors
  11690B Sunrise Valley Drive
  Reston, VA 20191-1409
  ph: (703) 453-1122
  fax: (703) 453-1133
  email: asne@asne.org

Asian American Journalists Association
  1182 Market Street, Suite 320
  San Francisco, CA 94102
  ph: (415) 346-2051
  fax: (415) 346-6343
  email: national@aaja.org

Associated Collegiate Press
  National Scholastic Press Association
  2221 University Avenue, SE, Suite 121
  Minneapolis, MN 55414
  ph: (612) 625-8335
  fax: (612) 626-0720
  email: info@studentpress.org

Associated Press Managing Editors Association
  450 W. 33rd Street
  New York, NY 10001
  ph: (212) 621-1838
  fax: (212) 506-6102
  email: apme@ap.org

Association for Education in Journalism and Mass Communication
  234 Outlet Pointe Road
  Columbia, SC 29210
  ph: (803) 798-0271
  fax: (803) 772-3509
  email: aejmc@aejmc.org

Association for Women in Communications
  780 Ritchie Highway, Suite 285
  Severna Park, MD 21146
  ph: (410) 544-7442
  fax: (410) 544-4640
  email: info@womcom.org

College Media Advisers
    Department of Journalism MJ-300
    University of Memphis
    Memphis, TN 38152
    ph: (901) 678-2403
    fax: (901) 678-4798
    email: rsplbrgr@memphis.edu

Columbia Scholastic Press Association
    2960 Broadway, CMR 5711
    Columbia University
    New York, NY 10027-6902
    ph: (212) 854-9400
    fax: (212) 854-9401
    email: cspa@columbia.edu

Dow Jones Newspaper Fund
    PO Box 300
    Princeton, NJ 08543-0300
    ph: (609) 452-2820
    fax: (609) 520-5804
    email: newsfund@wsj.dowjones.com

The Freedom Forum First Amendment Center
    1207 18th Avenue South
    Nashville, TN 37212
    ph: (615) 321-9588
    fax: (615) 321-9599
    email: info@fac.org

Journalism Education Association
    103 Kedzie Hall
    Kansas State University
    Manhattan, KS 66506
    ph: (785) 532-5532
    fax: (785) 532-5563
    email: jea@spub.ksu.edu

National Association of Black Journalists
    8701A Adelphi Road
    Adelphi, MD 20783-1716
    ph: (301) 445-7100
    fax: (301) 445-7101
    email: nabj@nabj.org

National Association of Hispanic Journalists
    1000 National Press Building
    Washington, DC 20045-2100
    ph: (202) 662-7145
    fax: (202) 662-7144
    email: nahj@nahj.org

National Association of Science Writers
    PO Box 890
    Hedgesville, WV 25427
    ph: (304) 754-5077
    fax: (304) 754-5076
    email: info@nasw.org

National Federation of Press Women
    PO Box 5556
    Arlington, VA 22205
    ph: (800) 780-2715
    fax: (703) 534-5751
    email: presswomen@aol.com

National Institute for Computer-Assisted
    Reporting
    138 Neff Annex
    School of Journalism
    University of Missouri
    Columbia, MO 65211
    ph: (573) 882-0684
    fax: (573) 884-5544
    email: info@nicar.org

National Lesbian and Gay Journalists Association
    1420 K Street, NW, Suite 910
    Washington, DC 20005
    ph: (202) 588-9888
    fax: (202) 588-1818
    email: info@nlgja.org

National Newspaper Association
    129 Neff Annex
    University of Missouri
    Columbia, MO 65211
    ph: (573) 882-5800
    fax: (573) 884-5490
    email: info@nna.org

National Press Photographers Association
3200 Croasdaile Drive, Suite 306
Durham, NC 27705
ph: (919) 383-7246
fax: (919) 383-7261
email: info@nppa.org

Native American Journalists Association
Al Neuharth Media Center
555 Dakota Street
Vermillion, SD 57069
ph: (605) 677-5282
fax: (866) 694-4264
email: info@naja.com

Poynter Institute for Media Studies
801 Third Street S.
St. Petersburg, FL 33701
ph: (888) 769-6837
fax: (727) 821-0583
email: info@poynter.org

Project Censored
Sonoma State University
1801 E. Cotati Avenue
Rohnert Park, CA 94928
ph: (707) 664-2500
email: project.censored@sonoma.edu

Quill and Scroll Society
School of Journalism and Mass
Communication
University of Iowa
Iowa City, IA 52242-1528
ph: (319) 335-5795
fax: (319) 335-5210
email: quill-scroll@uiowa.edu

Radio and Television News Directors Association
1600 K Street, NW, Suite 700
Washington, DC 20006
ph: (202) 659-6510
fax: (202) 223-4007
email: rtnda@rtnda.org

Society for News Design
1130 Ten Rod Road F104
North Kingstown, RI 02852
ph: (401) 294-5233
fax: (401) 294-5238
email: snd@snd.org

Society of Professional Journalists
3909 N. Meridian Street
Indianapolis, IN 46208
ph: (317) 927-8000
fax: (317) 920-4789
email: questions@spj.org

Southern Interscholastic Press Association
College of Journalism and Mass
Communications
University of South Carolina
Columbia, SC 29208
ph: (803) 777-6284
fax: (803) 777-4103
email: ebdickey@gwm.sc.edu

Student Press Law Center
1101 Wilson Boulevard, Suite 1100
Arlington, VA 22209
ph: (703) 807-1904
email: splc@splc.org

Glossary

A

Academics section – the part of the yearbook covering classroom and learning activities both at school and outside of school

Advance story – announcement-type story for coming event

Advertising policy – a written policy that details the publication's guidelines concerning ad sales and use in the publications

Advocacy editorial – editorial that interprets, explains or persuades

Agate type – the smallest point size in type a publication uses; traditionally used for sports scores and classified ads

Air – white space ("fresh air") around type and illustrations

Align – instruction to bring type into straight line

Alley – see **internal margin.**

Ampersand – symbol for *and* (&)

Anchorperson – principal person in charge of newscast

Angle – point of view from which something is written

Anonymous source – source whose name is changed or omitted in story to protect the source from harm or because the story's subject is sensitive or controversial

Aperture – the size of the opening on a camera lens

Art – illustration(s) to accompany stories or ads

Art head – specially designed headline that may break away from consistent typefaces or styles used in the rest of the publication

Ascender – stem or loop that extends above x-height of letters

Assignment book (sheet) – record of reporters' assignments kept by editor

Associated Press – cooperative wire news service owned by its member newspapers and radio and television stations. See **wire service.**

Attribution – statement fixing source of information in story

B

Backgrounder – a story or part of a story that provides information that explains events or reasons for news

Backgrounding – the process of reading and doing research in preparation for asking questions and interviewing sources for a story

Background lead – see **descriptive lead.**

Balance – in writing, refers to facts in stories being given proper emphasis, putting each fact into its proper relationship to every other fact and establishing its relative importance to the main idea or focus of the story; in design, refers to the weight of the page appearing even

Banner (streamer) – one-line head that extends across top of page

Bar – thick rule used for decoration or to reverse a line of text

Baseline – the imaginary line upon which all type letters sit

Beat (run) – reporter's specified area for regular news coverage; scoop or story obtained before other media can print or air it

Beat system – a plan to cover routinely all potential news sources in a specific area

Big on the body – typefaces with large x-height proportions to capital letters

Biweekly – publication that appears once every two weeks, as distinguished from semiweekly (twice a week)

Black letter type – commonly known as Old English typefaces, these types are of Germanic origin and are used primarily in newspaper nameplates or flags

Bleed – illustrations and type extended beyond regular page margins to outside page edges

Blur – in a photograph, indicates movement by the photographer during the exposure

Body type – type used for main text, as distinguished from headlines

Boldface (bf) – heavier, blacker version of type style

Book – in magazine terminology may mean magazine (as in "back of the book")

Border – line or frame that surrounds element in design

Bounce flash – diffused flash softened by aiming the direction of the flash at a low, light ceiling or wall and allowing the flash to shower the subject with light

Box – printed rule around story or headline or instruction to create it

Broadsheet – full-size newspaper, often measuring 14 by 21 inches

Budget – list of content for newshole (nonadvertising space) of newspaper

Bullet – visual or typographic device, usually at beginning of paragraphs or before items in list

Burning in – in a traditional darkroom or through computer imaging software, adding tone to an area of a print that would print without detail

Byline – author's credit printed with the story

C

Callout – see **pull quote**.

C and lc – capital and lowercase letters

Canned material – filler material, usually not local, used as time copy

Caps (uppercase) – capital letters

Caption – lines of text describing illustrations and photographs

Caption lead-in – see **catchline**.

Catchline – headline for cutline, usually used between photo and cutline. Also known as *caption lead-in*

CD-ROM – compact disc, read-only memory

Center of interest – a photographic compositional quality that makes it obvious why a photograph was taken

Center spread – two facing pages at centerfold of publication that are made up as one page

Chronological story form – a time sequence story form

Clarification – a follow-up item published after a story has been printed that needs a clearer explanation of facts

Classified ad – advertising in the section of a publication that classifies products and services under appropriate headings

Cliché – overused, trite expression that weakens the overall content of a story

Closed-end question – question that should be avoided in interviewing because it can be answered with a yes or no response

Clubs section – the section of a yearbook in which school organizations and their activities are covered

Coaching writing – a discussion and working relationship between a writer and editor to improve the writing process

Collage – art produced by pasting up a variety of elements into a single composition

Color separation – process of separating color originals into process printing colors

Column – see **grid**.

Column inch – unit of space 1 inch deep and one column wide, used primarily in measuring advertising space

Column rule – thin line separating columns of type

Commendation editorial – an editorial that praises the actions of a person or group of people

Community feature – a feature story that relates the school to parts of the community with ties to students

Comparison lead – a lead that compares time, size or culture, for example. See **contrast lead**.

Computer-assisted reporting (CAR) – the process of using online database research to supplement traditional reporting methods

Condensed type – narrow or slender typeface taller than its width

Confidentiality – protecting the identity of a source because of real danger that serious physical, emotional or financial harm will come to the source if his or her name is revealed

Conflict of interest – a reason to disqualify a reporter or a photographer from covering an event in which he or she has substantial involvement

Contact sheet – photographic print made from negative or positive in contact with sensitized paper

Continuous tone – photo image that contains gradient tones from black to white without use of screening

Contrast – the range of tones from white to black with all gray tones in between in a photograph

Contrast lead – a lead that contrasts time, size or culture, for example. See **comparison lead.**

Convergence – the evolution and blending of traditional media forms with emerging technology

Copyediting – the process of tightening and improving writing, checking for accuracy and style

Copyreader – person who corrects or generally improves material intended for publication

Copyright – a legal protection for original work that prohibits its use by someone other than the creator without permission

Correction – a revision published in the next edition of a publication after a story containing an error in fact has been printed

Courtesy title – the use of *Mr., Ms., Mrs.* or *Miss* along with the name of a person

Coverage – the range of pictures and verbal stories throughout a publication

Credit line – line giving source of picture or story

Crop – to eliminate areas of a photograph.

Cursive – type resembling handwriting but with letters not connected

Cut – in letterpress terminology, photoengraving of any kind

Cutline – see **caption.**

Cutoff rule – line across column separating text and advertising or between stories

D

Datebook – a master calendar of all school activities

Dateline – line at beginning of news story telling the point of origin (date is seldom included)

Deadline – time at which copy must be presented in order to be printed

Deck – see **secondary headline.**

Dedicated flash – a flash that coordinates with an automatic or program camera to determine correct flash settings electronically

Delete – to remove text (letter, word, sentence, paragraph or story)

Departmentalization – grouping contents of publication by subject matter

Depth of field – the range of focus from the foreground to the background present in a photograph

Depth reporting – see **in-depth reporting.**

Descender – part of letter that descends below x-height

Descriptive lead – a lead that describes the story's setting or gives details leading up to the story itself. Also known as *background lead*

Digital – words, pictures and graphics expressed in numerical form for use and output by computers

Direct address lead – a lead that temporarily speaks directly to the reader by using the second-person pronouns *you* and *your*

Direct flash – flash aimed directly at the subject from camera position

Direct quote – information from sources used in quotation marks because it contains their exact words

Display ad – an ad that displays, through type and illustrations, the product or service a merchant wants to sell. See **retail ad.**

Display type – type larger than body type used in headlines and ads; usually 14 point and above

Divider page – in a yearbook, a page or spread that introduces a new section of the book to the reader

Dodging – in a traditional darkroom or through computer imaging software, holding back light from an area of a print that would have blocked detail

Dogleg – column of type extending down page, not squared off under multicolumn headline

Dominant element – the largest element with the most impact on a page; a minimum ratio of 2:1 should be maintained in size to command dominant reader interest

Double spread (truck) – two facing pages made up as single unit

Down style – newspaper form of capitalization using minimum capital letters, primarily for the first letter and only for proper nouns following the first letter

DPI – dots per inch

Drop cap – large initial letter set in larger size than rest of text; appears at the beginning of text or at junctures throughout text

Dry offset – use of raised-image plate for direct printing on offset press without water dampening

Dummy – usually scaled-down layout showing format and general appearance of publication

Duotone – two-color halftone reproduction from a one-color photograph

DVD – a high density compact disk for storage of large amounts of data, especially high resolution, audio-visual material

E

Ear – space devoted to information at either side of nameplate

Editorial – the opinion of the newspaper as it appears on the editorial page; it appears without a byline and represents the views of the editorial board

Editorial board – on a high school publication, an editorial board is usually made up of editors of the publication who meet to make decisions about the publication's editorial policies

Editorial cartoon – distinctive art combined with a few words or a sentence or two that commends, criticizes, interprets, persuades or entertains as other editorial page content

Editorializing – inserting a reporter's or editor's opinion in a news story

Editorial of criticism – see **problem-solution editorial.**

Editorial short – a brief editorial of from one word to one or a few sentences usually grouped with other editorial shorts under a standing column heading

Em – unit of space equal in size to a square of any type size, approximately a cap M

En – one-half em

Endsheet – decorative and functional heavy paper that holds pages into book binding and that can be used for design elements such as yearbook themes or contents listings; end paper

Ethics – codes of conduct that guide journalists in the pursuit of truth and the news-gathering process

Expanded type – typeface wider than standard type of the same design (extended)

External margin – margin framing the page

F

Fabrication – creating a person, a situation, a dialogue, statistics or any pivotal or incidental information and passing it as real

Factoid – list or summary of facts

Fair comment – a defense against libel that allows a reporter and others in journalism to express an opinion about a matter of public interest

Fast lens – a lens with a large maximum f-stop, usually in the range of f/2.8 or larger; this lens allows more light to reach the film during exposure

Feature – story that goes beyond factual news reporting with emphasis on human interest appeal; element in story highlighted in lead;

item in newspaper such as cartoon and syndicated material supplied by "feature" services

Feature fact – the most important fact and the one that makes the best beginning for the lead of the story

Featurize – to write a news story with characteristics of a feature story

Filler – item, usually short, used to fill holes around stories and ads

Film speed – a number on a roll of film (also called ASA) that determines its sensitivity to light

Filtering system – a restriction placed on internet access

First Amendment – the part of the Constitution that guarantees freedom of the press

Fisheye lens – an extremely wide-angle lens that produces a photograph with a viewing angle of 360 degrees

Fixed focal length lens – a camera lens with only one focal length as opposed to a zoom, which encompasses a range of focal lengths

Flag – nameplate (or logo) of newspaper. See **masthead**.

Flat – single side of a printed signature containing half the pages of the signature

Flat light – light shining directly on subjects from in front that tends to flatten out the dimensions and details of the subject

Flopping/flipping – in photography, printing the picture opposite from its natural orientation usually so it faces into the page gutter rather than off. This process should be avoided.

Flush left or right – instructions to set type even with margins, left or right

Folio – page number

Folio line – type on each page giving name, date and page number

Follow-up story – a story that reports on an event after it has taken place

Folo (follow) copy – instructions to set exactly as copy reads, even in error

Font – see **typeface**.

Force justify – an alignment pattern that causes type to spread across a line width and leave

awkward white spaces between letters or words

Format – size, shape and general physical characteristics of publication

Four-color process – three primary colors plus black, which reproduce full-color spectrum

Fourth estate – term for journalism or journalists, attributed to Edmund Burke and first used in the House of Commons (the three original estates were nobles, clergy and commons)

Framing – using objects in the foreground or background to provide a natural frame around subjects in photographs

Freedom of information (FOI) laws – federal and state laws that allow all citizens access to a vast array of information

Future (book) – editor's calendar of upcoming events

G

Game story – a sports story in which the significant details, game summary and highlights, and player and coach analyses are presented on a timely basis

Gathering – assembling folded signatures in proper order. See **signature**.

Gaze motion – a clear and logical pattern of eye movement through a design

Glossy – photograph with glossy finish

Golden mean points – the intersections created when a composition is divided into the rule of thirds. See **rule of thirds**.

Graf/Graph – paragraph

Graphic – visual design device such as line, screen or art that enhances text and overall page appearance

Grid – geometric pattern that divides page into vertical and horizontal divisions and provides underlying layout/design structure. Also known as *column*

Grounding – anchoring visual or verbal content on the page so it isn't floating

Grounds – the three dimensions present and seen through the eyes that are compressed into two dimensions in photographs

Gutter – space between columns

Gutter margin – the space between two facing pages

H

Hairline – fine line stroke of type character (modern roman) or thinnest printing rule used for borders

Halftone – printing plate made by exposing negative through screen converting image into dots

Hammer headline – a short phrase or single-word headline with an accompanying, smaller headline underneath it

Hard news – important factual information about current happenings

Hardware – equipment that makes up computer system, as distinguished from programming for system (software)

Headbands – colored strips of fabric attached to the top and bottom of book binding to finish it

Highlights – the lightest areas of a photograph

Historical feature – a feature story that brings the past to life through coverage of a timely event

Historical present – use of the present tense in a headline to describe past events

Hold – instruction not to set into type or print in paper

Horizontal makeup – makeup emphasis on multicolumn headlines over stories displayed in rectangular forms

Hot type – refers to composition by linecasting machines employing molten metal

Human interest – emphasis (usually) on persons that seeks emotional identification with reader

I

Illustration – drawing, art, map or other form of nonphotographic material used in a publication

Impact – a photograph's power to stop viewers and engage them in its content

Imposition software – software that places page forms in order to be printed on single sheet to form signature with numbered pages

Indent – copy mark to set type certain distance from margin

In-depth reporting – single story, group of related stories or series resulting from detailed investigation of background information and multisource interviewing

Index – a complete, alphabetical listing of each person, club, event, advertiser and subject in the yearbook

Indirect flash – flash used off camera and aimed off subject so shadows fall outside the subject area

Indirect quote – a paraphrase of information from a source. It does not require quotation marks.

Infographic/infograph – short for *information graphic*; any chart, map, diagram, timeline, etc., used to analyze an object, event or place in the news

Informative feature story – a feature story in which readers are given information about ordinary topics that they may deal with each day, in and outside of school

Initial – large first letter of paragraph measured by multiple of number of lines that run around it (e.g., 36 point equals three lines of 12 point body). See **stickup**.

Ink jet printer – printer that sprays ink onto a printed page

Insert – material to be placed in story already written or set

Inset – picture or design carried within natural boundary of another reproduction

Internal margin – space also known as *alley* that appears between columns of type and in the gutter

Internet – system of computer networks all over the world that are linked together through telecommunications systems

Internship – working relationship in which student is hired for short period of time to perform professional responsibilities for publication or other media organization

Interpretative article – see **news analysis**.

Inverted pyramid – form of news story with most important facts first and remainder in order of descending importance; form of certain headline decks

Isolation elements – visual or verbal elements that are separated or surrounded by white space as a way to attract the reader's eye

Italic – variation of roman letters that slant to right

J

Jet printing – ink sprayed under pressure and droplets charged electrically and deflected by computer to form image

Jim dash – short, centered, thin-line rule used between headline decks and short related items

JPEG – a format derived from Joint Photographic Experts Group which is a standard for compression of digital images. JPEG format is a compression that loses small amounts of data with each opening.

Jump – to continue story in another column or page

Jump head – headline for portion of story from another page

Justification – adjustment of spacing between words and word divisions so that all lines of type are of equal length and align on both the left and right sides

K

Kerning – adjusting the space between letter pairs, primarily in display (headline) type

Keyword – use of specific words in internet searches that will yield necessary information

Kicker – short line above larger headline

Kill – delete (remove) paragraph story or advertisement

L

Ladder diagram – a chart showing a page-by-page delineation of a yearbook's content

Laser printer – a printer that uses a computer language to digitally render type and images on paper

Layout – drawing or sketch for piece of printing

lc – lowercase letters

Lead (*leed*) – opening words of story, usually summary statement of fewer than 40 words

Lead (*led*) – thin strips of metal used for spacing between lines; space between lines of type

Leading line – real or suggested line present in a photograph that leads the viewer's eye to the center of interest. See **center of interest**.

Legibility – extent to which line of type may be read in brief exposure. Important for headings. Compare with **readability**.

Letterpress – form of printing in which ink surface of type or plate is pressed on paper

Letterspacing – placing of space between letters of word

Libel – malicious defamation of person made public by any printing, writing, sign, picture reproduction or effigy tending to provoke him or her to wrath or expose him or her to public hatred, contempt or ridicule

Ligature – two or more letters cast together (e.g., ffi)

Light meter – a meter usually built into a camera that determines correct exposure based on available light and the sensitivity of the film

Lithography plate – plate with metal or stone surface carrying image. Water or acid separates the nonprinting (see **offset**) areas from inked surface.

Locator map – graphic map that helps readers identify the location of a place or event mentioned in a story

Logo – a visual brand or identifier

LPI – lines per inch

M

Makeup – assembling of type, cuts and/or ads on page

Market survey – a poll conducted by a publication's advertising staff to determine the buying habits of its readers

Masthead – identification statement of newspaper's vital statistics, usually on editorial page

Measure – width of line of type or page, usually expressed in picas

Modified news lead – a soft or indirect lead that can be more creative and less "formulaic" than traditional news leads

Modular – layout/design style that uses vertical and horizontal four-sided shapes, balanced informally, for all page elements. See **module.**

Module – unit or component of page set off by box rules or white space on all sides

Mondrian – page utilizing rectangles of harmonious shapes and sizes

Monopod – a single leg support used for stabilizing cameras when photographing with extremely long lenses

Montage – composite of several pictures, or parts of pictures, blended together

Morgue – newspaper reference library

Mortise – placing pictures so they overlap or touch

Mug shot – a small identifying picture usually cropped to show only the face or head and shoulders of a writer or person identified in a story

N

Nameplate – the name of the newspaper or publication as it appears on the front page or cover

Narrative – storytelling method of story development

Negative – negative image on transparent material used for printing positive picture

New journalism – fictional techniques applied to news events

News analysis – effort to explain "news behind the news." It approaches editorial form but does not involve deliberate value judgments. Also known as *interpretative article*

News brief – a story limited to one or a few paragraphs that may appear with other briefs

News elements – values that give news importance including timeliness or immediacy, proximity or nearness, consequence or impact, prominence, drama, oddity or unusualness, conflict, sex, emotions and instincts, and progress

Newsgroup – site on the internet where persons with similar interests can gather electronically and enter messages about related topics

Newshole – space left for news after ads have been positioned

Newsmagazine – a publication traditionally 8.5 × 11 inches in size

Newsprint – paper made from wood pulp and used by newspapers

News summary lead – hard news lead that gets readers immediately to the main point of an article

Novelty lead – see **oddity lead.**

Novelty type – typefaces whose appearance is visually augmented or quirky. The appearance may connect to the typeface's name

Nut graph/graf – summary paragraph located near the beginning of a story, usually identifies subject; also known as *focus graph/graf*

O

Obit – abbreviation for *obituary*

Objectivity – goal in newswriting of converting news event into precise, unbiased description

Oddity lead – a creative lead that succeeds in attracting readers because it is different, often using humor, a startling statement or an allusion. Also known as *novelty lead*

Offset – lithography; process in which image on plane-surface plate is transferred to rubber blanket roll from which impression is made on paper. See **lithography plate.**

Op-ed – opinion-editorial; refers to page opposite editorial page, usually devoted to analyses, opinion columns, reviews and special features

Open-ended question – question preferred during an interview because it elicits detailed answer and provides information for quotes

Open meeting laws (sunshine laws) – laws that require certain government agencies to open their meetings to the public

Opinion column – a column written to express the views of one writer. Opinion columns appear on editorial or opinion pages and appear under a column title

Optical center – point about 10 percent of page height above mathematical center, fulcrum for page balance

Outline light – light coming from behind a subject in a photograph that can provide a "halo effect"

Overlay – sheet of transparent paper placed over illustration, text, headline, photo or page background, giving printer special instructions on color application, screening and similar work

Overline – headline over illustration

Overrun – copies printed in excess of distribution needs

P

Pace – the rhythm in writing created by word choice, sentence length and construction, and paragraph lengths

Packaging – an arrangement of information on a page that may include visuals and alternative story forms accompanying a main story

Page proof – proof of entire page for checking before printing

Pagination – electronic design and eventual production of newspaper pages by newsroom editors

Panchromatic – film sensitive to all visible colors

Pantone Matching System – a patented color process allowing the selection of very specific shades and tones of color

Pasteup – composite page of proofs, artwork and the like, ready to be photographed for offset reproduction

PDF – portable document format, a native file format for Adobe Systems' Acrobat. In PDF format, data can be viewed independently of the original application software, hardware and operating system.

Perfect bound – a binding method in which strips of glue are applied along a flat gutter to hold the pages together

Photo credit – photographer's byline appearing with photograph

Photo cutout – cutting a photograph into the shape of some of its content and removing the background; also known as COB, cutout background

Photoengraving – process of making printing plates by action of light on film

Photojournalist – reporter who covers news and features with camera

Photo release – form for obtaining signed approval from person appearing in commercial picture or for picture possibly not privileged as news

Phototypesetting – preparing printing surface for offset reproduction by photographing letter images on film or paper, usually electronically, at great speed

Pica – printer's unit of measure, 6 picas to 1 inch

Pick up – instruction to printer to use material from earlier setting or issue

Picture editing – the process of selecting pictures for use in a publication

Picture package – a combination of two or three images from a single event or situation used with a caption to show different aspects of the event or situation

Picture sequence – a series of pictures of a singular subject or action

Picture story – a story told primarily through pictures with a short amount of text, full captions and a complete headline

Plagiarism – taking someone's words, art and other original work and passing it off as one's own

Plate – piece of metal or plastic carrying printing image on its surface

Point – unit of measure used principally in measuring type sizes in which 72 points equal 1 inch; printer's terminology for any punctuation mark

Point and shoot camera – camera with mostly automated functions that is simple to use and produces consistent exposures

Portrait section – a yearbook section featuring mug shots of individuals and school faculty and staff

PostScript – computer language invented by Adobe Systems

Presentation director – the designer in charge of the overall publication's design and look

Press release – stories prepared by individuals and organizations seeking publicity

Primary colors – in light: red, green and blue

Primary source – an eyewitnesses to an event or the creator of an original work – a physical or intellectual property

Print – a photograph

Printer spread – an arrangement of pages as they will be printed on a flat or signature

Prior restraint/review – reference by court of law prohibiting any future news or comment on case

Privilege – a second defense against libel that allows reporters to publish fair and accurate accounts of official proceedings, such as school board meetings and court proceedings, and reports, such as court records, without being overly concerned about libel

Problem-solution editorial – an editorial used when the publication's staff wants to call attention to a problem or wants to criticize someone's actions. Also known as *editorial of criticism*

Process colors – the four ink colors needed to reproduce color in a publication: cyan (process blue), magenta (process red), yellow and black

Profile/profile box – a type of feature story in which the writer captures a central focus of someone's life that others might find interesting or entertaining

Progressive margins – margins that are most narrow at the gutter and increase in size at the top, sides and bottom of the page

Proofreading – the process of checking for accuracy and necessary corrections in finished copy or pages before they are printed

Provable truth – the best and only absolute defense against libel

Public official/public figure rule – a defense against libel that allows reporters to publish stories about public officials or public figures in which actual malice would have to be proven by the persons bringing legal action against the reporters

Puffing – making reference to commercial interests in news or features

Pull quote – quote or short amount of text taken from the body of a story and reinserted, often in a contrasting way, to break large areas of text or to simply highlight it. Also known as *callout*

Put to bed – completing work of putting paper on (bed of) press for printing

Pyramid – ad arrangement on page, with wider ads at bottom and with peak of pyramid usually on the right

Q

Q and A – copy that features questions and answers in a dialogue format

Question lead – a lead that asks a question, often hypothetically

R

Rate card (schedule) – list of prices for ads of various sizes and length of run in a newspaper used as an aid by an ad salesperson

Readability – quality of type that determines ease with which it can be read in quantity; how well written something is, how easily read. Compare with **legibility**.

Reader advocate – a neutral party who investigates reader complaints and issues brief reports that will be published in a subsequent edition of the publication

Readership – measure of number of readers attracted to story or publication

Reader spreads – the natural flow of pages in a publication as viewed by a reader

Refer – cover or front page teaser that refers readers to inside content

Retail ad – an ad for a specific business. See **display ad**.

Retraction – printed statement correcting error made in earlier story (in libel case can help establish absence of malice)

Reverse – photo turned wrong face up in engraving process so that left side appears as right; type that prints white with background in black

Reviews – student critiques of entertainment in which writers offer their opinions about events that have already occurred or about new releases or issues

Revise – second proof of galley in which errors made in first proof have been corrected

Rhythm – in design, refers to the visual flow of a page

Rivers of white space – holes of white space inserted between text in poorly typeset copy

Robot – used by a search engine to locate web sites on the internet that fit a specific criteria and are then added to the search engine site database or list. See **search engine**.

Roman – type style of book-weight upright letters characterized by serifs. Compare with **italic**.

Rule of thirds – a photographic compositional framing technique in which the photographer divides the viewfinder into thirds both vertically and horizontally and places the subject along the intersection of one of the thirds

Running quote – multiple paragraphs of quoted material in succession with closing quotation marks omitted until the end of the quote

Run of the press (ROP) – color printing using whatever color the printer happens to have on the press, providing a less expensive color use

S

Saddle-stitching – a binding method in which staples are applied through the gutter of the publication

Sales call – a meeting between the publication's ad salesperson and a potential advertiser

Sans serif – type style without serifs

Scale – in design, the use of grids or columns that guide the designer in placing text and visuals

Scaling – determining new size of enlargement or reduction of original art

Scanner – input device for a computer that turns pictures and art into digitized images for editing and pagination on the computer

Scoop (beat) – important story released in advance of other media coverage

Scoreboard – a complete listing of a team's season including the opponents and outcomes of the games or competitions

Screen – pattern available on software or as an acetate transfer sheet that is used as background or is placed over type or another page element; glass plate or film with etched crosslines placed between negative and plate when making halftone; number indicating number of lines per inch in halftone (e.g., 65-line screen, 150-line screen)

Screened color – a percentage of color ranging between 10 and 100 percent used to lighten or darken the color

Script – typeface that resembles handwriting. See **cursive**.

Search engine – used on the internet to find information electronically through keywords

Secondary headline – a headline unit in a smaller type size than the main headline that provides details and amplifies the main headline for the reader. Also known as *deck*

Secondary source – a person with some knowledge of information but not from personal involvement; a published work that cites the words of others, work that has already been published in a primary source

Series reporting – stories broken into parts and presented over the course of several issues

Serif – type with small finishing strokes at the ends of main strokes of letters

Set solid – body text set with leading equal to the point size of the type; can result in letters touching

Shadows – the darkest areas of a photograph

Shallow depth of field – a photographic technique that allows one area of a photograph to be in focus while other areas are not, bringing the viewer's eye to the content

Sheet-fed press – a press that prints a single sheet of paper at a time

Shopper – publication with newspaper format devoted to advertising with very little news

Sidebar – a companion story to a main story; usually provides specific information about a narrowly defined topic related to the main story and is placed in a layout adjacent to the main story

Side light – light that illuminates the subject from the side and provides good texture and form

Side-stitching – a method of binding in which staples are placed in the sides of the pages, but not in the gutter of the publication

Signature – large sheet of paper printed with (usually) 4, 8 or 16 pages on either side and folded to form one unit of a book or other publication

Single-use camera – inexpensive camera with fully automated operation that is recycled by manufacturer after development

Slug – metal spacing unit 6 points thick; metal line from linecasting machine; words to identify piece of copy (guideline)

Small cap – a letter set to the posture of an uppercase letter, but to the height of a lowercase letter

Smythe-sewing – a book-binding method in which signatures of pages are connected by a heavy thread sewn across the forms and then glued to a gauze strip

Soft news – news in which the primary importance is entertainment, although it may also inform, and is often less timely than hard news

Source – information obtained from an interview with a person

Special edition/section – a published report of from one to several pages usually reserved for late-breaking news or special kinds of content

Sports section – the section of a yearbook in which organized or individual in-school and out-of-school athletic events are covered

Spot – short commercial or public service announcement over radio or television

Spot color – the use of a single color in addition to black on a printed page

Spot news – timely, important news

Spread – two facing pages

Spread unity – elements that visually connect two facing pages

Square serif types – typefaces with wide, blocky serifs attached to the stems of letters

Stand-alone photograph – a photograph that appears with caption information, but not necessarily with a story

Standard lens – a lens in the 50 mm range that reproduces a subject exactly as seen through the camera

Standing head – head that appears consistently in publications issue to issue and identifies content such as briefs and columns

Stickup – first letter of paragraph that rises above base of first line

String book – reporter's collection of his or her printed stories

Stringer – person who works casually or freelances for publications rather than working as a paid staff member

Student life section – often the first main section of the yearbook following the opening section. Coverage is provided of social activities and the discussion of issues of concern to teenagers.

Style manual – a list of writing conventions including abbreviations, punctuation and word selection that guides writers and maintains consistency in writing style throughout the publication

Style sheet – definition of type styles set for various information in a publication and applied consistently to type through a computer layout and design software program

Subscription database – an information source providing data for a price

Symposium interview – a feature story in which panels of students discuss timely topics of interest to readers

Synchro-sun flash – flash used as a fill light to balance shadows cast by natural light outdoors

Syndicate – company that provides nonlocal feature material

T

Tabloid – newspaper format that is about 11 by 17 inches

Tear sheet – sample of newspaper page, proof of publication to an advertiser

Teaser – graphic that often appears above the paper's nameplate on page 1 that promotes inside stories. Usually it is made up of a headline that teases the reader and some simple art or a photo.

Teen section – special interest newspaper section targeted toward student readers, often with contributions from student reporters and photographers

Telephoto lens – a camera lens that brings content distant from the photographer into the camera's range of view

Template – a skeletal page structure stored electronically in a page layout program allowing the designer to structure the page; can include type style sheets

Ten-second editorial – brief editorial comment presented in as few as two paragraphs

Text head – short, summary headline of from two to five words dropped into natural junctures in longer stories to help break up the text

Theme – a visual or verbal unifier that creates continuity throughout a yearbook

Theme development – the development of specific pages of the yearbook in which a word or visual theme appears in some repetitive form to link the designs

Thirty (30 dash) – symbol for end of story or almost anything else in journalism, including reference to journalists' obituaries

Thumbnail – miniature rough sketch of layout

Thumbnail cut – one-half column cut

Time copy – copy that may be run at any time

Time sequence – a chronological story form

Tint block – background of color for type or picture

Tombstoning – use of similar headlines side by side

Tracking – uniform kerning in a range of text

Transition – word or phrase that ties together paragraphs and develops story continuity

Transpose (tr) – to exchange the position of two letters, words or lines

Trend sports story – a sports story in which the writer covers a highlighted trend of a team since the time of the last publication

Trim – to shorten copy considerably by deleting unnecessary words

Tripod headline – a headline combining a large word or phrase followed by a two-line headline set in type half its size; both lines of the second part equal the height of the larger, opening words

Typeface – a range of type used for all the characters in one size and weight. Also known as *font*

Type family – a range of text in weights and postures for a particular typeface

Type wrap – type that contours to the shape of a picture; also known as *type runaround*

Typo – typographical error

U

UHF – ultrahigh frequency; TV channels 14 to 83 with limited range

Unity – in design, refers to a sense of continuity in use of type and column grids throughout a publication for consistency

Up style – copy for heads and body type set with maximum possible capitals

V

Videotext (teletext) – text without audio capacity, displayed continuously on TV screen as full page or as "scroll" with lines of stories rolling up from bottom of page

Vignette – cut in which background screen gradually fades away

Vignette lead – an anecdotal lead that relies upon a form of the storytelling method of story development

Visual continuity – design factors that keep a section of a publication coherent and unified

Visual entry points – a series of visual devices used by readers to enter content or pages

Visual hierarchy – an organized method of displaying information on a page, allowing a reader to understand the importance of the information by the size and weight of its headline(s) and its placement on the page

Visual redundancy – weak picture editing in which two pictures provide the reader with the same content or meaning

W

Washed out – a photographic print in which no pure black areas have been produced

Web – as in World Wide Web or the internet

Web master – the editor of an online publication

Well – U-shaped advertising area formed by running ads up both sides of page, or headline display area formed by running legs of type on either side of the headline

White space – the area of a page not filled with content; needed for balance in page design

Wide-angle lens – a camera lens in the range of 35 mm to 24 mm that gives a wider angle of view of a subject

Widow – partly filled line at top of column of type

Wirephoto – picture received electronically from distant point, usually by telephone line

Wire service – agency that provides information to member publications from across the world

Word processing – computerized method of typing and editing

Word theme – yearbook theme or unifier that is verbal and chosen because it is tied to specific events or issues related to the school community or to teenagers in general

Wrap – to continue type from one column to the next, as in "wrap around pix"

Wrong font (wf) – type of different style or size from that specified

W's and *H* – the what, who, where, when, why and how information that forms the basis for all stories

X

X-height – type dimension from top to bottom without descenders and ascenders

Z

Zoom lens – a camera lens that allows a photographer to use the lens between a minimum and maximum focal length range built into the lens

Z pattern – the pattern a reader's eyes follow as they move through a page entering at the top left, moving across, diagonally down and to the right of the page

Other Resources

For continued study of some of the topics covered in this edition, here's a list of books. The list is just a sampling, not a comprehensive compilation of journalism resources.

ADVERTISING

Blakeman, Robyn, *The Bare Bones of Advertising Print Design*. Lanham, Md: Rowman & Littlefield, 2005.

Shaver, Mary Alice, *Make the Sale!* Chicago, Ill.: The Copy Workshop, 2003.

ADVISING

Dvorak, Jack et al., *Journalism Kids Do Better: What Research Tells Us about High School Journalism in the 1990s*. Bloomington, Ind.: ERIC, 1994.

Hawthorne, Bobby, *Journalism: Teacher's Writing Manual*. Austin, Texas: Interscholastic League Press Conference, 2002.

Hinman, Sheryl and Tom Winski, *Journalism: Writing for Publication*. Villa Maria, Pa.: Center for Learning, 2000.

Kyker, Keith, *Educator's Survival Guide for Television Production and Activities*. Portsmouth, N.H., 2003.

Osborn, Patricia, *School Newspaper Adviser's Survival Guide*. West Nyack, N.Y.: The Center for Applied Research in Education, 1998.

BROADCAST

Kalbfield, Brad, *Associated Press Broadcast News Handbook*. New York, N.Y.: The Associated Press, 2000.

Schultz, Brad, *Broadcast News Producing*. Thousand Oaks, Calif.: Sage Publications, 2005.

Wulfemeyer, K. Tim, *Beginning Radio–TV Newswriting: A Self-Instructional Learning Experience*. Oxford, UK: Blackwell Publishing, 2003.

Wulfemeyer, K. Tim, *Radio–TV Newswriting: A Workbook*. Oxford, UK: Blackwell Publishing, 2003.

COACHING WRITING AND EDITING

Clark, Roy Peter and Don Fry, *Coaching Writers: Editors and Reporters Working Together*. New York, N.Y.: St. Martin's Press, 2003.

Fellow, Anthony R. and Thomas N. Clamin, *Copy Editors Handbook for Newspaper*. Englewood, Colo.: Morton, 1998.

Goldstein, Norm and Louis D. Boccardi (ed.), *The Associated Press Stylebook and Briefing on Media Law*. New York, N.Y.: Associated Press, 2005.

Kessler, Lauren and Duncan McDonald, *When Words Collide: A Media Writer's Guide to Grammar and Style*, 5th edn. Belmont, Calif.: Wadsworth Publishing, 2000.

DESIGN

Berry, John D., *Contemporary Newspaper Design*. New York, N.Y.: Mark Batty, 2004.

The Best of Newspaper Design, Society of News Design, Gloucester, Mass.: Rockport Publishers, annual.

Garcia, Mario, *Pure Design: 79 Simple Solutions for Magazines, Books, Newspapers and Websites*. St. Petersburg, Fla.: Miller Media, 2002.

Harrower, Tim, *The Newspaper Designer's Handbook*, 5th edn. Black Lick, Ohio: McGraw-Hill, 2002.

Krause, Jim, *Design Basics Index*. Cincinnati, Ohio: How Design Books, 2004.

White, Alex W., *The Elements of Graphic Design: Space, Unity, Page Architecture and Type*. New York, N.Y.: Allworth Press, 2002.

Williams, Robin, *Non-Designer's Design Book*. Berkeley, Calif.: Peachpit Press, 2004.

EDITORIAL AND COLUMN WRITING

Cardoza, Monica McCabe, *You Can Write a Column*. New York: Writer's Digest Books, 2000.

Casey, Maura and Michael Zuzel, *Beyond Argument: A Handbook for Editorial Writers*. National Council of Editorial Writers, 2001.

Hall, H.L. and Rod Vahl, *Effective Editorial Writing*, 4th edn. Iowa City, Iowa: Quill and Scroll, 2000.

Rystrom, Kenneth, *The Why, Who and How of the Editorial Page*, 4th edn. State College, Pa.: Strata Publishing, 2004.

FEATURE WRITING

Blundell, William E., *The Art and Craft of Feature Writing*. Plume, 1988.

Garlock, David (ed.), *Pulitzer Prize Feature Stories*. Oxford, UK: Blackwell Publishing, 2003.

Ricketson, Matthew, *Writing Feature Stories: How to Research and Write Newspaper and Magazine Articles*. St. Leonards, NSW, Australia: Allen & Unwin, 2004.

HIGH SCHOOL JOURNALISM

Ferguson, Donald L., Jim Patten and Bradley Wilson, *Journalism Today*, 7th edn. Glencoe, Ill. 2005.

Hall, H.L., *High School Journalism*, 3rd edn. New York, N.Y.: Rosen Publishing Group, 2003.

Hawthorne, Bobby, *The Radical Writer: A Fresh Approach to Journalism Writing for Students*. Minneapolis, Minn.: Jostens, 2003.

INTERNET

Harmack, Andrew and Eugene Kleppinger, *Online! A Reference Guide to Using Internet Sources*. Boston, Mass.: Bedford/St. Martin's Press, 2003.

Houston, Brant, *Computer-assisted Reporting: A Practical Guide*, 3rd edn. Boston, Mass.: St. Martin's Press, 2004.

King, Elliot and Randy Reddick, *The Online Journ@list: Using the internet and Other Electronic Resources*, New York, N.Y.: Harcourt College Publishers, 2001.

Poremsky, Diane, *Google and Other Search Engines*. Berkeley, Calif.: Peachpit Press, 2004.

INTERVIEWING

Brady, John, *Interviewer's Handbook: A Guerrilla Guide*. The Writer Books, 2004.

Metler, Ken, *Creative Interviewing*, 3rd edn. Needham Heights, Mass.: Allyn & Bacon, 1997.

JOURNALISM HISTORY

Lewis, Jon E. (ed.), *The Mammoth Book of Journalism*. New York, N.Y.: Carroll & Graf, 2003.

Newton, Eric (ed.), *Crusaders, Scoundrels, Journalists: The Newseum's Most Intriguing Newspeople*. Arlington, Va.: The Freedom Forum, 1999.

Satter, James, *Journalists Who Made History*. Minneapolis, Minn.: The Oliver Press, 1998.

Stephens, Mitchell, *A History of News*. Fort Worth, Texas: Harcourt Brace College Publishers, 1998.

PHOTOGRAPHY

Horton, Brian, *Associated Press Guide to Photojournalism*. New York, N.Y.: McGraw-Hill, 2001.

Kelby, Scott, *Photoshop CS Book for Digital Photographers*. Berkeley, Calif.: New Riders Publishing, 2003.

Kobre, Kenneth, *Photojournalism: A Professional's Approach*, 5th edn. Burlington, Mass.: Focal Press, 2004.

National Press Photographers Association, *The Best of Photojournalism, Newspaper and Magazine Pictures of the Year*. Durham, N.C.: National Press Photographers Association, annual.

Parrish, Fred S., *Photojournalism: An Introduction*. Belmont, Calif.: Wadsworth Publishing, 2001.

PRESS LAW AND ETHICS

Law of the Student Press, 2nd edn. Arlington, Va.: Student Press Law Center, 1994.

Monk, Linda R., *The Words We Live By: Your Annotated Guide to the Constitution*. New York, N.Y.: Hyperion, 2004.

Olson, Donna Lee, *Ethics in Action: Resources for High School Journalism Courses*. Iowa City, Iowa: Quill and Scroll, 2003.

Raskin, Jamin B., *We the Students: Supreme Court Decisions for and about Students*. Washington, D.C.: CQ Press, 2003.

REPORTING AND NEWS WRITING

Cappon, Rene J., *Associated Press Guide to News Writing*, 3rd edn. New York, N.Y.: ARCO Publishing, 2000.

Kershner, James W., *Elements of News Writing*. Boston, Mass.: Allyn & Bacon, 2005.

Knight, Robert M., *The Craft of Clarity: A Journalistic Approach to Good Writing*. Ames, Iowa: Iowa State University Press, 1998.

LaRocque, Paula, *Championship Writing: 50 Ways to Improve Your Writing*. Oak Park, Ill.: Marion Street Press, 2000.

Rich, Carole, *Writing and Reporting News: A Coaching Method*. Belmont, Calif.: Wadsworth Publishing, 2000.

SPORTS WRITING

Craig, Steve, *Sports Writing: A Beginner's Guide*. Shoreham, Vt.: Discover Writing Press, 2002.

Wilstein, Steve, *Associated Press Sports Writing Handbook*. New York, N.Y.: McGraw-Hill, 2002.

Index

Page numbers in *italics* refer to illustrations.